Mending Rips in the Sky

About the Title

Mohamed Aden Sheikh quotes, in Chapter Two, a traditional Somali proverb: "*Cir tarraray rag waa tolikaraa, Taako labadeede*!", i.e. when men of good will come together, they become so powerful they can even mend a rip in the sky. The editors thought this proverb would be an appropriate title for this volume of collected essays.

Mending Rips in the Sky

OPTIONS FOR SOMALI COMMUNITIES
IN THE 21st CENTURY

Edited by
Hussein M. Adam
and Richard Ford

The Red Sea Press, Inc.
Publishers & Distributors of Third World Books

11-D Princess Road
Lawrenceville, NJ 08648

P. O. Box 48
Asmara, ERITREA

The Red Sea Press, Inc.

Publishers & Distributors of Third World Books

11-D Princess Road
Lawrenceville, NJ 08648

P. O. Box 48
Asmara, ERITREA

Copyright © 1997 Somali Studies International Association (SSIA)

Book design & layout: Richard Ford
Cover Design: Aaron J. Wilson

Library of Congress Cataloging-in-Publication Data

Mending rips in the sky : options for Somali communities in the 21st
 Century / edited by Hussein M. Adam, Richard Ford.
    p. cm.
    Includes bibliographical references and index.
    ISBN 1-56902-073-6 (cloth : alk. paper). -- ISBN 1-56902-074-4
 (pbk. : alk. paper)
    1.Somalia --History--1991- I. Hussein Mohamed Adam. II. Ford,
 Richard.
 DT407.M46 1997
 967.73--dc21   97-10801
                                                                 CIP

Printed in Canada by Québecor

Dedication

to my family

I dedicate this book to my family. My wife, Fadumo M. Abdisalam, has supported me unselfishly during all the years that I served as the Founding President of the Somali Studies International Association (SSIA). My wife and elder children -- Ayaan, Farhan, and Guled -- played critical roles in the management and organization of the Fifth International Congress (December, 1993) as well as the Post-Congress Symposium (June, 1995). The other children -- Ubah, Zahra, and Mohamed -- have also contributed in both practical and emotionally supportive ways. The entire family also deserves my sincere gratitude and deep appreciation for their patience and support during the production of this book.

Hussein M. Adam

Foreword

In December, 1993, the College of the Holy Cross served as host institution to a world-wide group of scholars, ambassadors, political leaders, representatives of international relief and development agencies, and students who gathered on campus to grapple with social, political and economic problems confronting Somalia. They sought to assess the current situation and to suggest possible ways to restore order to that troubled nation and region.

December, 1993 was a contentious time in the life of the Somali people. The United States and the United Nations had intervened. News headlines were reporting the deaths of American soldiers, killed while attempting to keep the peace and provide relief for the suffering Somalis. Across the nation, diverse and strong opinions were voiced on how the US should respond. Should the US presence continue? If so, for how long? If there is to be a withdrawal, how will the US military extricate itself? And if they do depart, what will be left in its place to keep the peace and provide relief?

In the midst of these issues, the Fifth International Congress of the Somali Studies International Association convened. The presence of the Congress made the issues of Somalia come alive on our Holy. Cross campus. Our guests rendered the situation in Somalia a real life issue to be studied, assessed, and perhaps in some cases even acted upon.

It was a particularly appropriate time for Holy Cross to confront these and related questions. Why? Because 1993 marked the College's Sesquicentennial Year -- a year when time was taken to reflect on where the College had come from, what it had achieved in its 150 year history, and where it was planning to go in the future. As a highly selective, Jesuit, undergraduate, liberal arts college, Holy Cross remains strongly committed to providing an education for justice. It strives to educate "men and women for others;" men and women who will possess that quality of mind that is reflected in their respect for other points of view, and in their passion for truth; men and women who will bend their energies not to strengthen positions of privilege, but, to the extent possible, reduce privilege in favor of the underprivileged, the truly poor, the truly marginalized peoples of the world. Given these goals, a critical examination of fundamental philosophical and religious questions is integral to the Holy Cross liberal arts experience. Students and faculty are expected to ask: What is the moral character of learning and teaching? What are our obligations to one another? What is our responsibility to the world's poor, the powerless, and the marginalized?

During the Fifth International Congress, such questions took on a new and deeper meaning as students and faculty met our international guests, heard them speak, asked questions, and exchanged ideas. No longer were our questions merely academic. On the contrary, they were now associated with recognizable names and faces, and there was a growing awareness on our part that there was a rich culture at stake, and that we were now concerned with the fate of a living and suffering people. Holy Cross was challenged to live up to its mission to educate for justice.

The significant work that follows in this book is a compilation, elaboration, and assessment of the thoughtful papers, panel discussions, addresses and recommendations that were presented in the course of the proceedings. The diligence of Professor Hussein Adam, Associate Professor of Political Science at Holy Cross, as well as that of his colleagues whose efforts assured the success of the Congress has led to this publication. It is my sincere hope that those who will read and reflect upon this work will be moved to direct their energies toward the promotion of peace, reconciliation, justice and genuine hope in our troubled world.

Father John Brooks
President Emeritus
College of the Holy Cross
Worcester, Massachusetts

Preface

The grant made by the United States Institute of Peace to help finance the editing and completion of this important book represents one more step in the Institute's journey with Somalia. The initial step was a grant from the Institute, made in 1992 to St. Lawrence University, to finance a conference on the crisis in Somalia. The papers from that conference were later published in a book edited by Ahmed Samatar entitled *The Somali Challenge: From Catastrophe to Renewal.*

As the Somali crisis worsened, in October, 1992 the Institute organized the first of what became a series of conferences and workshops on Somalia. The Somali Study Group was formed after an initial conference. Over a two year period this Study Group prepared recommendations regarding international intervention in Somalia, as well as ideas about reconstruction and reconciliation. The Study Group was composed of Somali intellectuals and former Somali officials who were then residing in the US. I organized these meetings in collaboration with Ambassador Robert Oakley, former US Ambassador to Somalia and at the time Director of the Institute's Middle East Initiative. My other collaborator and close advisor was Professor Hussein Adam, a co-editor of this volume.

When President Bush made the decision to send US troops to Somalia to assure the safe delivery of humanitarian supplies, he chose Robert Oakley to be his special envoy to Somalia. The Somalia Study Group continued to meet and was able to communicate its recommendations to Ambassador Oakley.

In 1994-95 the Institute published two books that analyzed the UN and American interventions in Somalia. The first was by Ambassador Mohamed Sahnoun, who served as the Special Representative of the UN Secretary General in Somalia in 1992, entitled *Somalia: The Missed Opportunities.* Ambassador Sahnoun wrote this book while he was a Distinguished Fellow at the Institute. The second was a book by Robert Oakley and his deputy in Somalia, Ambassador John Hirsh, entitled *Somalia and Operation Restore Hope.* At the time these books were first published, the Institute organized public briefings on lessons learned from international intervention in Somalia.

In 1994 the Institute made a grant to the College of the Holy Cross to enable Hussein Adam to organize and edit some of the most pertinent papers presented at the 1993 meeting of the Somali Studies International Association. The product of that grant is this volume, which represents an important collective statement by Somali and Western intellectuals about the nature of the Somali predicament, as well as thoughts and recommendations regarding Somalia's future.

I wish to commend Hussein Adam, who is currently a Senior Fellow at the US Institute of Peace, and the other contributors to this volume for the important statements that this book makes about Somalia. The US Institute of Peace is proud to have supported and to be associated with this project.

David R. Smock
Director of the Grants Program
United States Institute of Peace
Washington, DC

Acknowledgments

This book would not have been possible without the help of many friends and colleagues. There is insufficient space to list all of them here, but the most important include the 400 individuals who participated in the Fifth Congress of the Somali Studies International Association, especially those who prepared and presented papers. The Congress itself was made possible through the generous support of the College of the Holy Cross which, in 1993, was celebrating its 150th year anniversary. The Congress became part of that celebration, including Holy Cross providing assistance in conference funding, facilities and meeting rooms, and costs of secretarial and logistical assistance.

In addition to Holy Cross financial help, dozens of students served as guides, registration aides, messengers, and computer assistants. Without this abundant support, the conference would not have been possible. Moreover, the administrative officers of the campus including food services, campus police, campus printing, and the office of grant support, under the direction of Professor Charles Weiss, were all of enormous help. In particular, we would like to single out Ms. Joy Bousquet, Secretary of the Mathematics Department, who typed almost every paper submitted as well as conference correspondence. She did all of this over and above her regular duties. Her tireless, rapid, and accurate work made possible distribution of papers at the conference and the follow-up symposium.

We would also like to thank Ms. Jean Evanowski, Secretary to the Department of Political Science, who answered phone calls and coordinated schedules and plans. Another indispensable partner in preparing for the Congress and in producing this book was Ms. Odile Hanson. She translated two of the papers from French into English. In addition, Ms. Tina Chen and Ms. Mary Boliver in the Office of Special Studies, organized funding, managed reservations, and supervised registration.

Beyond the conference was follow-up assistance and publication of this book. The United States Institute of Peace made a grant to cover costs of publication which has been deeply appreciated. At a time when many donor and funding agencies have adopted a "wait and see" attitude on matters relating to Somalia and Somaliland, the USIP has taken strong and bold stands on issues to keep people talking and to seek many different options to stimulate reconciliation and eventually rehabilitation and reconstruction of the war-torn land.

Also vital to the production of the volume have been staff and graduate students in Clark University's International Development Program. John King, Becky Turk, David Szczebak, and Femy Pinto -- all graduate students, and Liz Owens, Secretary in International Development, provided essential, professional, and timely assistance during the editing and formatting of the publication. Clark also helped with hotel accommodations and costs of preparation of the manuscript. For all of this assistance, we are grateful.

In addition, during the final stages, Jamie Frueh, Research Assistant at the United States Institute of Peace was an enormous asset in proof reading, typing the bibliography, and attending to last minute crises.

One editorial note is also necessary. In bringing symmetry to the chapters, we have tried, in-so-far as possible, to preserve the intentions and style of the author. Some chapters have end notes and bibliography; others do not. Some spellings vary from chapter to chapter, depending on local usage such as *khat* or *qaad* or *miraa*. And many of the spellings in the Somali language vary because of the considerable local variation in dialect, usage, and spelling. Preserving some of the variations, we feel, preserves the essence of the dignity and individuality of Somali society while, at the same time, bringing these differences together under a single cover and in a common purpose. We hope that this theme of diversity within a united front will have some adaptation to Somali society itself.

Hussein M. Adam
College of the Holy Cross
Worcester, Massachusetts

Richard Ford
Clark University
Worcester, Massachusetts

Table of Contents

An Introduction to the Fifth Congress

Hussein M. Adam
Congress Coordinator

On behalf of the Somali Studies International Association (SSIA) and the Holy Cross Congress Organizing and Advisory Committees, we welcome you to Worcester and the Fifth International Congress of Somali Studies (December 1 - 3) as well as to the follow-up panels within the 36th Annual Meeting of the African Studies Association (ASA), at the Westin Hotel, Boston, December 4-7, 1993.

Preparations for this Congress were begun during the 34th ASA meeting in St. Louis in 1991 as the unfolding Somali civil wars, famine, and US and UN humanitarian interventions attained staggering local and global implications during the course of our Congress preparations. This allowed us to attract a larger group of significant policy makers, voluntary relief/development organizations (NGOs) and other activists than was the case in our previous Congresses. Journalists have also given our activities more attention than in the past.

Among those who effectively helped me launch this project, permit me to thank the Congress Program Chair, Professor Lee Cassanelli and Publicity Chair, Professor Charles Geshekter. By phone, fax and during chance encounters at academic conferences, I have benefitted from consultations with many of you. I have also conducted fruitful consultative communications with Abdirahman Osman Raghe in Mogadishu and with the Hamburg host of the Second Congress, Dr. Thomas Labahn; with Professors Mao Awes and Bechtold at the University of Tubingen; also with Professor Annarita Puglielli of the University of Rome who coordinated the Third International Congress of Somali Studies in Rome. Let me recall that our practice is to include previous academic Coordinators in our International Executive Committee as Vice Presidents of the Somali Studies International Association (SSIA).

Since its founding, during the ASA Baltimore meeting of 1978, the SSIA and its affiliated branches have hosted five international congresses, including this one. A few years ago, a European Association of Somali Studies was formed in France and this September held an important conference in London attended by many in this audience. A number of the branches -- the German, British, Italian and North American for example -- issue regular or occasional newsletters and sponsor/endorse university-based publications.

The overall theme for this Fifth Congress is: *The Somali Crisis: Relief, Reconciliation and Reconstruction.* We are gratified that so many of you accepted our challenge, resulting in a substantial number of panels and round tables that directly address the Congress themes and subthemes. The Fifth Congress cannot help but specifically address issues of urgent interest and immediate concern.

The highlighted sessions of the Congress will focus on the international and Pan-African dimensions of the Somali crisis. One of our keynote speakers, Professor Ali Mazrui, recently wrote: "Three post-colonial taboos have been broken in the Horn of Africa in the 1990s. First there is the UN's temporary 'tutelage' of the Somalis to help them back to self government--the taboo of recolonization. Then there is the independence of Eritrea with the cooperation of the government in Ethiopia, of which it was once a province--the taboo of officially sanctioned secession. Third, there is the rest of Ethiopia groping for a federal constitutional order based on ethnic autonomy--the taboo of retribalization" (*Economist,* 11th September, page 28). Contradictory and challenging interpretations could be offered on the recent Somali tragic experience from a global and African perspective.

The Congress will encourage fruitful discussions/debates within a pluralistic framework. Let us strive to be analytical, to seek genuine understanding rather than make polemical judgments. Our policy recommendations -- based on sound analysis and reflected experience should be modest, cognizant of the fact that, ultimately, it is up to our people in Somalia/Somaliland to implement any that they so choose.

Somalia today is a house on fire and we could not isolate our professional Congress from the experiences of today's global "fire fighters and development facilitators:" the international and Somali non-governmental organizations (NGOs). We have scheduled several NGO round tables/forums on NGO perspectives on the Somali crisis, on institutional capacity building, on roles in relief, reconciliation and reconstruction and related issues and topics.

The pool of non-Somali, Somali scholars gathered here is relatively large and consists of many of the most famous names in the field. This applies also to the Somali scholars, activists and other professionals gathered here. There are many others in Somalia/Somaliland and in the diaspora who could not be with us. Nevertheless, practically all of us here have professional and personal networks with those who are not here tonight. It is within this sector of our civil society that one finds the training, experience and talents necessary to engage in program and project planning and implementation. A number of those present are actually engaged in revitalizing civil society through voluntary development organization (NGO) activities.

I humbly wish to remind the United Nations, and the United States in particular because of the critical role it is playing, that all people must learn to achieve peace, reconciliation and govern themselves by themselves. One cannot develop someone else, people must develop themselves. Somali talents lying idle at home and in exile abroad must be harnessed to reconstruct Somalia/Somaliland. International intervention can help or distort/hinder the process of organic self renewal. Attempts to govern the people and areas concerned without Somali involvement can be costly, not only to the Somali people, but also to the international humanitarian interveners as well.

Perhaps I need to clarify to our new participants and remind old members/supporters that the SSIA, as SSIA, does not take political positions. Individual members may do as they please on a broad range of issues. However, from our establishment in 1978, we decided to include the study of Somali life and culture beyond any specific state borders-- beyond Somalia into Djibouti, Kenya and Ethiopia for example. For this Congress we have papers analyzing Somali politics in Ethiopia, civil conflicts in Djibouti and aspects of the Somali diaspora in Kenya, Germany and Canada. The future praxis of the Somali people will decide whether there will be two states, a return to one state or a confederation of the two. As researchers we work with the given *de facto* situation and environment. A pragmatic stance allows us to get on with the business of research and analysis as we leave political rhetoric for the politicians gathered in Addis Ababa.

Let me repeat our sincere gratitude to the College of the Holy Cross and all the institutions/individuals listed in our acknowledgments -- especially students, secretarial staff, and administrators -- for having given the Congress project financial, material and moral support.

Let me conclude by recalling the aims of **The Somali Studies International Association.** During the November 1978 Baltimore Annual Meeting of the African Studies Association (ASA), a group of Somali and non-Somali scholars got together and established the Somali Studies International Association (SSIA), with the following objectives:

> - to promote scholarly research, both within and outside Somalia, in all areas and disciplines within the social sciences, natural sciences and humanities;

> - to encourage international cooperation and to facilitate the exchange of ideas among scholars engaged in research on Somalia and the Horn of Africa;

> - to organize international congresses on Somali studies and periodic panels at meetings of national and international associations and organizations;

> - to provide the general public with information on historical, cultural and contemporary issues in the Horn of Africa.

Again, a warm welcome to all! We are honored and pleased that you chose to meet here and to enrich us with your presence at a time when the College of the Holy Cross is celebrating its 150th anniversary!

Holy Cross and the Somali Studies Congress

Frank Vellaccio
Vice President Academic Affairs
College of the Holy Cross

Good evening. As Academic Vice President of the College of the Holy Cross, let me add my welcome to what I hope has been a chorus of welcomes to you. I want to thank you for attending and participating in this the Fifth International Congress of Somali Studies which the College of the Holy Cross, through the Herculean efforts of Hussein Adam, is privileged to host. As I am sure you have been told, this is one of a number of events we have had and will continue to have this year to celebrate our sesquicentennial.

Although 150 years is a relatively short span on the time-line of Western and Eastern civilization, it is a significant birthday for the College and a good portion of the US's 217 year history. From William McKinley through Kennedy to Bill Clinton, from slavery through the Civil Rights Movement to Rodney King, from the beginnings of the automobile through passenger airliner to space travel, from the telegraph through the telephone to the computer, from smallpox through malaria to AIDS, from pasteurization through quantum mechanics to solid state physics, from the Civil War through the World Wars to Desert Storm, from the formation of the South African Republic through apartheid to its end, from the philosophy of Karl Marx through the Soviet Union to the bombing of the Russian Parliament, from Dickens through Kafka to Toni Morrison, from Verdi and Wagner through Gershwin and Stravinsky to the Beatles and Pearl Jam, and from baseball through baseball to baseball we have existed. In this time, the College of the Holy Cross has struggled to liberally educate students to be leaders in business, professional and civic life, who live by the highest intellectual and ethical standards and has tried to do so in a way consistent with its founder's motto *Ad Maiorem Dei Gloriam.*

Few would disagree that colleges and universities like Holy Cross have played a critical role in the events and lives of the last 150 years both in this country and throughout the world. The children of this century and a half have been in their hands. In the past, when asked by a mother what a college or university can do for a son or daughter, higher education has always responded as Woodrow Wilson did as President of Princeton: "Don't worry Madame we guarantee satisfaction or you may have your child back." But today fewer and fewer people are satisfied with such a guarantee. Today higher education particularly in the United States is under scrutiny and criticism like it has never been before. People are appalled at the cost of colleges and universities and many are looking more for a certification process than an education. Books such as the *Closing of the American Mind; Profscam: Professors and the Demise of Higher Education;* and *The Moral Collapse of the University* echo, albeit often from different ideological stances, a chorus of disappointment and disdain for higher education. Much of the criticism is summed up in the indictment of the former Secretary of Education William Bennett when he says "Too many colleges and universities have no clear sense of their educational mission and no conception of what a graduate of their institution ought to know or be." Is such an indictment true of Holy Cross? We certainly hope not but the discussions we are involved in during this Congress remind us of the importance of continuing to ask this question, for if the business of education is not about addressing the culture, politics, literature and problems of Somalia, then we should not be in business.

Holy Cross, as a highly selective Jesuit undergraduate college, has tried to appropriate the best of secular higher education while responding to the challenge posed by its Jesuit heritage. It has been guided by Cardinal Newman's seminal work, *The Idea of the University* which curiously is itself nearly 150 years old. In many ways, then, to answer the question: "Is Holy Cross' mission relevant to contemporary society" is to ask: "Is what Newman had to say about the university still relevant today?" That Newman's work is considered by many as the most important treatise ever written on the idea of a university is no guarantee it isn't outdated. And although Holy Cross has had a rich and meaningful

150 years, that does not mean it is the place it should be today.

There is a parable about an absent-minded man which is relevant. It seems that among other things this man could never remember each morning where he had placed his belongings the day before. Each morning he spent a lot of time looking for his clothes, his shoes, the work he had brought home and even the breakfast dishes. All of this made him late each day for work, meetings and appointments. One day he had the idea to write down at night where he put everything before he went to bed. He wrote: "my jacket is on the chair, my shoes under the bed, my work on the desk," etc., and he ended, "I am in my bed." The next morning he awoke with the list still in his hand. He quickly got up and within minutes found everything he needed. He was overjoyed with the results and was ready to scream with joy to the entire world that he had found the solution to his problems when he read the last point on his list: "and I am in the bed." He quickly rushed to the bed but he was not there. He looked everywhere but he could not find himself. His joy was replaced with sorrow as he repeated over and over: "And I, where am I." As higher education gets better and better at what it does, has it lost a sense of where it is.

As we sit here and talk of what is, to this enclave, the affairs of the outside world, we should reflect on what Jaroslav Pelikan in his recent book *The Idea of the University: A Reexamination* calls "one of the most besetting vices of the university and yet at the same time one of its most charming characteristics, ... its quaint tendency to look inward and ignore the context of the society within which it lives and without which it could not exist." As Pelikan points out, this is not contradictory to Newman's educational philosophy, for an inherent part of his thesis was "that training of the intellect, which is best for the individual himself, best enables him to discharge his duties to society." And Newman goes on later in his thesis to say: "If then a practical end must be assigned to a University course, I say it is that of training good members of society. Its art is the art of the social life, and its end is fitness for the world." A similar position is expressed by Jacques Maritain in his text *Education at the Crossroads:* "It is the aim of education to guide man in the evolving dynamism through which he shapes himself as a human person--armed with knowledge strength of judgment and moral virtues--while at the same time conveying to him the spiritual heritage of the nation and the civilization in which he is involved and preserving in this way the century-old achievements of generations." It can be said then that Newman and Maritain believed the University served the greater society by educating its citizenry and served it best when it bestowed upon an individual not only a sense of duty to society but also the ability to help society.

Certainly situated in his world of justifying the need for a university in Ireland, Newman must have been concerned with the university's duties to society and not just the individual's. But it is tempting for us to believe that today's world is calling with a much louder voice and with greater needs than did Newman's. Today as we talk of the problems in the outside world and particularly in Somalia there is the tendency to feel this must be the most challenging and threatening time ever to pretend we can remain secure doing our work in this ivory tower. Yet the following passage from Jacques Maritain's *Education at the Crossroads* written in 1943 could have been written today:

> We come now to the special tasks which the present crisis of civilization and the conditions of the postwar world are to impose upon education. These tasks are manifold and momentous. As a result of the present disintegration of family life, of a crisis in morality and the break between religion and life, and finally of a crisis in the political state and the civic conscience, and the necessity for democratic states to rebuild themselves according to new patterns, there is a tendency, everywhere, to burden education with remedying all these deficiencies...In such a situation the duty of educators is twofold: they have both to maintain the essentials of humanistic education and to adapt them to the present requirements of the common good.

This is the challenge that higher education faced after World War II and which it faces today and which Holy Cross takes very seriously. Certainly to meet this challenge our ultimate objectives are clear, and it is hard to improve on Newman's original words which so artfully describe them (outside of using sex inclusive language):

University training ... aims at raising the intellectual tone of society, at cultivating the public mind, at purifying the national taste, at supplying true principles to popular enthusiasm and fixed aims to popular aspiration, at giving enlargement and sobriety to the ideas of the age, at facilitating the exercise of political power, and refining the intercourse of private life. It is the education which gives a man a clear conscious view of his own opinions and judgments, a truth in developing them, an eloquence in expressing them, and a force in urging them. It teaches him to see things as they are, to go right to the point, to disentangle a skein (skane) of thought, to detect what is sophistical, and to discard what is irrelevant. It prepares him to fill any post with credit, and to master any subject with facility. It shows him how to accommodate himself to others, how to throw himself into their state of mind, how to bring before them his own, how to influence them, how to come to an understanding with them, how to bear with them. He is at home in any society, he has common ground with every class; he knows when to speak and when to be silent; he is able to converse, he is able to listen; he can ask a question pertinently, and gain a lesson seasonably, when he has nothing to impart himself; he is ever ready, yet never in the way; he is a pleasant companion, and a comrade you can depend upon; he knows when to be serious and when to trifle, and he has a sure tact which enables him to trifle with gracefulness and to be serious with effect. He has the repose of a mind which lives in itself, while it lives in the world, and which has resources for its happiness at home when it cannot go abroad. He has a gift which serves him in public, and which supports him in retirement, without which good fortune is but vulgar, and which failure and disappointment have a charm.

As a Jesuit college we supplement Newman's objectives with the words of Pedro Arrupe former Father General of the Society of Jesus.

Today our prime educational objective must be to form men and women for others; men and women who will live not for themselves but for God.... men and women who cannot even conceive of love of God which does not include love for the least of their neighbors: men and women completely convinced that love of God which does not issue in justice is a farce.

If education accomplished the objectives of Newman and Arrupe, would not the task of this Congress be an easier one? This mix of knowledge and morality in students was what Elie Weisel, the noted author and holocaust survivor, addressed in a commencement speech he gave at Fairfield University:

Each of us must do something to improve the human condition. Each of us must save someone around us... You have been studying for the last four years. Now the time has come for you to care for your fellow man. Remember: Culture alone is not enough; knowledge alone is not enough. Knowledge without morality is sterile. Knowledge without an ethical imperative becomes inhuman. When I was younger than you, I saw killers kill hundreds of children, day after day. Some of them they buried alive. Others they burned alive. And these killers had college degrees; they had knowledge. They were educated. But they were devoid of the moral dimension.

This is the hope we have for the graduates of Holy Cross: that they will have the desire to make the world a better place, both morally as well as physically. But a heart is not enough when facing the problems the world presents today. They must have the abilities and characteristics that Newman summarized. What kind of educational process can produce the men and women of Newman and Arrupe? This is the work that must go on in this and all educational ivory towers. If we can be successful then there is hope that the Fifth International Congress of Somali Studies will not talk of relief, or reconstruction but of the benefits that have resulted from development.

Thank you and I wish you success in your individual and collective pursuit of truth.

SECTION ONE

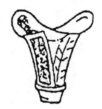

Theory
and Historical
Perspectives

Summaries: Section One

Ali A. Mazrui (Chapter 1) cites three paradoxes in the Somali tradition that have led to the current impasse: (1) governance systems of an ancient pastoral culture VS modern statehood; (2) tension between tyranny and anarchy; and (3) high emotions of nationalism and a low sense of nationhood. These underlying tensions, he argues, led to the explosions of the 1990s, in spite of strong cultural, religious, ethnic, and linguistic commonality. As these tensions lie mostly within the Somali culture, so, concludes Mazrui, must the solutions.

Mohamed Aden Sheikh (Chapter 2) laments that the only common element among opposition parties was animosity toward Siyad Barre. Upon Siyad's departure, the unity of the "opposition" melted. Sheikh argues that solutions must come through extended discussions, return of many of the Somali intellectuals who have left the country, and a compromise between those who seek total clan autonomy -- even though he sees such a position as unworkable -- and those who seek some form of modern federation. Men of good will, he concludes, can even "mend rips in the sky."

Ibrahim Megag Samater (Chapter 3) reflects back on the evolution and activities of the Somali National Movement (SNM). He argues that Somalia failed to transplant the liberal institutions of the state to meet African needs -- hence the collapse of the state and fratricidal killing and destruction which followed. He concludes that the present need is to find ways to resew the torn fabric of Somali society, whether under the umbrella of one, two, or even three different state structures.

Mohamed Haji Mukhtar (Chapter 4) traces the origins of mostly southern Somali political parties from the 1920s, commenting on the interaction among clan and colonial politics. He notes that as European influence receded, clan became an increasingly dominant. Given the present intensity of clan-based politics, he argues that some form of federation is the most logical first step to rebuild the Somali nation. His chapter dramatizes the depth and durability of the interface among clan, Somali politics, and European colonial interventionists.

Charles Geshekter (Chapter 5) comments on the evolution of the Somali dilemma. He finds four themes: (1) the European nation state as ineffective for modern Africa; (2) Cold War impacts on developing nations; (3) challenges facing African leadership; and (4) the role of local institutions in maintaining accountability. He concludes that UNOSOM was a "white warlord" spending $1.5 billion to feed itself. Little was left for the Somali people. He argues that the "Somali social fabric can only be stitched back together and ... rebuilt by Somalis, from the bottom up."

Lee V. Cassanelli (Chapter 6) urges that all Somali communities receive equal treatment. Citing the experience of "the other Somalis," he notes that the inter-riverine societies have been neglected, both in politics and in attention from the Somali scholarly community. He closes with an endorsement for ways that the Somali Inter-riverine Studies Association may be able to redress at least some of these "oversights."

Hussein M. Adam (Chapter 7) offers preliminary reflections on how four great political theorists of Western and Islamic traditions would have viewed the current Somali crisis. He concludes that Ibn Khaldun's concept of *asabia* (social solidarity) helps to explain how Siyad misjudged the cohesiveness of the traditional *asabia*; how the warlords continue to confuse and confront this traditional *asabia*; and how the fragile parts of the former Somali Republic, especially Somaliland, are experimenting with new forms of *asabia*.

CHAPTER ONE

Crisis in Somalia:
From Tyranny to Anarchy

Ali A. Mazrui

I. Introduction

Somalia, an important member of the international community, is disintegrating, and it is of vital necessity that it be rescued. It is a country of six to eight million people divided across clans and to some extent across regions. There are some differentiations in modes of economic production, but it is overwhelmingly pastoralist in character. The religion is predominantly Islam. It is a member of the Organization of African Unity, the League of Arab States, the Organizations of the Islamic Conference and the United Nations. The territory is about the size of Texas: 246,000 square miles.

Somalia has had an horrendous post-colonial experience. How could a people seemingly much more coherent and cohesive, much more homogeneous than most African countries, have descended to forms of behavior that are, to outsiders, almost inexplicable? The descent into desperation has a variety of causes and there are many villains. Some of the causes of collapse are recent, others have deeper historical and sociological reasons.

First and foremost there is the tension between an ancient pastoral culture and the demands of modern statehood. Second, there is a more typical post-colonial tension between the danger of tyranny and the danger of anarchy. Third, a paradox is evident in the Somali experience between high emotions of nationalism and a low sense of nationhood: the Somalis are capable of nationalist emotions, but they are not yet fully a nation in the sense of identity. Finally, there are the international and human consequences of the Somali crisis.

II. Historical Basis of Somali Society

First, broadly, as an interpretation of Africa's sociological situation, the continent is divided between lovers of land and lovers of animals. Lovers of land are cultivators, settled agricultural farmers. Lovers of animals are pastoralists, herding cattle, or camels, or sheep and goats. Lovers of land have demonstrated in Africa's experience a greater responsiveness to capitalism and the money economy. Lovers of animals have tended to be more resistant to the Protestant ethic and capitalist formation. Lovers of land have been more responsive to cultural westernization and Western education. Lovers of animals have on the whole been resistant to cultural westernization. Lovers of land have experience of statehood in some cases from precolonial days. Though not all lovers of land were formal states in Africa in precolonial days, many were. Lovers of animals, on the other hand, in precolonial days were usually members of stateless societies: tribes and clans. Lovers of land have sometimes had experience of elaborate political and social hierarchy even before the impact of the modern state. Lovers of animals, on the other hand, had ordered anarchy ruled through consensus rather than coercion.

In neighboring Kenya the best illustration of this dichotomy is not with our Kenyan Somali, but between the Kikuyu and the Maasai. The Kikuyu are lovers of land and are the largest ethnic community in Kenya. The Maasai are lovers of animals with doctrines and ideologies deeply influenced by a cattle fixation. The cattle of the world are deemed to be the rightful property of the Maasai people, just dispersed by the accidents of history. In the Horn of Africa the two contrasts could be between the Amhara, who until recently were the dominant ethnic group in Ethiopia, and the Somali. The Amhara, lovers of land, built a remarkable empire and had a monarchical dynasty which, according to their traditions started with King Solomon and the Queen of Sheba, and lasted 3,000 years ending in 1974. The Somali, on the other hand are, in our terms, primarily lovers of animals: sheep, goats, cattle, but especially the camel. They were, and continue to be, fiercely egalitarian and individualistic. In precolonial times Somalia was a nation without a state, a society without rulers. Its system of government was ordered anarchy -- order without government.

III. Colonialism and Notions of State

Then came European colonization and with it the ideology of the state. The ideology included concepts of territorial sovereignty and consciousness of frontiers and borders. For the nomadic section of the Somali pastoralists, this was often a severe constraint. The Somali people found themselves split five ways by the scramble for Africa: a fragment under the British in British Somaliland, a fragment under the Italians in Italian Somaliland, some under French sovereignty, others under Ethiopian sovereignty, and still others incorporated into Kenya. The people were split five ways and their flags reflect this in a five-cornered star. The new ideology of the state also replaced rule without rulers with colonial administrators. Paradoxically, the colonial partition both divided the Somali and united them. Colonialism did indeed fragment them, but they became more conscious of themselves as Somali people instead of as clans. Their resentment of partition and of domination kindled a new self-awareness; a new Somali nationalism was born, but was it nationalism without adequate national commitment?

The ideology of the state began to erode Somali skills of ordered anarchy: how to have order without government, how to have rules without rulers. Westerners had come with the so-called beginnings of a sovereign future state and, if Max Weber is right about the state being a monopoly of the physical use of force, the introduction of Western-style political systems was setting the stage for a possible clash of cultures of huge consequences in the future.

When independence came, it took the form of unifying Italian Somaliland and British Somaliland. Somali nationalism made the two halves want to unite, but was there enough national identity to keep them united? Nationalism is a form of infatuation which may be enough to make two halves propose marriage, even want marriage, even go into the ceremony of marriage. But nationalism on its own is not enough to keep the two halves married.

IV. Pitfalls of Independence

Although Somalia entered independence as a democratic system, it faced the two dangers of every post-colonial state in Africa and in the Muslim world. The danger of tyranny on one side and the danger of anarchy on the other. Every African country, every Muslim country has had to walk the tightrope: on one side the abyss of anarchy and on the other, the depths of tyranny. But in the case of Somalia, there was a different precolonial order. In precolonial Somalia there was very little government, or no government at all, and still there was order. This arrangement does not work in post-colonial conditions. Tyranny is centralized violence, either direct or structural. Anarchy, in conditions of post-colonial realities, is decentralized violence, sometimes politicized disorder, rebellion against regime. It can sometimes develop into ungovernability. Anarchy then becomes a synonym for chaos. It was not a synonym for chaos in precolonial Somalia. Tyranny can take the form of military rule, or it can take, in African and Muslim conditions, the form of a one party government or dictatorship.

In the case of Somalia, the tyranny matured in October 1969. Under General Mohammed Siyad Barre, the military took over. At first the regime combined tyranny with Somali nationalism. The nationalism included an attempt to reconquer the Ogaden from Ethiopia, inhabited by ethnic Somali, and the hope of reuniting Djibouti -- the former French Somaliland — with the new Somalia.

Siyad Barre tried to combine Somali nationalism with socialism and Islam. He strengthened relations with the Soviet Union and let the Soviets build a naval base at Berbera, a Somali port. Somalia was being turned into a massive collective armory. Barre undermined tradition further by substantially de-legitimizing the Muslim clergy, even executing some members when they protested against his reforms. Not all his reforms were bad; some were more pro-women than the clergy preferred. But a brutal modernization, even on the gender question, was not the right way to go about social reform. Executing dissenters was not the right approach toward securing legitimacy. He was sowing the seeds for future chaos. The religious base of Somali tradition was being eroded by the socialist tyrant in military uniform.

Siyad Barre's policies had elements in common with Pol Pot and the Khymer Rouge in Cambodia. Pol Pot wanted to agriculturalize the urban population, send them back to the farm, in a kind of brutal re-ruralization. Barre also wanted to agriculturalize Somalis, but not urban Somali; he focused on the Somali pastoralists. He wanted to take them from pastoral nomadism to the field for cultivation - a form of brutal modernization, a blow to the ancient ways of the Somali people.

V. Superpower Connection

Siyad Barre's friendship with the United States began during the Carter administration after Barre expelled the Soviets. In 1974, a revolution deposed the Ethiopian Emperor Haile Selassie who had been a great friend of the United States. Prior to this time, the US had a military base in Ethiopia and the Soviets enjoyed the hospitality of the Somalis next door. When Ethiopia's imperial system was overthrown, allegiances shifted dramatically; the superpowers swapped client states. Ethiopia, once America's client became a Soviet client; Somalia became American. The US thus inherited the Soviet naval facilities and North American arms now poured into Somalia.

Somalia has been a victim of both the Cold War and the end of the Cold War. During the Cold War the strategic value of Somalis to the superpowers was inflated. As a result the two superpowers poured armaments into that little country. Once again the stage was being set for the type of brutalization that tyranny at first unleashed and later, anarchy would exacerbate. When the Cold War ended, the strategic value of Somalia plunged like stock market prices on Wall Street at the start of the Great Depression. At one time it was a poor arid country but with a strategic location. In the global scheme of things, the two mighty capitals of the world -- Washington and Moscow -- were competing to make sure the country was in the "right" hands. Then suddenly the Cold War ended and that value plunged like a mighty dollar no longer mighty. Both the rise in inflated strategic value which took the form of arming it to the limit and the fall as a result of the Cold War were devastating for Somalia. No one cared enough to help prevent its disintegration.

VI. Who Should Help Somalia?

Ideally, Somalia should have been saved by fellow Africans - a kind of Pax Africana, Africans policing themselves or policing each other. It has been attempted in Liberia by a West African force drawn from several nations. At first it seemed that Africans had finally begun to police each other. Perhaps this was cause for celebration although for the time being the results are inconclusive.

A second preference would have been a rescue of Somalia by members of the Organization of the Islamic Conference (OIC), a kind of Pax Islamica. But even the few hundred Pakistani troops who are already in Somalia arrived under United Nations (UN) auspices. There has not been a rise to the trumpet call of the green flag of Islam.

A third preference for the Somali rescue would have been under the League of Arab States - a kind of Pax Arabica or Pax Arabiana. However, so soon after the Gulf War of 1991, the Arab states were rather cautious --though Egypt would have been prepared to contribute troops if it was realistic to create an Arab rescue operation. Somalis are not

Arabs; they are not native speakers of the Arabic language. They are, however, members of the Arab League and have been very close to the Arab world, culturally and economically, over the centuries. It therefore made sense for them to look to the Arab world for some kind of rescue.

A fourth preference would have been a truly multinational task force to both pacify and feed Somalia, a kind of Pax Humana which would combine troops from carefully and sensitively selected countries. What we have instead is a Pax Americana - a primarily American force. It is essentially Pax Americana with a UN fig leaf. However, it is Pax Americana with an important difference: at least in intention this military force is designed to save lives rather than to destroy them - which is more than we can say about Desert Shield/Desert Storm, the Reagan intervention in Lebanon, the US invasion of Grenada, or the US invasion of Panama. This is a qualitatively different use of American troops. President Bush described the Gulf War as a symbol of the New World Order. Actually there was nothing new about that particular massacre on the Gulf. It was decidedly part of the old order of warfare.

This could be a genuine rescue of Somalis. A rescue of a people who once had order without government, who now have neither order nor government, no food to eat and who need a response from the rest of our species. Basic tensions in Somalia may still need to be resolved. The tension between the residual culture of consensus and the new ideology of statehood. A balance, an equilibrium, a new form of reconciliation between Somali ancient culture and the demands of the modern state has to be worked out. The contending parties of the old order have to find a *modus vivendi*, a basis for accommodation. That tightrope of all post-colonial states in the Muslim world and in Africa will still be there. We still have to try to help Somalia deal with it just as we have to help Liberians deal with their situation.

VII. Ultimately Somalis Must Build the Nation

Somalia is that incredible entity: a nation with nationalism, but without a sufficiently strong sense of national identity to produce massive national commitment. It is like a family which sometimes has a sense of family consciousness, especially if it is defending itself against aggressive neighbors. At that point, a sense of family unity arises. Yet in daily life, they lack sufficient family cohesion. They quarrel and inflict pain upon each other. The Somali are like that family. Indeed, these are a people who are in many ways interrelated: they look alike, they speak almost alike, and they understand each other's sensibilities. George Bernard Shaw said that the Americans and the British were a people divided by a common language. What is tragically more true is that the Somali are a people divided by the same culture. The culture of the language of poetry, of religion, of clans, has moved in directions that are fundamentally divisive at the national front. The Somalis must consolidate nationhood and tap the fountain of nationalism, not just for defensive purposes, not just for oratorical purposes, not just in moments of anger, but in a behavior of sustained commitment. However, they need help right now before they can do that job. If the world cannot only feed the Somali children, but help the whole society back on its feet, then the concept of the New World Order would no longer be just an abuse of language, it would no longer be prosaic. If the world can get the Somali back on their feet, satisfactorily fed and well enough to help themselves, the triumph might deserve that most moving of all tributes - a powerful Somali poem to celebrate a human achievement.

CHAPTER TWO

A Few Words on Somalia's Crisis: The Need for a Responsible Answer

Mohamed Aden Sheikh

When the Somali Studies Symposium first opened at the Jubba Hotel in 1979, it was a cause of jubilation for many of us. Our aim for this international gathering could be summarized in these four points:

1. Given the expansion of the literacy campaign, it was the conviction of many among us that we definitely needed support from the international community. We thought the best way to obtain the support was precisely this kind of intellectual debate and assessment;

2. We were concerned that our cultural heritage risked disappearing -- the notable elders who were the true repositories of our cultural heritage were fading away -- while an attitude of indifference pervaded the youth and urbanized folk. It was high time that the orally-transmitted culture be transcribed. In this endeavor we definitely needed help and scholarly skills;

3. Somalia's doors would be opened to international scholars and learned people, thus letting them freely observe and closely study the

way of life. We could then assess the aspirations of the people and their chances for growth as a self-sustained nation;

4. A solid bond would be created between the international community of researchers and cultural institutions, and Somali researchers.

I am glad these few seeds have blossomed over the years, suffering and producing. I would like to express my deep thanks to all those who have kept alive this valuable instrument of culture, exchange and communication. But I am not sure that we Somalis have done enough or have always kept our initial commitment to stick to the Somali people's best interests.

It is this frustration that urges me to speak about the Somalis' situation today. Against the hope and deep feeling expressed in John Donne's poem: "Any man's death diminishes me, because I am involved in Mankind; and therefore never send to know for whom the bell tolls; it tolls for thee" -- the Somalis have proven that the bell tolls for someone else! Many knowledgeable people have determined that humankind has concerned itself with its capacity for violence and destruction ever since it began to reflect upon experience. "Pain and loss caused by aggressive acts," Dr. Prelinger wrote, "could well have been one source of contemplation, of questioning, and of notions of evil and hope for salvation." Somalis are still in search of this kind of contemplation, of this sort of notion.

I think the reason lies in the fact that since the aftermath of our independence we have relied on our "irresponsibility." We were irresponsible when it came to handling democracy in terms of social contract; irresponsible towards our educational system, economic development, in dealing with neighboring countries and in the ambivalence of our foreign relations in general. Almost everyone among us acted as if there would always be "someone" who would take care of our real or imagined problems. From that perspective, paradoxically, everyone thought of himself as master of his own destiny. As soon as the premise of our self-government was set, we thought we were smart enough to recapture severed relations with our respective clans, in order to win, rule and control, without bothering to share the burdens (and privileges) of "power" and not expecting to pay the inevitable toll.

After almost ten years this "irresponsible" management led to confusion and lack of credibility of our statehood. It triggered a coup d'etat that was enthusiastically welcomed by most, though nowadays, it seems that everyone is a stranger to these events. We depict them as the devil's concentration of wickedness, that we rightfully fought so long against, with so many risks. Yet we were all present there. And we did what we could to regain our breath. Most of our Somali countrymen and countrywomen had, for a short time, the dream of riding the early waves of enthusiasm. They worked hard in order to improve the situation of the country, from one of the world's least developed to a reasonably self-sustained nation. Alas, we lost the bet because we were again irresponsible enough to think that we were the exception to the rule: no African military ruler has ever led his country down the very difficult path towards true democracy.

It is easier for dictators to convince themselves that it is better to think on behalf of the people, for the good of the people, instead of letting the people express their feelings and choices directly. For the sake of unity, and out of fear of disorder and confusion, many of us worked with and tried to take advantage of what we used to call the "revolutionary process" in order to contrive new approaches and show new paths for development and growth to our deprived people. We created the monster who outmaneuvered us and apparently preempted most of our good intentions and the creative perspectives we hold and fought so long for, and paid so dearly for.

Once and for all we must recognize this simple fact and from here proceed not to rewrite Somali history as anyone pleases, but gather our forces and energies and stand up as responsible men and women so that we may regain our statehood. There is no point in arguing over recent history: there will be time for that and maybe others will do better. What matters now is that we all must face the reality of the tragic conclusion of Siyad's regime and its fateful consequences. But we are no better off in the hands of opposition forces, for two reasons:

1. In organizing themselves, they went centuries back into what we may call the clan's womb;

2. They have not been able to agree on anything but the toppling of the dictatorship.

Clearly that was not enough. Labeling themselves as Somali movements, patriots, salvation fronts, congresses and so on, they were anything but Somali national representatives. In fact, they did not represent even the clans or tribes that they were claiming to belong to. Army commanders, state officials, and some businessmen, none of them freely elected by an assembly of their own kinship, assumed the leadership of every segment of the old society. Whatever their hidden motives were, all of them stated that their objectives were simply to remove a hated and intolerable dictatorship, and re-establish unity and democracy in the country. If they were to be believed---and most people genuinely believed them -- there would have been no problem at all following the removal of the dictator and his followers. Instead, the worst of our problems were still to come, just after his departure.

Suffice it to say that all have suffered from that "liberation." People were not even allowed to bury their dead. They renounced their property. They lost their identity. They could not even save their own lives. Of course, nobody misses the defunct regime. But we ought to take note of the extremely desolate fact that since then the Somali people have only experienced chaos, devastation and loss. And by far the worst thing: the situation of "statelessness," which no other people in modern times have known. Citizens of other states cannot really appreciate the internal vacuum and the external difficulties that are involved. "Statelessness" doesn't only mean you jeopardize or lose your political sovereignty. It means much more. It means that you have been evicted from your house by unknown forces, for the most inexplicable and unexpected reasons, expelled from your country to nowhere in the world. You look behind you and see nothing but burning cities, schools, hospitals. You hear the screams of the dying and the hopeless.

I always thought that, in any event, a child, any child, could pass through the eye of a needle. The elderly and the sick too. But the innocent have been defiled and many Somalis have proven irrefutably that I was wrong. So, we lost not only our municipal records, our libraries, all our lives' documents, dear friends and relatives and places --- we lost part of our souls as well. In this insane fratricidal war, none of our national values, tribal heritage, religious teachings or political ethics have held fast by any degree. Perhaps we will learn, over the next decade, what a waste it all was. But still the questions stand: Why haven't those militarized clans, so badly misled, come up with a decent plan to get us through this mess? Why are they still warring and killing and raping after three years? Why should they have any sort of power? Is it true that uncontrolled gangs are just rummaging around, randomly plundering and sabotaging all peace efforts and goodwill missions? If that is the case, then we should mobilize everybody who condemns them, and combat them. But since mobilization is not happening, I have another theory.

Somali society has been completely blinded by a sort of abysmal rage and frustration. Whatever the small, urbanized section may think or do it seems powerless to cope with the human avalanche that besieged the cities and towns. This human avalanche was grouped in such a way as to guarantee itself some cohesion. There was a balance of clan connotation, but more in terms of clan-based grievances and demagoguery; a balance of resentment against neighboring clans over recent or ancestral feuds; but more than all this there was the violent need to destroy the central state, with its laws, police and army, and opulent cities, not just to change it. Especially the aggressive groups that seized the capital were earnestly working to get rid of the old order---yet they offered nothing new to take its place. Everyone was at a loss for what to do next.

The first worry was how to survive among this shambles and stick together. The international NGO's provided for that, bringing, sometimes unwillingly, needed foodstuffs. The international media bestowed on them the titles and the aura they needed to present themselves as the new masters of Somalia. And finally, the international community, after an unending huddling and bloody tug of war, considered them the only viable interlocutors in the peace-keeping process.

Their masterpiece accomplishment was the revival of clan loyalty that for most of us had been only marginally present in the political confrontation. They considered it a means of identification for the country folk. In an effort to demagnetize our collective national memory and historical struggle for independence and unity, and with the intention of restoring intense feelings of clanship, the aggressive warlords borrowed many of the works and publications on the myths and anecdotes of Somali genealogy in order to work out a renewed systematic pattern of Somali clan divisions. They came across certain publications in which some well-intentioned socio-anthropologists and political scientists argued that, after all, perhaps it would do better for the Africans to follow their old tribal-community pattern instead of this continuous trial and error to grasp the strange ways of Western democracy. That helped much in the creation of a clanomania mentality -- which seeks to redefine and reinforce the ancient tribal ties and boundaries in order to defend some vested interest of a few power-hungry men or greedy groups. That is why one often meets people who blatantly uphold their clan identity in opposition to national identity, and are so eager to support the self-righteous positions of their faction. But how can the Somali people be divided merely along patriarchal lineage? And where does the intricate mixture of maternal lineage end? What are the cut-off points? Can we realistically fathom a state based on one clan imposing its rule over the others? Or even a federation of clans? Three issues are highly relevant:

1. We know that the clan-based society is a politically male-dominated society: how will the advocates of the clan "constituencies" deal with the other half of society, the women?

2. We also know that there are many small clans that will not join other small clans as well as people who have their own ideas and

whose interests do not precisely coincide with those of the larger clans: what shall be done there?

3.   Then we come back to the question of responsibility: the clan-based society does not recognize the individual's responsibility. The clan, *en toto*, is responsible for any major wrong-doing perpetrated by any of its members. One can imagine the inevitable and intolerable consequences of a "straight-jacketed" justice such as the clans adhere to. To put it bluntly, it can never work.

I wonder, who is compelling us to be squeezed between giving loyalty to one of the clans, and winding up as stooges for a criminal warlord or follower of some fundamentalist fringe? We should know by now that none of these kinds of organizations or that sort of leadership will bring any benefit for our nation; nor will any of them last for long. Sure, many people, among them some Western scholars, are trying to attribute to one or another of the aforementioned actors on the Somali political scene a positive value that could lead to a viable, democratic development without deviating from the tradition of Western socio-political evolution.

Now that we find ourselves at the threshold of a new appraisal of Somalia's fate, what can we really do? The UN Secretary General has recently stated that he has but few options left: if the UN member states supply the necessary troops -- almost 25,000-30,000 men -- the policy of the UN's mission would remain essentially unchanged. Otherwise, he will only seek to keep the country's airports and ports open. Politically he might propose three different scenarios to the world body:

1.   Hand the country over to one or a coalition of tribal-military faction leaders, which would result in further regional and district fragmentation;

2.   Attempt to reinstate the old forms of inter-clan coexistence, renouncing any form of national structure and plunging the country into the obscurity of the obsolete values of tribalism;

3.   Appoint a commissioner, entrusting our people and our destiny to some foreign governor. We would be the first of all countries in the world to suffer this tragic and derisory fate!

Is this the end of it all? Of Somalia, of the Somalis and their culture and traditions? I just cannot believe it. I am well aware of the terrible circumstances that have forced many of us to flee our country. I also know that the world outside has not welcomed us warmly. To carve a small niche in any place is hard, sometimes impossible. Many of us have been humiliated, others persecuted and deported. We have often been made ashamed of being Somalis, of belonging to a country and people possessed of a single, wrong idea, that is capable of a single thing: killing each other, only to show its self-inflicted wounds and beg for a few sacks of rice from a world weary of charity and beggars.

That is why the overseas Somalis and their friends bear a great responsibility: relinquishing political inactivity and dissertations which are purely academic, theoretical. The international appeals and the lamentations of our people are useless at this point: we are the ones who do not want peace, who are not respecting deals, who kill anyone who wants to help! The very fact that many Somalis in the diaspora have tried their best to organize conferences, fora, meetings and sent messages to forward alternative approaches -- does not help much. At this time something more and something different is needed. First of all, it takes a personal and operative commitment. Somalia and the Somalis do not need weapons, much less armies. They must not argue over tribalism, regionalism or secession. In due time all this will be attended to. What Somalia needs now is an army made up of its best representatives: professionals, economists, farmers, teachers, health-care workers, jurists, artists and writers; Somalia needs all of them now, in these terrible circumstances, to prove to the world that it possesses a cadre of skilled, able persons, an intelligentsia capable of changing the fate of their country and filling the gap in the social fabric between the crude, pastoral mentality and the bogus leaders. We must weigh the possibility of returning to Somalia. Hundreds, thousands of us must return in order to strengthen and enhance the immense efforts made -- occasionally with the help of foreign friends -- by the few who have remained.

Is this utopian? Perhaps. Risky? Possibly. But let us also remember that our country is on the brink of being wiped off the world map, like the Assyrians and Babylonians. At least they left an intelligible trace behind them. What we would leave behind is just a huge trash-heap of questions. Let us also remember that nothing in the world has ever been achieved without the utopia of a few and the risk of many! This is more than a suggestion. Can we develop a "counter-exodus" program together, without ill feelings, without prejudice, and with all the goodwill which the dramatic nature of this situation calls for? "*Cir tarraray rag waa tolikaraa, Taako labadeede!*" i.e. men [of good will] can mend even a rip in the sky. I hope our gathering in this Fifth Congress of Somali Studies will help us in this endeavor.

CHAPTER THREE

Light At the End of the Tunnel: Some Reflections on the Struggle of the Somali National Movement

Ibrahim Megag Samater

I. Prologue

What follows is not a narrative account of the activities of the Somali National Movement (SNM) since the start of its struggle against the military regime of Siyad Barre. Nor is it an impartial academic evaluation of its performance and impact on Somali politics. It is not an analysis of the Siyad Barre regime or an examination of the role of external players in the Somali debacle. It is none of these and yet it is all of them. It is none of the above because it does not deal with each aspect with the necessary and sufficient depth and extent required for full treatment. It is all of these because these aspects of the Somali tragedy are touched upon in one way or the other.

This presentation is as its title says: reflections. And reflections by their very nature are untidy. They go back and forth in time and cross-sectionally across topics without any predesigned order. In this respect many aspects of the Somali problem are discussed. The zigzags in international policy towards Somalia, together with many false starts, are described. The experience and development of the Republic of Somaliland and its essential difference from the rest of Somalia is brought out. After a digression on the problems of politico-economic processes in Africa, a return is made to critical evaluation of the struggle of the SNM.

But there is method in the madness. In reviewing topics, the connecting thread is to seek those factors that were causal in the decay and destruction of the Somali state and the effect of that destruction on civil society. The seeking for causal factors itself means the identification of those elements essential for revival. In this search for casual factors, the torch light focuses on several dualities: dependence v. delving inward; authoritarian state power v. participatory democracy and traditional structure v. "modern" institutions. Even though all these dualities are interconnected, there is a contradiction -- complementary spectrum within each duality: in other words, a dialectical struggle.

There is a parable in Somali children's folklore about a race between a fox and a tortoise. Both finally reached home. But the fast fox, in its hurry, met with many obstacles, difficulties, and twists and turns. We may say that the fox's situation was a case of more haste and less speed. The tortoise, on the other hand, was definitely slow, but it reached home with steady and sure steps and with less damage. Can we take this parable as an illustration of the choices available to us in social change: depending on tradition itself for continuity (tortoise) or throwing the old overboard and welcoming the new with gusto? Or is a dialectical intermix better than the either/or?

The discussion of such matters in the text is conducted with specific reference to the practical struggle of the SNM -- as well as its vision. It is therefore neither a theoretical evaluation nor a practical account. It has a little of both, but it aims to sum up the experience in an introductory way!

Finally, I am not impartial. As one of the leaders of the SNM itself, I cannot be impartial. Irrespective of whether we in the SNM made mistakes or not, I cannot be impartial to the cause of liberation against dictatorial despotism and injustice. But this does not mean lack of objectivity. A partisan for liberty cannot do without a merciless search for truth. Impartiality is required of a judge in a judicial case. But historical causes require partisanship with objectivity.

II. Predilections of Policy

A cursory glance at the confusion and tragic complexity of Somali politics today may convince the observer -- and sometimes the participants -- of the impossibility of a solution. Many are persuaded to throw up their hands in despair. At the same time, many players plunged into the deep water of Somali politics with undue haste, only to pop up again and get out without giving the swim a try.

The pessimist has many points stacked in his favor.

1. The United States, the major power in post-cold war politics, led the international community -- that was moved by pictures of starving children -- into the quick plunge of Operation Restore Hope. The amassed technology, the number of troops, the apparent resolve, the pomp of the military machine, and the glitter of the media -- it was a big show, marvelous to watch. Nation after nation joined the bandwagon and declared its willingness to send troops to Somalia. For the general public of world opinion and specifically that of the United States -- uninitiated in the history and slippery politics of our small nation -- it was as if the international community had at last come of age. The cold war is over and peace is no longer endangered by superpower rivalry. As for local conflicts, the world can act, in a collective, multilateral fashion led by the only remaining superpower, to resolve them or at least contain them and prevent them from spreading and disturbing the larger prevalent peace. The humanitarian consequences of these local conflicts can simultaneously be dealt with in a resolute manner. Thus, the stage was set and Somalia became the prime test of the new interventionist mission[1] -- a contradiction in terms or the first installment of newspeak phrases of an Orwellian age -- which became mired in a local civil war, shooting and killing the people it was supposed to save, and destroying their homes. The interventionists just added a new name -- UN/US -- to the long list of the contesting so-called "Warlords." Finally, Operation Restore Hope ended up -- via UNOSOM II -- in debacle, as "Operation Despair Rescue."

2. The United Nations Organization, as the depository of the international community's collective wisdom and systems of action, has been bungling the Somali crisis from beginning to end. The day Siyad Barre was defeated, the UN bodies and staff fled as if they were part of his regime,[2] rather than staying and performing their expected duty of serving the people. If evacuation was dictated by reasons of staff

security, a rationale not wholly acceptable, then at least a stop-gap measure and a plan of return should have been put in place.

In lieu of a consistent policy and line of action, what we have witnessed on the part of these international organizations led by the UN is a mass of *ad hoc* activities moving like a pendulum from extreme to extreme. From the extreme of total neglect and abandonment there was a sudden move again to a position of over-involvement and domination. The mandate was no longer confined to the traditional functions of the UN and its related agencies, such as the delivery of humanitarian aid and peacekeeping. It now included forced disarmament of the factions involved in the civil war (in other words, direct intervention which, evidently, cannot be neutral), "guiding" or, to tell the truth, running the process of reconciliation and attempting to determine the shape and form of its end product -- a government of "national unity." The new concept of peacemaking was coined and the Secretary-General had to work hard to obtain new resolutions from the Security Council in order to obtain the empowerment necessary to implement these new burdens. In the meantime, the UN has to create its own special bureaucracy -- United Nations Operation for Somalia or UNOSOM -- to carry on administrative as well as judicial functions, because there is no "government." In other words, the UN put itself in the position of a new outside or colonial administrator after the collapse of the Siyad dictatorship until such time as a government of "national unity" is created. This aggressive interventionism on the part of the UN apparatus has been given a jolt by the withdrawal of American -- and later other western) troops early in 1994. But despite this shock, up to now, we see no sign of the UN apparatus abandoning its political interventionism. We see no indication of a broader and wiser policy with a long-term vision to replace the current *ad hocism.*

3. Last, but not least, the pessimist would point to the abysmal record of the Somalis themselves. For twenty-one long years, they have acquiesced to one of history's most horrible tyrannies. After the first few years of Siyad Barre's "revolutionary honeymoon," the nature of his regime became clear to all. By the end of the Somali-Ethiopian war of 1977-78, it became evident to all who could think clearly that the continued existence of this regime undermined the future existence of the nation itself. Somalis with conscience foresaw that if the regime were allowed to continue to pursue its policies unchecked, that by the time it is overthrown or it just comes to its natural end, there may be nothing left to save. They were, like the prophet Noah, crying at the deaf ears of their countrymen and the rest of the world, that the monster should be stopped

and the monstrosity put to an end.

Yet the reaction of their Somali countrymen was to cooperate in the continuation of their own oppression. They have allowed Siyad Barre to play on the characteristic rivalry of the clans so well that they were willing to be hoodwinked into bribery, cajolement and blackmail, even to bear arms against a so-called hostile clan. The fervent competition for the regime's favor reached such a pitch that any man of integrity who resisted the co-option risked imprisonment, the loss of life and property, or being labeled as a madman. Likewise, any group, clan, or region, attempting to safeguard its rights, protect itself or voice opinions for the better running of the nation's affairs risked genocide by the regime...with the apparently willing cooperation by the rest of the Somali community. It somehow escaped the attention of Somalis that the acquiescence -- if not downright approval and collaboration -- by the rest of the community in singling out a single section, clan, or region for persecution and genocide spelled the same fate for the rest.

Nonetheless, the end of the regime came through a combination of a number of factors. The persistence, to the point of death, of the minority that was leading the armed struggle against it, at last proved that the dictator can be opposed, resisted and finally defeated. The defeat of his army by the militants of the Somali National Movement and the total collapse of the governmental machinery in the North after 1988 encouraged the incipient opposition in the South to be braver. With some help from the SNM, the United Somali Congress (USC), representing the bulk of the population of the center from Galkacayo to Mogadishu and the Somali Patriotic Movement (SPM) of the Kismayo area were able to fan the flames of the armed struggle against Siyad Barre in the south. They were joined by the normally silent, but very large population, west of Mogadishu and all the way down to Kismayo. These people in the southwest, who were under-represented throughout all the regimes, now had the chance to participate in some real action determining their destiny through their organizations -- the newly formed Somali Democratic Movement (SDM) and a southern wing of the Somali National Movement (SNM).

By this time, the Siyad regime was near collapse. True to its nature, the dictatorship was unable to compromise. Whatever carrots it offered were either wrongly delivered, insufficient, or offered too late. Instead, it continued to alienate and antagonize ever newer elements of the society. The clever manipulation of the divisive clan structure of Somali society paid its final dividend of reducing the manipulator to what he really was -- a lonely madman. The international press, at this time, dubbed him the "Mayor of Mogadishu." The loss of the North, and the closure of Berbera port, the main exit port for Somali exports of livestock, put the regime in financial bankruptcy. At this time also, with the horrible massacres of Hargeisa and Burao becoming evident to the whole international community, those governments supporting the dictatorship could no longer do so brazenly and had to terminate their aid to him.

4. Whatever the cause may be, the pessimist would continue arguing -- whether through the sole action of the opposition, whether through erosion of internal and external support, or whether through old age and madness, the dictator was finally pushed out. But did the Somalis seize this long-awaited opportunity to engage, now that Siyad Barre was out of the picture? Did genuine reconciliation efforts pick up the pieces, rebuild the torn social fabric of their society, heal the wounds, and put their nation back on the road? The pessimist would give a clear and resounding NO. He would point to the horrible bloodletting that ensued after Siyad Barre, to the senseless fratricidal war of clans, to the unending victimization of the weakest, that finally led to the international intervention mentioned earlier. He would point to the inability of present Somali leaders and the so-called movements they represent, despite all the pushing and promoting of international organizations and friendly neighbors, to come to any sensible working arrangement of their affairs so far. He would point to the adamant refusal earlier in 1989 of the SNM, the USC, and the SPM -- the three movements who were conducting the armed struggle against the regime at the time -- of any and all initiatives at cease fire and dialogue between them and the Siyad Barre regime.

These movements, in those days, indicated the futility of any dialogue with Siyad Barre, their unwillingness to grant him on the table what he has already lost in the field, and argued instead the appropriateness of conducting any dialogue, compromise, and rearrangement of their future by the Somalis themselves outside the framework of the Siyad Barre regime. This looked like more than an empty promise when the three movements made a formal agreement in mid-1990 among themselves on the modalities of their cooperation during the struggle against the regime and after. Specifically, the agreement envisioned that after the overthrow of the dictator, the movement(s) responsible for the victory will form a government of national unity led by, but not necessarily confined to, them.

Despite the glimmer of hope provided by this agreement, the actual behavior of the signatory movements at the hour of victory -- the pessimist's argument continues -- was quite contrary to the letter and spirit of the agreement. Whatever the politics and internal pressures acting upon them, separately or concurrently, a faction of the USC formed a "government" of its own without consulting its partners and even parts of its most active wings. The SNM declared the separation of the North -- the former British Somaliland -- from the rest of the country and formed the Republic of Somaliland. The SPM, for a short while, fought against its former ally, the USC. The description of the subsequent melee need not detain us here.

The pessimists themselves can be considered to be of three types:

(a) Those who have given up hope that the Somalis can make their own history, and can come up with a solution to the crisis. This view looks for an outside solution and, in a nutshell, is calling for recolonization, with all the consequences this entails not only for Somalis, but also for the rest of Africa and other Third World countries wherever and whenever local conflicts become intractable.

(b) Those who despair of any solution from outside. This point of view considers the Somali clan structure, the political chess game that goes along with it, and the enigmatic nomadic psychology of the Somalis as too much of a puzzle for non-Somalis to tackle. Non-Somalis can play only a secondary, complementary role, but the initiatives have to be taken by the Somalis.

(c) Those who despair of both internal and external solutions. This point of view -- the most dismal -- waits for a miracle to happen. Well, "miracles" -- in the sense of the improbable -- do happen. But when they do, they demand as their prerequisite somebody who is willing to take the initiative, and who. despite the tremendous odds, perseveres with an unshakable faith in the pursuance of the vision. "Faith" as the old adage maintains "moves mountains."

Ironically, policy options recommended by the pessimist of the first type are the same as those preferred by the enthusiasts of the new global interventionism. Similarly, policy recommendations resulting from the pessimism of the second type more often than not coincide with isolationist views -- a sort of unrealistic *laissez-faire* attitude toward international relations. Since one or the other of these attitudes was predominant at any one time in international circles (as well as in sections of the Somali elites), we should not be surprised at seeing involvement alternating quickly between policy extremes of over-involvement to total neglect that made many of us giddy.

III. False Starts

In this presentation, we differ with all of the above conceptions and viewpoints as well as the lines of action that flow from them. We believe the Somali clan structure, and the politics it reflects, to be no more mysterious than other more or less "ethnic" systems pertaining elsewhere in Africa and Asia. It is a structure that can be studied (and has been studied), analyzed, and understood. As such, it is amendable to policy-making, though not totally malleable as some may think. The cultural, linguistic, and religious homogeneity of the Somali people is not a guarantee against conflict, but helps in understanding and facilitates matters of policy-making. Such analyses and understanding are not a monopoly of Somalis alone. Outsiders, unhampered by clan affiliation, can give objective and impartial analysis and recommendations, provided they have no axe to grind.

Useful foreign contributions to the present Somali crisis in the form of arbitration, encouragement of productive local processes, and material and humanitarian assistance are not only possible, but necessary at this critical stage in which Somali institutions either have broken down or are in an incapacitated state. Foreign players will range from private volunteer organizations, foreign governments, and international bodies acting either in concert or separately, though coordination will always be essential.

Yet despite this need for foreign involvement, the argument that Somalis themselves should provide the key to the solution of their problems is basically correct, simplistic as it appears. Here, the pessimist's second argument -- those who despair of outside contribution -- have more potency than the other pessimist's view -- giving up on Somalis to make their own history. If it is true -- which we hold to be the case -- that Somalis are primarily responsible for their debacle, with some foreign muddling and intervention of course, then the converse must also be true. In other words, the Somalis must also be responsible for the remaking of their society, with some foreign help along the way. Indeed, we would go beyond the "should" and assert that they are capable of doing so.

It is the main import of this article that the Somalis not only are capable of shouldering this responsibility, but are actually doing so even now. The very process of remaking Somali society is going on before our eyes if only we care to look. The tragedy itself and the debacle of the last few years give renewed opportunities for tackling many issues that were either missed or mishandled in the recent history of the nation.

Needless to say, the availability of an opportunity does not guarantee its correct utilization or that the attempt to do so would be successful. This would depend on many factors foremost among which are the attitudes adopted, and actions taken or not taken, by the actors concerned, both domestic and foreign. The point here is that the opportunity exists. If full advantage is taken of this opportunity, chances are that Somali society would be reconstituted for the better and may provide lessons for other societies where "ethnic" conflict threatens the existence of their nations as presently constituted.

The swift alternation between over-involvement and abandonment by the international community creates its own events that in turn produce their own effects and so on. By the time a chain of events plays itself out we are so far removed from the original positions with so much damage done and opportunities lost. Thus, a new drama is played over an already ongoing tragedy, with the result that the deeper undercurrents of the original tragedy are sometimes overshadowed by the new fanfare. It is this atmosphere that creates the present tendency to overrate what is happening in Mogadishu and its surroundings, and generalize it to the rest of the country. The scriptwriters and the *dramatis personae* of the new drama concentrate on their own scenarios and subplots to the almost total neglect of the themes of the major play. If the overt playing out of certain themes (or scenes) of the original play seem to contradict or threaten their performance, the danger has to be met either by elimination or assuming its non-existence.

Viewed in this light, the total silence on the causes of the Somali tragedy may be understood. The majority of Somali leaders and intellectuals, especially in the South, are not willing to deal with the present crisis as primarily a consequence of the past and, therefore, partly a consequence of their own actions and attitudes. The crisis is viewed simply as a conflict of clans and a struggle of so-called "war lords" over power, after the collapse of central authority and the departure of Siyad Barre. Similarly in the international arena, only the present conflict is discussed as if the genie suddenly popped out of the bottle and can suddenly be put back again if only these "leaders" could be brought together to reach an agreement. Nothing is said about the long years of stifling dictatorship in which the Somali state, social values, and the institutions based upon them were being gradually undermined, a process of destruction in which foreigners wittingly or unwittingly had their share. Nothing is also said about the equally long resistance to this nihilistic rule in which alternative options of organizing society were being tested.

Such questions as to why conflict among the various clans which throughout history was confined to particular localities at particular times, now took this form of gigantic national catastrophe, or why the political factions now existing are purely clan-based, whereas the political parties prior to the 1969 military coup were on the whole built on alliances across clans, are rarely raised, let alone investigated. Somali intellectuals who, on the whole, contributed little to the struggle against the dictatorship, show scarce interest, if any, in investigating the relationship between traditional clan structures and overall political development, or the consequences of politicized clanism. Such investigation would, hopefully, enable us to see whether, and how, the traditional structure can help reshape future institutions of the nation as well as being itself reshaped. Instead, they continue to bemoan the so-called overwhelming role of clanism while their actual behavior is more "clannish" in the political sense, than their ordinary nomadic clansmen. And to their final shame, they advocate shifting the responsibility of reconstructing their society to the international community, a recommendation which is only a measure of their own bankruptcy as a group.

This lack of seriousness breeds animosity to radical departures from the beaten path. We have mentioned earlier that during the reign of the Siyad Barre dictatorship any group raising opinions for the better running of the nation's affairs were marked out for persecution, while the rest of the population either acquiesced or cooperated in that persecution. The international community also adjusted itself to that atmosphere and cooperated accordingly. The present unwillingness to dissect the legacy of that regime or the hostile attitude adopted towards those who refuse to go along with the conspiracy of silence may be considered as a continuation of those previous attitudes. The road of self-analysis and self-correction was never paved with roses. It is always easier to repress painful matters and avoid going along uncharted territory, even though the correct path may be staring us in the face.

IV. The Unique Case of Somaliland

A most revealing illustration of this suppression of relevant matters is the almost total omission by the Secretary-General of the UN in his reports to the Security Council of the Republic of Somaliland and what is happening there, as if it did not exist. On the contrary, understanding the almost lonely and heroic efforts of the people of Somaliland at reconstruction as well as the reasons for the break away holds a major key to the larger riddle of Somalia. Several impartial observers have pointed to the relative stability of Somaliland. Inheriting a totally destroyed country, with almost nothing to build on, the people of Somaliland began literally to pull themselves up by their own bootstraps. They avoided major internal conflicts and man-made famines. Today, they feed themselves, have one of the lowest malnutrition rates in Africa, and are putting in place the future edifices of a viable system of governance.

In the south, in contrast, the major destruction took place after Siyad Barre fled and not in the struggle against him. Attempts at reconciliation most often give way to renewed waves of conflict, and famine, mainly man-made, reached the huge proportions that "justified" the intervention. Here, in this contrasting situations of two parts of the same previous country, may lie a lesson. Instead of studying the relevant success of Somaliland, encouraging it and drawing conclusions that may be of use to the south, as well as to the future of the whole, we find, on the part of both the southern elite and international bureaucracy, an unreasonable animosity towards Somaliland. Instead of giving a helping hand, the UN bureaucracy is bent on destroying Somaliland and nullifying the efforts of its people, as if a cancerous growth has to be eradicated. The southern elite, on their part, repeat phrases on the sacredness of Somali unity and the inviolability of the territorial integrity of the former Somalia, while their own backyard is burning.

Be that as it may, being misunderstood, isolated, or persecuted is nothing new to the Somali National Movement (SNM) and its leaders. As the political movement which bore the brunt of the struggle against Siyad Barre, it has learned how to deal with persecution, vilification, and isolation. As the political organ that gave birth to the democratic experimentation in Somaliland, and is still guiding it in more ways than one, it has learned how to forgive, how to compromise and accommodate, and how to relinquish state power when this is dictated by the principles for which it was struggling, even at the temporary cost of its own internal unity. While the so-called "war lords" in the South are at each others throats, the Somali National Movement (SNM) did not find it difficult to transfer state power even prior to the disarmament of its liberation forces and the armed militia of other clans who opposed it during its guerrilla warfare against the military dictatorship.

I can recall no other example of a liberation movement which won power through the barrel of the gun and which was simultaneously so uninterested in ruling with its gun. Even in those cases where the movement concerned was serious about the democratic transformation of society, elaborate measures were taken after victory to ensure that the victor in the armed struggle also remained so in the peace. This was done as if the accomplishment of the required social change could only be performed by that particular organization and no other. The result of this type of political engineering is the ossification of the revolutionary movement and the gradual loss of its originally genuine support. A good example of this type of development is the FLN in Algeria. In other cases, the victor in the revolutionary armed struggle refuses the participation as partners of other actors who were in the field -- irrespective of whether they were acting in parallel for the same goal or in opposition.

Sometimes it so happens that some sections of the society are unorganized during the struggle and support neither side. The victorious revolutionary movement then interprets that dormancy as tacit support to the enemy who now lost. This section now comes under suspicion and is prevented from acting as partners in the new democracy. The result in the two latter cases is an invitation to a new round of civil war either in the early stages of the victory itself or in the ensuing later years as a reaction to the increasing monopolization of power by the victorious group. In countries where political organizations are more or less co-terminus with ethnic groups, the explosiveness of this kind of situation needs no emphasis. Such may be said to be the case in Mozambique and Angola, where the ruling groups and the opposition are now in the different stages of learning the process of conflict resolution through dialogue after a lengthy period of painful fratricide.

The new experiment in South Africa, where the leading liberation movement, the African National Congress, came to power through a process of dialogue and reconciliation with its former enemy, is a promising, though untested, development. It augurs well for the future as a promising, less violent means of achieving freedom, justice and democracy. All men of goodwill cannot but congratulate and wish well the leaders of the ANC and others involved in this new experiment. Certainly, the ANC is not a newcomer in the struggle for justice. It is almost a century old and certainly much older than many liberation movements that came to power before it did. It therefore has accumulated plenty of experience, both of its own unique struggle and that of others, that can allow it to chart a new road. Specifically, the pitfalls suffered by the peoples of Africa who, after gaining freedom from colonial rulers did not realize true liberation but slipped back into the darkness of dictatorships and misery, are very instructive. That the monopolization of power by the successful movements played a critical role in the retrogression to the abyss cannot escape the attention of the newcomers.

I have no intention of putting the SNM on the same pedestal as the African National Congress. Certainly in terms of age, the long accumulated experience, the complexity of the issues involved in its past and present struggle, the importance of the country and theater in which it is operating, as well as the stature of its leadership, the ANC is a giant. Moreover, a lot of political organizations (liberation movements as well as established political parties) are eclipsed into dwarfs. In a comparison of this sort, the SNM would appear as the dwarf of the dwarfs. It belongs not only to a small country, but its support can be considered to be based mainly on one clan of that small country. It has no particular ideology that can, despite the smallness, give it luster. And in terms of leadership, it is a listless movement.

Some may even go further and accuse the SNM of being a visionless movement, without a program, without a disciplined cadre, and thus incapable of forming a cohesive administration that would fill the void. These critics would point to the record of its administration after liberation. From 1991-93, the paralysis and the civil strife caused the people to lose patience. They replaced the SNM's administration in early 1993, despite the wishes of the then existing leaders of the SNM.

Such criticism, we maintain, takes a superficial stand. It confuses the personalities of the leadership with the organic nature of the movement. On the contrary, we are here arguing that in these seemingly negative qualities lie the greatness of the SNM. As a movement that primarily drew its support from the narrow base of a clan it succeeded in bringing down the strong edifice of the national dictatorship. The so-called lack of ideology gave it independence and resilience. The absence of "charismatic" leaders and disciplined cadre is one of the ways in which it avoided the build-up of dictatorial tendencies within itself. If the Republic of Somaliland today enjoys relative stability within the context of conditions in the Horn of Africa, then we need to try to understand why. If the people of that small country are surviving through self-reliance, despite international boycotts and deliberate sabotage, then one should try to determine how they are doing it. And if the Somalilanders have found ways to reconcile their differences and reconstruct their society, then perhaps the rest of Somalia would benefit from knowing how it has been done.

The two parts of the former Somali Republic, i.e., the former British Somaliland and the former Trusteeship territory of Somalia, have had the same historical experience since their independence and union in 1960 until the overthrow of the last government of Siyad Barre. Could the different reactions of the two parts to the breakdown of the United Somali state be due to their different colonial experiences under the British and the Italians? Maybe, for the differential impact of the two colonial systems on the underlying traditional structure could have had different consequences. Could the different reactions be due to differences in the underlying traditional structure and cultural values? Unlikely, since the points of similarities in the Somali cultural milieu, irrespective of geographical location, overwhelm points of differences. But before one delves into that distant past, it is certainly more fruitful to look into the most recent past which just merges into the present.

While we do not deny whatever influences the above-mentioned factors may have, we maintain that the relative success of the Republic of Somaliland, as well as its weaknesses, are primarily due to the experience of the SNM in the struggle against the Siyad Barre dictatorship. How it handled (or mishandled) issues at hand; how it utilized or missed opportunities; and how obstacles either enriched or obscured that experience are all part of the essential record of achievement. If self-reliance, internal democracy, and resolution of problems through dialogue and compromise are the characteristics that today differentiate Somaliland from Somalia, it is because these qualities were learned and practiced by the SNM in the heat of the struggle for liberation. If it were not so, it would not have been easy for the movement to offer the hand of reconciliation to those who did not support it even prior to total victory. Nay, it would not have been easy for the militants of the movement to give safe passage to those Somali ex-refugees from Ethiopia who, through an ironical mutation of history, became part and parcel of the apparatus of the dictatorial regime and who, for all intents and purposes, replaced their former hosts.

V. Perspectives on African Development

In order to understand the experiences gained by the SNM during the struggle and to put these experiences in broader perspective it may be more useful to consider some issues fundamental to the crisis of underdevelopment in African countries. These broader issues impinge upon both economic policies and the system of governance at large. The failure of most African regimes, after the euphoria of the first few years following independence, in both economic performance and the democratic governance of their peoples, compel re-thinking these issues. For our purposes, these issues can be formulated as:

1. What is the most appropriate way to forge a nation? Is it through forcing a centralized state machinery or through the voluntary associations of the existing components of civil society?
2. What is the interplay between "modern" national institutions, such as political parties and state bureaucracy and traditional structures such as clan (ethnic) systems?
3. To what extent should one look inward or outward for the solution of one's problems?

These issues can be restated as the questions of dictatorship vs. democratic development, centralization vs. autonomy and self-reliance vs. dependency. No matter how they are phrased the essence remains the same; and the answering of one issue in a certain manner sets the pattern for the rest and forecloses other paths of development.

It is a well-known story that in the early decades after independence African governments pursued a statist approach in politico-development matters which relied heavily on foreign borrowing, not only capital and technical help, but even ideas and sometimes wholesale institutions. Since economic growth, as such, was perceived to be the magic key to the problems of development and since Africa lacked an experienced capitalist class with the wherewithal to carry on the process, the initiative was shifted to the state. The attraction of this approach to the new ruling elites was further increased by the example of the Soviet model where an apparently former backward country has succeeded in transforming itself through utilizing the state machinery.

The very words used, and naturally still in use, such as "development" "modernization," and "progress" assume moving from one stage to another. For the development experts of the time, and their African pupils, who were molded by the same educational process, this meant, implicitly if not explicitly, the attempt to emulate the attributes of the "developed" West. The attributes to be emulated include, of course, the political institutions, to the extent possible. The consequent development strategy thus gave scant attention to the real complexities of the societies that were to be developed. It goes without saying that, according to this attitude, African indigenous values and institutions are inimical to "development" as they are rooted in "backward" conditions. The corollary that development policy should be pursued, in spite of the people, follows immediately. The result of this attitude is the transformation of development policy into, in the words of a famous African writer, "an epic struggle, of the very few who know, to manipulate or coerce the many who are ignorant into a new and better mode of being in spite of themselves." Needless to say, all this obviates the essential in development, which is the learning process of the majority of the people. The sustainability of the development process in the longer run can be ensured through the commitment of the people to, their participation in, and their internalization of the requirements of that process.

But the state machinery available to Africans on the eve of independence was a colonial product, born out of a long history of oppression and ill-suited to purposes of genuine self-development. This colonial state was viewed by our people with suspicion, and rightly so.

They took refuge in strengthening communal and kinship systems. Hence the divergence between the interests of the state and its machinery on the one hand and that of civil society on the other. We know too well that during the early years of the euphoria of independence we did not question the relevance of the inherited state machine to our goals. Thus, we did not attempt to qualitatively transform it, but simply adopted it wholesale. Lacking the experience of its predecessor and burdened with an ever-increasing role, the new African state tried to fill the lacunae through expansion. Unable to deliver the goods and thus obtain compliance through meeting the genuine demands of the people, it tried to elicit such compliance through compulsion. With the degeneration of the early democracies into empty shells, authoritarian methods, one party systems, and military dictatorships became the rule. Because their authority is not based on the consent of the governed, these authoritarian regimes are, in fact, less authoritative. They, therefore, become increasingly concerned with short-term security matters rather than long-term development. Is there any wonder, then that the situation today in Africa is generally characterized by stagnation, corruption, repression, resistance, civil wars, and mass starvation?

The challenge to all Africans for the last decade and a half has been to pioneer an alternative path of development that leads away from this impasse and opens the door to real progress. Among the clear lessons is the realization that the present crisis in Africa is not only about economic matters but, on the contrary, involves larger political and moral issues. Overcoming the inhibiting legacy of the colonial state compels an inward-looking perspective that examines the present society and its mores for ways of transforming it. The first requirement in this self-examination for an alternative path is to find creative political initiatives for eliciting the necessary participation of the people. We have already seen the limits of elitist forms of democracy, i.e., those who imitate the West, as well as coerced forms of "mass mobilization" that only endorse what has already been decided by an authoritarian state. In fact, these are not two different and opposing forms of organizing society. On the contrary, they finally converge in the form of the authoritarian African state. This is not surprising since the content of both types is the dictatorial way of deciding for the people.

Both forms, i.e., elitist corruption of democracy and "socialist" coerced "mass mobilization," breed cynicism, further alienation from the state, and withdrawal into precolonial communal and kinship ties. These traditional structures themselves, have been affected by their long relationship with the colonial authorities. They cannot be considered pure. Yet they still command loyalty and respect. What is therefore required is an approach that integrates this cultural heritage into the formal political structure of the state. The state and civil society need not be hostile and juxtaposed entities. Instead democracy must be planted on the African soil. The specific forms of this democratic regeneration and the specific pathways to it -- whether peaceful or violent -- will vary according to the situation and the circumstances, but the need and necessity for it is clear.

Also certain broad features -- common to all working democracies -- can be outlined. First, there must be a limit to the arbitrary authority of the all-powerful state. Second, economic and political power must be shared and diffused throughout society, both horizontally and vertically. Third, the rule of law must be paramount and replace the whims of the holder of power. If these features appear to be the tenets of Western liberal democracy whose imitation by Africans we have considered to have failed, this should not be surprising. Indeed, we consider these broad features to be the essential contents of any democracy. It is the forms and the specific working details that differ according to the existing social context. It is easily forgotten, though Africanists all the time remind us, that precolonial Africa, surviving today somewhat in communal traditions, was rich in these broad features of a democratic society. After all, the all-powerful dictator, equipped with an impersonal machinery presides over the fate of society is a post colonial product. In precolonial Africa, councils of elders, chosen through lineage hierarchy or other means of popular suffrage, prescribed the powers of the ruler -- king or paramount chief, where there was one. Rules elaborated through wide discussions and codified in cultural heritage, religion, custom, and laws circumscribed the conduct of all -- young and old, rulers and ruled.

The integration of these democratic practices and values into the institutions of the modern state must start at the lowest rung. It is at the village level (where normal administration, social services, development programs and political matters can hardly be distinguished) that the training of the common people as citizens should begin. Freely chosen representatives at this level could form the first steps of a pyramid culminating at the national level. It is at the village, district and provincial levels that the communal, clan, ethnic interests can be coordinated, reconciled and combined with that of the nation at large. Traditional leadership structure goes down to the roots and can tap grassroots support. But if not corrected or complemented by cross-sectional political organization -- in other words where leadership does not depend on ethnic/clan loyalty alone -- then it is likely to give way to divisive and centrifugal forces.

The above general remarks apply with particular force in the case of

the Somali Republic. Inheriting two disparate colonial experiences, great
-- and commendable -- energy was spent in the early years in integrating
the different political, legal, administrative and educational systems. A
liberal constitutional parliamentary democracy was adopted. However,
this attempt at creating the new nation was based not only on the
inherited centralized structures of the colonial state but strenuous efforts
were applied to transplant all the institutions associated with liberal
democracy and move away from the traditional clan structure. The latter
as a precolonial institution, was considered primitive, anarchic, divisive,
with potential for savage clan-based fratricidal wars. As such the
traditional system was perceived to be the number one enemy of the goals
of national independence, i.e., social and economic progress, freeing the
individual from the shackles of the ascriptive bonds of tradition, and
fostering instead the foundations of the institutions of "modern"
nationhood with which free individuals can identify. (I recall, as an
active member of that special "tribe" of high school students, how in
those days we despised everything that had anything to do with "clanism"
and how emotional we were about matters of "nationalism" and
"independence.")

Indeed, attack on tradition was an integral part of the national
independence movement. Despite the veneer of seeking freedom from
the colonial yoke and its consequent domination of many aspects of social
life, the independence movement imbibed more values from its colonial
metropolitan adversaries than it rejected or wished to change. This
should not be surprising. Aside from whatever brainwashing there was
as a result of educational molding, nationalism, as an historical
movement, was a European phenomenon. Moreover, the concept of
nation-building, prevalent in those days and paraded as the quintessence
of research by political theorists, is the ideological heritage of Western
post enlightenment.

The Somali Republic like many others in the African continent, failed
in transplanting the liberal state. With the benefit of hindsight, this is also
not surprising. Traditions die hard, no matter what strenuous efforts are
expended in creating the new. After all, the cultural heritage of a people
cannot suddenly be revamped. Institutions that have served a purpose for
generations cannot just be outlived unless and until an alternative is found
that better serves those same social needs. Otherwise they will continue
to exist, albeit sometimes in a corrupted and destructive form. The new
laws and institutions of the liberal state could not easily and quickly
replace all traditional ones. Implicit in the concept of the liberal state and
its laws is the assumption that society consists of free individuals, with
basic rights and endowed with different talents. This assumption

underlies the rules of equality and even the ballot, the *sine quo non* of a liberal democracy, is based on that assumption.

One need not quarrel with these assumptions of liberal democracy. They are indeed necessary, but not sufficient for full democratic expression in African countries.

The missing link between the state and the individual is an intermediate category where the bonds of solidarity and human fraternity, so much neglected by liberalism but indeed essential for human survival and welfare, are nurtured. If in the industrial world this warmth of human solidarity and fraternal bonds is sought in organizations based on class, in the less developed world, specially in Africa, they are easily provided in ready-made form by ethnicity in the Somali case by "clanism." The extended family in the Somali case is the basic economic unit, adopted and adapted throughout the ages for the survival of its members. One family member may be a skilled worker in town, another a merchant, a third abroad in Europe or oil-rich Arabia, and another left to tend livestock in the hinterland. All their incomes buttress one another. As such the Somali extended family is a versatile system that is self-reliant, internally balanced and autocentric.

The Somali clan structure is a complicated pyramid with the extended family at its lowest form and a large, more or less political group claiming to originate from a single ancient ancestor at its pinnacle. Subclans in the middle echelons of the pyramid are most often more important for questions of survival and interest. I have no intention to go into a treatise about Somali clan organization and its functions. The simple point being raised here is that sometimes the extended family system may not have the carrying capacity to fully provide for the needs of its members in terms of security (economic and otherwise), emotional support and simple social interaction. Upper rungs in the pyramid are therefore called upon to supplement the efforts and resources of the extended family. The more difficult the problem to be solved in both extent and intensity, the higher the rung called upon. Most often the most important rung in these matters is the *diya*-paying unit of the clan. This is the unit that is responsible for injuries caused unto others by its other members. The other layers of the clan structure, most often dormant, are activated at times of stress, civil wars, famines or liberation struggles. In urban areas services that are normally provided in industrial countries by the state, municipalities, trade unions, cooperatives, etc., now become the function of the extended family and/or the clan in African countries. The need for clan solidarity, although assaulted in many ways by urbanization, becomes strengthened by it.

The consequence of these contradictory forces -- the inherited colonial state and the liberal laws adopted wholesale on the one hand, and the continuing need for clan support and solidarity on the other -- is a bifurcated society, with a non-integrated personality. This bifurcation is a breeding ground for corruption, misuse of power, manipulation of clan loyalty, mistrust among the clans themselves, and hence instability. The resulting disillusionment, right on the heels of the euphoria of independence, provided the fertile soil for the African coups. Whether, given sufficient time, these contradictions could have been overcome peacefully and democracy could have been workable is one of the "ifs" of history. The fact remains that in the case of Somalia the Siyad Barre military dictatorship came and completed the job of total disintegration. How it did so is an important subject by itself and need not detain us here.

VI. The Experience of the Somali National Movement Reviewed

The resistance to the dictatorship was affected by this historical background in more ways than one. The terror unleashed by the regime, the abolition of national representative institutions, and the transformation of the remaining state bodies into instruments of oppression and spying, left the extended family and the related clan network the only relatively safe haven. While this clan network had already, prior to the regime, built-in advantages for political organization, the behavior of the terroristic regime made it the only avenue for any opposition to it. Further, the clandestine nature of any opposition to the police state of Siyad Barre and the latter's manipulation of the clan structure, setting one clan against another, not only inhibited the building of bridges between incipient opposition groups, but succeeded in the displacement of any resentments against the regime into aggressions against other clans. Those who criticize the SNM for not starting off with a broader clan base, minimize this factor. There is no need here to recount in detail the efforts of the SNM to do so. These efforts did not materialize in substantial success in the early stages and are witness to the depth of the disintegration process wrought by the regime. Several factors are at play: the smaller bases of support in the center and the south of the country opened by the SNM in the early years; the *modus vivendi* with the SSDF before the latter's slip into dormancy; the active coordination and subsequent alliance with the USC and SPM; and finally the reconciliation process embarked upon on the eve of victory with those northern clans who opposed it all speak with eloquence of the sincerity of these early SNM efforts to broaden its base, despite the odds.

In the meantime the movement had to continue its work where it was most effective *vis a vis* the north of the country. The single-minded support given to the SNM by the Isaaq clan speaks only of the unevenness of the regime's oppression and its singling out of this clan in the mid and later 80s for particular persecution. The numerical strength of their support, and the uninterrupted nature of their habitat in the North, provided the SNM with ample opportunity not only to continue the valiant struggle with tenacity but also to experiment with ideas and forms that could lay the basis for alternative paths of governance and development. These forms and ideas, needless to say, were not ideological recipes, prepared by elites in the ivory tower, and experimented on an unsuspecting population. Rather they grew out of the practical needs of the struggle itself.

This does not mean that the struggle was visionless. Vision, there has to be. Otherwise it is almost impossible to move great numbers of human beings into action. The tremendous odds against which the SNM operated and the sacrifice it demanded from its supporters over an extended period of time could only be sustained by a vision of the future in which they believed. Some cynics maintain that hate also can move masses of people into action. They point to the Nazi movement, whose effectiveness has threatened the world for sometime, and the ever-present ethnic massacres in today's world. But, evidently, this cynical argument cannot be taken seriously. For one thing, occasional jacqueries should not be confused with sustainable movements. And those sustainable movements that have a large element of hate in their arsenal show it in their expressions and actions. The SNM definitely passes that test. As the saying goes, the proof of the pudding is in the eating.

The vision itself (from which programs of action are formed) is a mixture of ideal and the antithesis of the system one is attempting to change. Certainly hatred of the oppressive system and those who actively and willingly maintain it forms part of the driving motives of the fighter for change. But this is quite different from the kind of hatred alluded to by the cynic, for it is not directed against a particular ethnic group of tribe/clan or section of humanity. It is directed against an oppressive social structure whose removal is a milestone towards realizing justice. For this to be achieved it has to be accompanied by the articulation of the alternative, even if that articulation does not fall into any of the known ideological molds.

We have seen, in the preceding pages, that the oppressive system that evolved in Somalia -- and the rest of Africa in various different ways -- was characterized by an excessively centralized, dictatorial state, divorced from the traditions and historical continuity of the people it ruled. We have also touched upon the outlines of an alternative form of governance; one that integrates the state with civil society, is democratic and autocentric and decentralizes the arenas of action as much as possible.

This, precisely, is the vision which the Somali National Movement presented from its inception in its programs of action and which it attempted to practice while still conducting the armed struggle against the military regime. If this alternative vision was not very well-known outside its ranks, it speaks less of the limited ability of the SNM to propagate this vision than of the blinders inhibiting outsiders to see the actual truth. I say this with confidence, because even if we lacked the resources with which we could compete with the government in the propagation of our ideas, our actions and activities were an open book for anyone taking the pains look. Let us now take some of the main elements of the alternative path, discussed earlier, and which also inform SNM's vision and see what role these ideas played in the praxis of the SNM during the phase of the armed struggle.

If one were to single out a phenomenon in which the SNM is unique among liberation movements, past and present, it is the extent of its self-reliance. To be sure, all genuine liberation struggles have to strive for a measure of self-reliance if they are to achieve success. But, more often than not, it is almost impossible to do without some form of external support in terms of moral and material assistance. Specifically it is the material support that becomes a *sine qua non* in the case of armed struggles. To mobilize, train, supply, replenish and maintain fighting units is a very expensive affair. Expensive also, if only slightly less so, is the political wing with its far-flung cadres, internally and externally. A liberation movement, conducting an armed struggle, can hardly meet the total of these financial burdens from its own coffers. But the more it relies on external support for the sustenance of its operations and organization, the more it sacrifices its autonomy and independent decision-making. The tendency to be autonomous and independent and the need to seek outside support and allies and thus be part of a larger block is a contradiction that has plagued liberation movements throughout history. Rare is the movement that has found a judicious balance.

The SNM solved this dilemma by tilting towards total autonomy and facing the consequent risk. To be sure the SNM received assistance from Ethiopia in the form of sanctuary for its leadership, training bases for its fighters, and ammunition and fuel. Financial assistance from Ethiopia was next to nothing and even the ammunition and fuel were token contributions. Although this assistance was vital, especially in the early stages, in the long term it was small. The more valuable assistance from Ethiopia was the provision of sanctuary, not the material aspect. This help itself was not a one-way street. The presence of Somali opposition to the Siyad Barre regime in Ethiopia preempted the converse, while at the same time weakening the main threat to Ethiopia from the east. This mutual advantage had the additional strength of sowing the seeds of future peaceful cooperation between the two countries, instead of the then existing antagonism. Sensing this advantage, the Ethiopian regime was wise enough to avoid alienating the SNM by manipulation as much as the latter was careful in insulating its decision-making to itself.

In that Ethiopia was the only source of external assistance, the movement had to provide its own resources or perish. There was, of course, no lack of potential helpers. But the premium put on independence was such that the movement chose to eschew any and all aid that seriously affected its independent decision-making. The harm caused by Libyan cash to the sister and older movement -- The Somali Salvation Democratic Front (SSDF) -- was a clear enough warning. This choice of self-reliance by the SNM paid its dividends. It was compelled to raise cash from supporters abroad and inside the country. The fighting units were to be sustained by supporters in the areas where they operated. Foreign branches engaged in propaganda and diplomatic activity had to rely on their own resources.

All this meant that the rank and file as well as ordinary supporters could no longer be passive sympathizers. Instead, they were transformed into active participants. Thus the path of self-reliance easily led to the road of democratic decentralization. The people whom the movement were trying to recruit and commit to the struggle were already rebelling against a suffocating dictatorship. If they are to be convinced to give the best they have, even their lives, to the cause, they cannot be denied the freedom of choice within the movement. The people have to "own" their movement. One cannot claim to struggle for liberty and deny that liberty itself within their own ranks.

In the context of the struggle conducted by the SNM, the democratic practice expressed itself on two levels: (1) at the top organizational level where the higher leadership -- the Chairman, Vice Chairman and the Central Committee -- were elected in broadly representative Congresses, and (2) at the local level where branches in foreign countries and in the field put forth their own leadership. The most pressing matter is the relationship between the center and the localities. The centralization/ decentralization paradox bedevils not only liberation movements but most Third World governments as well. Central authority is a must if a nation has to exist as one. But how much power and responsibility should be devolved to lower bodies, outlying regions and the private sector, and how much power should be retained by central authorities, in order to attain a measure of both democracy and unity is a question not easily resolved. In the case of the SNM struggle, the wide geographic distances involving branches in many countries and field operations across the width and breadth of the country as well as reliance on own resources dictated autonomous activity and decision-making. This left for the center tasks such as broad policy formulation, overall coordination of the implementation, and contact with foreign bodies.

Since particular areas were more often than not occupied by particular clans or subclans, the policy of the movement's autonomous activity in reality translated itself into clan autonomous activity. We have seen in the earlier sections of this article that the post-colonial state failed to integrate traditional authority positively into the modern institutions of society. We have also briefly argued that this divorce between the state and civil society reached an extreme form in the former Somali Republic. Here, the solution to this dilemma of modern versus traditional authority presented itself before the movement in clear form by the exigencies of the struggle. Ironically, the clan organizational form became the vehicle for a revolutionary process of restructuring society. First, the solidarity it naturally provides became a safe haven for members from the state terror. Second, self-reliance itself means that the movement, instead of relying on outside supporters, relies on its people and hence on their local leaders and ways of doing things. There is a mutual feedback here between the movement and the ordinary peoples. The movement brought urban cadres -- the teacher, the army officer, the student, the medical doctor, the politician -- into the rural areas who then interact with the clans and their elders. Here, at the level of the fighting unit, the SNM found the opportunity of integrating traditional authority and methods into the democratic practices and needs of the movement.

These factors created opportunity to correct the mistakes of the past, make use of existing structures, and correct the divorce between civil society and the state. One of the tentative ideas that came about then was a greater role for the elders of the clans as autonomous decision-makers, and participants at various levels of the clan pyramid, parallel with and interacting with the various levels of the formal organization of the movement. The experimentation with the role of the elders was finally formalized in the form of the "*Guurti,*" that is, the senate or the council of elders, which is co-equal with the Central Committee, the legislative organ of the SNM. This parallel co-participation stretched from the lowest units all the way up to the highest level. We see, then, that the vision of an alternative path of governance replaced the centralized, dictatorial regime. The SNM provided an alternative system whose hallmark is participatory democracy from top to bottom. It was thus possible for it to carry over this tradition to a national level after victory, providing avenues for dialogue and compromise while state structures were still weak, culminating in the fora for consensus building such as the Borama Conference. And it is this that makes the vital difference between Somaliland and the rest of Somalia.

If there is any weakness in the performance so far, it is that the insistence on free decision-making and participation at all levels has sacrificed the need for discipline and obedience. This has weakened the formal organization of the SNM as a political organ. If this choice has enabled it to escape the appearance of dictatorial tendencies and "war-lordism," it has allowed the formal structures of the movement, as a political organ, to be diluted and absorbed by the traditional structures. Admittedly then, the experimentation for new forms has gone to the other extreme, tending to open the door for centrifugal forces since traditional structures by themselves cannot form the basis for a modern state. But this danger is not as great as it may appear to those who are not familiar with the depth of the changes wrought by the SNM struggle. It is precisely the decentralized forms and the actual democratic participation, especially that of clan elders, opened by the SNM that have minimized conflict within the SNM -- supporting Isaaq clans and between them and the others in the North by institutionalizing dialogue and compromise. Unlike the SNM, the other political factions in the south claiming legitimacy neither opened up such avenues of activity (at least on a stage comparable to that of the SNM) for the people they claim to represent, nor even conducted formal democratic congresses to legitimate their own leadership. Hence their inability to contain the situation after the breakdown of the Siyad Barre regime, let alone move it forward.

Moreover, those of us who are still optimistic enough to believe in progress also know that trends are never on a smooth, straight line. Like the business cycle, there are troughs and peaks, but the trend is upward with today's trough possibly higher than yesterday's low. If the abhorrence of the dictatorial centralized post-colonial state created in those who thought it a tendency toward too much freedom and reliance on the informal networks, I say proudly that this is good. There was need to restore these networks and legitimize them formally just as freedom was essential. With these firmly established the pendulum will swing back towards formal cross-sectional organizations. Reactivation of the SNM organization is a relatively easy matter and together with those other political organizations that are bound to come up in the present free atmosphere, political alliances across clans will be formed. The need is there and the ground work of dialogue and compromise has already been laid by the struggle of the SNM.

VII. Epilogue

The reader may be struck by the fact that I have said nothing about the important issue of dialogue and reconciliation between the north and the rest of the country, or more precisely, between the Republic of Somaliland and the original Somalia (i.e. the Trusteeship Territory before independence). It is not an oversight, but a deliberate omission, the reasons for which are simple.

First, if by reconciliation, we mean a return to the original union between the two parts, I am afraid it is now counterproductive to harp on that tune. Every problem, like an organism, goes through certain stages of a life cycle. There is the stage of early detection and prevention. There is the long middle stage of curative treatment, and there is the last stage of death and burial. A Somali friend once aptly remarked to a group that "the eggshell of Somali unity is now broken. We may talk about making a scrambled egg or an omelet out of it, but we cannot reconstitute the original broken shell!" Treating the problems that led to the separation was possible during the early and middle stages, but not now.

Second, this separation is not the result of manipulation by few politicians. Some people confuse the declaration of the Republic of Somaliland by the SNM in Burao on May 18, 1991 with the fact of separation itself. Separation was a political reality long before that. It is a consequence of an historical process whose two protagonists were the cruel persecution by the regime and the stubborn resistance of the persecuted. It is the culmination of the victory of that lonely struggle by the SNM for an extended period. Siyad Barre himself effectively sanctioned the separation and put the last nail on the coffin of the union by his bombardment of the cities of the north and the mass murder of their citizens which led to the fleeing of terrorized civilians into Ethiopia.

To ignore the victory, which to them is not only the downfall of the Siyad Barre regime, but also includes the separation itself, won by the people of the north with such superhuman sacrifice, or to treat it as non-existent, is foolhardy and borders on the callous. The Burao declaration only put the final touches on an already existing reality.

Third, the present use of "Somali unity" is a misnomer. The original meaning of unity for the Post World War II Somali independence movement was the liberation of the five parts into which the Somali-speaking peoples were divided by the colonial powers and their eventual inclusion under one nation state. When the Somaliland Protectorate gained its independence from Britain it had closer and more advantageous links with Djibouti and eastern Ethiopia than it did with Mogadishu. But it chose to sacrifice its newly won statehood and join the Trusteeship territory, without conditions, in order to lay the basis of the united state which the remaining three parts could later join. It is a well-known story how that Somali irredentism collided with the then existing international order, specifically how the neighboring countries and the Organization of African Unity, with the support of the rest of the international system, resisted any notion of revision of African boundaries on the basis of ethnicity. It is common knowledge how the pursuit of their goal of unity by the Somalis and the resistance of their neighbors to that goal caused instability in the Horn, including two major wars between the Somali Republic and Ethiopia, and the introduction of superpower competition and the arms race into the area, to the detriment of their peoples, especially the Somali people who, on all sides, bore the greater brunt of the havoc.

The upshot was the frustration of Somali unity, with Djibouti opting for its separate statehood and the borders with Ethiopia and Kenya remaining intact as left by the colonial powers. The marriage between the two original parts had became unworkable, Some of the reasons were touched upon in this presentation. Rather, the marriage had lost its *raison d'etre*. After great suffering and with Herculean efforts the people of Somaliland have restored the statehood which they both won and sacrificed in 1960. Moreover, they are willing to go about it through the internationally agreed methods of elections and plebiscites, even though they are by all logic entitled to it. What is indeed strange is that the international community -- as represented by the UN and other regional organizations -- which originally frustrated the Somali unity project, is now opposing the exercise of this legitimate right of self-determination and attempting to maintain and enforce an unworkable marriage and reconciliation and a now non-existent Somali unity.

Fourth, any process of reconciliation requires negotiation and dialogue between existing entities. The state of Somaliland, even though weak and not yet recognized by the international system is a *de facto* entity brought into existence by its own people. There is no such comparable entity in the south, i.e., the former Trusteeship territory, with which it can negotiate. Even the many factions have no legitimate standing (at least the majority of them) *vis-a-vis* the peoples they claim to represent in terms of democratic procedure. The proper course, dictated both by logic and justice, is to accept and assist the correct process of political development in Somaliland, while at the same time, encourage similar processes in the south until such time that a comparable entity appears with whom proper negotiations can take place. But, alas, we know this is not the policy at present pursued by the UN. Instead, it is following a policy of strangling Somaliland and enforcing the establishment of an artificial so-called "government of unity." It is a dead- end with more negative consequences and precious time lost.

In this analysis, I did not follow that beaten path with no exit. Instead, I chose to go beyond and beneath these superficial formulae. There is a Somali proverb -- "*Haani guntay ka tolanta*" — which literally means "a vessel is mended from the base upwards," but which can be roughly translated as "charity begins at home." In the spirit of this proverb, my approach was to understand what happened to the Somali way of living. The research and analysis required to reach this understanding is tremendous and lies before all of us. Yet from these simple reflections, one reaches the inescapable conclusion: that what happened is not a matter of an enigmatic primitive society gone astray. Neither is it a question of "warlord" versus chiefs. It is a matter of a system of governance that has gotten off on an early false start since the colonial days and ended up awry with the military dictatorship. The antidote to that system is its antithesis: an antithesis that can only be found through the practical activity of the people, enlightened by some vision.

I have tried to show the contents of that antithesis as well as the vision in the struggle of the SNM. What we need most urgently is to find ways of resewing the torn fabric of Somali society. Whether that resewn fabric is reconstituted under a single, two, or several states is for a free people to decide. But let us first build that freedom, not on shifting sand, but on solid ground. This is the road for sound reconciliation. And in this respect, the struggle of the SNM, and the present democratic experimentation in Somaliland, have something to offer. We are also willing to learn. But I doubt whether many in the arrogance-ridden UN system and the parrot-like singers of so-called unity in the south are really listening.

Endnotes

1. During the visit by President Bush to Somali to raise the morale of American soldiers on Thanksgiving Day and to present the olive branch of the new humanitarian mission to the starving Somalis, some American newspapers printed a story of the appearance of Jesus Christ (to both American soldiers and Somalis!) above a cloud of dust over the small town of Wanlawein. The authenticity of the story is not as important as the timing of the apparition. Have we reached the limits of propaganda gimmicks?

2. Whether or not, and how much, international organizations contributed to the longevity of the dictatorial regime, and to the misery of Somalians, is another topic outside the scope of our present story.

CHAPTER FOUR

Somalia: Between Self-Determination and Chaos

Mohammed Haji Mukhtar

I. Introduction

Somalia is not a state functioning under the rule of law. It is not even a country, but a patchwork of districts and regions caught up in different stages of lawlessness, anarchy and chaos. Each has different security needs, and each gropes for the restoration of normalcy and the return to civil law and order. Somalia is the only sub-Saharan country that has no working political, social or economic institutions. The anarchic factionalism of clan rivalry not only creates conditions of havoc and panic and traumatizes individual Somalis, but also calls into question whether or not Somalia still has a political identity. If it does, is there a Somali state, as is understood in modern parlance?

Many scholars and politicians believed that Somalia was ethnically homogeneous, with one language and religion.[1] How then could a society that has all these things in common, disintegrate and suddenly fall apart? What type of political organization can be offered in this type of society?

Before the arrival of colonial powers, the Somali peninsula was the home of several independent clans, each with fundamentally distinct languages and modes of livelihood. These clans inhabited separate geographical homelands. Traditionally, the three major clans; Reewin[2],

Irir and Darood have been divided into several sub-clans. The Reewin are composed of the Dighil and Mirifle; the Irir of Hawiye, Dir and Isaaq; and the Darood of Kablalah and Marehan. Most of the Irir and Darood are pastoral nomads who speak Maha, but most Reewin are agriculturalists who speak Mai, linguistically quite different from Maha.[3]

Historically, the Reewin occupy the fertile regions stretching from the Shabelle River in the north to Jubaland in the south. The Irir and Darood, due to their greater involvement in nomadism, are hard to localize. However, the homeland of some of the Irir is the northwestern region of former British Somaliland (Dir and Isaaq), where others such as the Hawiye occupy the central regions of Somalia. The Darood occupy the northeastern regions, southern Ethiopia and the area beyond the Jubba River in the extreme south of Jubaland and in northern Kenya.

The fall and partition of the Horn of Africa by British, Italian, and French powers at the turn of the century disrupted the socio-political life of the whole clan system. For example, the Italian colonial authority ruled both the Reewin clans and some of the Irir and Darood clans, while the British and French authorities ruled other Irir and Darood clans. Therefore, by the turn of the century, there were three Somalilands: British, French and Italian.

The British and the French-ruled clans were almost entirely nomadic and lived in the largely semi-desert areas of the peninsula. The Italians, on the other hand, recruited settlers to run agricultural plantations with forced labor to generate worthwhile sources of primary products for the mother country.[4] This harsh rule prompted Reewin resistance. The Jihads of Nassib Bunto, 1890-1905, and Sheikh Faraj, known as Gelle Baraki, 1920-1925, were the most famous rebellions.[5]

After these rebellions were suppressed, the Italians somewhat haphazardly created what they later called "La Grande Somalia." With the 1936 conquest of Ethiopia, the Somali Ogaden region was amalgamated with the rest of Somalia and governed from Mogadishu. The Italians brought almost all Somalis under one administration with their occupation of British Somaliland in early 1941. Thus, the Italians created the basis for pan-Somali nationalism.[6] From late 1941 to 1950, the British Military Administration (BMA) controlled all the Somali inhabited area of the Horn (except French Somaliland) with a conscious goal to create a "future united Somalia." This effort encouraged Somali political activity, especially those of an anti-Italian type.[7]

II. The Formation Of Somali Political Parties

Al-Jam'iyyah al-Khayriyyah al-Wataniyyah (JKW), the National

Benevolent Organization was a Reewin association that emerged under the Italians in 1920. It became a more progressive party, Hizbia Dighil Mirifle, (HDM) the Dighil and Mirifle Party, in 1947. The Reewin were energized by allied propaganda during the East Africa campaign "to free Somalis from Italian forces." However, the British administration in the Reewin regions was certainly as exploitative as the Italian. The British introduced the infamous "Teen" quota system which was even more exploitative than the Italian *cologno* system.[8] The second and third political organizations were the Patriotic Benefit Union (PBU), a Hawiye organization that sprang up in 1943 and the Somali Youth Club (SYC), which started as a trans-clan club, but turned into a Darood party in 1947 as the Somali Youth League (SYL).

The British administration supported SYL against HDM and PBU in the hope that SYL would support the British Trusteeship of the Horn of Africa. However, the British unwittingly assumed that the Darood were the majority clan in the Horn and dominated the membership and leadership of SYL.[9] This assumption caused considerable disenchantment with the British and thus blocked their colonial aspirations. In British Somaliland, the Isaaqs formed the Somali National League (SNL) in 1947, while Daroods of the region formed an SYL branch.

The repartition of Somaliland during the British Military Administration led to the Anglo-Ethiopian agreements of 1948 and 1954. These agreements returned Ogadenia, Haud and the Reserved Areas to Ethiopia, and, in 1950, the reinstatement of Italy as administering authority under United Nations' supervision.[10] Therefore, Somali political behavior, based on clan affiliation, had a new dimension.

The Italians had a clear mandate to foster the development of free political institutions and promote the development of the inhabitants of the territory toward independence so that an independent government could be formed within 10 years. Italy encouraged the establishment of a multi-party system, and more than 20 parties, mostly clan-oriented, sprang up. In the municipal, district and general elections from 1954-1960, the SYL and HDMS emerged as the most widely supported and powerful of the parties in Somalia. Two parties, the SNL and the United Somali Party (USP), dominated British Somaliland until its unification in 1960.

III. Problems of Independence and Unification

Unification radically altered the balance of power between opposing clan groups in the whole of Somalia. Despite the national jubilation and patriotic fervor that unification promoted, the breakdown in clan representation weakened the central authority of the new government. Before unification, the seats of the National Assembly in the south were proportionately divided among the three major southern clans: thirty Reewin, thirty Hawiye, and thirty Darood, irrespective of party affiliation. However, unification with the north diminished the political importance of the Reewin and offered both the Hawiye and Darood clans new importance through direct association with the Irir and Darood segments, Isaaq and Dir, and Dulbahante and Warsangeli. At this time, it was evident that the identity of the Reewin people was bound up with the HDMS party, and would never get support from the north. The Isaaqs also lost their dominant place in northern politics.

The unification sharpened regional cleavages between the north and south, reflecting different colonial legacies and cultural distinctions between the Reewin society in the south and the Hawiye-Darood-Isaaq in the north. The Reewin speak Mai, a different language from the Maha which most of the Hawiye, Darood and Isaaq speak. The constant infiltration of the pastoral Somalis from the north into the more fertile regions of the south inhabited by the Reewin further aggravated these disparities.[11] More importantly, the Reewin experienced discrimination in education and employment.[12]

The Reewin were clearly disenchanted with the national government in 1956 when the victorious SYL formed the first Somali cabinet which consisted of three Hawiye (including the prime minister), two Darood and one Dir. Though twenty of the sixty elected members of the legislative assembly were Reewin they received not one ministerial portfolio.[13] The Reewin therefore had no choice but to call for decentralization.

The Isaaqs strongly resented the national referendum of 1961 to legitimize the national constitution which almost half the northern registered voters opposed.[14] In December, 1961, northern military officers mutinied, and the two Isaaqi ministers resigned and, with others, formed the Somali National Congress (SNC), as an Irir solidarity party.[15] This represented a new attempt to capitalize on the ancient genealogical relationships of Isaaq, Hawiye and Dir elements in the government that opposed the Darood-led SYL.

The formation of the SNC radically altered the Darood and Isaaq loyalties to SYL and SNL respectively. In 1962, another party, the Somali Democratic Union (SDU), was also formed from the amalgamation of dissident Darood and Isaaq elements in SYL and SNL. All three parties -- SYL, SNC and SDU — now had strong adherents in both regions of the republic.[16] This left the HDMS confined to its traditional territory, relying on Reewin support. So these four parties shaped the political development of Somalia until the presidential election of 1967.

Due to new clan alignments in the aftermath of the 1964 general elections, the SYL became dominated by the Darood. President Osman's nomination of two successive premiers, Dr. Abdirashid A. Shermarke in 1960, and Abirizak H. Hussein in 1964, both Darood, confirmed the new development. The SYL, though winning only 69 out of 123 National Assembly seats in the 1964 election, co-opted through personal or clan allegiances, many members of other parties. In fact, 36 members joined the SYL immediately after the election. Among those who crossed the aisle was Mohamed Haji Ibrahim Egal, a former Isaaq leader of SNC.

The Darood-Isaaq alliance brought about the victory of Shermarke, a Darood, in the 1967 presidential election. After the resignation of the previous government, Egal was called to form a new government. For the first time a northerner, Egal, was Premier and a Darood, Shermarke President of the Republic.[17] These developments greatly reduced the significance of other political parties.

Between 1967 to 1969, Somali politics was characterized by considerable turmoil. Larger clan alliances, i.e., Dir-Isaaq-Hawiye, represented by the SNC, and the Reewin by HDMS, were split into smaller units. Even the Darood within the SYL became divided. Clan politics had fallen back to smaller lineage groups. This coincided with growing disillusion with the traditional campaign for the unification of the missing Somali territories, such as Ogaden, French Somaliland and the Northern Frontier District (NFD) of Kenya.[18]

The 1969 elections confirmed all these trends. More than 60 one-man lineage parties competed for the 123 seats of the National Assembly. The SYL won 73 seats, and the remaining 50 opposition members crossed the floor to join the SYL party, with the exception of one member, Abdirizak H. Hussein. Thus, for the first time in the history of the Somali National Assembly, all deputies belonged to one party, the SYL.

IV. The End of Democracy

The victorious SYL formed a government under the premiership of Ibrahim Egal, the second successive government formed by Egal and the fifth in the republic since unification. However, Egal's government was overthrown on October 21, 1969, immediately after the October 15 assassination of President Shermarke. This sealed the fate of democracy in post-independent Somalia. The country's executive and legislative organs were then replaced by 25 officers, headed by General Mohamed Siyad Barre, the Somali Revolutionary Council (SRC).[19]

The SRC declared its intention of wiping out the corruption and nepotism that had discredited the politics of the civilian era. Political parties were banned, and the constitution was suspended. From 1969 to 1976, the SRC maintained the absolute authority over the nation's political, economic, social and judicial affairs. However, in a move to restore a democratic framework in 1976, Barre created the Somali Revolutionary Socialist Party (SRSP) as a vanguard party with both civilian and military members.[20] Barre became the Secretary General of the party and head of its political bureau. Thus, the country remained under one-man rule until Barre was ousted.

The clan orientation of Barre's regime was evident from the beginning. The Darood elements (Barre's clan) became dominant in all aspects of Somali life. Eleven of the 25 SRC members were from the Darood clan as were also 36 of the 75 members of the central committee of the party. Major clans, such as the Reewin, were completely ignored in the composition of the sole executive organs of the nation. The historic rights of the land-tenure system were violated. Many Darood groups were transplanted to areas and regions outside their place of origin. Traditional Somali regions were fragmented and subdivided in an effort to implement the regime's long-term clan policies.

Barre relied on his immediate clan, the Marehan, and also established closer relations with the Ogaden (Darood), his mother's clan and the Dulbahante (Darood), the clan of his son in-law. Thus, Barre's inner circle of advisors were drawn from these three Darood sub-clans. The deprived Somalis referred to this state of affairs as MOD government (Marehan, Ogaden, and Dulbahante). In an attempt to demonstrate that Somalia was not governed by one man, Barre offered two constitutions, one in 1979 and the other in 1989.[21] The first only confirmed his authoritarianism and made Somalia a one-party state, whereas the second, though calling for a multi-party system, never materialized, as Barre was ousted before the national referendum could confirm it.

V. The Tragedy

The overthrow of Barre caused profound disintegration. The opposition groups were all clan-based organizations, each fighting for a particular clan interest. This is clear from an examination of the areas of their operation. Some of the groups have focused their activities on areas historically controlled by their respective clans. The Somali National Movement (SNM), operated in the Isaaq inhabited areas of northern Somalia; the Somali Salvation Democratic Front (SSDF) in Mudug inhabited primarily by Majerteen; The United Somali Congress (USC) in the Hawiye territory of the central regions; and the Somali Democratic Movement (SDM), in the inter-riverine regions predominantly populated by Reewin.[22] Other groups were fighting to maintain the *status quo* and defend the territorial gains from previous administrations since independence.

Efforts of these groups are clear in the invented regions of Somalia, particularly on the riverine and coastal areas.[23] These groups included: the Somali Patriotic Movement,(SPM), an Ogaden clan-based movement fighting in the Middle and Lower Jubba regions; the Somali National Front, SNF, (Marehan) in Gedo; and the Somali National Alliance, a USC faction (Habar Gedir), in the Benadir and Lower Shabelle regions. Note that none of the above three clans -- the Ogaden, the Marehan and Habar Gedir -- had historic roots in the regions they currently claim. The regions belong mostly to the Dighil branch of Reewin and pockets of non-Habar Gedir Hawiye clans. Historically, the Ogaden occupy the southern region of Ethiopia which is known as "the Ogaden;" the Habar Gedir reside in Mudug, as do the Marehans. The Somali opposition therefore, had only one common denominator: to oust Siyad. Beyond that, they had nothing in common, and, indeed, they hated each other as much as they hated Siyad.

Meanwhile, the country is undergoing abominable conditions, from humanitarian tragedy to political anarchy. Prospects for peace and national reconciliation are deadlocked, as was Somalia's clan politics. International communities were generally successful in their humanitarian efforts, but the most important and delicate question concerning the future governing system in Somalia has not yet been answered.

There is no doubt that there are individuals in the various groups fighting for power in Somalia, who are capable of providing enlightened leadership. However, the current political climate may not allow for such leadership to rise. The Gorbachevs of Somalia are buried in the rubble of rigid authoritarianism and despotism of the various political factions fighting for control of Somalia.

It is necessary, therefore, to consider a program of transition to peace, democracy and prosperity in the future Somalia which includes:

1. an immediate cease-fire by all warring parties to create an atmosphere of peaceful dialogue and conflict resolution;

2. need to address the problems of clan-based nationalism and civil war in a pragmatic procedure;

3. a federation based on territorial integrity to safeguard against the endless civil strife.

Centralization in government is a root cause of the Somali conflict. Today, part of the country is a self-declared republic, and the other is run by traditional local clan authorities. Much effort and time are expended trying to forge unity for a people who do not want unity. It is necessary, therefore, to consider the possibility of establishing a confederation or cantonization rather than a unitary state.

Finally, let me conclude with cautious hope and optimism. Recent events from around the world clearly show that the forces of freedom and democracy are overcoming the forces of despotism and tyranny. I am hopeful that the current generation of educated Somalis can take advantage of this historical challenge and opportunity to provide constructive leadership to free Somalia from the continuous fear, war and poverty it has recently endured.

Whether we will meet this challenge by taking a united stand against despotism and tyranny, or continue to be victims of fear, force and historical accident will remain to be seen.

Chronology of Events in Somalia

1869 - Opening of the Suez Canal and European involvement in the Horn of Africa.

1897 - Formal partition of the Horn actualized in various treaties between Britain, France, Italy and Ethiopia.

1920 - Formation of al-Jam'iyyah al-Khayriyyah al-Wataniyya in Somalia (JKW).

1935 - Formation of Jam'iyyat 'Atiyyat al-Rahman in the British Protectorate (JAR).

1936 - Italian occupation in Ethiopia and the establishment of "la Grande Somalia." This was the first time that Somalis in Ethiopia came under one administration with Italian Somaliland.

1941 - Italian occupation of British protectorate. This marked the inclusion of Somalis in the British protectorate in the Italian colony in the Horn.

1943 - Formation of Somali Youth Club, (SYC). 6 of the 13 founding members were Reewin, 4 Darood and 3 Hawiye.

1947 - Formation of Hizbia Dighil Mirifle (HDM).

1947 - Formation of Somali Youth League (SYL).

1948 - Withdrawal of Britain from Ogadenia and the incorporation of the region into Ethiopia.

1948 - Emergence of the Somali National League (SNL) in the British Protectorate.

1949 - United Nations resolution for the return of former Italian Somaliland to Italy as a "Trust" administration.

1950 - Transfer of authority from Britain to Italy for the administration of the "Trust Territory" of Somalia.

1950 - Baidoa Incident in which the Mirifle community in the city showed their disenchantment against the Darood elements brought by the previous British colonial administration.

1951 - Establishment of the first territorial councils in the "Trust Territory" of Somalia.

1952 - Kismayo Incident in which the Dighil community in the city expressed their resentment against the non-Reewin elements in the region.

1954 - First municipal elections in the "Trust Territory" of Somalia.

1954 - Assassination of Ustad Usman Mohamed Hussein, the president of HDM.

1955 - Somalization of administration in the "Trust Territory" of Somalia.

1955 - Annexation of the Haud and Reserved Area to Ethiopia.

1956 - First general election and the formation of the first legislative assembly in the "Trust Territory" of Somalia.

1957 - First legislative councils in the British protectorate.

1958 - Second municipal elections in the "Trust Territory."

1959 - Second general election in Somalia and the extension of the number of deputies from 60 to 90.

1959 - Transformation of the legislative assembly into a national assembly.

1960 - First general election in the British Protectorate.

1960 - Independence of Somalia and the unification of the two regions as the Somali Republic.

1960 - Formation of the first Somali government composed of both regions, with Abdirashid A. Shermarke as premier.

1961 - Referendum for the first Somali constitution.

1961 - First presidential election which Aden Abdulle Osman won as the first president of the Republic.

1964 - First general election after independence and unity.

1967 - Second presidential election, with Shermarke winning against Osman.

1969 - Second general election and the polarization of clan parties.

1969 - Coup d'etat in Somalia.

1972 - Writing of Maha in Latin orthography, thus relegating other major languages to a lesser status.

1974 - Signing of the Somali-Soviet friendship treaty and the establishment of Soviet naval base in Berbera.

1974 - Somali Republic joins the Arab League.

1976 - Formation of the Somali Revolutionary Socialist Party, (SRSP).

1977 - Somali National Army defeated, at the hands of the Ethiopians.

1979 - Referendum for the second Somali constitution.

1980 - United States took over the Berbera Base for use by the Rapid Deployment Joint Task Force (U.S. Central Command).

1988 - Uprooting and destruction of Hargeisa by Government forces.

1991 - Downfall of Mohamed Siyad Barre's regime.

1991 - Northern Somali region's call for secession and independence from the rest of Somalia under "Somaliland Republic."

1991 - Warlords turn the Inter-River regions into "the Triangle of Death."

1992 - Establishment of United Nations Operation in Somalia (UNOSOM I) to assist political settlements and national reconciliation.

1992 -International intervention in the Somali tragedy UNITAF to establish a secure environment for humanitarian relief operation.

1993 - Establishment of UNOSOM II for peacemaking in the whole Somali territory. Their mandate is to use force not only in self-defense but to pursue its mission.

1993 - The peace and reconciliation conference in Addis Ababa, Ethiopia.

Table 1. Results of General Elections in Somalia

Party	1956	1959	1964	1969	1980
Liberal Party		2			
Hizbia Dastur Mustaquil al Somali	13	5	9	3	
Somali Democratic Union			15		
Somali National League					
Somali National Congress			22	11	
Somali Youth League	43	83	69	73	
Somali Democratic Party	3				
Marehan Party	1				
Somali Revolutionary Socialist Party					171
Other*			8	36	
Totals	60	90	123	123	177**

*In 1969 there were over 65 parties competing in the general election and although 50 seats were won by non-SYL parties, those elected crossed party lines and immediately joined with the SYL with one exception.

** In 1980, the president appointed 6 additional deputies under his authority which he called "Patriots," making the total 177.

Table 2. Regions and Clan Base 1960-1993.

Original Region(Total 8)	*Clan Base	Present Region (Total 18)	*Clan Base
Alta Jubba	1	Bay	1
		Bakool	1
		Gedo	1,2
Bassa Jubba	1	Jubadda Hoose	1,2,4
		Jubadda Dhexe	1,2
Benadir	1,4	Benadir	1,2,3,4,5
		Shabellada Hoose	1,4
Hiran	4	Hiran	4
		Shabellada Dhexe	1,4
Mudugh	2,4	Mudugh	2,4
		Galguduud	2,4
Mijurtinia	2	Bari	2
		Nugal	2
		Sanag	2
Northwest	3	W. Galbeed	3
		Awdal	5
Northeast	2,3	Sool	2
		Toghdeer	3

* 1. Reewin   2. Darood   3. Isaaq   4. Hawiye   5. Others

Table 3. Results of Somaliland General Election (1960)

Party	Seats
Somali National League	20
United Somali Party	12
National United Front	1

Table 4. Clan-Based Opposition, November 1993

Name	Clan Base	Area	Leader
Somali Afrikan Muki Organization	Jareer	Lower Shabelle, Lower & Middle Jubba	Mohamed F. Abdullahi
Somali Democratic Alliance	Gadubursi	Borama	A. Haji Hersi
Somali Democratic Movement	Reewin (Dighil)	Benadir, Lower Shabelle, Lower & Middle Jubba	Ali Ismail Abdi
United Somali Congress (SNA)	Hawiye (Habar Gedir)	Mudug	Gen. Mohamed Farrah Aidid
Somali National Front	Darood (Marehan)	Gedo Mudug & Lower Jubba	Gen. Omar Haji Mohamed
Somali National Movement	Isaaq	Northwest	Mohamed Ibrahim Egal
Somali National Union	Reer Hamar	Benadir	Mohamed Rafi Mohamed
Somali Salvation Democratic Front	Darood (Majerteen)	NE, Galgaduud, Nugal, Mudugh & Kismayo	Gen. Mohamed Abshir Mussa

Southern Somali National Movement	Dir	Lower Shabelle & Jubba	Col. Abdi Warsame Isaaq
USC	Hawiye (Abgal)	Galgaduud, Middle Shabelle & Benadir	Mohamed Qanyare Afrah
United Somali Front	Isse	Awdal	Abdurahman Duale Ali
United Somali Party	Darood (Dulbahante, Warsangali)	Sool, Sanaag	Mohamed Abdi Hashi
Somali Democratic Movement (SDM)	Reewin (Elay)	Bay, Lower Shabelle	Col. Mohamed Nur Alio
Somali Democratic Movement (Bonkai)	Reewin (Mirifle)	Bay, Bokool, Gedo	Abdulahi Mohamed Idris
Somali Patriotic Movement	Darood (Awlihan)	Lower & Middle Jubba	Gen. Aden Abullahi Nur
Somali Patriotic Movement (SNA)	Darood (M. Zubeer)	Lower Jubba	Col. Ahmed Omar Jess

Endnotes

1. Touval, Sadia. 1963. *Somali Nationalism*. Cambridge: Harvard University Press. Lewis, I.M. 1982. *A Pastoral Democracy*. New York: Africana Publishing Company, and Castagno, A. 1964. 'The Somali Republic' in James S. Coleman and Carl G. Rosberg (eds.) *Political Parties and National Integration in Tropical Africa*. Berkeley: University of California Press.

2. The *Reewin*, pronounced and ascribed mistakenly as *Rahanweyn* or *Rahhanwein*, are one of the largest groups in the Somali Peninsula. They occupy an area that extends from the Shabelle River in the east and Kenya in the west; the Indian Ocean in the south and southern Ethiopia in the north. They are agro-pastoral and speak a language of their own known as *Mai* (Maay or Maaymaay). Modern linguistic studies suggest that *Mai* is one of the oldest languages in the Horn of Africa. See: Lewis, H. 'The Origins of the Galla and Somali.' *Journal of African History* 7, 1966,

pp. 27-46. Unlike the nomadic clans of Somalia where political identity is based on genealogical lines, the *Reewin* developed a political structure that transcends lineage systems to a system of territorial identity. Terms like: *Reer Bay* (people of the Bay), *Reer Dhooboy* (people of the Dhooboy), *Reer Ghedo* (people of the other side of the Jubba River), *Reer Maanyo* (people of the sea) -- just to mention some -- explain how territorial identification is important in the *Reewin* political structure. For further details see: Cassanelli, *The Shaping of Somali Society*, pp. 15-25. The best general overview of *Reer Goleed* (people of Gosha) see: Menkhaus, Kenneth J. 'Rural Transformation and the Roots of Underdevelopment in Somalia's Lower Jubba Valley.' Ph.D. Dissertation, University of South Carolina, Columbia, 1989. pp. 16-40. With regard to their political thought see: Mukhtar, M. 'The Emergence and the Role of Political Parties in the Inter-river Region of Somalia.' *Ufahamu*, Vol. XVII, No. 2, UCLA 1989, pp. 75-95.

3. Mukhtar, Mohamed H. 1989. 'The Emergence and the Role of Political Parties in the Interriver Region of Somalia from 1947-1960 (Independence).' *Ufahamu*, Vol. XVII, No. 2, Berkeley: UCLA Press, p 82.

4. Potholm, Christian P. 1970. *Four African Political Systems*. Englewood Cliffs, NJ: Prentice Hall, Inc. p. 185.

5. Mukhtar, Mohamed H. 1983. 'al-Sumal ao-Itali Fi Fatrat al-Wisayah Hatta al-Istiqlal 1950-1960' (Italian Somaliland from Trusteeship to Independence, 1950-1960.) Ph.D. Dissertation, al-Azhar University, Cairo. pp. 7-9.

6. Hess, Robert L. 1966. *Italian Colonialism in Somalia*. Chicago: The University Press. pp. 175-6.

7. The Four Power Commission of Investigation of the Former Italian Colonies, Vol. II. 'Report of ex-Italian Somaliland.' 1948. p. 21.

8. Pankhurst, Sylvia. 1951. *Ex-Italian Somaliland*. London. pp. 230-243.

9. Castagno, A. 'The Somali Republic.' *Ibid.* pp. 522-23.

10. Details about the Anglo-Ethiopian Agreements, see: The test of the protocol in W/O 230/238/4628, Fol. 607/B, 1948. With regard to the Haud and the Reserved Areas issue, see: Drysdale, John. 1964. *The Somali Dispute*. Frederick A. Praeger. 1964. London. pp. 74-87. Information related to the Italian return, see: *UNGA, Resolution 289* (V), Nov. 21, 1949.

11. Lewis, I.M. 1967. 'Integration in the Somali Republic.' in Arthur Hazelwood (ed.) *African Integration and Disintegration*. London: University Press. p. 276.

12. Petition from the Central Committee of HDM to the UN Advisory Council, *T/Pet. 11/583*. August 26, 1955. The petition was signed by all Reewin members in the Territorial Council.

13. Castagno, A. 'Somali Republic', *Ibid*. p. 532.

14. Lewis, I.M. 'Integration in the Somali Republic.' *Ibid*. p. 274.

15. Lewis. *Ibid*. p. 274.

16. Potholm, Christian P. *Four African Political Systems*. *Ibid*. p. 203.

17. Lewis, I.M. 1972. 'The Politics of the 1969 Somali Coup.' *The Journal of Modern African Studies*. 10, 3, p. 397.

18. Bayne, E.A. 1969. 'Somalia's Myths are Tested.' American University Field Staff Report. Vol. XVI. No. 1. pp 7-10.

19. Lewis, I.M. 'The Politics of the 1969 Somali Coup.' *Ibid*. p. 401.

20. Nelson, Harold D. 1982. *Somalia. A Country Study*. Washington, DC: U.S. Government Printing Office. pp. 158-88.

21. Nelson, Harold D. (ed.). *Somalia. Ibid*. p. 188. Further attempts at constitutional reform, see: Makinda, Samuel M. 1993. *Seeking Peace From Chaos: Humanitarian Intervention in Somalia*. Boulder: Lynne Rienner Publishers. pp. 22-23.

22. Daniel Compagnon. 1990. 'The Somali Opposition Fronts: Some Comments and Questions.' *Horn of Africa*. Vol. XIII, No. 1 & 2. pp. 31-34.

23. There were eight regions in the Republic until the early 70s, but due to Barre's clan-oriented policies, the country was divided and redivided. By 1980, there were 18 regions. See Table 2.

CHAPTER FIVE

The Death of Somalia in Historical Perspective

Charles Geshekter

I. Introduction

The United Nations proclaimed 1993 the "International Year for Indigenous Peoples." Somalis called it *dad cunkii*, "a time of cannibalism," as their country degenerated into a murderous mayhem that destroyed the infrastructure of the nation. In 1992-93, Somalia became a metaphor for political disorder where over 300,000 Somalis died of starvation, warfare, or disease. Habitat deterioration, a militarized society, and the breakdown of social discipline constituted a culture of war and an economy of death.

The UN spent $4 billion in 1993-95 trying to rescue Somalis from the carnage of clan antagonisms that dismembered the country into semi-autonomous regions. Peace-keeping initiatives and large-scale humanitarian intervention were futile amidst the fratricidal battles that consumed Mogadishu. The ultimate symbol of the failed Somali state, the capital of Mogadishu was detached from wider Somali political culture which functioned away from the capital where people insisted, "no more Mogadishu." Without coherent objectives, a unified command, or realistic timetables for its exit, UN forces occasionally devastated Mogadishu even more, where 35% of its one million people could not provide themselves with basic necessities. Botched attempts to administer Mogadishu through a strategy of military intervention prompted Somalis to view the UN as little more than a successor to Mohamed Siyad Barre, the despised military dictator who ruled Somalia from 1969 to 1991.

However, it was not true that "failure in Mogadishu will mean failure in Somalia."[1] Away from Mogadishu, inter-clan fighting subsided and armed militias were much less in evidence by 1996. Pasture lands improved with good rains and reduced livestock. Working well without external interference, a succession of local power bases had emerged. Starvation had largely disappeared, hundreds of thousands of children were immunized, livestock exports increased, and schools reopened.[2] While the capital remained racked by anarchy and spasmodic violence, eighty miles away in Baidoa - Somalia's "starvation capital" in 1992 - local citizens and French UN troops celebrated a festive 1993 Bastille Day with parades, luncheons, and a soccer match.[3]

It is part of Somali culture to care about the specific part of the country where one lives. With local identity and a sense of community among kinsmen narrowly conceived, rebellious clan factions were unwilling to accept a singular rule of law from any central authority. Mogadishu holds little positive importance for most Somalis, whose country is a glaring example of "subnational factions in permanent rebellion against uniformity and integration...at war not just with globalism but with the traditional nation-state."[4] In the two decades that followed independence in 1960, Somalis considered nationalism a force for integration and unification. After the events of the past fifteen years, however, they remember their national government as a divisive force that provided no one with a safe environment.[5]

The disintegration of Somalia raised policy questions about the culture of power in the modern state, the definition of good governance, the principle of national sovereignty, and the concept of "humanitarian intervention." The meddling of foreign powers accelerated Somalia's collapse. But one cannot blame Somalia's misery on external exploitation or multinational conspiracies, and then exonerate its own inept leadership, weak political institutions, or warring local parties. To assume that Africans are forever victims merely perpetuates colonialist notions of an inert, helpless Africa. The post-colonial Somali elites misgoverned Somalia.[6]

In 1989, British journalist Richard Dowden observed that it was "bitterly ironic that Somalia, the only nation in Africa with one ethnic group, one culture, one language, and one religion should be the most deeply divided of the continent's fifty-two fractious countries. The Somali nation has broken down into its tribes and there is little trust between them."[7] To a certain extent, Somalia was a unique African country because its people generally spoke the same language, practiced a similar way of life, adhered to the same religion, shared a common culture, and even bore physical resemblances. So why were Somali leaders such poor stewards of their own patrimony? Since the rehabilitation of Somalia must begin there, a re-appraisal of Somali homogeneity is a good place to start.

This apparent unity overlooked heterogeneous Somali experiences and deep-seated clan differences that no colonial or post-colonial government ever managed to reconcile within a national entity. Authority was dispersed in traditional Somali culture; the modern Somali state concentrated it. In the disemboweled Somali state, obsolete institutions and idealized concepts helped destroy the country.

In the late 20th century, the international community consists of an industrialized core of social democracies and a non-industrialized periphery of vulnerable people who face ecological collapse and the disintegration of local authority.[8] The core states sustain their domination over peripheral economies through local elites which maintain the relationship "internally by exclusion or by manipulation of domestic social forces."[9] The global civil society takes this existing order as something to be made to work more smoothly, not something to be criticized or changed. Marxist and liberal predictions that ethnicity and primordial loyalties would disappear as a result of modernization now seem premature or the opposite of what actually happened. Cultural unity may be insufficient to prevent the demise of contemporary states beset by the centrifugal forces of separatism, movements of ethnic rage, and religious fundamentalism.[10]

Popular insurrections in Somalia that challenge the legitimacy of a central state suggest it has become less useful to think in terms of the nation-state now than at any time since World War II. Similar forces imperil adjacent countries of the region. This essay suggests that Somalia is an exceptional case rather than a precursor for several reasons: (a) the decentralized democratic politics of traditional Somali conflict resolution; (b) its multiple colonial traditions and regional sub-cultures; and (c) an indigenous social order that shrewdly manipulated foreigners for domestic gain.

On the other hand, Somalia may be treated as a case study that illustrates four wider themes: (a) the fragile, incoherent, divisive nature of the state in modern Africa; (b) the long-term effects of the Cold War on a place where it was fought by proxies; (c) the crisis of governance and leadership in Africa; and (d) that without responsive, accountable political institutions, a common language, culture and religion cannot guarantee national cohesion.

II. Kinship, Culture, Somali Values, and Islam

Somalis have inhabited northeast Africa for over 2500 years. The semi-arid environment permits cultivation in the southern inter-riverine area and at the extremities of the northern mountain range. However, the mainstay of Somali life until the mid-20th century was nomadic pastoralism, a system of resource management based on a delicate balance of animal movements whose success required freedom of mobility to locate precious grazing and water. Ten years ago, 65% of Somalis practiced nomadic pastoralism, the highest percentage of any country in the world.

Their ingenious engagement with a harsh environment helped make Somalis what they are. The Somalis' lineage segmentation, where one had neither permanent enemies nor friends, produced a mercurial political style captured in the Bedouin proverb: "my brother and I against my half-brother; my brothers and I against my father; my father's household against my uncle's household, our two households (my uncle's and mine) against the rest of the immediate kin; the immediate kin against non-immediate members of the clan; my clan against other clans; my nation and I against the world."[11] But arrayed against this hoary stereotype of Somalis as bellicose people there were the equally revered and widespread qualities of kindness, hospitality, generosity, tenacity, courage, and humor.[12]

Somali clan distinctions reflected historical experiences and social class differences. In the southern inter-riverine area lived the Rahanweyn and Dighil farming communities, less aggressive clans who spoke a distinct Somali dialect called *mai*. The Darood clan families who surrounded the Rahanweyn long despised them and treated them as second class people, even during the three decades of modern Somali independence. It was no coincidence that the farmers around Baidoa and Bur Hacaba suffered the worst atrocities by Darood and Hawiya militias in the mayhem that followed the overthrow of Siyad Barre in 1991.[13]

The Benadiri Somalis along the southern coast are cosmopolitans in towns like Brava, Merca and the oldest sections of Mogadishu (*Xamar Weyne*) established over 600 years ago. These sea-oriented, mercantilist communities maintained rich traditions in the material arts.[14] Somalis would often invoke inter-clan stereotypes and assert hierarchies of nobility against the so-called "Bantuized Somali" communities of southwestern Somalia, some of whom descended from liberated East African slaves from the 19th century.

Somali nomads could be notoriously prejudiced against darker skinned people against whom they hurled racial slurs. In 1992, a nurse with Save the Children Fund was shocked to hear some Somalis sneer that they would "rather see our children starve than feed alongside these smelly Bantu."[15] Clan distinctiveness, nomads versus farmers, and racial conceits were disquieting factors beneath the public relations image of a homogeneous Somali nation.

The competition for resources implied that one group's gain was at the expense of another's in a zero-sum game of sub-clan power. In harsh times, the circle of trust contracted, excluding those who were genealogically distant. Sub-clan unity was maintained by respecting equality among members who gained equal access to the means of livelihood by which justice was measured. Somalis are proud people for whom acknowledging the need for help comes hard. The "Somali pastoralist's view of himself [was] never to accept to be below others or subservient to anybody, except to the Almighty."[16]

Pioneering Muslim missionaries came to the Somali lands as early as the 12th century. As Sunni Muslims of the Shafi' rite, Somalis are united by the egalitarian message of Islam that inspires dignity and courtesy towards others. They embrace Islam as symbol of self-esteem and personal responsibility. Islam in Somali culture is dominated by religious scholars and charismatic preachers affiliated with Sufi *tariqas* (brotherhoods). The political activism of Islam was mitigated by the dispersal of power among clan elders who accommodated Islam through localized political contracts and relied on men of religion to judge cases of Shari'a law.

Amidst the current chaos in Somalia, a new puritanical Islamicist movement called *Al-Itixaad al Islami* ("Islamic Unity") resorted to simplified rhetoric that fed on the dire conditions of poverty and a yearning for law and order. Through sermons and social assistance (such as clinics and schools), *Al-Itixaad* became a potential rallying point for Somalis exhausted by the factionalism that destroyed their country. Known popularly as *Al-Ikhwaan* (the "Brethren"), the movement attracted Somalis who sought reassurance in a rigid code of conduct. When *Al-Ikhwaan* members warned that food or other goods stolen from their owners are *xaaraan* ("unholy things"), they appealed to urban dwellers terrorized by thieves and bandits. On the other hand, the Mogadishu warlords were hostile to anyone who preached against their staples of booty, cigarettes, and qat.[17]

In the long run, *Al-Itixaad* will remain primarily a nuisance to

Somalis who are vulnerable to emotional blackmail if accused of infidelity to Islam. Since *Al-Itixaad* is financed and equipped from sources in the Sudan and Iran, some Somalis suspect it seeks to "Arabize" them. Somali fears are reinforced whenever *Al-Itixaad* condemns the Somali veneration of Sufi saints as a form of idolatry and forbids pilgrimages to their shrines. Somalis are deeply attached to local saints whom they praise for their piety or venerate for mystical intercessionary powers. Some devotees of local saints in Somalia believe that three visits to the tomb of Sheikh Maddar outside Hargeisa are the equivalent of one visit to Mecca and hence earn one the title of hajji, a designation which Arabs would, of course, repudiate. Such cultural practices are an important part of rural social life which enable Somalis to resist the blandishments of *Al-Itixaad*, another way that Somali culture limits the role of Islam as a supra-national force.[18] Despite strong links to the Arab world, Somalis do not consider themselves "Arabs," with whom their relations range from ambivalence to hostility.

Notwithstanding the Somalis' reluctance to be called "Arabs," Somalia joined the Arab League in 1974 to gain geo-political advantages. In the mid-1980s, classes that taught Arabic to Somali adults were still noticeable around Mogadishu. Somali workers expelled from the Gulf states and Saudi Arabia prior to Operation Desert Storm and subsequently limited amounts of Arab League relief aid provided over the past decade seemed to embitter Somalis towards Arabs. When the UN dispatched Pakistani peacekeepers to Mogadishu in 1992, Somalis scorned them as people who "have nothing in common with us whatsoever except for the spices they use in their food."[19] In June 1993, forces of warlord Mohamed Farah Aidid ambushed and killed twenty-four Pakistanis, then mutilated their bodies in a defiant act to brand them "infidels" unfit for acceptance into heaven. Somalis joke that they're not Arab enough for Arabs and not African enough for Africans, leaving them somewhere in between, a "stepchild to either culture."[20]

III. Somali Nationalism

In the pre-colonial era, communitarian kin ties and not a centralized state maintained the customs of Somali civil society. Somalis exploited the meager resources of the region through decentralized processes of political and marital alliances that inhibited national consciousness. Within the fragmented Somali nation, colonial traditions further accentuated regional distinctions. In response to international trade opportunities, some Somalis thrived and others did not. In Somalia as elsewhere in Africa, colonial regimes generally "exploited tensions among these groups to enhance their own power; existing differences were sharpened by the uneven impact of social and economic change. Ethnic groups became `advanced' or "backward," rich or poor as the internal realities of Somali society grew more heterogenous.[21]

Somalis considered European colonial administrations as alien and undemocratic and equated them with the term "oppression" (*gumeysi*). Indigenous towns that were commercial or religious in nature were called *beled-salaama* (peaceful places) as distinct from 20th century urban areas that came to be known as *beled colaadeed* (city of strife), *beled gaalaad* (city of infidels) or *lama degaan* (cursed place). Rural dwellers were often contemptuous of city folk. By the 1960s, Somalis scorned urban bureaucrats as lazy, unproductive siphons "who sat around so much they made their chairs tired." Somali pastoralists treated city dwellers with suspicion and dread, and traditionally abandoned towns thought to be cursed with bad luck.[22]

As an external institution, the colonial state concentrated economic opportunities and material resources in places that Somalis feared and despised. The historical basis for the Somali national state was opposite that of Europe where capitalism first emerged through civic social institutions and where centralized government became a legal instrument to correct inequalities and imbalances. Throughout the colonial period, some sub-clans benefitted from the colonial presence because they were better positioned by pre-colonial social arrangements to take advantage of opportunities afforded by collaboration. Even though Somali civil society existed without the need for a pan-Somali state, the Somali nationalist agenda extolled after 1945 complementarity and insisted on homogeneity.

The late 19th century colonialist division of the Somali range lands among Britain, France, Italy, and Ethiopia had contributed to a national sense of resentment. In the 1940s, the first modern Somali political organizations, the Somali Youth League and the Somali National League, made political freedom and territorial unification their primary objectives. The fragmentation of the Somalis was considered a "wound" inflicted by Christian strangers who had "dismembered" the Somali lands. The main intellectual goal and common denominator for advocates of Somali national consciousness was unification under a single Somali state. Without a whole Somali nation, Somali identity was deemed incomplete. Somali nationalists insisted that only a central state could restore the territorial integrity of pastoralist rangelands and unite its people under one independent Somali government.

An educated Somali class resorted to rhetorical devices, poetic exhortations, and mass organizations to mobilize people. The quest for territorial re-unification became the sine qua non of Somali nationalism, a political imperative that supported irredentism and led Somalis "to misapprehend the world outside their own lands and customs, [and] to see it in terms of fanciful concepts."[23] At independence in 1960, the five-pointed star on the new Somali flag symbolized the search for "Greater Somalia," a future state that would re-unite all five Somali-inhabited territories to make a homogeneous nation whole once again. In a thoughtful analysis of the *siinley* poetic duels of the 1970s, however, Ali Jimale Ahmed warns that since "no one has documented a chronology of Somali national consciousness beyond what seems to be its genealogical manifestation, we cannot really demonstrate that all Somalis saw themselves as one people (including Reewin [Rahanweyn], Barawa, Gosha, Boni) before colonialism [emphasis in original]."[24]

During the 1950s, Somalis rallied under the banner of anti-colonialism. Popular support for reunification campaigns to create a "Greater Somali" identity became an "underlying spirit of national unity which, under severe provocation, unleashed considerable emotion."[25] Amidst the era of African decolonization, the Somali Republic was formed on July 1, 1960 when the ex-British northern and the ex-Italian southern regions united to form a national state that presided tenuously over the fissionary tendencies of clan society.[26]

When African countries emerged from colonialism in the 1950s and 1960s, they agreed to maintain the boundaries established by European administrations. It was thought that strong governments would engineer development programs, initiate social reforms, and create political structures imbued with a sense of national unity. Inside those boundaries, ethnic groups competed vigorously for privileges that came from affiliation with the government in power. Whichever group controlled the capital city with all of its real and symbolic power, was the one that received critical external assistance, especially during the decades of US-Soviet rivalry in Africa.

Although many northern Somalis in the former British Somaliland supported the 1960 union with ex-Italian Somalia, the two territories had been individual colonial states for over fifty years and had grown institutionally and historically distinctive. Once political independence and partial reunification were achieved, Somalis began to squabble among themselves. Regional sub-cultures, aggravated by social class competition, festered over the next twenty years to eventually produce domestic conflicts as lethal as those anywhere in the world.[27] Communal ties became the basis for post-colonial competition over public patronage and international aid and struggle ensued among the Somali ruling class that "invented clanism as a means of mobilizing the population while its members competed to capture the state in order to enrich themselves."[28]

The Somalis' colonial experiences under British and Italian rule produced different concepts of accountable governance, financial systems, and commercial opportunities. Some cynics have called Italy a country run as a protection racket, where the clientelism built into everyday life spread money around so that every state job belonged in some way to a political party.[29] The southern Somali elite adapted to this system while northern Somalis from a British colonial tradition considered themselves alien to that sort of governmental system. When social class differences, clan particularism, and distinctive colonial histories were manipulated and aggravated by the Siyad regime over a twenty-year period, the result was economic discrimination and genocidal madness comparable to the ethnic cleansing that overwhelmed Yugoslavia in 1992-94.[30]

As a focal point for superpower rivalries, independent Somalia relied on an international dripline that provided the external subsidies and loans needed to run its government. With its predominantly rangeland ecology and low population density, the country had few economic prospects to sustain itself and imported everything from tractors to needles. Somalia developed into a client state and an international supplicant under Siyad Barre who used its strategic location to play the superpowers against each other: the US against the USSR, the USSR against China, and moderate Arab states such as Egypt and Saudi Arabia against Libya and Iran.

Somali governments allowed the country to become a playground for Cold War maneuvers. The economic and military aid supplied by the Soviet Union and the US to buy Somali friendship was often squandered by unaccountable public sector officials who institutionalized corruption without moral discipline.[31] Somalia was nicknamed the "graveyard of foreign aid," the country with the highest per capita rate of foreign aid in Africa, where the state became a conduit that transferred wealth from western countries and the USSR to a new national clan of Somali bureaucrats.

The post-colonial Somali state shifted disputes over resources to a non-nomadic venue where differences in educational and economic opportunities and the control of funds hardened into differential access to power. Those who jockeyed to control Somalia gradually became a "state clan" that depended on foreign expertise to run its administration, on external aid for development projects, and on foreign loans to cover recurrent costs. Public institutions decayed as civil servants supplemented salaries through legalized corruption.[32]

Presiding over a society where agro-pastoralists ignored fixed boundaries and whose traditional political economy depended on a dispersion of resources, Somali leaders were obsessed with changing the existing boundaries of northeast Africa to concentrate Somalis under a single government. Unification into an even "greater Somalia" remained the central moral institution of its national consciousness. Thus, Somalia became the type of country that Stanley Hoffman called a place where the "subjective self-image that citizens have of their nation, which often selects only some features of the national identity, or distorts them or invents new ones" turns nationalism into "an ideology, [and] a program of action that sets goals and, more often than not, defines and defies enemies."[33]

To maintain the fiction of a unified Somalia devoid of internal (or sub-ethnic) conflicts, Mogadishu administrators routinely decreed harmonious communal goals for the Somali people among whom no divisions could be acknowledged. Political analysts of the 1960s and 1970s may have noticed few differences among a poor Rahanweyn inter-riverine farmer, a wealthy Isaaq livestock exporter, a Bravan weaver, and a Habar Gedir camel herder, but Somalis knew all about them. Obsessed with remaking the past to suit their contemporary image, modern rulers tried to ban Somalis from verbalizing clan affiliations. Mocking such commandments, Somalis would facetiously ask each other, "what's your ex-clan?"

The original Somali constitution of 1960 proclaimed the country would "promote, by legal and peaceful means, the union of Somali territories." This foreign policy marooned Somalia outside mainstream African politics where upholding the boundaries inherited from the colonial period were considered a sacred principle.

Somalia further isolated itself from post-colonial Africa by condemning neighboring Ethiopia, which Somali leaders branded a "black colonialist power" at a time when Africans equated colonialism with the European variety. The Pan-African Movement of Caribbeans, black Americans and Africans living away from the Horn had long rhapsodized about Ethiopia "as a solid island of freedom in the stormy waters of colonial aggression" and revered its legacy as "an impregnable rock of black resistance against white invasion."[34] Emperor Haile Selassie parlayed this mystique about Ethiopia with his own shrewd diplomatic skills in having Addis Ababa chosen as the headquarters for the new Organization of African Unity in 1963.

Unlike the pan-Africanists, Somalis rarely had illusions about symbolic Ethiopia as they primarily recalled adversarial relations with the armed forces of its colonial state that had occupied the Ogaden. To non-Somalis, the Greater Somalia rhetoric seemed unjustified and deprived the country of supporters in Africa and abroad. Somali governments had neither been able to secure regional peace nor create domestic social justice, so when the country disintegrated in 1991-92, the OAU deserted it. In an ironic reversal in 1993-94, the UN actually invited Ethiopian and Eritrean leaders to help fashion an "African solution to an African problem."[35]

IV. Centripetal Military Force in a Centrifugal Culture: 1969-91

Nine years of democratically elected Somali governments ended in October 1969 when General Mohamed Siyad Barre established a military regime, ostensibly to end internal bickering over the country's direction. For a few years, his socialist-oriented, developmental dictatorship provided relatively creative rule. It embarked on administrative reforms and crash campaigns of mass literacy, drought relief, and educational development. By 1975-76, however, it had degenerated into a personality cult based on nepotism and military repression. While civil servants were drawn from throughout the country, key military positions and government posts were assigned to members of Siyad's Darood sub-clans, primarily the Marehan, Dulbahante, Ogaden and Majerteen.

The regime generated huge amounts of regulatory red tape that created fertile grounds for official corruption. The economic mainstays of livestock and agriculture remained primarily in private hands. Siyad's mother was from an Ogaden clan and by 1976 he sought its independence from Ethiopia and amalgamation with Somalia. In 1977, three years after the overthrow of Emperor Haile Selassie amidst the tumultuous socialist revolution in Addis Ababa, Siyad dispatched Somali army regulars to help local insurrectionists "liberate" the contested Ogaden. The initial euphoria of Somali victories evaporated into a humiliating defeat when the Soviet Union rushed military advisors, troops and equipment to aid Ethiopia.

The military debacle of 1978 shattered all hopes for achieving a Greater Somalia and signaled the demise of pan-Somalism. Betrayed by their socialist allies, Somalis bitterly criticized Siyad's leadership for bungling the "liberation" venture and soon turned against each other. An attempted coup, poorly organized by disaffected Majerteen military officers, resulted in the frightful reprisals of a scorched earth policy against the northeastern region by Siyad's state security agencies. The Majerteen became the first clan to desert the regime and to mount an open insurrection when Colonel Abdullahi Yusuf defected from the Somali army in 1978 to establish the Somali Democratic Salvation Front (SSDF). By 1981, the national state called Somalia began to die a slow, agonizing death.

Fleeing retaliation in Ethiopia, over 500,000 refugees entered

Somalia in the early 1980s, many of them Ogadeni guerrillas armed with modern weaponry. In northern Somalia, grazing disputes between Ogadenis and Isaaq herders boiled over into antagonisms over rural/urban lifestyle differences. Terrorized by a veritable "foreign" army of occupation composed of Darood clansmen, the Isaaq bitterly complained throughout the 1980s that armed rural Ogadeni refugees together with poorly-paid Marehan and Dulbahante soldiers provoked and encouraged by Siyad behaved in a despicably "un-Somali and un-Islamic manner." They raped women, murdered unarmed civilians, and prevented families from conducting proper burials.

Siyad repressed criticism of the widespread atrocities in the north and disallowed any discussion of them; throughout the 1980s his base of support narrowed severely as Somalia's death spasms intensified.

The military mentality of hierarchy and infallible commands was the antithesis of the principles of Somali pastoral democracy whose philosophy and machinery of government were based on consent and lengthy discussions. The military regime required obedience not agreement, demanded secrecy not candor, and relied on propaganda not information. Somali traditional values were eroded by a dictatorship that appointed people based on loyalty and servility, not competence.

Siyad tried to eliminate the customary practice of making "blood payments" (livestock transfers) to effect legal settlements, rewarded clans for their loyalty to the "Siyadist Revolution," and appointed mediators to replace the elders as liaisons between lineages and the government. Siyad removed significant decisions from public review, muzzled the press, and jailed dissenters. The regime preached national unity, but waged cultural war against its critics, primarily members of the Isaaq and Majerteen clans. The army swelled from 20,000 troops in 1973 to 120,000 in 1983, making it the second largest military force in sub-Saharan Africa.

The military government took inter-clan fights to new heights, producing a disequilibrium that could not be contained in any way familiar to nomadic culture. Somali political culture never adapted to the modern political apparatus of a commandist state. With its unusually low ratio of population to land in this largely nomadic society, the absence of effective political centralization left open the possibility of segmentation into familiar social clusters. As Siyad's military government controlled less and less of the countryside, Somalis sought the safety of their lineages and sub-clans for survival. By the mid-1980s, popular anger took the form of withdrawal from a government that was dying from within.

Accountable to no one, the repressive military lords under Siyad Barre equated criticism with treason. Communal strife and discord intensified; opposition groups formed along clan lines, often led by disgruntled officials who were unable to articulate any comprehensive national policies. The institutional weakness of central authority, the widespread availability of firearms, and the lack of strong, well-organized opposition parties produced the warlordism of bandit gangs that maintained security and threatened outsiders. Somali mafia-style protection rackets contributed to the economy of the warlords. Mostly ex-supporters and "dubious relics" from Siyad's regime, they thrived on livestock deals, drug trafficking, weapons procurement, and the theft and redistribution of food aid.[36]

An obsession with weaponry - small arms, grenades, land mines, semi-automatic weapons, tanks - laid the groundwork for a culture of war and an economy of death. Two decades of ruthless repression emptied Somalia of national political leaders, leaving military thugs and gangsters in towns, while clan elders and religious figures struggled to maintain a semblance of social order in rural locales.

Amidst the growing political disarray of the 1980s, analysts typically characterized Somalia as economically hopeless. They advocated austerity measures to cut government expenditures, devalue the currency, and liberalize markets. The economist Vali Jamal, however, reconceptualized the World Bank's statistics to show how such evaluations underestimated the nutritional value of milk in Somali diets (vital in a pastoral economy) and ignored the economic impact of overseas remittances earned in Arab states (thirteen times the Somalia-based wage bill) that were sent home through informal channels.

Describing Somalia as an "unconventional economy," Jamal demonstrated how Somali civil society managed to endure through a web of obligations in which lineage loyalties operated on a smaller, more intimate stage.[37] Resilient and adaptable, Somali families provided a social security and welfare system that re-distributed resources even as the national Somali state was entering its final death throes.

A 1987 International Labor Office study characterized Somali families as "multi-occupational, even multi-national production units. Most townspeople have kith and kin in the nomadic and farm sectors and most have at least a distant relative in the Gulf countries." The Somali clan system was the conduit for the transfer of remittances through several hands, an economic lifeline that could stretch from overseas workplaces in Britain, Italy, Kuwait, and Saudi Arabia "to a nomadic family grazing their livestock across the border in Ethiopia."[38] The ILO offered an admittedly low estimate that Somalis earned $700 million in the Gulf states in 1985 and remitted $280 million (30%) to Somalia. The ILO concluded that the 200,000 Somalis working in the Middle East "had far-reaching consequences for levels of living, domestic economic development and management of the economy."[39] These overseas Somali workers remain critical factors when analyzing the economic prospects for separate autonomy movements in northern and northeastern Somalia.

Somalia was not a pristine society "uncontaminated" by the modern world. Rather, it had been internationalized, thanks to the Somalis' own 20th century diaspora that reached nearly every continent.[40] Somalis initiated overseas work and sent home earnings to families with whom they retained emotional and financial ties. Somali travelers admitted that wherever they went, "they never left home." Their money was passed back to kinfolk through the integrity of couriers, fellow clansmen who formed an indispensable "Somali Savings Bank" sustaining an overseas trade and cash nexus that escaped the controls of a central government.

Somalis were both sophisticated and isolated. Somalia was a country of paradoxes where naive nomads mingled among urbane world travelers. Female genital mutilation was still performed on nearly all Somali women. Yet literary, urban Somalis knew all about Shakespeare, whom they humorously called "*Sheikh Subeer.*" And the BBC's Somali language broadcasts generated a response of 1000 letters a month from Somali listeners around the world.[41]

Somalia never developed an ample number of competent, disciplined cadres with the administrative training and technical strength necessary to manage development projects. The inability of the government to provide minimal national services undermined political stability. By the 1980s, absenteeism and embezzlement were widespread in the civil service. The government rarely invested funds in productive capacities and had no "maintenance mentality." A former Chief of Protocol at the Foreign Ministry recalled that officials would "use a building until it collapsed for lack of maintenance and care, then just move to another one. This is why we could not even retain what was left behind by the colonial powers."[42]

The Somali national state was poorly grounded in the sentiments of the general population except with regard to external threats. Somalia operated without a standardized education system to link a modern culture or to transform Somalis into a national citizenry. The revolutionary transformation of the Somali language in 1972 provided the country with a unified educational system that lasted fifteen years, enough for one generation of Somalis to use common texts and syllabuses.[43]

Beyond the redemption of the Somali lands, there were few national objectives that Somalis could agree upon. Relationships became expendable once clan lines were crossed. Theirs was an ethnic nationalism directed against external enemies and internal scapegoats as a means of mobilization, an imagined community that remained, by definition, exclusively Somali. Supraclan solidarity was a function of common resistance to non-Somali colonizers. Beyond that however, inter-clan differences were as deep as cleavages anywhere in Africa. In truth, Somalia was a multi-cultural state.

In northern Somalia in the 1980s, the Isaaq clans confronted a massive influx of Ogadeni refugees from eastern Ethiopia whom Siyad encouraged to loot property, attack people, and destabilize cities. An instrument of suppression, the Ogadenis and the regular Somali army were viewed as alien forces sent to oppress the Isaaq. Clan animosity intersected with class antagonisms as rural Ogadeni clansmen harassed Isaaq entrepreneurs with a visceral hatred, convinced that their wealth and urban commodities were undeserved. The Isaaq tell pathetic stories about Ogadenis who stole modern household appliances from homes in Hargeisa, Borama and Burao, then retreated with their "trophies," expecting them to work in remote pasture lands devoid of electricity.

In a horrific frenzy between 1988-90, the Somali government murdered 60,000 civilians in the northern towns, destroyed buildings, poisoned wells, and planted one million land mines to climax the most repressive regime in Somali history.[44] Net foreign aid donations to Somalia from 1985-1990 exceeded $1.4 billion, of which northerners received 7%, even though their 3 million people were 35% of the population. Any semblance of Somali political unity vanished under the lethal attacks on the north as ethnic nepotism was marked by criminal vengeance.

The final collapse of a central Somali government in 1991 removed the last obstacles to the formation of new regional polities that sought self-preservation against these alienating circumstances. In the northern part of the country, the declaration of independence by "Somaliland" on 18 May 1991 culminated decades of economic discrimination and suffering that hardened into a regional, clan-based identity. The Isaaq communities throughout the Burao-Berbera-Hargeisa triangle demanded secession as the first step towards regional self-reliance. There was a coalition of reasons for their unprecedented action: 1) Islamic leaders and elders supported the Somaliland National Movement (SNM) with food and recruits; 2) the Isaaq used overseas remittances to acquire weapons for protection; and 3) their cultural alienation from rural Ogadenis and the army of Siyad Barre convinced them that "separation is viable, union is a liability."

Although weak and inexperienced, the fledgling Somaliland Republic has been activated by Somalis eager to stake out new collective boundaries for themselves. Since the central Somali government offered them no defense, the Isaaq combined local traditions with their own modern experiences to resurrect a polity based on the boundaries of the former British Somaliland Protectorate. Elders and religious leaders organized the distribution of food relief, adjudicated disputes, and recruited fighters for the SNM. By late 1995, Somaliland was headed towards a form of consociational democracy which recognized that ethnic or clan identities should be considered for membership in a government while "civil and military appointments combine proportionality with merit criteria."[45]

By 1991, all traces of a Somali patriotism upon which to base a unified country had vanished. The union of northern and southern Somalia was seen as a thirty-one year marriage that turned so acrimonious that it left almost no redeeming features and hence ended in bitter divorce. As most policemen will attest, family disputes are usually the deadliest.

V. End of the Cold War, End of Somalia

The vagaries of the Cold War and Siyad's shrewd domestic manipulation of clan configurations help to explain the durability of his regime. By exploiting Cold War rivalries, Siyad managed to acquire the capacity for repressive action but was unable to manage social forces or direct economic development. The destructive consequences of the Cold War remained visible everywhere in immense stockpiles of weapons available at bargain prices: 106mm recoilless rifles, semi-automatic assault rifles, grenades, rocket launchers, tanks, and land mines.

The end of the Cold War was pivotal to the timing of the final disintegration of Somalia. The country ceased to function once the West, no longer needing to compete diplomatically with a defunct communist bloc, grew tired of propping up a government unable to maintain itself. The collapse of Somalia was the result of internal centrifugal forces that coalesced in 1991 when the West abandoned Somalia to its own devices.[46] Without mineral resources, opportunities for capital investment, or even geo-strategic allure, Somalia was relegated to "a larger basket of African countries facing progressive strategic marginalization."[47] The United States made little use of its Horn facilities during the 1991 war with Iraq and the former Soviet Union abandoned all interest in the region. After visiting Somalia in June 1992, US Senator Nancy Kassebaum claimed that "if the Soviet Union still existed today we would never have allowed Somalia to disintegrate this way." In fact, Somalia's slide towards death had been underway long before 1989.

Denied injections of foreign funds and unable to inspire his countrymen, Siyad Barre had become just the "Mayor of Mogadishu" where his narrow clan-based government brutally tried to maintain its shrunken power base. Mogadishu became the final arena in the struggle to topple Siyad Barre as his well-armed supporters degenerated into kleptomaniacs whose desperate attempts to preserve their power led them to destroy the urban infrastructure of roads, communications systems, and government ministries.

In late 1990 rebels swarmed into Mogadishu forcing the man whom Somalis contemptuously called Afweyne ("Big Mouth") to flee the city concealed in a tank on 27 January 1991. In an ironically symbolic twist, the American and Soviet Ambassadors were airlifted from Mogadishu aboard the same US helicopter to an aircraft carrier that was part of the force assembled for "Operation Desert Storm."

Two generations of Somalis had failed to provide the country with political or intellectual leadership. As demoralized civil servants fled abroad, they left a ransacked infrastructure and an administrative legacy of unscrupulous practitioners. All semblance of government collapsed. Inter-clan atrocities turned Somalia into a lethal place without schools, prisons, courts, police, or diplomats where public property was destroyed, copper wires and water pipes dug up and sold, and foreign relief personnel killed. In this "writhing nest of tribal gangs," there were no centralized political forces left with "the credibility, imagination, and capability to disarm the population and start the peace process and reconstruction."[48] Amidst the ruins of Mogadishu and nearby towns, looters and killers conducted sadistic military missions for food, fuel, bullets and qat. The remnants of Siyad's forces retreated through the Bay and Juba regions, Somalia's richest farming areas, with their Hawiya enemies in pursuit. Factional fighting subjected the region to a scorched earth policy as rival militias mercilessly preyed upon the agro-pastoralist and nomadic communities.[49]

While the United Nations, the US and the Arab League focused on Iraq throughout 1990-91, the anarchy of the post-Siyad era distinguished Somalia as a place in dire need of assistance which the Red Cross called "the worst humanitarian disaster in the world since 1945." After its central government disappeared, southern Somalia was overwhelmed for two years by famine, disease, and murder before the world's centralizing institution, the United Nations, intervened in late 1992.[50]

VI. UNOSOM: A Return to Centralization?

Somalia became a violent crucible where disorder at the center of its state compelled people to construct decentralized polities on its peripheries. While ostensibly designed as a humanitarian operation to save lives, the United Nations Operations for Somalia (UNOSOM) tried vainly to re-establish centralized power. Its predecessor, the Unified Task Force (UNITAF) led by American marines in Operation Restore Hope, was in military command from 9 December 1992 until 4 May 1993 when it handed over command to UNOSOM II. UNITAF and UNOSOM filled the Somali power vacuum by suddenly injecting and deploying a vast amount of force and financial aid.

Without a consensus on what to do, the UN instinctively sponsored negotiations between Somali factions in attempting to resurrect a national government. Because it considered territorial integrity non-negotiable, the UN was disinclined to address the questions of Somaliland or Majerteenia where separatist organizations depended on local autonomy and the peace-making initiatives of sub-clan elders. If the UN planned to rehabilitate the old Somali state, it would need to occupy the country for many years in some neo-colonial form of trusteeship, a prospect that no one was willing to acknowledge.[51] Of course, no one would publicly admit that "Somalia" was dead and that a corpse cannot be revived.

To whom were UN relief agencies accountable? Collective security works when a major power undertakes that responsibility. International organizations lack the autonomy to articulate collective purposes and mobilize resources to implement them. The fusion of humanitarian relief, peacekeeping, disarmament, and political reconciliation that would lead to the re-emergence of stable conditions for a national government was a combination of contradictory objectives. While the concentration of armed force is a basic military principle, the distribution of humanitarian aid required a dispersion of personnel and resources. Clustering Somalis into aid stations protected relief workers from attack by local armed bands and facilitated the feeding process, but it severed the victims' connections with their agro-pastoral kinfolk. According to a report critical of UNITAF, "by supplying more free food to the towns, there is less incentive for the displaced to leave. As a result, people may be remaining in displaced camps longer than would otherwise have been the case. These camps are prone to epidemic disease. The intervention may have thereby contributed to death rates remaining high."[52]

With no clear command structure for its administrative role in Somalia, the UN's humanitarian assistance became secondary to military objectives, thus opening rifts with the technical relief agencies concerned with the practical problems of everyday life. The UN was hampered by bureaucratic bickering, overt hostility toward Somalis, poor political intelligence, and misguided attempts first to rehabilitate warlords into political leaders and then later by efforts to imprison them. Somalis wondered if the UN was an occupation force that intended to turn the country into a trusteeship run by foreign experts and young westerners.

Throughout the 1990s, the real unsung heroes were the experienced Somali doctors, nurses and public officials who, left jobless or seriously underutilized by the UN, courageously stayed in Somalia and risked their lives to help the starving or wounded.

A foreign force sent to protect Somalis never should have become the object of their rage. The liberal rules of engagement that permitted helicopters to attack control-and-command centers seemed more designed for inner city combat than for humanitarian relief. At its height in mid-1993, UNOSOM consisted of 25,000 military personnel, 8000 logistical support staff and 3000 civilians at a cost of $1.5 billion, of which only $9 million (half of 1%) was earmarked for civilian police. When Somalis learned how much the UN would spend on its operations, they swamped officials with job applications. As few Somalis got UN jobs, many charged that UNOSOM suspiciously resembled the Siyad regime by intercepting funds from abroad. Somalis around Mogadishu viewed the UN's multinational bureaucracy that was backed by armed forces who fired on civilians, as the "New White Warlords," just another faction siphoning off money. Eventually, even American military officers adopted the Somali view of the UN bureaucracy as a "self-licking ice cream cone."[53]

Tragic ironies and coincidences abounded. For instance, the increasingly isolated UN Special Envoy, retired Admiral Jonathan Howe, rarely left his armed compound throughout 1993-94, confined there like Siyad Barre had been to his own fortress at Villa Somalia in his final months. In tit-for-tat assaults against warlord factions, the UN demolished Mogadishu property in a manner reminiscent of the way that Siyad's besieged forces in their final months directed heavy artillery attacks on "hostile" civilian neighborhoods.[54]

Somalis often disdained the outsiders who came to "rehabilitate" their country. Yet their long dependency on external aid seemed to convince Somalis that if they could continue to manipulate foreigners then, with little effort or accountability, money and goods would fall from the sky. Somalis became resentful supplicants consumed with a crippling sense of entitlement, but with little compulsion to express appreciation. Somalia had lost all sense of national cohesion or concern for the well-being of its people. No intellectual clarity, ideological principles, or political will existed to resurrect a national government. There was no formal police force, no salaried civil service, no central pool of taxes, nor any banks, telecommunications or public utilities. It may be possible to rebuild a functioning nation-state out of an assemblage of loosely federated communities but any form of compulsory reunification would provoke uncontrollable revulsion in the north.[55]

Many experienced civil servants remain tainted by their service in Siyad's regime and cannot be expected to return even if security and peace prevails. Hundreds of thousands of educated Somalis who reached adulthood since the 1960s have dispersed around the world. A broad-based administration that was relatively free from clan loyalties eventually might be able establish a mutual trust network among regional groups; it is unlikely that anyone can re-establish the government machinery needed to mobilize the return of overseas Somalis. Those US and UN officials who tried throughout 1993-95 to identify charismatic leaders who could "unite" the country only "showed how little [they] learned from Somalia's recent past - not to mention its history of supporting other `strong leaders'."[56]

Frank Crigler, the next to last U.S. Ambassador to Somalia (1987-90), identified the fatal flaw at the heart of the concept of peace-enforcement by pinpointing a lesson of 20th century geo-politics which he termed "the notion that peace can be imposed on a reluctant and notoriously proud people at gunpoint and that the social fabric of their nation can be rewoven at the direction of outsiders."[57]

With no history of accountability at the seat of government in Somalia, the militarized culture personified by Siyad Barre had forced people back onto their family connections. After the annihilation of lives, property and livestock throughout the country, Somalis "retreated into the succor of their clans" to identify with their respective territories and to initiate self-help schemes free from state interference.[58] Somalis trust themselves, not the government, to solve problems. Somalia dissolved into segmentary divisions whose northern and northeast "clan structures reveal the positive side of traditional society" where Somalis do business with people they trust.

The Somali social fabric can only be stitched back together and then a set of regional polities rebuilt by Somalis, from the bottom up. No cease fire imposed from the outside, no government structure erected by international personnel will survive the withdrawal of those forces. Do Somalis have the right to establish their own political standards and social mores free from outside dictates? Can ethnic consciousness or kin corporatism transcend clanism to provide a renewed political program? Elders know how to equitably settle disputes but not how to form embryonic governments. The *guurti* ("council of elders and judicious persons") are informal institutions with a single focus - conflict mediation - whose expertise does not extend to the machinery of a nation-state where one selects the best qualified people for positions. Somali elders lack knowledge "of the scholastic ingredients of the expertise expected of the managers of a state" and do not have the breadth of vision necessary to create nascent political parties that would contest elections and then form a national government.[59]

In Somali family networks, everyone cooperates to restrain the transgressions of one's kinsmen to minimize the chances of retaliation that often leads to widened conflicts that could engulf everyone. Sub-clan loyalties comprise a jigsaw puzzle across the countryside where each village has checkpoints and every family has high-velocity rifles. John Drysdale, a British ex-colonial officer who served as a UN political advisor in 1993 has noted:

> The Somali clan system cannot be eradicated because it is the one and only safety net for those who lack financial independence. Without a clan there is a frightening insecurity. A clan is similar to a large club of like-minded, trustworthy members; each of whom collectively offers other members, inter alia, insurance cover against hard times and without a premium. There is no age limit and no selection process. It is the birthright of those who see themselves as an elitist group of people each bearing a distinctive pedigree. No wonder boys and girls, at a tender age, have to recite without hesitation their genealogy along the male line to a distant patriarch, some twenty even thirty generations back. Membership is secure for life (even in death the clan or sub-clan buries them) and in return for solidarity, loyalty to the point of sacrifice is expected and is freely given.[60]

There may still be attempts to resurrect the former Somali state along federal or consociational lines. Before doing so, one must acknowledge that local Somali politics are rooted in consensus and decentralization, while two generations of Somalis experienced modern government as a heavily centralized, unaccountable system. How can the centripetal requirements of modern government be linked to the centrifugal ethos of the Somalis' multi-layered system? The thought of locally responsible government seems novel to many Somalis especially since the "opportunity to recast the system has only arisen out of such complete destruction of society and economy. Had any vestige of a working government remained, it would probably have been rapidly strengthened by the UN and other aid agencies who channeled resources to it."[61]

To assist regional administrations, relief agencies and NGOs should avoid grandiose plans, focus attention on sustaining Somali-inspired programs, and enter partnerships only with those organizations to re-establish social services. This means giving priority to supporting initiatives by Somali elders, religious leaders, voluntary organizations, women's groups and professional organizations in areas which have already established relative tranquility. The smaller NGOs without top heavy structures, like Médicins Sans Frontières or Partner Aid International, function best when their grants can be matched either with locally generated revenues or with recruited labor. They should assign priority to police recruitment, telecommunications repairs, renewal of water supplies, the restoration of veterinarian services, the re-opening of schools, and making road improvements. They can assist in the emergence of a new paradigm in which institutions, norms and social policies serve and nourish Somali ideals.

Wherever Somalis have already created interim security councils that grapple with disarmament, they deserve considerable support in the restoration of an infrastructure. The involvement of the pragmatic Somali relief organizations is critical for reconstruction. According to a specialist on relief operations, "it has been repeatedly demonstrated that if civilians have ownership over relief or development programs, they will protect them."[62]

The escape from the Somali disaster is through the self-administration of elective assemblies and traditional bodies. Between August 1992 and May 1995, numerous clan and inter-clan conferences were convened which resulted in numerous agreements. The shift away from centralized authoritarianism suggests that Somalis are looking for salvation in local democratic arrangements headed by delegates who are adroit at settling disputes without resort to government mediators. The next few years will see the resuscitation of old techniques as a defense against assaults on one's political and cultural being as well as novel combinations. Although these autonomous actions can be over-romanticized, multilateral organizations like NGOs and UN must adjust their policies away from incoherent state actions and recognize the validity of community self-help efforts. There is no way of knowing what the future holds. Despite the uncertainty as to how much restructuring lies ahead, no new Somali national state will re-emerge.

VII. The Rage of Conflicting Political Discourses

The domestic antagonisms that destroyed Somalia reflected a clash of political discourses.[63] Civil servants and educated Somalis had accepted the bureaucratic premises of the 20th century, the perspective that nationalism was necessary for entry into the modern world of progress, reason and development. This "modernist" agenda was embodied in the Somali constitution that insisted on the reunification of divided Somali territories as the theoretical bridge linking nomads with city dwellers. Through their appropriation of government resources, bureaucrats became a state "clan" that was divorced from pastoral production strategies, yet dependent on expatriate consultants and externally conceived development projects.

In practical terms, the power and wealth that derived from control of an undemocratic central administration was tied to a large public sector whose intricacies mystified most Somalis. The neglect of the nomadic majority in development schemes and a regional bias against the ex-British northern region widened the gap between citizen and government.[64] Somalis who were unfamiliar with the language and procedures of the new bureaucracy were excluded from modern visions of progress; eventually they came to constitute another discourse, one of rage and disenfranchisement. Rural dwellers and impoverished urbanites felt they bore the burden of supporting a ruling elite. Their alienation became a visceral antagonism towards the expatriates who lavished Siyad Barre with aid, most of which Somalis suspected got diverted into private accounts.[65]

The "cannibalism" that preceded and followed the collapse of the Somali government released a torrent of pent up frustrations. Displaced rural youth without city-skills and urban youngsters with no future prospects formed armed gangs that relied on violence to survive.[66] These gangsters, petty thieves and drug addicts were collectively known as *mooryaan*, a Somali term for a nasty, blood-sucking tick. Their frenzied race to loot property was called *bililiqo* ("to swallow evil things"). Scornful of agriculturalists and manual laborers, the marauders descended on farms and towns to plunder all kinds of material wealth. They ransacked Mogadishu by exercising pastoralist-style proprietary rights, squatting in houses that weren't theirs, contemptuous of written niceties like legal documents or deeds. They killed the occupants of a home to appropriate it, like pastoralists seizing pasture land.

Asserting themselves through the opportunities created by the death of the Somali state, these Somalis destroyed libraries, educational facilities, the post office, and stripped buildings down to their electrical fittings and window casings. They demolished every Mogadishu monument that had been built to commemorate Somali nationalism. "The rich and rulers had their day," a *mooryaan* boasted. "Our day, for us, the poor people, has come, and with these *qori* (rifles), we will take whatever things we want."[67]

Somali children have routinely witnessed beatings and robberies, and seen the power that accrues to teenagers with guns. Their drawings and makeshift toys reflect an obsession with weapons. "Their values will never be the same - family values, religious values, community values," said Willi Huber of the Austrian aid group SOS-Kinderdorf. "With smaller children, it may be easier. With bigger children, it's not so easy. You have a big social disaster on your hands."[68]

The raiding parties that terrorized populations and created thousands of refugees had no programs, no ideologies and no hope of taking over the country. They simply were prepared to kill and loot. Their discourse of rage reflected an ominous trend that undermines efforts to build democratic institutions and create confidence in the modern state. Hardly unique to Somalia, similar sentiments are noticeable in such diverse countries as Rwanda, Zaire, Liberia, and South Africa.

Despite the demise of apartheid, the typical South African township teenagers with no education, no possessions and no future prospects had become street thugs, determined not to suffer their parents' humiliations. The student wing of the African National Congress initiated Operation Barcelona in 1993 that encouraged youngsters to destroy government vehicles and property in support of striking teachers.[69] In Liberia, many victims of its calamitous civil war were specifically "people of means, targeted because they wore fine clothes, or lived in nice houses: government functionaries, merchants, and especially [people] known for their entrepreneurial skills."[70]

VIII. Conclusion

For the country with the largest nomadic population in the world and a dispersed political economy, attempts to impose a centralized government dependent on external support could only be maintained through the "coincidence of tyranny with external military patronage."[71] Three decades of unaccountable decision-making alienated Somalis from formal government processes. Beneath its surface unity, a ferocious competition was unleashed for spoils that spawned nepotism and clannishness. Somalia degenerated into a predatory state that became "a government at war with its own people." The government had a considerable capacity for exercising despotic power to repress Somalis, but it could not inspire them. Now that its central government has disappeared, the post-colonial Somali nation-state has been exposed as an artifact, a political fiction, just another "lame Leviathan."

By 1996, Somali politics were in transition between a turbulent past when its national government had sought to expand its post-colonial boundaries and an uncertain future when it seems likely to fracture into smaller units. A legacy of inherited colonial borders contributed to its foreign policy misadventures and the nature of its post-colonial governments stymied attempts at reconciliation among its diverse domestic ethnicities. The Somali national state that once struggled so hard to reconfigure international boundaries of the Horn now faces the prospect that its own internal boundaries will undergo further realignments.

These are not years for optimism about Somalia. Ken Menkhaus, an American political scientist who worked for UNOSOM, remembered the country as a fundamentally different place a few years earlier when "one could walk, day or night, anywhere in the city or countryside with virtually no fear of robbery or physical assault. Though the government in Somalia in the 1980s was repressive, the people were quite friendly and kind. If given the chance...the Somali people will shake off this violent chapter in their history and rebuild the civil society, the `pastoral democracy' they once had."[72]

Somalis less sanguine about their future may recall a poem composed a century ago by Sheikh Gabiou which ended with these lines:

> Before the end of the world
> The Somalis shall be divided in three:
> One will live in a palace surrounded by his guards,
> One will continue living in the bush drawing
> > sustenance from the sale of milk,
> > which he will carry to town in his tunji,
> One will die in the dusty street crying
> > "Somalia!"[73]

A state called "Somalia" was born on July 1, 1960. It died on January 27, 1991. The culture, economy, and social arrangements of its Somali-speaking people, however, remain vibrant and alive. Somalia offers an opportunity for new thinking about local governance that breaks decisively from old assumptions. The rehabilitation of Somali civil society must start with a decentralized, confederate arrangement of clans, not with an attempt to resuscitate a failed state.

There is no "solution" to Somalia because only puzzles have solutions. Somali reconstruction will be a political process negotiated through imperfect settlements, acceptable compromises, and partial victories that do not adhere to fixed timetables.

Whenever historians gather to debate the meaning of the 20th century for Somalis or when international advisors assemble to recommend political "solutions," they should consider an aphorism by the Russian medievalist, Vassily Kluchevsky: "History teaches nothing. It only punishes us severely for not learning its lessons."

Endnotes

1. Karl Maier and Richard Dowden, "Talk, Don't Shoot, in Somalia, " *The Independent* (13 July 1993), p. 6.

2. Angus Shaw, "Somalia Rebuilding Outside Mogadishu," *Sacramento Bee* (22 July 1993), p. 11.

3. Richard Dowden, "Mortars and Wine in Tale of Two Cities," *The Independent* (15 July 1993), p. 8.

4. Benjamin R. Barber, "Jihad versus MacWorld," *The Atlantic*, (March 1992), p. 59.

5. Kenneth Parker, "Home is Where the Heart...Lies," *Transition*, #59 (1993), p. 71; and Nurrudin Farah, "A Country in Exile," *Transition*, #57 (1992) pp. 4-8.

6. Mahmood Mamdani, *Citizen and Subject: Contemporary Africa and the Legacy of Late Colonialism* (Princeton: Princeton University Press, 1996); Jean-Francois Bayart, *The State in Africa: The Politics of the Belly* (New York: Longman, 1993); George B.N. Ayitteh, *Africa Betrayed* (New York: St. Martin's Press, 1992); Douglas Rimmer (ed.), *Africa Thirty Years On* (London: Heinemann, 1991); The Carter Center, *Beyond Autocracy in Africa* (Atlanta: The Carter Center, 1989) and *African Governance in the 1990s* (Atlanta: The Carter Center, 1990) provide comparable examples from across Africa.

7. Richard Dowden, "Somalia is Disintegrating into Anarchy," *The Independent* (10 October 1989), p. 5. Twenty years ago, the Somali poet Mohamed Warsame "Hadrawi" composed a song that depicted Somalia as a slaughtered camel beset by vultures grabbing pieces of its carcass.

8. The broad theoretical and historical dimensions are explored in Samir Amin, *Empire of Chaos* (New York: Monthly Review Press, 1992).

9. Robert Cox, "Multilateralism and World Order," *Review of International Studies*, Vol. 18, #1 (1992), pp. 173-74.

10. Crawford Young (ed.), *The Rising Tide of Cultural Pluralism: The Nation-State at Bay?* (Madison: University of Wisconsin Press, 1993); and "Reconstructing Nations and States," *Daedalus*, Vol. 122, #3 (Summer 1993).

11. Said S. Samatar, *Somalia: A Nation in Turmoil* (London: Minority Rights Group, 1991), p. 25. See also Halim Barakat, *The Arab World: Society, Culture, and State* (Berkeley: University of California Press, 1993), especially Chapter Nine, "National Character and Value Orientations."

12. For an introduction to Somali humor, see Charles Geshekter and Said Ahmed Warsama, "An Introduction to Humor and Jokes in Somali Culture," in R. J. Hayward and I. M. Lewis (eds.), *Voice and Power: The Culture of Language in North-East Africa* (London: SOAS African Languages and Cultures Series, #3, 1996), pp. 141-53.

13. For instance, the Hawiya clan family is divided into sub-clans: Abgaal, Habar Gedir, Murursade, and Hawadle. Each of these further sub-divides into sub-sub-clans, e.g. Habar Gedir include the Saad, Saleban, Sarrur and Ayr sub-sub-clans.

14. Examples of Benadiri jewelry, weaving, and handicrafts are handsomely photographed in: Clara Manca, *Somalia: Monili ed Ornamenti Tradizionali* (Roma: Istituto Italo-Africano, 1989); and Kathryn S. Loughran, *et al.* (eds.), *Somalia in Word and Image* (Bloomington: Indiana University Press, 1986).

15. Quoted in Sam Kiley, "Elders Find Rich Pickings Among Misery of Camps," *The Times* [London], 31 August 1992.

16. Mohamed Abdillahi Rirash, "Somali Oral Poetry as a Vehicle for Understanding Disequilibrium and Conflicts in a Pastoral Society," *Nomadic Peoples*, #30 (1992), p. 118.

17. On the other hand, the late warlord Mohamed Farah Aidid once made the ludicrous assertion that Somalia was the birthplace of most Muslim saints making it "the only place where Islam is practiced in its pure form." Roland Marchal, "Le Developpement d'un mouvement Islamiste en Somalie," *Bulletin du Centre D'Analysis et de Prevision*, #54 (Winter 1992/93); Jennifer Parmelee, "Radical Islam on March in Horn of Africa," *Washington Post* (18 November 1992); Terry Leonard, "Fundamentalists Speak to Somalis Weary of War and Lawlessness," *Associated Press* (12 January 1993); and Abdirisaq Aqli, "Historical Development of Islamic Movements in the Horn of Africa," paper presented to European Association of Somali Studies Conference, University of London, 23-25 September 1993.

18. According to I.M. Lewis, among northern Somalis, "the characteristic religious expression of social identity at the level of the clan takes the form of an annual celebration in praise of the clan ancestor." Among the sedentary southern Somalis, "the corresponding rite of clan identity is...a collective rain-

making ritual (*roobdoon*)" without the intermediacy of ancestors. I.M. Lewis, "Conformity and Contrast in Somali Islam," in I.M. Lewis (ed.), *Islam in Tropical Africa* (London: Oxford University Press, 1966), p. 262. Other pre-Islamic Somali practices include: 1) *cashar* (medication) where one writes Koranic verses in charcoal on a board, then mixes them into milk which is drunk to cure sickness; and 2) *shardi* (pledge) where one promises to give a she-camel or money as a gift to the gatekeeper at a venerated Sheikh's tomb in return for having one's prayer for a particular favor answered, e.g. a family member cured of illness or given protection during a long journey.

19. Liz Sly, "Somali Mission of Mercy Could Become Bloodbath," *San Francisco Examiner* (29 November 1992). Somali disdain for Punjabi sepoys extends to other cultures as well. Somalis sometimes show conceit towards members of groups whom they consider formerly enslaved. See also, E.R. Turton, "Somali Resistance to Colonial Rule and the Development of Somali Political Activity in Kenya, 1893-1960," *Journal of African History*, Vol. 13, #1 (1972), pp. 117-43; and Richard Dowden, "Out of Somalia: People of Poetry Who Love to Fight," *The Independent* (26 October 1993), p. 12.

20. Said Samatar, "Somalia Is a `Stepchild' of Two Cultures," *New York Newsday* (11 January 1993), p. 17.

21. Aristide Zolberg, "The Specter of Anarchy: African States Verging on Dissolution," *Dissent*, Vol. 39, #3 (Summer 1992), p. 309. A compelling analysis of the process in Somalia is: Ahmed I. Samatar, "The Curse of Allah: Civic Disembowelment and the Collapse of the State in Somalia," in Ahmed I. Samatar (ed.), *The Somali Challenge: From Catastrophe to Renewal?* (Boulder: Lynne Rienner Publishers, 1994), pp. 95-146.

22. These town/countryside distinctions are effectively shown in a novel by Farah M.J. Cawl, *Ignorance is The Enemy of Love* (London: Zed Press, 1982).

23. Amin, *Empire of Chaos*, p. 110.

24. Ali Jimale Ahmed, *Daybreak is Near...Literature, Clans, and the Nation-State in Somalia* (Lawrenceville, New Jersey: Red Sea Press, 1996), p. 113.

25. John Drysdale, *The Somali Dispute* (London: Pall Mall Press, 1964), pp.165-66.

26. The new Somali anthem, *Soomaaliya Ha Noolaato* (Long Live Somalia) had only a title, no words and was composed by an Italian. Mohamed Osman Omar, *The Road to Zero: Somalia's Self-Destruction* (London: Haan Associates, 1992), p. 49.

27. Scotland was another example (of many) where union actually exacerbated old prejudices. The Scots reinvented their identity in the mid-18th century in "response to the dilemma of maintaining a national identity as a stateless nation." Keith Brown, "Imagining Scotland," *Journal of British Studies*, Vol. 31, #4 (October 1992), pp. 415-25.

28. Abdi Ismail Samatar, "Structural Adjustment as Development Strategy? Bananas, Boom, and Poverty in Somalia," *Economic Geography*, Vol 69, #1 [1993], p. 35.

29. Jane Kramer, "Letter From Europe," *The New Yorker* (21 September 1992). Metternich had called Italy not a country but a "geographical expression." This could apply equally to Somalia. Italian political patronage once played a major role in the determination of radio and television jobs, professorships, and even the string sections of symphony orchestras. Strikingly similar arrangements prevailed in Somalia under the dictatorship of Mohamed Siyad Barre.

30. Basil Davidson, *The Black Man's Burden: Africa and the Curse of the Nation-State* (New York: Times Books, 1992), p. 281 shows how, when mutual ethnic respect gave way to crude chauvinism, it destroyed Yugoslav federalism where "the principal reason for failure lay in the persistence of a single party authoritarianism unable and unwilling to reform itself."

31. Said Samatar, "The Search for Political Accountability in African Governance: The Somali Case," in Carter Center, *African Governance*, pp. 165-68.

32. An excellent analysis of this historical process is: Abdi Samatar and A.I. Samatar, "The Material Roots of the Suspended African State: Arguments from Somalia," *The Journal of Modern African Studies*, Vol. 25, #4 (1987), pp. 669-690. For a critique of bureaucratic excesses and government unaccountability, see Jama Mohamed Ghalib, *The Cost of Dictatorship: The Somali Experience* (New York: Lilian Barber Press, 1995).

33. Stanley Hoffmann, "The Passion of Modernity," *The Atlantic* (August 1993), p. 103.

34. Quotations from S.K.B. Asante, *Pan-African Protest: West Africa and the Italo-Ethiopia Crisis, 1934-41* (London: Oxford University Press, 1977), pp. 16-17, 215. The contrast between symbolic and real Ethiopia is discussed in Charles Geshekter, "Anti-Colonialism and Class Formation: The Eastern Horn of Africa Before 1950," *International Journal of African Historical Studies*, Vol. 18, #1 (1985), pp. 1-32.

35. George B.N. Ayittey, "An African Solution for Somalia," *Wall Street Journal* (7 October 1993), p. 12.

36. I.M. Lewis, "Misunderstanding the Somali Crisis," *Anthropology Today*, Vol. 9, #4 (August 1993). The Chinese "warlord" was a regional militarist who, by virtue of his capacity to wage war, exercised effective governmental control over a well-defined region by means of a military organization that obeyed no higher authority than himself. Warlords desired to see China re-unified and denied that their actions were responsible for its fragmentation. They were a "conservative phenomenon [that] protected the region by detaching it from the turbulent state." J.A.G. Roberts, "Warlordism in China," *Review of African Political Economy*, #45/46 (1989), pp. 26-33; James E. Sheridan, *Chinese Warlord* (Stanford: Stanford University Press, 1966); and Diana Lary, *Region and Nation* (Cambridge: Cambridge University Press, 1974).

37. Vali Jamal, "Somalia: Survival in a `Doomed' Economy," *International Labour Review*, Vol. 127, #6 (1988), pp. 783-812; "Nomads and Farmers: Incomes and Poverty in Rural Somalia," in Dharam Ghai and Samir Radwan (eds.), *Agrarian Policies and Rural Poverty in Africa* (Geneva: ILO, 1983), pp. 281-311; and "Somalia: The Gulf Link and Adjustment," in K. Raffer and M.A. Mohamed Salih (eds.), *The Least Developed and the Oil-Rich Arab Countries* (New York: St. Martin's Press, 1992), pp. 128-152.

38. John Drysdale, "Somalia: The Only Way Forward," *Journal of the Anglo-Somali Society*, Winter 1992/93, p. 6.

39. Somalia's export-oriented economy of labor and livestock must be situated within the Middle Eastern regional economy to appreciate how the fall in oil prices, slowdown of the construction boom in the Gulf, and the consequences of Operation Desert Storm affected separatist movements in the country. International Labour Office, Jobs and Skills Programed for Africa [JASPA], *Generating Employment and Incomes in Somalia* (Addis Ababa: International Labour Office, 1989), pp. 25-26, 166-67.

40. The topic is investigated in Charles Geshekter, "Somali Maritime History and Regional Sub-Cultures: A Neglected Theme of the Somali Crisis," paper presented at the New Directions in Maritime History Conference (University of Western Australia), 6-10 December 1993.

41. The author wrote a series of newspaper articles about this phenomenon: Charles Geshekter, "A Country of Paradoxes: Somalis are Both Sophisticated and Isolated," *St. Louis Post Dispatch* (15 December 1992); "Exiles Are Distant Hope for Somalia," *San Diego Union-Tribune* (24 January 1993); and "The Future of Somalia Isn't in Mogadishu," *Sacramento Bee* (27 October 1993).

42. Omar, *Road to Zero*, p. 151.

43. Hussein M. Adam and Charles L. Geshekter, *The Revolutionary Development of the Somali Language* (Los Angeles: UCLA African Studies Center, Occasional Paper #20, 1980).

44. Daniel Compagnon, "Somaliland: Un Order Politique en Gestation?" *Politique Africaine*, #50 (Juin 1993), pp. 9-20; Gerard Prunier, "A Candid View of the Somali National Movement," *Horn of Africa*, XIII, #3-4/XIV, #1-2 (1990-91), pp. 107-120; Chris Searle, "Agony and Struggle in Northern Somalia," *Race and Class*, Vol. 34, #2 (1992), pp. 23-32; and B. Rajagopal and Anthony J. Carroll, "The Case for the Independent Statehood of Somaliland," unpublished paper, Washington, D.C., May 1992. A monthly news magazine about Somaliland (in English and Somali) is *Warsidaha Somaliland* [available from 7 Havelock Road, Southall, Middlesex UB2 4NY England].

45. Ahmed Yusuf Farah with Professor I.M. Lewis, *Somalia: The Roots of Reconciliation* (London: ActionAid, 1993); and Hussein M. Adam, "Somalia: Militarism, Warlordism or Democracy?" *Review of African Political Economy*, #54 (1992), p. 23.

46. James Kamusikiri and Steve Iman (eds.), *Eastern Europe and the West: Implications for Africa* (Los Angeles: UCLA African Studies Center, 1990).

47. Stanley Foundation, *Changing Realities in the Horn of Africa: Implications for Africa and U.S. Policy* (Muscatine, Iowa: The Stanley Foundation, 1991), p. 5.

48. Abdi Samatar, "Social Decay and Public Institutions: The Road to Reconstruction in Somalia," in Martin Doornbos, *et al.* (eds.), *Beyond Conflict in the Horn* (Trenton: Red Sea Press, 1992), p. 215; and "New World Disorder," *The New Republic* (21 September 1992).

49. This is explained in Africa Watch, *Somalia Beyond the Warlords: The Need for a Verdict on Human Rights Abuses* (New York: Africa Watch, March 1993) and "A Special Report on Somalia," *Africa News*, Vol. 37, #7-8 (January 3, 1993). An outstanding collection of essays on the politics of land tenure and access to resources in the inter-riverine area is: Catherine Besteman and Lee V. Cassanelli (eds.), *The Struggle for Land in Southern Somalia: The War Behind the War* (Boulder: Westview Press, 1996).

50. Many reasons, besides humanitarian relief, have been offered to explain the intervention: 1) protect future oil reserves; 2) contain Islamic fundamentalism; 3) demonstrate peaceful uses for Western military forces; 4) privatize

international assistance through NGOs; or 5) use the UN as a surrogate for American imperialism. For a sample of explanations, see Stephen Rosskamm Shalom, "Gravy Train: Feeding the Pentagon by Feeding Somalia," *Zeta Magazine* (February 1993), pp. 15-25; Ray Bonner, "Why We Went," *Mother Jones Magazine* (March/April 1993), pp. 54-60; Alex de Waal and Rakiya Omaar, "Somalia: Adding `Humanitarian Intervention' to the U.S. Arsenal," *Covert Action*, #44 (Spring 1993), pp. 4-11, 53-54; James Petras and Steve Vieux, "The Somali Invasion," *Lies of Our Times* (January-February 1993), pp. 14-16; Charles Geshekter, "Taking Issue on Somalia," *Lies of Our Times* (June 1993), pp. 25-26; Noam Chomsky, *The Prosperous Few and the Restless Many* (Berkeley: Odonian Press, 1993), chapter 4, "Photo Ops in Somalia"; Michael Maren, "The Somali Experiment," *Village Voice* (28 September 1993); Sidney Blumenthal, "Why Are We in Somalia?" *The New Yorker* (25 October 1993), pp. 48-60; Mohamed Sahnoun, *Somalia: The Missed Opportunities* (Washington, D.C.: U.S. Institute of Peace Press, 1994); and John L. Hirsch and Robert B. Oakley, *Somalia and Operation Restore Hope* (Washington, D.C.: U.S. Institute of Peace Press, 1995). A valuable, annotated bibliography is Walter S. Clarke, *Humanitarian Intervention in Somalia Bibliography* (Carlisle Barracks, Pennsylvania: U.S. Army War College, 1995).

51. Laurence Martin, "Peacekeeping as a Growth Industry," *The National Interest*, #32 (Summer 1993), pp. 2-10; and Jeffrey Clark, "Prelude to Disaster," *The Humanitarian Monitor*, #1 (June 1993), p. 3-6.

52. Rakiya Omaar and Alex de Waal, *Somalia: Operation Restore Hope: A Preliminary Assessment* (London: African Rights, May 1993), p. 17.

53. Michael Maren, "Somalia: Whose Failure?" *Current History* (May 1996), p. 202; Patrick Gilkes, "From Peace-Keeping to Peace Enforcement: The Somalia Precedent," *Middle East Report* (November-December 1993), pp. 21-24.

54. When Howe posted a $25,000 reward for the arrest of Mohamed Farah Aidid, the wily warlord offered the same bounty for the capture of Admiral Howe! Such wild west amateurism replicated the tragedy of July 1989 when Bishop Salvadore Colombo was murdered in his Mogadishu cathedral. Siyad offered a $10,000 reward for information on the killer. Critics sneered that Siyad valued the life of one infidel more than the thousands of Somalis killed by his own forces. A few days later, an anti-Siyad group announced it would pay *$20,000* for information on the identity of whoever claimed Siyad's reward! For military perspectives see: "Somalia and Operations Other Than War," *Parameters: U.S. Army War College Quarterly*, XXIII, #4 (Winter 1993-94); John G. Roos, "The Perils of Peacekeeping," *Armed Forces Journal International* (December 1993), pp. 13-17; and "Mission to Somalia," *Joint Forces Quarterly* (Autumn 1993), pp. 37-70.

55. I.M.Lewis and James Myall, *A Study of Decentralized Political Structures for Somalia: A Menu of Options* (London: London School of Economics and Political Science, 1995) offers policy makers theoretical political options.

56. Omaar and de Waal, *Somalia: Preliminary Assessment*, p. 33.

57. T. Frank Crigler, "The Peace-Enforcement Dilemma," *Joint Forces Quarterly* (Autumn 1993), p. 67.

58. John Drysdale, *Somalia: Problems of Rebuilding a Nation* (Hove: Quantum Books, 1992), p. 7.

59. Yousuf Duhul, "Somali Tribal Tangle: Tribal Solidarity vs. the State," unpublished paper, London, June 1993, p. 22.

60. Drysdale, "Somalia: The Only Way Forward," p. 6.

61. Susan Johnson, "Where There is No Government," unpublished ActionAid Report, London (May 1993), p. 4.

62. Gayle Smith, "Somalia: Examining the Military Option," *The Humanitarian Monitor*, #1 (June 1993), p. 8.

63. A brilliant analysis is found in Ken Jowitt, *New World Disorder: The Leninist Extinction* (Berkeley: University of California Press, 1992). Eric Hobsbawm, "Barbarism: A Users Guide," *New Left Review*, #206 (July /August 1994), pp. 44-54 agrees with Michael Ignatieff's explanation that atrocities are committed by "young males between the ages of puberty and marriage, for whom no accepted or effective rules and limits of behavior exist any longer." See also, Ralph Peters, "The New Warrior Class," *Parameters: U.S. Army War College Quarterly*, Vol. XXIV, #2 (Summer 1994), pp. 16-26.

64. Martin Doornbos, "Pasture and Polis: The Roots of Political Marginalization of Somali Pastoralism," in John Markakis (ed.), *Conflict and the Decline of Pastoralism in the Horn of Africa* (London: Macmillan, 1993).

65. For a perceptive description and analysis of Somali-expatriate misunderstandings, see Anna Simons, *Networks of Dissolution: Somalia Undone* (Boulder: Westview Press, 1995), pp. 3-27.

66. Omar and de Waal, *Somalia: Preliminary Assessment*, p. 26.

67. Ahmed Artan Hanghe, *The Sons of Somal* (Cologne: Omimee Publishers, 1993), p. 52. Mohamed M. Afrah, *Mogadishu: A Hell on Earth* (Nairobi: Copos Ltd., 1993) is a grisly, eye witness account of the 1991-92 savagery. An assessment of the formidable task of restoring Somali material culture is Steven A. Brandt and Osman Yusuf Mohamed, "Starting From Scratch: The Past, Present, and Future Management of Somalia's Cultural Heritage," in Peter R. Schmidt and Roderick J. McIntosh (eds.), *Plundering Africa's Past* (Bloomington: Indiana University Press, 1996), pp. 250-59.

68. Keith Richburg, "Famine, War in Somalia Creating `Lost Generation'," *San Francisco Chronicle* (15 September 1992), p. 8. See also, "SOS Children's Village, Mogadishu," *Journal of the Anglo-Somali Society* (Autumn 1993), pp. 26-29.

69. The warlords (or ward bosses) of Natal have been compared with 14th century Italian *signori* or 20th century Chinese warlords and Colombian druglords. Their mixture of terror and patronage, private militias, and protection rackets are fueled by unemployed, illiterate gangsters called *comtsotsis* whose activities resemble those of the Somali *mooryaan*. Bill Berkeley, "The Warlords of Natal," *The Atlantic* (March 1994), pp. 85-100.

70. A Liberian who heads a relief organization in Monrovia agreed that decades of inequity and oppression left people deeply enraged. "I identified with those crazy people," admitted Blamo Nelson. "Behind those masks is a mad, horrified people. The country is in a knot. So many people have so much blood on their hands that few are likely to disarm and risk having to answer for what they have done...A generation of children has been brutalized,... educated in little except tribal hatred." Bill Berkeley, "Between Repression and Slaughter," *The Atlantic* (December 1992).

71. Zolberg, "Specter of Anarchy," p. 309.

72. Ken Menkhaus, "Some Points on Somali Culture and Suggestions for Troop Comportment in Operation Restore Hope," unpublished paper (5 December 1992).

73. Quoted in Jeanne Contini, "The Illiterate Poets of Somalia," *The Reporter*, Vol. 28, #6 (14 March 1963), p. 36.

CHAPTER SIX

New Directions In Southern Somali History: An Agenda For the Next Decade

Lee V. Cassanelli

I. Introduction

Over the past several years, as most of you know, there has been a great deal of discussion about the need to tell the world about "the other Somalis," those who live along and between the two rivers. Today we see one outcome of that discussion, a conference devoted to the inter-river region: to its peoples and cultures, its history and its current condition, its problems and prospects for the future. As I mentioned to some of the organizers, I have some reservations about the wisdom of dividing Somali studies along regional lines, and I will share these with you in just a minute. But I have no reservations at all about the importance of studying this neglected area of Somalia; and I commend all of you for your commitment to opening up this new frontier of research, not just for the sake of Somali studies, but for African studies as a whole.

I do not have to remind you that I am really an outsider, though I think many Somalis now regard me as "one of those Southerners, one of those "Maay people," because I once wrote a book about southern Somali history. You know how Somalis have a way of identifying foreign scholars with the regions or clans they study (e.g., I.M. Lewis -- a Northerner, and especially a Dulbahante), just as they identify certain UN agencies and NGOs with certain clans according to the people they employ or work with (e.g., the organization Irish Concern in Mogadishu is considered part of the Hawadle, AICF/France is Sheikhal, and so on!). So, I have acquired a clan-family identity, whether I wanted one or not! But as a scholar, and an historian, I have a commitment to my profession as well as to my clan family, and my agenda will always be different from those of my Somali colleagues. But discussing different viewpoints is what scholars and intellectuals should be about; the goal should always be to further our understanding, not simply to promote our cause.

You are all familiar with the reasons for the relative neglect of Somali inter-riverine societies in modern scholarship, especially studies published in English. Ever since the publication of Lewis' *Pastoral Democracy*, Somalia has been characterized as a pastoral society, and there continues to be a special fascination with the nomadic way of life -- even though it no longer represents the predominant Somali life style. It is also the case that, until recently, most research on southern Somalia was done by Italian scholars whose publications were not widely-read outside of Italy. (Much of this Italian scholarship is very important, and really ought to be reread by the new generation of inter-riverine specialists. I'll say more about this in my comments during the first panel, if there's time.)

A third factor that contributed to the academic marginalization of southern Somalia was the development of a written Somali language, which is based on the northern and central dialects. The consequence has been the neglect of the substantial linguistic and literary traditions of the inter-river area, which are based on several distinctive dialects collectively known as *af-maay*. Despite the efforts of a few Italian and Somali scholars to record the poetry, proverbs, and traditions of *af-maay* communities, there is little question that the riverine region has been a distinctly secondary field in the study of Somali language and literature.

I also see another factor at work in the public neglect of inter-riverine Somalia, and that is the scarcity -- until very recently -- of scholarly contributions from Somali intellectuals of the region. This is not so much the result, I believe, of an absence of historical consciousness within inter-riverine society, nor of a shortage of potential scholars. Rather, it is a result of the limits of educational opportunities in the recent past, and also of a kind of reticence to speak out publicly, a sense of privacy on the part of inter-riverine intellectuals, that has certainly not been characteristic of educated Somalis from other regions. There is little question that inter-riverine people -- and especially speakers of *maay* --

have not been fairly represented in the major cultural and educational institutions that have had the responsibility for preserving and disseminating the Somali heritage. There was discrimination, to be sure, in the Somali Academy and in the Ministries of Education and Higher Education. But it seems to me that there has also been a reluctance on the part of southern Somalis to engage in research and writing about their part of the country. It is almost as if the inter-riverine community had to undergo the trauma of war and displacement, to become aware of the need for investigating and publicizing its own very rich and diverse traditions. It is now late, but not too late, to do something about this.

II. The Inter-riverine Studies Association (ISA): Prospects and Potential Problems

The gathering of this group represents an important step in redressing the imbalance that has characterized Somali studies in the past. But in seeking to correct this imbalance, we must be careful not to reproduce old patterns of learning or to create new problems for ourselves and for the next generation of scholars. Let me offer some ideas for your consideration.

First, we should learn from the experience of the Somali Studies International Association that was founded in 1978, and that has done a great deal to promote knowledge about Somalia both in the academic community and among the wider public. There have been many positive features of the Association: its openness to Somalis of all clans and regions, both inside and outside the country; its remarkable record of meetings sponsored every three years since 1980 on three different continents; its attempt to promote dialogue with government officials, NGOs, and development organizations; and the recent efforts of its leadership to give a greater voice to women and to Somali students and young people who are not yet official "scholars," but who care deeply about the future of Somalia.

On the other hand, despite the accomplishments of the SSIA, Somali studies has continued in my view to suffer from several limitations, and we can also learn from these. Among the most important limitations are: (1) the tendency for Somalis to look inward: to study primarily the problems of their own clans, and to want to hear only about the problems of their own clans; (2) the tendency to see scholarship primarily as a tool of politics, as a vehicle for challenging other groups and for promoting the interests of their own; and (3) the tendency for Somalis of whatever clan or region to think about Somalia in isolation. There has been a reluctance to study issues in a broader comparative context that includes other African societies and other developing countries. Somali scholarship has been extremely introverted, and this has contributed to its isolation academically and intellectually.

The ISA has a wonderful opportunity to take Somali studies in new directions. But it can only move in new directions if it doesn't become captive to the attitudes and frameworks of the past. Yes, it is important to remedy the ignorance about inter-riverine history and culture; but in doing so, we must not perpetuate the narrow partisanship that sees our culture, our language, our heritage as better or richer or of greater value than some other groups. I know it is tempting when trying to overcome the prejudices of the past to fight back with angry scholarship, especially when a community's dignity or even survival are at stake. But if we are to communicate our concerns, we must do so in a way that permits further dialogue, not one that cuts it off. When we challenge previous interpretations, we must do so with evidence and arguments that remain open to future reinterpretations.

One goal of this conference certainly is to redress the balance of power in Somali studies. But we must also strive to communicate with the wider world of Africanist scholars. The question they ask is, Why should the world care about the Digil Merifle, or the Benadiri, or the Bantu communities of Somalia? My answer would not be, because other Somalis have ignored us, and have tried to write us out of history. Rather, my answer would be because the study of inter-riverine Somalia can teach us a great deal about the issues that concern Africanist scholars at large.

For example, studying the Maay language can help linguists sort out the history of the spread of Cushitic languages in northeast Africa. Studying the towns and cultures of the Benadir can bring new perspectives to the very rich and well-established historiography of the East African Swahili coast, in which many scholars around the world are interested. Inter-riverine Somalia perhaps has more in common with the rest of East Africa than it does with the pastoral Somali regions to the north. For example, the mixed farming and herding economies of our region are far more typical of other Kenyan and Tanzanian peoples than is the pure nomadic culture of Lewis' Somaliland. Studying how inter-riverine Somalis use their environment, allocate their labor, build territorial alliances, and inherit property would be of great comparative interest to scholars studying similar phenomena elsewhere. As a final example, the cultural and linguistic diversity of the south, where communities of Oromo, Arab, and Bantu origins have been incorporated over time into Maay-speaking communities, offers valuable insights into an historical process that finds many parallels elsewhere in Africa and America.

My point here is that the ISA has the opportunity to bring Somali studies into the mainstream of African studies. It can become an effective model for other Somali scholars, as long as ISA members look outward and not inward; as long as they engage intellectually with theories and debates from other parts of Africa, and not simply fight intellectual battles within Somali studies.

I've said enough. This is a welcome and exciting occasion, and I look forward to the day when library shelves on Africana are full of books and articles on inter-riverine Somalia. The seeds of some of those books and articles will, I feel certain, be sown here today.

CHAPTER SEVEN

Hobbes, Locke, Burke, Ibn Khaldun and Reflections on the Catastrophe in Somalia

Hussein M. Adam

I. Introduction

Professor Ali Mazrui once argued that there are at least five ways to utilize political theory:

- treating it as a form of intellectual exercise like abstract mathematics
- analyzing it in search of a personal message to guide one's life
- examining it for the sake of historicity
- studying it as part of intellectual history
- tearing the ideas away from their historical context and applying them to another situation

This paper explores applications of several classical political theorists, analyzing their work to consider how they might have assessed a contemporary African predicament, the catastrophe in Somalia. These political theorists may be read profitably because they reflect as well as transcend their age. They represent a fascinating mixture of the old and the new, the parochial and the universal.

II. The Catastrophe in Somalia

Somali society is made up of six clan-families subdivided into clan, subclans, sub-subclans, all the way to lineages and extended families. Four of the six -- the Hawiye, Darood, Isaaq and Dir -- are pastoralists; the Digil and Mirifle (Reewin) are agropastoralists. In addition, Somalia has ancient city dwellers and farmers of Bantu origins who live beyond the Somali clan system. The boundary lines of the post-colonial state did not coincide with traditional clan territories. As the politics of the Siyad regime, especially in the later years, became increasingly clan oriented, the discontinuity between traditional identities and the boundaries of the state became pronounced.

As the Somali state disintegrated in the 1980s and finally collapsed in 1991, the resulting situation produced not only a staggering human tragedy but also the need for a revised political theory. Given that Africa may enter the next century facing many conflicts between traditional civil societies and the relatively recent post-colonial state, aspects of the Somali tragedy and attempts at state restoration may well mirror Africa's needs in the 21st Century. Africa will enter the next century confronting the deeper question which involves the compatibility between ancient African civil societies and the relatively recent post-colonial state. Somalia is the pioneering example of total state collapse. This is a consequence of the extent and sharpness of the mismatch between the post-colonial state and the nature and structure of Somali pastoral and agropastoral society. The heavy handed, centralized Siyad Barre military dictatorial regime became the perfect agent to ignite the implosion of the Somali state. On the positive side, there is a glimmer of hope that Somalia might also be the first to experiment with novel principles of restructuring state/civil society relationships.

Somalia is about to enter its fifth year without an international recognized polity; no national administration exercising real authority; no formal national legal system; no banking and insurance services; no telephone and postal systems; no national public service; no reliable, organized educational and health systems; no national police and public security services; no electricity or piped water systems. In southern Somalia in particular, disruptive violent bands of armed youths have perpetuated a state of episodic chaos and semi-anarchy. "Although Somalis have had to contend with many a hard time before, the present is exceptional in both intensity and pervasiveness."[1] Catastrophe is characterized by a constellation of crises whose impact has led to depletion of the material, moral and intellectual resources of Somalia.

Somalia today presents a country with two differing political cultures: the south where armed strongmen dominate the political landscape, the so-called warlords including Ali Mahdi Mohamed (northern Mogadishu), General Aidid (southern Mogadishu and parts of central Somalia), General Morgan (Siyad's son-in-law controlling the souther town of Kismayo) and Colonel Omar Jess (controlling south-eastern areas surrounding Kismayo). The second are the northeastern and northern parts of the country which have enjoyed relative peace and stability. Former British Somaliland has established its own Somaliland Republic with a separate government which enjoys *de facto* but not *de jure* recognition. The British had ruled Somaliland through indirect rule which strengthened the role of traditional religious and secular elders.

III. Thomas Hobbes: State of Nature and Political Absolutism

Given Hobbes' argument on need for a strong state, the southern Somalia situation vindicates his bleak description:

"Whatsoever therefore is consequent to a time of war, where every man is enemy to every man ... In such a condition, there is no place for industry; because the fruit thereof is uncertain: and consequently no culture of the earth ... no arts; no letters; no society; and which is worst of all, continual fear, and danger of violent death; and the life of man, solitary, poor, nasty, brutish, and short."[2]

In Hobbes' view, men (and women) are considered in their separateness as atomic particles where every individual served as his own judge.[3] As atoms bounce back and forth within physical matter, so individuals interact with each other as each goes his or her own way as they pursue individual ends. However, in the historical Somali state of nature, people could not only be reckoned with as individuals but, more importantly, as communities. By ignoring the legitimacy and importance of human associations between the individual and the state, Hobbes was working with an imaginary vision of society, unlike that of Plato, which he criticized. He made the same mistake that other Western theorists made for the next two centuries. The anarchy of Somalia is an anarchy of warring social groups -- clans, subclans -- rather than an individualist "war, where every man is enemy to every man." Anarchy involving social groups provides individuals with relative havens of security, mixed with moments of conflict and danger.

In contexts where human associations intermediate between the individual and the sovereign, the fear of death becomes motive to establish a state. The idea of social stability being maintained between social organizations of less extent than the state was utterly alien to Hobbes' frame of mind. Somali society, especially in the northern regions, also shows how absolutely inescapable is the authority of tradition and custom (*xeer*) in the functioning of society. In this and other respects, Hobbes' theory represents a clear triumph of logic over common sense. The June - October 1993 war between General Aidid's Habar Gedir (Hawiye) clan and the United Nations/United States forces showed that, notwithstanding Hobbes' one-sided conception of fear and self-preservation, political groups stress other values as well: self-sacrifice, sympathy, compassion, group solidarity, pride and vanity.

Southern Somalia does not appear to be moving toward establishing sovereignty by institution or covenant in which people come together voluntarily to establish a political contract. There are, however, a number of pretenders (the warlords) who have fought to take over by conquest -- sovereignty by acquisition. It does not look like any of them would succeed in conquering all the others since allegiance and legitimacy is fragmented into clan cleavages. This has created a situation unimagined by Hobbes: decentralized absolutism. Hobbes insists that a man is obliged to preserve his own skin and permit others to do likewise. The law of nature forbids a man to do that which is destructive to his life. Those chafing under destructive warlord violence might seize on this as an indirect defense of rebellion. The concept of decentralized sovereignty is utterly alien to Hobbes' frame of mind. Yet, if southern Somalia is to evolve from petty predatory sovereignties to a large-scale sovereignty, it would likely do this within the framework of divided federal sovereignty. Hobbes, on the other hand, insists that the alienation of power to the sovereign must be unified, centralized, absolute and irrevocable, without conditions.[4]

IV. John Locke: State of Nature and Social Contract

Locke was interested in making a case for legitimacy of a government that either had been or would be born of rebellion. Locke recognizes that no paper prescription can provide an absolute guarantee against arbitrary government. What recourse do the people have in contingencies such as these? According to Locke, in all such cases, the only recourse is an "appeal to heaven," that is, to arms. The people of the self-declared Republic of Somaliland could argue that they followed

Locke's advice in tolerating injustices while searching for nonviolent means to redress the situation. When they finally decided to "appeal to heaven," they shunned recourse to the politics of revenge practiced in the south and conducted a restrained and considered revolution for the restoration of proper balance in the body politic by reclaiming their original 1960 sovereignty.

Locke's depiction of man in the state of nature is far removed from the rapacity of Hobbes's natural man. It is the picture of man as a sociable, rational being, living in harmony with his fellows. Locke postulated a state of nature regulated by laws derived from God, a state of nature in which men were equal and free before the Lord and each other. Locke also states that his natural man ought "as much as he can to preserve the rest of mankind."[5] Locke's conception of the state of war approached Hobbes' anarchic state of nature and approached the situation in southern Somalia. In northern Somalia, state collapse did not lead to widespread clan warfare. Instead, the protective role of the Islamic religion and of relatively vital traditional law *(xeer)*, contributed to relative peace and stability. The active and prominent roles played by clan and religious elders in adjudicating individual and group disputes have maintained a society of rules without rulers, statelessness without anarchy. The historicity of Locke's state of nature is approached therefore, by Somaliland where life is not filled with the stark terror it was for Hobbes, only with a series of "inconveniences." Originally, in Locke's state of nature, executive power of the natural law was vested in every individual; in Somaliland's relative statelessness, it is vested in clan and subclan elders who enjoy respect and moral influence, not coercive power.

For Somaliland, the urge to create a sovereign partly arises from experiences living in one form of a state or another since 1960. They also hope to win international recognition and attract official external assistance. Some of them argue, should they fail to win international assistance, they would be in a better position to negotiate for sovereignty within a federal or confederal system. Locke rejected the mystique of divine rights as well as the fear of death and argued that man came out of a state of nature to form government by mutual consent of naturally equal men. This societal contract conception lies at the heart of traditional Somali political thought and experience.

When the Siyad military state collapsed in January 1991, northern Somalis convened a grassroots congress in Burao in May 1991 during which they proclaimed independence for their Somaliland Republic. By mutual consent, they also created a supreme legislative body, divided into a council of elders *(guurti)* and a popular chamber; and an executive power headed by a president, vice president and cabinet built on clan diversity and representation.

The current situation is one in which, with a full collapse of the state, Somalis have been obliged to rely on traditional *xeer*. There are earlier precedents such as occurred in the sixteenth century when the Islamic state of Adal collapsed. From its coastal capital of Zeila, its famous leader, Ahmed Gurey waged several successful wars against the Christian Abyssinian kingdom. In 1542, Gurey's Christian enemies defeated his armies, leading to the decline and collapse of Adal. Oral traditions record the recurrent wars, famine, chaos and banditry (*shifta*) that followed. A common response to the decline of public law was to revive and revitalize the *xeer*. The Isse clan (Dir clan-family) in particular produced an elaborate constitution (*Xeer Cisse*).[6] The constitution bound together six subclans -- three related by blood kinship and three "adopted." Having lived under the pluralistic state of Adal, they decided to transcend the concept of kinship based solely on "blood." Although blood kinship is pervasive, Somali genealogies also reveal examples of kinship by "contract" and through "fictitious" stories of origin.

These are examples of a rational social contract used to create "kinship." All six subclans came to constitute the Isse clan through this legal instrument -- all of it composed in poetic style to assist memorization. It was decided that the traditional clan leader, the *Ugaas* (other Somalis use *Suldan* or *Boqor*) would be chosen from the numerically smallest subclan of the six which happened to be of the three "adopted" subclans in the original contract. The leader is a first among equals. The constitution provides detailed provisions concerning choosing the right *Ugaas* as well as dethronement. A non-threatening subclan was given, through the *Ugaas*, special prestige, recognition and responsibility in adjudicating claims and disputes objectively and fairly. It is claimed that this specially crafted social contract carried the Isse through the chaos and turmoil of the sixteenth century and continues to minimize and resolve intra-Isse conflicts. The *Ugaas*, like other Somali traditional leaders, presides over the decision-making body or assembly, the *shir,* which is open to all adult males of the clan. Since the decision taken would bind the whole *shir*, including opponents, the good leaders seek to accommodate the opposition along consociational practices to avoid pressures that might later divide the group. Above all, given the cultural obsession with pride, every effort would therefore be made to avoid a loss of face. Here is a deliberate effort to create a sovereign who does not dominate or terrorize society, unlike Hobbes' Leviathan, a product of logic and mathematical reasoning.

Reconciliations legitimize and facilitate political cooperation.

Northerners have taken a grassroots approach to the process. Traditional secular and religious (local) elites, modern elites, representatives of non-governmental organizations and ordinary citizens have participated in peace and reconciliation conferences held in virtually all the main towns: Berbera, Burao, Sheikh, Hargeisa, Erigavo and Borama. Elders play a leading role. This approach has won the support of most non-Isaaq clans and the SNM was therefore able to transform Somaliland from a clan into a multi-clan or territorial project. The trust and social solidarity being created rests on multi-clan foundations. There are three Somali clan-families represented in Somaliland -- the Isaaq (the largest) and parts of the Dir (Isse and Gadabursi) and Darood (Dulbahante and Warsangeli) clan families. The Isaaq clan-family is itself subdivided into at least six clans. Locke never made it clear whether men suddenly or gradually consented to live in a common society. History shows that the Somaliland social contract is being forged in stages. For example, the Borama peace and reconciliation conference lasted from January until May 1993. At first, it set out to reconcile outstanding clan conflicts and on March 30th adopted a communal and territorial Peace Charter.[7] The Borama conference went on to provide a more detailed social contract in the form of a National Charter, adopted on May 3, 1993.[8]

As a result of the agreement, several steps toward reconciliation, disarmament, and rehabilitation have taken place. For example, according to a mid-April (1994) report, the following heavy weapons have been surrendered and assembled in Hargeisa: thirty-eight "technicals" mounted with anti-air guns, twenty three tanks, five multi-barreled rocket launchers, thirty-five artillery pieces, assorted missile systems and ten tons of munitions. Several "technicals" have already been dismantled and are now back in civilian use. The 4th, 88th and 99th (former SNM) brigades based in Hargeisa have completed disarmament of heavy weapons at Washadda Kabka. To the west of Hargeisa, the 5th and 99th brigades have assembled their weapons at Gaalah. Military units in all parts of Somaliland have assembled their heavy weapons at designated assembly points.[9] Reliable external assistance could speed up this process of disarmament and demobilization, based upon the following NDC guidelines:[10]

- Disarmament and demobilization will be voluntary;
- Disarmament and demobilization programs will be universal, that is, open and equally accessible to all military groups;
- The demobilization program will be nationally coordinated;
- The demobilization program will be locally implemented;
- All military groups will be entitled to representation.

V. Edmund Burke: On History and Political Community

Edmund Burke's advocacy of monarchy and aristocratic rule would be alien to Somali political thought and experience. However, Burke's other political reflections may offer insights when applied to the Somali predicament. His concept of social order did not depict a series of separated, atomized individuals because he believed in a familial basis for social organization. When the sovereign violated citizen rights, Burke felt that an oppressed community could, by political revolution, overthrow the tyranny. The conditions for such a withdrawal of trust were prolonged and excessive abuse, with no prospect for improvement, under pressure so heavy that no delay was possible.

Had he witnessed Siyad's brutal military dictatorship unleash prolonged violence against the Somali people, Burke might have been moved to remark as he did when discussing the American Revolution that "revolts of a whole people ... are always provoked." Nevertheless, the violent excesses in southern Somalia would cause him to recall his condemnation of the French Revolution. He would probably admonish southern Somalis for choosing to "act as if you had never been molded into civil society and had everything to start anew." Authority, he would assert in regard to so-called warlords, has been placed in the hands of men "not taught habitually to respect themselves ... intoxicated with their unprepared greatness."[11]

Burke, unlike Hobbes and Locke, saw man as a group creature and a familial being and regarded speculation about him in a condition of isolation as unrealistic and dangerous. He would, therefore, view with sympathy Somalia's social diversity based on clan, subclan and lineage segmentation. Clans cannot simply be wished away. The current situation represents a basic realism that clans exist and they need to be harnessed and modified to promote positive political developments. The myth of a united, centralized Somalia has been broken and the country, if it is to be united again, can only be brought together on a federal basis. In Somaliland, the attachment to clans is tolerated, not to sow divisions, but to strengthen ties between clans and create multi-clan coalitions that give meaning to a new form of social solidarity. The love for clan and love for country are not mutually exclusive, as Burke explained long ago:

> To be attached to the subdivision; to love the little platoon we
> belong to in society is the first principle (the germ as it were) of
> public affections. It is the first link in the series by which we

proceed toward a love to our country and to mankind."

Somaliland has decided to utilize its traditional Somali law (*xeer*) together with Islamic law and modified British colonial law as the basis of its new legal system. The utilization of traditional Somali law would please Burke who observed: "for people will not look forward to posterity who never look backward to their ancestors." The creation of a formal council of elders (*guurti*) in the Somaliland legislative body is probably the first time such a measure has been taken in post-colonial Africa. Somaliland elites have decided, finally, to reconcile the old folkways, wisdom, and experience of clan and religious elders with some of the newer forms of government. In this matter, they have the authority of Edmund Burke:

> "... when ancient opinions and rules of life are taken away, the loss cannot possibly be estimated. From that moment we have no compass to govern us; nor can we know distinctly to what port we steer."[12]

VI. Ibn Khaldun: Social Solidarity ('*Asabia*) and State Formation

Ibn Khaldun attributed the origins of states, including large and powerful ones, to a key factor he called '*asabia* which may be roughly translated into "social solidarity," "group feeling," or "group consciousness." A primary source of social solidarity is the group to which an individual feels most closely attached, namely his clan or tribe, the people with whom he shares a common descent.[13] However, in political terms, social solidarity can be shared by people not related to each other by blood ties, but by long, close contact as members of a group or organization. This Afrocentric thinker has the advantage of focusing on the sociology of groups rather than on the psychology of isolated, atomized individuals.

This is a fertile concept that invites cross-breeding with the Somali experience. Earlier in this century, Somalis were galvanized by a potent Islamic Jihad, an anti-colonial crusade led by the Sayyid Mohamed Abdulle Hassan. The Sayyid waged wars against the partition and colonial occupation of Somali territories by the British, Italian and Emperor Menelik's Ethiopian forces. Religion is a powerful cement that can fortify tribal or clan solidarity. The combination of religious and clan solidarity produced a formidable movement that waged wars between 1899 and 1920. Apart from unrelenting colonial warfare (including the unprecedented use of war planes in 1920), the movement also suffered from the introduction of clan nepotism and some bias toward luxury -- the seeds of its eventual decay and disintegration.

The modern Somali nationalist movement saw the rise of two main political parties -- the Somali Youth League (SYL) in the south (Italian Somaliland), and the Somali National League (SNL) in British Somaliland. The two main parties agreed to seek independence followed by unification. The SYL essentially represented a Hawiye-Darood coalition while the Isaaq dominated the SNL. Since these three, plus the supporting Dir clan-family are essentially nomadic or pastoralists, we may conclude that the 1960 Somali state was formed by a pastoral *'asabia* or social solidarity. This was obvious to the Somalis, to borrow Professor Mazrui's phraseology, who loved both the land and animals -- the agropastoral Digil clans, those who love the land -- Bantu Somali farmers, and those who live in ancient parts of the coastal cities who love trade and crafts. The agropastoralists formed their own Somali Independent Constitutional Party (HDMS) which, as late as 1958, forcefully reiterated its position: "the party has become convinced that the only method of unifying the Somalis ... is through a federal constitution which accords full regional autonomy."[14]

Ahmed Samatar notes 'that the Somali state has died three times -- as a regime, as an apparatus, and as an idea of group consciousness, or what Ibn Khaldun calls *'asabia* ... the remaking of each element of the state will demand tremendous effort." Samatar then goes on to suggest "three possible sources for the generation of a new *'asabia*: Somali kinship values, Islamic principles, and secular thinking and experimentation." [15] Somalis are in the process of experimentation, searching for a restored sense of social solidarity. However, this is taking the form of creating decentralized *'asabia*s: in Somaliland, on the basis of mutual consent, the social contract approach; in southern Somalia, through powerful individuals manipulating clan solidarity to impose their social cohesion alternatives on the population. If there is to be future cooperation, then creative federalism and coalition building will have to emerge.

VII. Conclusion

The main object of this paper is to assess whether ideas of Hobbes, Locke, Burke and Ibn Khaldun help comprehend the Somali catastrophe, on one hand, and on the other, whether the Somali crisis can throw new light on their theories. In our view, this has allowed us to analyze and explain the Somali situation in a more interesting manner than if we had resorted to a straight-forward, narrative account of the events. Hobbes's state of nature resembles the situation that unfolded in southern Somalia following the complete collapse of the Somali state. The difference is that the violence involved social groups rather than isolated, atomized individuals. In these areas a decentralized Leviathan (an oxymoron according to Hobbes) has arisen by conquest rather than mutual consent. Locke's kinder and gentler state of nature seems to be reflected in the situation in northeastern Somalia and, especially, in former British Somaliland and now the self-declared Republic of Somaliland.

Hobbes used the imaginary concept of the social covenant to transfer power to an absolute monarch; Locke intended to use his imaginary contract to transfer power from the monarch to the parliament. In Somalia's past and contemporary situation, the social contract is a historical process involving grassroots conferences. In Somaliland this social contract process has resulted in a peace charter as well as a national charter setting up a new, embryonic state with separate legislative, executive and judiciary powers and functions. There is a rediscovery of the value and utility of traditional law *(xeer)*. The legislative body has two chambers, one of these, the council of elders *(guurti)*, consists of seventy-five clan and religious elders -- the traditional elite usually ignored by Africa's modern elite. Edmund Burke would be pleased by this instance where the modern elite cooperates with the traditional elite in constructing the future while respecting traditional law and the past. Burke would also not find contradiction between the love of one's clan and the love for the nation.

Ibn Khaldun's concept of *'asabia* is fertile enough to explain critical aspects of Somali politics, perhaps because it evolved from nomadic societies. The Sayyid, at the turn of the century, forged a potent clan and religious *'asabia* that bordered on fanaticism, thereby sowing the seeds of its own destruction. The Somali nationalist *'asabia* believed in a centralized state. It sought to unite all Somalis -- including those in Ethiopia, Kenya and Djibouti -- into one unitary state. Failure to achieve its maximum objectives resulted in electoral chaos, corruption and elites living in luxury. Once fractured, the nationalist *'asabia* could not survive and the military took over the reigns of power in 1969. Military General Siyad Barre utilized the military's organizational based *'asabia* to install what was, in the early years, a relatively popular rule. In its early stages, the state reflected a sense of cohesiveness and comradeship -- as people addressed each other as Jaalle, "comrade." Siyad went on to make his power absolute and sought to have his son inherit the presidency, establishing a dynasty which is a taboo concept in Somali political discourse. The desire of the President and his clique to gain exclusive control over all the sources of power and wealth brought a conflict between the Siyad dynasty and the men whose '*asabia* sustained it. Siyad's attempts to impose clan hegemony and the poisoning of clan relations within the armed forces, civil service and society at large provide the seeds of the regime's eventual decay and total disintegration. Siyad was chased out of Mogadishu by the raw '*asabia* of armed young warriors, compact and cohesive, recruited from rural clan hinterlands where the concept of social solidarity is still strong. The post-Siyad situation is complex, presenting a dual scenario: in southern Somalia where strong men are attempting to impose their own versions of '*asabia*; and the northern Somaliland Republic, where they are experimenting with a democratic social contract as a basis for a new national '*asabia*.

Endnotes

1. Ahmed I. Samatar, *The Somali Challenge - From Catastrophe to Renewal?* Boulder, Colorado: Lynne Rienner Publishers, 1994, p. 8.

2. Thomas Hobbes, *Leviathan.* New York: Collier Books, p. 100.

3. William T. Bluhm, *Theories of the Political System.* Englewood Cliffs, NJ: Prentice Hall, Inc. 1965, p. 270.

4. *Ibid.* p. 275

5. *Ibid.* p. 311

6. Ali Moussa Iye, *Le Verdict De L'arbre.* Dubai: International Printing Press, 1991.

7. *Axdiga Nabadgalyada Ee Beelaha Soomaaliland* (Peace Charter), Boorama, 03/30/1993 (mimeographed).

8. *Shirweynaha Guurtida Beelaha Soomaaliland* (National Charter), Boorama 04/25/93 (mimeographed).

9. Jeremy Brickhill, *Disarmament and Demobilization in Somaliland.* (Northwestern Somalia) 22 April 1994, (mimeographed).

10. National Demobilization Commission, *The Policy of the NDC: Discussion Paper No. 1.* 6 June 1994 (mimeographed).

11. Various Burke citations are found in Alfred Cobban, *Edmund Burke and the Revolt Against the Eighteenth Century,* New York: Macmillan, 1929; Ali Mazrui, *On Heroes and Uhuru-Worship.* London: Longmans, Green and

Company, Ltd, 1967; and Lee Cameron McDonald, *Western Political Theory.* New York: Harcourt, Brace and World, 1968.

12. Edmund Burke, *Reflections on the Revolution in France.* New York: Liberal Arts Press, 1955, p. 89.

13. Ibn Khaldun, *The Mugaddimah -- An Introduction to History.* Princeton: Princeton University Press, 1981, p. xi.

14. Cited in Saadia Touval, *Somali Nationalism.* Cambridge: Harvard University Press, 1963, pp. 96-97.

15. Ahmed Samatar, *op. cit.*, pp. 12-13.

SECTION TWO

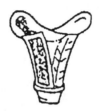

Kinship
and
Clans

Summaries: Section Two

Abdalla Omar Mansura (Chapter 8) explores Somali genealogy to document that the clan system, unlike what is commonly assumed, is based on much more than simply blood lines. He asserts that clans are the product of nomadic and pastoral lifestyles and have developed intricate social and political relationships responding to the particular challenges of such livelihoods. Need for defense, water, pasture, and security led to a series of fluid alliances. Clans, he concludes, are a product of shifting economic and political expediency and should not be confused with any permanent or static social or political structures.

Bernard Helander (Chapter 9) analyzes kinship and its relations to the present clan structure using the Rahanweyn as an example. He finds, first, that the Rahanweyn are themselves a melting pot, incorporating many groups. Second, he observes that villages, not clan, form the core of the social and therefore political unit of the people. Finally, he argues that their clan structure assumes a form comparable with a federal government in which the center assumes some responsibilities but that most day-to-day duties continue to reside with the villages. He believes the Rahanweyn social structure offers useful lessons for other Somalis.

Mohamed-Abdi Mohamed (Chapter 10) projects that the function of the Somali clan system has changed dramatically in the 20th century. Whereas the initial pastoral needs for defense and mutual help were the original incentive for clans, by the 1990s, the clans evolved into a "system of exclusion in which the strongest dictate their rules, and crush and isolate the weakest." He argues that the future of Somali society lies in reconstructing the precolonial nation, not the clan-based expediency that has emerged in the last decade. He distinguishes between natural kinship and politicized clanism.

CHAPTER EIGHT

Aspects of the Somali Tribal System

Abdalla Omar Mansur

It is clear to everybody that clanism is one of the root causes of Somalia's destruction and is still one of the main obstacles for the restoration of the Somali state. Therefore, in my opinion, it is necessary to analyze and understand various aspects of this social disease in order to attempt some kind of remedy.

For nearly fifty years it was taboo to mention the names of the Somali clans in public, and yet at the same time the base and reality of Somali politics rested on the clan system. In preparing for Somali unity, in a modern state without tribal barriers, the Somali Youth League (SYL) tried to abolish the traditional, segregational use of clan labels. Thus people, especially in the urban areas, used to answer "I am Somali" for the traditional question "who are you?" intending "which clan do you belong to?" This habit was continued even after independence. Then a new form for asking a person his clan developed: "What is your ex?" meaning "Now we are all Somali, but what was your ex-clan?" This form was used in a confidential manner, never in public, although in the political scene there were more than sixty parties considered anti-national, since they were representing the various clans and sub-clans, bearing false labels, like the national, patriotic, or democratic party, etc., with the same hypocrisy used today by the present fifteen factions.

Following the antitribalistic principles of the SYL, the military regime (1969), had brought back into use capital punishment in the place of "*diya*-paying" because the members of each subclan were linked traditionally by virtue of their collective obligation to pay or receive compensation for murder and other injuries. Actually this principle of individual responsibility for murder has also led to feuds and bloody revenges. Another significant step that the military regime implemented against tribalism, especially in its first five years, was to engage unemployed urban youths, mostly intellectuals excluded by the tribal system, for a series of public works. The rest of the story is well-known, and need not be elaborated here. After Somali's defeat in the Ogaden War, Siyad Barre, the man responsible for instigating the worst tribalism to keep his power, actually facilitated the clanist movements, to complete the destruction of Somalia in their search for power and clan-hegemony.

The aim of my paper is not to talk about the present Somali political system, but to elucidate some aspects related to the nature of Somali clan families in order to make some reflection on an aspect of Somali culture. Doing this, I realize that I am breaking the old rule of hypocrisy which lasted for half a century.

According to the tradition, the Somali nation symbolically consists of a vast genealogical tree. Nearly all Somalis descend from a common founding father, the mythical Hiil (father of Sab and Samaale), to whom the Somalis trace their genealogical origin. At the same time, a widespread Somali belief says that most of them descend from the Qurayshitic lineage of the prophet Mohammad. The clan families which have high regard for this claim are: Darood, Isaaq, Ajuraan, Shikhaal, Geledi and a few others.

Now let us divide the genealogy in two parts. The first part concerns the connections between the forefathers of clan families and the Qurayshitic family. The second part concerns the forefathers and their descendants. By analyzing the first part we come across many contradictions. For instance, as for the forefather of Darood there are more than seven different versions of his genealogy up to Aqil bin Abitalib. Another example can be that of the Shikhaal's subclans (Qudhub, Looboge, Gandershe). They have a common Arab ancestor Faqi Cumar, but each subclan has a different genealogy for the same ancestor.

Before World War II, a Somali community mostly from Somaliland, created in Kenya the "Isaaq Sharif Community," claiming that their ancestor was the cousin of the prophet Mohammad, in order to obtain the best treatment in that multiracial society. In fact, there was discrimination by the British colonial authority in Kenya regarding European, Asiatic and Bantu people. The Somalis preferred to be considered as Orientals, but the local Indian community refused this claim. Therefore, some Somali Muslim erudites tried to justify the legend of Arab origin. They fabricated the genealogical connection between the forefather Sheekh Isxaaq and the cousin of the prophet, Ali bin Abitaleb. In 1948 this new genealogy was published in a book printed in Cairo, and this seems more careful than the one of Darood, since it coincides in some way with the genealogy of one of Ali's descendants. Anyhow, all these facts tend to show that this part of genealogy is fabricated.

Now, is this claim of Arab descent originally due to the aim of getting high social status, to gain political advantage, as Isaaqs have had tried to do? And why do all these clans descend exclusively from Qurashitic lineage, and no single genealogy claims origins from other countries like Yemen, Egypt and Persia, with which Somalis have ancient and long historical relations?

We can find the answers to these two questions in the Somali legends which talk about charismatic Arab sheikhs who made alliance with the local people, and became their ancestors. For instance, the legend of Darood. He was expelled from Arabia and, seeking refuge, he arrived at the Somali coast. He dug a well beside a large tree. Then he was discovered by Dir's daughter, Doombiro, who was shepheding her flock.

He watered her animals at his well. Noticing that the stock had been watered, Dir followed his daughter and discovered the stranger. Darood quickly closed the well with a large stone and climbed up the tree. The chief, Dir, and his followers sought Darood's aid after unsuccessful attempts to reopen the well, but he refused to come down until the chieftain promised him his daughter in marriage. The chieftain allowed him to descend by taking him on his own shoulders. From this marriage, the Darood clan family descended.

The following story illustrates the Islamic cultural background as shown in a tale about Moses. After escaping from Egypt, Moses found two sisters near a well. The girls wanted to water their flock, but the well was covered by a very heavy stone that could not be removed by less than four to six people. Moses removed it by himself and helped the girls to water the flock. The father of the sisters, Shuayb, gave him one of them in marriage.

In this Islamic version of Moses's story, an important element of the legend is lacking: the "man in the tree," which we can find in another Somali story. One day, a stranger was discovered by Faaduma the daughter of Jembeelle Hawiye, while she was grazing her flock. He was sitting in the branches of a tree. He refused to get down until she called her people, then he asked three things: a hundred camels, a slave, and Faaduma in marriage. Moreover, he had to climb down onto the back of a man. All his conditions were accepted. From this marriage, the *Ajuuran* clan descended.

This story is very similar to that of some groups of Afar society, retained by themselves as Nobles which are called Asaimara. They claim descent from a common Arab ancestor who was discovered by local tribes in the branches of a tree from which he was induced to descend only when the autochthones had agreed to accept him as chief and had made a fitting gesture of submission. The Asaimara descended from his intermarriage with the indigenous local population.

These two stories, which are less Islamized than the first one, lead us toward African culture, where we find the mystery of the tree and the reason for which the local population was so eager to form an alliance with the strangers accepting all their conditions. Among the peoples of Oromo (especially Borana and Guji), Sidamo Janjero, Bako and others living in southern Ethiopia, in the area of the lakes, which is supposed to be the homeland of Eastern Cushitic speaking peoples, the story is frequently of a clan ancestor, king, or priest, endowed with supernatural powers, descended from the sky and discovered by the local people sitting in a tree. In this case, the sky is considered as God. In the Oromo language, the sky and God are the same word: *Waaq*. Before the coming of the Islamic and Christian faiths to the Horn of Africa, the Eastern Cushitic-speaking peoples had an ancient common religion, which is still professed by the Borana while it is hidden through assimilation process in the new faiths adopted by the other populations. One of the most characteristic elements of such religion is connected with the notion of the sky-God, called Waaq. This name is still used as God by the Oromo, Konso, Burji, Haddiya, Tasmai, Dasenech, Arbore, Elmolo, Bayso, Rendille, Dahalo and Somali, all of them speaking Eastern Cushitic languages except Dahalo. A group of these populations (Borana, Konso, Sidamo, Haddiya Tasmai and Afar) still consider the same kind of trees as sacred. For instance, the sycamore is Borana's temple. They believe that Waaq sometimes descended on that tree. And this belief is another characteristic element of traditional religion.

Another Somali tradition that shows the merging of African and Islamic culture is the rite that the Somali women during their seventh or ninth month of pregnancy, called *kur or madaxshub*. The invited women pour abundant oil on the pregnant woman's head, invoking Eve or Fatima, the daughter of the prophet, in order to safeguard the woman during delivery. This rite is not a part of Islam, it has root in the cult of Goddess of Fertility and Maternity practiced by the Borana women in the same way. Here, Fatima is a covering name for the ancient Goddess Ateta, as the Arabian descendent was for the heavenly origin.

Now let us see the second part of the genealogy. Here the phenomenon of merging is more pronounced, although it seems to be less confused than in the other part. Even in this part the ancestors of clan families represent a critical point. The forefathers that bear Islamic names such as Fiqi Cumar of Sheekhaal, Ibraahim of Ajuuran, Cumar Diini of Geledi and Sheekh Cabduraxmaan Darood, all married girls with Islamic names Faaduma Mahdiyo, Faaduma Jambeelle, Caasha, and Doombiro. Even this last name seems Arabic since it resembles the name of the wife of Imam Ahmed Ibrahim Al-qasi, Dalombiro bintu Maxfud (in Futux-al-Xabasa). Now, how is it possible that these wives maintained Islamic names if they belonged to the local people who had been converted only by their husbands? If the answer is because their names were changed by the sheikhs after conversion, why did their sons not bear the Islamic names?

The names starting from the sons of all ancestors up to the nearly tenth generation have obscure meanings because they belong to a remote linguistic stratum and they certainly are not Islamic. After that generation the fusion of Islamic names with those of Somalis began. This implies that the greatest number of Somalis seem to have converted to Islam by nearly the fifteenth century, induced, probably by the Audal Kingdom, one of the greatest and powerful Islamic states that existed in the Horn of Africa from fifteenth to sixteenth century. How does one explain that in several clan genealogies the name *Waaq* appears only at the initial point of Islamic names? The theoforus names (names of persons that contain divinity names) are very common among all the Semitic people from the antiquity until today. So the Islamic tradition has introduced this form of name. For instance BiddeWaaq is a translation of the Islamic name Cabdullaahi (the servant of Allah). Here the name *Waaq* no longer represents the traditional meaning *"Sky-God,"* but *Allah.* Even this novelty underlines the previous thesis about the Somali Islamization period.

If we continue to analyze the genealogy of each clan we discover another very interesting thing. The genealogy is not the crucial element for determining belonging to a clan family as it is believed commonly. For example, Xawaadle, Gaaljecel Degoodi and Cawrmale usually are considered to belong to the Hawiye clan family but, genealogically, they are not. The Xawaadle clan descended from Mayle Samaale and the other three clans from Gardheere Samaale. Other groups under the same condition are the Garre and Dabarre clans which are considered to belong to the Digil clan family, but genealogically descended respectively from

Garre Samaale and Maqaarre Samaale.

These changes, mostly concerning the subclans, are recent. But also, in a remote time, the clan families and clans had been formed by the fusion of different peoples, even non-Somalis. For instance, in the sixteenth century Shihab ad-Din chronicle (Futux Al-Xabasha) distinguish explicitly the Somali clans (Geri, Mareexaan, Harti, Misirre and others) from the Xarla clans (Barata, Barzara, Yaqula, Gaasar and others). But today, the few people of Xarla remaining in the Harar area appear to be already assimilated by the same Somalis and included in their genealogy, becoming Xarla Koomba Kablalax Darood.

In conclusion, the sayings cited above, and many others, highlight the fact that the Somali tribal structure is not based typically on a blood relationship, but rather is the fruit of nomadic pastoral life. The necessity of defense, the need of pasture and water-induced flexibility, including even the severance of kinship ties and the movement to new territory resulted in the formation of new alliances, and later, clans.

A great deal of Somali genealogy and clan systems is a product of fabrication, rather than of organic blood descent. In other words, this tribal system, which is the result of an historical phase in which the society, the way of life and the economy were different, cannot be consistent with present social needs. Therefore, it does not seem logical to me that one should remain prisoner of this archaic system that has been practiced by nearly all the people of the world.

Bibliography

Abdalla Omar Mansur, (1980),*La storia della religion e tradizionale dei cusciti*, [The History of the Traditional Religion of Cushitic Speaking Peoples], Tesi di Specializzazione, Universita di Roma, La Sapienza.

Abdalla Omar Mansur, (1988), *Le lingue cuscitiche e il Somalo* [The Cushitic languages and Somali], Italian translation by C. Serra Borneto, "Studi Somali 8" 127 pp. Rome.

Cerulli, E. (1957), *Somalia: scritti vari editi e inediti*, Roma.

Lewis, I.M., (1955), *People of the Horn of Africa*, London.

Luling, V., (1988), "The Man in the Tree. A Note on a Somali Myth." in Puglielli (ed.) *Proceedings of the Third International Congress of Somali Studies*, Roma.

Mohamed Abdi Mohamed, (1990), *La Somalie aux hautes*
  periodes, These pour l'obtention du Doctorat, Universite de Franche Comte.

Shihab ad-Din, *Futuh al-Habasha* (Arabic version written in XIV century.)

Informants and consultants:

1. Ibrahim Cali Xasan (a Dir elder)
2. Cali Ibrahim Aadan (a Reewin elder)
3. Maxamed Cabdi Maxamed (an eminent Historian)
4. Cabdullahi Farax Caseyr (doctor)
5. Mussa Maxamed Nassir (lecturer)

CHAPTER NINE

Clanship, Kinship and Community Among the Rahanweyn: A Model for Other Somalis?

Bernhard Helander

I. Introduction

This paper seeks to outline the basic principles of clanship among the Rahanweyn. The purpose of this exercise is to demonstrate how members of Rahanweyn clans assign a restricted set of functions to clanship and also have other social idioms as regulatory principles for their social life. This particular social formula, I shall argue, is part of the reason why inter-clan strife is relatively more rare among the Rahanweyn than among other Somali groups of clans. Generally acknowledged as "peace-lovers," the Rahanweyn could provide a useful example for other Somalis in search of ways to reshape their traditions.

Whereas it is well-known that many Rahanweyn clans, due to the adoption of strangers, have a slightly different and more heterogeneous character than many other Somali clans, the very nature of these differences are less well understood. The Rahanweyn conception of clanship may be described as a cultural principle that serves to regulate and adjust processes of sociability into an ideological framework that is influenced by, what I shall call, "standard Somali" notions of descent, but that also has its own distinctive traits. The most important difference from the rest of Somalia is probably that clanship among the Rahanweyn does not seek to be a totalizing social idiom. On the contrary a remarkable feature of the Rahanweyn society is its ability also to allow other forms of sociability.

The Rahanweyn clans have many times been presented in the anthropological literature as a kind of social melting pot (see Lewis 1969; 1993). While the very notion of society as a melting pot has seen much recent criticism in the society that gave birth to it -- the United States of America (Kivisto 1989) -- not least in view of increasing segregation of different immigrant groups,[1] there are obvious merits of this representation of the social character of the Rahanweyn clans: Rahanweyn clans have a very high proportion of immigrant members who, despite their original descent from other clans, are fully integrated into their host clans' solidarity. However, while the notion of a melting pot correctly portrays the proportion of immigrant or adopted members in the clans, it may also obscure the particular social and cultural mechanisms of the Rahanweyn's form of clanship that, as it were, has facilitated the emergence of melting pot-like clans.

Among the many and varied models that the Rahanweyn themselves have of their society, the idea of this group of clans as a confederation has always figured prominently. According to this version, the very name Rahanweyn would derive from the words *raxan* and *weyn*, literally "crowd-big." On a mythological level this version of the meaning of Rahanweyn is supported by myths that describe the entire subdivision of Rahanweyn clans into two larger subsections known as Sieed and Sagaal (the Eight and the Nine) as based on confederation rather than descent. Similar myths also exist within single Rahanweyn clans. However, concurrently with views that focus on the federational links between clans and their sub-groups, there are also local models of the Rahanweyn society that seek to emphasize the descent links that various groups can trace to common ancestors. According to these models, the very idea that the name Rahanweyn is derived from the term *raxan* (crowd) is wrong since the Rahanweyn dialect (*Af May*) does not even contain the x-sound (an unvoiced pharyngeal fricative) of the standard Somali. Rather, proponents of this model argue, Rahanweyn derives from the name of the ancestor of all Rahanweyn clans, a certain *Ma'd* (or Mohammed Reewin). Recently, this usage has achieved increased prominence in scholarly circles so that some writers no longer talk of Rahanweyn but prefer the term "Reewin" instead (cf. Mukhtar 1993; Kuusow 1993).[2]

In dealing with Rahanweyn models of their own society, it would be grossly inaccurate to give prominence to just one type of model. As I will show, both the federational or melting pot model and -- at least from a "standard Somali" point of view -- the more conventional descent-based model are equally applicable and equally justified as representations of the Rahanweyn society. This paper provides an overview of those aspects of Rahanweyn clanship that I perceive as vital and special for their form of society. However, I do believe that the importance of this overview goes beyond a mere addition to the ethnographic record.

At this particular point in time, when the Somali society has all but ceased to exist, and at a moment when Somalis live through what might possibly be the greatest crisis their society has ever faced, I believe it essential to make available positive aspects of their traditional forms of organization that might possibly serve to help them in overcoming some of the acute difficulties they are facing. While I do not argue that the Rahanweyn should serve as a model for the entire Somali society, there are nonetheless important lessons to be learned by a closer scrutiny of their form of organization. What I will do here is to bring up some themes of the Rahanweyn's social organization and highlight those aspects that I see as both different from the other Somalis and that may have something positive to offer as inspiration or as model.

I have so far talked of the Rahanweyn as if they constituted a homogenous unit, but of course that is not so. Although there is a sense of over-all Rahanweyn unity, based, among other things, on their common forms of attachment to land, their combined reliance on agriculture and animal husbandry, the pride they have in their dialect, and, to some extent, their shared forms of Islamic worship, the Rahanweyn remain divided into some thirty clans of varying size. While I shall continue to speak rather broadly about the Rahanweyn here, I must acknowledge that, although supplemented by impressions from other parts of the "inter-river" area, my paper is primarily based on fieldwork among one Rahanweyn clan, the Hubeer of Ooflaawe, some eighty kilometers west of Baydhabo.

In brief, there are four different aspects of Rahanweyn clans that I perceive as radically different from the standard Somali version of clanship, and somehow define the traits of their mode of sociability:

1. The status of adopted members within their host clans;
2. The nature of *diya*-paying groups and settlement of *diya* payments;
3. The social and cultural role of marital ties;
4. The importance given to the villages and towns as a form of

community, partly independent of clans.

In the following sections, I shall briefly describe each of these points and then finally seek to further validate my point that the experience of the Rahanweyn in building functioning inter-clan communities could serve as an example for the Somali society at large.

II. The Status of Adopted Members within their Host Clans

The Rahanweyn clans contain a high degree of adopted members. Most Somali clans, both in the north and south, have means that facilitate weak groups to become incorporated and protected among more powerful groups. Yet, the Rahanweyn differ, both in the extent to which this is carried out and in the relatively secure status that adopted or incorporated members enjoy within their host clans. In some Rahanweyn clans, there are indications that the number of adopted members actually exceeds the number of the real members of that clan. Lewis mentions that in 1962, not one of the twenty-two chiefs of the Eelay clan were of original Eelay descent (1969:69);

> Indeed, so many layers of foreign settlement have been deposited by successive waves of immigrants that in a great many clans the original founding nucleus ... has not only been vastly outnumbered but has eventually withered away altogether [Lewis 1969:68].

It needs to be underscored that migration and resettlement are fundamental strategies in the Rahanweyn's agro-pastoral mode of life. In fact, to some extent it may be argued that the possibility of changing one's clan membership through adoption is a requirement for their form of subsistence to function properly. A household or a small lineage may, by moving to a new area, enjoy circumstances that are much more in line with their particular needs. Thus, although Rahanweyn clans do contain large numbers of members from the other Somali clan-families, the bulk of migration and adoption take places among Rahanweyn clans. The fact that migration and resettlement throughout the entire inter-riverine area have been going on for several hundred years also means that most families have relatives spread out among a large number of clans. As I have shown elsewhere, such relatives often serve as mediators between someone seeking to become adopted and the clan (cf. Helander 1994). This system of maintaining vital, personal networks which transgress clan boundaries resemble that recently described by Günther Schlee among the Rendille, Gabbra, Sakuye and some Somalis in northern Kenya (Schlee

1989). It can also be argued that the such cross-clan kinship links serve to mitigate inter-clan warfare.

The institution of adoption among Rahanweyn clans is usually known as *sheegad*, a term derived from the verb "to say" or "to tell."[3] It is not unlikely that this term itself derives from the ceremony that formerly newly adopted members of a clan had to go through, during which they pledged allegiance to their new host clan and swore to contribute loyally to payments of blood wealth and to fight alongside their new clansmen if it should become necessary. The remarkable thing with the *sheegad* institution is that the adopted members do not become second class citizens within their host clan. Over time, most adopted groups and individuals tend to become fully integrated within their host communities.

The Hubeer often use a slightly different terminology to distinguish the adopted from the real members of the clan. While those who acquired clan membership by birth are simply called *dhalad*, "born," the adopted are called *dhaqan*, "culture." The implication being, of course, that the adopted member have become Hubeer by conforming to local cultural standards.

There are no restrictions of either economical or political nature imposed upon the majority of adopted members. As long as they fulfil their obligations to the adopting clan, they are free to buy and sell property. They tend to take full part in community affairs of all kinds. They can and do compete to become elected to the posts as *suldaan* or *malaq*, the leader for a clan or lineage. In brief, it is very hard to tell who is adopted and who is a real member because in all respects the adopted members lead lives very similar to the other members of the clan.

III. The Nature of *Diya*-paying Groups and Settlement of *Diya* Payments

One of the most substantial requirements that the adopting clans will put on people aspiring to clan membership is that they take full part in the settlement of *diya* payments as members of the new clan.[4] However, although most adopted members abide by this condition, that does not make them sever their links to their clans of birth. As I have described elsewhere at some length, adoption is usually the final outcome of a long and gradual process of transferring oneself and one's household into a new area. Even generations after such a move, children will be taught their real genealogies by their mother, not the genealogy of the lineage that has adopted them. An adopted family may also still retain claims on inheritance within their clan of birth. Yet, when such a family faces demands of *diya* payment they are expected to turn to their host clan for support, not to their clan of birth. And the expectations are, naturally, even higher for such a family to contribute to payments that their adopting clan is facing.

This may seem awkward from the perspective of many other Somali clans. The "standard Somali" principle is that descent determines membership in a *diya*-paying group. The mutual responsibility that members in such a group have serves further to strengthen the descent ties. However, among at least the smaller Rahanweyn clans, the clan as a whole serves as one large *diya*-paying group. It is also often the case that a household's contribution to a fine is, to some extent at least, negotiable and therefore determined largely on an *ad hoc* basis. Certainly, no one can, in the long run, afford to abstain from participating in the payment of the clan's collective debt. Yet the system is so flexible that someone in difficulty can be granted exemption. It can sometimes also happen that recently adopted members will be asked by their clans of birth to contribute to their *diya* payments. Such demands may be difficult to avoid because the very nature of clanship ties among the Rahanweyn is that one should try to keep future options open, and showing solidarity with one's clan of birth will maintain the possibility to move back. The basic rule, however, is that one contributes to the *diya* of one's host clan because it is frequently only as a member of this *diya*-paying group that one can claim rights in agricultural land within the clan's territory.

It may sometimes be more difficult for adopted members to get a fair share of the blood wealth payments that the clan receives. This problem usually affects recently adopted members and relates to the fact that the bulk of *diya* payments actually take place between subsections of the clan. Although it would be rude to question the loyalty of a recently adopted member vis-a-vis the adopting clan as a whole, the lineage or subsection to which one formally belongs may still regard the new member with a certain amount of reserve. This will also affect their readiness to part with incoming compensation to someone that has not yet earned their full trust.

IV. The Importance of Marital and Matrilateral Ties

The Hubeer recognize two distinct types of adopted members. One is called *dhuhul* ("charcoal"), and refers to groups that have made a more or less formal agreement with the clan to become adopted. While that may have been more common in the past, the largest category of adopted members are called *dhareer* ("saliva"). This is usually explained as referring to the growth of social ties that emerge from eating together and having one's saliva mingled on the common plates[5] . In reality this group consists mostly of men and women who have been able to use their marital ties with the clan as a means to becoming accepted as a clan member.

Again, from the perspective of other Somali clans, this is a most unusual way to make political use of marriage ties. For instance, among the northern Somali, a marriage to a woman in another clan creates a bond between the parents-in-law, and a woman from another clan can be used as a messenger to her own clan in times of warfare. But the very idea that a marriage constitutes a possibility for the husband or wife to change his or her own clan allegiance is indeed unique to the Rahanweyn.

However, the Rahanweyn appear to go even farther than that because the ability to use marital ties as an entry ticket to clan membership is paralleled by a distinct set of cultural ideas. Although the evidence is not conclusive, it appears that they do give a much higher recognition to matrilateral and affinal ties within their notions of human procreation and individual identity. They tend to see a human being as constituted by "hard" paternal substance like bone, and "soft" maternal substance like blood. On a social level, this idea is represented by the lineage called *laf* or *ray* ("bone" or "testicle") and the affinal relatives that they refer to as *hidid*, meaning "vein" or "root." Given the hard/soft dichotomy in which the idea of the respective parental influence is cast, and bearing in mind that a lineage is "a bone," it is hardly surprising that adopted members are sometimes described as "cartilage." "Adopted members are like the soft cushions between bones," as a Hubeer man put it to me.

It is important to understand that the whole social system of the Rahanweyn is framed in an ideology and symbolism that not just sees assumption of a new clan identity as something one is forced into by economic necessity or production needs. Rather, I think it can be argued that it is the distinct ideological properties of the Rahanweyn system of clanship that to a large extent has facilitated the melting pot character of the Rahanweyn social fabric. In other words, Rahanweyn clans do not represent a corruption of Somali ideals but have their very own distinct and ideologically coherent system of clanship, based on their own cultural premises, but very much related to the "standard Somali" type of clanship.

In the Rahanweyn system of clanship, it is therefore possible to "become" the member of another clan. It is difficult to say at what stage these changes shift from being a matter of political convenience into being regarded as an integrated aspect of personal identity. However, as the following discussion (recorded in 1989) illustrates, adoption can actually mean that such a change eventually takes place, although it may be debated. The woman in the following discussion originally traces descent from the Geelidle clan and is married to an Hubeer man. The other woman, B, is also of Geelidle descent although divorced from her Hubeer husband who has left the area. Since she is now living independently and runs a small tea shop, she never attempts to conceal her original Geelidle descent.

> A: I am Geelidle and my children are Hubeer (*ana Geelidle aha ii ariikey Hubeer aha*). God makes me both those clans *(lamaada qabiil Ilaaiyaa oo weli)*.
> B: How can you be (*see ku ete*)? You are Geelidle (*Geelidle waaye*)! How can you be both (*lamaada see ku ete*)?
> A [Pointing to her right and left side]: This side is Hubeer and this side is Geelidle (*tan Hubeer ii tan Geelidle*). I am not telling lies, I am really [like that] (*been mikiin sheego haye foola in aha*)!
> B: How are you that (*may, ada entee ku etee*)? Of which Hubeer are you (*Hubeer entee ka etee*)?
> A: Me? I am Hubeer, I am Abow Ibraahim and Abow Aamin (*Anuva? Ana Hubeer aha, Abow Ibraahim ii Abow Aamin aha*).
> B: I don't want to hear your sheegad-status (*Sheegad mal fadow*).
> A: I am not sheegad, I am real, why [do you ask] (*Sheegad mi ki ihii, foola aan aha, may*)?
> B: But which are you then (*Entee ku etee, laakiin*)? The children I gave birth to, how can I say I am of their clan (*Ariika ana dhalley yee sheegadey reed*)?
> A: I can say! If I can't say I belong to the clan of my kids what clan can I say I belong to (*Sheegadee! Unugii ana dhalleyba hoo sheegada waaye, may sheegadee*)? I am Hubeer and I am Geelidle, forget about what B is saying (*Ana Hubeer aha Geelidlena aha, B warshe uskudhaf*)!

V. The Importance of the Local Community

Perhaps the most remarkable feature of the entire Rahanweyn social fabric are the villages. Villages have a mode of sociability on their own that is only partly related to the type of relations that exist within the clan. Villages among the Rahanweyn are tightly-knit communities that often host settlers from many of the clans' constituent lineages. Villages are the real foci of Hubeer political and social life. It is within villages that relationships and cooperation are forged. Ironically, the importance the Rahanweyn attach to their villages fit rather well with the anti-tribalism rhetoric of the former military regime, and the village committee-system promulgated by Siyad Barre was probably no where adopted with the same enthusiasm as among the Rahanweyn. In the pre-Siyad times, villages of the inter-river area did not have any type of institutionalized leadership. Even then, however, villages constituted a distinct arena for social interaction with established cooperation across lineage boundaries.

Most villages among the Rahanweyn have a similar appearance. A village square in the center is surrounded by restaurants and shops that sparkle with commercial activities. The center is surrounded by a densely inhabited zone, outside of which lie the farms of the villagers. Within the cultivated zone there are occasional homesteads. The agricultural resources existing in an area are generally seen as belonging to a specific village rather than to a clan. Although the larger zone in which a village lies is identified with a specific clan, it is the villages and its resources that attract new settlers who subsequently may seek to become adopted by the clan. Although smaller villages may have members that come only from one subsection of the clan, the larger villages are regularly composed of many different sections of the clan and frequently members from completely unrelated clans too. It should be emphasized that the seeds for the Rahanweyn social formula are therefore distinctly urban or semi-urban because it is within their most densely-settled communities that the spirit of inter-clan cooperation is most highly developed.

There is a distinct field of social relations that stem from the Rahanweyns' attachment to their villages. First, villages provide households with a sphere of cooperative networks for labor sharing and provides access to water. All such relations, that I have described more fully elsewhere (Helander 1988, 1994), have the village, rather than the clan, as their point of reference.

In this way, an individual has at least two sets of relationships to other people within the clan: with other villagers he or she shares, e.g., reciprocal labor sharing arrangements and interests in water reservoirs and wells. With the members of the clan, the same individual shares interests in the common defense of the clan's grazing lands and, more importantly, interests in the equitable distribution of, and responsibility for, payments of blood wealth.

For the adopted members, there can sometimes be a third set of relations, namely those to the members of their own clan of birth. Within that clan, a person may still have, for instance, interests in unsettled inheritance and it is often through one's clan of birth that payments of bride wealth (*fad* or *yaraad*) are channeled. If large numbers of members from the same original clan become adopted into the same host clan, they often tend to form a sub-lineage on their own within the clan that has adopted them. As the above discussion between the two women illustrates, the ties to one's clan of birth can, when juxtaposed to those of one's host clan, give a slightly confusing impression.

However, there is little doubt that at least from the perspective of daily subsistence, it is the villages that play the most significant role for the Rahanweyn. Most Rahanweyn actually choose to identify with the village of residence rather than with their clan. A Rahanweyn individual on a visit somewhere outside of his home area would only exceptionally mention the name of his or her clan but rather describe themselves as a villager from a named village. The Hubeer prefer to describe themselves as the *reer Ooflaawe*, the people of Ooflaawe which is the name of the area they inhabit.

As organizations, the villages differ from the clans in more than failing to invoke descent as a constituent principle. Village life among the Rahanweyn tends to have ideals of its own, often influenced by and coached in an idiom of religion. Village life is dominated by principles of good neighborliness and inter-clan solidarity rather than the assertion of clanship ties. In fact, in many settings of everyday life in a Rahanweyn village it would be considered rude to, at least openly, treat the members of one's own lineage differently than other villagers.

There are disadvantages with the Rahanweyn's focus on the village community above that of the clan. It can be argued that it was partly due to their extremely weak clans that the Rahanweyn so easily fell victim to the disasters of the civil war (Helander 1992). Unused to large-scale warfare, and largely unprepared for it, many Rahanweyn were simply unable to defend themselves against the attacks from other militias.

VI. Conclusion

I have argued that the Rahanweyn's form of clanship differs in some marked ways from that of many other Somali clans. I have pointed out that although membership in their clans is based on descent, one may become a member through adoption as well. One of the most common ways of achieving that is by relying on one's affinal ties with a clan. This, I have said, constitutes a radical break with the Somali notion that a wife from another clan can be helpful in providing a link or dialogue with that clan. In the Rahanweyn version, inter-clan marriages may open the door for membership in the clan of one's spouse..

The importance of clanship for the Rahanweyn is limited to a few important functions. It provides members with an overall security in times of conflict, and it provides a system for handling blood compensation. However, beyond that, clanship is not the chief regulatory principle of social affairs that it generally tends to be in other parts of Somalia. A Rahanweyn individual will primarily turn to his or her village for support in everyday affairs. It is also the village which seems to provide people with a sense of identity. It is within the mixed-clan environment of a village or town that a person's status and prestige is settled by one's ability to live up to the obligations imposed in lateral networks for labor sharing and other forms of cooperation.

It may be suggested that the Rahanweyn's mode of sociability rests on three sets of organizational principles: clanship, the institution of adoption and village membership. As I have shown, each one of these principles affects the other but it is the combined effect of all three that has contributed to give the inter-river area its very distinct social character.

What can one say is the lesson of all this for other parts of Somalia? Certainly the fact that there exists a community spirit independent from that vested in one's clan is not unique to the Rahanweyn, although it is certainly more emphasized among them. I think that the key to their- - as it may appear -- social success, lies entirely within their business-like approach to the functions performed by the various sets of social relations to which they belong. It would seem that the way they regard clanship in relation to other types of social relations is extremely pragmatic. They seem to view the clan as a form of federal government, ideally good for purposes like defense and social security but not at all an appropriate organization when it comes to more everyday matters. And it is by restricting the importance of clanship to deal precisely with, as it were, federal issues that they have been able to form tightly-knit communities with members from different clans and within which clanship plays a very restricted role.

As I have repeatedly pointed out, there are differences in the way the Rahanweyn conceive of and act within their social universe, in comparison to other groups of Somali clans. But at the same time, the ingredients to their particular social formula are present also in other parts of the country and it would therefore not be beyond imagination that other groups of clans start looking towards the achievements of the Rahanweyn. In fact, the awareness of the Rahanweyn social model appears to be spreading among many other Somali groups. The Hawiye, for instance, sometimes talk of the two different types of relations that one might have to the Rahanweyn and call them *Sagaaro gad* ("the buyers of antelope meat") and the *Eelaay wiiq* ("those staying with the Eelaay"). During the recent civil war, when a group called the Southern Somali National Movement was formed, some Isaaq clan members in the north thought this to be an indication of large numbers of Isaaq living as adopted members among the Rahanweyn.[6]

It is my hope that at this point, when a great number of Somalis have expressed the need to take a close look at their own traditions with the aim of rebuilding, and perhaps reshaping, their society, the Rahanweyn's social model may offer some inspiration for those aspiring to construct a society characterized by cooperation and peace.

Endnotes

1 . Cf. Simon Jenkins's brilliant assessment of the Los Angeles riots as "a melting pot that bubbles over", *The Times*, August 18, 1993.

2 . In this paper, however, I shall stick to the conventional usage and speak of Rahanweyn. The term *Reewin* seems to give undue attention to the descent-model of the Rahanweyn society, at the expense of the confederational character of their society.

3 . Throughout this paper I deliberately use *Af-May* terms and spelling.

4 . *Diya* is an Arabic term that most Somalis seem to prefer over the Somali word *mag*. Both, however, mean" blood wealth."

5 . I. M. Lewis, personal communication.

6 . Mostly, however, the SSNM was made up of Dir clan members.

Bibliography

Helander, B. 1988. "The Slaughtered Camel: Coping with Fictitious Descent Among the Hubeer of Southern Somalia." Unpublished doctoral thesis, Uppsala University.

----- 1992. "Who is Starving?" *Somalia News Update*, 1 (28).

----- 1994. "The Hubeer in the Land of Plenty: Land, Labor and Vulnerability among a Rahanweyn Clan." in C. Besteman and L. V. Cassanelli (eds.) *Production and Politics in Southern Somalia*. Boulder: Westview (in press).

Kivisto, P. 1989. "Introduction." in P. Kivisto (ed.) *The Ethnic Enigma*. Philadelphia: Balch Institute Press.

Kusow, A. M. 1993. "The Somali Origin: Myth or Reality?" Unpublished paper presented to the *Fifth International Congress of Somali Studies*, Worcester, Massachusetts.

Lewis, I. M. 1961. *A Pastoral Democracy*. Oxford: Oxford University Press.

----- 1969. "From Nomadism to Cultivation: The Expansion of Political Solidarity in Southern Somalia." in M. Douglas and P. M. Kaberry (eds.) *Man in Africa*. London: Tavistock.

----- 1993. *Understanding Somalia: Guide to Culture, History and Social Institution*. London: Haan Associates.

----- 1994. *Blood and Bone: The Call of Kinship in Somali Society*. Trenton, NJ.: Red Sea Press.

Mukhtar, M. H. 1993. "Somalia: Between Self-Determination and Chaos." Unpublished paper presented to the *Fifth International Congress of Somali Studies*, Worcester, Massachusetts.

Schlee, G. 1989. *Identities on the Move: Clanship and Pastoralism in Northern Kenya*. Manchester: Manchester University Press.

CHAPTER TEN

Somalia: Kinship and Relationships Derived from It

Mohamed-Abdi Mohamed

Contrary to the European's notion of kinship, which limits the family group to the closest members, Somalis will grant the title of relatives to remotely related people and even to people with whom they share only the bonds of the clan or the tribe. In fact, Somalis have developed an entire network of "family relations" which allows each individual to have an identity, to be acknowledged and identified, and that he can use according to his needs and circumstances.

A first analysis would lead to a belief that this network of "family relations" is based on the father's bloodline which determines the notion of clan or of tribe. In fact, things are more complex. Relationships with the mother's side also play a part. The kinship system is therefore double.

Studying the kinship system over the last half-century demonstrates its evolution. That very evolution led to the current crisis: the Somali family system not only determines the behavior of individuals, but also that of groups, and it plays an important role in the history of Somali society. Many suggest it is the kinship system that is largely responsible for the horrors committed during the current civil war.

This fact being established, can we continue to fight, and to commit robbery, murders, and massacres in the name of a clan which most likely does not truly exist? If a solution can be found, what is to prevail? Social kinship, meaning the totally unrealistic clan system? Or family kinship, meaning the ties born out of marriage -- the alliance systems? How does one establish peace? What type of democracy should be rebuilt, once peace is back?

I. The Somali Kinship System

Before getting into the core of the subject, let us establish some definitions and prerequisites:

1. **Somali** is a term referring to the Somali ethnic group whose territory encompasses Somalia, half of the Djibouti Republic, the entire Eastern Ethiopia (the Ogaden and Haud region) and the Northern part of Kenya (region of the Northern Frontier District).

2. **Somalia** refers to the Republic of Somalia, founded in 1960, thanks to the unification of the Italian colony (Somalia Italiana) and the British colony (Somaliland).

Right away, we are looking at the division of the Somali ethnic group, first, into several colonial administrations, and then into several states. Once the ethnic group has been broken up, can we still treat it as one or should we, from the start, separately consider the groups engendered by the division? Can we still talk about one Somali ethnic group or must we talk about Somali ethnic groups?

Starting from the premise that an ethnic group is made of individuals sharing the same culture, that is to say the same language, history, customs, religion and beliefs; I consider that the unity of the Somali ethnic group is still alive in spite of its being divided into several states.

Besides, I believe the old model that defined the Somali ethnic community, the one which existed before the huge colonial upsets, is still maintained and reachable through oral traditions since those traditions are everlasting and are an integral part of the Somali culture.

The workings of Somali society are rather complex but are essentially based on four pillars:

1. A social system based on kinship (*xigto*),

2. A lexicon of laws that we could call "social morals"- generated by the social system and controlling it (*dhaqan*),

3. Religion (*rumeysi*), monotheistic or not, which, in addition to its spiritual side plays a regulating part in Somali society and

4. A state system (*dawlad*) whose function has evolved considerably in the course of the last century.

The first three elements are ancient and are explained, based on what they used to be before colonization. The last one has appeared only since colonization. Explanations of these four pillars follow.

A. Kinship

The kinship system (*xigto*) is a twofold organization of society. First, it gathers individuals from the Somali ethnic group (nation) into families (*qoys*) or family cells. It places the families into extended families (*reer*) which include the descendants of a close ancestor (grand or great-grandfather) and their relatives. These extended families are in turn grouped into lineages (*jilib*), the lineages into sub-clans (*laf*), the subclans into clans (*golo*), the clans into clan families (*tol*), and the clan families constitute the nation (*qaran*). Each grouping is built around a common ancestor, called the *xigaalo*. It corresponds to the genealogies and the lineages on the father's side. It allows each individual to have an identity.

Onto that vertical system of kinship is grafted a horizontal system of alliances, based on marriages, the *xidid*. Marriages are usually not allowed within the narrow sphere of the extended family. In order to create an alliance, the wedding must take place between people outside the sphere of endogamy. It means that the two prospective spouses must share no kinship ties over seven to ten generations in the best of cases. Several marriages thus taking place between two groups (extended families or clans) bond them in a durable fashion. Then they share pastures, water holes, and support each other. Exceptions to those rules are found mainly on the coast and in cities.

Beside its vast kinship system (*xigto*) with its multiple vertical and horizontal ramifications, Somali society has developed, in the very bosom of the system, a division into age and sex classes (*gado iyo dhaddig labood*), which define each individual's role in society.

All individuals belonging to the same age and sex class, beyond family and hierarchical relationships, hold the same duties (*xil*) toward the group they belong to and derive the same rights (*waajib*) from it. For instance, young men between the ages of fifteen and twenty-two (*gaashaan qaad*), must protect the territory and the property of the clan and keep herds away from base camps during seasonal migrations.

Although guided by an older man, they enjoy a good deal of freedom. The *jilib culus* and the *oday*, men forty years of age or more, help the chief or the nominal head of the clan in ruling the community. They are advisors or wise men who are listened to and respected. Their prestige comes with a certain wealth but their responsibilities are very heavy, mainly during a conflict with a clan or a neighboring group, for they will be judged on their ability to resolve the conflict in a manner which will be fair and honorable to their community.

The division in age classes is pretty much the same among men and women. Their numbers are identical, although the age limits between the two classes are slightly different. Before they are seven years old, children of both sexes live with their mothers and around women. This is the only time when the distinction between boy-girl (male-female) is slight. Circumcision for the boys and excision (*gudmo*) for the girls are highly symbolic rites of passage which are their first steps toward aduthood. No more running around naked, and the boys must not stay with the women. As soon as they are *gudmo*, the boys participate in the men's activities and share their meals. Beyond the symbolic age of seven, the children's upbringing is separate, depending on their gender. In the same fashion, their roles in society will be different later on. The women are the engines of economic life but nonetheless have no voice in the management of the community. They can state their opinions during public debates but cannot make decisions. They thus seem treated as inferiors but they are protected and respected, for the relations of alliance depend on them. In fact, the social organization into age and sex classes is found in the entire Somali ethnic group, independent of clan or tribe. It is a horizontal, egalitarian system which evens out hierarchies.

The *xigto* is recreated at the level of soil or space occupancy. Indeed, each group, whether it is simply a portion of the *xigaalo* or the result of a *xidid* alliance, owns a territory, with camps, pastures and water holes. The territory is subdivided into smaller and smaller units, corresponding to more and more restricted circles of people. The terms that are used do not only designate camps of various sizes, but also the camps and the land belonging to them, due to the fact that the camp inhabitants use it. These lands are therefore grazing grounds, water holes, and cultivated fields. From the smallest to the largest, the territories are called: *qoys*, *jees*, *reer*, *duddo*, *qayro*, *beel*, *qaran*, the first one corresponding to the land allotted to a *qoy* family (father, mother and children), and the last one to the entirety of the Somali territory (meaning populated by Somalis). But the terms in the middle can be related either to corresponding levels of the *xigaalo* (*reer*, *jilib*, *laf*, *qolo*, *tol* in the same order), or to associated groups of individuals (outside marriage, but for some reason or other, is *bahayisi*) or allies (*xidid*). In wartime, when the families who are usually living in small isolated groups gather together for better protection, the terms *reer*, *duddo* and *qayro* can also take on the more restricted sense of camps. Of course, the implied connotation of "entrenched" camp is one whose size is greater. For example, a *qayro* can include several thousand *aqal*, tents made with animal skins and straw, circular and topped with a rounded roof, typical of nomads.

Some categories of people are excluded from the Somali kinship system. These include marginal castes. Their members, who cannot own any valuable land or herds (cattle and camels), have master-client types of relationships with the "noble" Somali, i.e. nomadic pastoralists. The latter protect them in exchange for services rendered. According to a study I conducted some years ago, the caste members in question are either the descendants of previously noble groups who were defeated and had fallen after a war against another group, or descendants of the first inhabitants of the Horn, or possibly the descendants of slaves brought to the Horn to work the land by the Arabs who are settled on the coast, mainly in the south. Marriages between caste members and nobles are forbidden and used to be punishable by death.

The social organization is thus complex, combining patriarchal lineages, alliances through marriage, age and sex-based classes and the land distribution system. Such an organization could not function without rules.

B. Social Morals

The *dhaqan* is the Somali social code. On one hand, it is based on traditions, *caado*, and on the other hand on customary rights, *xeer*. This code of values sprouted from the complex Somali social organization and was created to exercise control over it. Traditions greatly influence the functioning of society: numerous activities are performed mechanically, without comment or revolt, as if they could not be done any differently. Questioning them is unthinkable.

Customary laws manage relationships between groups, from the smallest to the largest. They constitute a huge collection of laws, all oral until very recently, grouped by themes (for example, *dhiig* for assault and battery, *shaqo*, work regulations, *dagaal*, rules for war and peace, *dhaqan*, civil rights governing marriage and property). These laws are common to all the tribes, with a few small variations, as opposed to classic cases (*sooyaal*). When a new issue arises, one must then propose a new law. The resolution of that particular case will serve as jurisprudence (*ugub*).

The tribunal (*guurti* or *guddi*) is composed of a judge and jury, all chosen according to their knowledge of customary laws. All are mature men belonging to the most respected age groups (*jilibculus* and *oday*), less often they are *gadhmadoobe*, gathered in assemblies (*shir*). But, depending on the seriousness of the conflict and the kinship between the two parties involved, the number of jurors varies. When a conflict places two important groups in opposition, an equal number of jurors is selected from each group. But if the conflict is too serious, they can be chosen among a third group uninvolved in the conflict. That third group then plays the role of mediator (*ergo*) and welcomes on its territory the two adverse parties to whom it grants protection for the duration of the trial.

On the contrary, most typical cases which do not threaten good relations with neighboring groups, that is, conflicts within a community, are resolved using more simple means. Sometimes, only the chief (*boqoor, garaad, ugaas*) of the community and his judicial advisor (*xeer beegti*) take care of them.

Although Somali people fancy themselves free of all constraints, and although they are undisciplined and anarchistic to the point of temerity, they submit to the laws dictated by the sages gathered in *guurti* (council or tribunal). They know very well that they could not survive in the harsh climate of the African Horn without individuals and various communities helping one another and getting along.

C. Religious Morals

The *dhaqan* is reinforced by *religious morality,* whether those moral rules were decreed by a monotheistic religion or other cultural practices. The beliefs (*rumeysi*), whatever they might be, engender a moral code based on the fear and respect of God or the gods and spirits. That moral code offers a wide array of divine commandments that the believers must respect, commandments whose spirit is close to the social code (*dhaqan*). The moral code thus overlaps and completes the social code and allows Somali society to run smoothly.

D. The State

The fourth pillar on which Somali society rests is the *state (dawlad)*, though one must make a distinction between the state in the modern context and the state as conceived in the old days. The old Somali social system never held the notion of a central power until colonization, with the exception of a few small kingdoms mainly established along the coast. Asking the chief of the tribe to take action was relatively rare and was limited to the most serious cases. The chief, assisted by seven counselors, delegated a great deal of his power to the chiefs of factions and clans.

Colonization and decolonization gave birth to a modern Somali state, founded on a constitution, a standing army and a police force. The modern state formulated its own laws, but time proved that its real influence was limited to the cities. Outside the cities, people have preserved their traditional system of government.

II. Relationships Inside Somali Society

As we have seen, the *xigto* and the *dhaqan* are the foundations which allow Somali society to function, the *rumeysi* having only a reinforcing role and the *dawlad* playing a limited part. A study of the *xigto* shows that individuals can have their own identity or find their place in Somali society in various ways. Besides their own genealogy (*xigaalo* system), they can claim an alliance (through marriage: *xidid*) as their role in the community depends on the age class they belong to. All relationships that they can share with the members of their community and with outsiders are fashioned by tradition (*caado*) and customary laws. Let us examine three cases in particular:

A.   About Lineages and the *xigaalo*

A man can deal with another person in different ways. His attitude may vary according to the clan or tribe that person belongs to. If he is facing a man from the same *reer,* he will show him the respect due to his rank or age. On the other hand, if his interlocutor belongs to a neighboring *reer,* he can either treat him as an equal or brother (*ina adeer*: cousin), thus taking into consideration the fact that they are both issued from the same ancestor, close or remote. Or he can emphasize their being different. In fact, it all depends on current or future circumstances. It is wiser to treat one's neighbors well. Who knows if tomorrow they might not be needed. That mode of reasoning is positive for it promotes solidarity and views the community and more generally, society, as forming one unit.

On the contrary, the downward reading of patriarchal lineages and carrying that system to its extreme, divides the nation (the ethnic group) into smaller and smaller groups until they finally are reduced to a large mass of individuals, without family or social ties. That constitutes a system of exclusion, which, in recent years, has been applied beyond reason. In such a vision, all relationships with others are conducted on a basis of rivalry and difference. There is no social coherence. The *xigaalo* system is therefore a double-edged sword whose anarchical use, outside the rules of the customary rights system, finally led the Somalis into a civil war.

One thing the Somalis have forgotten today is that the system of patriarchal lineages is not an immutable one. No Somali can be certain that the genealogy he claims links him to his real ancestor. Indeed, for various reasons (distance, war, the necessity for a larger territory, fear of another group with expansionist tendencies, dissidence within the tribe), a group such as a clan, can separate from its mother-tribe and form, alone or with other groups (case of *Ismadhaxal*), a new tribe or associate with another tribe (*soo raac*) or ask it for asylum (*magan gelyo*). Depending on the cases, it is a *sheegad* or a *tolow*. According to the circumstances, the groups that separate from their mother-tribe "renounce their blood and their specific traditions." If they reject them, they then adopt those of their new tribe.

Somali society is thus a dynamic one, breaking up and rebuilding itself constantly, depending on the times, the circumstances, and the needs of the various communities. No Somali can therefore be absolutely certain of the identity of his ancestor. And, as a consequence, there is no reason for "xeno-clano-phobic" sentiments.

B. About the *xidid*.

The *xidid* is the system of alliances sealed by marriages between two clans. Somalis practice exogamy and the prospective spouses must not share, with rare exceptions, a close common ancestor. These alliances result in the distribution of pastures and water holes and in the sharing of long and painstaking tasks.

Several marriages between two clans strengthen their alliance. But the latter must be treated gingerly. It would not do to jeopardize it by behaving improperly. That is the reason why relations between in-laws are based on a great and mutual respect and on a constant exchange of courteous gestures. The couple who represent the tie between the two clans are the most put upon. Neither one of the two spouses must fail to fulfill his or her duties toward the in-laws. The husband, under no circumstance, can either offend his wife's family or raise his voice against one of its members. Being a man, he has to be able to control himself, whatever the circumstances might be. If he fails, he is obligated to make amends as soon as possible, by paying a fine which is higher than the fine one must pay when insulting a non-relative. His spouse, as well, must be courteous and helpful to her in-laws, all the more because in most cases she will have to leave her family behind and come live with her husband's. If she treats her in-laws with humble respect and works for their well-being, and her husband wishes to divorce for personal reasons, he can be forced to leave his family while his wife, who will have been adopted in a way, will stay. Also, he can simply be forced not to divorce in order to avoid all disagreement between the two families.

C. The *xigaalo* and the *xidid* — an Example.

An offended man can ask his paternal family (*xigaalo*) to support him and to help him avenge himself. He can count on them for he is issued from "the same blood." His offense becomes the clan's. But he cannot ask for that kind of help from his mother's side of the family or his wife's family. Although they are allied, they have no blood obligations. In only one case could they fight together, and that would be if their herd were stolen. In fact, a man's relationship with his father's side of the family (*reer adeer*) and the one with his mother's side (*reer abti*) are very different. When dealing with the paternal family, he will always have to show that he is strong, virile, ready to do anything to defend his clan; when dealing with the maternal side, in particular, his uncle, his mother's brother, he will be able to let himself go, express his feelings and his doubts, or ask for advice. As far as his in-laws are concerned, he shows them respect and never reveals his problems. Such a complex mechanism evolved during the last century under the influence of colonization and because of the political choices made by those in power.

One observation from an anthropological point of view: *xidid* and *xigaalo* are words borrowed from tree terminology. *Xigaalo* designates the visible part, the trunk and the foliage. Starting from the trunk, or foundation, which symbolizes the patriarchal lineage, the branches and all their ramifications represent the ancestor's descendancy; *xidid* stands for the roots, *xidid* alliances are therefore considered as secret alliances, hidden, discrete, but strong and vital to the life of the tree.

III. The Impact of Colonization and Independence.

A. A Brief Look at History

The arrival of colonists suddenly brought turmoil to the Horn of Africa. The coastal peoples, willingly or under pressure and force, signed the first commercial agreements and treaties with representatives from European powers such as France, Italy, and England. The Somali territory was split between the three powers who managed portions of it, very unequal in size. Soon, Menelik, who crowned himself king of the kings of Ethiopia, claimed the entire Somali territories as his kingdom. His successor, Haile Selassie, through secret agreements signed with England, obtained the Haud and Ogaden provinces in 1948 and 1954. Later on, the Northern Frontier District was placed under the authority of a newly independent Kenya. Only Somaliland and the Somalia Italiana colonies were spared such distribution and were able to regain independence and reunification.

All through the colonial era, the authorities exploited the fact that the Somali ethnic groups were composed of many tribes and clans. Basing their actions on stories told by European explorers, the Europeans developed a management strategy that played on internal Somali divisiveness. Explorers had labeled Somalis anarchistic, undisciplined warmongers, cruel, ever ready to fight at the slightest provocation, but also organized in rival clans. The explorers, in fact, only related to epiphenomenons — appearances. The governors of the Somali provinces manipulated clan rivalries to the point of causing clan wars, whose flames they cleverly kept on fanning. The European colonial officers therefore provided weapons to the clans who became their allies, and warlike relationships developed between those clans and the ones who refused to accept the foreign presence and submit to it. Inter-clan rivalries crystallized.

During that time, the Somali were exposed to their first known form of a central state. Indeed, the ancient Somali social system was based on distributed power, with the exception of a few small coastal kingdoms. Having to appeal to the chief of an entire tribe was relatively rare and was limited to the most grievous cases. The chief, assisted by his seven counselors, delegated a large part of his powers to the chiefs of factions and clans. Independence in 1960 was a reality only for some Somalis, those from the provinces who consolidated and formed the Republic of Somalia. As for the others, they remained under foreign domination.

Colonization and decolonization brought forth a modern Somali state, whose foundation is a European-style constitution. The modern state decreed its own laws but the passing of time proved that its real power remained in the cities; the country dwellers kept their traditional system of managing their affairs. However, that system was greatly modified because of tribal wars and is going to undergo, again, substantial transformations due to the governments in power.

In the Somali constitution, a fact is stated plainly -- the Somali state will endeavor to free the other Somali provinces from the colonial yoke using all legal means. But when those means fail, the state will then help the Somali liberation movements in these regions, FLSO or WSLF (Ogaden), FLCS (Djibouti) and FLNFD (Kenya).

The military regime which took power in 1969 also used the constitution as a means to rebuild the Somali nation, along with eradicating tribalism. Legal means failed in 1976-77 and Somalia attempted to retake, by force, the Ogaden. That attempt fell short, just like the previous ones.

That sort of failure and the broken alliance with the USSR created numerous enemies for Siyad Barre, in the midst of the *intelligentsia* as well as among the population. From that time on, feeling continually threatened, and desirous to stay in power, Barre turned to tribalism. He kept all leftist intellectuals likely to oppose his policies away from power. Other intellectuals, who had a certain tribal prestige, were opportunistic and were in full agreement with Siyad Barre, replaced the previous ones.

Everywhere in Somalia, tensions between clans arose. Mengistu Haile Mariam's regime made the most of the problems between clans to oppose Siyad Barre and defeat Somalia. Clan-affiliated parties appeared, supported by Ethiopia. For its part, Somalia supported the Liberation Front for Western Somalia (Ogaden) as well as the Liberation Fronts for the Abbo Somali (Oromo), for Eritrea and Tigre that constantly attacked Mengistu's regime. That way, through the fronts, the two governments of the Horn confronted each other.

The clan fights went on for several years, weakening Siyad Barre's government. On the other hand, Mengistu's regime was destabilized by the war in Eritrea and Tigre, by the Oromo revolt, and by the FLSO/WSLF guerilla warfare.

In an effort to save their own positions, the two dictators, Siyad Barre and Mengistu Haile Mariam, met in 1986 and discussed agreements of mutual non-intervention in each other's affairs. On April 6, 1988, they signed a peace agreement which allowed Mengistu to empty the Ogaden of army reserves in order to send help to Eritrea and Tigre where the situation was desperate. The treaty led Siyad Barre to believe that the clan affiliated parties, deprived of Ethiopia's support, would collapse.

But neither of them could stop fate in its tracks. The revolutions, of an ethnic nature in Ethiopia and a clanic nature in Somalia, revolts which these rulers themselves had set in motion, became more and more pressing. A collective popular upheaval set the two countries afire and overthrew the two military leaders. But if in Ethiopia the conflict was resolved, such was not the case in Somali where the war still goes on.

B. Analysis

Conducting a study of the kinship system over the last half-century shows its evolution as a movement which was partly responsible for the current crisis. The huge mutations which the Somali people have experienced in the course of this century and, since Independence, have modified their established values.

The pastoral clan system -- a system of a balanced but perpetually evolving society -- existing at the beginning of colonization, has slowly changed into a "modern" clan system of exclusion, in which the strongest dictate their rules, and crush and isolate the weakest in the name of their given clan affiliations.

Although there is no such thing as a "pure clan" in the sense of "a group of male individuals issued from the same ancestor or limited group of ancestors," those who created the theory out of thin air had only one goal -- dominating and crushing the peoples in their power. That was an easy way for them to get rid of undesirable peoples. They only had to cause dissensions between the clans and then make sure to revive them regularly.

The clan wars born in that fashion were responsible for a tremendous number of victims. They were more deadly because the fighters were using modern weapons supplied by the colonists, weapons which allowed killing even from a great distance. Children, pregnant women, and elderly people were also killed, contrary to the old days when war was a man's affair. Customary laws, which, until then, had always been able to resolve dissensions in a manner fair to all involved became incapable of finding satisfactory solutions. Customary rights thus lost part of their influence on the population and that opened a door inviting future transgressions.

The clan theories, used by all the clan leaders to avenge their honor, evolved naturally, creating a more and more powerful system of exclusion. The entire Somali tribal system was based on alliances, mutual help pacts, persistently sealed by marriages, and constantly questioned when they proved unsatisfactory. It was in a state of permanent evolution, due to the fact that it was always being built and rebuilt

Such a change between the clans, meaning the birth of new clan theory, along with the disappearance of old alliances and mutual help pacts, also affected the behavior of individuals to the point that what was previously forbidden now became a new "virtue." For instance, marriage, which used to be a way of forming alliances and thus of strengthening bonds between clans (exogamy) slowly became more exclusive, meaning that wedding among clan members took place more frequently (endogamy); what used to be forbidden became the norm, such as marrying the paternal uncle's daughter.

Moreover, customary laws lost more and more respect. First, unable to solve the issue of clan wars, it was then cast aside, considered obsolete by the first Somali government that wanted to impose modernity and progress, notions that its members had learned when studying in European schools.

They wanted to apply a system of government based on European conceptions. But in the end, they failed to get the Somalis to understand it. People only saw it as a tribal system on the scale of a state and as an administration whose function was paralyzed at all levels by corruption. The new state, therefore, had nothing to offer them in exchange for the customary laws whose use it had forbidden.

That first Somalia, born with Independence, can be called a democracy as far as it was founded on a multi-party system and freedom of speech. But in reality, that democracy, designed according to a European model, was totally unsuitable to Somali people. The military men who came later were quite welcome, for their initial political program was clear, simple and answered Somali aspirations:

1. Rebuilding of the great Somali nation, dismantled by colonization;
2. Cleansing the administration;
3. Eradicating tribalism through new laws whose goal was to limit the tribes' power;
4. Promulgating laws limiting the impact of traditions (equality between men and women, for example); and,
5. Simultaneously, giving new value to Somali culture by means of its language, its folklore and the cult of Somali heroes.

Siyad Barre's accession to the presidency and his increasing taste for power caused the initial program gradually to lose its substance. Within a few years, things were back to where they were when the civil government left. Corruption had settled in again and was led by men directly connected to the government; tribalism had also made a full comeback, orchestrated by Siyad Barre and his men.

The Somali people lost a good deal of their social references and found few new ones to replace the old. But by comparison with the previous situation, the gap, opened between the population and its ancient traditions, had widened even more. Islam, which had until then always provided a haven, had been banished by the military regime, the reason being the espousal of communist theories on one hand and on the other hand the *imams'* daring disapproval of regime's use of power. Siyad Barre installed a dictatorship, created a private police force, censored the press, and tolerated no freedom of opinion. All these facts, accumulated since the constitution of the Somali state, have presented their many obstacles to the creation of Somali democracy and have caused the

Somali kinship system to degenerate, leading to the civil war that broke out in December 1990.

III. Suggestions for Peace and Democracy:

A. About Peace

It is mandatory to admit, first of all, that Siyad Barre's dictatorship and his armed opponents, organized in clan factions, are the ones responsible for the tragic situation in Somalia. To obtain a durable peace, it is necessary to stop all hostility and all rivalry to gain power, and to open a dialogue for peace negotiations. One must create a representative transitional government and get ready to organize short or medium-term elections. But even before installing a democratically elected power, one must work for the recognition of human rights and reestablish freedom of opinion.

B. About Democracy

The trauma of the last ten years has tarnished and devalued all moral values, both traditional (*xeer* and *caado*) and religious (*rumeysi*). It has erected, instead, genealogical clan bonds (*xigaalo*). The breaking up of society into smaller and smaller entities, down to the individual, has produced a fierce individualism and created an outrageous system of exclusion. The meltdown of the social structure engendered severe identity problems among Somalis and led, finally, to civil war.

That war is often understood as a clan conflict on a large scale, but it is not. Rather, it was born out of the very destruction of the social fabric as a whole, of the *xigto* and the laws that made it function, a fabric that gave everyone an identity, a place and a social role. It is the vanishing of codes to which people could refer themselves that brought forth a profound identity crisis.

Today, one talks about bringing peace back to Somalia and creating a democratic state. But is not the underlying concept of a state one of European style democracy? Does not that European concept imply equality for individuals but also, ironically, reduced civic responsibilities on the part of these same individuals?

We have previously observed that neither the civil government's constitution nor that of the military regime, each with its own legislation, were adapted to Somali society and culture . I believe that in Somalia -- and it may be the case in many African countries -- one is wrong to impose a European model of democracy on the traditional system.

In fact, the issue is now to find another form of democracy which must have its roots in Somali culture. A democracy which is not born out of the culture, the life-style, the mentality and the environment in which a people lives, is not suitable to that people. It is not about nostalgia, going backwards, but about adapting old models to today, giving them renewed value and reviving them while improving them.

It is in its culture that Somalia can find a new form of state management, by bringing back and rewriting its historical "pastoral democracy" system. It can be summarized succinctly as:

"the more powerful a man is, the greater his responsibilities toward his fellow citizens," or, *"the more rights a man enjoys, the more duties he has."*

Such a democratic system of balance between rights and obligations is most likely the best adapted to African cultures and particularly to the Somali one, for it corresponds to the ancient model of the traditional chief, who, while he enjoyed many privileges, as a counterpart, had to carry the burden of great responsibilities on his shoulders.

It is nonetheless inconceivable to bring back all traditions and all ancestral customary laws. First, a good number of them have disappeared. Second, one must not re-establish the system of exclusions from the old social organization (caste system, inequality between sexes). The clan and tribal theories also must be opposed. We showed that they were built on the *xigaalo* but were pulled out of the complementary social and legal contexts. We also demonstrated that the *xigaalo* was not a static organization, composed of immutable affiliations, but instead a dynamic social system in permanent evolution because of its multiple recompositions. Democratization must start with a nationwide active awareness of the clan theories and their impact on everyday Somali life.

Maybe it is necessary to bring back traditional chiefs at the level of the villages and the small towns, and to find their equivalent for larger structures. The presence of an elected head of state would become necessary to represent the country abroad, but his role might be very limited inside the country. Managing it should be entrusted to an assembly of sages and of traditional chiefs or their equivalent. Lastly, the regions should be able to rule themselves, the central government's role being to divide the national wealth and to even out the inequalities deriving from the geographical conditions of these regions.

SECTION THREE

The Civil War, Human Rights and Minority Issues

Summaries: Section Three

Shamis Hussein (Chapter 11) argues that the present dilemma of Somali society resulted from an inability of the "opposition groups" to diffuse conflict, along with a misunderstood or even hidden agenda of the intervening international organizations. She suggests that the UN and other international missions, designed originally to stop violence, resulted in a new form of external subjugation and dominance -- a situation which Somalis would never accept. The external mission failed miserably with regard to promoting reconciliation.

Roland Marchal (Chapter 12) studies the urban Mooryaan in Mogadishu. Best defined as "young looters," the Mooriyan have greatly expanded their influence and control in Mogadishu. Given disruptions of the last seven years, many people have flocked to urban areas to obtain food and services. Marchal considers the relationship of the Mooryaan to this new, emerging, and basically amoral urban culture -- crime, changing role of elders, dress, role models, drugs, women and more -- to conclude that the Mooryaan have created a new urban life style that functions independent of the traditional clan structure. He also notes differences among various layers of the Mooryaan groups.

Omar A. Eno (Chapter 13) writes about the discrimination to which the inter-riverine Bantu/Jarer people have been subjected. He notes how the Bantu Somalis have contributed to all parts of the nation's economic, political, and cultural history yet receive few benefits in return. Given this tradition of discrimination -- Eno calls it apartheid -- the Jarer have absorbed more than their share of hardships during the civil war. He urges that the new, post-Barre Somalia be one in which all genders, ethnicities, classes, and cultures be treated equally. He closes noting there is urgent need to focus on minority rights.

Amina Sharif Hassan (Chapter 14) traces the history of the Somali people and nation, noting their importance in the region for at least two millennia. She observes that the Siyad government passed many laws, such as the land registration reform laws, that contradicted these traditions and also benefitted a few Somalis at the expense of the majority. These changes were especially onerous to the inter-riverine Bantu Somalis about whom Omar Eno (Chapter 13) has also written.

CHAPTER ELEVEN

Somalia, A Destroyed Country and A Defeated Nation

Shamis Hussein

Preface

Since the overthrow of the Barre regime, the Somali situation has shifted from one of outstanding optimism to great pessimism. The political inadequacies of Barre's opposition groups suggest a Somali inability to diffuse conflict. Having ignored the region for a long time, the media suddenly picked up on the starvation which was occurring in the Baidoa region and demanded action. The United Nations Security Council authorized the humanitarian intervention and peace enforcement in Somalia. The executive power given to the UN US-led forces in Somalia is the first of its kind in the history of the UN operations in conflict areas of the world.

The aim of this study is to present what the international community and the media, intentionally or unintentionally, have overlooked as the root causes of the Somali crisis. I also attempt to address the other side of Project Restore Hope's mission in southern Somalia and to give an understanding of the Somali diaspora beyond the connotations of clanism.

Some of the material in this study is extracted from a manuscript to be published soon and two papers that I presented in Oxford: one for a peace project at St. Antony's College, Oxford University and the other one for the United Nations branch in Oxford. I have been prompted by the polarization of Somali clanism as the trigger and sustainer of the

Somali civil war. One is also aware that the voices of the Somali people against interventionism are acute, though not well-organized for various reasons. I, therefore, attempted to express the Somali viewpoint on interventionism and the United Nations.

I am very grateful to Omer A. Ali, a Somali chief executive officer for Dar-Al-Maal-Al-Islam (DMI) Bank in Switzerland and the Bank for sponsoring me to undertake a few months research on the Somali crisis. I would like to thank all the Somalis who gave me interviews during my visits to the Horn of Africa including Kenya (in 1991-1992 and 1993). I am also very grateful to Peter Roth (a United Kingdom barrister who was a convener of the Wilton Park special conference in cooperation with the Development Studies Association on legal aspects of humanitarian assistance and intervention) for inviting me to participate in the above mentioned conference on 2nd July 1993. I wish to record my gratitude to all speakers and participants including international lawyers and jurists, in particular Jan Eliasson (United Nations Under-Secretary General for Humanitarian Affairs) and Ambassador Mohamed Sahnoun (the Algerian former Special Representative of the United Nations Secretary General). I very much appreciated Ambassador Sahnoun's discussion on the Somali crisis which gave me insights into the United Nations approach. Finally, my sincere thanks to all my friends, Somalis and non-Somalis, who contributed to this work in many ways, in particular Hirit Belai who took the trouble of typing this work and Tal Michael for help in editing. The responsibility for any mistakes in this work is mine alone.

I. Introduction

Somalia is one of those places where history continues to dominate contemporary politics. The Somali Horn is a crossroads to the continent of Africa, Asia and Europe. The extension of the Red Sea which separates Arabia from Africa marks the geological rift which starts with the Jordan Valley and the Dead Sea, proceeds to Wadi-Al-Arab to the Bay of Aqaba at the head of the Red Sea. Cape Guardafui juts into the Indian Ocean and extends to Kismayo. Before the last millennium, Somalia played a significant role in the events of ancient civilizations. While she attracted the traffic of the shipping lines of the three continents, she was also valued as a spiritual place by the ancient Egyptians and the Israelites, among others. The ancient Egyptians used to call Somalia the "Land of Gods" and the products which they used to mummify their dead were mainly imported from the present day Somalia. The Greeks, Phoenicians and the Romans all had their contacts with the region. To the Romans, Somalia was known as "Terra Aramatico."

In more recent history, the Turks, Portuguese, Chinese and Persians had trade links and other influences with the Somalis. For instance, the word Mogadishu is said to be a Persian word for the Seat of the Shah. Nevertheless, because of the geographical proximity, the Arabs in the Arabian Peninsula must have had the closest socio-economic relations with the people of the Horn. Somalia is rich in antiquity, and although it has not been mined, possesses valuable mineral resources. The Somalis form a single ethnic group. They all speak the same language (Somali, a Cushitic language), practice the same religion (Islam) and belong to the Sunni sect of the Shafiya rite. It is believed that the Somalis are the only fully homogeneous groups in Sub-Sahara Africa and they were classified as a nation prior to the modern state system. There is a school of thought which suggests that the Cushites in Egypt are dominated by the Arab Semites, and those of Ethiopia are also politically dominated by the Semiticized Cushites of Abyssinia. With the exception of what was then French Somaliland (Republic of Djibouti), Somalia today constitutes the only nation-state of Cushitic speakers.

Traditionally, Somalis are considered to be a democratic and an egalitarian society. Clans are represented by *sultans or ugaas, boqoor, garaad, beeldaje* and *islaw* — titles given to heads of clans -- who are born orators and acquire a high efficiency in the art of argumentation and debate in clan councils. Every adult male had a say in the clan affairs but only the able and the respected individuals' views were taken into further consideration. Prior to independence, the Somali society was shaped into four classes:

1. The **nomads** who depend on their livestock and animal husbandry;
2. The **settled groups** who were found in the coastal areas and the river areas and were mainly farmers and brokers;
3. The **traders** who trade between the coastal towns and the hinterland down to the interior with the nomads;
4. The **lower caste** groups comprised of the *yebir, midgan* and *tomal*.

Physically, the lower caste groups do not look different from the other Somalis, but they had different social status and were not mixed in marriage with the other Somalis. The *yebir* group were occupied with leather work, e.g., saddlery, scabbards, shoe making. The *midgan* were normally armed with small daggers, bows and poisoned arrows; they engaged in hunting and mainly collected myrrh and frankincense for which the land of Punt was famous. The *tomal* were the blacksmiths. They engaged in iron work and fashioned all kinds of traditional arms.

However, it is worth noting that the status of the lower caste people had improved in the post independence years. When Somali National Irredentism strengthened in the sixties, the Somali lower caste groups were metaphorically known as the Somali Six. The other five being Somali Ethiopia, Somali Djibouti, Somali Kenya, former British Protectorate (Somaliland) and the former Italian colony of Somalia. Subsequently, lower caste groups job segregation decreased, but there has not been tremendous improvement in their social status up to the present day.

II. The Background

The present day destruction of Somalia has its root causes in the dismemberment of the Somali territory during the colonial period. This led to the various entities: Somaliland, Somalia, Somali Republic and Somali Democratic Republic. In the intervening years, the European powers divided the Somali-speaking territories into five parts: the British Somaliland Protectorate, the Italian colony of Somalia, French Somaliland, the two adjacent parts to Ethiopia (Ogaden, Haud and the reserved area) and Kenya (Northern Frontier Districts - NFD).

The three European powers, France, Italy and Great Britain all made territorial concessions to the Abyssinian King Menelik. As Mr. Rodd of Britain states in a letter to Lord Salisbury after ceding a portion of Somali territory to Menelik in 1897:

"In a view of the great difficulties I have had to encounter,
including moral pressure, while the French had but a few weeks
ago accepted so conspicuous a curtailment of their protectorate
claims on Somali coast. I trust that your Lordship will
consider that the arrangement is as satisfactory one as we
are entitled to expect."[1]

However, in 1963, the British transferred another portion of Somali territory to Kenya when the latter achieved its independence. In the decolonization period, it was the British Somaliland Protectorate that first achieved independence on 26 June 1960. This was a separate political entity for four days. Then in July, 1960, the Italian colony of Somalia achieved independence. The same day the two Somalias united and formed the Somali Republic. The new Republic adopted a light blue flag with a five pointed star in the middle. The star was the symbol and reminder of the division of the Somali territory and the embodiment for the search for greater Somalia. The last Somali civilian government was overthrown on 21 October 1969 by a military coup d'etat, under the leadership of General Mohammed Siyad Barre (MSB). The military government changed the name of the Somali Republic to the Somali Democratic Republic. Nevertheless, in the post-independence years Somalia's successive governments vigorously engaged in the search for a "Greater Somalia" and the liberation of other Somalis who remained under the jurisdiction of non-Somali authorities.

During those years there has been an evolution in the formation of classes and ideologies: classes based on education and economy and ideologies based on intellectual affiliations. For instance, Somali students got scholarships from the then Warsaw Pact countries, the West, the Middle East, in particular from Egypt, Syria, Lebanon and Iraq. Somali students were also sent to China, India and North Korea. Therefore, the scholarships that were given to the Somalis by those countries have contributed to improvement of the nation's literacy and the formation of different ideologies among Somali scholars.

III. What Prolonged the Somali Civil War

In order to understand what prolonged the Somali civil war and why is there no central government after two years of Barre's removal, it is useful to reflect on the Somali nation's experience of war. The Somali nation has experienced three main types of wars:

A. Traditional War

Traditional wars took place between clans and were commonly triggered by confrontation over wells (drinking water for livestock), camel raids, and women. Clan disputes were settled by the *sultan, boqoor, ugaas* and *garaad* who practiced the *sharia* law and the *xeer* (customary law).

B. National War

National wars are those in which the adversary is an outsider (non-Somali). For example, wars of independence and regional wars such as the wars between Ethiopia and Somalia in 1964 and 1977-78 (Ogaden wars).

C. Civil War

Civil war differs from traditional war as the government wages war against its own citizens and clan scores are settled under the umbrella of the state. National and civil wars were fought in an indiscriminate manner; they also bred national catastrophes and could be termed as modern wars. While the traditional war was settled by the *sultan, boqoor, ugaas* and the *garaad*, the national wars were also manageable. For instance, in the wars of independence, the Somalis were generally regarded as resistors par excellence.[2]

Somalia was the first African country to experience an air strike against them during the colonial period. The British Royal Air Force was used twice to bombard the Somalis, first in 1920, against Siyad Mohammed Abdullah Hassan, called "Mad Mullah" by the British, who fought against the British rule for a period of twenty-one years. The second occurred when the Somalis refused to pay the stock tax introduced by the British authorities in the former Somaliland in 1921. Nevertheless, the stock tax was violently opposed by the Somalis and was finally dropped by the British authorities. Thus, Somaliland remained a protectorate, unlike the Sudan and Aden, which were both British colonies. One of the reasons for the slow pace of European penetration in the Horn was the determined Somali resistance that colonial forces encountered in many areas.[3]

According to Lord Mountnorris of Britain, the British were then more interested in Berbera than in Aden as the following quotation indicates: "Mountnorris... discovered a very large annual market, an affair as it was called at Berbera, and in 1808 he urged the British government to occupy Aden, in order to exploit the trade of Berbera."[4] Lord Mountnorris' statement contradicts the view in the modern history of Somalia which suggests that the British were not interested in Somalia, but were only there to supply mutton to their garrison in Aden. The above quotation suggests it was Somali vigilance and the resistance to foreign intervention that curtailed colonial ambitions to their country. On regional war, the Somalis managed to regain the Ogaden, Haud and reserve areas, during the course of the 1977-78 total war with Ethiopia. It was the Soviet and Cuban participation in the war that enabled Ethiopia to regain the Ogaden region. Therefore, a reflection of the Somali nation's war experience indicates that they (the Somalis) have been able to execute and to contain traditional and national wars.

In retrospect, there are two main factors that have prolonged the civil war in Somalia. The first is Siyad Barre's governing methods and their impact on Somali social trends; the second is the role and degree of third party involvement in Somali internal affairs. As readers may know, Barre was a brutal dictator. To many Somalis he was of the same ilk as the fascist government of Italy which he served as a young man during the

Second World War. While his atrocities against the Somali people are well-documented by various international organizations, it is worth drawing to attention the style of his government and how he held on to power for twenty-one years: Barre used the policy of divide and rule, magnifying clan distinctions for political ends.

When Brigadier General Mohamed Ainanshe, Colonel Salad Gubeere and Captain Abdulkadir Deel were executed in 1972 by Barre's government, the then President Barre entered a meeting with his fellow clansmen and said:

"Comrades, Sultan, the other Darood subclans, for example the Majerteens, are power thirsty and I do not want them to be part of this business. The Ogaden and the Dulbahante are poor nomads. I will accept them as soldiers. They will defend the revolution. The Isaaq are cunning. I warn you of their conspiracy. They were responsible for the defeat of Mohamed Abdulleh Hassan by the British in 1920. They are infidels as the Ogadens call them *Gaalka lidoor*. I will drive them out of the government positions. The Hawiye will be busy with their agriculture and they will never realize what is happening."[5]

With that approach, Barre also victimized various sectors across clan groups within Somali society. They are comprised of four groups:

1. The traditionally respected figures in the clan hierarchy known as *sultan, boqoor, ugaas, aqiil* (in which the position and the title is to be inherited by the male lineage of the family);
2. The intellectuals and highly educated individuals;
3. The *Ulama-Al-Diin* who were the religious leaders;
4. The financially well-to-do groups who were mainly the traditional traders and business owners.

These four were described by Siyad Barre as enemies of the revolution. Subsequently the positions of *sultan, boqoor, ugaas* and *aqiil* were undermined and replaced by government-appointed Nabaddoon who played an intermediary role between the government and the clan. The intellectuals who opposed government policies were imprisoned or executed, causing many educated Somalis to flee overseas. Those of Ulama-Al-Din who recited the Quran and renounced the Presidential Decree on Family Law were executed in 1975. The execution of the ten sheikhs was a severe blow to the rest of the Ulama-Al-Din. Traders and business owners were accused of being a privileged petty *bourgeoisie* and an obstacle to equality and wealth distribution. Some of them had their agencies nationalized -- in particular, the shipping agencies. Others were frustrated and thus, lost interest.   Consequently, a newly rich group emerged whose wealth was extracted from donor's aid to the country. This encouraged nepotism and the misuse of national resources. Barre therefore challenged the tradition, culture, principles and values of the Somali people.

In the process of disordering Somali society, Siyad Barre did not simultaneously antagonize the major clans.   Instead, he singled out individual clans at different times. As a result, the opposition groups based on clan affiliation were formed at different times and had different grievances that bred differences in agendas. Therefore, after the removal of Barre's regime it became difficult to obtain a coherent political organ to replace him and resume the government as had been the case during the overthrow of the civilian government in 1969. The situation inherited from Barre's regime had been retrogressive. As the Somali proverb says, *ayax teeg eel se reeb* (the locust is gone but has left behind the eggs).

III. The Role of Third Parties in the Somali Civil War

The Somali civil war erupted on 27 May 1988, when the Somali National Movement (SNM) launched a surprise attack against Barre's troops in the then Northwest of the Somali Democratic Republic. The SNM defeated and contained the government troops before the intervention of the USA. The latter had a military base on the Somali coast at Berbera.

US military assistance valued at about $1.4 million arrived on June 28, 1988 at the port of Berbera. The lethal arms came at a critical point in the war and were used to regain control of the land, including Hargeisa which the SNM controlled from May 31 to July 13, 1988 Furthermore, in a controversial action that had the effect of boosting the Somali government's military capability in the northern war zone, an American military team repaired the Somali army's communication site at Hargeisa, which was damaged in the fighting. US policy appeared to reinforce Siyad Barre's harsh retaliation...[7] As a result the SNM and the Isaaq clan were badly shaken by the ferocity of the government response.[8]

The US intervention in Somalia's internal conflict not only prolonged the Somali civil war but it contributed to the death of many and the flight of about 500,000 civilians from their homes to Ethiopian refugee camps. The number continued to increase and was estimated to have reached about a million. Furthermore, many Isaaq Somalis were displaced within the Republic's existing boundaries.

Paradoxically, successive US governments declined to supply arms of an offensive nature to Barre's regime when engaged in a conventional war of two armies with the Ethiopian regime. The US government continued even to monitor the degree in which the Somali government was passing arms and military equipments to the Somali guerrillas, who were fighting in the Ethiopian border area. The Somali government was therefore constantly reminded by the US that the arms that were supplied to them were meant only for defense and should not be used otherwise.

The governments of Italy, Saudi Arabia, Kuwait, Iraq, Egypt and the United Arab Emirates all adopted a position of strong support to Barre's regime against the Somali people. However, no government had a more tremendous impact on the manner in which the Somali civil war was executed and on its outcome than the USA. It is therefore clear that third parties have continuously challenged the right of the Somali people to depose an unpopular regime. It was the disturbance of the internal balance of power and the US assistance to Siyad Barre that enabled him to prolong his rule.

IV. Humanitarian Intervention - Peace Enforcement

There is a significant difference between humanitarian assistance and humanitarian intervention. It is understood that intervention evokes interruption and affects the sequence of events. Therefore, humanitarian intervention might incorporate military intervention and empower the intervener. Humanitarian assistance, however, enables the assisted to improve his or her situation.

> "The UN charter, particularly Article 2 (4)and 2 (7) on humanitarian intervention...contained no explicit provisions permitting either the organization itself or its member states, individually or collectively, to take forceful action even in extreme situations to compel a recalcitrant state to comply with its human rights obligation."[9]

In the light of the New World Order however, in 1991 the UN member states debated on the capacity of the organization to coordinate humanitarian assistance. Subsequently, on 19 December 1991, the General Assembly adopted Resolution 46/182. As a result, in March 1992, the Secretary General established the Department of Humanitarian Affairs.

> "...the resolution (46/182) will always need to bear in mind, that is, at all times United Nations Humanitarian Assistance will be provided in accordance with the principles of humanity, neutrality

and impartiality. The sovereignty, territorial integrity and national unity of states will be fully respected. Assistance will be provided within the consent of the affected country and in principle on the basis of request from the country."[10]

According to the Under-Secretary General for Humanitarian Affairs, Jan Eliasson, the United Nations has the unique mandate to address the root cause of a crisis and to respond to prevent and react to emergencies effectively and in a timely fashion. In any event the Somali situation passed the preventive stage. When Siyad Barre was ousted in January, 1991 the staff of the UN agencies, international NGOs and foreign embassies were all evacuated from Somalia. Even though some international agencies, in particular the ICRC and MSF, returned to Somalia, the UN staff in Somalia were stationed in Nairobi. According to a UN official in New York, "Mogadishu was unfit for humans." Nevertheless on 23 January 1992, the Security Council adopted its first resolution on Somalia, Resolution 773. The initial objective was to provide humanitarian assistance to the Somali people. Since then, the United Nations has adopted various resolutions on Somalia, each time extending the organization's aims and objectives in Somalia.

For instance, Security Council Resolution (SCR) 751, of April 24, 1992 was passed in order to monitor the then March cease-fire in Mogadishu, between the warring factions of General Aidid and Ali Mahdi. The first contingent of troops were fifty military personnel who were to observe the cease fire. There was also an understanding to send more troops to escort the relief supplies and protect the relief workers. But they never materialized and in July 27, 1992, SCR 767 was passed, for the deployment of the troops who were to protect the relief supplies. Nevertheless, the five hundred Pakistani troops who were the first foreign troops to enter Somalia, were sent in September 1992. The earlier resolutions also included the imposition of an arms embargo in Somalia, though nothing has been done about an arms embargo and disarmament in Somalia. In Bosaso (Northeastern Somalia) a captain of a Pakistani ship carrying arms to Bosaso was spotted conversing with the UN command of the Pakistan contingent in his own language.

On 12-13 October, 1992 a special coordination meeting on humanitarian assistance for Somalia was convened in Geneva, Switzerland. In that meeting, Ambassador Mohamed Sahnoun, an Algerian diplomat who was appointed special representative of the Secretary General Dr. Boutros Boutros-Ghali in April 1992 to Somalia, stated:

"A whole year slipped by whilst the UN, the international community, save for the International Committee of the Red Cross and few non-governmental organizations, watched Somalia descending into this hell."[11]

In the October conference mentioned above there were 350 delegates representing eighty-nine countries, fifteen NGOs, fifteen UN organizations and special agencies, five international organizations and the International Committee of the Red Cross. The only Somalis who were allowed to attend were representing these bodies rather than the Somali people. The conference was aimed at donors, and was rather like a doctor's prescription for an absent patient.

The Ethiopian delegate, perhaps not appreciating that Somalis had not been invited, said:

"Somalis are proud people and the untold human tragedy should not be allowed to take this pride. Somali values and legitimate concerns should be accorded serious attention and consideration. In this regard, Somalis should be consulted. Involving neutral Somalis in the process of reconciliation and in the delivery of humanitarian assistance is necessary because their input can help the effectiveness of both processes.[12]

The Egyptian delegation also emphasized the need to respect Somalia's sovereignty and territorial integrity. Nevertheless, the office for the United Nations operation in Somalia (UNOSOM I) was established. However, what began as humanitarian assistance grew to be humanitarian intervention, peacekeeping and peace enforcement.

"Peacekeeping" has no legal foundation in the United Nations Charter. The first peacekeeping operation was authorized by the then Secretary General Dag Hammarskjold. It was unique and was created for the Suez Crisis in 1956 which resulted in the attack of Egypt by France, the United Kingdom and Israel which the Security Council failed to condemn, since both France and UK are members of the Permanent Five of the Security Council.

V. Unilateral Intervention and the UN Mandate

It has been mentioned that, because of US rejection, the January and March 1992 Security Council Resolutions on Somalia were weakened. Apparently the US airlift of supplies to Somalia in August 1992 was prompted by political considerations -- to help the Bush presidential election campaign. It started as a military operation and was approved by the civilian-controlled USAID's Office for Foreign Disaster Assistance in November. The US proposed the SCR 794 on 3 December 1992. The Bush Administration also offered US troops and invited other UN member states to contribute. The US made a condition: retaining the military command of the UN troops.

The United Nations endorsed the US condition and on 9 December 1992 the deployment of the 30,800 member US-led United Task Force to Somalia began. As the UNITAF troops landed in the Somali soil it was then under the command of the US Marine General Robert B. Johnson. About twenty-three other nations accepted the US initiatives in Somalia. Some sent military contingents, others contributed financial assistance. The Security Council Resolution 794 has non-humanitarian dimensions. The resolution reinforces the United Nations operation in Somalia (UNOSOM I) which was to be responsible for the coordination between humanitarian assistance, recovery activities, political constraints and security operations. Although the US-led UNITAF formally handed over its operation in Somalia to UNOSOM II on 1 May 1993, it soon became apparent that UNOSOM II was taking its direction from the US authorities in the country. Other members of the UN peacekeeping force, notably, Italy, Germany, Saudi Arabia and Kuwait, strongly protested the US domination of the operation. The Italians, who had a 3,300 member contingent, had a confrontation with the US military in Mogadishu. According to the Italian Defense Minister, Fabio Fabbri, most of the eight hundred Italians in Mogadishu would join the rest of the Italian contingent in the north of southern Somalia (Hiran Region).

As the Mogadishu situation deteriorated "the illegality of this action becomes clear from the decision taken recently by the European Parliamentary Assembly in Paris which declared itself innocent of the worsening roles of the international forces in Somalia."[13] The staff of the international NGOs, in particular Save the Children Fund and MSF, did not fail to express their concern over the change of the humanitarian assistance to a military operation.

Since the disintegration of the Soviet Union, the US has emerged as a monopower and potential intervener. Nevertheless, it is obvious that the US is losing its grip as a world power, but certainly in different fashion from her former adversary, Russia. For instance, its indecision and inactivity in crisis areas like Yugoslavia, Afghanistan, and its lack of success in brokering a Palestinian-Israeli peace is in stark contrast to the recent help given by the Norwegians. Furthermore, it has its internal difficulties both economical and social. "The US has a huge debt, four trillion dollars, which is three times that of the Third World countries put together...Research institutions in Los Angeles and New York indicate that the US has the highest crime rate in the world, indicating a terribly violent society."[14]

In a changing world what will be the role of the United Nations? It is understood that in the New World Order or Disorder the role of the General Assembly in conflict areas vis-a-vis between nations or within nations is weakened, while that of the Security Council is overwhelmingly strengthened and exercised. For this, appraisal of the Security Council's apparatus raises questions about the body's accountability as it is not democratically represented. The political selectivity of the potential intervener in choosing its geographical area for intervention under the auspices of the Security Council is also apparent. Military maximization in Somalia and its reverse approach in Bosnia Herzegovina enunciate the UN criteria of neutrality and impartiality. The Security Council's complacency in the continuation of ethnic cleansing in Bosnia highlights the ethical deficit of its powerful member states.

VI. Somaliland and the United Nations

When the center failed to hold, the Somalis in the north decided to dissolve their part of the unitary state that was formed on 1 July 1960. In May, 1991, leading representatives of Somaliland clans and various cross-sections of the political and social groups held a national conference in Burao Town (90 miles from the main port Berbera). Abdirahman Ahmed Ali, then the chair of the SNM, a former Somali Ambassador to The United Arab Emirates, the German Democratic Republic (GDR), Ethiopia, and Sudan was elected president of the state. A two year transitional government was formed. Alongside the government, a council of elders, known as "the Wise Men" (*Guurti*) was established, including *sultan, ugaas, aqils.*

The new government inherited a war-devastated region that lacked basic infrastructure, a terrain full of mines, voluntary returnees that comprised of war disabled, widowed and orphaned, and an impoverished community. Under the circumstances, the administration appointed all major ministries, opened a central Bank in Berbera, and made the latter a free port. For about eight months there was total stability in Somaliland. The Somaliland *de facto* government sought help from the international community but no aid was forthcoming. Instead, the international community continued to give *de jure* recognition to the former Somali Democratic Republic that ceased to operate and whose capital Mogadishu, lacked a municipal government.

At that time, the stability of Somaliland seemed precarious for the

UN and a hot potato for the international community. It was a dilemma because, on one hand, they did not attempt to separate it from the rest of Somalia; on the other hand, it was stable and was not a threat to peace and security. Nevertheless, the Security Council never failed to put Somaliland in the general pool of Somalia. When UNOSOM staff in Mogadishu initially visited Hargeisa, Abdi Waraba (the Hyena), a member of the Somaliland Elders Council, told them "we hear in Europe that an eighteen year old girl has the right to choose whether to stay or not with her own parent. Are you suggesting that the people of Somaliland have no right to elect the government of their choice?"

At any rate, the only help which reached Somaliland was mainly from Somalilanders in the Middle East who comprised the Ta'abir group (intrepid pioneers) and the petty *bourgeoisie*. Berbera port became the only source of income and the center of attention in this unemployed community. The good behavior of the Berbera depended on their own good will as they were not accountable to any institutions. Consequently, the government's effectiveness decreased, and fighting between militia groups started. Ironically, the militia feuds received wider media and better attention than the previous stability. However, the Somaliland Elders Committee managed to contain the occasional feuds among clans in Somaliland.

They began their peace efforts, starting in neighboring grazing areas and seasonal villages, and then moving into small towns, main towns and then the city. The final meeting of Somaliland elders was held in Borama, (northwestern Somaliland), beginning on 24 January 1993. It was a follow-up of an earlier meeting in Sheikh (50 miles from Berbera) which issued a 19 point formula for peace on 5 October 1992. The Borama conference was expanded. More than 700 persons attended and discussed revenue collecting, a disbursement mechanism, a civil service structure, and, above all, bringing militia under the organized command of some form of Somaliland army.

The Borama conference was changed to a national conference as the two years transitional government came to an end in May 1993. While the conference was on, the United Nations and UNOSOM representatives in Somaliland declined to give any assistance to the Elders Committee conference. Paradoxically, however, UNOSOM Hargeisa delivered an invitation addressed to individual clans and clan members to attend a UN sponsored conference in Addis Ababa. The second invitation was addressed to the Somali National Movement by UNOSOM to attend the Addis Ababa conference. But the Somaliland Elders Committee rejected both invitations outright because they felt that UNOSOM was polarizing them and that the UN had an ulterior purpose in ignoring their peace efforts. In the third invitation UNOSOM addressed the invitation to the Somaliland Elders Committee and explained that the first session of the Addis Ababa conference would be a humanitarian conference. Then the Somaliland Elders Committee sent representatives and demanded that they would remain observers on political issues since they were holding their own conference inside Somaliland.

At the Addis Ababa conference on 11 March 1993 the representative of the *de facto* Somaliland government stated:

"In Somaliland there is poverty but there are no starving masses, there is no famine and there is no civil war... (or) conflict that could not be resolved locally. The country and its people represent no threat to the other peoples in neighboring countries. The question is therefore - does Somaliland need, as the UN Secretary General seems to insist, the large scale deployment of multinational forces to prevent "starvation, restore peace, and initiate processes of reconciliation and mediation between many factions" plus hordes of incompetent civilian personnel "to run the country in view of the prevailing chaos and lack of any form of centralized authority or institution?" Or is it that Somaliland needs a more realistic, more informed, more imaginative, more enlightened and less humiliating form of assistance which would focus and address the genuine problems of the country? Should the people of the country and their leadership be consulted or is it that the UN Secretary General, Dr. Boutros Boutros-Ghali knows best?"[15]

The Somaliland representative in the conference, while admitting the existing difficulties in Somaliland, emphasized the priority needs and called for international assistance but not military intervention. The Elders Council in the Borama meeting sent a protest note on this matter to the Chair of the UN Security Council. In the Borama conference, in May, 1993 a new president was elected, President Mohammed Ibrahim Egal. The latter was the last prime minister of the last Somali civilian government. In June 26, 1960, Egal had been the head of the Somaliland state that lasted only four days. Egal studied political science and was the only Somali politician to use a policy of *detente* in the early sixties when the then new republic found it difficult to solve the issues of "Greater Somalia," with its neighbors. When elected, Egal reaffirmed Somalilander rights of self-determination without losing sight of its inherent Somali connections.

After two years and few months of a *de facto* government in Somaliland, the United Nations remained unenthusiastic in its efforts. In principle, several UN agencies (e.g., UNHCR, UNICEF, FAO, WFP, UNDP) and UNOSOM opened offices, but there was no significant implementation of projects. UN agencies and international NGOs in Somaliland carried out many fact-finding missions in all fields, and substantive reports have been submitted. But none of these has been implemented. Professor Bulaleh of Somaliland stated: "The Somaliland people are tired of the fact finding missions. People came from overseas to collect data ... yet nothing is forthcoming; they do not even bring us copies of their reports."

In stark contrast to Somaliland, the UN in general and the UNHCR in particular, implemented about 250 quick-impact projects around Siyad Barre's home areas, which included Garbaharey, Luuq and Bardhere. In Somaliland there has not been a systematic de-mining program. There are anti-personnel mines, anti-tank mines and hand grenades. Anti-personnel mines are to be found in the shade trees and the water holes in the nomadic areas as well as the urban areas and main roads between towns and villages. According to Rimfire International, the minefields in Somaliland are among the worst that they have ever seen. However, there have been continued problems between Rimfire and its local employees.

There are normally not more than fourteen Rimfire expatriates in Somaliland. The company operates only in the Hargeisa area and employs about 450 locals. For the two years during which they have been in Somaliland, Rimfire has been at odds with their local staff. Yusuf Gabobea, a war veteran in Hargeisa stated,

"First, they did not bring any sophisticated equipment in explosives disposal and mines, so the method is very slow, very much like the previous manual standard we were using prior to their arrival. Second, they do not give insurance and protection allowance to the local staff and pay very little. Third, they do not spread their resources to other areas. Fourth, they do not admit that the job is enormous for one company and have made no request for a joint venture with other international companies.

Ahmed Ali, a young militiaman expressed his view about Rimfire and said the following: "From what I know, all Rimfire does is to complain about vehicle looting; of course some young men do loot vehicles because we have lost respect for these agencies. All that this foreign clan in Somaliland does is to do nothing except collect information, even though they were given different assignments. They all dig for problems in this devastated country and become anthropologists. If you ask me, this foreign clan involves rapacious people who suddenly found open doors."

Hussein Abdi, a Somali businessman who is the founder of the Ruga village near Mait, made the following statement:

> "We Somalis have been defeated, but we manage to follow world events. So we came to know that the international community has raised a lot of money in the name of the Somalis and as one can see there is not even a typewriter in this village. Our hopes have been raised and this has undermined the sense of nationhood and engagement in self-help schemes. If only they can stop all this noise, Somalis seem to survive in situations that others often see as hopeless."

Halimo Ali in Lasanood town stated "The UN did not even provide transport to the Somalis in Luboye to bring them to Las-Anood and no UN aid has reached this region so far." Therefore, as one can conclude from these interviews and many more that have not been mentioned in the report, the UN's unpopularity in Somaliland is acute, mainly because of UNOSOM's failure to deliver its promises and its lack of transparency.

VII. Aidid and the United Nations

General Mohammed Aidid was a founding member of the United Somali Congress (USC) that was formed in 1989. Prior to that he was the Somali Ambassador to India. Aidid is a bright soldier, he studied in the Italian Military Academy in 1954 and also completed a police course. In 1958, he was appointed Chief of Staff at the Military Training Center in Mogadishu. He then took a three year course at the Soviet War Strategic Academy in 1963. Aidid was renowned for his military capabilities. In 1971, Siyad Barre imprisoned him for six years as he perceived of Aidid as a threat. Aidid was released from prison in the course of the Ogaden war of 1977-78 in which his skills were needed.

In 1990, Aidid was elected Chair of the USC. He then established good relations with the Somali Patriotic Movement of the south, led by General Mohammed Omer Jess and the Somali National Movement in the northwest, then under the chairmanship of Abdurahman Ahmed Ali. Shortly after the collapse of Barre's regime the confrontation between Aidid and Ali Mahdi began. Both men are from the Hawiye clan, one of the three major clans in Somalia, the other two being the Darood and the Isaaq. Ali Mahdi is from the Abgal subclan of the Hawiye that resides in the county of Mogadishu which was the capital and the seat of the dictator, Siyad Barre. Unlike his rival, Ali Mahdi does not have academic qualifications. However, his business thrived in the latter part of Barre's regime. He owned restaurants and has Italian business connections. After the overthrow of Barre's government and departure from the capital, Ali Mahdi proclaimed himself President of the Somali Democratic Republic, without consultation with any of the existing opposition groups, even though tacitly he was a USC man, being a Hawiye.

In his first national televised speech in Mogadishu, Ali Mahdi failed to refer to the historic endeavor of non-USC Somalis with Siyad Barre and began to say "Thank God the one-year struggle with Siyad Barre is over and we finally drove him out of Mogadishu....". While that reinforced the northern Somalis' skepticism against a Mogadishu administration, the political difference between Aidid and Ali Mahdi climaxed. Subsequently, the conflict between the Habar Gedir (Aidid's clan) and the Abgal (Ali Mahdi's clan) heightened. The rest of the Hawiye were on the periphery. In November 1991, the fierce fighting within the USC erupted. The looting, counter-looting and the ravaging of Mogadishu city took place. Non-USC Somali civilians in Mogadishu and nearby were also targeted, such as the traditional urban traders of Mogadishu, known as Xamaries and Darood civilians whom they (the USC) failed to distinguish from supporters of Barre's regime. Consequently, the lawlessness spread and victims increased. In such circumstances, many observers began to doubt Aidid and Ali Mahdi's power over their men or, for that matter, their clan.

A national catastrophe in Somalia became eminent. Initially, Aidid was not against UN humanitarian assistance to Somalia. But he was concerned about humanitarian intervention encapsulated with military intervention. Aidid demanded a consent and transparency in the UN criteria of intervention. In contrast to Aidid, Ali Mahdi who was enjoying *de jure* recognition from the Italians, among others, welcomed intervention indiscriminately, with the hope that his presidency will be legitimized by the interveners. Aidid's skepticism of the UN began when James Jonah, then Assistant Secretary General visited Mogadishu in January 1992. Mr. Jonah, after a meeting with Ali Mahdi, hastily described Aidid as "an obstacle for progress." The rumor that Ali Mahdi maintains good relations with Siyad Barre's remnant and with Italian politicians in Rome persisted. When the UN humanitarian assistance began, the Kenyan police in Nairobi caught a UN-chartered plane carrying supplies of money and uniforms to Ali Mahdi. Aidid then attempted to blockade further UN supplies to Somalia and began to denounce the UN involvement in Somalia.

However, when Ambassador Sahnoun visited Somalia in July, 1992, he did not remain a detached UN technocrat, nor did he favor any of the warring factions, but clearly felt the magnitude of the human sufferings in Somalia. Ambassador Sahnoun was aware of the enormous task ahead of him, describing the Somali situation as a "broken porcelain pot." With that understanding, Ambassador Sahnoun managed to reach various sectors of the society, while not ignoring the leaders of the warring factions. As a result, he won the trust of most groups. Sahnoun, not being satisfied with the UN and some of the Arab states' approach to the Somali crisis, publicly criticized the UN and the Arab League. The Secretary-General Boutros Ghali, who is both an Arab and the head of the United Nations, responded with a letter to Sahnoun, the contents of which caused the Ambassador to resign on October 26, 1992. Aidid was said to have felt comfortable with Ambassador Sahnoun and was able to confess to Sahnoun that he was not in full control of his men. Nevertheless, the resignation of Ambassador Sahnoun and later promotion of Mr. Jonah, further infuriated Aidid and indeed many who followed events in Somalia.

When the foreign troops landed on Somali soil, Aidid welcomed them unenthusiastically. Their objectives were as blurred as he might have expected. There was no policy of disarmament and the young men slipped their weapons to the interior, while the leaders of the warring groups were allowed to remove their weaponry from the areas of UNITAF presence. At the October, 1993 Geneva conference, it was agreed that a Somali reconciliation conference would take place in Addis Ababa. The conference took place in January and was followed with another in March, 1993, also in Addis Ababa. While Aidid was at the March conference, General Mohammed Hersi (Morgan), the son-in-law of Siyad Barre, captured Kismayo, in spite of the presence of UN troops. That damaged the image of UNITAF UNOSOM in Somalia even further.

However, it is worth noting that the undeclared UNISOM II war in Mogadishu was not between the Habar Gedir subclan of Hawiye (Aidid's clan) and the UNITAF. It had much wider implications. General Aidid represents the Somali National Alliance (SNA), which is a pact between four Somali organizations: the United Somali Congress (USC); the Somali Patriotic Movement (SPM), and the Southern Somali National Movement (SSNM), chaired by Colonel Abdi Warsama Isaaq. Furthermore, General Aidid and General Abdullahi Yusuf, leader of the Somali Salvation Democratic Front (SSDF), entered a peace agreement and have improved relations between their groups. The SSDF was the first organization to oppose Siyad Barre. Abdulahi Yusuf, a founding member of the SSDF, was imprisoned by Siyad Barre. Aidid's opponent organization is the Somali National Front (SNF), under the leadership of General Morgan. While Morgan represents the remnant of Barre's regime, Ali Mahdi and General Mohammed Abshir now support him.

The SNA disapproved of the UNOSOM activities in southern Somalia. They broadcast their UN protest from Mogadishu radio on 5th of June 1993. UNITAF attacked the radio station and in the ensuing fighting, twenty-three of its Pakistani troops were killed as were a number of the Somalis defending the station. The following night the UN US-led forces continued aerial bombardment of Mogadishu. The US singled out Aidid from the rest of the leaders of the many factions from his opponent Ali Mahdi. The people of Somaliland demonstrated against the UN-US led attacks in Mogadishu in which Aidid was described as the UN's most wanted man. Somalilanders expressed their support for him and made it clear that he was welcome in Somaliland, should he find it necessary and that no state or international body can abjure rights which do not belong to them. It is existing international law that gives the Somalis in Mogadishu the right to protest the UNOSOM-UNITAF presence in their homeland, whether by radio broadcast, leaflet or demonstration.

VIII. The Mission That Lost Its Meaning

Use of force by the United Nations in a situation where international peace and security (or that of neighboring countries) is not threatened is illegal under international law. The UN/US-led forces in Somalia conducted a full military operation combining land, sea and air forces. After the 5th of June, the US began an air raid on the city of Mogadishu. As a result, many Somali civilians were killed and citizens of Mogadishu suffered a continuation of the US air raid the following night. President Clinton described the action as intended to create havoc for the thug, by which he meant General Aidid, the leader of Somali National Alliance. The undeclared war between the Somalis in Mogadishu and the US continued. On the 17th of June US gun ships attacked the once famous Mogadishu hospital, Digfer, built by the Soviet Union in the 1960s. Once again, the victims were civilian patients.

The UNOSOM forces failed to refer to the general convention of rules of war that gives the hospital a protective status. The UN US-led forces in Mogadishu claimed that attacks against the UN forces were launched from the hospital and that weaponry was kept in Digfer by Aidid's supporters. The Somali Director of Digfer, Dr. Mohamed Fuji, responded that the only weapons inside the institution were antibiotics and other medical supplies. On the 12th of July 1993, three US Cobra gun ships raided a house in a residential area in Mogadishu, where Somali intellectuals and community elders were holding a meeting to explore avenues of achieving peace in southern Somalia. Seventy-three Somalis were reported killed and hundreds wounded, among them respected elders and professors. On the same day, four foreign journalists were killed by an angry Somali crowd.

On 24 August 1993, the deputy head of the UNOSOM II, Ambassador Lansana Kouyate, said that everything possible was done to bring about a political solution to the conflict in the south of Mogadishu. Nevertheless, General Aidid still had a bounty of $25,000 on his head. However, on the 1st and 16th of July 1993 the authorities of the Italian contingent in Mogadishu informed their US colleagues that they had contacts with Aidid. Ironically, the US authorities in Mogadishu rejected the Italian initiatives on both occasions.

That led the Italians publicly to disagree with the US approach. The military operations and the arbitrary shelling of Mogadishu continued: a particularly embarrassing incident occurred on 30 August when a building used by the United Nations Development Program was assaulted by elite US forces and eight UN employees including a Canadian and an Irishman were tied up and taken away.

The US failed to curtail the use of its sophisticated computerized weaponry against the defenseless Somalis who did not even have a regular army. In addition to the air raids, hundreds of Somalis were killed in local incidents, and many wounded in the hands of the UNITAF forces. The UNITAF crimes against the Somali civilians include indiscriminate rape, torture and continuous civilian harassment. They have engaged in house-to-house searches, destruction of buildings and house furniture and floors, allegedly searching for arms. According to Somalis in Nairobi who fled from Kismayo, the Belgian troops were the worst criminals: they went to the river areas and drowned women, children and men in the rivers (seven Belgians are currently before a court in Belgium as a result of this incident). The Italian magazine *Epoch* claimed in its June 1993 issue that the Italian contingent in Somalia had used methods of torture contradictory to its status as a civilized nation, thus dishonoring Italy. It added that the last time that Italians applied this method of torture was during the Second World War in Yugoslavia.

The pictures in the magazine include Somali men hooded, with head, hands and legs tied back together and lying on the hot sand with no top. Each Somali man is carried by several army men who use gloves when tying them. In another picture of these men, a hooded man is lying on the ground, fastened by a rope tied to a vehicle. This torture episode took place in Adanyabal in Abgal region (Ali Mahdi's clan) and indicates that the Somali citizens are subject to UNITAF/UNISOM crimes.

Under the circumstances, Somalis remain bewildered. There is no independent body to investigate, or monitor UNITAF's crimes in southern Somalia. While the Belgian and Canadian authorities have taken action following well-publicized events, no international tribunal has intervened so far. While Somalis were initially complaining of local looting they are now witnessing international looting.

In Spring, 1993, the UN Environmental Program in Nairobi revealed that European companies were dumping toxic waste in Somalia's territorial waters. Also, illegal fishing has been reported. In April, 1993, Somali fishermen captured two Pakistan fishing dhows by using machine gun and heavy weapons mounted on small boats. The captain of the dhows was killed by the Somali fishermen; the 19 crewmen were taken to Bosaso. Italy, Taiwan, Japan and Greece are among the illegal fishers along the Somali coast. It was Green Peace International that extended a helping hand to the local fishermen who have been complaining of this illegal fishing. In May 1993, Greenpeace International paid a two week visit to the Somali coast of Bosaso. The organization used light aircraft and local boats in Bosaso and detected six vessels by ship radar stationed at night in rich fishing grounds near Bosaso. The organization is demanding an immediate moratorium on all foreign fishing in Somali territorial waters, calling for the UN to do something about it.

In early June, US marines made a surprise raid on the northern shores of the Somali coast near Bosaso. The latter is an ancient coast known to the Greeks as Mosullon and the Semites used to call it Bandor Khasim. There are a number of shipwrecks in the area which have aroused interest among archaeologists and it is thought that there may be much of value in the area. The incident raised questions as to what exactly the US marines were doing in the area. The Somali territorial waters are subject to illegal fishing, unprotected ecosystems, marine pollution and waste dumping. On land, Somalis in Mogadishu reported looting of historical sites, in particular, Burhakaba in the Bay region. Bur Eibe and Bur Hakaba are other areas where there are vulnerable historical sites first recorded by Miss Thompson as related to the Fayuun Bur culture of Egypt. There have also been reports from Mogadishu that Somali children have been smuggled from the country and that in the feeding centers, Islamic and Christian teachings have competed with one another..

In short, the mission that was to save the Somalis from civil war and the ills it caused, has turned out to subjugate them in an unprecedented manner. As described in earlier sections, the US strongly supported Barre's regime when it was engaging in genocidal war against the Somalis in the northwest. This has obviously raised questions in the minds of many Somalis as to what the real aims of the United States in Somalia may be. Though any speculator will not be envied, nevertheless, there have been different schools of thought developed in the course of "the Restore Hope fiasco."

One school of thought suggests that the US intervention in Somalia was not a premeditated act. It was prompted during the Bush presidential campaign and was meant for the American audience. President Clinton continued for the same reason and the Democrats in the US are not renowned for tackling foreign issues successfully. Another school of thought argues that it is because of oil potential on the Red Sea coast of Somalia and off shore that US oil companies are encouraging their government to rebuild Somalia and bring in a government of their own choice.

A third school of thought believes that the US intervened in Somalia in order to preempt a spread of Islamic governments in the Horn, taking account of the Sudan situation. Finally, the fourth perspective holds that because of the disengagement of the cold war, humanitarian intervention with a hidden agenda of colonization would be the new doctrine for a potential intervener. Therefore, since the opportunity presented itself, Somalia became a testing ground.

Whatever the reason, it is obvious that the US was overly ambitious as an intervener in the Somali crisis. Mogadishu became a more slippery ground than the US might have contemplated. Furthermore, the meticulous absence of indigenous people in the decision-making process in their homeland, provoked repercussions and resentment towards UNOSOM/UNITAF forces.

There was/is an acrimonious debate among Somalis over the US antipathy towards Islam. Traditionally, Somalis have not politicized religion. It was understood that a good practice in Islam was to help one to be a better person and more disciplined. Therefore, concern arose in Somali circles as to why the religion they have practiced since the seventh century has to worry the United States. It is a fact that since the arrival of the UNITAF/UNOSOM force in Somalia, Islamic theology gained credence as the best resort to organize a shattered society; a unifying force against an intervener who intentionally or unintentionally damages the likelihood of progress in the Somali crisis. There are three main Islamic groups that propose an Islamic state in Somalia: the Muslim Brotherhood, who are moderate in politics; the Jihadish, who have strong views on self-defense, national defense and reprisal; a new Islamic group that adopts tough measures on political issues. Traditionally, however, Islamic suffism (mysticism) has been and remains to be most popular in Somalia (notably the Tariiq Qadariya, Salihiya and Ahmediya).

If, however, humanitarian intervention is a pretext for a hidden agenda of colonization then the US administration must think again. Any colonial agenda will be self-defeating since it will strengthen resistance, probably based on an Islamic identity. Should the prospect of oil and mineral resources in Somalia have led the US to military interventionism in Somalia's moment of dismay, then they (the US) will earn the resentment and contempt of the Somali people. A Somali woman who fled from Mogadishu and is now living in Djibouti stated the following: "I heard that they (the US) are suffering a Desert Storm syndrome. *In shallah* they will suffer a Restore Hope syndrome." At any rate, the US administration pursued the wrong course in the Somali crisis. It is vital for them to review their aims and objectives in this corner of the African continent.

IX. The Shattered Society of Somalia: What Can Be Done?

Somalia today is a shattered society. The entire social fabric has disintegrated, its citizens dispersed and its community beleaguered by the UNITAF/UNOSOM rules of engagement. It has been argued that Somalia's mischief is self-inflicted. However, while the international media, among others, were portraying Somalis as "dangerous, looters, drug users *(qaat)* and bandits," other Somalis were collecting their thoughts and forming their opinions. Their verdict is:

1. Throughout the periods of foreign intervention in the Horn of Africa, the Somalis have been victims of third party involvement. It goes way back to the dismemberment of the Somali territory, in which its legacy embodies the regional territorial confusion that prevails in the Horn of Africa and near...

2. A decade of superpower squabbling, fueled the colonial inherited problems.

3. Where Somalis contributed such as Siyad Barre and the present day leaders of the warring factions, it became apparent that they have been empowered by interveners, who continued to marginalize the productive sectors of the Somali society. In short, the regional and the local power equilibrium has been continuously disturbed.

X. What To Do With A Shattered Society

First, what not to do is to try to bring the Somalis under a UN trusteeship, for the simple reason that it is out of date. Somalis in the south were already through a UN trusteeship in 1950 under the Italians. Furthermore, people fought for independence, achieved it and thus enjoyed independence. As readers may remember, civil wars do happen and it is a human global factor not unique to the Somalis. Should anybody try to turn the clock back, it is obviously not going to work. As early as 1895, Captain Swayne of Britain wrote "...He [the Somali] sees too much of the European weaknesses and as a result of the familiarity, he loses his respect for them." To cite an instance of the familiarity which breeds contempt, Aden Somalis have been known to call visitors from passing ships "damned fool passengers." Captain Swayne continued to say "whatever faults a Somali may have, lack of intelligence and, what for want of an English word may be called *savoir faire,* are not [among] them." Therefore, Somalis did not pay allegiance to the European powers in the 19th century, and to expect them to adhere to UNITAF/UNOSOM rules and regulations now is unwise.

Second, since evidence suggests that the international community contributed immensely to the wider spectrum of the country's political and socio-economical disarray, their contribution to alleviate the human suffering and alike in Somalia is by all means welcome. From the point of view of the Somalis, positive suggestions to help Somalia's shattered society include:

1. (a) To help the productive sectors of the society through helping their people. For instance, instead of bringing a non-Somali nurse from abroad, employ a local nurse; her family will share the salary with her and her patient will not need an interpreter.

(b) Instead of sending international experts who can't operate in what they believe is a dangerous area, engage local experts who are prepared to take the risks.

To cite an example of the above: The representative of the World Health Organization in Somaliland is stationed in Nairobi. According to him, he cannot live in Somaliland because there are no decent lavatories. For this, while he remains in Nairobi, he gets a hardship fund among other allowances. In Somaliland, there are indigenous doctors who remained in the country, and who have gained tremendous experience in the conditions of the civil war. They have carried out operations in the most hazardous circumstances, using torches as the only source of light. Why not encourage and give assistance to them?

2. While helping Somalis, through Somalis, set up a monitoring group comprised of Somali professionals (based on the relevance of their qualifications) and non-Somalis, who can monitor and follow up implementation of projects and sustainability, perhaps through the office of Humanitarian Affairs and Emergency Relief.

3. Set up a review body to assess the good use of donor's funds.

These three points are neither complex nor complicated. The treatment is not exotic and it accommodates the patient. It is certainly less expensive than the UNITAF /UNOSOM operation fiasco. Somalis are not short of human resources, but obviously the community has been shattered by the magnitude of the suffering.

The Somali Horn has endured several curses in the course of known history and its people will survive the current disaster. The Somali country is destroyed, the Somali nation is defeated, but the Somali people remain defiant and confident.

Endnotes

1. Somaliland Foreign Affairs Dispatches, No. 6. Mr. Rodd to Marquess of Salisbury, received May 1897.

2. Turton, E.R. "Somali Resistance to Colonial Rule and the Development of Somali Political Activity in Kenya 1893-1960. Article in *The Journal of African History*, volume XIII, Cambridge at the University, 1972, Page 121.

3. Lee Cassanelli. *The Shaping of Somali Society: Reconstructing the History of a Pastoral People: 1600-1900.* Philadelphia: University of Pennsylvania Press, 1982, page 183.

4. A.M. Brockett. *The British Somaliland Protectorate to 1905*: Thesis, Lincoln College, Oxford 1969, p. 14.

5. Ahmed Omer Askar. *"Sharks and Soldiers."* Printed in Finland, 1993.

6. Hussein A. Bulhan. "Why Somalis Flee: A Review of the Gersony Report", October 1989, Page 23. See also more on the Gersony Report of February 1989 by the United States Department of State's Bureau for the Refugee Programs.

7. Jeffery A. Lefebure. *Arms for the Horn, U.S. Security Policy in Ethiopia and Somalia 1953-1991.* Published in University of Pittsburgh Press 1991, Page 242.

8. *Ibid.*, page 243.

9. Richard Lillich . *The Development of Criteria for Humanitarian Intervention.* A paper presented at Wilton Park, Special Conference, Legal Aspects of Humanitarian Assistance and Intervention. 2-4 July 1993, Pages 3 and 4.

10. Jan Eliasson. *The World Response to Humanitarian Emergencies.* Council on Foreign Relations 15 September 1993.

11. Mohamed Sahnoun. UNOSOM Statement at the Coordination Meeting on Humanitarian Assistance to Somalia. Palais Des Nations, Geneva. 12 October

1993, page 1.

12. Mohamed Abdi. Statements by the Head of Ethiopian Delegation at the Coordination Meeting on Humanitarian Assistance for Somalia. 13 October 1993, page 9.

13. Ridah M. Larry. "Lions in Somalia, Chickens in Bosnia." Saudi Gazette 23 June 1993.

14. *African Event Journal,* vol. 8, No. 8, August 1993.

15. Hassan, Osman. " A Statement of the Government of Somaliland": At the donor's conference in Addis-Ababa, March, 1993.

Bibliography

Ahmed Omer Askar. *Sharks and Soldiers.* Printed in Finland, 1993.

A.M. Brockett. *The British Somaliland Protectorate to 1905.* Thesis, Lincoln College, Oxford University, 1969.

African Event Journal. Vol. 8, No. 8, 1993.

Eliasson, Jan. The World Response to Humanitarian Emergency. (Presented at the Council on Foreign Relations, 15 September 1993).

Hussein A. Bulhan. Why Somalis Flee. A Review of the Gersony Report. October 1993.

Hassan Osman. A statement of the government of Somaliland at the Donor's conference in Addis-Ababa. 11 March 1993.

Human Rights Watch. Human Rights Watch and The UN Field Operations. Printed in the USA, June 1993.

Jeffery A. Lefebure. *Arms for the Horn US Security in Ethiopia and Somalia, 1953-1991.* Published by the University of Pittsburgh Press, 1991.

Lee V. Cassanelli. *The Shaping of the Somali Society. Reconstructing the History of the Pastoral People: 1600-1900* Philadelphia: University of Pennsylvania Press, 1982.

Lillich, Richard. *The Development of Criteria for Humanitarian Intervention.* A paper presented at Wilton Park, special conference on legal aspects of Humanitarian Assistance and Intervention, July 4, 1993.

Mohamed Abdi. Statement by the head of the Ethiopian delegation at The Coordination Meeting on Humanitarian Assistance for Somalia. Geneva, Switzerland, October 13, 1993.

Ridah M. Larry. "Lions in Somalia Chickens in Bosnia." Saudi Gazette 23 June 1993.

Somaliland Foreign Office Despatches: No. 6, Mr. Rodd to Marquess Salisbury, Received May 1897.

Sahnoun, Mohamed. Statement at The Coordination Meeting on Humanitarian Assistance to Somalia. Palais Des Nations, Geneva, Switzerland, 12 October 1993.

Turton, F.R. " Somali Resistance to Colonial Rule and the Development of Somali Political Activity in Kenya, 1893-1960." Article in *The Journal of African History*, Vol. XIII, Cambridge at the University Press, 1972.

Yogesh K. Tyagji. *The Changing Picture of International Peace and Security Under the UN System: Iraq, Somalia and Beyond.* A paper presented in Wilton Park special conference on Legal Aspects of Humanitarian Assistance, 4 July 1993.

CHAPTER TWELVE

Forms Of Violence And Ways To Control It In An Urban War Zone: The Mooryaan In Mogadishu

By Roland Marchal[1]

"Wallee ma qabowdo oo looma dego qiyaas, qorey Jiibkiyo raggii qaadan jiray Shilkaha, qorraxda iyo oonka nimankaan ka qoomameyn, qaroonkii gumarka nimankii quwaaxi jiray, mujaahid qallalan intuu qowga saaranyahay, Agoonka qaawaani intuu qeyladii ku jiro, qabriga kii galay intii uu qurbaan ka helin, wallee ma qabowdo oo looma dego qiyaas" [2]

The fall of Siyad Barre's regime did not bring the traditionally ritualistic and cathartic dimension inherent in the collapse of most dictatorships. There was no popular celebration in which all members of opposition parties came together to plan and develop a governance strategy for the new regime; there were no national celebrations taking place in all corners of the country to immortalize the revolutionary heroes and to name them to positions of lasting honor for the new nation. Instead there was almost immediate dispute among different opposition groups, not based on partisan views or feelings about governance models but based on clan identification. These disputes were punctuated by several violent incidents, some of which qualify as full-fledged massacres.[3] However, these "new" styles of post-revolutionary behavior may be growing more common, as witnessed in Ethiopia in May, 1991, at the time guerillas entered Addis Ababa or, at the other end of the continent, in a Liberia freed of Sergeant Samuel Doe. This new style of post-revolutionary behavior suggests need for reflection on the importance of the sequence of events in more contemporary political phenomena. If rejoicing is not in order and if the defeat of a dictator and his subsequent flight is no longer a "victory," then there is a possibility that the democratic illusion in certain violent revolutions has considerably diminished. This is so both because the consensus of the opposition may wilt upon "victory," and because the experience of using guns may call for a new vision for those who have learned to use them.

Even if the Somali case is not as special as one would think, the path taken by the armed opposition against Siyad Barre was profoundly original, and becomes the object of a unique reflection. It may become a scenario more believable in tomorrow's Africa than in today's. Proof is, in the months following the peaceful departure of the old general's partisans from Mogadishu, combat between different factions of the opposition gathered within the United Somali Congress (USC) flared up several times (April, June, September). Then between November, 1991 and March, 1992 it took an even more radical and destructive form.[4] In fact, the capital had become, since the end of January, 1991, the reserved domain of militias who were recruited from among the family of Hawiye clans, even though the population remained more heterogeneous. The Daroods[5] linked to the old regime had not yet fled the capital and other clan groups such as the Reer Hamar, Bantu, Rahanweyn, Dir, and Isaaq, continued on in Mogadishu in abundant numbers for some months.

Political competition was taking place mainly among the Hawiye, between Ali Mahdi Mohamed, the USC Mogadishu, self-proclaimed (on 28 January 1991) interim president and General Mohamed Farah Hassan Aidid. Aidid had directed the largest armed faction, from Ethiopia, called USC Mustahil, working with at least two other fronts: the Somali National Movement (SNM) of Abdirahman Ali Tur hegemonic in Somaliland; and the Somali Patriotic Movement of Omar Jess whose clan definition (and thus territorial definition) was evolving during this period.[6] For example, when Jess arrived in Afgoye, in early February, 1991, his fighters came from small Dir, Hawiye and Ogadeni clans. That struggle for power was based on clan alliances which have remained constant up to the present time. In each of the confrontations in the capital, factional polarization assumed forms of involvement in the battle which were clearly more diversified. Anyhow, each group tried to present a vision of its behavior during combat which could appear rational from the point of view of the clans as well as from a political perspective.

Those teleological analyses and the permanent rewriting of history linked to the relative fluidity of the political situation have increased the difficulties foreign observers experience when trying to understand the situation. These outside perceptions, however, continue to be built largely on contradictory rationales. First, there is a moral standpoint which cannot avoid contesting the "hostage status" of a large fraction of the civilian population, held under the sway of leaders who certainly showed little humanity during the massacres of Darood populations in January and February, 1991; this moralistic vision stresses the anomy of the situation in Somalia and emphasizes its intolerable pathology without, however, taking into consideration the concrete processes of the confrontations and without criticizing the factual reconstructions to which they lead from the part of the involved Somali actors.

There is also another kind of logic which suggests that these battles are in congruence with the existence of two factions who fight, as such, for goals that can be identified[7] in a traditionally structured political field. By thus objectivizing the militias or the fighting groups, one loses again the essential dimensions of the Somali crisis, the fluidity of military alliances and the relative disconnection between expression through war and political ideology. That particular contradiction in the modes of analysis was poorly handled by most of the journalists and the diplomats involved in the situation. They were torn between two visions: one condemned the "madness" of the faction leaders; the other observed factional leaders using violence and power in calculated ways. Yet neither vision assessed the importance of the "little wars" and of the extremely precarious control that the political leaders were able to exercise, often after the fact, over a group of armed actors.

This article provides a first account of the preliminary results of research concerning the forms of violence and their control in Mogadishu since the revolution. Although some of these assertions may be refutable, this study highlights several themes. First, the violence is not as anomic as it appears, and it remains globally regulated by socially identifiable codes and strategies. It is indeed quite fascinating to examine the thousand and one identification procedures worked out by the fighters to make it possible for them to defer a real armed conflict, while at the same time claiming their rights over some goods or stressing the necessity of respecting agreements made at the level of the subclans, of the clans, even (more rarely) of the political leaders.

It also shows several main facets of the social reality in Mogadishu. On one hand, it demonstrates the existence of a crisis experienced by the young, and made even more acute by massive migrations and by the leaders' inability -- at all levels of power -- to come up with the hint of a solution. For example, young looters, the Mooryaan, upon hearing on the radio a description of the Los Angeles riots in May, 1992, found themselves quite on the same wavelength and started dreaming of their great journey to the States to join their "brothers."[8]

On the other hand, violence also is the expression of a Somali historical legacy that could be linked to two sources, each profoundly distinct. One such force is reaffirmation of a "looting culture" tied to some processes of retraditionalization of Somali society, due to specific social dynamics. The second is the legacy of Siyad Barre's regime manifested in two ways. The first is confusion between private and public property, confusion that he never stopped cultivating. The second views war as a way of seizing bounty, from the beginning of the confrontations in the northern part of the country against the SNM during the 1980s.

Looking at it that way, one should analyze the demonstration effect probably played since the Ogaden war -- a uniformed "delinquency," of which the sadly famous "Red Berets" and other militias were nothing but the ultimate expression. The fact that the recruits for these supplementary groups, mainly Marehan from the Central region, had immediate access to material goods (Land Cruisers) and symbolic gain (officer ranks in the army) influenced many Habar Gedir adolescents who migrated to the capital in the late eighties.

Finally, if these two dimensions of the Somali crisis are not socially questioned today, it is also because Mogadishu is the location of a fight which goes beyond factional confrontations to deal with the nature of the territory. What should be the newcomers' status? Must they be welcomed by the "traditional" city inhabitants who also claim their rights to victory and therefore, hardly consider seeing their usual upper status over the migrants be questioned. This last aspect is, in the time-frame starting with the United Nations intervention in March, 1992, one of the strongest sociological logics of the armed conflicts in a number of southern Somalia towns such as Merca, Kismayo, or El Bur.

The Mooryaan Phenomenon: An Historical Overview

The term "Mooryaan" designates the looter and is, in fact, applied today to those young boys, chewing *qaat* and carrying weapons as tall as themselves, who indulge regularly in "delinquent" activities. But it is necessary to measure this social phenomenon which can hardly be reduced to such a stereotype, although, like all cliches, it contains some undeniable truth.

The word "Mooryaan" was used for the first time in December, 1990 in an official political speech given by Ahmed Jilow, then chief of the political police (the sadly famous National Security Service, NSS) in the Benadir region, before he became one of the most listened-to advisers of Ali Mahdi. Jilow explained that the problems and social upheavals the capital was experiencing were acts of the "Mooryaan" and that he was going to use all possible means to reduce that kind of delinquency. This type of declaration established a public justification for the attack, launched on some of the capital's zones where many Habar Gedir lived, starting with a part of the Wardigley district, Tokyo. Here youths had formed gangs which had little purpose other than looting. Yet it served as a political justification to attack the adult Habar Gedir as much as the youth gangs. Siyad Barre's forces used the excuse of the insurrection to bombarded that part of the city, which, in addition, had the misfortune of being located below the Villa Somalia where the old dictator had established his entrenched camp.

Undoubtedly, awareness of and action to curb the violent activities of the youth gangs was justified. They were not only urban marginals, like ones born out of similar crises elsewhere in Africa, but the youth also had played a significant role in spreading hostile propaganda and taking part in small interventions against the regime since 1988.[9] In that sense, the regime was perfectly clear in identifying the real actors of the first subversive acts in the capital. But because of its own paranoia, the Barre regime showed itself incapable of limiting the assault. The massacre of some fifty Isaaq youth on Jezira beach in June, 1989 is typical of such blind acts of repression to exterminate the people causing social agitation, but striking a totally incorrect targets[10].

In order to understand the deeper motivation of these actions, one must go back to events in the early 1980's. From the end of 1982 until 1984, the Habar Gedir Salebaan were opposed to the Marehan — Siyad Barre's clan -- for reasons that are not completely clear. It is equally certain that the radical opposition to the regime was already fierce, for the Somali Salvation Democratic Front (SSDF) had not yet imploded under Colonel Abdullahi Yussuf's command[11] and many a Salebaan who had taken arms sought refuge in Ethiopia in the midst of the SSDF movement. Siyad Barre's army showed little humanity in the repression. Numerous families were separated, with adult men in Ethiopia or in the bush, and women and children finding shelter in the capital.

Those are the children, resourceless most of the time, who become members of gangs, living off odd jobs, both legal and illegal. They tended to congregate in the Hamar theater area and around the cathedral, inside the capital's historic district. In 1987, young Habar Gedir Saad, fleeing similar oppression from militia in the Galkayo zone, joined with the youth gangs in Mogadishu. However, it would be inaccurate uniformly to attribute such marginality to the Habar Gedir alone. For instance, several gangs of Abgal adolescents would meet regularly at the Lafole Hotel.

The term "Mooryaan" is interesting to study since its meaning, continuing to the present time, is subject to heated debate. For some, it designates a parasite worm living in the human body, especially during the rainy season. One must take note of the fact that this explanation is identical to the one given for the term "Jirri" which designates the same social group, but among the "Majerteen," mainly in Kismayo and Bosaso. In the north, the Isaaq use a different expression, though it is just as evocative: "day-day." It can be translated as "those who burrow" in order to find food or cars.

There is another explanation for the term which is also deserves consideration. It is a distortion of the word *mooriyaan* which supposedly belongs to the Central region dialect (the Habar Gedir region) and designates the very poor, the "bums" who used to sleep next to the pens where cattle were resting at night, in order to find heat and a modest protection. The term would have become obsolete toward the end of the Italian administration.

Each explanation presents a certain coherence, beyond the strictly linguistic aspect, and makes a choice difficult. The first allows us to understand why this term appears not solely among the Habar Gedir. The second allows a better understanding of the violent reaction among the adult Habar Gedir upon hearing Ahmed Jilow's speech. They reacted by identifying themselves with the youths who were explicitly threatened.

If the term had lasted, it might have been possible to propose a time-frame as a dynamic structure of social transformation. One can distinguish four groups (three permanent or semi-permanent) that coexist more or less until today. But their numerical importance has varied because of the losses in the 1991 battles, fought mainly against Siyad Barre's partisans in southern Somalia, for the "Mooryaan" can also prove to be good fighters.

The first group is the one of the "founders" whose previous activities we have mentioned earlier. Those were living, indeed, in a relatively well-defined area of the city. One can offer several distinctive characteristics. First, they were heavy users of drugs. Today, it is hard to know exactly which narcotics they used, a kind which may have been fairly sophisticated[12] such as cocaine. We are sure of one fact: they never stopped using a mix of *qaat*, various amphetamines and tranquilizers[13], whose effects were thus greatly intensified. During the first days of the Mogadishu battle in December, 1990, such a habit gave them the courage necessary to fight alone, in unequal conditions, without ever backing off in spite of extremely heavy losses. Such tactics were surprising, given the superior firepower and military equipment of Siyad Barre's troops.

These groups, or what was left of them after a few days, also took advantage of the combat to acquire many weapons and soon became "over-armed." They lived, together with their girl friends, in houses that they had "liberated." All members, independent of gender, wore gold chains, rings, and ear-rings, a fact which was rather a sign of urbanization, as opposed to the nomad populations who arrived after the fighting had begun. In the same way, they had a greater appreciation for imported products and their choices of clothing were clearly linked to models from the West. For example, they would call themselves Rambo or Clint Eastwood or they would wear wigs and sun glasses. This behavior emulated the West where it was stylish to wear such outfits.

Their space was also made functional. If they left their new property, it was usually for the purpose of doing something illegal. If not, they stayed at home, chewing *qaat* or entertaining their girlfriends. The women's status was varied as well. Some remained tied to the group for the sake of drugs, although the drugs they used did not cause significant dependency. There also were the "war prisoners" about whom one does not know much. According to some interviews, [14] the majority of the girls were Isaaq (and had migrated to Mogadishu because of the war in the north) or from Reer Hamar. But the explanation is weak. It would also seem that the internal structure of the female group remained "traditional" in the sense that there was a fairly well defined hierarchy in the group, based on age rather than on their relationship with the looters. Clan origin was not a fundamental factor of differentiation. Instead these gangs were founded much more on personal affinities. One mentions these "founders" in the past tense, because the group was greatly affected, numerically, during the combat between December, 1990 and September, 1991. The losses were considerable and some opted for safer activities (though often still illegal) no longer "at the front" as had been the case during the heroic period. Examples of the "safe" activities included trade in relief supplies, recycling of stolen goods, and fence many "liberated" products..

With the recurrence of combat and the continuing migrations into the capital, other groups of a slightly different nature appeared, demonstrating the considerable social transformation underway in southern Somalia. A crucial issue is the organizing principle of these new groups as looting had become the dominant mode of earning a livelihood. Undoubtedly, the manner in which international aid is going to be poured into the country will constitute an essential factor in a restructuring the social order.

Three other groups can be identified in the current era, which, if they existed before, were only minor organizations. The first "new generation" group differs from the original unit on several levels. These include its mode of formation, location, internal functional mode, relationship with space as well as with other congregations. One is mainly dealing with young people, living in the same district, who have acquired the habit of gathering and talking while chewing *qaat*, and who decide to launch themselves into some adventure. Once they have accomplished their task (attack on a house, a gas station, a convoy of food supplies) they part so often that the group's identity is constantly changing. These are not clearly defined gangs, but instead, temporary associations built around short-term actions. It is thus rare that such gang members will live together. Some remain in houses, eventually shared with persons not belonging to the group. Others live relatively well, inserted into the homes of relatives or friends, even in some cases with their own families. Those around them are in no way ignorant of the criminal nature of their activities, but remain quiet or close their eyes to them because they derive marginal benefit from the illegal acts. To oppose such actions would put the fragile equilibrium of the household in danger.

In this last case, it is interesting to underline that those close to the Mooryaan emphasize the intensity of their psychological conduct, described as deviant. Supposedly drugged to the point of madness, these young men found that the trauma of the war rendered them uncontrollable, even by their closest relatives.[15] However, certain testimony gathered from persons of the same generation gives a definite shade to this highly pathological description. If everything is a matter of scale, one may say that this new generation is more traditional in its relationship to drugs. They certainly chew *qaat* frenetically, but are not seeking, at least for the moment, harder drugs and make only limited use of volatile mixes with tranquilizers.

Another notable difference, in comparison with the first group, is that these young people do not automatically have recourse to stabilized sexual behavior. The spectacular evidence of the number of rapes in Mogadishu bears this out. Yet once again, one must remember the capacity for exaggeration, because sexual perversion is also, in a relatively prudish[16] society, a symbolic expression of social anomie. What is more, by isolating these Mooryaan from the rest of the population, one creates a social group which can potentially become a scapegoat upon which to lay the blame for the current crisis and the inability to surmount it, while, in fact, they represent only one facet of it.

A third grouping has an even more fluid nature. It may happen that some youths live together around (and on) a technical -- an armored vehicle or a Toyota upon which is mounted a 105 mm recoilless gun. These people are therefore mainly fighters and live primarily on the resources allocated by their subclan or, more rarely, by the faction of the USC to which they swear allegiance. But it happens, just as often, that one morning, for a minimal reason or an unplanned contingency, they fall into urban banditry and set themselves to pillaging various places in a relatively systematic manner. The goods thus gathered are immediately resold to merchants, often of the same subclan. But they are not professional bandits and their relationship with their bounty is of a relatively different nature.

A fourth grouping of an even more evanescent nature is tied to the tradition of rioting. The groups riot in order to demonstrate the intensity of a demand or a dissatisfaction and always wind up finding overstocked shops or overly furnished offices. A simple verbal quarrel suffices to launch them into an intense debate over the redistribution of wealth. What is notable, in several actual cases mentioned in interviews, is that at the heart of the desire for pillage, lies the idea that the contested goods had been ill-acquired and that the confusion between private and public interests could not always be in favor of the same people. An example of Somali redistributive democracy!

The interviews, conducted over several periods, also shed light on other dimensions of that reality. It allows us to stress both the evolution of mentalities and maybe even the transformation of its sociological framework. One can discuss them on three different levels: (1) the urban/nomad relationship; (2) control by elders; and (3) the question of loot. It is striking to observe that, after the relative normalization fostered by the involvement of the United Nations and the growing presence of NGOs in Mogadishu, beginning in March, 1992, those interviewed placed more emphasis on the nomadic background of the young bandits than they did a few months earlier.

Several explanations may be given. On the one hand, the amelioration of the situation from the political and security points of view -- relative though it may be -- reduces the possibility of an armed confrontation where the Mooryaan would have a protective as well as a predatory function. With peace, one forgets the security they provide at certain moments. On the other hand, it is certain that urban culture was more marked in the first generation than in those which followed it.[17] One can see, as an indication of poverty, albeit relative, in which many

Mooryaan continue to live.

Another issue is the relationship with the elders, a delicate question which cannot be described in a general fashion. Indeed, according to some, the Mooryaan appear to acknowledge some notables and, in a way, grant them the status of privileged interlocutors with whom all internal clan problems could be examined. In fact, the situation is much more complex, including within the Habar Gedir subclans from which the majority of today's looters come. The situation depends on the degree of unity -- i.e. personal friendships or political convictions -- among the people responsible for "strategic" linkage who will know how to confront the problems that divide them, including: the blood-price for a murder, the restitution of loot coming from close lineage, etc. In a more generic fashion, it is conceivable for a notable to debate the young bandits on political issues -- having something to do with sending a contingent to war against the fallen dictator's forces, or to their native region to consolidate the subclan's security. But the problems linked to the Mooryaan's primary activity cannot be confronted head-on, for the notable would then risk losing the social recognition with which his community as a whole, endowed him. If the merchants, who often are elders at the same time -- even if it goes against the idealized image -- often know how to manipulate ambiguity with real talent, the religious ones, for instance, are under the obligation of remaining inflexible at the risk of provoking protests, since what is socially acceptable on the part of a merchant is not so from the part of a man of religion.

On a related theme, there are important dimensions on the radical modernization of customary laws which some clans have undertaken to face the new, urban situation. One becomes aware, once again, of the extreme heterogeneity of the different clans in their conception of the law and of a recomposition of the social order.

The last aspect is not the least significant. It is related to the attitude toward the bounty. We have underlined the extent to which pillage goes back to a cultural strata which is meaningful in terms of rights of war -- or of feud, since the Somalis do not really make a qualitative distinction between the two terms.[18] But one should also wonder about the deep-rootedness of certain delinquent habits: the Mooryaan, since 1989, would systematically steal the foreigners' four-wheel-drive cars to make propaganda against a hated regime, but also with the goal of furnishing material to the guerillas. It is furthermore significant that these initially very selective thefts spread -- in 1990 -- to the wealthiest strata of the Somali population in Mogadishu, accompanied with a clanic[19] or populist rhetoric. If one now wonders about the relationship with loot, or more accurately about the possibility of returning loot, i.e. the capacity to recover one's goods, one must face again a more complex reality of the Mooryaan phenomenon.

With the very first generation, things were relatively simple: one knew where they lived, and the only problem was identifying the leader with whom to negotiate to recover their stolen property and even to prevent theft altogether. [20] In the same way, if we look at the soldiers operating a technical car, social control can be exercised with relative firmness on two other levels: the eventual restitution in relation to the payment of blood-price if the adventure cost lives, and the concrete capacity to recuperate stolen goods. For example, if it is fuel, it may have been immediately bought again by a group of women who try to sell it in small quantities on the streets.

It is mostly with the "second generation" that the problems developed more crudely and violently since its structure is based on more functional relations than the other groups's: their leaders are leaders only in a given conjecture and because of often very rational motivations (ability to provide the weapons, knowledge of the setting for a potential hold-up, proven mafia competence).

In conclusion, it may be interesting rapidly to emphasize certain parallels with the description Howard Becker attempted, several decades ago, in a work that has remained justly famous[21]. First, one may question the validity of a sequential model and the notion of career in the constitution of the Mooryaan. In a way, it is war itself, as a durable phenomenon, which offers the best path for the transition from occasional occurrence to a more constant form of deviance. The collapse of the state apparatus in December, 1990, is but the visible moment in a process already in place for several years. Also, the incapacity rapidly to reconstruct a legitimacy necessary to maintain social order, will modify, in the space of some months, the type of delinquency and the procedures of reversibility.

At the same time, it is reasonable to assume that this behavior is based on acquiring a sub-culture organized around pillage.[22] Nonetheless, the evocation of a "subculture" remains problematic in many respects, to the extent that this latter is hardly homogeneous. While it can be characterized by generic elements that are relatively simple and barely discriminating, it is more often a subculture incredibly diverse in its makeup. At the same time, at least at present, it is not certain that the deviant identity, to use H. Becker's term, dominates all the other identifications. This is perhaps one of the most original dimensions of the Somali case, even if the propensity to social control fluctuates rapidly. An interesting dimension can be briefly suggested by asking about the variety of the processes by which this sub-culture is constituted, in the image of the analysis of marijuana smokers or of jazz musicians, attempted by the American sociologist. For example, within the pillage culture, the constant use of *qaat* evokes certain new expressions and attitudes among the Abgal Mooryaan. These seem to indicate a process of imitation in relation to their Habar Gedir counterparts which raises the behavior to the level of the fighters as a whole. If that were founded, it would prove the fact that whatever the generalization of the phenomenon might be, it would have kept an obvious Habar Gedir imprint. It would also be wise to underline the Mooryaan's taking over the old places of the ruling class. They meet their girl-friends at the Jezira bar and have a taste of the good life. Is it a retrospective irony or a more complex phenomenon of resocialization?

Finally, one could wonder with some pessimism about the existence today of those whom H. Becker calls the "moral entrepreneurs," meaning those who should play an essential part in the creation of new social norms defining deviance. If that figure of a moral entrepreneur can raise new questions, one could also wonder about a symmetrical dimension studied, for instance, in the Lebanese or Irish [23] context in which one considers what part the Mooryaan play (or played) in the reformulation of identities and of the clan sub-cultures beyond the field of their immediate function?

Endnotes

1. The information upon which this work is based has been gathered during several periods of time spent in Somalia in August/September, 1991, March, 1992, August/September, 1992. The author wants to thank the CREDU in Nairobi and the Quai d'Orsay Centre d'Analyse et de Prevision, for their technical help. He alone claims responsibility for the analyses presented here. He would also like to acknowledge his intellectual debt to people who, regardless of their own political choices, have helped him considerably in meeting some of the actors of the Mogadishu drama. A first version of this text was presented at the conference "Etat, Territoire, Ethnicite" organized by Politique Africaine in Bordeaux, on November 12 and 13, 1992. The author also benefitted from Daniel Compagnon's critical remarks; may he be thanked for them.

2. This is part of a *baraanbur* (i.e., a woman's poem) sung by Mme Dhoofa. Here is an approximate translation: " There will be neither peace nor tranquility as long as there will be no solution for the soldiers and the militia who go around carrying weapons, those who did not complain about the sun and their thirst, they who gnawed on roots to relieve their thirst. There will be no peace as long as the mojahedin, reduced to skin and bones, will be burnt on rocks, as long as naked orphans will scream with hunger and as long as the ones dead for the cause will not

find eternal rest. I swear that there will be neither peace nor tranquility as long as ..."

3. Siyad Barre, seeing the end of his reign getting near, did not hesitate to use any imaginable means to form an alliance with the Darood which could have allowed him to engage in one last battle, with a chance of winning: massacres of civilians, geared to create counter-attacks which rallied behind him some Darood otherwise little inclined to identify with a regime they found really too predatory; distribution of weapons and money, etc...

4. See my article "War in Mogadishu" *Politique Africaine* #46, June, 1992, 120-126.

5. We will not discuss here the merits of this affirmation that has worked well, socially, precisely because Siyad Barre had his heart set on creating such a division in the capital's population. Nonetheless, it would be a mistake to see it exclusively as the strategy of a dying regime: the divisions were deep already, but could have found another field of expression beside war and community slaughter.

6. Traditionally, this front is seen as an Ogadeni front in the image of its leader's clan belonging. But this identification remains subject to questions until today, for a number of reasons. On one hand, at certain times, Dir and Rahanweyn fighters joined this movement which was perceived as an effective ally of the USC in their fight against Siyad Barre (particularly in January-February, 1991). On the other hand, this organization, more than others, seems to have used mandatory conscription of the Bantu and of the youths from other small clans, who, in order to survive, had to accept being involved in the war. Behind such a fluctuating reality, there is the issue of the place of the Ogadeni on the Somali territory and the fact that its political and military representation testifies to the precariousness of its status: among the three Ogadeni leaders still politically active in September, 1992, only the current vice-president of the republic in the Ali Mahdi government is of Somali origin (from Afmadu), the other two, Omar Jess and Gabyow are respectively from Ethiopia and Northern Kenya.

7. Even though their reality was a fleeting one, like the pseudo "attempted coup" by General Mohamed Farah Aidid in September, 1991, in a city where the ministers' offices no longer had windows.

8. Mogadishu interviews, August, 1992.

9. Interview with Mohamed Abdi Arush "Bile", who was leading one of these groups before being forced into exile in Ethiopia, then in Turin, Italy, in July, 1992.

10. According to Mohamed Abdi Arush, Siyad Barre's regime thought that his group was Isaaq and those murders were thus aimed at suspects and potential opponents (interview, Turin, May, 1991). Some observers propose another

explanation of the massacre, more directly linked to the events which were taking place, at the time, in the Somali capital.

11. For an historical view of this period, one can consult the work of J. Markakis, *National and Class Conflict in the Horn of Africa*, Cambridge, Cambridge University Press, 1987, and the pioneer article by D. Compagnon, "The Somali Opposition Front," *Horn of Africa*, vol. XIII , #1 & 2, 1990, which remain, given the lack of other studies, the only coherent source of information about this movement.

12. Siyad Barre's first spouse, the famous Khadija, would have been implicated in hard drugs trafficking, but Somalia, at the time, seemed to be rather a transit location than one for consumption. From the overthrow of the regime until March, 1992, in spite of many rumors, it seems unlikely that local comsumptiom would have substantially increased, given the low incomes. One can worry more about the current era when a sizeable portion of the money poured in by the international community is diverted by this group, either by directly looting aid funds or renting cars, or selling products that were previously stolen, etc...

13. Some Somali doctors make references to an explosive mixture of Benzodiapin and ephedrin to which they supposedly add some kind of stimulant (caffeine, and/or *qaat*), interviews, March, 1992.

14. Interviews with various women, September, 1992. According to the same sources, these young girls would also have fought beside the Mooryaan around the Leonardo da Vinci high school, near the current residence of a subclan head, Ali Ougass.

15. Thus this tragic anecdote: a gang of Mooryaan had taken over a house during the battle of Mogadishu. Besides stealing, they also protected some members of their subclan who were living close by; at the end of the war, they received money to leave the premises and give the house back to its owner. Unfortunately, the agreement was concluded without the participation of one of them who had already gone to Kismayo, looking for new bounty. His loot gathered, he came back to an empty house and settled in it again, forcefully. His close relatives, turning out to be incapable of reasoning with him, offered a solution: either to wait for the return of the then absent owner, or to have the unruly adolescent shot, leaving the choice up to some subclan notables...

16. It certainly used to be less so than today. But one should not forget to analyze all the moralizing rhetoric, often heavy with sexual connotations, which has developed for the past year and a half. It would also be necessary to tie this emphasis of rhetoric about sexual corruption to society's attitude faced with the remnants of women's modernized judicial and practical status, changes that took place during Siyad Barre's period of liberalization in the mid-eighties (such as, in the course of interviews with highly politically minded women, hearing criticisms about mini-skirts and the hot nights in Mogadishu).

17. Thus this other anecdote: One day, the Mooryaan broke into a house and demanded the owner's money. She belonged to their clan. The latter said that she has spent all her money having the house built, buying rugs, furniture, etc... The young people, both naive and profoundly astonished, then uttered: "but why did you do that? We never needed all that..."

18. See I. M. Lewis, *A Pastoral Democracy* London: Oxford University Press, 1961, 242.

19. Meaning " the rich must pay more than the poor and their money also comes from Siyad Barre" (an argument whose moral dimension must not be overestimated); or "your subclan will pay you back, it is urgent to use your wealth now, for the sake of the war" (an argument whose financial efficiency one must not overestimate)!

20. But obviously, there is no shortage of more or less savory cases. In September, 1991, some Abgal Mooryaan were intent on pillaging a repair station in Shibis; the Abgal inhabitants tell them to go away, since the owner of the station and those of most of the cars belong to the same clan. Alas! our young warriors made them into Habar Gedir to gain clan justification. In one word, if the clan did not exist, it would be necessary to invent it.

21 H. Becker. "Outsiders" *Etudes de Sociologie de la Deviance*, Paris, Editions A.-M. Metaille, 1985.

22. See H. Becker *op. cit*, 53-54.

23. Elizabeth Picard, "Milices Libanaises et Paramilitaires Irlandais: de la Mobilisation du Groupe a l'Invention de Son Identite", Conference: "Les Identites et le Politique," CERI, March 26-27, 1992.

CHAPTER THIRTEEN

The Untold Apartheid Imposed on the Bantu/Jarer People in Somalia

Omar A. Eno

I. Introduction

The objective of this paper is to emphasize the perpetual and persistent atrocities committed against Bantu/Jarer people in Somalia. I appeal to every civilized person to join me in the struggle to end the long-standing and ongoing racism and discrimination which have caused untold suffering to Bantu/Jarer people since Somalia was founded. This paper will also unveil some crucial information that has always been kept obscure and ambiguous to the outside world. The formidable history of Somali Bantu/Jarer people has been deliberately distorted and made insignificant by every Somalia autarchy, as well as callous Somali scholars, who have deliberately contributed to misleading foreign writers. Therefore, I feel obliged to debunk all the mythic history against Bantu/Jarer, and to uncover the untold apartheid imposed on Bantu/Jarer people in Somalia.

Bantu/Jarer tribes are the natives and landlords of what was previously known as the Shungwaya-land, the inter-riverine areas of Juba and Shabelle in Somalia. Bantu people are a sedentary tribe living on the banks of both the Juba and Shabelle rivers. They are predominantly an agricultural community, less interested in a nomadic life. These are the real authentic Africans of Bantu origin and residents of Inter-riverine areas. Their physical features are of a typical African, such as: flat nose, thick hair, dark skin, strong, healthy, and a muscular body that makes obvious the differences between the Bantu/Jarer and other Somalis.[1]

Bantu people have contributed greatly to the struggle for Somali independence, like any other Somali tribe, and we hoped for a positive outcome after independence, since Abdulkadir Sheck Sakawadin was one of the founders of the freedom fighting party, the SYC (Somali Youth Club), which later became the SYL (Somali Youth League). Mr. Sakawadin is of Bantu origin, but he and his family never received respect and recognition as a national hero and as one of the pioneers of Somali independence. His rejection was related to his race.

After many years of violence, fighting, and guerrilla war against the Italian fascists, southern Somalia finally obtained its independence from Italy on July 1, 1960. It was the dream of every Somali, as well as the international community, to see Somalia stand up on its own feet and function as a healthy nation. We (Somalis) expected our independence would prove to the rest of the world that Somalia is prosperous, with wise and versatile leaders, capable of contributing to the development, progress, welfare and solidarity of our nation.

A great upheaval occurred after independence and everything turned contrary to our expectations. New methods of tribalism and hooliganism have emerged owing to the greed for power of other tribes.[2] We have been and still are being discriminated against in Somalia, publicly and privately. We have been systematically alienated by every Somali regime in academics, politics and economics, and often exploited as the cheapest labor force. We have been denied our Somali identities and human respect; we have been prejudged and categorized as *Adoon* (slave), low class humans who lack the capability of normal thinking and reasoning, which undermines our general competence and dignity.

The Bantu have suffered right from the beginning. We have been suppressed and oppressed, robbed, raped and killed. We have been deprived of our civil rights as Somali citizens by every Somali regime from independence until the present. We have been stigmatized and undermined as inferior to other Somalis, yet we have never been given any eligibility for opportunities in Somali society. However, those of us from Bantu/Jarer tribes who tried to demand our rights, equal distribution of opportunities in the system, and balanced power among tribes, have been preposterously humiliated by every Somali authority. My experience in Somalia has been that we (Jarer) did not need to commit a crime of any kind, because, being a Jarer itself is a crime.

Bantu people and their land have become a core target of many clans in Somalia, who have deliberately imposed blockages and obstacles on my people's economic advances in agriculture, small business, decent employment, and education. We, the Bantu, are still being oppressed in every aspect of our lives because the nefarious Somali system exists to exploit us, forcing us to live as a submissive clan, not entitled to live comfortably, while many other tribes lurked behind lucrative businesses and prominent positions. We (Bantu) are not identified by our rightful names or the real tribe that we belong to, instead we are labeled *Adoon* (slave). We (Bantu) are cynical toward every Somali system because we have become strangers in our homeland after being kicked left and right, in an eternal daily dilemma that makes our lives insignificant.[3]

II. How the Somali System Crippled the Jarer's Economic Advances

As mentioned earlier, a massive number of Bantu people depend on agricultural activities along the banks of the Juba and Shabelle rivers. Although agriculture has been the backbone of Somalia's economic growth, Somali authorities have deliberately denied my people any allocation of proper agricultural tools and equipment, such as tractors, trucks and irrigation machinery. If Bantus were given proper tools and farming equipment, they would establish themselves economically within the Somali economy. The Somali regime did not favor Bantu advancement. Therefore the Bantu were denied systematic assistance. So, they were destined to depend on their hoes and manual farming, limiting the volume of their production capacity, whereas the other tribes, who did not have the skills and capability of farming, were given all the governmental assistance. The Bantu are unable to compete economically and feel very frustrated because of the unfair subjugation.

As for the Bantu who resided in large cities in Somalia, they have experienced a different kind of daily oppression. They are not allowed to hold any prominent position in the Somali economy. Being Jarer automatically outlaws their eligibility, based on their tribal status. They are second class citizens, employed as cheap labor, only able to afford a century-old wattle and daub house to live in.[4]

III. How Somali Authorities Destroyed the Education and Future Development of the Bantu Children?

The educational system for Bantu children in the inter-riverine areas has been cleverly designed by Somali bureaucrats. Their intention is to maintain illiteracy in the Bantu communities, thereby restricting their access in the institutional administration. Before Siyad Barre's regime, the Somali hegemony had set up the educational system in a way that did not favor the Inter-riverine communities, since all the secondary schools, as well as most intermediate schools, have been deliberately centralized in Mogadishu and other cities in southern Somalia. A Bantu farmer was forced to send his children to Mogadishu and support them there for the course of four to seven years to complete higher school education. While other regions were provided with easy access to the educational system because higher schools were built in their neighborhood within walking distance. That is why statisticaliy 98% of Bantu young men and women are today stuck with primary school certificates only, because their parents could not afford to maintain them in the cities to complete their studies.

In 1969, Siyad Barre's regime emerged with a new system full of tricks to disable the educational advancement of Bantu and the inter-riverine people. He authorized the building of a few intermediate and secondary level schools in the inter-riverine areas. But the catch to Siyad Barre's system was making people believe that he was dedicated to assisting their children at any cost. To my surprise, research statistically proved that 99% of the students that Siyad assisted were from other tribes. Once again, we (Bantu) had been intentionally left unqualified to enroll in Somali universities and polytechnics. The few Jarer who have been accepted into limited faculties at the universities had to bribe authorities with large sums of money, equivalent to their life savings.

The Ministry of Education in Somalia used to receive scholarships from all over the world, particularly from the European Common Market and the United States. The Jarer never benefitted from these scholarships. Instead, we were allocated a very low percentage of the scholarships to the Soviet Union, especially in the military field, because there was little demand to study in the Soviet Union. It is really painful and disgusting to experience such discrimination and segregation in our own homeland. Further injustice and control restricted Bantu/Jarer enrollment in the faculties of medicine, engineering, and law. Obstacles and barriers have prevented Bantu/Jarer academic advancement, which is why I have come forward to speak out. The time has come to unveil the truth and inform everyone about our (Bantu/Jarer) sufferings in order to avoid a similar catastrophe in the future.[5]

IV. How the Bantu/Jarer were Alienated from the Circle of Somali Politics

As we all know, politics is a tough and dirty game that requires a lot of financial funding. The occupants of the Central region have control of

Somalia's treasury. They have become the sole political power. The ruling tribe has totally monopolized Somalia's political policies. The government pledged free financing within their party/tribe to ensure reelection at Somali taxpayer's expense. Within the Bantu tribe there is little financial stability to support a party to represent the Bantu people.

Another political disaster, partiality aimed at the Bantu and the inter-riverine people, was the allocation of seats for members of parliament. Statistics from the United Nations show that the most populated regions in Somalia are inter-riverine and coastal areas, yet they were allocated the least number of seats. This misrepresentation is another important issue that needs to be addressed in the present reconciliation process in Somalia. Bantu/Jarer people in Somalia have been intentionally prevented access into the political arena, so that no one will represent the Bantu/Jarer, leaving us without a political voice.

After Siyad Barre's regime was removed from power, it was the hope of every Somali to establish a better government since every Somali tribe had contributed to ousting Siyad Barre. To our despair, the result has not been freedom, but replacing one tribal dictatorship with yet another tribal dictatorship. Genocide and slaying began on innocent people that engulfed the whole of the Southern region of Somalia, claiming the lives of approximately 400,000 Somalis. We did not fight to overthrow Siyad Barre and his government of dictatorship and tribalism to have another tribe take his place and continue the injustice. I wonder who will be left to be governed in Somalia, if half of our Somali people have already been murdered and the other half are in the process of being murdered.[6]

We all know that throughout the centuries, Somalia has experienced complex historical migrations that involved people of many different origins (Somalis, Arabs, Bantu, Oromos, etc). This process has created an interplay of different cultures that has shaped Somali society and created a non-monolithic culture. These cultures had a mutual influence and somehow shared and assimilated values from one another. Nevertheless, in the present Somalia, it has been established that there are four main cultures and traditions, each one related to a particular socio-economic orientation and ecological adaptation, and each one having equally contributed to enrich the present Somali culture. These cultures are: pastoral, agropastoral, agrarian, and a mercantile culture.

Unfortunately, there is a tendency to reduce these cultures into one and define the whole Somalia as having only one culture, namely a pastoral culture. This misrepresentation neglects not only the rich culture and traditions of the riverine and coastal regions, but reduces the strengths of Somali culture. The reason for this neglect stems from three main factors:

1. The Somali Academy of Science and Literature working on a given political directive has always promoted the notion of Somali cultural homogeneity, dismissing anything that may prove otherwise, such as diversity. Hence, only the pastoral culture is celebrated, and the rest rejected.

2. All research on southern Somalia was done by Italian scholars (E. Cerulli, Colucci, Grotanelli, etc.), whose publications are not widely read in the English-speaking world.

3. The development of the written Somali language, which is based on the northern dialect, has also led scholars to focus on the literary and poetic traditions of the north and central regions, leaving the riverine and coastal regions as a secondary field for the study of Somali literature.

I think that what some Somali scholars have termed as "Somali Prussianism" or "Camel Complex" -- a superiority complex -- validates only that which belongs to the pastoral tradition and is not beneficial to the development of Somali culture as a whole. It is time for us to learn from this multicultural country the celebration of every culture which ultimately is a strength.[7]

Saving our existence, dignity and integrity is more important than the fictitious homogeneous misrepresentation of the previous constitution's mission statement. Our freedom of association does not include the imposition upon us of old guard misrepresentation. We are aware of those campaigning behind the scene against our commitment to amend this presently misleading mission statement. It's not a divine law that cannot be tampered with.

It is our duty to educate the misinformed that we are not members of the same ethnic, linguistic background. It is also our responsibility to correct past mistakes and be proud of our diversity. Accepting *the status quo* is a violation of, for example, the "Canadian Charter of Rights and Freedoms." But the bottom line must be clear -- our right to our own identity, integrity, ethnicity is sacrosanct. "Inclusion of false homogeneity is not absolute." We are not going to accept genocide of our culture, identity, dignity, ethnicity, and languages.

While it is difficult to conceive of any limitation on homogeneous ideas, the same cannot be said of homogenous impositions, notably when they impact on the fundamental rights and freedom of others. There is an impingement upon the Somali Arab settlers, Bajunis, Barawans, Bantus (the indigenous farming community), Mashunghulis, Jarer (the polytechnic people). All the above-mentioned belong to this Association.

There is no *Adoon* (slave) or *Bilis* (free) or reverse racism *Gibilcad* (light-skinned). We are all equally elected to do our duties to respect one another regardless of our race, religion, creed, ethnicity, culture, tradition, or gender.[8]

V. History

Before I start my analysis, I would like to stipulate and separate between two different histories that have always been connected by many Somali scholars with their intention to mislead the general public. The Waziguwa Bantu or Gosha are the sedentary people of Kismayo and its surroundings. Therefore, although Waziguwas are Bantu originally, they have no historical connection with the other Bantu groups from Shungwaya or inter-riverine areas, because the Waziguwas or Gosha history in Somalia falls in a period of 450 years ago while the history of the Wa-Nyika[9] from Shungwaya in Somalia falls over 1,000 years ago. Waziguwas are originally a diaspora from Tanzania, while the Wa-Nyikas are natives and autochthonous of inter-riverine in Somalia.

The Waziguwas clearly maintain the tradition of their province from Tanganyika. They say that they abandoned their original homes and headed toward the coast during the days of their great grandfathers because of persistent drought in Tanganyika. The most important leaders from their hometown during those days were called Semdiri and Mabewa. In Dar-es-Salaam the fathers of their grandfathers met with the Arabs. The Arabs outsmarted them by promising to transport them to other fertile land, where drought had never been experienced. The Arabs boarded about 400 Waziguwas on a boat, among them were men, women and children, and ferried them by sea and off-loaded them in the ports of Barawa, Merca, and Mogadishu. Here the Arabs left the Waziguwas in the subjugation of Somalis. However, the Arabs promised the Waziguwas that they were coming back to pick them up, but never showed up. (During my interview, when I questioned my informers and asked them how long ago this event took place, they proved to me that they had no ideas of the exact time. At first they told me they lived in the Juba region about 450 years ago, but when I asked who was the King of Zanzibar by then, they replied he was Sayyid Bargash!) The Waziguwa depended on the Somalis and confirmed to me they remained under the Somali tutelage for not more than two years. Since the Somalis were tyrannizing them, they escaped through the bushes of the mainland, trying to return to their original hometowns of Tanganyika.[10]

Even following their escape, the Somalis came to fight them, and kept on coming to fight them several times, (which means the Somalis intended to recapture the escaped slaves.) At last the war against the Somalis came to an end and the Waziguwas continued to live in Goshaland because of their glory over the Somalis after a long duel of at least ten battles. The Waziguwas had won the war under the leadership of Mkoma and killed the Somali leader Sheikh Mohamed (but the Waziguwas used to call him Sheikh Mambulo).

The Bantu from Shungwaya are also called Wa-Nyika and they fragment into twelve tribes:

1.	Mdigu	7.	Mkamba
2.	Msamba	8.	Mribi
3.	Mlungu	9.	Mgibana
4.	Msifi	10.	Mtaita
5.	Mgiryama	11.	Mkadiyaru
6.	Msuni	12.	Mdara

VI. The Black Bantu in Mogadishu

Al-Dimasqi gave Mogadishu the name of Black Bantu. I already emphasized in one of my other writings that traditions and vestiges are proving that the present southern Somalia was first inhabited by Bantu (Zenji), then by Galla and finally by Somalis. It is evident that during the time of Al-Dimasqi, Mogadishu was still an Arabian colony and a city for Bantu.[11]

Before and at the time of the arrival of the Digil and Rahanweyn confederacies in southern Somalia about the end of the fourteenth century, the Bur country was inhabited by a group of people known as the "Loo Medo," who were most probably Negroid and would appear to have shared the country with the Ma'adanle, a group of Hamitic Ajuran, and Galla elements - the Galla Wardai. Eile tradition says that at one time they themselves inhabited the whole of the country in the region of the three Burs -- Bur Hakaba, Bur Degis and Bur Eibe -- but were driven out of the first two areas by the Elai and Helleda.

Any attempt to explain Swahili history must note first that all traditions of Swahili migration, since the earliest coherent records, involve movements from north to south. Apart from very localized phenomena, there are no traditions of major movement from south to north. By the sixteenth century or thereabouts, the focal point of the remaining Sabaki peoples in Somalia had shifted south because the Pokomo, Mijikenda and Bajuni, had been forced out by the Orma at that time. All have traditions of coming from "Shungwaya," which is usually placed on or around the Juba River. The Barawanese stayed on in Barawa. Some northern Bajuni clung on to the Somali coast, mainly by dint of temporary evacuation to the offshore islands. Also left behind were scattered Bantu-speaking (Sabaki) farmers along the Juba and Webi Shebelle rivers.[12]

Most scholars agree that the earliest riverine cultivators were ethnically distinct from the Cushitic-speaking Somali. They appear to represent the remnants of the northernmost extension of Bantu-speakers who migrated into the adjacent regions of East and Central Africa during the first millennium A.D. Their physical features distinguish them even today from most of the pastoral Somali, although centuries of intermarriage have blurred these distinctions in most of southern Somalia. Most of the farmers have taken on the Somali culture -- they speak Somali, they are Muslims, and they maintain genealogies, usually linking them to Somali ancestors. Nevertheless, until recently, they were considered inferior to the "pure" (*Bilis*) Somali, both because of their agricultural pursuits and their presumed racial origins.[13] For all we know, the future of the group (Bantu) as an entity ethnically and culturally distinct from the dominant Somali may well have been in grave danger from the moment the Italian administration withdrew from Somaliland in 1960.

According to their origin, we may distinguish two types of Somaliland Bantu. To the first belong those tribes (e.g. Gosha) who grew out of cores of fugitive slaves, either run-away or liberated, who have been transported this far north in the course of the 18th and 19th centuries. Previously their home would have been Tanganyika, their affinity Yao, Zegua, etc. To the second group we may reckon those tribes in all probability represent remnants of a pre-Somali population going back to the first millennium of the Christian era.[14]

VI. Conclusion

As I indicated clearly in the first part of my paper, we (Bantu) became the hardest hit by discrimination, racism, unfairness and lynchings that were reinforced by every Somali autarchy and its loyalists against Bantu people. A new era emerged when a few selfish and greedy warlords emerged, who are on a power trip and claimed the lives of about 400,000 helpless Somali -- most of them women and children from inter-riverine areas. They will be remembered eternally by every genuine Somali community, and one day justice will be served.

Although Somali scholars and authorities utterly denied our identities as the natives and landlords of the inter-riverine zone in Somalia, yet time and history will tell as Professor Mukhtar mentioned in the conclusion of his paper *Islam in Somali History* on page 33:

> " Although Somalis claim they are homogeneous, the exact origin of their race remains mysterious. I believe for a fact that there are many reasons why Somali scholars had to lie and connive about the culture and tradition of Somali Bantu as well as the inter-riverine tribes in general."

There were essentially three main reasons:

1. To reinforce the Somali myth of homogeneity and the myth of all Somalis as nomads.

2. To impose the customs, traditions, language, and culture of the dominant tribe upon every other Somali tribe.

3. To divert the world's attention and focus to their specific regions in order to obtain recognition and acceptance as the legitimate Somali historical regions.

As Cassanelli said in his book *The Shaping of the Somali Society* (page 28), efforts have been made to discourage scholars from studying other Somali themes. Valuable sources for the study of Somalia's past were ignored, among them, Arabic, Italian, French and German sources, as I pointed out in this study. The oral tradition of non-nomadic Somalia was deliberately denied, and their languages were not studied. Historical sites were set up where there were no signs of history. Religious heroes were made up where the practice of Islam has been insignificant. The aim was, under the guise of nationalism, to safeguard the interests of particular clans and renounce others' aspirations.

Today, the international community and other scholars are now astonished at the fatal historical error narrated by Somalis and some foreign writers regarding Somali homogeneity. How is it possible to commit such atrocities and genocidal actions that engulfed the whole nation of Somalia if we are really homogeneous! As far as slavery is concerned, it was justified by scholar Vinigi Grottaneilli of how the Waziguwas were deceived by the Arabs and their immediate struggles after realizing that they were trapped as slaves. Therefore, I recommend the following as the solution for Somalia:

1. An immediate and thorough disarmament is indispensable, yet it should not be implemented unilaterally. Instead, disarmament should engulf every arsenal of every callous warlord, otherwise the credibility and effort of United Nation's auxiliaries will be in vain.

2. The reconciliation process must be reinforced although it is one of the most complicated and delicate segments of the whole peace process, because there are unhealed wounds of killing, rape, torture, robbery and destruction engineered by a few ruthless warlords. Most of the ordeal in Somalia has been experienced by innocent people and harmless tribes who did not participate in the atrocities of power struggles, therefore their hatred, grudge and mischief cannot be reconciled easily. War victims have lost faith, human dignity and self-esteem in any system, so inclusion of every tribe in the process of reconciliation is pivotal.

3. A carefully designed approach of governance in Somalia is necessary, although it is not an easy task to accomplish, because almost every Somali is perplexed and ambiguous about the issue of governance. In my opinion, I suggest that every tribe must be included in the process of governance in order to obtain a balance of power. Therefore, governance should start on the level of regional and provincial autonomy, otherwise we will be doomed to more destruction and havoc in Somalia.

4. Somalia needs to build a unique kind of constitution that accommodates all important and relevant requirements of our lives. So, in the process of building a new constitution, people of all ages and genders, from all locations must be included in the discussion in order to construct a comprehensive, consistent, concise, coherent, and convenient constitution. The creation of this constitution may be composed of a combination of three elements: the Islamic religion, the cultural traditions from different Somali communities, and some clauses from the global system.

Endnotes

1. Interview with Halima Essow, an elderly Bantu woman in Afgoi, July, 1993.

2. Interview with Mahdi Mohamed Isse, a major in the Somali army and a professor in the Military Academy in Mogadishu, July, 1993.

3. Interview with Mohamed A. Enow, a Somali journalist in Nairobi, July, 1993.

4. Interview with Ahmed Ali Ibrahim, agricultural consultant, July, 1993.

5. Interview with Mawlid Maani, Secretary-General of the Somali African Muki Organization (SAME.) in Somalia, July, 1993.

6. Interview with M. Arbon, President of SAME. in Somalia, July 1993.

7. Abdurahman Sheck Isse, a Somali scholar based in Toronto.

8. Shariff Aidaruse, president of the Somali-Canadian Association of Waterloo Region.

9. Bantu, Jarer and Wa-Nyika are the same people, but different names are used.

10. Grottanelli, Vinigi L. 1953 *Geografia Helvetica.* Vol. 8, pp. 254, 25.

11. Enrico Cerulli. *Somalia, Scritti Vari* edited in Editti Vol. I pp. 44, 256.

12. Chittick, H. Neville and J.E.G. Sutton. 1983. *Azania Journal of the British Institute in East Africa.* Vol. XVIII, pp. 127, 139.

13. Kopytoff, Igor. 1989. *The African Frontier.* pp 218.

14. *Bulletin of the International Committee of Urgent Anthropological and Ethnical Research.* N. 3, 1960 pp. 28-29.

CHAPTER FOURTEEN

Somalia: The Forgotten People

Amina Sharif Hassan

I. Preface

The Somali peninsula is a region of great importance. For centuries, it has been the focus of outside world powers, from the ancient Egyptians, who called it "God's Land," to the late-nineteenth-century European empire builders. Recently, there has been a contest between the United States and the Soviet Union for military bases and other strategic stakes in the Horn region. "Conflicting nationalism and incompatible territorial claims (for example those between Ethiopia and Somalia), together with a simmering residue of religious antagonisms, further compound the problem of the superpower competition. Of late these factors have combined to make the Horn of Africa one of the world's principal trouble spots."[1]

Some Somalis also have ambitions similar to those of the colonialists for the riverine and inter-riverine area. Their actions are similar to those of a colonial power in search of economic resources and the desire to monopolize the region for group and/or tribal interests, even though they have no socio-economic roots with the indigenous ethno-cultural groups in the area. The ethnocultural groups from this region see no difference between internal and external colonialists.

This matter has compelled some people to write about Somalia in order to unveil the truth and discuss the nature and the cause of the instability of southern Somalia. Although the English proverb says: "the squeaky wheel gets the oil," the Somali people say that "justice is slow and it creeps as a turtle and when it comes no more, injustice will exist."

II. Introduction

In 1885, the Italians went to Somalia looking for rich and fertile land to exercise their farming expertise and business objectives in order to exploit the virgin and untouched resources in the Somali peninsula. All their efforts were focussed on the coastal cities and towns so as to penetrate the hinterland. These towns and cities were mainly located in the southern part of Somalia, in particular, the Benadir ports (Mogadishu, Merca, Brava, Warshikh, and Itala -- called Adale or "Cadale") and Kismayo, present capital of the Lower Jubba region. Ibn Battuta, a well known Islamic traveller, in a 14th century tour of the Somali coast before Europe occupied the region, said:

> The ruler of Mogadishu was a Berber (Somali) sultan who spoke Somali and Arabic with equal ease. Ibn Battuta seemed to have been astonished by the wealth of Mogadishu. Of particular interest was his description of Mogadishu as an "extremely large city." Ibn Battuta (who hopped about cities in the Muslim world from Tangier to Cairo to Damascus to the great urban centres of the Central Asia) was unlikely to have been sentimental or exaggerate what constitutes an "extremely large city."[2]

> Other than the fact he was a Berber (the familiar term of medieval Arabs for Somalis and related peoples) who spoke the Benadir dialect of Somali, we do not know much about this ruler, his ethnic affiliation, or his relationship with the hinterland tribes. He may have belonged to one of the Hawiye clans, such as the Abgaal, who predominated in the Mogadishu area by this time or the Ajuuraan dynasty, whose sultan was to be established in the Lower Shabelle valley a few centuries later.[3]

The people of this region were independent for many centuries. Their lifestyle was nomadic and were semi-settled. They traded, farmed and reared animals and practiced shifting cultivation since meat, milk and agricultural produce were and still are very essential for their staple food. The Somali tribes were headed by chiefs (or *Malaaq*). *Islaw* is the title given to persons for their courage in rescuing their companions during war. This is inherited by all patrilinear descendants originating from the first *Islaw*. They all will be called "*Islaws*." as it is a title for a tribe leader and for a noble person.

An *Islaw* will have a major responsibility in the community. The eldest carries the responsibility of each leading *Islaw*. The rest of the males in the family will be *Islaws* of a lower status and will have less or even no responsibility. Every *Islaw*, whether a leader or not, is expected to behave in a dignified manner in public. Other titles include *Ugaas, Sheikh* or religious members of the community, the *Imam* and sometimes Sultans are also known as leaders for a variety of neighboring tribal communities in Somalia. Although this relatively hierarchical social structure was highly respected among the Somali natives of these regions, people, at the same time, had the freedom to state their views and were listened to with respect. Decisions were reached in a democratic way because rulers were not able to impose orders on their Somali followers without their consent. The leader could suggest his concern to the people. Somali customary laws (*heer* or *xeer*) guided all societal relations. The *Heer* were a mixture of religious and societal norms which people established in their gatherings, like "blood compensation"[4] for minor injuries or death and related incidents.

The values in cash or in kind were set up to compensate for death or other crimes according to the Islamic law. The amount varied among the different tribes. The most important factors considered were the manner of the presentation according to the norms of the society and the four *Fataha (afar Fataxa)*. These two factors were more important than any material value. The final consideration was the material value of compensation. Marriage dowries were dealt with in a similar fashion. The *Fataha* was recited after each agreement by everybody attending the meeting. Nothing was recorded in writing but each and every time the parties recalled how a previous problem was resolved and how incidents of a similar nature were dealt with in the past. This *Heer* or *Tastuur* was applied consistently under all governing systems in the history of southern Somalia. While the different governing systems had their specific laws to maintain law and order, they placed emphasis on the Somali *Heer*. The *Heer* was frequently exercised by Somalis, for instance during the Omani rule of the pre-colonial times, as well as during the Italian occupation of Somalia. The Somali *Tastuur* or *Heer* was considered in the following manner during the Italian colonial period:

> To protect the traditional rights and power of the chiefs, the Italian administration recognized as valid not only the Muslim Shari'a but also Somali customary law (*tastuur*) which occasionally differed from Muslim practice outside Somalia. The sole restriction on this general practice was the requirement that the native law administration by the Cadis be compatible with the fundamental principles of Italian law".[5]

Immigrants who belonged to tribes from other regions were required to obey the rules of the natives of southern Somalia. Since they were fewer in number they were considered as members of a subclan. In order to maintain security and survival, the host tribe was responsible for assisting them in settling in the country and in starting agriculture, as well as protecting their interests. New members were also expected to participate in the required communal duties. This type of assistance and facilitation for integration is practised in southern Somalia, the riverine and the inter-riverine areas. The outsider who integrates into the community is given free land for home building and a rented piece of farm land. This rented land is called *Doon fuul* and may be used within the community but not owned. The outsiders, regardless of their tribes and origin, were protected in the same way as natives of the community. In contrast, the Europeans who came to this region of Somalia, and particularly the Benadir ports, experienced hostility throughout the 19th century. The Somalis were attacking anyone who landed on the coast.

An example would be the war between the Italians and the Biamaal tribe. For example, the war between the Wa'adaan and the Italians at Lafoole, which resulted in the killing of Antonio Cecchi, an Italian explorer, on 26 November 1896. In 1924, the Italian governor ordered the disarming of the Somali tribes of the Upper Webi Shabelle region. Most of the Somali leaders accepted the order but Sheikh Hassan Haji of the Gaaljeel (Gaaljecel) replied:

> I do not accept your order. We will not come to you at any cost because you have broken our pact. All our slaves escaped and you set them free. We are not happy with the antislavery order. We abandoned our law, for according to our law we can put slaves into prison and force them to work...
>
> The government has its law and we have our laws. We accept no law other than our own. Our law is that of God and his Prophet. We are not like other people; you have not seen any of our people enrol in Zaptie' (Sabddio)[6]. Not one...
>
> If you come to our land to make war, we will fight you in every way, just like we fought the Dervishes. God has said: The few can defeat the many. The World is near its end; only 58 years remain.....We do not want to stay in this world; it is better to die following the Muslim law. All Muslims are one.[7]

The struggle continued through the years. Rebellions against the Italian colonialists erupted, depending on the evolution of Somalia as a nation. In the mid-19th century, Chief Hassan Geddii Abtow, heading the three Mataan Abdulle of the Abgaal tribe, was asked to take a census on his tribe and later to report the results to the Italian ruler in Mogadishu. When the time came for him to report, Chief Hassan brought with him three bags (about 50 kg each) of Wambo[8] seeds and told the Italian governor: "this is the census of the Mataan tribe as I asked each and every one of them to put one Wambo seed into the sack". This was an act of resistance to the Italian occupation. There were many examples of resistance to the domination of the riverine and inter-riverine region such as those of Nasiib Buunde, Abdullahi Isse, and others. Women were also part of this resistance. Several of the most notable were: Hassanai Owbakar (Hassnai Bandiiro), Gura Bilaal, Fay Jeelle and Timiro Ukaash (Cukaash).

On 1 July 1960, Italian Somaliland became independent and united with British Somaliland, forming the Republic of Somalia. This independence was the fruit of the struggle made by several political parties against the Italian and British colonialists. These parties were different in their orientation which varied between tribal, regional and national interest. The first democratically elected head of state was President Adan Abdulle Osman. The second was President Abdirashid Ali Sharmaarke. The latter was killed in his homeland by an armed soldier.

At the beginning of the first Somali government formation, tribal representation was put into practice. Although it was not balanced, the cabinet was made up of four Daroods, three Hawiye, two Isaaqs and three Digil. Many tribes were unaware of the value of participating in the government and did not foresee how decisions made in the parliament would affect their interests. All tribes were enjoying an old fashion liberty and independence. They were landlords, many thought that their local tribal authorities were strong enough to protect them from any outside influence. Such independence did not last long.

The nature of the government representatives was based on tribal origins. Each representative was only working toward his tribe's interest. Some nationalists surely lost the game, but the challenge was still there to reach decisions with majority concerns. So, many Somalis boycotted, rather than accept such unbalanced government.

In 1969, the last parliamentary election occurred in an illegal way, as some of those who were announced as winners were dismissed and substituted by others who were not. An example of this is former MP *Islaw* Isman Nur, who was from the SYL party and the last Minister of Finance, Sufi Omar Karani, who was from the "*Xisbiyo.*" Both were from the Afgoi district. Such actions and many of a similar nature created mistrust and confusion in the Somali nation. As a result, President Sharmaarke was killed on 15 October 1969, during a tour of northwest Somalia. In 1969, the indigenous people of southern Somalia were still in full control of their own property -- in particular the landlords and native tribal local authority systems were still independent, as their rights were practically untouched or were still recognized. On 21 October 1969, the military assumed power as General Salaad Gabeyre was officially named the "Father of the Revolution," and later General Mohamed Siyad Barre became head of the Revolutionary Supreme Council. In 1972, three officers were executed: General Salad Gabeyre Kediye, General Mohamed Aynaanshe and Colonel Abdulqadir Dheel, the last having been out of the military and government circle for some time before his execution.

Many others were put in jail and freedom of speech and the press suspended. Many National Security Services staff of especially favoured tribes were recruited to carry out specific tasks which imposed unaccustomed humiliation and widespread oppression and human rights abuses on the people.

Afkaga hayso ama Afgooye Aad.[10] This expression which means 'keep your mouth shut or go to Afgooye' became a warning to many Somalis after the former MP Faarah Golaley expressed it. Afgooye, at that time, was the town where all the cabinet ministers and members of parliament of President Sharmarke's government were jailed. This regime taught many Somalis that nobody had the right to comment or criticize whatever actions and policies the Barre regime applied or invented, no matter how harmful it was to the nation.

II. The Siyad Regime and Oppression of Southern Somalia

Some of the major oppressive measures of Barre's regime were imposed on the riverine and inter-riverine regions of southern Somalia and in particular, the farmers and farming land. An example of these oppressive measures was the price fixation policy for all grain produced in these regions. This policy led to the formation of the grain marketing board. The board was supposed to act as a price regulatory measure in order to protect farmers and consumers from middlemen. At high market price, the grain marketing board was supposed to put more grain on the market by selling its buffer stocks and at low market prices, the board was supposed to buy grain from the market until the market price stabilized.

But instead, the marketing board worked against the farmers and the consumers by escalating prices, and nothing became stable at market level as the farmer became the main sufferer. All grain had to be brought to the Agricultural Development Agency (ADC), the agent assigned to collect all produce. Any farmer who did not bring his produce to ADC was punished and later fined. It was forbidden for the farmer to store even one sack of grain for his own consumption. The price received by the farmer from the ADC was only seventy shillings per quintal of grain (So. Sh. 70/quintal), whereas the farmer had to buy grain from the market at two hundred and fifty shillings per quintal (So. Sh. 250/quintal). To discourage the native traditional farmer, the government started to import bad quality (in respect of the consumers taste) maize (*galey jalaleey*) at one hundred and fifty Somali shillings per quintal (So. Sh. 150/quintal). The price to the local farmer remained only So.Sh. 70/quintal. At the same time, the price of all other products increased sharply. As a consequence, many dryland farmers were unable to continue farming and left their land in order to earn alternative income for survival, while those with irrigated plots changed over to cash crops, such as vegetables or melons as these crops were not under government control.

In 1975, the land reform legislation (Law no. 73) was decreed. This act was aimed specifically at the farmland of southern Somalia and did not give consideration to the indigenous system of land owning. Further, the people were not consulted and their right to own land was not considered. This legislation placed all land under state ownership. Individual plots were limited to 30 hectares if the farm was rainfed, and 60 hectares if it was irrigated which meant landowners would lose their land if they owned more then what the law allowed. Many farmers were unsuccessful in registering their property because of the bribes, corruption, and clanism. Those who survived paid huge bribes and gave up part of their land and most probably gave up other important assets, and later became victims who were earmarked to pay continuous bribes.

Some of the details follow:

> The largest round of land alienation occurred in the 1980s, using the
> provision of the 1975 land reform as a pretext. This "land looting"
> was more comprehensive and far -reaching than any that had gone
> before; it reached even the most inaccessible areas along the two
> rivers. Again, land was acquired by a mixture of purchase, bribery,
> threat and outright violent seizure.[11]

Many of the indigenous farmers did not understand what the
legislation was about, and those who understood thought it was a means
to loot their land but had nowhere to seek help. Before this legislation,
all land was owned by a tribe or clan, and individual tribe members
inherited farmland, the heritage being passed from generation to
generation -- sometimes for as long as 1,000 years. It is apparent that
such legislation was regressive, since it did not consider the pre-existing
systems of land ownership in the region or the rights of the indigenous
people. Similar laws were also applied to urban land. Almost all
agricultural land was handed over to newcomers who had not previously
owned land and who replaced the original farmers, especially the small
farmers.

An example of this was the Crash Program and the *Waaya-arag* who
were exclusively soldiers recruited outside the farming region and placed
in the agricultural area, even though they were government soldiers. The
aim was to make them adopt the farming system and convert them to
farmers. At first, the land was taken for public purposes, as the original
owners were removed and left landless without any compensation -- such
as new skills training, cash compensation or job creation programs. So
many farmers left agriculture without the knowledge of how to survive
outside the farming environment. Many of these people became poorer
and worked as labourers for those who looted their land. Others left the
area and moved to cities, where they formed ghettoes. Examples of these
looted farms are found along the Shabelle river such as the Ilanley
(Cilaanley) and(Abti Rabe farms, now known as the Tobacco Farm
Project. Other farms taken include: Jail Farm *(Beerta ciidanka asluubta)*
and the Mareerey aw Hassan Community farms, known as Afgoi-Mordile
project or (LIBSOMA).

There are many other areas along the Shabelle (like Kurtunwarey and

Sablaale of the Settlement Development Agency). Farms looted along the Jubba river include the Mugambo Irrigation Project, Fanoole Rice Farm, and Jubba Sugar Project. In the process, thousands of farmers lost their land. These farms were taken as state farms. Later the beneficiaries were non-indigenous government officers or urban people who had no experience in agriculture. Besides land confiscation for state farms, there was the farmland enquiry rush in the Ministry of Agriculture. Many government ministers, high military officials, government civil servants were sent to districts and towns to look for a farm space. Farmland was registered for the new applicants, regardless of whether it was in production or not -- many farms which were under full production were registered to new applicants and their original owners kicked out. These incidents became common in the riverine area.

The so-called new farmers had access to bank loans and all subsidies on imported agricultural machinery, vehicles for agricultural use, all agricultural inputs (seeds, fertilizers and fuel) etc. However, these credits and imported agricultural subsidized goods were not used for agricultural purposes. Instead, most of it went to commercial or other sectors of the economy. Little land was reclaimed, the rest was abandoned and left without cultivation. The indigenous people were prohibited from using the land for their own production. Meanwhile, the original owners were settled in the villages beside their looted farms and were watching helplessly, as the government system was hostile to the indigenous farmers. The actions mentioned above were reported thus:

> Taking advantage of new land registration laws and seeking to profit from the rising value of riverine land,(especially due to expectations that the Bardhere Dam Project upriver would bring the entire region into intensive development, speculators claimed thousands of hectare of land traditionally farmed by riverine villages, transforming many smallholder farmers into landless rural wage-labourers or share-croppers.[12]

Italian colonialists exploited this region; however, it did not seem to matter whether or not the colonists were from the same culture as the natives. This same issue was discussed in another paper:

> Some of the largest instances of land looting were on government

projects, such as the huge irrigated sugar and rice farms of the lower Juba. In theory, compensation was paid; in practice, it did not reach the farmers who had lost their land.[13]

The Middle and Lower Shabelle regions shared this importance with the Jubba valley region of Somalia, but the Shabelle farmland was more accessible and closer to Mogadishu than the Jubba land. It became also a target for government officials, civil servants, and all of Barre's family and relatives, as well as his favourite tribesmen, whom he brought from Geddo, Ethiopia, and the central regions of Somalia to protect his power. He offered them good government positions, free land, power and huge wealth that they never earned. Further, they did not use it in economic ways, wasting most of it on luxurious travelling to Europe and North America. After looting and exhausting the Shabelle land, they moved farther south to the Jubba valley. The Ministry of Agriculture facilitated and legalized the land looting process through the Department of Land and Water. It issued ownership documents on the basis of political recommendation, tribal recognition, and power considerations. The Ministry neglected the indigenous owners of land, even though many had inherited it over several generations before Siyad Barre came to power. In the eyes of the people, possession of an ownership document from the Ministry of Agriculture did not translate into true ownership. Even though the indigenous owners had no formal documents, their oral traditions and the lore of the villages and towns had "recorded" the "real" background and property deeds of their fellow *paiezano*.[14]

In 1988, the government escalated its campaign of asset confiscation and began to plumb the region's productive potential to enrich its supporters. The state strategy included "loans" for agriculture, fishing boats, and even building tourist hotels. The Mareehan were able to acquire land from the state , who "owned" the land, especially that rented by Gosha (Bantus) or from merchants.[15]

This is but a brief overview of the plight of the forgotten Somali farmers of the riverine and inter-riverine regions.

Endnotes

1. D. Laitin and S. Samatar. *Somalia: Nation in Search of State*. Boulder, CO: Westview Press, 1987.

2. D. Laitin and S. Samatar. *Somalia: Nation in Search of State*. pg. 15.

3. *Ibid.*

4. This is the value in kind or cash payed to compensate for criminal acts, in particular, bloodshed, injuries or death which occurred between tribes, subclans, or families of the same clan.

5. Robert L. Hess. *Italian Colonialism in Somalia*. pg. 109.

6. *Sabddio* was a Somalized term for Zeptie referring to the Italian soldiers who were ethnic Somalis.

7. Robert L. Hess. *Italian Colonialism in Somalia*. pg. 151.

8. *Wambo* is commonly grown and used for eating only by the Abgaal tribe during war times or drought. The size of this cereal seed is very small and approximately equal to one fifth of a sorghum seed.

9. *Xisbiyo* was the Hisb Dastur Al Mustaqbal.

10. An expression used by Mr. Faarah Gololey.

11. *Land Tenure, the Creation of Famine, and Prospects for Peace in Somalia*. Discussion Paper No. 1. October 1993 African Rights.

12. *Report on An Emergency Needs Assessment of lower Jubba Region (Kismayo, Jamame, and Jilib Districts), Somalia*. Submitted to World Concern. By Kenneth Menkhaus, 1991.

13. See African Rights, Discussion Paper No. 1, October 1993 Page 5, Para 3.

14. Paiezano is an Italian word which means people from the same town or village.

15. See page 11 in *The Gun Talks Louder than the Voice: Somalis Continuing Cycle of Violence,* by John Prendergast, Center of Concern; July 1994.

SECTION FOUR

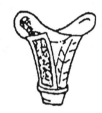

Political and Economic Analyses and Strategies

Summaries: Section Four

Mohamud A. Jama (Chapter 15) charts the political history of the Somali state, noting the particular impacts of the multiple colonial masters. The horrendous toll of the Siyad dictatorship, writes Jama, was simply one more chapter in the exploitation of the Somali people. He sees that the most likely solution to Somali society's present impasse is some form of external initiative, working closely with all the local leaders, He notes that an effort by the Government of Djibouti showed promise but did not have appropriate follow-through mechanisms or money in place and therefore floundered. A combination of a local initiative with strong international agency backing might provide the right combination to reach a settlement.

Ahmed Ashkir Botan (Chapter 16) suggests that the current structure of clans and alliances in place in the post-Siyad years "has nothing to do with traditional Somali tribalism." He states that the traditional clan structure held two fundamental tenets: collaborative security and individual identification,. He sees the present use of clan autonomy as a perversion of the clan's original purpose. He calls for a restructuring of a national government which will have formal and systematic modes of decentralized, federal type decision-making, yet not one that simply allows a clan to rule a region. He concludes, spelling out the conditions and possible terms within which such decentralization could allow for meaningful participation by all interested parties.

Jamshid Damooei (Chapter 17) analyzes the economic situation of the post-civil war years. He notes that the previous backbone of the economy was agriculture and livestock. Excessive interference in these sectors by state controlled agencies and politically powerful individuals disrupted the economy and was one of the factors leading to the political crisis of the 1980s. He closes with a number of specific recommendations aimed at rebuilding economic capacity, creating a climate conducive to economic stability, sectoral rehabilitation, and financial planning.

CHAPTER FIFTEEN

The Destruction of the Somali State: Causes, Costs and Lessons

Mohamud A. Jama

I. Introduction and Proposed Framework for International Mediation

In January, 1991, Somalia's autocratic ruler, General Siyad Barre was toppled in a month-long insurrection in the capital. In 10 of his 21 year rule, Somalia had been in the midst of an increasingly bloody civil war. Over the last three years, the civil strife expanded from its core in the north to the central areas of the country and then leap-frogged to the deep south to culminate in a crescendo of battles in the capital.

The armed resistance movements opposing Siyad Barre's regime comprised three groups: the Somali National Movement (SNM) with broad following in Northern Somalia (Former British Somaliland); the United Somali Congress (USC) and the Somali Patriotic Movement (SPM) in Southern Somalia (Former Italian Somalia). In September 1990, the three movements agreed on a coordinated military strategy and, in principle, to form a coalition government after the fall of the regime.

On January 27, 1991, three days after storming the presidential palace, a faction of the southern-based United Somali Congress announced the appointment of its leader as an Acting President and the formation of an interim government consisting of a Prime Minister and a 26 member cabinet. The other two resistance movements and a faction of the United Somali Congress, including its chairman, quickly rejected the appointment of the Acting President and the legitimacy of the interim government.

By mid-February 1991, the SNM quickly expanded from its rural strongholds in the northern provinces and gained control over most areas of the north. On February 27, the SNM convened a Preparatory Conference of Northern provincial representatives. The Preparatory Conference was followed by a six-week, broad-based consultative conference of provincial leadership groups. The conference proclaimed the return of Northern provinces to the independent juridical status of June 1960 and the reestablishment of a sovereign "Republic of Somaliland" in the north.

All efforts to reconcile the rival factions of the USC or to negotiate an agreement between the interim government, and the other two resistance movements failed. In the last such effort, in July, 1991, the interim government convened a National Reconciliation Conference hosted by the Government of Djibouti. While some representative of the anti-USC factions participated in the conference, the northern-based Somali National Movement refused to attend. The conference endorsed the leadership of the interim government which, in return, agreed to a distribution of the major offices of the government among the participating factions. In September, 1991, the interim government announced the establishment of an 83 member cabinet. The reappointment of the Prime Minister and the composition of the new cabinet intensified dissent within the USC but also prompted most of the participants in the Djibouti Conference, with ties to the anti-USC southern alliance, to denounce publicly the interim government.

Although there is broad sympathy for the USC among the constituency of the SNM, some of the other Northern provincial factions allied with the SNM are either hostile to the USC or more sympathetic to a looser form of association between the north and south than are most supporters of the SNM. The fragility of the security in the north, as a result of the destruction of the infrastructure and economic hardship, continues to inhibit the northern leadership and puts at risk the compromises negotiated at the Consultative Conference of provincial delegates.

Almost a year after the collapse of the Barre regime, civil strife continues, adding to Somalia's tragedies of the past ten years. Past efforts to mediate reconciliation failed because these efforts focused on finding limited interim solutions and were seen as an attempt by the interim government to seek international endorsement and use that endorsement as a basis of gaining domestic legitimacy and advantage over other parties. The success of the interim government in gaining endorsements for its political strategy from the Organization of African Unity, the League of Arab and the Islamic Conference reaffirmed these anxieties. In contrast, the United Nations limited pronouncements to appeals for humanitarian assistance and is therefore the most acceptable mediator.

This paper briefly describes the historical background of the Somali state, assesses the human cost of two decades of autocratic rule and its legacy, and concludes with a summary of the lessons to be learned from Somalia's experiment with political integration and autocratic rule. These lessons are suggested as guiding principles in the search for a political solution to the civil strife.

II. An Overview of the Contemporary History of Somalia

Pre-independence, pan-Somali national movements were formed to reverse seven decades of colonial rule and partition into three separate colonial territories and parts of two others. The colonization of Somali territories and partition into British, Italian and French was both competitive and collaborative and continued up to the decade after the Second World War. In the only colonial effort to form Greater Somalia, Britain sought to unify the Somali territories it occupied during the war -- southern Somalia and the Ogaden in Ethiopia -- with the Somali territories under its rule - northern Somalia and Somali-inhabited districts in northeastern Kenya. Having failed in this effort, Britain agreed, in 1948, to return southern Somalia to Italy, under United Nations Trusteeship, but retained Somali-inhabited areas in Kenya as part of its East Africa territories. In successive moves in 1948 and 1954, Britain similarly completed the divestiture of areas which it retained from Ethiopia after restoring that country's Emperor to power. In so doing, Britain restored the prewar-war colonial partition of Somali-inhabited territories. In contrast, the French sought to minimize the Somali character of its enclave, French Somaliland, which it renamed French territory of Afar and Issa. After independence in 1976, the Territory was again renamed the Djibouti Republic .

A. Pan-Somali Nationalism and the State: 1945-1969

The contemporary Somali state was formed on 1 July 1960, following the independence and unification of the British and Italian Somali territories. The Act of Union, agreed to by the respective parliaments of the two newly independent states, affirmed the political aspirations of the pan-Somali national movements. These movements, formed during the two decades following the end of the Second World War, were driven and inspired by the succession of territorial changes, in which every major Somali clan found itself divided among two or more colonial territories. In 1943, the Somali Youth League was formed in the southern territories. In the British-administered northern areas, opposition to territorial changes culminated in the establishment of the Somali National League in 1948 and the National United Front in 1954, on the eve of the final transfer of some of the British Somaliland's rangelands to Ethiopia. The nationalist movements first sought the reintegration of territories ceded from the British and Italian territories, but later expanded their demands to independence and unification.

The Somali state from its inception in 1960, as an independent state, pursued the return of ceded territories as its principal objective. The successive civilian governments of the 1980s supported pan-Somali nationalist movements in Ethiopia, Kenya and Djibouti. Periodic clashes between the security forces of these states and their largely nomadic, Somali populations, especially in Ethiopia and Kenya, kept the political passions in Somalia at a high level, encouraging successive governments to seek a strong military capability to back its territorial claims.

Despite the broad support to pan-Somali nationalism, political parties of the new state degenerated into regionally-based electoral factions which were dissolved after elections only to mushroom in larger numbers in Somalia's clan-driven competitive multi-party democratic system of the 1960's. In the last free elections held in March, 1969, over 80 such factions contested the elections in which about half of the incumbents were defeated.

B. The Military Regime: Strategies of Governance and Repression

On October 21, 1969, a military junta of 24 military officers, led by General Mohamed Siyad Barre, staged a *coup d'etat* and formed a military government under a Supreme Revolutionary Council (SRC). In its first declaration, the SRC claimed it acted to end corruption and tribalism and promised an early return to civilian rule through fair and free elections. A year later, during the first anniversary of the coup, the SRC proclaimed the adoption of Marxist-Leninist ideology and, in 1974, signed a treaty of friendship and cooperation with the Soviet Union. During the 1970's, the Soviet Union expanded its military assistance, started in the 1960's, and helped Somalia develop the largest mechanized military force in Subsaharan Africa.

In 1976, General Siyad Barre formed a Soviet-style single party, the

Somali Revolutionary Socialist Party (SRSP) and assumed the title of General Secretary and Chairman of the Politburo of the party. In 1979, he introduced a draft constitution which institutionalized both the junta's apparatus and practices and the SRSP as the only legitimate party. The draft constitution was approved in a referendum in which Siyad Barre's government claimed to have received more than 99 percent approval rate of the electorate. This was followed by elections to a national assembly, whose members were nominated by the politburo, approved by the central committee of the party and elected as a single list of uncontested candidates. The Assembly, in turn, elected General Siyad Barre as President. This process was repeated every four years.

This controlled process of self-legitimization coupled with an expanding second tier political leadership and progressively intrusive intelligence and internal security services throughout the 21 years of General Siyad Barre's rule was to define both the character of the regime and opposition to it. Perception of dissent from the regime's authoritarian policy prescriptions led to periodic purges of officials. The mildest expression of disaffection also led to detention. All of these tendencies were to lead to Barre's reliance on a clan-based Praetorian guard and a network of advisors and managers whose corruption and mismanagement were condoned as a reward, in return for their continuing loyalty.

C. Opposition to the Siyad Barre Regime

By the end of the 1970's, political attitudes had become polarized, setting the stage for both opposition to the regime and its survival strategies. In the first serious challenge to the regime, a group of army officers organized an abortive *coup d'etat* in April, 1978, a month after the end of the Somali-Ethiopia Ogaden war. In 1979, some of the leaders of the coup who escaped, and their supporters formed the Somali Salvation Democratic Front (SSDF), the first of four clan-based opposition groups in Ethiopia. Despite its clan base, this group attracted many left-wing activists of the Barre regime who opposed the war with Ethiopia and Siyad Barre's reversal of Somalia's alliance with the Soviet Union. The SSDF further received considerable military and financial support from Libya and the then left-wing regime of South Yemen, both of whom supported Ethiopia during the Somali-Ethiopian war. In 1982, the SSDF mounted an Ethiopian-backed attack in the central provinces of Somalia which the Barre regime successfully used to portray itself as threatened by pro-Soviet forces.

By the mid-1980's, the SSDF was caught in the growing rift between Ethiopia and Libya. Its military style leadership and close association with left-wing regimes also reduced the willingness of other opponents of the regime to support the SSDF. All of these developments intensified conflict between the clan-based military leadership and the left wing faction of the SSDF. In 1985, three key left-wing leaders were assassinated and the Ethiopian security forces arrested most of the other faction, including the leader of the SSDF.

During 1979-1981, northern opponents of the regime organized a network of highly decentralized committees inside the country and among northern exile communities. These committees were formally constituted, in April 1981, as the Somali National Movement (SNM). The SNM quickly developed as the organizational framework for the pervasive northern disaffection with the Barre government. In 1982, after riots and sustained anti-government demonstrations in the principal northern cities, many northern army officers and some of the internal activists escaped across the border to Ethiopia and started to organize armed militias among the northern nomadic population which straddle the Somali-Ethiopian border. The Executive Committee of the SNM similarly moved its political headquarters to Ethiopia while most of the leadership of the north were arrested or escaped to join the leadership of the SNM. These developments were to shift the center of northern opposition to Somali-inhabited areas in Ethiopia. Throughout the 1980's, the SNM operated from camps in these areas and became the principal opposition to the regime.

From 1982 to 1988, the SNM fought a cross-border war with the regime's security forces. The Government responded with curfews and economic sanctions against northern cities and reprisal attacks on border villages and across the border in Ethiopia. By early 1988, both the Barre and the Mengistu regimes were confronted with desperate military situations and growing internal political upheavals. To stave the collapse of their regimes, the two leaders met in Djibouti and agreed to end their support to their respective domestic opponents. The agreement allowed the Mengistu regime to shift its forces on the Somali border to northern Ethiopia and Siyad Barre to return from Djibouti to the north to demand from the local leadership an end to SNM activities or face destruction.

A month after the formal signing of the Somali-Ethiopian agreement, the Ethiopian security forces asked the Somali National Movement to suspend its operational base in Ethiopia. In May, 1988, the SNM launched an all-out desperate attack against the regime's forces in the two principal cities in the north. The attack triggered uprisings in most of the northern provinces. By some estimates, about 50,000 northern civilians were killed. After three months in which most of the two cities were destroyed and the urban population sought asylum in Ethiopia or in their traditional rural homelands, the security forces regained control of the cities but abandoned the countryside to the Somali National Movement.

Over the two years following the May, 1988 upheavals in the north, civil unrest and opposition to Siyad Barre's regime escalated in the south. By early 1989, two new southern-based opposition groups were formed. In July, 1989, Somalia's capital, Mogadishu, saw three days of demonstrations. These demonstrations and the summary executions of several hundred civilians triggered an end to most international support and assistance which had helped sustain the regime. Alarmed by these developments, the regime freed most of the political prisoners and encouraged external mediation efforts between it and the opposition, which the principal armed opposition groups dismissed as a scheme to regain international assistance.

III. The Costs of Dictatorship

A. The Human Cost

After 21 years in power, Siyad Barre's regime came to an end, but left behind destruction, retribution and upheaval. About a million of Somalia's seven million people are languishing in remote villages or desolate refugee camps in Ethiopia, Djibouti and Kenya. About half of these are new refugees, whose numbers continue to grow as a result of the continuing civil strife among rival factions in the southern provinces.

Electricity, water supply and telephones ceased to operate everywhere in the country and have yet to be restored. In the capital city, these hardship coupled with lootings, armed robberies and now the violent clashes between rival factions of the United Somali Congress have disrupted the sporadic deliveries of humanitarian assistance on which most of the population have become dependent. Mogadishu, a once-peaceful, sprawling coastal capital city has disintegrated into feuding rival villages, caught in a cycle of factional raids, counter-raids and reprisals, and atavistic inter-communal violence.

In provinces north and south of Mogadishu, a similar process of strife and destitution is underway. Most of the civilian population have retreated to provincial towns and villages in traditional homelands, creating temporary concentrations of the displaced and destitute in areas without basic infrastructure or access to services. These concentrations of displaced people, victims of civil strife, also fuel the continuing cycle of violence. In order to gain protection, communities of internally displaced people organize or provide recruits and support to tribal militias. These forces in turn have become the nucleus of clan-based factions and have transformed most of the countryside into battle grounds. In parts of the south, the relatively more organized and better armed anti-USC subclans prey on the weaker ones, in some instance to the point of genocide.

In the northern provinces, more than a million impoverished and destitute people have returned to cities in ruins which had been systematically looted, dismantled, and then heavily mined. Most of these people are returning from villages and rural areas, which were for a decade targets of Barre's brutal and bloody rural counter-insurgency. Others are coming back from refugee camps in Ethiopia or from the southern provinces, to which they migrated decades ago, having left behind most of their assets and in most instances robbed of their last belongings in their arduous journey to the north. The rest of the civilian population in the north, approximately two million people are in villages and impoverished rural communities or in provincial towns, where all of the basic services collapsed or never existed.

B. The Political Cost

The Dissolution of the State

Almost a year after the overthrow of the Barre regime, Somalia remains not only in ruins but ungovernable as well. Both are legacies of two decades of dictatorship. From the start, the appointment of an Acting President and the composition of the government he formed was seen as a power grab by the Mogadishu faction of the USC leadership. The other factions of the USC leadership objected to the appointment of the Acting President without consulting the other two resistance movements. Most of the southern anti-USC groups rejected the legitimacy of the interim government. The SNM similarly dismissed the authority of the USC to appoint either an Acting President or form a government and proceeded to consolidate its control in the north. Later, the interim government sought to accommodate its critics and opponents by calling for a national conference in Mogadishu to appoint a transitional government. This was also declined by the SNM and all other southern factions opposed to the interim government.

With the failure of their efforts to agree on a common strategy, the two rival leadership factions of the USC pursued competing strategies. The interim government intensified its contacts with exile groups, allied with anti-USC forces, and relaunched its reconciliation conference. Some of the exile groups attended the conference, held in Djibouti during April, 1991. While the conference did not lead to a political reconciliation, the participants agreed to attend a second conference in Djibouti a month later. During the April conference in Djibouti, the USC faction opposed to the interim government sent its forces to occupy Kismayo, which was until then the center and stronghold of anti-USC forces in the south, including remnants of the forces of the former regime. The USC forces, under the command of the USC Chairman and the principal opponent of the interim government within the USC, regained control of Kismayo.

These parallel efforts of the two USC factions in Mogadishu have had mixed results. The initial success of the USC military campaign enhanced USC's claim as the dominant post-Siyad force in the south. The campaign also weakened the credibility of the leadership factions of the anti-USC forces who participated in the first national reconciliation conference in Djibouti. The Djibouti Accord sponsored by the interim government, on the other hand, set the stage for renewed conflict among the USC factions. The ensuing factional strife sealed the fate of the interim government but also increased northern resolve to chart its own course and the anti-USC southern alliance to maximize its political goals, thereby creating the conditions for a continuing political stalemate and the dissolution of the state.

A Legacy of Factionalism

The current factions in Somalia's political landscapes are rooted in Siyad's strategies of selective but alternating repression of different clans and subclans. The interplay of strategies of repression and responses produced differentiated provincial patterns of support to different leadership groups. These were the source of cleavages among the regime opponents, and have now become the source of the post-Siyad civil strife.

The USC and anti-USC factions in the south and the SNM in the north illustrate this legacy. In the south, two rival alliances of provincial factions are locked in a continuing civil strife. The USC militias who assumed power in the capital are organized and led along provincial (subclan) constituencies. Its leadership comprises three factions that competed for influence, even prior to the January, 1991 insurrection: a Rome-based group, which organized the first committee of the USC; an Ethiopia-based group, which established the armed wing of the USC and advocated collaboration with other armed resistance movements; and the Mogadishu group, which competed with both factions and advocated national dialogue among themselves, the regime and armed insurgencies. These initial differences in orientation have reemerged and reinforced competition along provincial subclan leadership factions, with the leadership of the Ethiopia-based group opposing the interim government formed by the Mogadishu faction. The Rome group competes with both while mediating between the two factions during violent clashes.

Five other groups, allied or opposed to the USC, operate in the southern region. The leadership of one of them, the Somali Democratic Movement (SDM), did not significantly participate in opposing the former regime, but has cooperated with the USC since the collapse of Barre regime. Its constituency, the most sedentary among Somalia's communities, was often a target of forceful conscription into the security forces of the former Barre regime. The constituency of the second faction, the Somali Democratic Union (SDU), supported the SNM before the latter's proclamation of the abrogation of the Act of the Union and now cooperates with the USC in the south. In recent months, the traditional settlement areas of the constituencies of both political factions have become targets of the anti-USC alliance, including militias loyal to Siyad Barre's.

The remaining three factions, nominally allied and, like the USC, organized along subclan provincial constituencies, cooperate in opposing the USC and others. While linked by kinship ties, the three factions were formed under different domestic political circumstances in which their present leadership was divided over opposition and support to the former regime.

The Somali Salvation Democratic Front (SSDF), defunct since the mid-1980s, has been reactivated after the collapse of the Barre regime. Its current leadership include three different factions: former SSDF leaders who remained in exile, proponents of reform and dialogue with the former regime; and some former leaders of the Barre regime. The SSDF forces and supporters encompass all of these elements. Some of its forces consist of units recruited by the Barre regime from former SSDF militias after it became defunct. The latter units, led by some of Siyad's most loyal commanders, including his son-in-law, were especially active on behalf of the Barre regime both in the north during 1985-1990 and in the final battle for the control of the capital. Large segments of SSDF's current leadership and constituency in the central and the coastal areas in the Northeast did not support the SSDF during the early 1980s nor did these constituencies actively support the Barre regime. But during 1989-1991, militias from these areas became progressively engaged in regime-inspired bloody tribal feuds with militias and tribal constituencies of the USC. The inter-communal violence continued after the collapse of the regime.

The second anti-USC faction, the Somali Patriotic Movement (SPM), was formed as a result of dissension within the regime in early 1990. In January and February, 1990, two units, one in the north recruited from among the Somali refugees from the Ogaden province in Ethiopia and the other in the south, mutinied. It's southern faction, with principal support in parts of Kismayo province and from co-kinsmen in Kenya, remained isolated from its northern counterpart in the Ogaden. The northern, refugee-based wing had a loose alliance with the Ethiopian-based faction of the USC and the SNM. In the last days of the Barre regime, militias of the Mogadishu faction of the USC, which formed the interim government, attacked forces of the northern wing of the SPM outside the capital. The leadership of both factions of the SPM regrouped in the south after Siyad Barre's overthrow. The SPM is currently led by its southern wing which gets support from its kinsmen in Kenya.

The leadership of the refugee-based faction, with support among kinsmen in the Ogaden, has shifted its attention to participate in the political developments in the newly established Somali province in Ethiopia of which its constituency is part. Ironically, the Ethiopian action may have helped create opportunities for cooperation among the very clan constituencies on opposing sides of the civil war in Somalia. The most immediate impact of this reconciliation, if it materializes, is likely to be in northern Somalia, where a sizable proportion of its population and about 300,000 northern refugees straddle both sides of the Somali-Ethiopia border. The third anti-USC faction in the south is the Somali National Front (SNF), formed by an alliance of Siyad's critics within his subclan. The SNF leadership seeks to prevent its anti-USC allies from entering into a pact with the USC, at its expense. It is led by two former Generals from Siyad Barre's subclan who are opposed to any future role for the Barre family. The SNF, while distancing itself from the Barre family, must also find accommodation with his loyalists. Siyad Barre is, however, unwilling to leave the leadership to his former critics within the subclan.

While organized as a network of kinship-based provincial communities, each of the anti-USC factions pursued variations on a dual strategy: first, of maximizing cleavage within the USC by supporting the USC faction leading the interim government and second, opposing the USC to maintain its cohesion and cooperating militarily with commanders of Siyad's former forces while rejecting Siyad's return to power.

IV. Political Factions and Provincial Communities

Competition within the grand alliances is just as intense as that among the clan-based alliances. It fuels the internal conflict within the USC and competition among the anti-USC alliance and reflects the inability of the two southern alliance systems, the USC and the anti-USC, to develop formal organizational structures. Instead of a formal structure, both rely on *ad hoc* committees whose membership is unstable and which can be convened by any group of notables not accountable to any other body.

The search for reconciliation will require -- of both the USC and the anti-USC alliances -- an agreement on a decision-making structure, including procedures for consultation with traditional provincial (clan and subclan) leadership. An agreement on formal organizational structures and transparent decision-making procedures will not only enhance the credibility of the leadership of the two alliances but will also establish a framework for resolving internal disputes and negotiating, ratifying and implementing negotiated agreements among themselves and with their counterparts in the north.

The political factions illustrate the dual leadership functions of Somalia's clan system: of producing a relatively traditional provincial leadership with a grassroots following and an urban clan leadership without a stable constituency. Somalia's clan system can be used to facilitate inter-communal harmony or intensify conflict among urban leadership factions. Political consensus can therefore be only maintained through an alliance of urban leadership accountable to provincial constituencies.

The Somali National Movement developed an elaborate leadership structure combining these dual functions. This allowed it to develop political consensus and grassroots support. The key element in both types of leadership is its representativeness and proportionality. In early February 1991, the Executive Committee of the SNM invited leadership groups not represented in its decision-making structures to an All-Northern Preparatory Conference. The conference, attended by both leadership groups of all northern provinces/clans, agreed on a number of measures designed to consolidate peace. The conference also called for a broad-based leadership meeting of all northern communities to review, among other things, the North-South 1960 Act of Union.

The All-Northern Provincial Conference, convened at the end of April, 1991, recommended the expansion of the Central Committee of the Somali National Movement. The Committee expanded its membership, elected a President and a Vice-President and approved a broad-based 17-member cabinet incorporating all provincial northern communities.

One of the fundamental weaknesses of provincial-based leadership was its lack of a system of political accountability to broad-based constituencies. A second flaw was the lack of hierarchy in leadership among leaders representing parallel communities. Both intensify the factionalism and the vulnerability of leaders to rivals from their own constituencies.

V. Strategies for Promoting Peaceful Settlement

A. Issues and Challenges

The post-Siyad political stalemate has added to Somalia's humanitarian tragedy, thus creating the conditions for an escalating cycle of political violence and civil strife. In the southern half of the country, the civil war remained unabated. Tens of thousands of people have died in the last six months, as a result of the clashes among rival factions of the USC in Mogadishu, the capital, and between the USC and its opponents in the south.

The remnants of the Barre forces expelled from the northern provinces moved to the central provinces and established an alliance with other anti-USC forces in the south. This alliance of anti-USC forces also initiated a campaign of terror in the inter-riverine areas and rural areas on the Kenya-Somalia border areas, outside the control of the USC.

All of the civilian populations throughout the country face extreme hardship and destitution. None of the political factions can cope with the plight of the millions of destitute civilians. The current situation in Mogadishu is especially alarming, with nearly ten thousand people reportedly killed in the latest fighting among USC factions. In the north, food supplies to Somali refugee camps in eastern parts of Ethiopia have also been interrupted as security conditions worsened in areas around the camps. Another half million displaced nomadic population which sought safety across the border in Ethiopia are also affected by disruptions of food supplies in Somali-inhabited eastern province of Ethiopia. Both refugee and the internally displaced population in Ethiopia have started to return and are beginning to form encampments around the cities where the institutional and management infrastructure to cope with this large influx of destitute people is lacking. All of these factors create the conditions for large scale famine, which, without an organized humanitarian international response, can and may undermine the fragile peace achieved in the north.

A recent assessment of the United Nations Food and Agriculture Organization, conducted prior to the latest developments, estimated that nearly 4.5 million of Somalia's 7 million are at risk of starvation. But the report concluded that assistance cannot be organized unless the security situation improves. Without a political settlement, the security situation is unlikely to improve. Consequently, greater suffering and loss of life seem inevitable.

By December 1990, all foreign diplomatic missions had left the country. The United Nations humanitarian organizations were evacuated to Nairobi, Kenya. The absence of diplomatic missions and United Nations organizations leaves to a small number of nongovernmental organizations the difficult task of informing the international community and providing, as well as monitoring assistance to the millions of displaced victims of a bloody civil war. The ambiguous status of Somalia's sovereignty, in the light of the competing claims, now further severely limit the country's capacity to attract international assistance and, therefore, the access of the refugees and displaced civilians to humanitarian international assistance.

An end to the political stalemate and humanitarian tragedy requires active international participation in the search for a peaceful settlement. Only the Government of Djibouti formally attempted to assist the factions in achieving a political settlement. But this effort failed for three reasons: the SNM and other leadership groups of the northern provinces were preoccupied with their own reconciliation and did not participate in the conference. None of the southern delegates to the conferences had a credible mandate from their political faction, or from the provincial constituencies they were seeking to represent. Finally, the conferences produced neither a vision for the country as a whole nor a realistic political strategy of achieving reconciliation in the south. Instead, the agreement reached at the final meeting confirmed initial perceptions of the Djibouti Conference as an attempt by the leadership of the interim government to seek international endorsement and through this gain domestic legitimacy.

B. Framework for a United Nations Mediation

International mediation efforts, under the sponsorship of the United Nations, can succeed if structured:

1. to mediate an agreement between the northern and southern provinces on an interim arrangement to be the repository of Somali sovereignty, and;

2. to promote agreements on a coordinated but parallel transitional framework for a political settlement.

The principal obstacle to a United Nations mediation is the tendency of the international community to give quasi-legitimacy to any faction controlling Mogadishu, the capital. The linking of legitimacy to participation in an international mediation process can enhance United Nations efforts and serve as a catalyst for negotiated agreement on an interim arrangement to be the repository of Somali national sovereignty.

An agreement on an interim arrangement will facilitate Somalia's capacity to enter into a legitimate partnership with the United Nations and other international humanitarian efforts. It will, however, leave the future relations of the northern and southern provinces and the future structure of government within each, to the outcome of the parallel transition negotiated by the parties. A coordinated parallel transition to a democratic government in both the north and south will also allow each of the two parties to assume responsibility for internal political reconciliation and the rehabilitation of their economies and institutions.

To facilitate an agreement on a political settlement of the civil strife and political stalemate, member states of the United Nations are called upon:

1. to reaffirm the right of the Somali people to freely determine and decide on a framework for a durable solution to the civil and political strife;

2. to call on the leadership of the north and south in Somalia to enter into negotiations on a transitional framework for ending the civil strife and the consequent humanitarian tragedy.

3. to request the Secretary General to assist in negotiations among all the parties to the conflict and propose ways in which the United Nations and the international community can assist in monitoring the implementations of agreements on a political framework for transition, including assistance in the holding of free, fair and democratic elections.

4. To request the United Nations system and its specialized agencies to assist in the emergency rehabilitation and restoration of the basic infrastructure and services, to enable the Somali people to cope with all aspects of the humanitarian tragedy.

An international mediation initiative, if coupled with provisions for the United Nations to monitor the implementation of agreements among the parties, will help overcome the principal obstacle to negotiation, distrust among the factions, and elevate the discussions by shifting their focus away from factional rivalry to building broader alliances.

VI. Somalia's Political Experiments

A. Lessons Learned as Guiding Principles of a Settlement

Somalia needs a political vision. It deserves from its leaders and people, in the north and south, a commitment and a long-term program to restore peace and stability, instead of short-term strategies, designed to maximize factional advantages and clan appeal. The failure of the interim government reflects the futility of any factional effort to reproduce a clan-based leadership as a framework for national reconciliation. Such strategies foster intra-factional rivalry and violence.

The current intra-USC violence illustrates the vulnerability of other alliances to similar risks. An escalation of leadership rivalry within each of the two other alliances into violence will not only impede but derail the re-establishment of democratic representative institutions, which are the only viable long-term political solution to the civil strife.

In searching for a solution, the leadership groups must understand the lessons to be learned from the failure of Somalia's experiment with political integration and two decades of autocratic rule. Such an assessment can be a framework for selecting transitional strategies and determining the future relations of the north and the south and structure of the Somali state.

The principal lessons from three decades of independence include:

1. Political integration of the north and south failed. The Act of Union instituted a national assembly by combining the northern legislature of 33 representatives with a Southern Assembly of 90 representatives. These disparities, entrenched in the Act of Union, transformed the integration into a process of political incorporation. From the start, the southern provinces with 73% of the National Assembly and 60 percent of the population were able to dominate the political process and allocate for themselves both the Presidency, the Premiership and key cabinet posts. These disparities inherent in the 1960 Act of Union encouraged the neglect and dissolution of northern institutions and infrastructure.

2. Pan-Somali nationalism provided the impetus for the initial integration and the high valuation of a large military force, which inspired Somalia's external military alliance, first, with the Soviet Union and later, with the United States. Both proved conducive to dictatorship and instability.

3. Two decades of corrupt tribal autocracy destroyed the institutional foundation of the Somali state and weakened the broad appeal of the pan-Somali nationalism. The future stability and unity of Somalia will depend on the capacity and willingness of the current leadership groups to agree on and build the foundation of a new and more pragmatic political and institutional arrangement to replace pan-Somali nationalism.

4. Force of arms cannot be a substitute for an enduring political solution. Two decades of the Barre regime proved that. But periodic popular mandates through free, fair and democratic elections can sustain stability and the legitimacy of the state. A new form of political association, in which the north and the south each has its distinct legislative institutions and executive powers, is likely to be an adequate safeguard against the reintroduction of the autocratic rule. With such devolution of authority and substantial decentralization of provincial administration in both regions, the prospect of imbalances within and between regions will be diminished. Political parity between north and south in a new association will be essential to the legitimacy and future stability of the new association and the capacity of its institutions to perform crucial functions.

5. Lineage-based organizations -- clans, subclans and extended families -- are integral parts of Somali society. Such constituencies are tailor-made for any organizational venture but are as much sources of mutual support and collective action as they are sources of cleavage and leadership factionalism. The enigma of lineage-based groups is the unity of groups on means and instrumental objectives and their inability to achieve unity of purpose and long-term goals. This enigma is evident in the ability of clan-based political factions to mobilize their respective constituencies in overthrowing the Barre regime and their willingness to support the views, interests and political stance of lineage-based leadership factions at great costs to clan constituencies.

6. The challenge to Somali society is to find strategies for organizing solutions to shared problems as a framework for horizontal integration of provincial communities with similar interests and problems. What Somalia needs is a leadership capable of articulating the common interests and shared goals of these communities.

B. Implications for the Horn of Africa

Any assessment of Somalia's prospects and future must also include an evaluation of the implications of the radical political changes in the countries of the Horn of Africa. Indeed, strategies for building the foundations for democratic political systems, in each of these countries are likely to succeed to the extent that they are able to respond collectively to the challenges and the opportunities for regional cooperation. A coordinated international framework for supporting regional stability and cooperation can enhance the search for a durable solution to the region's political upheavals and its recurrent humanitarian tragedies.

Both in Somalia and the region as a whole, humanitarian emergency assistance in the past had been vulnerable to misuse and diversion for other purposes. Somalia's humanitarian tragedy equally poses a challenge to the management of international humanitarian assistance. A clear commitment by the international community to assist in achieving a political settlement in Somalia can create the conditions for providing humanitarian assistance to the victims of the civil strife. Such a commitment will also reinforce broader regional stability and create opportunities for an enduring solution to the region's vulnerability to a recurring humanitarian crisis.

CHAPTER SIXTEEN

Somalia: Regional State or Cantonization of Clans?

Ahmed Ashkir Botan

I. Introduction

Somalia is situated in the eastern-most corner of Africa, known as the Horn of Africa. It includes an estimated population of 7.5 million[1] and occupies 632,000 square kilometers of territory. Somalia is rich in natural resources, both on land and at sea. Agriculture and livestock are potential areas for development as well. However, such economic potential has never been tapped for two reasons: poor administration on the part of the various governments; the lack of technical know-how and capital for investment. Somalia may be rightly considered one of the poorest nations on the face of the earth.

Somalia has always been considered an exception with regard to the rest of Black Africa on account of its extraordinary ethnic, cultural, religious and linguistic homogeneity, and it is for this reason that Somalia, prior to its independence, was referred to as the "nation without a state." On this, Ali Mazrui, in his famous work entitled *The Africans*, writes: "Most other African countries are diverse peoples in search of a sense of national unity. The Somali were already a people with a national identity in search of territorial unification."[2] This ethno-cultural peculiarity has always been a great source of national pride and heritage, a jealously guarded bond uniting the Somalis.

But over the past three years, this peculiarity has ceased to exist. The homogeneity has been shattered into a thousand pieces, in hundreds of clans and factions. The destruction has led to the inevitable consequence of the dissolution of the state and nation, a veritable collapse of Somali society into the worst kind of ill-fated and exploited tribalism. Those who had come to know Somalia and its people are still today at a loss to believe the havoc wrought by such an incredible social upheaval in a country so admired and hailed for its exceptional unity and cohesion. Many Somalis themselves are literally shocked at the devastating intensity and the scope of Somali social disintegration. In this state of shock it is, or has been until the present, impossible for the Somalis to devise a remedy or come up with a plan that might put an end to this tragedy.

Some Somalis, among whom the actual authors of the destruction may be counted, consider the breakdown of the Somali social fabric a completely natural and inevitable phenomenon. They argue that tribalism is inherent to Somali social organization, and as such, must be duly taken into account when formulating the conception of any Somali state and in the subsequent distribution of state powers. Backed by a host of foreign sociologists, anthropologists and "experts," these designers of a new tribalism seek to interpret every manifestation of life in Somali society from a purely tribalistic point of view.

No one denies that tribalism has, for centuries, been the basis of Somali social organization and that this is part of Somali cultural tradition. But the type of tribalism currently fomenting in Somalia has nothing to do with traditional Somali tribalism.[3] In fact, traditional tribalism, despite defects and limits intrinsic to its nature, such as the absolute irresponsibility of the individual and the position of inferiority to which women are delegated, contained (and still contains today in areas inhabited by nomad populations) two main functions:

Collective Solidarity: The group defends its members in case of outside aggression and gives both material and moral support in times of difficulty and need. In other words, the group provides those social functions that in modern society are furnished to the individual by institutions like the health care and insurance industries.

Individual Identification: The majority of the Somalis lead a nomadic life, in continuous migration. The individual has neither an identity card nor a fixed residence. The only possible way to identify oneself is through declaration of clan membership. Belonging to a clan is for the individual a sort of identity card, a way in which one may be recognized. This type of tribalism constitutes no threat to the existence of the state and national unity. It is a primitive form of socio-political organization that all societies have passed through over the course of social evolution and development. However, though it is no threat to state and nationhood, such a system cannot co-exist with the realities and needs of the socio-political organization of the modern state.

A politicized tribalism must, however, be considered a very real threat to the existence of the state and national unity. Politicized tribalism was introduced into Somalia and efficiently made use of by colonial powers that sought to undermine existing social cohesion and snuff out the movement for national independence. Once independence had been achieved, politicized tribalism was the key to success of the governing elite's struggle for power. Tribalism of this type serves only to create and secure the position of the ruling elite. Dominant positions in political, economic and cultural spheres may be obtained through the fostering of politicized tribalism. Struggles for power inevitably provoke conflicts that are apparently tribal in nature, but in reality are between rival factions of the elite. On this, Claude Riviere writes: "The conflicts assume a character of struggle between political factions bidding for power, rather than of a tribal nature. The most acute conflicts arise not so much between classes but between elites that possibly make use of ethnic arguments, inasmuch as these serve their interests."[4] It goes without saying that the ruling elite and contenders also rely heavily on the lack of formal education and political awareness of the masses.

Politicized tribalism as an instrument in the struggle for power may have its own logic, but it is unjustifiable in that other, more suitable ways and means of conceiving politics and tribalism exist. Disintegration of society should not be the desired goal of any political system, even more so in areas that contain different ethnic groups and antagonistic tribes. Conflicts are manipulated to serve the power struggle of the elite. Politicized tribalism, however, loses any objective logic in a socio-cultural context of homogeneity, which is the case of Somalia. It serves only a handful of greedy, power-hungry and unscrupulous men.

In Somalia, the first signs of this phenomenon, as implemented by Somali nationals, came after the realization of the Somali constitution, in the mid-fifties, and thereafter grew into the sure-fire method of crooked governing that Somalia has since come to know. Every clan stakes its claim to adequate representation in government. Power is thus strictly divided according to the dictates of clanism. Since high government positions are awarded not on the basis of competence and capacity but rather on the basis of clan membership, every political leader or state functionary holds steadfast to his position and becomes irremovable. He utilizes power and public funds as if they were his own private property and lavishes favors and benefits upon members of his clan in order to create a solid base and continued clan support. This new type of tribalism has seeped into the nerve center of state organization and corrupted the distribution and management of public power. Political tribalism has become the standard practice in the governing of Somalia.

The great Somali poet, Cali Sugule with particular foresight, disillusioned by the behavior of the governing class, warned the Somalis and especially their leaders, of the grave consequences that their tendency to mix state affairs with tribalism would surely produce, in his poem entitled *Dhagax iyo dab*:

> *Dhagax iyo dab layskuma dhuftee kala dhowraay!*
> *Wax ka dhigan dowladnimo gabiil dhexagalee kala*
>   *dhowraay*
> *Kala dheer labaduye!*[5]

(Throw not the stone into the fire/keep both of them far apart!
Government mixed with tribalism is so/keep both of them far
      apart
The two of them cannot get along/keep both of them far apart.)

Given the current situation in Somalia and the catastrophic results that the beleaguered politicization of tribalism has produced in this country, we cannot but marvel at the accuracy of the poet's prophecy, but unfortunately, the fulfillment of this prophecy has been so utterly devastating, the consequences so despairingly tragic, that not even the poet himself could have imagined such an outcome.

In fact, the various groups of elites, in vying for power, transformed a people's war against a dictatorial oppressor into a tribal civil war. In time, the dictatorship could have been dismantled by means less cruel, with less tragic consequences. The tragic consequences of this civil war, the total material and moral destruction of the country, the deep lacerations cut into the Somali social fabric and the systematic atrocities committed against the weak and innocent, could not have been better described than by another great Somali poet, Yam-Yam, in his well-known poem entitled *Bandhigga tiiraanyada*,[6] an extremely efficient and exact, but profoundly sad, overview of the war.

II. De Facto Clan Cantonization

One of the most dramatic consequences of this senseless war, certainly the most tragic as far as Somali unity is concerned, is the splitting up of Somali national territory into a cantonization of clans. Indeed, clans and sub-clans have delineated boundaries according to population concentration. A zone is cantonized by a clan whose members make up the majority of inhabitants in that zone. The ruling clans enact a sort of ethnic cleansing in an attempt to rid their canton of members of rival clans. Sadly, the atrocities committed evidently seem to be on a par with the horrors witnessed in former Yugoslavia. Whole groups of people considered to be members of rival clans have been massacred or driven from lands where they have lived for generations. Minority groups not linked to any of the belligerent clans have been forced to flee from cities and villages in which they were born, after having suffered every type of imaginable violence and robbed of their every possession.

Within the clans themselves, things are not much better. According to the atomizing logic of tribalism, each clan is divided into sub-clans and families. Each sub-clan or family claims the right to control that portion of the clan's territory considered to be its own. There being no centralized power to coordinate and control these subdivisions, each tends to be totally disconnected to the others; each acts more as a sovereign state instead of a region that is part of a unified state.

III. The Addis Ababa Conference and Regional Autonomy

Attempts have not been lacking to put an end to this tragedy. From the onset of the war, many well-meaning Somalis, aware of the uselessness of the war, the futility of the motives which caused and have perpetuated it and above all the dramatic consequences that have been the result, have attempted, in collaboration with the United Nations and the international community, to convince the contenders to abandon the idea of exercising military might and meet with one another at the negotiating table so that differences may be resolved through dialogue and mutual understanding. Notable efforts have been made in organizing peace conferences, meetings, seminars and debates both inside the country and abroad.

Among these various attempts, at center stage was the peace

conference held in Addis Ababa in March, 1993, on national reconciliation of Somalia. Although the accords signed by the various factions have never been respected and plans agreed upon never put into action, the conference can claim responsibility for an idea of fundamental importance and extreme danger, or rather the proposition of regional autonomy. Its importance lies in the fact that just as the concept of regional autonomy has been applied and developed elsewhere, so too, in Somalia could regional autonomy form a basis for the necessary growth of a nation and the development of a lasting democracy. On the other hand, it appears to have been an extremely dangerous proposal in that if the concept of regional autonomy is interpreted in the wrong way, it risks sending the country into even greater confusion by abetting the anarchy that already rules Somalis and furthering the socio-political disintegration.

We must then explore the essence of regional autonomy. What are its strong points? What are its limits? Are we talking about true autonomy or a simple decentralization of administrative powers? The terms of the Addis Ababa accord are not such as to provide explicit and clear responses to these questions. Neither the location nor the situation was suitable enough for undertaking a more thorough and detailed study of a concept as complex as regional autonomy.

At times the accord itself creates confusion and contributes to the unsureness with regard to an eventual Somali interpretation of regional autonomy. For example, the accord establishes a direct link between regional councils (highest authority within each region), UNOSOM II and related organizations.[7] It concentrates power in the Provisionary National Council, even though this is a clear denial of territorial autonomy.[8]

What's more, from discussions I have had with many of the accord's designers, it is clear that there is no consensus among them on how to interpret the concept of autonomy. Some have no idea what regional autonomy really means, how far it should be extended or how much it should be curtailed. For others, autonomy is synonymous with sovereignty and the sphere of competence of the autonomous region must be without limits. In the end, few were able to relegate regional autonomy to its rightful place within the unified state that consists of a federation of regions. As can be seen, among the Somalis utter confusion reigns when any attempt is made to understand and interpret the concept of regional autonomy. A confirmation of this rests in the fact that by now drafts of regional mini-constitutions, statutes and laws have begun circulating, in which each author puts forth his own version of regional autonomy as he pleases.

At this point, doubt may arise as to whether adoption of regional autonomy was put forth by a Somali mind. Regional autonomy seems to have been nurtured elsewhere and then "suggested" to the Somalis, perhaps by the usual African "experts" who have always asserted that the key to understanding life in Africa is purely tribal. If ours is to be an autonomy conceived by the minds of the "experts," we can be certain that it will give political legitimacy to the cantonization of established clans. Therefore, we are not dealing with a recognized autonomy of a territorial community and its politico-institutional organization, but rather with autonomy attributed to a clan. Clans represent only parts of a community, with the exclusion of those who are not members. It would not be an original attempt at overcoming the modern concepts of territoriality since a return to the primitive concept of pitting stronger clans against the weaker represents a giant step backwards. What's more, regional autonomy based on the cantonization of clans finds no place among conceptualizations of governance, as set forth in modern political theory.

But perhaps a closer examination of the terms of the Addis Ababa agreement might render a politico-institutional picture less pessimistic and confused than we have thus far seen. In fact, in Section IV, regarding the workings of the transition period, the agreement establishes, among other things, a decentralization of power, while at the same time underscores the necessity of safeguarding the integrity of the Somali state. Now, if the integrity referred to in the agreement is meant not only as Somalia's territorial integrity, but also as the integrity of the Somali state's sovereignty, then inside Somali national territory there cannot and must not exist other, extra-state entities that claim the right to govern. It may be understood that the regional autonomy referred to in the agreement is the legal, political instrument destined to create decentralization of power to further democracy, before the politico-institutional backdrop of the unified state. In other words, the Addis Ababa conference seems to have expressed the political will of the Somalis, sealed in the agreement, to proceed towards the reconstruction of their state on a regional basis, maintaining, of course, the principle of the unified state.

The desire to democratize political power in Somalia may be considered at the crux of an even larger, Africa-wide movement. After decades of monarchies, military dictatorships and single party governments, 1989 marked the beginning of the manifestation of a strong desire for change and an irresistible push towards democratization throughout Black Africa. All agree upon the relentlessness of and the necessity for democratization in the political and economic life of the continent so that peoples may be lifted out of the endemic economic and social backwardness that has plagued them.

If, however, on one side the will to democratize seems decided and uniform, the debate as to what kind of democracy is anything but peaceful. Some maintain that Africa must come up with its own form of democracy, adapting democratic principles to its cultural traditions. Others feel that such an idea threatens to break down society and could spin out of control. Still others shout the impossibility for Africa to, in this precise historical moment, install a true democratic system since the prerequisites for the realization of a democratic system are lacking, such as a minimum economic development and adequate educational systems.[9]

Whatever outcome these ideas, the most relevant and encouraging news is that Africa itself is convinced of the undeniable necessity of this process and of the importance of taking those crucial first steps towards this goal. Democratization should take the form of an even distribution of power from the center to the confines of each country's borders, a decentralization of power. Since skepticism about and mistrust of federalism are still rampant in Africa, especially in countries where the nation-state has been created artificially (which is the case of the overwhelming majority of African nation-states today),[10] the most appropriate instrument for the realization of decentralization and thus democratization of the continent's political and economic life is seen as regional autonomy.

As early as 1990, a new, amply democratic constitution had been written, which restored the multi-party system (Arts. 8 and 18), the mechanisms and laws of a market economy (Art. 40), free, direct elections (Arts. 15, 58/1 and 79/1) and, for the first time in Somalia's history, a vast decentralization of administrative powers (Art. 101). They were formidable instruments of democracy which, together with a little political foresight, could have led Somalia, despite resistance of the regime in power, to a real decentralization of power and a true territorial autonomy, while at the same time safeguarding the country against the tragic situation which has befallen it.

IV. The Inherent Difficulties of Implementing Regional Autonomy in Somalia

As I have said, proposals for regional autonomy in Somalia, made at Addis Ababa, are as confused as they are open to the most differing interpretations. In particular, it is unclear whether it should be autocracy or true autonomy or, simply a decentralization of administrative powers that receives political sanction.

Confusion regarding a politico-juridical concept of such importance and complexity as territorial autonomy was inevitable in the socio-political chaos and anarchy in which Somalia finds itself. In fact, in a situation of total disintegration, no constitutional charter exists which, *a priori,* recognizes the constitutionality of autonomous local powers, nor laws designed to define and limit those powers. There are no manifestations of autonomy such as statutes and regional laws (on rights of minors, for example). Owing to this lack of tradition or experience with autonomy, the idea of regional autonomy could have done no less than add fuel to the already blazing inferno of confusion.

Given the current situation in Somalia, the recreation of a state and the implementation of its authority, as well as the signing of a new constitution, will take time. Until such matters are resolved, any attempt at foreseeing how Somalis interpret regional autonomy will be guesswork. But let's suppose, for a moment, that we are dealing with authentic and full autonomy, an autonomy that comprises all the extensions appertaining to local autonomy: normative, organizational and political autonomy. Now let's try to single out the areas of greatest difficulty in present-day Somalia evolving into a transformed state. Three areas are of particular interest: political-juridical; techno-economic; and lack of an autonomist tradition.

A. Politico-Juridical Difficulties

The total undoing (political, economic, social) brought about by warring clans has left the country without any unified political direction, void of national institutions which normally foster and apply such direction. In the absence of the state and its institutions, contending clans control their own portions of national territory. Within these territories, the clans enforce their own "laws" which mainly coincide with the desires and capricious will of the clan leader. The clan leader often plays on typical clan sentiments to create the base for his rise to power. As already mentioned, clans that constitute the majority in a given region consider regional autonomy as a type of complete sovereignty of the clan itself. Accordingly, clans take it for granted that within their region they may behave in any way they choose and enact whatever laws they like. In short, clans claim unlimited jurisdiction within their regions.

In such a situation it is obvious that political autonomy means not the power of politico-administrative direction on the part of the local entity, regulated by the laws of the state, but rather an unlimited political "freedom" beyond the control of the state. In this situation, the power of normative autonomy is conceived not as a power subordinate to the system of laws that govern the country, but as an autonomous power in the most reduced sense of the word.[11] These few observations show us how in the context of socio-political disintegration, where the life of the country has been profoundly poisoned by a terribly politicized tribalism and clan mania, the chances of efficiently implementing regional autonomy appear remote.

B. Techno-Economic Difficulties

Somalia is one of the poorest countries in Africa. With the onset of war, this poverty has been intensified, turned into sheer misery. Economic and social structures once existent in the country have been completely destroyed. The economic potential of Somalia is enormous with respect to its population density, but technical know-how and investment capital are lacking. A huge effort is needed to rebuild the country economically. Investments of every kind (domestic and foreign) are required as well as a pool of human resources of Somalis and expatriates, possessed of the technical training necessary to take on this enormous job.

Any Somali human resources, already insufficient to meet the needs of the Somalis, have been dispersed throughout the four corners of the world and, for Somalia, are wasted. Many capable people have been assassinated; many others incorporated (often reluctantly) into international organizations, foreign academic institutions and other sectors in order that they may provide for themselves and their families. Out of necessity, many are forced to work in jobs for which they are over-qualified, or that are unrelated to their professions. The few capable persons remaining in Somalia live as outcasts whose lives are in constant danger.

The return of professional Somalis is of vital importance to reconstruct the country, for they represent the only segment of Somali society capable of reasoning in terms of state and nation, capable of advancing proposals of nationwide democratic development. No clan (or region under the control of a clan majority) could bring back its dispersed nationals, much less offer them the means to work in peace; just as no clan could conceive of a broad plan of regional or national development or furnish the necessary means for the realization of such a plan.

The only entity which can conceive of a national plan of broad, harmonious economic development, facilitate the return of the dispersed Somalis and design structures to assure the success of such a plan is the nation-state. The state would be ruled by a democratic government and legitimized by the consensus of the national community. Of necessity, it would be non-authoritarian, strong-willed and possessed of the power and necessary capabilities that would make democratic development a reality in Somalia.

C. Lack of Autonomist Tradition

There has never existed an autonomist tradition in the history of Somalia. From a society in which power was once totally decentralized, Somalia, at least in theory, became a national community governed by a centralized power. Neither the colonial power nor the various national governments that followed ever granted any autonomy to the outlying regions, much less decentralize power. On the other hand, there have never been Somali political, philosophical or juridical movements with autonomist leanings, as have been conceived, developed and implemented in other parts of the world. This explains the reign of total confusion with regard to the idea of regional autonomy in Somalia and why the concept of regional autonomy is so open to interpretation among the Somalis. On top of all this we must acknowledge the lack of schooling among the vast majority of Somalis and consequently their political immaturity.

Such grave shortcomings assure that selection of local groups, founding of political associations and determination of who will govern the country will be made, not on the basis of a political or ideological platform, but simply on the basis of clan orientation. In circumstances such as these, every democratic instrument -- political parties, free elections, majority rule, recognition of the right of opposition, protection of minority rights -- loses any real worth and meaning.

For all the motives and difficulties summarily recounted above (and others not mentioned) I am of the opinion that, given the current state of affairs, a real and authentic regional autonomy cannot at present be implemented in Somalia. Forcing its implementation today, in light of what we assume to be the prevalent attitude, would constitute a real danger to the eventual existence of a Somali state and Somali national unity.

I realize that these difficulties pose an obstacle to the efficient implementation of autonomous structures. But in themselves they do not constitute evidence that autonomy is not possible. It is not enough to say, however, that autonomy in Somalia today is merely hindered by difficulties running rampant through a nation. At present there is not only a lack of an historical context capable of accommodating regional autonomy, but also the inherent, concrete danger that the concept might wind up so contorted that its implementation could only complete the disaster that Somalia has lived through until now.

V. Administrative Decentralization

Just as Somalia has had no experience with regional autonomy, administrative decentralization is also unknown. The country's administrative organization remained more or less what Somalia had inherited from the colonial powers. It included national territory divided into regional zones; provincial districts headed by regional governors; and district commissariats directly appointed by the central power and therefore subordinate to the central power.[12] All state functions were central. Regional and district functionaries followed orders and directives from the central power.

To introduce, for the first time in the history of the country, a system of administrative decentralization is no easy task. Decentralization is a complex political problem that involves a transfer of governing functions to the outlying areas of the country. Decentralization is generally thought to be a more efficient, and better way of satisfying public needs than a system based on centralization of political power. Advantages considered inherent to a decentralized system of administration, according to the most widely accepted beliefs, can be summarized as follows:

- it permits a more direct and thorough understanding of the problems that need solving and the needs that administrative action must meet;
- administrative action focuses on specific local needs, offering relatively flexible bureaucratic solutions;
- citizens become more involved since decentralization favors direct contact with those who govern them, and benefit from a more efficient system at their service;
- with strict regard to politics, decentralization is an instrument of democratic education, both because it stimulates and heightens a sense of responsibility on the part of local administrators and because it allows for the possibility of continuous control and solicitation on the part of the governed.[13]

In my own modest opinion, absolute priority must be given to the reconstruction of the state and the improvement of its institutions and juridical system, and consequently, to the recovery of national unity. Once law and order have been restored within a framework of a unified state, Somalia must proceed towards the introduction of a system of administrative decentralization aimed at improvement of the state's administrative services. As far as what type of decentralization to adopt, the system should, in the initial stages, encompass a mandatory regionalization for the identification of functions to be decentralized and a hierarchical regionalization in order to assure unified direction.

In the next phase, when the country's political situation appears more tranquil and state institutions more solid, forms based on more self-sufficient decentralization will be called for. These new agencies would educate citizens about the role of government and instill in them a sense of responsibility inherent in maintaining democracy. The combination of growing institutional strength and formal educational programs would clear the way for "the rise and assertion of local autonomies and self-government."[14]

VI. Towards A Hypothesis of A Confederation of States of the Horn of Africa

At a historical moment in human evolution when nations are trying to join together and unite, Africa proceeds in the opposite direction. Everyone, including the most powerful nations, is in search of new economic aggregations, new political unions, new forms of cooperation to defend against outside aggression and the evils lurking about in the modern world (or perhaps to better influence the outside world). But not in Africa as this novelty seems to be "not for her." Africa seeks to divide, to cut her own throat, disintegrate and atomize even further.

Africa appears headed toward political and economic disintegration, social dispersion and dissolution of the state. She is crumbling under the pressure of various forces. Sub-nationalism, ethnism and tribalism, real or imagined, have proven themselves to be the most efficient instruments in promoting disintegration in Africa. Political alienation has grown from the murky depths of an inexhaustible well of malfunctioning institutions, rampant corruption, systematic violations of human rights, and deaf-eared denials by those already in power.

So, while the rest of the world is coming together, uniting and gaining strength, Africa is sinking its roots ever deeper into more minute and futile particulars: ethnism, tribalism, clanism. The continent slides further and further down until the social body becomes atomized and reaches a point of total disintegration. The inevitable consequence visible today are that Africa exists physically on the map. But from political, economic and social standpoints, Africa has ceased to exist. It is already dead and gone from the Earth. So dramatic is its current marginal role that a few years ago a scholar of Third World problems was moved to write, "if the African continent was to be swallowed up by the waves and vanish from the face of the earth, it is likely that no one would notice, since African trade constitutes just two percent of the world market."[15]

If the whole of Africa is worth so little or nothing, what is a mere ethnic group worth? And a tribe? A clan? Can this social atom so tenaciously fought for be worth anything with respect to the whole? If these questions were given their due attention, Africa, mistreated and derided, would not be in the tragic shape it is today. It is time to eliminate these useless divisions and their harmful disintegration. It's time to think out ideas and to work out plans for economic and cultural cooperation, while we set aside for the moment political questions. In particular, we need to begin thinking and elaborating a plan of wide, concrete economic and cultural cooperation between the states and peoples of the Horn of Africa. We could start by opening up national borders to allow the free circulation of goods and persons. Later, common economic and cultural organs and institutions could be established.

Once rancor and reciprocal differences have been removed, and economic and cultural links strengthened, the next phase, this time political, could be undertaken. The elaboration of an approximate plan could lead to a confederation of the Horn of Africa. No easy task, mind you, and not a short-term project! But it can and must be done. We must begin thinking and offering up ideas. Conviction and perseverance are necessary, the conviction that a confederation is the only possible road for survival.

VII. Conclusion

The introduction of local autonomy in Somalia is an irrevocable necessity and a mandatory step towards democratization. But this cannot happen through improvisation and hastiness. Due to its importance and, at the same time, its complexity, autonomy must be studied and understood correctly. For autonomy to become a reality, ground must be cleared and the political, economic and social situation of the country made accommodating. Citizens must be educated so they know the meaning of autonomy and how it fosters democracy. We should remember that in those countries where regional autonomy has evolved from a centuries-long tradition, research is still underway to refine and adapt the form best suited to each juridical orientation. Autonomy, being the last stage democratization, necessitates meticulous preparations and an ever more in-depth study. We must make wide use of others' errors yet avoid the application of models whose experiences are not in line with our needs, and thus, inapplicable to our reality.

Some argue that unless we start from the beginning, it will be impossible to reconstruct the state in Africa, and this includes Somalia. This is precisely why we must acknowledge the urgency of the need to decentralize power, which means: federalism, regionalism and other forms of local autonomy. Yet, the so-called "experts" on African affairs cannot see past their generalizations. They interpret every manifestation of life in Africa in terms of particularisms and their particularist approach.

How is it possible to go back to the beginning as our point of departure? There's a catchy rhyme in Somalia today that efficiently sums up the situation: "Somalia and I against the world. My clan and I against Somalia. My family and I against the clan. My brother and I against the family. I against my brother!" To the African "experts," those vast repositories of truth and knowledge about all things African, a better response cannot be given than that of Dr. M. Aden, when he says:

"However positive values may be attributed to Africa, however the road to African democracy may be re-examined by anthropologists and researchers, no matter how it does or doesn't mimic the western model, the 'statute of the clan' does not win out as a possible direction for growth. On the contrary, it is this mentality that furthers the breakdown of society into micro-communities in opposition to the world around them, by virtue of doubtful common descent, kinship and blood relationships; and it only serves to propagate backwardness, in permanent opposition to growth."[16]

Endnotes

1. An actual census has never been taken in Somalia, due to the difficulties connected with tracking down a population that is to a large extent, nomadic.

2. Ali A. Mazrui, *The Africans*, 1986, p. 71.

3. It would be more appropriate, in the case of Somalia, to speak of clanism or large extended families, inasmuch as the Somali all belong to one single tribe, subdivided into clans of large extended families; we however, shall continue to use the term tribe as it is commonly used today.

4. Claude Riviere, "La Contradizione Irrisolta tra Etnicismo e Coscienza Nazionale", in *Politica Internazionale*, n. 2-3, February-March 1987, p. 19.

5. "Cali Sugule", in *Dhagax iyo dab*, Mogadiscio, 1967.

6. Cabdulgaardir Xersi Yam-Yam, Bandhigga tiiraanyada, Addis Ababa, 1993.

7. Addis Ababa Agreement, Section IV, March 3, 1993, p. 5.

8. *Ibid.*, p. 4.

9. See AA. VV., Dossier, "Africa's New Democracy", in *The Courier*, n. 138, March-April 1993, p. 62.

10. See Irma Taddia, "Il Problema della legittimita' Politica e le Formule Federali", in *Politica Internazionale*, n. 2-3, February-March 1987, p. 37.

11. See M.S. Gianinni, "Autonomia Politica", in *Enciclopedia del Diritto*, Milano, 1959; Staderini, F., *Diritto degli Enti Locali*, Padova, 1991.

12. See "Ordinamento Amministrativo per la Somalia Italiana", in *R.D.*, July 4, 1910, n. 562.

13. See, among others, R. Lucifredi, under "Decentramento Amministrativo", in *Nuoviss. Dig. Italiano*, 1960, vol. II, p. 248; F. Staderini, in *Diritto Degli Enti Locali*, cit.

14. F. Staderini, *Diritto degli Enti Locali*, cit.

15. G. Smussi, in *Terzo Mondo Informazioni*, n. 8, October 1990, p. 21.

16. M. Aden, in *Arrivederci a Mogadiscio*, 2nd ed., Edizioni Associate, Rome.

CHAPTER SEVENTEEN

Analyzing Somalia's Past and Present Economic Constraints and Opportunities for Creating a Conducive Economic Environment

Jamshid Damooei

I. Introduction

This paper is a study of the past and the present economic problems in Somalia. It highlights the impact of the political developments of the last three decades in the creation and escalation of the country's economic problems. The study looks at the present economic situation to find the principal causes of the emerging economic problems during the last three years. The study shows that several factors may have contributed to the escalation of the current economic crisis. They range from the bottlenecks caused by the ongoing civil war to the shortcomings emanating from the current emergency operation of the international NGOs, bilateral donors and the UN system. This study aims at providing policy solutions that are practical and implementable within the present economic and political climate of Somalia.

II. The Origin and the Recent Political History

There are different suggestions by scholars which indicate that the Somali identity and its settlements in the Horn of Africa date back some 2,000 years. It is known that the early Somalis and their contemporary descendants have had a common language and a highly decentralized way of life (pastoral). In the early days the pastoralist economic structure was communal. This meant that every household or family was an autonomous unit containing an entire economy and forming an independent center. This social formation later developed into groups which were related to each other, particularly in times of need, in the form of clan affiliations. Despite the homogeneity of the Somali society, the division of people into clan and sub-clan families has always played an important role in the politics of this country. The other important element in the politics of Somalia is its Islamic religion. These two elements together with the politics of foreign interests shaped the nation's recent political history.

After the official unification of northern and southern Somalia on July 1, 1960, Somalia became a republic. The new constitution provided for: a head of state to be elected by the 123 members of parliament every six years; the presidential nomination of an executive prime minister who would appoint the cabinet from the leading parliamentary party, subject to the majority vote of the National Assembly; and the election of deputies every four years. The constitution also empowered the president to appoint five justices to the Supreme Court. As for the rest of the country, eight administrative regions run by governors and thirty-six districts were created. Both regional governors and district commissioners were to be appointed by the central government's Interior Ministry. The above-mentioned political setup lasted almost a decade. In the pre-dawn hours of October 21 1969, the armed forces took over the power in the country. This military take-over opened a new chapter in the life of the newly independent state of Somalia.

One of the most important events making a significant impact on the contemporary politics of Somalia was the breakout of the Ogaden War in late 1976. The Western Somali Liberation Front (WSLF) took offensive in the Ogaden in late 1976. The movement received help from the Somali government which had military ties with the Soviet regime. By the end of July, 1977, the Ethiopians conceded control of Ogaden with the exception of the three cities of Jigjiga, Haraar, and Dire Dawa to the WSLF. This led to a full-scale war between the two countries. As the USSR made its support for the Ethiopian side apparent, its relationship with Somalia strained. In March, 1978, the Somali government announced the withdrawal of its forces from the Ogaden. This war left deep divisions in the internal politics and damaged the economy to a great extent. It brought the involvement of the government during the war under question. It caused discussion among the different ranks of the army during the *post mortem* of the war. This led to disagreement between different clans.

The Soviet exit from the economic, military and political scene of Somalia set the stage for greater involvement of the USA. The Somali government came to the American government for military and economic assistance. The US military assistance to the Siyad Barre regime eventually totaled $200 million, and the economic assistance exceeded $500 million.

Siyad Barre's increasingly brutal and discriminatory regime led to a 1978 coup attempt and the eventual formation of Somali National Movement (SNM) in 1981, among the northern clan of Isaaq. The SNM soon began raiding government facilities. This provoked a violent response from Siyad Barre and he bombed the regional capital of the Isaaq, Hargeisa, killing thousands and pushing hundreds of thousands (along with the SNM) to Ethiopia. Despite the brutal response of the government, the apparent weakness of the regime to calm the resurgence encouraged other clans to take arms against Siyad Barre. In 1989 the United Somali Congress (USC) was formed from the Hawiye clan. The struggle against the regime gradually developed to the center and the south of the country. Increasing military and political coordination among the president's foes finally eroded his power. He fled Mogadishu in January, 1991.

Shortly after the downfall of the regime, disagreement among the USC forces surfaced. Part of the troops under the command of General Farah Aidid chased Barre's army out of the capital city. The other segment under the control of Ali Mahdi Mohamed remained in the city and declared a new government. In the north, the Isaaq clan formed an independent Somaliland Republic, a state which continues to remain unrecognized, internationally.

At present, there is no functioning government in Somalia. Ali Mahdi's claim to power is not recognized except by his own followers who only control the northern section of Mogadishu. Various clan militia turned on one another, effectively dividing the country into 12 zones of control. The dispute between Mahdi and Aidid eventually developed into a full scale war in November 1991. This war was finally ended by a UN brokered cease-fire on March 3, 1992. Later in 1992, the continuation of drought forced increasing number of Somalis from their land to cities in search of food, exposing them more directly to violence. The plight of Somali people was brought to the world's attention in the latter part of

1992. This resulted in the military action by the UNITAF and the formation of UNOSOM I and II.

III. The Society

One of the striking features of Somali society is the homogeneity of Somali culture. Somalis have a common language, a similar way of life which is predominantly pastoral, a common political culture, a profound Islamic heritage and a deeply held belief that nearly all Somalis descended from the same source and are therefore drawn together by kinship and genealogical ties.

The emphasis on pastoralism in Somali life does not mean that there are no other influences emanating from other elements in Somali society. The culture of southern Somalia and places such as Gabilay and Borama in the northwest has a strong agricultural component. In these areas, power and prestige do not relate to the size of peoples' herds, but instead is determined by the ownership of land. This tradition of an agricultural economy gives southern Somalia some distinct cultural characteristics, which explains the political position of many clans whose economic base is agriculture. Furthermore, chiefs of agricultural clans exercise real authority compared to the chiefs of pastoral clans who merely play a ceremonial role and are actually powerless. It is also important to know that although clan loyalty is a general characteristic of all Somali clans, genealogical relations do not play as crucial a role in defining a group's corporate existence in settled communities as they do among pastoral societies. In a pastoral society, the place of an individual in a group in relation to the larger society is primarily determined by blood ties, whereas economic interests and spiritual primacy play an important part in agricultural clans.

There are four major branches of lineage systems in Somalia which are predominantly pastoral (Dir, Darood, Isaaq and Hawiye) and two which are mostly agricultural (Digil and Rahanweyn). The curious nature of Somali segmentation is that while they are drawn together based on their cultural solidarity, they are also turned against each other on the basis of their clan interests. In order to understand this puzzling situation better, one has to look at an individual's hierarchy of loyalty to his/her clan and the larger family. A person gives political allegiance first to his/her immediate family, then to his immediate lineage, then to the clan of his lineage, then to a clan-family that embraces several clans, including his own, and ultimately to the nation that consists of a confederacy of clan-families.

It is important to know that for centuries there has not been any centrally controlled ruling body in Somalia. The confrontation between the ancient lineage structure and the emerging state power began in the post-colonial era, following the Italian Trusteeship. The administrative structure after independence was based on the colonial experience. One of the early acts of the independent state was to codify fundamental legislation outlawing clans as units in political matters. This has always been a highly sensitive issue because it touches upon the very existence of the state. The irony is that despite such intention, the composition of the civilian and the military government that ruled the country since independence has been based more on clan coalition than on individual leadership ability or other professional merits.

IV. The Economy Before the Recent Crisis

A. Production Sectors

Agriculture is the most important sector in the Somali economy and includes livestock, crop production, forestry and fisheries. In recent years before the present upheaval, the sector accounted for nearly 65% of GDP, 95% of exports and about 80% of employment. The performance of the sector largely depends on the climate and the amount of rainfall.

Livestock is the backbone of Somali economy. Somalia has been one of the major producers of livestock in Africa. According to statistics (published by the Department of Planning and Statistics of the Ministry of Livestock, Forestry and Range in cooperation with GTZ) in 1990 Somalia owned 43% of camels, 2% of cattle, 10% of goats and 5% of sheep for the entire continent of Africa. The major proportion of the sheep and goats is produced in the northern part of Somalia. Cattle are predominantly produced in the central, southern and Trans-Juba areas. Camels are produced in all four regions (North, Center, South and Trans-Juba).

Pastoralism is by no means a mere symbol of Somalia's pre-colonial past. It remains the most vibrant sector of Somalia's economy. Trade of live animals has been the prime source of foreign currency earning for the country. International commerce remained a central occupation in the Somali economy. Many Somalis have taken advantage of the massive profits of the oil exporting countries on the Arab peninsula and sought jobs in these countries. The remittances from Somali workers, traders and seamen elsewhere have always been a traditional part of the Somali economy. Remittances from the Gulf countries are a recent phenomena which date back to the late 1970s. Estimates of remittances are different and the gaps between them are rather wide. A consolidated estimate by

JASPA put it close to $ 370 million in 1984/85.

Crop production is another vital source of economic activity for contribution to GDP, creation of employment, stimulating exports, and emphasizing future development and promotion of exports. Somalia's major crops are maize, bananas, sorghum and rice. Export of bananas has been the second most important item in the total exports of the country. Agricultural activities are built on relatively abundant resources in relation to the population of Somalia.

In general, the overall performance of crop production in Somalia has been low. The low productivity is due to a number of reasons including outmoded production techniques, lack of proper infrastructure and man-made irrigation systems and the small size of the domestic market. There have also been legal problems concerning land tenure and ownership of water and water rights.

Somalia has a coastline of 3,300 km and access to rich fishing grounds in the Indian Ocean and the Gulf of Aden. Recent studies showed that Somalia could produce 180,000 tons of fish per year. In 1989, the total catch was around 21,018 metric tons or about 11.7% of its estimated potential. The gap between the potential and effective production indicates existing possibility for enhancing the future contribution of this sub-sector.

The previous government of Somalia was eager to explore possibilities for the development of the country's mineral resources. This effort was particularly concentrated on exploration of oil and natural gas deposits. Occurrences of valuable metallic and nonmetallic mineral resources have been identified but not in commercially viable quantities.

Manufacturing industries have been stagnating if not declining during the 1980s. Public industrial enterprises had dominated the manufacturing sector in the past. The problems with these industries were many, including: use of obsolete equipment, shortage of raw materials, fuel shortages, frequent and often prolonged power failure, lack of foreign exchange to purchase imported inputs and finally and most important, weak management.

B. Poverty

There have been several studies of poverty in Somalia which have come to different results. The differences are in part due to the disagreement in the conceptualization of poverty in Somalia.

In the rural areas, most studies show that the terms of exchange between the farmers and nomads over the years moved in favor of nomads. On the international market, the price of livestock has been on the rise due to the oil boom (increase in the meat consumption) whereas the reverse had been true for the price of crops. On the domestic front, the livestock market had been free, whereas the crop market had been subject to government regulation.

On the issue of urban poverty, the findings indicate that between 1970 and 1986, average wages increased six fold, while private sector wages did somewhat better, showing an increase of 7.7 fold. In the same period the general level of prices increased 35 times. The gap between the price increase and the wage increase became much worse in the last three years of the previous regime. These studies show that in 1986 the average wage would have bought one-third of the minimum needs of an average family. The situation turned much worse in the last three years of the previous regime for which there are no figures.

Based on the above figures, one should expect to see a massive increase in poverty. However, Jamal, in his study for ILO/JASPA(1989), concluded that such a tremendous increase in poverty did not happen because (a) wages became a fraction of total income, and (b) remittances increased. Most government officials could expect to supplement their salaries with various types of allowances.

Finally as Jamal (1989) pointed out, the real tragedy of Somalia's recent experience is that, while the country, especially Mogadishu went through boom conditions, it did not develop. Adult literacy, primary school enrollment, infant mortality and occurrence of infectious diseases hardly improved. Instead, the infrastructure stagnated and the industrial sector declined. The country went into a spending spree. Unfortunately the spending never provided the basis for the country's long-term development.

C. Economic Development and Public Policies

Public policies to foster economic growth in Somalia appeared as the most important challenge to the new independent government of Somalia in 1960. The first Five-Year Plan (1963-67) was developed despite the shortcomings of both professional planners and technical people who could design and carry out the plan and the information on the structure of the economy. By the end of the plan in 1967, only half of the expenditures were made, the foreign aid commitments were not put to the service of the plan. To remedy this, a short-term plan was developed to fulfill the gap (1967-70). The most significant change resulting from this plan was the increase in public employment.

The strategy of the government at the time was to play the two superpowers against each other and refuse to make it clear whether it adhered to socialism or capitalism. The result was that Somalia received the highest amount of per capita economic assistance of all Sub-Saharan African countries. In the 1960s, Somalia received $90 per capita in foreign economic assistance, about twice the average for Sub-Saharan countries. This helped to pay for a host of new parliamentarians and ministers who led comfortable lives in Mogadishu and a 500 percent increase in the size of the Somali army.

President Siyad Barre declared Somalia a socialist state a year after his successful *coup d'etat*. As a consequence, a much greater proportion of the Somali economy came under the control of the government. Therefore, banks, insurance companies, petroleum distribution, schools, and sugar refining plants were nationalized and national agencies were created for construction of materials and foodstuffs. At the same time, the President assured small businesses and camel owners that their activities and properties would be protected as they are counted as workers rather than capitalists. He also left banana plantations to private ownership, making both important items of exports remaining in the private hands. The creation of cooperatives became a cornerstone of the program to build a socialist economy.

The evidence presented in many studies shows that during the period of 1969 through 1974, some parts of the Somali economy were invigorated by the state ideology, self-help schemes and the belief that hard work and vision can succeed. By the mid-1970s and particularly since the Ogaden war, the situation changed. Government control over the economy in a constructive way declined and corruption and mismanagement began to replace vision and enthusiasm. The 1980s reveal a period of disappointment and disaster for the Somali economy. A great proportion of the burdens of such setbacks falls on the shoulders of the government and the system of governance pursued by the former regime. The mismanagement of the economy over time created severe economic imbalances in the country.

Somalia is a country with great economic potential, such as vast fertile land, considerable unused surface water resources, unexploited marine resources, a rich tradition of livestock production and untapped mineral resources. As indicated, with the exception of the early years of the previous regime, the last two decades showed a continuous decline in the overall performance of Somalia's economy. The bulk of food consumed in Somalia had to be imported from foreign countries. The existing data on Somalia's past foreign trade shows that the import of cereals to Somalia increased from 42,000 MT in 1974 to 343,000 MT in 1986, indicating an increased dependency on food aid from donor countries.

The entire Public Investment Program (PIP) used to come from donors on a two-year interval, through a Consultative Group meeting arranged by the World Bank. The counterpart funds generated in Somali shillings against the flow of foreign aid were used to finance the Government contribution for its entire development program and even for a major part of its recurrent budget. Tax revenue has always been an insignificant part of government fiscal resources to finance its budget. While the ratio of soldiers to teachers and military expenditure to spending on the social sector in Somalia remained second highest among the entire developing countries in the world (UNDP Human Development Report, 1992), Somalia had very little financial resources of its own.

The structural adjustment program in Somalia had a history of over a decade before the recent crises. This policy was supported by two consecutive stand-by arrangements with the IMF. The aim was to stimulate domestic production, slow down inflation and create a sustainable external position over the medium run. The perceived objectives of the adjustment were to increase the aggregate supply and at the same time reduce the domestic aggregate demand. These policies were on a stop and go basis. The overall impact has been hard to measure. The following policies and actions may have contributed towards the creation of a number of macroeconomic imbalances, overall economic degeneration, and social decay:

1. Pursuing a policy of price controls, particularly for agricultural products. This policy caused misallocation of resources through creation of price distortions.

2. Creation of a variety of public enterprises in different fields of economic activities. A widespread mismanagement in these enterprises caused inefficient production practices, burdening the national economy and causing a continuous financial loss for the Government.

3. Disregard for provision of social services and creating a declining trend for human development and public welfare.

4. Unsound fiscal policy through a continuous policy of having budget deficits, allowing a declining trend in meeting government spending through tax collection and excessive expenditure for military purposes.

5. Pursuing an inappropriate monetary policy responsible for fueling inflation. The prevalent credit policies failed to stimulate the production sector. Instead, it became a major facility for a handful of

currency speculators and merchants who took great advantage from the existing market distortions in the foreign exchange market.

6. Following a policy of overvalued exchange rates for a long time and creating a further misallocation of resources as a consequence.

7. Adopting a policy of government subsidies for political reasons at the expense of causing economic distortions in a number of areas of economic activities.

8. Pursuing a policy of almost total disregard for poverty alleviation and provision of a safety net for the poor.

9. Pursuing a policy of divide and rule among the different clans, showing no tolerance for any opposition to the rule of the central government and letting nepotism and political favoritism prevail. This caused the majority of Somali people to be marginalized and disenfranchised.

V. An Assessment of the Present Economic Conditions

A. Production, Trade and Employment

The last three years of civil war caused extensive social and economic upheaval, massive population displacement (internal as well as external), near total destruction of the already fragile infrastructure, and a deep sense of distrust and suspicion among the different centers of political power in the country. The waves of destruction, looting and civil anarchy left few places of business or means of production unaffected. However, there is a general belief, at least among the business circles in Somalia today, that the future economy will be one controlled by the private sector, uninhibited and free from a central control.

At present, the most critical economic issue of Somalia is its high rate of unemployment. The limited activities of foreign relief agencies are the important sources of employment in Mogadishu and other major cities. Destruction of agricultural production has created a similar depression in the rural areas.

The civil war caused serious damages to the industrial establishments in Somalia. Damage is likely to have been less among the privately-owned factories (bottling, construction materials and furniture) which were protected by their own owners. A small amount of construction materials and furniture are currently produced by the small-scale industrial sector. Domestic and international trade has experienced a severe setback due to a number of reasons. They are lack of security, fall in domestic production and destruction of financial institutions. There is, however, an active presence of Somali traders in a number of centers such as Mogadishu, Hargeisa, Bosaso, and Berbera in the country and in Nairobi and Djibouti outside the country.

B. Analyses of the Current Economic Trends

In the absence of any functioning government (at least in the south and the center of the country) the existing economic trends are caused by the spontaneous change of the economic environment, the role of the functioning private economic agents and the operation of active donors, foreign NGOs, and the United Nations system.

Economic distortions stemming from current emergency operations are often referred to as elements impeding the free interaction of market forces in an economy. It is often regarded as policies pursued by governments or certain businesses leading to a misallocation of resources and the unavoidable occurrence of social costs in the form of loss of welfare to some groups in that economy. In the case of Somalia, the source of the existing distortions should be traced in the working of donor agencies, NGOs, the UN system and the Somalis themselves.

A simple analysis of the decisions taken and modalities and mode of operations followed by the UN and some non-UN emergency institutions suggest that they have effectively pursued the following objectives:

1. Provided free food to those in danger of starvation at a generous level of safety and assurance.

2. Taken steps to insure the continued availability of food, perhaps at a "reasonable" price to many people in the major population centers.

3. Created, where possible, a financial scheme that can finance some public works, such as running of schools and provision of health care in some areas.

4. Placed emphasis on self-sustainability of operations where emergency assistance is currently allocated.

5. Used cost-effectiveness as a guiding criterion for deciding who will provide services for the emergency operations, rather than a system that provide Somalis with a greater advantage.

6. Tried to be seen as impartial to different factions of disputing clans even at the risk of creating disadvantage in business for some Somali business people.

Most of the above-mentioned objectives simply explain the difficult nature of emergency operations in Somalia. It also suggests that there may be a social cost stemming from a number of decisions taken by the operating system in Somalia. While avoiding the negative effects of some of these policies appears politically cumbersome and indeed extremely difficult to measure, there are reasonable grounds to suggest a careful revision of a number of these decisions.

C. Monetization of Food Commodities

WFP (World Food Program) and some NGOs have taken steps in selling food at wholesale prices and using the money to finance public works. The intention of creating job opportunities has been in the minds of the management of these organizations. Despite the good intentions, in reality the situation may be very different and the policy may create more unemployment than jobs. Although it is difficult at the present time to back any analyses with reliable data, the following effects of monetization seem quite apparent:

1. Prices of agricultural products (main food staples) have fallen sharply. Some farmers prefer to store their harvest rather than selling it at the market prices. This may affect their decision on what and how much to produce for the next agricultural season.

2. Cheap food has changed the terms of trade to the disadvantage of the farmers and to the advantage of the livestock owners. With the price of food so depressed, the livestock owners can now sell fewer animals as the proceeds of their sale will be sufficient for their needs. As a consequence a restrained supply of livestock has pushed up its prices further.

3. Importers of food are equally constrained to bring food to Somalia as their most competitive prices will still lie well below the wholesale prices of the monetized food. Lack of ability to compete may have the following reasons: a) High risk of importing and selling food in the local market by the private sector. Loss of merchandise will not put WFP or an NGO out of business and therefore they do not have the same perception; b) There are considerable economies of scale that the large international organizations enjoy which are not

comparable with the operation of a private company in Somalia; c) Private companies work on the basis of the profit they expect to receive and not the social objectives that international organizations often pursue; d) Furthermore, private firms have to include all the direct and indirect costs that they have in their business activities (including information costs), whereas international organizations are more likely to omit certain costs because of the nature of their activities.

D. Non-existence of Somali Sovereignty

Many Somalis in and outside the country are complaining about the growing scope of foreign companies operating in Somalia and benefitting from the vacuum created by the lack of any national government. These companies have access to international financial intermediaries which is not available to Somalis; they are less likely to be accused of clan affiliation than the Somali-owned companies; and they do not pay any tax or duties that otherwise have to be paid to the host country, which is indeed a loss of social welfare to Somalis.

On the other hand there are many examples showing that the cost of operations, particularly that of security, is much higher for these companies. This suggests, that an internal system of counter balancing the existing unequal condition has emerged. However, the long term consequences of such phenomenon are alarming.

E. Establishing Binding Precedence for Future Economic Concerns

Organizations involved in the emergency operations have taken decisions that may go farther than dealing with the immediate economic and social situation in the country. For example, on a number of occasions, NGOs introduced fees for certain services in an effort to make those operations self-sustaining (fiscal autonomy and direct cost recovery seem to have been generally accepted as the most important features of a self-sustained activity). In other cases, the pay for certain professions has established the prevailing rates in those areas. Decisions on issues such as free health care or free schooling or standardized pay for certain jobs are those made by a sovereign nation. In the case of Somalia, much ground has already been broken and some precedents already established. To reverse some of these situations will be extremely difficult should the future freely-elected Government of Somalia decide to do so.

F. Institutional Constraints and Bottlenecks

The extent of destruction in Somalia goes far beyond the physical infrastructure of the country. Somalia as a nation has been isolated from global economic institutions. This has rendered high transaction costs to many economic activities that Somalis may pursue in their country. Main areas of such institutional vacuum are:

1. Lack of financial intermediaries capable of keeping savings, extending credit, arranging for letter of credit and transfer of payments for internal and external trade.

2. Lack of any public sector institution providing administrative services and facilitating support for the work of the private sector.

3. Lack of legal provisions and binding law to regulate economic activities and absence of a free and fair economic environment for production and trade: this may prevent many investment decisions that the private sector may wish to take but consider risky in the absence of knowing the future legal constraints.

G. Lack of A Financial Intermediary System and Central Banking

Somalia has neither a central bank nor a network of any official intermediary. Transactions are done on the principle of a direct exchange of cash. Savings cannot be kept in any deposits. According to some businessmen interviewed by the author in Mogadishu in June 1993, the cost of safeguarding the means of payments in some transactions may exceed 15% of their entire value. In transactions involving transfer of payments from the country to abroad and vice-versa, Somalis are forced to bear a much higher cost of physically taking the hard currency to the seller than having it sent through a reliable banking network. Letters of credit cannot be opened and Somali exporters have to take a chance of not getting paid for the commodities sold to their partners in other countries. The latter has already caused a great loss to a number of livestock exporters during the previous season of export.

Lack of a central bank and any banking system has created a potentially volatile situation for the Somali local currency (Somali Shilling = SoSh). The importance of a stable monetary condition and the fact that setbacks are more than likely to happen which will cause serious problems in the country's macro-economy, have come to the forefront of some international concerns, namely UNOSOM.

The Somali shilling has had an interesting cycle of change during the last three years. Its value shrank at a high rate during the early days of the current upheaval and then stabilized for the major part of 1991. The value of Somali shilling fell considerably during 1992 following the outbreak of fighting in Mogadishu. At some point it reached over SoShs 7,500 to the US dollar, which was nearly seven times lower than the rate at the end of 1990. With the start of new emergency operation, the value of the Somali shilling rebounded considerably and stood at a rate close to SoShs 4,000 to the dollar in late May/early June, 1993. There are minor differences in the market exchange rate based on the large or small denomination of the bills and payment of cash or a bank cheque. These differences explain the existing transaction costs prevailing in the current market setting.

In the absence of any direct government intervention in the currency market, or impact of its fiscal management, the value of the Somali shilling is, more than anything else, linked to the level of commodity transactions in the market as well as the structure of the currency exchange market. The structure of the exchange market in Somalia shows little evidence of a collusive behavior. The major buyers of Somali shillings are the United Nations Organizations and some NGOs. The purchases are done through auction arrangements. Dealers and brokers can compete for the sale of the currency. There are, however, reasons to believe that only a few can arrange the exchange of the large sums of hard currencies.

Whether arrangements for the exchange of large sums are done under some collusive agreement is hard to judge with certainty. The resumption of trade and other productive activities will certainly have an important effect on the future exchange rate. Assuming everything else remains the same, the value of the Somali shilling becomes stronger as the volume of trade expands. Besides the impact of new imports or increase in the domestic production, there may be movements of local currency from the regions to the main currency markets. Little is really known about the real potential of these "off-shore" centers and the extent of their true effects in the future.

The function of a central bank as a monetary authority in creating an elastic currency (establishing a mechanism that can change the amount of currency in circulation, on the basis of the need for it) is a major constraining factor. The necessity of such an arrangement will be felt more strongly as the operation in Somalia moves from emergency to the stage of rehabilitation and reconstruction. The level of the Somali Shilling in the country may, at present, be sufficient as we see a relative stability in the market exchange rate. This is due to the considerable fall in the level of economic activities at present time. As rehabilitation begins and domestic production resumes and foreign trade expands there will be a dire need for flexibility in the level of money supply. The money supply can be considered in either form of its narrow or broad definition. It is obvious that inability to secure an appropriate response in the money supply will cause a recessionary pressure and a hampering effect on the progress of the recovery.

A major negative impact of not having a banking system is the erosion of any official credit activities in Somalia. This is particularly felt in areas where the need for seasonal credits has been significant, such as agricultural activities and export of livestock during the Haj season.

H. Lack of Public Sector Institutional Services

Government services are essential for smooth conduct of production and trade activities in a country. This becomes even more important in the context of a developing country such as Somalia, in which the private sector is unequipped and ill-prepared to take advantage of the existing domestic and international potentials. The most tangible areas are those relevant to collection and dissemination of business information, maintaining commercial links with other countries and regions and providing support for domestic production through appropriate policy interventions by the line ministries.

I. Lack of Any Reliable Legal Framework

There are a number of investment areas where the private sector can be gainfully engaged. Nonetheless, the uncertainty of what may later develop has prevented any action on the part of the private sector. At the same time there are questions and legal issues pertinent to the daily affairs of business people in Somalia. The institutional vacuum on legal matters has hampered any progress which, in turn, has added to the cost of doing business in Somalia.

VI. An Outline for Creating a Conducive Economic Environment for Rehabilitation and Reconstruction

A proposed outline for reconstruction and rehabilitation of Somalia may contain three major sets of policy interventions and rehabilitation provisions.

A. Immediate Regeneration of the Economy

There should be a joint effort with the participation of Somalis, international organizations and the donor countries to assess the current economic situation with the objective of immediate regeneration of the economy. This may involve taking the following steps:

1. Appraising the economic impact of commodity monetization on production and trade by trying to measure the overall social welfare effects of such intervention at present and in the near future.

2. Evaluate the effectiveness of the currently used concept and measures of self-sustainability in the form of direct cost recovery by charging fees for services, at present or for future consideration.

3. Look into the existing problems and seek ways for a wider use of Somali business entities for absorption of a greater proportion of relief, emergency, military and future rehabilitation of financial expenditures of international organizations and donors.

4. Assess the working of commodity markets in the major cities and their linkages with the regional urban markets.

5. Conduct a detailed study of the current exchange market in Somalia with a view of predicting how it may evolve as reconstruction gets underway, production expands and domestic and foreign trade grow in the near future.

6. Assess the existing donor coordination and its effectiveness in getting the possible optimum results and seek ways for its improvement.

7. Examine possible methods of generating income for public works in the absence of a formal and sovereign government.

8. Identify possible procedures for establishing the necessary public institutional services for the interim period for the normalization of life in Somalia.

9. Propose ways to benefit from active and continuous participation of Somalis in all aspects of designing and administrating relief as well as recovery efforts at present and in the near future.

10. Propose ways to arrange basic financial facilities for external trade, such as opening of LCs and enabling traders to transfer payments and keep deposits with a financial intermediary.

11. Seek ways to perform a limited role of a central bank in areas of exchange intervention, if needed, and influencing money supply if it becomes an unavoidable necessity.

12. Make concrete suggestions for direct intervention to assist the needy and the poor in all areas and regions.

13. Make proposals in dealing with special issues in Somalia, such as reintegration of "Boy Soldiers," assistance to informal sector and credit facilities to small farmers, women heading single families and urban poor.

B. Creating A Conducive Economic Environment for Rehabilitation and Recovery

There is a dire need to assess the prospects of creating a sustainable macroeconomic framework that can promote a successful implementation of the rehabilitation and reconstruction in the medium term. The focus of such effort should be to assess the need and propose the mechanism of establishing a macroeconomic environment conducive to promoting free and fair trade, encouraging domestic investment, attracting direct and joint foreign investments, facilitating efficient operation of exchange markets, enhancing the operation of financial markets, establishing an efficient public sector financial structure compatible with a probable decentralized government power and administrative structure, and, most importantly, setting in place a mechanism of direct intervention that can alleviate poverty in Somalia. The main components of such interventions are:

1. Make an assessment of the possible mechanism of generating public revenue in the form of direct and indirect taxation, import duties and other means of revenue collection such as fees for public services and so on.

2. Examine financial intermediaries, in the form of a commercial banking system or other temporary arrangements for establishing special financial account arrangements to facilitate transfer of payments for domestic and international trade, and for safe-keeping deposits in local and hard currencies.

3. Examine the extent of needs for central banking based on the specific required functions of a central bank in Somalia during the rehabilitation phase. Propose the specific institutional arrangements for the fulfillment of these functions or rehabilitation of a Somali Central Bank if a National Government is established.

4. Evaluate the establishment of viable and self-sustaining credit schemes for production and trade as well as looking further into the

future creation of specialized banking in Somalia. The proposal here should also indicate how similar schemes can be developed to assist the credit needed in housing and resettlement activities.

5. Propose ways to assist the informal sector in Somalia. This is currently the most active sector in providing jobs for many people in Somalia. Identify schemes to provide gainful employment for special groups such as women who head single family households, boy soldiers, and urban poor.

C. Building National Capacity

Building national capacity in Somalia is an effort to enhance the absorptive capacity of Somalia's economy for a successful implementation of its near future rehabilitation and reconstruction program. It should be viewed as setting in motion a process that can enhance the ability of Somalis to take advantage of the opportunities available to them for the betterment of their lives. This means empowering people to take charge and determine their destiny in a framework that they find most suitable. The role of international donors is to facilitate such a process. Fostering a sustainable human development process is in the heart of such development.

It should be realized that human development is not limited to social sectors (health, education and nutrition). While human development focuses on developing capabilities of people, it also places great importance on how these capabilities are employed. Therefore, free participation in social, political and economic decisions-making is vitally important.

Human development does not have a generic agenda for every country in the world. Each country should have its own. Indeed, Somalia must have its own focus and put people in the center of its own agenda for economic development. Such processes must be extended to all ranges of needs and ambitions of the country. In the case of Somalia this should constitute an open-ended process for inclusion of national aspirations and desires over time.

D. The Structure

It has been pointed out earlier that since independence, there has been a government superstructure with non-traditional characteristics and inspired by colonial administrative modes. It has also been argued that the political power despite such administrative structure was formed on the clear basis of clan coalition.

In order to overcome the existing "institutional vacuum" we need to concentrate on the resumption and restructuring of three important institutions. These are the political, legal and civil institutions. Creating and strengthening national capacity will ultimately mean training people who will become qualified professionals, decision-makers and managers capable of running their country efficiently in all aspects of political, social and economic lives. But such a system can only be viable if it is self-sustained. The commitment should come from the country itself. In the case of Somalia, the pertinent components for developing the necessary framework will entail developing the required financial capacity, mobilizing the necessary productive base and optimizing the use of the existing human resources.

E. The Approach to National Capacity Building

In the absence of any functioning government in Somalia the program can embark on an approach that can be perceived as realistic (i.e. implementable, based on the existing constraints), compatible with the existing political environment, and in conformity to the principles accepted by the community of donors and reflected in the ensuing international gathering on the rehabilitation of Somalia. In essence, the approach must generate a process of national capacity-building capable of fostering a sustainable economic development in Somalia. The outline of such an approach may entail the following:

1. Pursue a policy of creating a decentralized and at the same time broad-based institutional foundation in the design of the necessary entities. A decentralized and broad-based political and administrative power structure for the future Somalia may be justified on the grounds that: a) the traditional structure of Somali society and the political development of the last three years indicate that a decentralized power base is the most likely scenario to be followed, b) empowering people to take charge setting their own destiny and having political freedom are the unavoidable ingredients of a successful strategy for strengthening national capacity in a country, and c) decentralization of political power does not necessarily mean weakening of national unity. It merely means, in most cases, a more efficient method of governing a society by the people who are bound together by the virtue of their own culture, social heritage or economic considerations.

2. Encourage institutions that contribute to the strengthening of political freedom by emphasizing personal security for peaceful political activity, prevalence of rule of law, freedom of expression and legal guarantees for economic and political participation of all people.

3. Promote the role of the private sector by enabling it to acquire a higher degree of professional competence and managerial capabilities.

4. Put greater emphasis on the utilization of internal resources in all areas for capacity-building. This is an important element contributing to the creation of a self-sustained program.

5. Avoid committing Somalis to developing activities which are beyond their institutional, technical and financial capacity in the foreseeable future.

6. Seek tangible social benefits in excess of the social cost of every project, and pursue a well-justified order of preference for implementing different needed projects/activities, as the available resources are scarce. In certain cases, there may be justifiable ground for simply looking at cost recovery as a selection criterion. Cost recovery should be regarded as an important element of self-sustainability.

7. Address the historic imbalances in the allocation of resources for the development of the regional capacity.

8. Reach all segments of society and create greater opportunity for the lower strata, in particular women, returning refugees and other specially deprived groups, to be able to fully participate in the process.

9. Consider safeguarding the environment as a necessary element in sustainable development. In the context of Somalia, the abject poverty of the overwhelming majority of its population is the biggest threat to the environment.

F. The Areas of Capacity-Building

Building national capacity in Somalia is a formidable task. It has to fill a large gap, created not only by the ruins of the last three years of civil unrest, but by the neglect of decades of its governing administration. These areas include the following:

1. **Political Institutions**: Political participation of people in the governance of their own country/community is a crucial prerequisite for achieving a higher degree of human development. Building political institutions for Somalia is not to design their future political ideology, as this is a purely national matter for the Somalis to decide in a democratic environment. Political institution-building in the context of this program is to help build institutions for: a) representational arrangement at community, local and national levels, b) media ownership and management, c) assisting the establishment of entities which aim at defending and preserving the right of individuals and groups to free non-violent political participation.

2. **Legal Institutions**: Rule of law is an essential component of a civilized society. The prevailing anarchy in Somalia eroded the basis of any written law in the country. In certain areas, lawlessness caused a rebuke of the long-held traditions of clans which governed their people for centuries. Among the many existing problems, the lack of a constitution for the country as a whole is a major stumbling block. Nonetheless, stopping and doing nothing is a greater problem. The building of legal institutions requires a great deal of information in every aspect of Somali society which can be provided by Somalis themselves. The task of the institution- building in this area can focus on: a) legal provisions and institutions that can safeguard people as individuals or groups against misdemeanors, offenses, felonies and crimes committed against them in every community across the country, b) legal provisions and institutions that can safeguard economic interests of people as individuals or groups against fraud, physical and other kind of damages committed against them. A more elaborated legal system that can tackle freedom of economic participation may be developed later within the framework of a future constitution, c) helping to rehabilitate the law enforcement units in every community, d) legal provisions and technical assistance to Somalis in laying the technical foundation for the preparation of a provisional constitutional framework for the reconciliation process as well as helping to lay down the eventual constitution of the country after the general election.

3. **Civil Administrative Institutions**: Somalia, for years, relied on the direct services of foreign experts in the administration of civil institutions. The transfer of human skills and know-how was therefore rather slow and troubled by a growing brain drain. The

events of the last three years worsened the situation to an unprecedented level. The task of reconstruction and rehabilitation of civil institutions involves: a) institutions of public administration which embrace the development of public sector administrative machinery and training of their technical staff in all levels of local, regional and later at the national level, and b) private sector management and professional development institutions which tackle the development and training qualified, professional managers and other technical expertise of the non-governmental sector for the present and the future Somalia.

4. **Financial Institutional Development**: This is an area deserving immediate attention which, in part, has been explained in the previous section of this paper. Lack of financial institutions has crippled business activities, inflicted damage to the production capacities in rural and urban sectors and made it impossible to have any regular and systematic public service delivery as there has not been any public revenue generation to secure such services. The areas of reconstruction and rehabilitation of a viable financial structure include: a) public revenue-generating institutions at all levels of community especially local, and later at the national level, and b) institutions tackling financial intermediation, provision of credit for investment in all areas of production and trade, and safekeeping of savings.

5. **Social Sector Institutional Development**: Improving social sector takes the center stage in any Human Development Program. The current situation in Somalia is desperate. However, the history of neglect extends to the entire period of the 1980s. Deterioration of health, decline in the school enrollment, reduction in the number of caring teachers and the fast erosion of all means of social safety nets happened during the 1980s. Rebuilding social institutions requires a major mobilization in Somalia and includes:

a) rehabilitation of educational institutions at all levels of primary and secondary schooling, both general and technical. This involves a thorough review of the most urgent needs as well as institution-building for the longer term. The institutional building involves educational management (retraining teachers, mobilizing communities in understanding the concepts of community ownership and management, and helping communities to establish community based-education committees), restoration of primary and secondary schools and resumption of the activities of adult schools. On a more medium-term basis the reconstruction of local and regional education authorities can be envisaged. An interesting idea put forward by UNESCO has particular importance to Somalia in every region. This is the idea of developing "Peace Education." This plan would create hope and confidence in the future instead of fear and despair and replace dialogue for aggression and hostilities. The work involves formation of youth clubs, orientation of youth to have positive attitudes, and teaching the younger generation about the values of peace, conflict resolution, human rights and rights of the child, and environmental education.

b) rehabilitation of Technical Training Institutions which are a part of the general secondary education system. For Somalia there is a great need for restoration of such schools. They include technical schools and vocational training centers. In both kinds of schools, emphasis should be placed on developing courses in areas that Somalis needs. Curriculum development, technical teachers' training and building educational managerial skills are among the most important areas for such a challenge.

c) rehabilitation of post-secondary institutions involves opening of technical and managerial schools and universities. This is a longer term program which can be tackled at a regional and national level later, as the country returns to a normalcy.

d) rehabilitation of health, sanitation and nutrition institutions at all community levels, local and regional. The already fragile health manpower received a bigger blow during the ongoing crisis. The immediate area of attention is to utilize the existing Somali manpower in various professional areas which may be scattered in various regions disproportionally. The areas of capacity building should focus on strengthening the technical staff for provision of essential health care services to regional hospitals, mothers and children centers (MCH) and health posts. Strengthening the existing and developing further capacity for the management and coordination of health services is another important task. Rehabilitation of institutions for provision of potable water and sanitation facilities and training of experts and engineers is an important area of immediate attention. Training community water care takers is a vital step that will have significant positive effect on the sate of the health of Somalis in every area.

e) strengthening community capacities at the local and regional level to deal with social emergencies. This calls for putting in place provisions that can deal with poverty alleviation. In terms of training, there is a tremendous need for training community social workers and other technical staff that can provide services for the deprived strata of the society. The relevant areas for the immediate future include strengthening the existing and establishing new institutions for reintegration of "boy soldiers," assisting single women heads of families, orphans and other socially disadvantaged groups.

VII. Conclusion

The objectives and principles of national capacity-building in Somalia have been highlighted in the foregoing sections. The approach, as explained, is to create a framework for human development programs compatible with the evolving social and political conditions in Somalia. The central issue in having a successful program is the "relevance" and the "pragmatism" pursued in laying down the provisions for its implementation. A Human Development Approach, as previously argued, should not be seen as a mere training program. It is to set in motion a process that in time can create an environment conducive to emergence of an equitable economic growth. The program thus relates to the economic, social and political policy agenda in the country as well as trying to prepare people to be technically more productive. As there is no national government in Somalia which could take charge of developing a national strategy, one has to rely on a collective effort of donors and international organizations to design the program with the central involvement of Somalis.

Bibliography

Berry, L. and I. Johnson. 1983. "The Republic of Somalia." International Development Program of Clark University. USA.

Jeffrey Clark.1993. "Debacle In Somalia." *Foreign Affairs* Washington, DC

Jamshid Damooei . 1991. *An Outline for UNDP Fifth Country Program: A Medium-Run Program (1991-1993).* New York: UNDP.

--------- 1993. *Moving Towards Creation of a Conducive Economic Environment for Reconstruction and Rehabilitation in Somalia.* New York: UNDP.

Hossein Farzin, Y. 1988. *Food Import Dependence in Somalia.* World Bank Discussion Papers No. 23, Washington D.C.: World Bank.

Reginal Herbold Green. 1993. *Somalia: Towards Reconstruction, Rehabilitation, Restructuring.* New York: A Report Prepared for The UNICEF.

N.L. Hicks. 1978. "Poverty and Basic Needs in Somalia (mimeo)." Washington D.C..

M.J.Hopkins. 1978. *Somalia and Basic Needs: Some Issues.* World Employment Program Research Working Paper No. 3-32/wp 8. Geneva: ILO.

IFAD. 1979. *Report on the Special Programming Mission to Somalia.* Somalia.

ILO. 1989. *Generating Employment and Incomes in Somalia: Report of An ILO/JASPA Inter-Disciplinary employment and Project-Identification Mission to Somalia.* Addis Ababa.

V. Jamal. 1981. *Nomads, Farmers and Townsmen: Incomes and Inequality in Somalia.* Addis Ababa: ILO Working Paper. JASPA.

David D Laitin, and Said Samatar. 1987. *Somalia: Nation in Search of a State.* UK: Westview Press.

I.M. Lewis. 1988. *A Modern History of Somalia; Nation and State.* Boulder, CO: Westview Press.

Satish Mishra. 1993. *Finance, Banking and Economic Regeneration in Somalia.* Nairobi Kenya: REDSO\ESA\APD, USAID.

Ministry of Planning. 1990. *National Account Aggregates* (1977-1989). Mogadishu Somalia.

Abdi I Samatar. 1989. *The State and Rural Transformation in Northern Somalia.* USA: University of Wisconsin Press.

Ahmed I. Samatar, 1988. *Socialist Somalia: Rhetoric and Reality.* UK: Zed Books.

Tyler. 1983. *Somalia: Case Study On Rural Poverty.* Rome: FAO, WCARD In-depth Studies No.7.

UNECA. 1993. *ECA's Agenda on Emergency, Humanitarian, Rehabilitation and Reconstruction Affairs.* Addis Ababa Ethiopia.

UNDP. 1991. *Development Co-operation Report: Special Report* (1989-1991). New York

UNDP. 1991. *Report on the Needs Assessment Mission to Somalia.* Nairobi Kenya.

UNDP. 1992. *Human Development Report.* UK, New York: Oxford University Press.

UNDP. 1992. *Major Conference Issues and Consultations.* Addis Ababa Ethiopia.

UNESCO. 1992. *Somalia Crisis: The Challenge to Education.* Somalia.

UNICEF. 1993. R*elief and Rehabilitation Program for Somalia.* New York.

USAID. 1993. *From Relief to Recovery.* Washington D.C.

Thomas Vietorisz. 1987. *Regional Variation, Economic Specialization and Income Distribution in Somalia.* Somalia: USAID.

World Bank. 1990. *Somalia: Crisis in the Public Expenditure Management.* Washington D.C.

World Bank. 1987. *Somalia: and Public Enterprise Reform.* Washington D.C..

SECTION FIVE

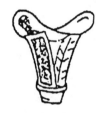

Toward
Reconciliation and
Conflict Resolution

Summaries: Section Five

Mohamed M. Sahnoun (Chapter 18) was Special Representative to the UN mission in Somalia in 1991 and 1992. He describes, from a first-hand perspective, how his strategy had been one of working within the context of the Somali political reality. Under his guidance, the UN had established four decentralized zones, based in Bosaso, Berbera, Kismayo, and Mogadishu. These points were to form the core of both relief distribution as well as political rehabilitation. Yet the inertia of the centralized UN management systems thwarted success. As a result, local initiatives foundered while central management disintegrated into clan-based and warlord-driven conflict. These organizational obstacles precluded implementation of Sahnoun's plan and, toward the end of 1992, he resigned. In retrospect, Sahnoun argues that the decentralized approach -- to pluck feathers "one at a time until the eagle ultimately cannot fly," was the only possible way to neutralize the warlords. He also points to missed opportunities (before 1992) when international intervention could have proven more effective.

Ahmed Yusuf Farah and I. M. Lewis (Chapter 19) present results of a survey carried out in 1993 in "Somaliland." They review causes of the conflict as well as traditional means of dealing with such issues, noting the persistent role of lineage elders, using dialogue and the social pressure of the clan, to resolve disputes. They conclude that the extensive and time-consuming methods of dialogue implemented by the elders of Somaliland are living proof that dialogue does work and that there is a substantial role for these techniques in other parts of Somaliland/Somalia.

Abdi-asis M. Mohamed (Chapter 20) follows on the theme of Farah and Lewis in Chapter 19, noting similar efforts underway in the Northeast. He finds that reliance on elders has, as in Somaliland, enabled the Northeast to establish a cease-fire and begin rebuilding. He identifies progress on a number of fronts, yet finds that basic and major needs still exist, including health, water, veterinary medicine, housing, regional administration, and economic institutions. Throughout his article he cautions that the violence and disorder in the south not be allowed to pull humanitarian and rehabilitation assistance away from the Northeast, where it will have far higher impact on creating sustainable results.

Ann and Robert Seidman (Chapter 21), drawing on their extensive experience in Africa and Asia drafting legislation and creating constitutions, consider what processes may be needed among Somali communities. They suggest three: (1) a theoretical framework; (2) a problem solving methodology known as ROCCIPI -- rules, opportunities, capacities, communication, interests, processes, and ideologies; and (3) a democratically supported participatory methodology to provide Somali leaders with both theory and a practical methodology to accomplish their tasks of creating a new constitution,. The article sets out splendid guidelines for leaders to consider as discussions take place over what structures and processes will be included for Somalia/Somaliland.

CHAPTER EIGHTEEN

Prevention in Conflict Resolution: The Case of Somalia

Mohamed M. Sahnoun

The framers of the UN Charter were keen to provide the international community with a document which would provide ways and means for peaceful solutions to all disputes, including conflicts within states which could become a threat to peace and security. Only in exceptional situations does the Charter advocate the use of force. Even then, a number of precautionary measures--such as economic sanctions--are clearly spelled out before taking action by air, sea, or land forces.

Article 33 of the Charter, which is central to the architecture of the document, reflects this preoccupation for peaceful solution in the following words:

> The parties to any dispute, the continuance of which is likely to endanger the maintenance of international peace and security shall, first of all, seek a solution by negotiation, enquiry, mediation, conciliation, arbitration, judicial settlement, resort to regional agencies or arrangements, or other peaceful means of their own choice.

Chapter VIII of the Charter which deals in three long articles with regional arrangements underlines further that member states shall make every effort to achieve peaceful settlement of disputes through regional organizations before referring them to the Security Council.

The United Nations and regional organizations should have cooperated closely long ago to put in place a monitoring system in different subregions of the world which can alert the headquarters of a pending crisis and make suggestions on how to avert a larger conflict. This early warning system is still missing. Preventive action must indeed rely on permanent structures and adequate human resources. In addition, statesmen with a long experience in negotiating peace should be available on short notice to undertake specific mediation operations as special envoys of regional organizations and when necessary of the United Nations.

What is required at the early stage of a crisis is prompt availability of these resources for mediation and conciliation, and for large humanitarian intervention. This availability should be, first, at the regional level, and when these regional efforts have produced little or no result, the matter should then be addressed by the appropriate structures of the United Nations. Where the ingredients of a serious crisis are already evident, the international community should act and act quickly. The concern about forcible intervention, in both *humanitarian* and *political* fields, is demonstrated and translated into action as soon as possible as required again in Article 33 of the UN Charter. It would not have to conflict either with the principle of sovereignty. The issue is prevention through an early diagnosis of the situation followed by mediation, or conciliation, and appropriate humanitarian assistance. It might involve, at a later stage, pressuring the parties concerned and, if necessary, gradually escalating these pressures. The use of armed forces will become exceptional.

In addition to the members of the United Nations, the Secretary-General himself is authorized to bring "to the attention of the Security Council any matter which, in his opinion, may threaten the maintenance of international peace and security." This disposition of the Charter was rarely used by Secretary Generals in recent history. Yet it is clear that by referring to any matter here, the drafters of the Charter had broadened the scope of the Secretary General's mandate and allowed him to make the necessary appreciation of whether and when specific situations warrant the attention of the Security Council, and to consequently address the matter to the Council. It implies that the Secretary General is entitled to make the necessary investigations and to assess the different ways and means to resolve an issue well before it evolves into a dangerous conflict. There is clearly a tendency today on the part of the Secretary General to rely too much on peace-keeping forces and not on prevention. In fact, the agenda for peace actively advocates this approach.

It is our belief that if the international community had intervened earlier and more effectively in some of the conflicts we see today, much of the catastrophes that have unfolded could have been avoided. In theory, there should have been no shortage of actors who could have intervened to mediate the conflicts that engulfed Somalia. Somalia is a member of the League of Arab States, and the Organization of African Unity. During the Carter and Reagan administrations, Somalia was also a close ally of the United States and of the West, receiving hundreds of millions of dollars in American economic and military assistance. Somalia also retained good relations with the former colonial powers of Britain and Italy, two important members of the European Community. Finally, Somalia was of course a member of the United Nations. Any one of these actors could have offered their services as mediators or supported the mediation efforts timidly undertaken by neighboring countries at various times. Sadly, none of these nations or institutions, all supposedly "friends" of Somalia and its people, moved to help her in her hour of need in a timely and efficient way. When the international community finally did begin to intervene in early 1992, hundreds of thousands of lives had already been lost.

Let us examine three specific instances in recent Somali history which clearly identify typical crisis situations where the international community might be called upon to intervene.

I. The Uprising in the North - A Regional Disaffection

Although Somalia had known several periods of unrest since its independence in 1960, the first crisis occurred when a large uprising took place in the north in May-June, 1988, that ultimately led to the nation's disintegration. The uprising was fueled both by clan-based rivalries and by political/economic considerations. The northern part of Somalia, home of a large clan, the Isaaq, as well as other smaller tribes, came to resent the leadership of the southern tribal groups, which they consider to have monopolized political power since Siyad Barre took over in a coup in 1969.

The inhabitants of the northern regions clearly perceived themselves to be wronged and without the possibility of democratic redress. The revolt was led by the Somali National Movement (SNM), an opposition group rooted mainly in the area. Governmental forces unable to prevent the uprising, unleashed a bloody repression against the civilian population using aircraft and heavy weapons. At the time, Amnesty International denounced the systematic torture of prisoners by the government security forces, and human rights organizations around the world protested the repression. One would expect that in the absence of a democratic mechanism in the country allowing for corrective measures, the international community would come to the rescue of the victimized population, by putting stronger pressure on the Government and proposing its acceptance of mediation. It did not, and this represents the first missed opportunity.

II. The Manifesto - A National Protest

In May 1990, exactly two years after the beginning of the uprising in the north and as armed opposition spread significantly to other regions of the country, a manifesto signed by 144 well-known and moderate political leaders was published in Mogadishu calling for a national conference to reconcile the various movements and ethnic groups. The group blamed the government for the atrocities committed during the war, suggested the abolition of repressive laws as a sign of government sincerity, and called for a multiparty system and constitutional changes, and also for a national reconciliation conference which would form a caretaker government and prepare elections. There were some limited foreign diplomatic demarches in support of this move. US Secretary of State James Baker stated in a meeting with the Somali Prime Minister that the US bilateral assistance to Somalia would be suspended until the Mogadishu government demonstrated proper respect for human rights.

But there was no concerted action on the part of the international community. In fact, the United Nations began to evacuate its personnel from Hargeisa and elsewhere in Somalia as early as the summer of 1988 for safety reasons. Neither the United Nations nor the regional organizations were providing any leadership for serious mediation efforts, and the fragile and isolated endeavors of some governments could not have any impact. Siyad Barre's government responded to the manifesto appeal by arresting many of the leaders, including the former president of Somalia, Abdullah Osman. This was the second missed opportunity.

III. The Fall of the Siyad Barre Regime - A Country Without a Government

By this time, the conflict was spreading throughout the country and

Siyad Barre could only, on the one hand, appoint new prime ministers and promise democracy, and on the other hand, unleash the worst reprisal ever against his own people. On January 5, 1991, in the midst of the final preparations for Desert Storm, the US had to dispatch helicopters from two amphibious carriers near Somalia to rescue American and other foreigners from Mogadishu. Siyad Barre himself finally fled Mogadishu on January 27, 1991 with his supporters. Somalia was then without a government, and the major insurgent movements controlled the capital.

A few timid attempts at mediation were then initiated by some governments in the region. One serious attempt at reconciliation between the different factions was undertaken by the Djibouti government from July 15-21, 1991. With the support of some governments of the region, a meeting of several parties was held at Djibouti and a partial agreement was reached on the steps to be taken to promote peace and democracy. Unfortunately, the results of this conference were not endorsed by all the parties.

Clearly, the organizers of the conference lacked experience and could not exert enough pressure on the parties to the conflict. The government of Djibouti had requested the support of the United Nations but it was turned down with no explanation except that the matter was too complicated. Had the United Nations, together with the regional organizations, been involved in the preparation of this meeting, this reconciliation process could have gotten off to a good and serious start. It was the third missed opportunity.

Because of the failure of this attempt at reconciliation in Djibouti and the absence of any other important alternative, the Somali factions were left to themselves and soon intra-clan fighting began in Mogadishu. This battle laid to waste large areas of the city in November and December, 1991. Estimates of deaths through March 1992 ranged as high as 30,000. It was the worst part of the civil war. I sincerely believe we could have avoided it.

IV. The United Nations Security Council Decision in 1992

When our UN delegation arrived in Mogadishu on our first mission in March, 1992, the city was nearly deserted. Despite several cease-fire agreements however, fighting was still occurring periodically around the city. These skirmishes looked almost grotesque in view of the overall tragedy which the people of Somalia as a whole was experiencing: chaos everywhere, the total collapse of all administrative structures, and, above all, the horrendous humanitarian disaster. At least 300,000 people had died of hunger and hunger-related disease in the country as a whole and the figure would be much higher if those tallied as casualties of the repression and the civil war are added in. Some 70 percent of the livestock had been lost, and the farming areas had been devastated, compelling the farming community to seek refuge in remote areas or across the border into refugee camps. Some 500,000 people were in the camps in Ethiopia, Kenya and Djibouti.

The UN team and Mogadishu-based NGOs had limited resources with which to work. Yet they were expected to help supply food, care for the sick, provide administrative expertise and coordination for relief operations, work to restore infrastructure, and of course, mediate clan disputes. There was no military option in the initial stages. The UN mission had to rely, to a large degree, on moral suasion to get things done.

Gradually, skirmishes in Mogadishu were receding. The Somali people viewed the arrival of the first UN teams as a sign of interest in their fate. They could not understand why the United Nations and all its agencies had been keeping a distant and suspicious stance towards Somalia when their needs were so obvious. They could not but compare the United Nations to other charitable institutions and non-governmental organizations (NGOs), which spared no effort to rescue the starving and the sick and to provide essential relief. The means of the NGOs were limited, but their goodwill and their courage were admirable. Largely thanks to them, in March 1992, the population began to gradually return to Mogadishu, as well as to other big cities and villages. Despite deep-seated grievances and distrust of the United Nations, the Somali leaders agreed to deal with the institution. After long and patient discussions, we were able to win back their trust. All accepted, in principle, as early as March, 1992, the deployment of security forces for the protection of emergency relief workers. They also agreed to a UN mediation effort.

All of these leaders, however, insisted on the need to launch an urgent and large humanitarian assistance operation as well as an important recovery program. They were very concerned that they would lose control of some of the young militia who might join other unruly youth already engaged in looting. Since arms and ammunition were easily available, this was justifiably the biggest concern. It was estimated that more than 40,000 weapons had been abandoned by the former Somali army as the civil war reached its peak in January, 1992, and forced the troops to disband. Many Somali leaders had requested UN assistance in disarming the population. However, the Somalis would voluntarily bring in their weapons only if the food basket was sufficiently attractive. It was also necessary to use some forms of inducement such as temporary employment or other activities. None of these was available.

Had the assistance, both military and humanitarian, been forthcoming in the way expected in Somalia by relief workers and Somalis, it would have greatly contributed to create an atmosphere propitious to dialogue and compromise. Not only was the UN assistance program very limited, it was also so slowly and inadequately delivered that it became counterproductive. Fighting erupted over the meager food supplied. While the ICRC and all NGOs did their utmost to enhance their programs and ventured deep inside Somalia to provide emergency relief to the population despite tremendous danger and difficulties, some UN agencies were arguing that the security situation did not allow a large presence, or sometimes even any presence at all, of their staff or their structure.

Our argument was that one should break the vicious circle. The scarcity of food deteriorated further the atmosphere of security which already prevailed within the country. Our assessment of food requirements for the whole country, including refugees, was a minimum of 50,000 MT per month, which, for a period of six months beginning in January and ending in June should have amounted to 300,000 MT. By mid-July the World Food Program (WFP) had delivered, by its own admission, only 18,857 MT out of 68,388 MT pledged by the same organization in January, 1992.

Other UN agencies, except for UNICEF, did not fare better in this emergency relief operation in the first six months of 1992. In fact, most of them did not even maintain offices in Somalia, their representatives preferring to remain in Nairobi or Djibouti. By comparison, the International Committee of the Red Cross (ICRC) brought, between February and June, 1992, a total of 53,900 MT of food into Somalia through twenty different entry points by sea, air and overland across the Kenya-Somalia border. This is almost three times as much as the UN. The ICRC operated four hundred kitchens feeding over 600,000 people in Mogadishu and six other towns. These community kitchens provided up to two cooked meals daily. The ICRC also handled the distribution of food to several hospitals in various cities and sustained four daily rotations of airlift delivery from Mombasa (Kenya) to Mogadishu, Belet Weyn, and Baidoa. In the face of this tragic situation, I made an urgent appeal to donor countries to involve themselves directly in the delivery of food to Somalia through airlift operations.

It was clear that by then the Somali society had largely broken down and there were only a few safeguards remaining on which we could rely. What sustained our hope was the encouragement we had received from the elders in all the regions as well as some former social, political, and administrative officials including former police officers and women leaders both at the national and community level. They were approaching us sometimes with tears in their eyes offering to work closely with the United Nations to bring Somalia out of the mess.

Despite previous bitter experiences, all had given their consent to work with the United Nations and regional organizations for a comprehensive solution. The interim president, Ali Mahdi, whose faction (USC Manifesto Group) was in control in north Mogadishu agreed with us that he would resign his position as soon as we could announce a date for a meeting with other Somali leaders. This was important for progress, given the hostility towards him or, more precisely, towards his claim to be the acting head of state.

Our delegation pursued a strategy of putting the clan system to work for Somalia. Agreements among local elders helped gradually to reduce the fighting and allow food deliveries into the interior of the country. After arduous discussions and with the help of the elders, we arranged a deal with Ali Mahdi and General Aidid and other faction leaders for the deployment of five hundred Pakistani peacekeepers in Mogadishu. Despite recurrent problems, the port was open and distribution through it was established.

By the middle of October, 1992, all faction leaders of the different regions and community elders had given their assent for a national conference whose objective would be to exchange views on the process of national reconciliation. The President of Ethiopia, Meles Zinawi, acting as president of a committee set up by the heads of state of the Horn of Africa to deal with Somalia, proposed to hold this conference in Addis Ababa, which we agreed should be in January, 1993.

In the meantime, we had proposed to divide Somalia into four zones to encourage decentralization of all operations among the four areas which would include Bosaso (NE), Berbera (NW), Kismayo (South) and Mogadishu (Center). This decentralization would have made both UNOSOM and relief agencies less dependent on the conditions prevailing in Mogadishu and promote the new regional leadership so badly needed by Somalia. This proposal was endorsed by Security Council Resolution 767.

Unfortunately, several serious problems created by wrong and unjustified moves of the UN management both at headquarters and by some representatives in the field continued to hamper our efforts. First, despite significant contributions made by donor countries, most UN agencies were not able to fulfill their pledges and organize a massive emergency relief operation in the way this was done in Ethiopia in the early '80s or even in the Biafra war in the late '60s.

Second, the UN agencies would hardly leave Mogadishu, Nairobi and Djibouti, and the tendency to centralize everything in Mogadishu became clearly a feature of UNOSOM operations. We had practically no response whatsoever to our numerous requests to the agencies to fill the posts and responsibilities allocated to them in the four different zones indicated above. So delivery of emergency relief and rehabilitation operations continued to concentrate on Mogadishu giving General Aidid and his allies a certain leverage. This also undermined our efforts to organize the grassroots structures in the local communities within the regions.

Third, most agencies were reluctant to coordinate seriously their activities with us, which would have helped enhance the security measures envisaged. We proposed to use monetization of a reasonable percentage of the food delivery to encourage cooperation from the local merchants. These merchants were prepared to use their influence to check the activities of the armed looters and the mischief of some of the militia leaders. It is clear that ultimately these merchants had to make some deals with the looters which encouraged the latter to increase their harassment of the relief work.

Fourth, we proposed to the agencies to harmonize their payment rates for services and the use of facilities, and a number of other steps which would have greatly limited the ability of the militia and the looters to affect our operations. But most agency representatives seemed to resent any authority except their own headquarters and coordination became an impossible task. Although looting was still limited in October 1992 to 10 percent of the delivery, according to ICRC, and 15 percent according to WFP, it could have been reduced further if these steps had been taken.

Fifth, the bureaucratic approach of the UN headquarters in New York tended to ignore our advice and our warnings in sensitive matters related to security. It took much time and difficult negotiation for our team to reach an agreement for the deployment of five hundred UN troops for the security of humanitarian assistance, and we were hoping they would be deployed right away. After all, this was just a small battalion. There is no doubt that, had these five hundred troops been fully deployed as late as a month after the agreement, that is the beginning of September, it would have made an appreciable difference in the environment. The bureaucratic delays and the skirmishes at headquarters between different departments led to total confusion as to the priorities. Five hundred troops had not even arrived when an announcement that over 3,800 troops will be sent to Somalia was made in New York! This statement was made without informing the UNOSOM delegation in Mogadishu, the leaders of the neighboring countries, and worse, without consulting the Somali leaders and community elders as we had done before.

Sixth, as the United Nations began to gain the trust of the warring parties and acceptance and sympathy among the people, we learned that a Russian plane with UN markings, chartered by a UN agency, had delivered currency and military equipment to the north of Mogadishu, apparently to the troops supporting interim president Ali Mahdi. This, of course, infuriated his arch-rival, General Aidid. Much of the trust which we had built up over the months was seriously eroded. Suspicion against all UN personnel in Mogadishu was spreading. This rekindled an old perception of many Somalis that the United Nations, and some countries, were biased in favor of the acting president. The UN Office of Legal Affairs suggested that an investigation be carried out in Nairobi. This was important to show the good faith of the United Nations to all concerned including the Somali population and the governments of the neighboring countries, especially because there were indications and rumors that more than one such flight had taken place. In fact, late in October another Russian plane crashed in Northern Mogadishu on an illegal flight, also carrying suspicious cargo. What is incredible is that although the UN name and reputation were at stake, no serious investigation was undertaken and no legal action for redress had been pursued.

These are only a few examples of the important organizational obstacles we found in our way while attempting to address the issues of starvation and civil war in Somalia. Our hope was that with the personal support of the Secretary General we would ultimately tackle these difficulties and gradually create an environment for serious peace talks not so much between the faction leaders as between new leaders being promoted by the grassroots process well under way.

The untimely announcement by the Secretary General that the United Nations would send in additional reinforcements, without proper consultation, and my resignation led to a rapid deterioration of the security situation in Mogadishu and elsewhere. Somali armed groups began to harass the relief efforts more actively. Although the ninety day plan of April 1992 had given way to the one hundred day plan for accelerated relief deliveries to Somalia approved on 12 October 1992, a UN report on the plan dated 3 December 1992 stated, "some 38 days into the program, it is clear that while much has been accomplished, even the short-term needs are not being met." Out of a target of 100,000 MTs, between October 12 and December 3, the World Food Program only delivered 18,900 MTs of food supplies. Shortfalls in assistance continued to be manifest and the security situation deteriorated markedly. Estimates of the amount of food being stolen ranged now from as low as ten percent to as high as 80 percent. The US government used the higher figure as part of the justification for Operation Provide Hope.

By all accounts, in March 1993, Operation Restore Hope had largely achieved the main purpose assigned to it. Starvation and famine were broadly checked, and the situation was gradually returning to normal in the region most affected, the Southwest. In Mogadishu itself and in conferences in Addis Ababa, spectacular reconciliations have taken place between former enemies thanks to the efforts and also the initiatives of the President of Ethiopia as well as the other leaders of the Horn of Africa. It is with this background in mind that we can ask the question: should the US forces involved in ORH or some of them have remained in Somalia under the UN management and implement what appears, to say the least, to be an ambiguous UN/US strategy? My answer is clearly no! It was a mistake to leave a large contingent of US forces to provide the UN with important logistical and lethal support and maintain a high US profile in the commanding heights of the UN superstructure.

ORH was a remarkable intervention warmly welcomed by all Somalis across the board including Farah Aidid and the SNA (Somali National Alliance) and it did achieve all its aims. Some mistakes might have been made here and there, but they are insignificant in view of the overall success of the operation. Ideally, the US forces should have left totally in April 1993 when ORH had formally ended.

Some token logistical support could have been envisaged for few remaining UN forces. But this should have been done *within a clear strategy defined together with the Somali themselves, the President of Ethiopia and the neighboring countries, as well as the Organization of African Unity.* In fact, the UN should have been only one of the partners whose role was to continue to provide security and coordination of the emergency relief and the rehabilitation program in very limited areas leaving the political reconciliation and the stabilization to the Somalis, who had already agreed to a minimum plan in Addis Ababa and the neighboring countries, especially Ethiopia.

The confusion is due to an ill-prepared and largely subjective strategy which today requires a full investigation by the Security Council. The UN Secretariat pushed through policies and moves not even discussed with the Somali in all regions and not cleared with the neighboring countries. For example: a decision to disarm one clan and not all clans at the same time is a recipe for continuous civil war in the country. A move to take over and shut one radio station belonging to one clan and not all radio stations of all clans at the same time is totally unwise. To leave the Pakistani forces in Mogadishu despite several incidents was a terrible mistake. To look for quick fixes as political solutions, without taking into account the local realities is nonsense. These were, unfortunately, some of the features of the UN strategy and no wonder that it failed. Animosity very quickly prevailed and this is not surprising with the background of suspicion I described earlier.

These liabilities in the overall strategy were further compounded by reactive and unfair decisions taken after the confrontation in May-June 1993 between UN forces and Somali armed groups in the South of Mogadishu. After the June 5 ambush where twenty-three Pakistanis lost their lives, Aidid was declared guilty, forty-eight hours after the event, without proper investigation. An all-out offensive was launched not only against him but against the clans and subclans allied within the SNA. The destruction and the casualties which resulted are known to all of us. The wounds will not heal easily.

For Somali culture, clans fight for survival constantly because of the difficult and fluctuating environment. Their culture, their poems, their history is full of examples of clans who have disappeared from earth because they were unable to protect their interest through the total solidarity of all the members or because of bad leadership.

It would have been much wiser to gather a maximum of arguments proving the guilt of Aidid or anyone else, and then persuading the elders and other subclan leaders of the need to cooperate with the UN in bringing the culprits to justice. This works in Somalia because the tradition itself requires stern measures for manslaughter and to put the highest priority for collective undertaking on the matter.

The UN Secretariat had been alerted of all these elements long ago. I was forced to resign because I could not understand why people in New York who knew nothing of the realities in the field would make hasty and uncalled for decisions and persist in having them implemented, despite evidence of misjudgment and strong objection of the people in the field.

It is unfortunate that members of the Security Council tend to rely solely on reports submitted by the Secretary General and, except from inputs and instructions they receive from their countries, which by the way have no embassy in Mogadishu, do not look at other sources of information. Why does the Security Council not hold hearings where distinguished diplomats and scholars could give useful evidence to complement and check what it might learn from the Secretary General. In case I was requested to give such a testimony, which I was not, I will remind the Security Council that I had objected to a rapid build-up of the forces in Somalia, back in August, 1992 and that I insisted, as I insist today, that we should give the maximum chance to the political approach to resolve the pending issues in Somalia. The situation is largely stabilized in most regions of Somalia and it is almost suicidal for any clan to attempt to invade another clan's territory. The UN forces were initially deployed in Somalia for a very clear and limited purpose, that is, to ensure the security of the emergency relief. It is because they were gradually deviating from this role that many Somalis were persuaded of the existence of a hidden agenda.

The best way to check and neutralize the warlords is to do what Somalis have always recommended to me: that is, plucking feathers one at a time until the eagle ultimately cannot fly. I convinced Aidid to sign three agreements with the UN by putting pressure on him through the elders of his own clan and other community leaders. He was much weaker at the time than he is now, while community leaders were gradually asserting their authority with our encouragement.

I would also suggest that we should proceed the way we proceeded in Cambodia. Let the US, Canada, Ethiopia and others monitor the political solution without being militarily engaged -- the way France and Indonesia sponsored the peace process in Cambodia which led to the Paris accord. The peace agreement itself will determine the role and the magnitude of the UN peacekeeping forces to be deployed in Somalia. Meanwhile, these forces should be drastically reduced and the original mandate of securing the emergency relief and rehabilitation program, in specific areas be reconfirmed. I believe that if these few steps are taken, a totally new atmosphere will be created much more propitious for a serious dialogue between the different clans and the different regions. Force had become a logic in itself and those who foolishly were pushing for more build-up of the forces without any kind of strategy bear a heavy responsibility in the tragic events of the last months in Somalia. The UN should learn a lesson from the Somali tragedy.

CHAPTER NINETEEN

Peace-Making Endeavor of Contemporary Lineage Leaders in "Somaliland" (Northwest Somalia)

by Ahmed Yusuf Farah and I.M. Lewis

I. Objectives

1. Generate adequate and reliable information that can help ActionAid manage better its present and future reconstruction and development work in "Somaliland."

2. Share with other interested NGO and multilateral organizations ActionAid's positive experience of working with the elders in Erigavo region, where the organization operates reconstruction activities in the areas of water supply and animal health.

3. Review the political processes documented by I.M. Lewis (1961) in his classic work *A Pastoral Democracy.* This was made imperative by the paucity of serious contemporary anthropological studies on the northern Somali society. Compared to similar societies in Sub-Sahara Africa, this northern, primarily nomadic

society remains the least documented. Moreover, working in an unstable situation requires a clear understanding of the local politics of the project area in particular and the wider social context in general.

4. Produce an updated study on the traditional system of governance, by examining the changes that took place in the contemporary post-independence period (1960-1993).

5. Explain the security differences between the relatively peaceful study area and the troubled south.

6. Explore the relevance of traditional political leaders for consolidation of peace, reconstruction and institution-building.

II. Methodology

This survey of the northern peace conferences took a period of four months to complete. It started in June, 1993, in London, with a two week review of the literature. The bulk of the recently produced relevant material was found to be prescriptive, and based mostly on superficial, quick studies, or speculating on the causes of the crisis. Shortage of reliable, recent and in-depth sociological data became apparent from the literature survey. This influenced the decision to use I.M. Lewis (1961) *A Pastoral Democracy* as a point of departure for the field survey.

Under the supervision of I.M. Lewis, A.Y. Farah (a northern social anthropologist), undertook a six week field trip in Erigavo (three weeks), Hargeisa (two weeks) and Awdal region (one week) in the self-proclaimed "Republic of Somaliland." The researcher would have liked to observe a peace conference in full swing, since participant observation is an important anthropological technique of data collection. Unfortunately, the researcher was denied the opportunity to participate in the Erigavo conference, which was first scheduled to take place on the tenth of April and wrongly assumed to take place sometime during the trip, but was delayed several times during the survey period.

The raw data presented in the study, was obtained from several sources. Ensuing legal agreements between reconciling parties, were collected and studied with the help of the local authorities of Somali customary law (*xeer*). Most of these were kindly provided by Abdi Abdillahi, a graduate of the Lafoole College of Education, who was actively engaged in the secretariat work for the peace functions of the *Guurti* of "Somaliland." The Sultan of the Eastern Habar Yonis in

Erigavo issued the bilateral agreements between his clan and neighboring Warsangeli and Dulbahante clans. A former secondary school classmate, Jibril in Erigavo, provided the treaty of the Eastern alliance. The Rer Nur past and present petitions, were obtained from the *Guurti* of Rer Nur lineage of the Gadabursi and Mr. Khayre Hussein.

Valuable information was also collected through informal and open discussions the researcher had with lineage leaders at various levels of political segmentation, and other social groups (intellectuals, modern politicians, poets, religious men and women) who have participated in most of the peace conferences. In addition, the researcher enjoyed an illuminating video show on the Borama conference, which was organized by the Somali Relief and Rehabilitation Association in Hargeisa.

III. Synopsis

A. Social Organization

The three clan families that live in the north are: Dir, Isaaq and Darood. The largest of these, the Isaaq, live in the central part of the self-proclaimed "Somaliland." Dir groups of Gadabursi and Issa live to the west of the Isaaq, and the Darood groups of Dulbahante and Warsangeli inhabit their traditional territory east of the Isaaq.

The elaborately segmented patrilineal descent formation of the northern Somali society subdivides the major groups into varying segments at different levels of political grouping. In a pervasive agnatic context built of elaborate segments, the structurally and functionally important points of cleavage are: "clan-family," "clan," "primary lineage" and "*dia*-paying group." The latter group is the most stable political unit, which guarantees the Somali security of his life and property. Apart from the agnatic principle which binds close kinsmen in this corporate group, its endurance is further enhanced by the collective obligation to pay and receive blood compensation *dia*. Though susceptible to manipulation by reckless personalities, the fluid segmentary social system of the northern Somali society has the capacity to place each and every kinsman in a *dia*-paying lineage where his basic rights are guaranteed and obligations defined.

B. Traditional Sources of Power and Authority

Today, the highest level council of elders is known as *Guurti*. Headed by clan leaders (Sultans), the Guurti consists of a body of elders, which represent the lineages of the clans. Most commonly, a significant number of these representatives are *dia*-paying group leaders, *Akils*-"Local Authorities." The *Guurti* of the clans and large subclans attend to the internal affairs of the groups and represent them in inter-clan, regional and national peace conferences and other matters of wider common interest. The *Guurti* of the clans are commonly townsmen who live in the urban centers dominated by their respective groups. However, they are tied to their rural kinsmen by agnatic bond and common treaty. They also typically own livestock in their home areas. This economic interest enhances social ties between kinsmen in urban and rural domains.

Participation in the northern peace conferences included politicians, military officials and professionals who served past regimes. While they used some modern style conference techniques, participants from traditional lineage *ad hoc* councils (*shirs*) and prominent adult men of the concerned parties injected many traditional procedures into the conference. The *Guurti* played a central role in the peace process, which harnesses the services of the sacred authority of the religious leaders and persuasive power of the distinguished poets. Perhaps linked to the natural demographic growth, our study found that political offices had proliferated among the clans in the study area. Most probably, this was also fostered by the need of the clans and subclans to assert independence in a situation of turmoil and uncertainty with an explicit tendency to search for solutions in the traditional lineage structure, given the absence of effective modern law and order authorities.

C. Types of Conflict

The three main types of conflicts discussed in this section are: pastoral conflicts over range lands, conflicts over arable land in settled areas, and politically instigated conflicts that chiefly resulted from competition for political dominance and access to limited resources among major Isaaq groups. Pastoral and sedentary conflicts are more pronounced in areas with multi-clan composition, e.g., Erigavo and Gabiley districts respectively, as well as among Isaaq and non-Isaaq groups. Burao (Habar Yonis and Habar Jelo) and Berbera (Habar Yonis and Iisa Musa) conflicts in 1992, exemplify politically instigated conflicts.

Pastoral conflicts over basic resources whose distribution are determined by environmental factors appear relatively easier to resolve than disputes over arable land in settled areas. Investments made by holders in arable land make this fixed property valuable. Also such property is usually scarce, particularly in Borama and Gabiley districts that have a relatively prolonged history of settlement and cultivation in the north. These factors and the different clan origin of local groups involved in dispute make the resolution of such conflicts more difficult.

1. Techniques of Peacemaking. Traditionally, to seal a peace treaty, women were sometimes exchanged. This was done in some of the major peace agreements in "Somaliland." Introduction of unprecedented rules contributed to peacekeeping. To dissuade armed militias from seizing the herds of opposing groups, the elders decreed that the responsibility of paying damages inflicted by armed groups should be shouldered by the immediate relatives of the perpetual offenders.

In reconciling embattled clans, the central *Guurti* used the services of distinguished leaders, including poets and religious men. Reconciling parties were encouraged to make peace themselves in order to avoid futile and protracted litigations and also to make enduring agreements

2. Constraints on Effective Peacemaking. The traditional system of governance that relies primarily upon the moral authority of lineage leaders and the good will of their kinsmen, has limited power to effectively maintain peace and prevent the occurrence of crime and violence. Clan-based armed militias pose the greatest threat to peace and stability. Yet, despite improved relations between clans, chiefly as a result of the elders' peace movement, inter-clan suspicion still lingers. This is hindering demobilization and disarmament which indeed is the expressed wish of every person in "Somaliland."

3. Achievements. The sustained effort of the lineage elders, firmly established an encouraging tendency, in which peaceful dialogue is a favored means to settle legitimate grievance in lieu of the use of force. Individual acts of violence are constrained not only by legal rulings which place increased responsibility upon the offender, but also by the predictable condemnation of agnatic kinsmen and the opposition of implicated social units. Legal contracts promulgated through a series of peace conferences, presently define political and socio-economic relations between local clans in contemporary northern Somalia.

IV. Conclusions

Using I.M. Lewis' *A Pastoral Democracy* (1961) as a point of departure, A.Y. Farah has conducted a brief field survey of current political processes and local level peacemaking in Somaliland (North-west Somalia). During the period of Scientific Socialism in Somalia, the military government claimed that it had abolished clanship and similar claims have been rather wistfully made by various Marxist writers on Somalia. Others have asserted that the traditional clan system and the system of lineage governance which I.M. Lewis analyzed in 1961 no longer exist. Our findings are entirely contrary. Lineage elders are alive and well and positions of lineage leadership, far from disappearing, have actually proliferated over the last thirty years.

In the wake of the overthrow of Siyad's regime in the north, in the absence of any effective centralized successor government, the lineage elders have been propelled to the center of the political stage. Although they are often based in towns, the elders (in principle all married men) are deeply involved in the rural, predominantly pastoral society and typically own livestock. Today, as in the past, they deliberate policy and make decisions for these groups at extremely democratic meetings in which now, as before, oratory and poetry play important political roles.

In inter-group peacemaking, which was our central concern, wives are regularly employed as intermediaries and ambassadors since intermarriage between clans is a general feature. As in the past, we found that in a number of cases the collective exchange of women in marriage was employed to seal peace treaties between previously hostile clans and lineages. This was over and above the solemn oaths which were sworn by signatures in the presence of the traditional men of religion (*wadaads*) who opened and closed the peace conferences with their blessings and readings from the Qoran. The terms of peace agreements were set out formally as traditional contracts or treaties (*xeer*), and included the usual Somali provisions of compensation for death and injury in subsequent breaches of peace.

The supreme achievement and symbol of the vigor of these traditional grassroots political processes is demonstrated in the appointment by the peace elders of the new "Somaliland" government. This is a remarkable climax of these local-level peace initiatives and proof of the vitality of the "pastoral democracy" which has, in effect, replaced "modern" political activity which our findings testify. With regard to the continuing strength of traditional political processes, two developments are important to note. First is concentration of collective responsibility within the close family of the miscreant who persistently breaks the peace and attacks the property or person of others, without the authorization of his kin group. In some cases, persistent offenders have been executed by their own kin. This is a very significant innovation aimed at countering the unauthorized violence of freelance bandits (the "*deydey*"). Of similar importance in peace negotiation, is the use of local radios to communicate with estranged or hostile groups and persuade them of the good intentions of the negotiations.

When we contrast the effective, low profile, locally-based, and inexpensive northern Somali peace process with the expensive, externally directed and less successful peace initiatives in the south, a number of factors seem to be involved. There is, first, the general and genuinely popularly rooted desire for peace in the north, associated with the ultimate goal of international recognition. Although both north and south are plagued by "freelance" bandits, there are no significant power-hungry warlords in the north, vying for control on the scale witnessed in southern Somalia. Although three different families of clans are represented in "Somaliland," they are not locked in a desperate power struggle with ramifying implications for other communities. The relative success of northern peacemaking highlights how the presence of such bellicose figures impedes peace and reconstruction. It is also evident that the concentration of aid resources in one place (Berbera in the north, Mogadishu in the south) is a potent stimulus to conflict.

In summary, our short study shows clearly how the "bottom-up" road to peace and reconstruction works in Somaliland. The government formed by the SNM guerilla movement which liberated the north-west in 1990 could not achieve popular support and withered away. It was left to the local clan elders to weave a web of peace and inter-clan relations from the grassroots. This is a slow process. Yet two years from its commencement, the elders achieved success. Peace in Somali society, of course, is a relative matter in this essentially warrior society of pastoral nomads. It is unrealistic and ethnocentric to expect a complete absence of conflict and raiding in Somali society. The most that can be hoped for is that institutions capable of resolving conflict should be in place and functioning. This is the situation today in the north, and it will obviously be improved further as the demobilization of armed bands proceeds. We also emphasize the importance of effective communications among clans -- the persuasive power of peace poetry and the use of radios in negotiations as prelude to actual meetings between groups. Finally, it is striking how the over-concentration of relief supplies in one area, in the absence of generally agreed plan for inter-clan distribution, fuels competition and conflict.

This modest success story, despite, rather than because of UN or other foreign intervention, highlights the effectiveness of low-level, grassroots peace negotiation. It needs to be replicated in the northeast region which has similarly, by its own efforts, achieved a comparable degree of harmony. The situation in the south, obviously, also urgently needs to be examined. Although the UN appears to have facilitated some local peace initiatives outside Mogadishu and is currently promoting the formation of local and district councils, we do not know to what extent these are genuinely representative of local clan interests nor do we yet understand whether they can form part of a wider, popularly supported, governmental organization.

V. Policy Implications

The northern peacemaking model indicates the significance of traditional systems of governance in chaotic situation of utter failure of the nation state's machinery of law and order. Given the dismal record of the modern state in Somalia and in Africa in general, the notable peacemaking role of northern elders highlights the potentials of native political institutions in unstable contemporary Africa. The remarkable peacekeeping effort embarked upon by the traditional lineage leaders, is rightly identified as a notable achievement at this critical period. The realized fragile peace not only restrained freelance violence and inter-clan strife, it restored a sense of hope and confidence, which were affected deeply by the prolonged social upheaval. Eminent leaders and ordinary people derive from this fluid achievement a sense of pride. The situation in the north is frequently compared to the less stable south which is thought of as a source of Somalia's tragedy.

The grassroots northern peace initiative needs encouragement and support. Desperately needed external assistance for massive reconstruction, which could not proceed without restoration of stability, should be handled carefully. External assistance should be timely, measured and appropriate. This is necessary in preserving the self-help effort of the local peace initiative, while, in the meantime, supplementing it with additional, required resources. Traditional peacemaking is resilient but cumbersome. Hence, it can accommodate extensive cash and kind assistance without any predictable improvement in its nature and outcome. Few of the series of the peace conferences gratefully received dry ration and limited cash for transport, fuel and other necessary items.

The elders' peace duties should not be considered as a panacea that can solve prevailing security problems in Somaliland. The relentless effort of clan leaders, which reached its height in the peace and state formation conference held at Borama, raised the expectations of the people, who are desperate to see positive developments which might bring international recognition and solve the vexing security issue. The elders' moral and customary skills are not good enough at preventing the occurrence of violence and warfare. The authority they have had in reconciling estranged groups is not efficient, for it ultimately depends upon consensus and persuasion techniques of traditional peacemaking. This leads one to suggest that elders' peace prerogatives should be examined in the wider context -- the formation of modern law and order institutions, which are needed to supplement the law and order responsibilities of lineage leaders.

The elders' peacekeeping functions are indispensable in the short term, until effective law and order are put in place. To displace their traditions with an exclusively modern system of governance denies the natural role of elders, which could have drastic repercussions if the modern system collapses. Professionals and civil servants of the failed state tended to de-emphasize their significance in the modern state. Reconstruction of modern and basic infrastructure is clearly needed. But given the scale of destruction, this will take time and substantial resources, most of which are now lacking in the war-torn "Somaliland." Presumably, limited resources and expertise should be targeted in reconstructing vital ministries, e.g., finance, interior and security. The task of reconstructing basic services should start at the district level rather than from the top. This approach is attuned to the decentralized system of governance which is enshrined in the interim national charter formulated by the elders in the Borama conference.

The elders can play a vital role in the creation of a modern local system of administration. Without the support of the lineage leaders, any imposed system of governance has little chance to survive. Elders should also be consulted in balancing the representation of local groups in the administration. Equitable distribution of political and economic resources is very important, since competition for access to resources between rival groups and appropriation of resources by particular groups, were foremost among the factors which instigated the civil war.

Failure of the SNM interim administration to undertake meaningful attempts to organize the triumphant guerillas into regular security forces led to loose and disenchanted armed bands. This encouraged freelance banditry and fueled political bickering among rival groups in the administration. This enhanced the elders' moral authority, whose sustained peacekeeping endeavor reached its height at the Sheikh conference of November, 1992, which successfully reconciled the Habar Yonis and Iisa Musa clans. To consolidate their peace duties, the elders placed the control of the armed militias under the political leadership of kin groups. This has the implication of actively involving the elders in the expected disarmament and demobilization of the armed militias.

CHAPTER TWENTY

How Peace is Maintained in the Northeastern Region

Abdi-asis M. Mohamed

I. Introduction

The Northeastern Region (NER) is a geopolitical term covering four provinces: Bari, Nugal, Mudug, and part of Galguduud. Garowe, the capital of Nugal, was chosen to be the seat of the NER administration. The estimated population is 2.5 million (65% women and children).

Since the fall of Siyad Barre's regime in January 1991, Somalia has spiraled deeper into violent, political fragmentation and social and economic chaos. What began as a loosely concerted struggle against a regime, quickly deteriorated into a contest between rival clans, accompanied by indiscriminate killing.

In addition to the high toll of dead and wounded, large numbers of people have been displaced and dispossessed by the conflict, many of this people returned to NER seeking safety with their lives.

A. Displaced People

The people of the NER are suffering from the effects of two simultaneous conflicts: the hostilities between the SSDF and the USC, and the fighting in Mogadishu. Both have displaced large numbers of people, many of whom have sought refuge in the NER. Over 300,000 displaced people with a large proportion of women and children have become an unbearable burden to an already destitute community.

The strain of supporting these extraordinary circumstances has placed the population of the NER under considerable stress, and threatens to overwhelm what fragile mechanisms the people have managed to develop. In some places, the displaced outnumber the inhabitants: government buildings, hospitals, and schools are filled with squatters.

Galkacyo, the capital of Mudug region, has suffered widespread damage from the war. About 20% of the buildings have been destroyed, and another 10% badly damaged. These are mainly government buildings, including the bank and schools. Many businesses and stores have also been deliberately burned with goods inside. Most buildings around the central market were also destroyed.

In addition, Galkacyo has suffered widespread looting. Roofs, doors and windows have been taken from many government and private buildings and electricity cables systematically stripped. As a result many residential buildings have been destroyed.

On 21 December 1991, the NER, under the leadership of former police chief, Mohamed Abshir Muse, established an autonomous administration. The main brains behind the administration were the traditional leaders, including elders chosen for their talent, *Ulema* (men of religion), intellectuals, and politicians. They have established a functional administration at regional, district and municipal levels, with recognizable lines of responsibility and accountability. The leaders of the NER justified their move because of the collapse of the central government and the need to create self-reliance and self-defense.

II. Brief History of Traditional Authority

Before the creation of the modern state, the Somali political authority was spread through the community as a whole. Somali egalitarianism is encapsulated in the fundamental social value that every man has the right to have a say in communal matters. The issue is discussed in the institutionalized *shir* (assembly). After deep discussion and analysis of the matter, a decision in the *shir* is decided by consensus.

This is what is known as pastoral democracy, a democracy where everybody has the right to take part. The clan-head presides over the assembly of elders but does not make decisions. All adult males, especially the elders, are empowered by a contractual treaty to direct the policies of the lineage.

The peace achieved in the NER reflects the traditional Somali democratic values. The opposite of this situation we can see from other parts of Somalia, e.g. the Mogadishu conflict, where the traditional institutions have collapsed. The method used by NER leadership can be an answer to the rest of Somalia as stated by Mohamed Sahnoun, former UN Special Representative to Somalia, in his speech in Geneva in 1992.

III. Humanitarian Situation

The international community, foreign governments, UN agencies and NGOs should be very careful not to encourage, unintentionally perhaps, Somali disunity, distrust, further instability and, as a result, cause more damage by unbalanced and biased aid or support for some regions or factions over others. More attention for one region is bound to be seen as favoritism for that region. This could cause further atrocities among various Somali clans. For example, if a region is well provided with food and medical supplies by the relief organizations, as has happened already, while the other regions receive little to no assistance, what will be the feeling and reaction of the latter?

International relief organizations almost ignored and excluded the Northeastern region from its relief and rehabilitation programs. The people of the NER find this attitude of the international organizations and governments difficult to understand. Some regions will, of course, be more in need than others, but it is a matter of degree. Furthermore, those who are creating instability should not be rewarded and those for peace and unity penalized.

IV. Medical Situation

The health system in NER has suffered many years of neglect under Barre's regime and has almost entirely collapsed. The two hospitals built by the Italian cooperation in Garowe and Bosaso were never completed, leaving non-functional structures in both places. Elsewhere, health care facilities were destroyed (Galkacyo, Jariiban, Buursalax). Most functional hospitals are nothing more than free accommodation for their patients, who receive little, if any, care at all.

Health staff are generally available. The NER administration has taken steps to identify doctors and nurses now present in the NER (as well as trained professionals) and has registered them in case of need. The administration has also identified other professionals living in Kenyan refugee camps and has requested assistance with their repatriation.

At present, the health care structures of the NER are unable to cope with most needs, including:

1.Treatment and management of war-wounded;
2. Maternal and child health care (including EPI);
3. Basic community health care;
4. Prevention and management of epidemics/outbreaks;
5. Collection and collation of health-related data.

V. Maternal and Child Health Care

Children under five and pregnant mothers are at high risk. Under five mortality runs at about 25%, while maternal mortality is about 10%. Aborted pregnancies are also common and widespread. Mother and child health care is virtually non-existent in the NER. Systematic vaccination has not taken place in the region since 1978, leaving children vulnerable to the main killer diseases.

A. Community Health Care

Malaria is second to war injuries as the most common cause of sickness and death, and it reached almost epidemic proportions in some areas of the NER. Waterborne diseases, diarrhoea, tuberculosis, and various respiratory tract infections are common and go largely untreated. The vast majority of the people have no access to a functioning health post.

B. Epidemic Prevention and Control

Outbreaks of typhoid and hepatitis (identified as Hepatitis E by the ICRC) have killed several hundred people over the last two years. NER health officials presently lack any capacity of surveillance, identification, or response in case of further problems. Recently, in 1994, there were cholera outbreaks and many people died, but international response has been inadequate.

VI. Environmental Problems

The NER faces environmental disasters both in the sea as well as on land. The region's unexploited and abundant resources have attracted many international companies to fish around the NER using internationally banned fishing methods which have incurred heavy loss of marine life. Toxic wastes were also reported to have been dumped in Somalia.

The latest report available from the area highlights large-scale deforestation caused by cutting down trees for use as charcoal which has high demand in the Middle East.

VII. Fourth Coordination Meeting on Humanitarian Assistance for Somalia

Participants at this meeting (held in Addis Ababa in December, 1993) agreed that the Somali people needed security, maintenance of law and order, and representative and accountable institutional structures. The participants, furthermore, agreed that rehabilitation and reconstruction assistance can and will be invested in those areas where stability and security have been attained and where the involvement of elders, indigenous NGOs, and representatives of the international community are allowed. The people of the Northeastern region already fulfilled all these conditions but international organizations and governments still ignored their needs.

The meeting focused on three main areas facing the Somali people and their international partners:

1. The continuing emergency needs;
2. The process towards reconstruction and rehabilitation;
3. Economic management and governance.

The representatives of the international community reaffirmed their commitment to provide unconditionally essential emergency assistance to vulnerable groups, especially children.

Further, the meeting underscored the importance of the Somali community being involved in identifying and assisting vulnerable groups and it stressed that emergency measures should be consistent with longer-term concerns of sustainable action.

VII. Recommendations

On the rehabilitation of the regional economy, the people of the NER are determined to pick up the pieces and rebuild their lives as best as they can. They have resources like livestock and livestock by-products, fisheries and valuable natural gums.

Priorities of these communities include needs assessment and preliminary feasibility studies. Financing and expert advice on the following essential public services and principal productive economic activities are vital and necessary ways to start the process:

1. Medical services: hospitals, clinics, vaccinations, nutrition;
2. Veterinary services: animal disease control, vaccinations etc;
3. Water services: urban and rural water facilities (i.e. boreholes, catchments, reservoirs) by solar, wind, generators, etc;
4. Electricity: towns and economic villages by solar and generators;
5. Education: reopening of schools -- primary and secondary;
6. Housing: low-cost projects in view of the new refugee influx;
7. Rehabilitation of roads, telecommunications, ports and airports;
8. Bosaso port: provision of handling equipment and storage;
9. Reestablishment of the regional administrations;
10. Reestablishment of financial institutions and small businesses.

Bibliography

Amnesty International. "Somalia, A Human Rights Disaster." August 5, 1992.

Addis Ababa Declaration of the Fourth Coordination Meeting on Humanitarian Assistance for Somalia. December 1, 1993.

Bradbary, Mark. INCS-UK, "Fact-finding Report to Northeastern Region, 1991."

Cabdisalam M. Ciise-Salwe. "The Collapse of Somali National State: the Colonial Factor." Paper presented at the conference on *Paix et Reconstruction en Somalie*, in Paris, 15-17 April 1993, p.6-8.

Mohamed Abshir 'Walde', Jama Ali Jama, 'The Northeastern Region of Somalia, A Profile'.

MSF-Holland. "Report of Fact-finding Mission to Northeastern Region. December 7, 1991."

Sahnoun, Mohamed. Former UN Special Representative to Somalia, speech in Geneva, 1992.

CHAPTER TWENTY ONE

Creating a Democratic Law-Making Process in Somalia

Ann Seidman and Robert B. Seidman

I. Introduction

After three decades of political independence, Somalia's national fabric lies in shreds. Years of violence have destroyed any semblance of effective national government. Yet achieving peace and writing a new constitution comprise only the first steps Somalis must take together to increase incomes to improve their quality of life. To bring about the massive social changes required, they will need to draw up and enact a vast array of institution-transforming laws and build a new legal order competent to make and implement them. For this purpose, they need a law-making process that will facilitate meaningful and democratic participation of the mass of the population. That calls for a legislative theory to assist them in grounding their new legislation on reason informed by experience.

Adopting a problem-solving methodology, this paper argues: first, the explanation for the failure of Somalia's post-independence government lay in its inherited institutions, including those supposedly dedicated to making laws; to change those institutions requires a whole gaggle of new, institution-changing laws. Second, for structural reasons it seems likely that in the new Somalia, as in most countries, meaningful democratic participation in law-making will not likely take place in parliament, but, if at all, in the processes of conducting research and drafting the detailed provisions of proposed laws. Third, a democratic law-making process requires that the participants' effectiveness depend not on their political power, but on the persuasiveness of the data and reasoned arguments they advance. That requires institutionalization of research and drafting processes guided by a legislative theory that, in the law-making process, facilitates the use of reason informed by experience. Fourth, to demonstrate the possibility of such a theory, the paper illustrates how one might use it to guide the design of legislation to assist Somali farmers improve their productivity, incomes, and quality of life. Finally, it proposes some steps the new Somali government might take to institutionalize participation in those segments of the law-making process that take place outside Parliament.

II. Somalia's Inherited Governing Institutions

A. Traditional Clan Systems of Governance

Like those elsewhere, traditional Somali institutions arose in response to historically-specific challenges. At one time, they may have served adequately. Without radical adaptation, however, only by chance would they adequately address radically different circumstances.

For centuries, traditional Somali clan leaders had ruled their extended clan communities in ways that fostered internal cohesion, protecting their members' lives and work and their participation in trading networks that extended as far away as China . Traditional clan institutions and laws emerged historically out of an economy based on relatively low levels of technology, with historically-shaped structures for interacting with the outside world. Traditional clan governance rested on patriarchal rule by elders, within whose ranks a certain limited 'democracy' existed. Often, they made clan law without even consulting lesser clan members. Almost always, their councils excluded women.

Twentieth century challenges differed completely from earlier situations which had produced the clan system. Now Somalis had to cement the changing larger regional economy into the global specialization and exchange system in ways that could benefit most Somalis. For that, the institutions of the clan system seemed ill-adapted. The institutions imposed by the departing colonialists, however, also proved incapable of dealing with development's imperatives.

B. Colonial Rulers

For almost a century two colonial powers (the British in the north, Italians in the south) ruled Somalia. They imposed on the pre-existing clan institutions two sets of centrally-controlled, thoroughly undemocratic law-making processes. Although somewhat different, both shaped new institutions to coerce Somalis into international patterns of specialization and exchange. Those institutions served, not the Somalis' but their own interests, shaping each part of what later became Somalia into a bifurcated economy.

As elsewhere, its colonial rulers shaped Somalia's government and associated institutions to facilitate the growth of 'modern' export enclaves. Through those enclaves, their metropolitan firms exported Somali crude materials to their home-based factories, imported manufactures into Somali markets, and siphoned out the resulting investable surpluses. Outside these enclaves, life changed little. To govern the hinterland, both British and Italian colonialists happily suffered the clan system and traditional laws and customs, while favoring those traditional leaders who most helped the colonialists to develop this distorted growth pattern.

C. The Independent Government

The newly independent Somali nation launched itself, complete with a parliament and the other *de rigueur* trappings of the post-colonial third world state. Behind that facade, it retained the essential features of the economic and even the political institutions the former colonial rulers had imposed. In effect, the new, formally independent government replaced two sets of external political rulers with a congeries of conflicting old and new elites.

Under the western parliamentary system established at independence, successive governments did little to change the inherited colonial capitalist trade and financial institutions. Those institutions geared the Somali economy into a one-sided relationship with fluctuating world markets dominated by transnational firms. They produced not development but, instead, persistent economic dependency, instability and poverty, an important cause of the breakdown of the fragile western-style political system. They kept most Somalis desperately poor.

The new constitution pasted over these old institutions provided a facade of democratic elections through which quarreling elites vied for popular votes. (Some 62 parties actually emerged! Davidson, 1992) Most contested for political leadership, not to transform the inherited institutions which impoverished most Somalis, but to win state power's lucrative plums. From whatever party, the new lawmakers neither opened doors to inputs from the mass of Somalis, nor restructured the institutions that left disarticulated 'national' export enclaves dependent on unstable world markets. Instead, pursuant to the conventional wisdom of neoclassical economics, they urged Somalis to produce more for export in order to earn the foreign exchange and government revenues that financed imported goodies for the rich and powerful.

To ordinary Somalis, the multiparty conflicts that repeatedly replaced one group of elites with another meant little. Many welcomed Siyad Barre's 1969 bloodless military coup. Under a rubric of 'socialism' that promised stability and, for the majority, an improved quality of life, that coup installed a dictatorship. No more than his predecessors did Barre attempt fundamental transformation of Somalia's economic or political institutions. Over the next decades, employing ethnic/clan differences to divide and suppress opposition to maintain power, Barre relied heavily first on Soviet and then US military aid. When the Cold War collapsed, cutting off his external military support, Barre fled his increasingly well-armed opponents.

In post-Barre Somalia, especially in the south, Somalia's people found themselves victims of military thrusts by clan-based 'warlords' seeking to control the national government. With seemingly unlimited access to modern weapons, the detritus of Cold War 'Great Power' competition, they wreaked havoc, killing and maiming thousands. They destroyed production, trade and financial networks so that thousands more -- including children and women -- starved. They largely destroyed the colonially-instituted -- and barely changed -- 'national' trading and financial institutions that tied Somalia into an externally dependent pattern of international specialization and exchange. They destroyed as well practically all the inherited institutions that comprised the patched-together Somali national state.

By 1994, partly clan-based grassroots, partly top-down international pressures set the stage for new governing structures. In the north, to resolve local conflicts, clan elders fell back on traditional political and legal systems. Eventually they agreed to a new set of parliamentary institutions, with legislators elected indirectly through the clans. In the South, UN troops and big power pressures applied carrot-and-stick diplomacy to bring clan leaders together in Addis Ababa. There, primarily to facilitate the peaceable resolution of the all-pervading military conflicts, they agreed on a transitional national council (TNC) based on regional representation, and a Commission to draw up a constitution.

Assuming such a new governing body is established, it would face the necessity of transforming the economic and political institutions that had for so long condemned the majority of Somalis to a life of wretched poverty. Three decades of post-independence governments had dismally failed that task. That constituted a failure of their inherited law-making system.

D. Law and Institutional Transformation

Somalia's constitutional commission must create a government to monitor its economic, political and social institutions and change them in ways likely to increase productivity, incomes and quality of life of people in today's high-tech, closely knit world. The commission cannot simply go back to the traditional clan-based systems of governance. Those systems lack the capacity to meet challenges so different from those that excited the clan system. Only serendipitously could the clans address the challenges of development in ways likely to benefit the mass of Somalis. Yet without the establishment of appropriate industrial, trading and financial institutions to facilitate the introduction of 20th Century technologies in industry and agriculture, the Somali majority can have little hope of escaping subsistence-level poverty.

Governments change institutions through the exercise of state power. By definition, institutions consist of repetitive patterns of behavior (Homans, 1967). Governments exercise state power by directing citizens and state employees to behave in certain ways. Those directions they embody in normative rules -- statutes, decrees, fiats, laws. To say that Somalia's post-colonial governments failed to transform colonial capitalist institutions reports their failure to use the legal order to change those repetitive patterns of behaviors. Laws trigger the activities of the legal order. Somalia's dismal post-colonial history reflects a pervasive failure of its law-making system to generate laws appropriate to bringing about institutional change.

As a key element for ensuring people-oriented development, Somalia's new government must empower the people in all aspects of its new law-making process. Without popular participation, law-making inevitably becomes an elite and ruling class monopoly. As has every modern constitution, Somalia's new constitution will no doubt lodge law-making power with an elected legislature. Alone, however, no matter how fair the elections, that does not ensure adequate popular participation in the many step law-making process required to shape Somali institutions appropriate to today's increasingly interrelated and complicated world.

III. Legislative Theory and Methodology

People-oriented development, elected representative assemblies, and rule-by-law require genuine democratic participation and legislative theory that makes possible justifications based on reason and experience. Positivist philosophies and pluralist and public choice political theories deny the possibility of that kind of theory. Contesting that claim, this section sketches such a theory; the next illustrates how it might work (Seidman and Seidman, 1994).

Preliminarily, that legislative theory rests on a recognition that law constitutes an organized polity's primary instrument for social change. That, of course, does not imply that lawmakers at will invoke the law to change social behaviors. Law has its limits. Only at peril may a lawmaker ignore those limits.

No more than elsewhere can Somalia's new governors pass laws that can successfully command farms to increase their yields per acre, or factories to produce more output per dollar invested. They can only pass laws that aim to change the behaviors of the relevant social actors: farmers, factory managers, workers, and the officials responsible for implementing those laws. That underscores the limits of law. The definition of institutions as repetitive patterns of behaviors becomes a reality check: To transform institutions, lawmakers can, at most, attempt to use the legal order to alter the norms that shape social actors' behavior patterns -- and on that endeavor, law imposes limits.

An adequate legislative theory should guide law-makers in that enterprise. Here we propose a legislative theory consisting of three elements: a methodology, instructions on the use of grand theory ("perspectives"), and a set of categories ("vocabulary").

A. Methodology.

In the literature, two alternative methodologies predominate. One, ends-means, rests on philosophical positivism, with its disjuncture between values and facts. In effect, positivism instructs law-makers to determine their ends by searching either their own values or those of their constituents. (In practice, of course, a politician who wants to stay in office pursues ends that harmonize with the values of the politically powerful.) Reason informed by experience becomes relevant only in searching for the appropriate means to carry out the predetermined ends. Save to the extent that groups in civic society have political power that the law-makers must respect, ends-means instructs lawmakers that they can and should turn a deaf ear to popular inputs to the determination of policy ends. Even in democratic polities, the determination of ends becomes a struggle of interest groups to impose their ends upon the polity, the 'mobilization of bias.' In the sense of empowering the powerless, popular participation remains restricted to the means of attaining the victors' pre-determined ends.

In contrast, the problem-solving methodology rests on the notion that propositions about matters of fact ("is" propositions) and normative ("ought") propositions constitute a continuum (Dewey, 1916). It proposes an agenda for justifying normative propositions in terms of reason and experience, requiring research to gather relevant evidence at each of four steps:

1. **Difficulty**: A statement of the social problem, and the identification of the role occupants and their behaviors that comprise it.

2. **Explanations**: The formulation and validation of explanations for the role occupants' behaviors (including, where relevant, propositions concerning the behavior of implementing institutions).

3. **Solutions**: (a) The development of a legislative program (including appropriate implementation provisions) that, given probable social costs and benefits, seems likely at least cost to overcome the causal factors identified by the warranted explanation; and (b) the drafting of the required bill.

4. **Monitoring and Evaluation**: The timely evaluation of the social impact of the law (required by a provision in the law itself), thus making likely the introduction of necessary revisions, in light of experience.

The logic of problem-solving rests on its second and fourth steps: Explanations which identify causes constitute the logical link between the perceived social problem and the legislative solution. Monitoring and evaluation constitute the logical link between the existing legal order and the identification of a social problem. Law-making never 'solves' a social problem, it can, at best, chip away at it.

The problem-solving methodology calls for the use of reason and experience at every stage. These include: putting forward educated guesses (hypotheses) about whose and what behaviors constitute the perceived social problem, and finding evidence to warrant those guesses; generating and testing causal explanatory hypotheses; devising solutions and assessing evidence on their social costs and benefits; and developing monitoring systems and capturing evidence about how, after its enactment, the new law works. That does not mean that problem-solving is not value-driven. Discretionary choices abound at every stage. Perspectives guide those choices; in problem-solving, grand theory serves that purpose.

B. Perspectives: The Function of Grand Theory

Researchers may guide the discretionary choices problem-solving requires in either of three ways: By their domain assumptions (that is, the -- usually unexamined -- baggage of valuations and propositions about what makes the world go that we all carry with us) (Gouldner, 1970:49-51); by ideal types or 'visions' that incorporate assumptions of what constitutes the good society (e.g., Weber 1930; Stokey & Zeckhauser 1978); or by grand theory, that is, large scale explanations of the world, such as Adam Smith's explanation for mercantilism, or Karl Marx's explanation for nineteenth century capitalism. Of these, only grand theory consists of propositions in principle susceptible of empirical warrant. To the extent that researchers guide their discretionary choices by grand theory, they can justify those choices ultimately by reason informed by experience. Only persons with political power can challenge a law-maker's domain assumptions or vision. Anybody with better data or better reasoning can challenge a grand theory. The use of grand theory to guide the discretionary choices required by problem-solving makes possible popular participation on a basis other than political muscle.

C. Categories

Finally, an adequate legislative theory must provide a set of categories to assist in structuring the research process at each of the problem-solving methodology's four stages. Those categories necessarily focus on behavior of a law's addressees in the face of a rule of law.

The simplest model of people behaving in society consists of individuals and collectivities making choices in the face of a range of constraints and resources thrown up by the objective and subjective environment (Barth 1966). In the case of a law's addressees, that environment includes the law itself, the expected behavior of the implementing agencies, and all the non-legal constraints and resources of the social actors' country- specific circumstances. The model emphasizes that to explain why a set of role occupants (farmers, employers, workers, etc) behave as they do in the face of existing law, requires understanding, not only the law itself, but also the time- and place-specific constraints and resources of their environment. To alter the constraints and resources likely to affect role-occupant behaviors, implementing agencies may impose sanctions. These may include, not merely punishments or rewards, but other conformity-inducing measures as well (for example, roundabout or educational measures) (Seidman, 1978).

Law and development studies (Seidman 1978; Seidman and Seidman 1994: Ch. 6) suggest seven categories of possible factors likely to influence role occupant and implementing agency behaviors: *The Rules*, which may prescribe appropriate behaviors, or provide opportunities that make some behaviors more advantageous to the role occupant; the role occupants' and implementing agency's respective *opportunities* and *capacities* to behave in conformity with the existing law; whether the law has been *communicated* to them; their *interests* in conforming; the *processes* by which they decide whether or not to obey; and their *ideologies*, that is, the values and attitudes which may influence their behavior. Broadly construed, these categories subsume all the categories of possible explanations for role occupant and implementing agency behavior when faced by a rule of law. (The mnemonic ROCCIPI, from the first letters of their names, helps to remember them.)

To draft laws likely to change relevant behaviors requires: (1) generating possible explanatory hypotheses suggested by reviewing these categories in light of the researchers' grand theory; and (2) research to capture evidence to test those hypotheses. Only if laws address the real causes of the behaviors that comprise social problems can the laws contribute to eliminating those social problems. The ROCCIPI model categories provide a research agenda for transforming policy into law. Thus the theory guides the research. A problem-solving methodology, the use of grand theory to guide research, and categories defined by the triangular model of behavior in the face of law and the ROCCIPI agenda. These constitute a legislative theory that at each step may guide the use of reason informed by experience. The next section illustrates how that theory might facilitate structuring a participatory law-making process for drawing up a legislative program. As an example, we discuss a bill to establish an agricultural extension service -- a likely priority for any new Somali government.

IV. An Illustration: Drafting an Agricultural Extension Law

To illustrate the use of the proposed legislative theory, this section examines how it assists in structuring a research agenda looking to the formulation of a law to reestablish a Somali agricultural extension agency. The proposed law must include detailed provisions on a variety of topics: for example, how the proposed agency will relate to the farmers; processes for recruiting and training its staff, and for guiding extension agents in assisting the farmers to increase productivity and incomes; and the means of financing the revitalized service.

The proposed theory suggests examining the factors likely to influence the behaviors of the relevant sets of role occupants and implementing agencies in connection with these various issues. This section first discusses the necessity of participation in that research by the actors whose behavior constitutes the social difficulty that excites the legislation, and briefly discusses available research techniques. Second, it explores the social problem in terms of the actors and behaviors that comprise it. It then invokes the categories of the triangular model and the ROCCIPI research agenda to suggest a way of structuring participatory investigations into the causes of the problem. Finally, it makes some brief observations on the sort of legislation likely to be required.

A. Research and Participation

1. *Research and participation*. For two reasons, research of the sort appropriate to drafting laws to transform institutions requires participation by the actors in the relevant institutions: (a) The research aims to provide evidence as to the scope of the difficulty and the validity of hypotheses explaining the behaviors of the relevant role occupants, the farmers and the actors in the existing implementing agencies. Clearly, for that purpose, they themselves constitute the greatest available reservoir of knowledge about their own behaviors and the constraints and resources of their own environments. Their participation in the research becomes not merely a matter of satisfying a ideal of participation, but a matter of ensuring adequate inputs to the research.

(b) By participating in the research, those affected by the problem -- in our illustration, the farmers and agents -- begin the process of changing their behaviors. They acquire new skills to help solve their own problems. They come to understand better the nature and causes of the difficulties they confront, enabling them better to participate in finding solutions. Implementing agents become sensitized to their 'clients" difficulties, as well as stimulating them to improve their own work (e.g., Klitgaard 1991). In a word, the social actors' participation in the research process facilitates their empowerment.

2. *Available research techniques*. For law-making purposes, researchers may use various techniques to formulate hypotheses and gather evidence to test them. These range from focus group discussions to large- scale or sample surveys. Focus group discussions produce not

quantitative but qualitative analyses, but, in most cases, drafting legislation calls, not for aggregated quantitative data, but for evidence relating to qualitative relationships. Focus groups only involve a few participants (preferably under 15). At much lower cost than broad surveys, they permit greater in-depth discussions of the causes and the possible uses of law to change problematic behaviors.

On the other hand, a well-designed survey can provide quantitative data. While desirable, time and other constraints frequently leave lawmakers no option save to rely on qualitative evidence. Competent law-making rests on evidence; large quantitative aggregates of data may provide a valuable means of checking the validity of analyses derived from qualitative case studies. If time or financial constraints render large-scale surveys impossible, case studies may nevertheless provide some of the evidence required.

Whatever the techniques used, as their first task researchers will find it helpful to engage those affected in discovering the nature and scope of the social problems at hand: Whose and what behavior constitute the social problem that the proposed agricultural extension bill must address?

B. The Behaviors that Compromise the Difficulty

Part of the explanation for the widespread rural poverty lies in relatively low agricultural productivity and poor distribution channels. The behaviors of two sets of role occupants apparently comprise that social problem: the agriculturalists and whatever agencies now purport to assist them to increase their productivity and sales. For the purposes of this illustration, the primary role occupants analyzed comprise sedentary farmers, a high proportion of whom live in southern Somalia. To increase their productivity, improve their incomes, and improve their quality of life, these Somali farmers must behave in different ways from how they have in the recent, if not the longer run, past.

As the first step in the law-making process, ideally researchers should engage them in analyzing whether their present ways of farming constitute a social problem. Better than others, they can elaborate how years of violence disrupted the historically-evolved institutions that earlier facilitated the sale of their crops in national and global markets. They could describe, if they still farm at all, the extent to which most farm families produce barely enough food crops for their own subsistence. Researchers could help them relate this to whatever national statistics exist as to agricultural productivity and sales and their impact on national development.

Researchers must take into account relevant differences among different groups of farmers: large employers, subsistence farmers and landless laborers; farmers who produce primarily for export and those who produce domestically-consumed crops; and male farmers and female farmers. To learn about their differing behaviors, researchers try to ensure adequate representation of each of these strata in focus groups and survey samples.

The second set of role occupants comprise the existing agencies (not only public but also private actors whose cooperation farmers need to increase productivity and sell their produce: NGOs, private sellers of fertilizer and equipment, wholesalers, money lenders and bankers. Researchers should engage them, too, in assessing the extent to which their role falls short of that required to enable the farmers to increase their productivity and sell more.

After engaging farmers and others in identifying the actors and their behaviors that comprise the difficulties the proposed agricultural extension law must address, the researchers should then encourage them to assist in investigating the causes of those problematic behaviors.

C. Explanations: Using the ROCCIPI Agenda for Participatory Research

Discovering the causes of the problematic behaviors calls for generating explanatory hypotheses and capturing data to test them. In focus groups, researchers together with participants might generate explanatory hypotheses by systematically reviewing the explanations suggested by experience or offered by alternative grand theories with respect to each of the ROCCIPI categories. This will help them to consider the full range of possible causes. Focus groups' case studies or other qualitative investigative techniques can also help in capturing the evidence necessary to assess those hypotheses' likely possibilities. Surveys might help to gather more extensive quantities of data.

Experience elsewhere suggests the following kinds of questions based on initial hypotheses to guide the gathering of specific evidence to explain farmer and agency behaviors:

1. *Primary role occupants:* the diverse strata of farmers. Rules: Within what relatively formal framework of law (both norms promulgated by the state, and those of customary law that the state, in some sense, recognizes as legitimate) do each strata of farmers now make production choices? How does that framework affect those choices? Do those rules establish an agency and prescribe agency behavior likely to channel farmers' choices in ways that will enhance

productivity? What kinds of discretion do the existing rules permit the farmers and the agency officials? (In general, the broader the discretion, the more likely that the role occupant will make their choices not in light of the public interest, but in light of their own interests and ideologies).

Opportunity and capacity: Do each of the several strata of farmers have access to and the skills needed to utilize productively enough well-watered land? credit? inputs? markets (including processing, storage, transport facilities)? appropriate technologies? Do they know about all of these?

Communication of law: Do farmers know the formal rules within which they must choose their different courses of action?

Interest: Are prices of crops high enough and those of credit, transport, and manufactured goods (farm inputs and consumer necessities) low enough to reward farmer for risking labor and land in expanding crop production? Do women receive payments for the farm work they do?

Process: Do existing agencies engage farmers in decisions relating to improving their opportunities and capacities? Do women participate in decisions concerning farming work? Do farmers make production decisions privately, or in public discussions led by a knowledgeable agricultural extension officer?

Ideology: Are (as urban elites often assume) male and female farmers 'backward' (i.e., risk-averse)? or, in light of fluctuating crop prices, weather risks, and other farming variables, do they exhibit a justified caution? How do traditional value-sets affect farmers' production decisions. Do patriarchal values keep women from participating fully in farm activities?

As groups of farmers discuss these questions, the researchers should request them to assess the extent to which available facts support the alternative explanations they propose. The researchers might engage the groups in formulating broader surveys to gather further relevant evidence.

2. *Existing agencies purporting to assist farmers.* Existing agencies may not adequately assist farmers to increase productivity and incomes. To improve their performance, or replace them by a more effective agency, researchers must first determine why.

Like all implementing institutions, these agencies constitute complex organizations. The model of a decision-making organization suggests that the range of their decisions (and therefore their behaviors) respond to their input, conversion, output and feedback processes. Those processes consist of sets of role occupants who make decisions in the face of formal and informal rules addressed to them. How they decide to behave depends on those rules and all the other non-legal constraints and resources in their environment (Fig. 3). Combined, these various role-occupants' behaviors determine how an extension agency, as a complex decision-making institution, 'behaves.' For example, someone decides which groups or strata may provide inputs into the agency's decision-making processes: urban elites or farmers? large or small farmers? export crop or subsistence farmers? men or women? Someone decides what sorts of information the input channels will accept: Information about distributional effects, or only about productivity? About productivity, or only about efficiency? About institutions, or only about incentives? Whom and what the agency hears inevitably influences what and whose problems the agency seeks to solve, and how it goes about solving them. How and why do the role occupants who make these decisions behave as they do?

The same sorts of questions guide enquiry about feedback processes, that is, the processes by which the agency learns about the consequences of its decisions. If the agency personnel who elicit feedback processes listen only to large farm owners, agency decision-makers who implement the conversion processes will learn only how those large farmers assess the program. If its agents make special efforts to get the opinions of poor female farmers, it may hear a very different story. Worst of all: If the agency personnel permit senior agency officials to hear only success stories, the agency will not likely make many urgently required changes.

The conversion processes, that is, the working rules by which the role occupants process inputs and feedbacks into a decision about what the agency should do, will also affect the agency's 'behavior.' If the working rules specify that the agency may not supply assistance to farmers with less than 5 hectares, then it will necessarily neglect poor subsistence farm families. If the working rules require that farmers produce titles to their land before the agency will help them obtain credit, then many farmers will automatically prove ineligible. If the rules require written decisions with reasons publicly promulgated, decisions may rest less on political preference or plain corruption than if decisions remain secret and without justifications. If the rules require decisions by a single official, results may differ from decisions by a panel of three, five or more.

The behaviors of still another set of role occupants, the agents who work directly with the farmers in the field, of course play a major role in determining the implementation of agency decisions. For example, if the agents almost all comprise men, experience suggests that, although women do most of the food farming, they will almost never talk with female farmers.

In other words, to explain adequately the existing agencies' behaviors, ideally the researchers should investigate the causes of their behaviors, at least working with focus groups involving all these several sets of interacting role occupants. A review of the ROCCIPI agenda in a focus group involving extension agents, for example, might raise the following kinds of questions:

Rules: Do the relevant existing rules set forth clear criteria and procedures for agents' performance of their stated tasks? The legislation creating the extension service (if any) likely describes those tasks only in broad terms, leaving it to the agency itself to formulate more detailed regulations for the behaviors of its agents. The participants should examine those regulations: Do they specify the qualifications the agents must have? Do they adequately spell out their responsibilities? How many and what types of farmers should they work with? What kinds of information should they provide to the farmers relating to cultivation of particular crops? appropriate kinds of farm inputs? the availability of credit? the possibilities for transport? storage? processing and selling the crops? Do the rules spell out the range of procedures they should employ in working with farmers, for example, as individuals or in cooperatives? Obviously, the rules must give the agents some discretion to work creatively to help each farmer or group of farmers find solutions to their particular problems; but simultaneously, they must provide sufficiently detailed guidelines to ensure that the agent fulfills at least a minimum of the specified tasks.

Opportunity and Capacity: Does the agency employ enough agents (including women) to serve the needs of all the farmers? Do the agents have the necessary training and resources to perform their prescribed tasks? For example, do they know how to help the farmers to learn by doing, rather than simply lecturing at them? Even more elementary, do they have the means of transport to get out to the farmers' homes? Are their caseloads sufficiently small to enable them to visit farmers as often as good extension practice requires?

Communication: Any effective agency must inform its agents of the rules that purport to govern their behaviors. How do they do that? Do the administrators just hand the agents a list, or do they engage them in discussions about the rules' significance? Exploration of this question tends to merge with an analysis of the process by which the agency reaches its decisions, an issue discussed more fully below.

Interest: Do agents have adequate incentives to work with all the farmers -- not just the wealthy male land owners -- in the ways the rules prescribe? At the most elementary level, do they receive adequate pay? Beyond that, do the agency administrators or the farmers provide the agents with sufficient recognition for doing a good job? What punitive sanctions exist for an agent's failure to carry out their tasks? Do the local farmers have a voice in an agent's continued employment?

Process: How do agents decide which farmers to help and in which ways to help them? Do the agency administrators make the decisions behind closed doors and simply dictate the rules to the agents, or engage them in deciding what tasks they should perform and how they should perform them? Do the administrators involve the agents together with farmers in a public process of making those decisions? and if so, which farmers? Do they encourage the agents to develop participatory processes for involving the farmers in explaining and solving their own problems?

Ideology: Do the agency's administrators believe that the agents should work only with larger 'progressive' farmers? Do the agents believe that small farmers and female farmers can, if given adequate assistance, farm effectively?

These kinds of questions clearly reflect concerns suggested by various grand theories: the incentives likely to motivate agents; the special problems of women as farmers; the stratification that persists in most farm communities. As much as possible, the questions asked should generate evidence to assess the most likely explanations for the agents' behaviors. As the agents discuss these questions together with representative groups of farmers, they will likely gain greater insight into the causes of their own behaviors.

C. Drafting the New Law

The third step in problem-solving comprises the development of a legislative program and the actual drafting of provisions for a new law. For that law to alter the behaviors that constitute the social problem, self-evidently it must address the causes of those behaviors revealed by the warranted explanations for them. Especially, it must specify the processes for implementing the new law. A law with inadequate implementation becomes no more than symbolic (Edelman, 1964;

Gusfield, 1963). The phrase, "It is a good law but badly implemented" misstates the problem; a badly implemented law is a badly drafted law.

Here again, representative groups of those affected should participate in helping to propose possible solutions. In particular, they should take part, in light of their own constraints and resources, in assessing the probable social costs and benefits of alternative possible measures for overcoming the causes identified in each ROCCIPI category.

It seems likely that a new extension law for Somalia ought not try to detail the specific tasks of the responsible implementing agents. It might more felicitously set forth their qualifications, and the criteria and procedures that the extension agency should follow in formulating the specific rules defining the agent's detailed tasks. Above all, the law should require that those decision-making procedures remain open and accountable to those affected; and, wherever possible, those affected -- agents as well as farmers -- should participate in the process of formulating those rules. As a bare minimum, the agency should publish the draft regulations and hold well-publicized public hearings on them in locations where all strata of farmers can attend. Sometimes, agencies in other countries invite the public to submit written comments, but given most poor Somali farmers' literacy levels, the legislation should provide better methods of soliciting their opinions.

The development of a democratic law-making process, however, cannot stop with the enactment and implementation of the law. The law itself must incorporate provisions to ensure adequate feedback.

D. The Necessity of Feedback

As its fourth step, the problem-solving methodology requires that the bill contain provisions to institutionalize monitoring of laws, once enacted, to assess their social impact. For two reasons, this step, too frequently neglected, constitutes an indispensable step:

1. Laws-in-action frequently dictate changes because the law-in-the-books do not appropriately alter addressees' behaviors. The research may have failed to identify all the factors that caused the initial problematic behaviors, and therefore the new law did not adequately address them; or the amount of research required -- even though narrowed by the ROCCIPI agenda -- may have proven to be too extensive to complete before enacting urgently required laws.

2. Circumstances always change. This generates new constraints and resources that influence the role occupants' behaviors. A law

becomes out-of-date even as the legislature enacts it.

Only on-going monitoring and assessment of a new law's social impact can ensure timely revision of its provisions to overcome newly-identified difficulties. As earlier observed law-making begins with a negative evaluation of the present situation -- and that includes the existing law. In turn, that occasions a perceived need for new law, ushering in a new law-making cycle. Effective popular participation in government requires participation by the people affected -- in this case, particularly the farmers and the extension agents -- in monitoring the implementation of law.

Following the four steps of the problem-solving methodology and using the ROCCIPI categories, this section has proposed a research agenda as the basis for a sound agricultural extension law. Like the legislative theory on which it rests, at each step, that agent invokes reason informed by experience. To the extent that it does that, it helps to make possible democratic participation in the law-making process that grounds proposed new laws in reason informed by experience.

V. Summary and Conclusions

This paper employed the problem-solving methodology to suggest the first steps required for introducing a democratic law-process in Somalia. It first explained the collapse of Somalia's post-independence government ultimately by its inability to transform Somalia's economic and political institutions into ones capable of dealing effectively with modern conditions. Since law comprises an organized polity's primary instrument for changing institutions, the failure to transform those institutions constituted a failure of Somalia's law-making institutions. Law-making institutions dominated by the rich and powerful will grind out new laws that favor the rich and powerful. For Somalia to have a law-making process that favors the mass, the mass must, in some sense, control it.

A genuinely participatory law-making process cannot merely respond to the claims of power. It can empower the powerless only if law-makers listen to arguments derived from reason informed by experience. To counter positivist denials of the possibility of doing that, the paper proposed a legislative theory that used reason informed by experience to guide a democratic law-making process. That theory rests on the premise that social problems and social institutions, alike, consist of repetitive patterns of of social actors (role occupants). To change problematic institutions, new laws must seek to alter or eliminate the factors that cause those role occupants' inappropriate behaviors. To specify a new law's provisions, therefore, requires research to gather evidence at each of problem-solving's four stages of analysis, each resting on a bed of data: The difficulty, in terms of the behaviors that comprise the social problem; explanations for these behaviors; a proposed legislative solution; and monitoring and evaluating implementation.

Only when armed with sufficient evidence in relation to these four steps can lawmakers claim to have grounded their proposed new laws in reason, informed by experience. A set of categories -- denoted by the mnemonic ROCCIPI -- subsumes all the factors likely to influence relevant role occupants' behaviors in the face of a law. Thus it comprises an agenda for generating hypotheses, which in turn direct the researchers search for data.

To illustrate the possibility of using that legislative theory to structure a democratic law-making process, the paper focused on the problem of re-establishing an agricultural extension program for Somali farmers. It underscored the point that only by involving the relevant social actors could the research process likely discover all the relevant known evidence. Engaging them in the process, furthermore, would help to empower them to play a greater role in finding their own solutions.

Finally, the paper suggested that Somalia's new government might immediately take two steps. First, it could establish guidelines stipulating a law-making process that incorporates maximum feasible popular participation, and justifications for legislation that depend on reason informed by experience. Second, it should ensure the training of government personnel in an adequate, truly democratic legislative theory and methodology.

Together, these two steps might set the new government of Somalia on the path towards creating a democratic, participatory law-making process designed to meet the Somali population's basic needs.

Bibliography

Bachrach, Peter, and Baratz, Morton S.. 1963. "Decisions and Non-Decisions: An Analytical Framework." 57 *American Political Science Review* 632.

Barth, Fredrik. 1966. "Models of Social Organization." Royal Anthropological Institute. Occasional Paper 23. Glasgow: The University Press.

Benda-Bechmann, F. 1989. "Scapegoat and Magic Charm: Law in Development Theory and Practice", 28 J. Legal Pluralism and Unofficial Law. Quoted in Kulcsar, 1992:232.

Buchanan, James M.. 1972. "Politics, Property and Law: An Alternative Interpretation of Miller v. Schoene." 15 J. *Law & Econ.* 439.

Dahl, Robert. 1956. *A Preface to Democratic Theory.* Chicago: Univ. of Chicago Press.

Davidson, Basil. 1992a. "Africa: The Politics of Failure" in Ralph Miliband and Leo Panitch (eds.) *The Socialist Register.* London: Merlin Press.

Deutsch, Karl. 1961. "Social Mobilization and Political Development." 55 *American Political Science Review* 493.

Dewey, John. 1916. *Essays in Experimental Logic.* Chicago: Univ. of Chicago Press.

_____. 1925. "Logical Method and Law." 10 Cornell Law Quarterly, 17.

Edelman, Murray. 1964. *The Symbolic Uses of Politics.* Urbana: Univ. of Illinois Press.

Gouldner, Alvin. 1970. *The Coming Crisis of Western Sociology.* N.Y.: Basic Books.

Gusfield, J. 1963. *Symbolic Crusade: Status Politics and the American Temperance Movement.* Urbana: Univ. of Illinois Press.

Homans, George Casper. 1967. *The Nature of Social Science.* N.Y.: Harcourt, Brace and World.

Igben, M.S., ed. 1988. *The Nigerian Farmer and Agricultural Institutions.* Ibadan: Nigerian Institute of Social and Economic Research.

Kalyalya, D., K. Mhlanga, A. Seidman, and J. Semboja. 1986. *Aid and Development: A Pilot Participatory Learning Process.* Trenton, NJ: Africa World Press.

Kautsky, J. H. 1962. An Essay in the Politics of Government. In J.H.Kautsky, ed. 1962. *Political Change in Underdeveloped Countries: Nationalism and Communism.* N.Y.: Wiley.

Kesselman, Mark. 1982. "The State and Class Struggle: Trends in Marxist Political Science" in Bertell Ollman and E. Vernoff. 1982. *The Left Academy.* N.Y.: McGraw-Hill, p. 82. Reprinted in Cantori & Ziegler 1988:112.

Klitgaard, Robert. 1991. *Beyond the State versus the Market in Economic Development.* San Francisco: ICS Press.

Kulcsar, Kalman. 1992. *Modernization and Law*. Budapest: Academiai Kiado.

Markakis, John. 1990. *National and Class Conflict in the Horn of Africa*. London: Zed Press

Morgan, David L. 1988. *Focus Groups as Qualitative Research*. London: Sage Publications.

PRA, 1989. " An Introduction to Participatory Rural Appraisal for Rural Resources Management." Worcester, MA: Program for International Development, Clark University, and Nairobi, Kenya: National Environment Secretariat, Ministry of Environment and Natural Resources.

Schaffer, B. B. 1969. "The Deadlock in Development Administration" in Leys, Colin (ed.) 1969. *Politics and Change in Developing Countries: Studies in the Theory and Practice of Development*. Cambridge: Cambridge Univ. Press:177.

Schoepf, Brooke Grundfest. 1992. "Gender Relations and Development: Political Economy and Culture" in *2lst Century Africa*.

Seidman, Ann and Robert B. Seidman, 1994. *State and Law in the Development Process: Problem-solving and Institutional Change in the Third World*. London: Macmillan.

Seidman, Ann *and* Frederick T. Anang, eds. *21st Century Africa: Towards a New Vision of Self-sustainable Development in Africa*. 1992. Atlanta: Crossroads Press 1992.

Seidman, Robert B. 1978. *State, Law and Development*. London: Croom-Helm.

Stokey, Edith, and Zeckhauser, Richard. 1978. *A Primer for Policy Analysis*. N. Y.: W. W. Norton.

Trubek, David and Mark Galanter. 1974. "Scholars in Self-Estrangement: Some Reflections on the Crisis in law and Development Studies in the U. S. " [1974] *Wisc. L. Rev.* 1062.

Weber, Max. 1930. *The Protestant Ethic and the Spirit of Capitalism*. Tr. Talcott Parsons. London: George Allen & Unwin.

SECTION SIX

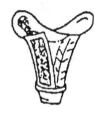

Reconstruction - Straws in the Wind

Summaries: Section Six

Hilarie Kelly (Chapter 22) considers the role of local women's organizations in rehabilitating Somali society. Inspired by experience living among Somali women in Kenya, she notes the women's groups untapped capacity, competence, and ability to accomplish amazing tasks. Her recommendation, based on this research, is that those concerned with Somali rehabilitation place greater attention on how rural women have organized themselves in the past, especially at local and grass roots levels, to solve problems.

Abdirahman Osman Raghe (Chapter 23) traces the evolution of Somali NGOs. He notes that the primary impetus was the crisis following Somalia's defeat in the Ogaden war (1987-88). A flowering of NGOs followed, including several donor umbrella projects. While the NGOs faced many problems -- staffing, training, registration, and banditry -- many have survived and are now poised to play important roles in policy advocacy, the delivery of services, and grassroots empowerment. While local capacities are still weak and funding sources limited, the author concludes that NGOs are among the few hopes for bringing civil society to a rehabilitated Somali society.

Abdullahi M. Ahmed, Ranieri Guerra, and Augusto Pinto (Chapter 24) propose a means to restore health services to an ailing people. They consider facilities, staffing, repatriation of overseas Somali health professionals, equipment and supplies, and activities, including a breakdown of duties, based on the level of responsibility of a particular health facility. While they make no specific mention of organizations that would finance such efforts, they conclude with a call to the "international community" for such help.

George Urch (Chapter 25) presents a plan for education, similar to the health plan in the previous chapter. It includes emphasis on teacher education, administration, institutions, staffing, and external assistance. He notes that Lafoole College of the Somali National University is well-suited to the challenge, though it will need considerable financial support to take the necessary steps.

Richard Ford (Chapter 26) presents a case study based on field work carried out in the Northeastern region in 1994. The case offers a concrete methodology that enables local communities to analyze their own data and create community-based action plans. If Somalis's longer-term governance models are to include formal structures for decentralized participation and decision-making, then methods such as those which Ford describes would be essential to systematize and scale-up local action plans into regional and perhaps national participatory development plans.

CHAPTER TWENTY TWO

The Potential Role of Women's Groups In Reconstruction

Hilarie Kelly

I. Introduction

Somali society has undergone tremendous upheaval in recent years, affecting Somalis both within the former republic and outside. The current challenges to the Somali community are many and will have to be addressed in creative ways on many levels. The purpose of this paper is to generate discussion on the potential roles of women's groups in the reconstruction of Somali civil society.[1] Some observations are made about locally-based women's groups as problem-solving institutions in other communities that have also faced serious crises of survival. Future research, I suggest, should include an examination of how women's groups have continued to function both within the former republic and among Somali women who live elsewhere.

II. Locally-Based Somali Women's Groups

In the past, Somali women in both rural and urban areas have organized local groups, such as the *Abay siti* (religious devotional groups) and *hagbad* (rotating credit associations), which can transcend family, clan, and even ethnic ties.[2] These groups provided a framework for women's cooperation, particularly in terms of sharing resources and vital information on strategies for survival and improved welfare. Such groups are not inconsistent with Somali religious beliefs and traditional, family-oriented values. Women's groups thus represent a pre-existing organizational resource for the social and political reconstruction of Somali society, in addition to the male elders who are often mentioned in policy statements and in the media as traditional and legitimate leaders.

This paper is inspired, in part, by research conducted in Kenya, where a traditional, pre-Islamic women's group (*gaas eyba*) within the Orma community was revitalized as an Islamic institution under the influence of Somali neighbors during a critical and hazardous period in Orma history following a series of political and natural disasters that decimated the community.[3] Throughout this period, dating from the turn of the century to the present, the Orma community negotiated its way into a national and international commercial economy at the same time that it negotiated relations with various and sometimes competing political forces, including the Zanzibar Sultanate, British colonial authorities, Italian colonial authorities, and eventually the post-colonial states of Kenya and Somalia. Although the Orma situation is not identical to that of the Somali, both communities have faced the necessity of reconstructing civil society after epic catastrophes: the Orma at the beginning of the 20th century, the Somali at the end of it. In the Orma case, women's groups have played a role in this process.

The traditional *gaas eyba* of Orma women functioned as a women's council or moot with special sacred and judiciary duties and powers. As with men's councils, these women's councils could be small in scale, occurring among a few women in an isolated, nomadic hamlet, or they could be much larger, involving all women resident in a fortified village during a time of war, or even involving women from throughout the entire community during the octenniel assembly open to all Orma, when the laws of the *gada* system were reiterated. Significantly, all of these demographic units, regardless of size or scope, are referred to as *warra*, an organizational concept analogous to the Somali *reer*.

As the Orma community converted entirely to Islam, women found themselves increasingly peripheralized by the way men monopolized the mosque and other public arenas of Islamic influence. Neighboring Somali women often joined Orma women in group meetings, sharing their ideas on the particular ways that women might observe Islam. Orma women now sometimes refer to their *gaas eyba* as "our mosque," and the meetings now commonly feature *Abay siti* hymns.[4] The participation of Somali women in these local Orma women's groups facilitated amicable relations between the two communities. This was an important accomplishment, given that the two communities had sometimes been at war in living memory, and given that the Kenya Government both in colonial and post-colonial times has sought to drive a wedge between these two communities in order to prevent possible "irredentism."

Somali historian Amina Adan has written about the evolution of some Somali *Abay siti* groups into *hagbad*, rotating credit associations, a process that was beginning to occur among the Orma as well by 1986. She implies that women who participated in such groups were those who then became active supporters of national political movements. The Orma and Somali situation thus demonstrates the dynamic potential of such women's groups to adapt to changing circumstances and needs.

III. Women's Groups and Problem-Solving

The principal recommendation of this paper is that more attention should be paid to how Somali women organize themselves, especially at the local level, to solve the various problems -- great and small -- of their daily existence. Further, it is important to observe more carefully the various ways in which women articulate with men, not only as individuals but also collectively, to avoid such debacles as those faced by the United Nations while trying to organize district councils that include a minimum of one woman each. Somali women in many localities may already be working within their own groups or networks to resolve local problems. (Many assertions have been made to this effect by Somali women abroad.) It may be advantageous to recognize these women's collective efforts as well as the leadership capabilities behind them, and to encourage these groups or, at the very least, not undercut them. This approach would not preclude the establishment of gender-mixed councils by any means, but it would do more to accommodate the multiplicity of leadership roles and problem-solving strategies available in the Somali community, especially in terms of established gender role differences and the importance of "grassroots" participation.

This paper is not based on field research into Somali women's groups, nor is it based on any review of the literature on this topic. It would be extremely useful to see such material assembled together, and to forward it to the relevant policymakers. This would be an appropriate agenda item for the Somali Studies International Association to pursue. However, the Somali population is not entirely homogeneous, in spite of many common bonds, and the functioning of women's groups may be especially sensitive to various local circumstances. Hence, the available material is probably as yet somewhat limited. To appreciate the potential for locally-based women's groups to help solve the problems of the wider community, we may learn something by looking at some examples outside of the Somali community.

Orma women's groups (*gaas eyba*) have provided them with a mechanism for organizing cooperatively to cope with challenges to personal, family, and community survival.[5] One advantage of these groups is that they have always been regarded by men as well as women as having a legitimate and sacred mandate to promote harmony and fertility for the entire community. In recent decades, the social stresses of increasing sedentarism have contributed to the popularity of these groups in areas where Orma families are now more-or-less permanently settled in large numbers. As a forum for women to discuss the behavior and misbehavior of both women and men, the *gaas eyba* provides women with an acceptable, collective means for expressing both approval and disapproval.

The *gaas eyba* acts as a pressure group, using moral suasion and even physical or economic sanctions to encourage women's obligations to assist each other in time of need. Meetings facilitate the organization of cooperative work parties (*dado*). Such actions contribute to family welfare, as women's workload has actually increased with sedentarization, economic diversification, and commercialization. Furthermore, increasing wealth disparities and the gradual alienation of male labor and economic responsibility from the conjugal family has left many women, children, and elderly people vulnerable to poverty, so that mutual assistance obligations among women can at times offer an important safety net when other social welfare institutions fail or are non-existent.

As in the past, the *gaas eyba* continues to enact socially-approved sanctions against extremely abusive husbands. Wife-beating and other forms of physical coercion used by men against women are a fundamental and highly sensitive issue in Orma gender relations (Kelly 1992). In 1986 the hottest topic of discussion in many local *gaas eyba* meetings was the Kenya Government's widely advertised campaign to discourage wife-beating. The consensus seemed to be that while the government's moral support was certainly appreciated by women, the *gaas eyba* was actually a more locally effective tool for negotiating, not only with offenders but also with the councils of Orma men, which are also called *gaas eyba*, a term that simply means "shade of prayer," referring to the fact that council meetings usually take place under shade trees and are sanctified by prayer.

The Orma women's *gaas eyba* has shown some potential for facilitating women's involvement in local development and politics. One group organized a pre-school to introduce their children to Swahili vocabulary and numeracy, pooling their resources to support a local, educated young woman as the teacher. In 1979, many Orma women used *gaas eyba* meetings to pool their otherwise limited knowledge about upcoming elections and the population census. The traditional *gaas eyba* was always linked to women's dairying, facilitating cooperative labor and sharing networks. As commercial milk sales have become an important feature of sedentary life, the *gaas eyba* has become an important forum for working out complicated rules regarding milk sales, including issues of quality control to keep market prices high, and regulation of price structures and credit arrangements. There is a considerable literature on women's self-help groups in Africa, delineating their instrumentality and pointing out the formidable constraints on their long-term efficacy.[6]

Public health projects throughout the world often focus on women, especially in their reproductive roles as mothers, and many projects actively solicit the support of local women, especially those in leadership roles. Health is one major domain of continuing concern in Africa, and within that domain one of the issues requiring attention is AIDS prevention. In 1992, the World Bank identified the former Somali Republic as one of twelve African countries that are a high priority for preventive action on AIDS, *not* because of HIV prevalence (which was low in Somalia), but because of relatively high STD (sexually transmitted disease) prevalence in urban areas, which is a known avenue for future HIV infection. Because of the social dislocation that has occurred in this region of Africa, two decades of rapid urbanization, and the flow of Somalis in and out of Kenya and other parts of East Africa where both STD and HIV rates are high, there is a possibility that HIV infection rates will rise in the Somali community in the future. For a variety of cultural reasons, open discussion of this issue can be difficult, creating a barrier for appropriate preventive measures, including basic education. Because AIDS in Africa is primarily a heterosexual disease, it would be appropriate to elicit suggestions on prevention from both women and men at the "grassroots" level, and to involve local groups as much as possible in preventive action. Women's groups such as the *Abay siti* and *hagbad* are potentially important resources in this regard, as members may circulate vital information and support in a relatively non-offensive, non-intrusive manner.[7]

Precedents for this kind of women-based, local approach exist elsewhere. One example is a successful project carried out by Planned Parenthood in the Hispanic community of East Los Angeles.[8] The project, which has previously been implemented in Mexico and Hispanic neighborhoods of Arizona, recruited local women and trained them as *promotoras* -- educators of what is neutrally called "reproductive and family health." The women address a variety of topics, including the culturally-sensitive but urgent issues of contraception, domestic violence, and HIV/AIDS risks. The underlying message of the *promotoras* is that Hispanic women, by necessity, must "take charge" of their lives more than in traditional settings because current pressures on family and community life require them to do so. The *promotoras* meet with small groups of women (usually ones they know personally) in private homes. Group members range in age from teenagers to elders in their 70's. Hispanic parents who are uncomfortable with "outsiders" discussing sensitive issues with their children in public areas, such as schools, find it more acceptable that *promotoras* from their own local community discuss these same sensitive issues with their daughters in home-based settings. Melinda Cordero, the Coordinator of the program for Planned Parenthood in East Los Angeles, says that maintaining intergenerational ties and communication appears to be especially important to the women participants, who continue to value family and community cohesion.

Surprisingly, little resistance to the *promotoras* has come from traditionally-minded male authority figures, who stereotypically expect women to defer to men in these matters, or from the Catholic Church, which has a very conservative stance regarding sex, contraception, and gender roles. Normally hard-to-reach, young male gang members in East Los Angeles have approached the *promotoras* for information on contraception and HIV/AIDS, and even asked them for condoms. Ms. Cordero noted that the only objection she had ever heard from men in the community was that they did not want to be left out of the process; consequently, a local man was recruited and trained as a *promotor*, and he has held meetings with community men, through which he plans to recruit additional *promotors*. The program is basically an "each one teach one" model of community development and empowerment.

While the *promotora* project was initiated by Planned Parenthood and not by pre-existing local women's groups, and while there are many differences between the Hispanic community and the Somali community, this example, nonetheless, demonstrates some of the potential for local, women-centered initiatives to creatively address some difficult problems. Many among the Hispanic population now in the United States come from families dislocated and torn apart by warfare in Latin America. In the Somali situation, as with the U.S. Hispanic population, it may not be reasonable to expect that "traditional" leadership (if this is taken to mean only patriarchal and gerontocratic forms of leadership) can unilaterally solve all the urgent problems facing the community.[9] Somali women and young men who became disconnected from their immediate families and the control of elders (who were themselves disempowered by instability in some areas) may not necessarily submit without comment to the authority of those elders now.

IV. Limitations

Limitations on the potential for women's groups to participate meaningfully in reconstruction include the fact that these groups tend to be very small-scale and have a limited focus. Not all Somali women were inclined to join *Abay siti* or *hagbad* groups even before the current crisis. In the past, many scholars viewed local women's groups, especially those with religious components, as trivial, vestigial, reactionary, etc. Nonetheless, there is now a considerable literature showing that women's groups, including such Somali variants as *zar* and *rohan*, are amazingly resilient and enduring, and some have evolved into fairly practical organizations with broad replicability. For example, Kikuyu women in Kenya originated the idea of *mabati* groups, in which neighborhood women, sometimes from different ethnic groups, pool their resources to install durable, galvanized iron roofs on each others' houses. (The roofs reduce the risk of house fires and facilitate rain water collection, thus reducing trips to distant wells or streams.) Such groups are now found throughout rural East Africa.

Another limitation of locally-based women's groups concerns their sometimes parochial themes. For example, the *Abay siti* groups in some locales may possibly remain simple vehicles of religious devotion, and not evolve into more problem-oriented organizations such as the *hagbad*. While some observers, Somali and non-Somali alike, are uncomfortable with the possibility that Islamic "fundamentalists" could become more powerful in this region, it should be recognized that Islam is still important to the majority of the population. Attempts to peripheralize Islam could actually provoke a backlash.[10] In Kenya, some Somali women's groups with religious themes have turned to "fundamentalist" causes, while others have been devoted to various *sufi* ideals, and still others have become fairly ecumenical and broadly civic-minded. The role that Islam will play in the process of reconstruction is still unclear, since the Somali community is not necessarily united on this issue.

Another limitation of the role of women's groups in reconstruction stems from the way traditional gender roles seem to discourage sustained and decisive action by women on any significant scale. As mentioned above, the United Nations has insisted that at least one woman be included on every district council, as these are formed to meet UN requirements for forthcoming aid. Predictably, this policy has met with limited success. The *Wall Street Journal* reported that:

In one district, when the UN refused to back down on
the issue, the 21 men balloted among themselves - the
loser giving up his seat to his wife" (Oct. 15, 1993).[11]

In a situation where the UN-proposed representation will inevitably
be more limited than many Somalis might like (only 21 members per
district) and feed into a still more limited hierarchy of administration (i.e.,
the regional councils, composed of only three representatives from each
district therein, and a transitional government), it is not surprising that the
competition for council membership has encouraged influential men to
ignore the call to include a woman. And is a one-woman minimum
requirement per district really sufficient to insure women are represented
in the democratic process or is this just tokenism and "window dressing?"
In this context, the actions of the men described in the news article were
not undemocratic; the wife they selected may very well do a fine job,
given the limitations of the imposed role. While it is certainly worthwhile
to encourage democratic leadership and the inclusion of women in civil
administration and government, the actual model being imposed is
probably too simplistic and insufficiently sensitive to the political
processes already at work in reconstruction. Furthermore, the model
ignores women's on-going, self-initiated contributions to community life.

V. Conclusion

To address the current Somali crisis, it is important that we
acknowledge the existing "grassroots" institution-building strategies
employed by all segments of Somali society, including women. In the
past year we have heard countless recommendations from various
policymakers and "experts," widely repeated in the media, that legitimate
Somali leadership resides in "the elders." But who are "the elders?" Are
they only men, and only old? Somali traditions suggest that leadership
qualities of various kinds have long been recognized to exist in many
forms:

- among the wise "old" men who have survived long enough and
  productively enough to establish their own lineages;
- among the influential men in their prime who wheel and deal in
  property and social capital;
- among young men who exhibit resourcefulness and courage, often
  in the face of terrible hardship;
- among the articulate and sharp-witted and among the pious of both
  genders;

- among women who have mastered the exacting social requisites of daughter, sister, wife, and mother with grace and wit;
- among women who excel in household management and the education of children;
- among women who skillfully mediate between fathers and sons and between their affines and their natal families (advancing the honor of both);
- among women who productively and resourcefully manage the resources of male kin as well as their own;
- among women who perform critical tasks in livestock management and farming, often during lengthy absences of male relatives;
- among women who take on the care of the sick, the disabled, and the enfeebled elderly;
- and among women who cooperate with each other to create the domestic comforts prized by all.

At this point in history, the reconstruction of Somali civil society will require leadership from all these valuable resources.

Endnotes

1. This is a discussion paper, not a data-driven research report. The author has not visited Somalia since 1980, and has not been in East Africa since 1986. Furthermore, the author's research and experience has been primarily with the Oromo and Somali communities of Kenya.

2. I am grateful to Somali historian Amina Adan for sharing with me a manuscript she wrote that included some information on this topic (Adan n.d.:19-24). She wrote:
"The Somali nomadic woman who was settling in a town and did not have the hard work of pastoral life to busy herself, of course, felt the monotony of her new life. Perhaps she remembered the congregation of *kebed* making and *saar* dancing [and] she created for herself an institution which is a blend of Islam and older Somali tradition."
The *kebed* is a decorative and highly functional mat made for paneling the walls of traditional nomadic homes. To make one is a task requiring the cooperation of many women. Nomadic Orma and Wardey women also make such mats. The *saar* spirit possession dance has been discussed by I.M. Lewis (1971). I witnessed rural Somali women in Kenya engaged in *Abay siti* gatherings too, so it is not only an urban occurrence. Its practice has probably been facilitated by the phenomenal growth of small towns and the mobility of the population between rural and urban environments.

3. The Orma are among the most southerly of the Cushitic-speaking Oromo peoples, most of whom live in Ethiopia. (Only the Waata, an Oromo caste of former hunter-foragers who now live separately and independently of the Orma, live further to the south.) The ancestors of the Orma migrated out of south-central Ethiopia at least 500 years ago, moving into northern Kenya and southern Somalia, especially along river courses (permanent and seasonal) that permitted cattle pastoralism. They have lived in close contact with various Somali communities in these areas since that time. As Somalis began to outnumber Orma in the area between the Juba and Tana Rivers, especially since the mid-19th century, the Orma, who continued to live there, were clientized and were acculturated as Somali, while those living south of the Tana River retained their Orma identity. Somali often refer to Orma as Wardey. See Kelly, 1984, 1988, 1992.

4. The same "*Abbay sittidey*" hymn from southern Somalia noted by Giorgio Banti was taught to the author by Orma women in *gaas eyba* meetings in Tana River District, Kenya. See Banti's brief comments, transcription, and Italian translation of this hymn in his chapter on scripts ("Scrittura") in *Aspetti Dell'Espressione Artistica* in Somalia, Annarita Puglielli (Ed.), Universita Di Roma "La Sapienza" 1988:24-25. Several Orma women explained to the author that the hymn had first been taught by immigrant Somali women who had attended *gaas eyba* meetings to establish goodwill and address mutual concerns. During the time of the author's field research (1978-1981; 1983; 1986), however, Somali women were rarely observed attending.

5. See Kelly 1992 for a detailed discussion of the history of the Orma women's *gaas eyba*.

6. See, for example, Staudt 1978-79, Hay and Stichter 1984.

7. Western-educated Somalis can avail themselves of some rather different venues for exchanging information and support on this sensitive issue. A North American magazine produced by and for the Somali community carried a letter from a female reader to an advice columnist concerning the possibility that the woman's sexually active fiancé might bring to the marriage a risk of HIV infection. The male columnist responded appropriately (if briefly) from an epidemiological perspective, but one wonders how much this really helped the woman negotiate with her fiancé, who had denied any risk, regarding potential dangers and workable courses of action (IFTIN, vol. 1, no. 1, Feb. 1992:9).

8. A story was broadcast about this project on National Public Radio on June 12, 1993. I contacted Melinda Cordero, Program Coordinator for Planned Parenthood in East Los Angeles, who had been interviewed on the program and I spoke with her at length. I am grateful for her cooperation and assistance. N.P.R. transcripts and further information about the project are available.

9. See Zavella (1989) for a discussion of the emerging perspectives of Mexican-American women on changing leadership roles in the family and community.

10. The term "fundamentalist" is somewhat problematic, since it originated in English language usage as a reference to certain sectarian issues specific to Euro-American Christianity, and because the term is used too uncritically to refer to a wide variety of Islamic opinions and movements. UCLA historian Dr. Nikkie Keddie prefers the term "Islamism" in preference to "fundamentalism," because this captures the popular spirit behind many such movements.

11. I thank Dr. Charles Geshekter for sharing this information with me and for contributing comments to the development of this paper.

References

Adan, Amina n.d. "Somali Women From 1800 to the Present." Paper written for Dr. Chris Ehret, University of California, Los Angeles.

Banti, Giorgio. 1988 "Scrittura." In *Aspetti Dell'Espressione Artistica in Somalia.* Annarita Puglielli (Ed.), Universita Di Roma "La Sapienza" 1988:24-25.

Hay, Margaret Jean and Sharon Stichter, eds. 1984 *African Women South of the Sahara.* New York, Longman.

Kelly, Hilarie. 1984 "Orma-Somali Culture Sharing in the Juba-Tana Region." In *Proceedings of the Second International Congress of Somali Studies,* vol. VI, Thomas Labahn, ed., Helmut Buske Verlag, Hamburg, Germany: 13-38.

_____1988 "The Emergence of a Pastoral Women's Collective." Paper presented at the African Studies Association meeting, Chicago, Illinois.

_____ 1992 "From *Gada* to Islam: The Moral Authority of Gender Relations Among the Pastoral Orma of Kenya." Ph.D. dissertation in Anthropology, University of California, Los Angeles.

Lewis, I.M. 1971 *Ecstatic Religion.* London, Penguin Books.

Staudt, Kathleen A. 1978-79 "Rural Women Leaders: Late Colonial and Contemporary Contexts." *Rural Africana,* no. 3:5-21.

Zavella, Patricia. 1989 "The Problematic Relationship of Feminism and Chicana Studies." In *Across Cultures: The Spectrum of Women's Lives.* Emily Abel and Marjorie L. Pearson, eds. Women's Studies (special issue) vol. 17:25-36.

CHAPTER TWENTY THREE

Somali NGOs: A Product of Crisis

Abdirahman Osman Raghe

I. Background

Similar to the non-governmental organizations (NGOs) of many other societies, Somali NGOs were born as a product of crisis and as a perception of need by an individual or a group. Their background is not in general terms different from the history of the first generation of the international NGOs that were rooted in the humanitarian tragedies of the major world wars. Most of the organizations that existed before World War II were largely an outgrowth of missionary activities, whereas immediately afterwards, a new breed of secular NGOs started offering relief to the war-torn victims and later emerged as non-profit making relief and development organizations.

From the social and political contexts, NGOs vary from country to country. Even those operating under the same social and political contexts show marked differences in their size, programs, governance, etc. (Asfaw, 1992, p.6). Somali NGOs, as a new phenomena, have their commonalities and differences accordingly. Their course of evolution and development also reflects the popular socio-economic process in the country.

In Africa and the rest of the Third World, indigenous NGOs have emerged parallel to the public and private sectors as well as a movement to support and facilitate grassroots initiatives, groups and associations. Their sustainability and economic independence from the international resource agencies and NGOs was always questionable due to inherent fund raising and professional weaknesses.

The emergence and perception of Somali NGOs as a product of crisis is not different on their level from the background described above. The Somalia NGOs could be considered mostly the product of the tragic consequences of the 1977-78 Somali-Ethiopian War and the 1991-1993 civil war in Somalia. The Somali local NGOs could serve as a vehicle of the people's aspirations for democratic change if trained, coordinated and also facilitated to develop as a sector.

By definition, NGOs "are in general, private non-profit making organizations that are publicly registered..... whose principal function is to implement development projects favoring the popular sector and which receive financial support" (Leilah Laudim, 1978, p. 30). Berhe, in his paper on African indigenous non-governmental organizations, maintains that the term NGO "refers to African indigenous grassroots associations, people's organizations, citizens' groups, relief, development, research and advocacy agencies, trade unions and independent women's, youth and intellectual groupings" (Berhe, 1992, p. 2). Some other authorities also talk about membership NGOs that "provide services and employ staff but are owned by those who should benefit from the services that organizations provide" (Fowler, et al, 1992, p. 8).

Berhe, Fowler and colleagues opt for a definition broad enough to include groupings outside government structures and political parties (Asfaw, 1993, p. 4). According to some expatriate staff of the United Nation Operation for Somalia (UNOSOM) and the international NGOs during 1991-1993, an "NGO in Somalia is an unlucky term." The number of the local NGOs in Mogadishu at this time was mushrooming like wildflowers after the rain, without the necessary links into the real background of their growth.

In the absence of a government and any other viable relief support mechanisms in this country during the civil war, the emergence of local NGOs for various reasons including political motivation must be taken into account. In the middle of the civil war and beyond, the dynamics of this society already started as self-motivating trends. Privatization and development of civil society groups have, somehow, taken modest steps in most of the Somali regions. Today, there are contradictory processes underway all over the Somali territories. Besides the political fragmentation and deadlocks at the top, the social and economic changes by the people have already taken their course. We already have private communication groups, private businesses, private airlines, service companies, private development, joint ventures, NGOs, etc. However, this progress is risk-prone.

Somali local NGOs must be encouraged with the necessary institutional building capacities as a new sector for micro-development, social advocacy, empowerment, and re-education for the community's self-help and self-reliance. Already, the active and capable LONGOs (Local NGOs) could be identified through their experience and track record.

II. Somali NGOs (1980-1990)

Following the Somali-Ethiopian war of 1977-1978, the influx of half a million refugees into Somalia attracted many international NGOs into relief projects and programs among widely-distributed refugee camps in the country. Larger concentrations of camps were placed in the northwest/Somaliland and the Hiran Regions. As a result, the experience of the NGOs' humanitarian operations benefitted some of the local Somali intellectuals and professionals.

The National Refugee Commission (NRC) acted as the local coordinating body of refugee operations and also the counterpart of the UNHCR. All the agencies' and NGOs' efforts in the camps were directed by this commission. The field or camp level leadership structures at the refugee camps referred their day-to-day activities and needs to the regional refugee commission, under the national umbrella (NRC). In connection with this work, I would like to pay tribute to the late General Manager of NRC, Mr. Yusuf Abdi Shirdon, a known honest nationalist who passed away as a victim of the civil war.

Previously, Somalia had experienced poor relief infrastructure and a lack of national mechanisms to implement and facilitate relief programs. The distribution of the relief supplies to the vulnerable groups in the event of a disaster, such as drought, remained a less tangible task. The traditional structures in the rural areas were utilized to support the relief programs, due to lack of local NGOs or effective local volunteer groups such as the Somali Red Crescent Society. However, the present political hostilities and their consequences are beyond the limits of traditional challenges and could not be dealt with sufficiently, using these previously effective mechanisms.

In addition to the crises which sparked the emergence of Somali NGOs, frustrations resulted from government institutions or public sector development since independence in 1960, and have contributed also to the need for Somali NGOs in the country. Like other communities in Africa and the Third World, the Somali nomadic, farming and fishing communities had self-help traditions of their own in their socio-economic activities. Back in the 1960s, the idea of grassroots, self-help groups and activities was conceived in some parts of Somalia/Somaliland to maintain feeder and longer earth roads and to address problems of land erosion and sand dune encroachment.

As early as the 1980s, the "Rural Development Strategy" was set to serve as the guideline for micro-development initiatives in the country. The Rural Development and Planning Department of the Ministry of Interior was responsible for the technical facilitation of the agencies, NGOs and donors through the regional and district development structures. The physical implementation and the translation of that strategy into tangible projects and programs must be questionable. However, the setup as outlined above has at least helped the Somali NGOs to establish a formal line of relations with the government.

Basically, two of the initial Somali NGOs were established as a product of the 1977-1978 Horn of Africa crisis and as a result of the only official option: the Somali Unit for Research, Emergencies and Rural Development (SURERD) and HAQABTIR were Oxfam-America and ILO-supported indigenous initiatives. Others, like ADAMIGA, DARYEEL, DEGAAN, etc. that followed suit, have also shown their capacities as capable local NGOs. For instance, SURERD, also a product of the Somali Studies International Association (SSIA) experience in Somalia, was able to address some project needs for both refugee and non-refugee Somali communities such as Sheikh Bananey of the Bay region and Sheikh Omar-Elberdale of the Gebiley district as well as some traditional and farming communities like Gendershe (Weaving Community) and Bal'ad of the lower and middle Shabelle regions respectively.

SURERD's objectives, in brief, were to stimulate and respond to the aspirations of self-help and self-reliance groups in the rural communities of Somalia. By 1984, pipeline projects in SURERD's plan of action included more than thirty-six community-based projects. Besides Oxfam-America, other international NGOs and agencies had project cooperation or partnership with SURERD such as the German Agro-Action and USAID. This NGO was successful in promoting rice production in the Jowhar area of the Middle Shabelle region.

In view of the above background, a good number of local NGOs have emerged and operated in Somalia during the last ten years of the previous regime (1981-1991). The number of the local NGOs was growing rapidly on an imitation basis before tough criteria for registration was set by concerned government departments and the international donor agencies.

The USAID PVO development project, the UNDP capacity building umbrella mechanism and the UN Emergency Unit were in operation before the total collapse of the Somali state in the 1990s.

The USAID PVO project which was fully operational by 1986, was a partnership effort between the Ministry of Interior (Rural Development Department) USAID, US international NGOs, the Somali communities. Under this project, a Management Unit for Support and Training (MUST) served as a catalyst between the parties in partnership. MUST also provided support to the joint committees to discuss and decide upon the submitted projects for funding from the project's two grant resources. The Experiment in International living, a US NGO, was involved in some of the project's components such as MUST development and the training of Somali NGOs. Chapter I and II of the project's operational manual contain the criteria set for local NGO registration.

Responding to the natural and man-made emergencies, two capacity building projects were finalized with UNDP: (1) the UN Emergency Unit which was based at UNDP HQ in Somalia; and (2) the disaster preparedness umbrella mechanism which would have been placed at the Ministry of Interior. This umbrella mechanism would have established other units at the appropriate ministry such as agriculture, livestock, land and air transport, etc. The UN Emergency Unit which was operational in 1989-1990 at the UNDP HQ, Somalia, would have played a major role in establishing the preparedness unit and training of its key staff.

This project would have facilitated the inter-ministerial and technical official committees for disaster situations to undertake their responsibilities better. The central mechanism to the Ministry of Interior was also designed to undertake information gathering and dissemination for both early warning and setting of action plans for the disaster situation in the country. This would have benefits also for the relief operations of the international and local NGOs in Somalia.

A Somali NGO forum was also in the formation stage during this period. There were problems of structure, funding and leadership that slowed down the establishment and functioning of that forum as a central unit for NGO development. The incompatibility of such a forum as an emerging force or movement with the past regime's dictatorial policies was apparent. Yet, there were serious attempts to launch it during the 1980s.

The NGO movement is relatively young in Somalia/Somaliland. During the past regime, efforts aimed at establishing self-help organizations were immediately frustrated through high handed action or imprisonment, especially in the Northwest/Somaliland. The case of "UFO," a voluntary intellectual group in Hargeisa who served six years of imprisonment at the isolation East German-built Labatan-Jirow jail, near Baidoa, during the 1980s could be raised as a concrete example of the past regimes' police policies against the development of voluntary civil society work and groups. The same group of intellectuals have successfully achieved their NGO vision, founding the Somali Relief and Rehabilitation Association (SORRA) which now works in Somaliland.

The political and security environment of the country during the period referred to was considered critical. NGO operations were exposed as well to the negative impact of the past regime like all other sectors of society. However, the international and local NGOs were able to face the challenges and to continue a level of their activities and efforts accordingly. Once again the purpose of taking note of these projects and activities is both as a background of the local NGOs evolution and to provide for a future vision.

Following the outbreak of the present crises through 1991-1993, most of the former NGOs were either displaced or had disappeared due to the deadly security environment and political fragmentation caused by the civil war in this country.

III. Somali NGOs (1991-1994)

Somalia, with a history of both natural and man-made disasters, has experienced for the past four years (1991-1994) an unprecedented humanitarian tragedy and political crisis, including a bloody civil war. The consequences and devastations of this civil strife were compounded by the collapse of the Somali state and institutions. As said earlier, almost all the previous Somali NGOs were displaced. The traditional mechanism in the rural areas to support and facilitate the international efforts was also affected, disrupted and displaced.

Therefore, besides the serious challenges posed by armed banditry around the humanitarian relief, the total lack of available local capacities such as grassroots committees, self-help groups or NGOs put more burden on the interventions of the international agencies and NGOs. Even during normal times, a project or program without the recipients' participation in some form would, for sure, end up falling below its original objectives and strategy. This is a fact generally faced by the UNOSOM operations in Somalia to date.

In addition to the humanitarian crises and as an alternative to public sector development that gave birth to the previous Somalia NGOs in 1980s, the absence of the public and private sectors as well as other feasible local capacities because of the present civil war has exposed a visible vacuum. The local NGOs have then to fill the vacuum and stand for the popular aspirations of both relief and development in cooperation with the international community's efforts. The active portion of the Somali local NGOs have shown their voluntary and non-profit capabilities and commitment in their operations.

Hence, with the collapse of the state institutions and infrastructure in Somalia due to the civil war, many kitchen and orphanage arrangements were introduced parallel to the international agencies and NGOs operations during 1991-1993. The ICRC, as a war mandated body, has been the primary organization involved in distributing relief food up to mid-1993 and even when the UN agencies were largely absent from Somalia after 1991 because of security concerns. The United States has been the largest bilateral donor, providing over US$ 210 million of humanitarian assistance, including 300,000 metric tons of food aid. Most of this was channeled through non-governmental organizations (NGOs). Among these NGOs, the ICRC has been the most active recipient spending 30% of its global budget on Somalia (*Africa Today*, 1993, pg. 57).

During the ICRC period, kitchen and orphanage organizers for the displaced persons (mainly women and children) received help. Yet few Somali NGOs were eligible under the ICRC registration regulations for food and other relief supplies, or even for small projects such as sanitation, etc. The ICRC, in partnership with the Somali Red Crescent Society (SRCS), was able to operate under a background of political and security arrangements and with greater tolerance for the day-to-day looting and diversions of its resources.

However, in the midst of the chaos which prevailed through many areas of Somalia, ICRC and the international NGOs, with the support of the UN, have continued to work with Somali local capacities and professionals whose contributions were limited to humanitarian activities such as health and food distribution, in addition to other activities such as sanitation, water, etc. Besides ICRC, other international NGOs such as CARE, SOS, IARA, SCF, CRS, etc, were also in operation with a lower profile in the country through 1991 and partly 1992.

The few Islamic NGOs and agencies that operated along with ICRC and other NGOs through 1991-1992 have proven very effective at grassroots levels. Most of their target areas were religious institutions and groups as well as education and health needs. Currently, some of the previous education and health structures are partly run by Islamic groups with support sources from such organizations. There are no real answers as to their impact at this point.

Under the United Nations Operations for Somalia (UNOSOM I), the consolidated Inter-Agency 90 day Plan of Action for Emergency

Humanitarian Assistance to Somalia was launched on April 14, 1993 and the previous 100 Day Action Program for Accelerated Humanitarian Assistance for Somalia on September 28, 1992 were the two principal humanitarian plans set forth for action in Somalia during this period. Their level of concrete performance as two country-wide sanction plans was locally questionable in terms of tangible projects or programs.

According to the 90 Day action plan document, under Section V, coordination mechanism (97), "Key to the 90 Day Plan is the recognized coordinating role of the United Nations and the increased active presence of the United Nations agencies in Somalia. The security of the UN personnel and the delivery of the humanitarian supplies through safe corridors were heavily considered in this plan. To support the important work of the national and international NGOs and to ensure that there is close cooperation amongst all partners involved in the implementation of humanitarian assistance in Somalia, the United Nations coordinator for humanitarian assistance will undertake to hold regular meetings with all members of the NGO community."

Besides the above, regular meetings for NGOs with the UNOSOM Humanitarian office, UN coordination was expressed through the provision of identification cards for the international staff of both UN and NGOs as well as some of the local NGOs registered with UNOSOM. The criteria and procedures for registration was initially under less well-presented requirements. At later stages, the conditions for local NGO receipt of UNOSOM ID and Registration included at least, a letter of support from one international NGO, receipt of the local NGO's last quarterly report of activities, and physical inspection of its office premises.

For the local NGOs, the UNOSOM identification card proved essential for the international NGOs and UNOSOM contacts. It also allowed possession of arms against banditry actions and the facilitation of free movement through key infrastructure such as the ports, airports, checkpoints, international NGOs and agencies premises, etc. Indirectly, both of the above two UNOSOM requirements have also encouraged the promotion of the professionals' containment within the NGOs work.

The four main objectives of the accelerated 100-Day program were:

1. to strengthen the on-going activities of the United Nations and NGOs and to accelerate their expansion to people presently not receiving adequate assistance and to geographical areas not yet covered by relief efforts;

2. to implement relief and recovery objectives;

3. to nationalize coordination and management of the activities of the United Nations system, NGOs and others through collaborated arrangement;

4. In light of the above, to determine the financial resources which are immediately required for submission to the donor community.

On the outset of this program, the elements of relief, rehabilitation, reconstruction, security operations and political reconciliation were seen as inseparable. Despite the increase of UN diplomatic activities inside and outside the country, security constraints, political deadlock, and the consequences of famine and drought continued through 1991-1992.

Under Section VI, coordination Para. 55 of the 100-Day program, "United Nations in Somalia will fall under the overall coordination of the UN Secretary General's Special Representative for Somalia. In his capacity as head of UN Operations for Somalia (UNOSOM) the special representative is responsible for the coordination between humanitarian assistance, recovery activities, political constraints and security operations."

Before the end of this program, the media turned the international community's attention to the plight of Somalia's civil war, famine and drought victims. By this move, the no-win case of UNOSOM I, at least throughout 1992, was broken by the US-led multinational forces (UNITAF) under Operation Restore Hope. Beyond a doubt, the Operation Restore Hope has left a successful record on the aspect of humanitarian intervention among its original tasks.

During that period, another event that brought visibility to Somali NGOs was the broad-based principle adopted by UNOSOM for the mobilization and convening of the humanitarian and political reconciliation Addis Ababa conferences between January 4-7 and 7-15, 1993 respectively. Many local NGOs, both old and new, that were considered as participants by UNOSOM for these conferences, also had in mind opportunities for rehabilitation projects that would be offered to the local NGOs for their implementation. A good number of NGOs have been accommodated under this broad-based outlook which led to political controversy with almost all of the various factional leaders.

The same scenarios have also taken place in terms of local NGO participation in the Addis Ababa humanitarian and political conferences between March 11-13 and 15-27, 1993. Along with the local NGO participants, these conferences also included women and traditional leaders. In both conferences, the social groups have, together, taken common positions in the form of a pressure group towards dialogue and political reconciliation by the warring factional and movement leaders.

Somali NGOs had a leading role in this effort, shown in the concerns which they presented in common statements in each of the humanitarian conferences (January and March 1993 respectively).

Somali NGOs are among the most accessible means to express civil society's capacity for free organizations. The Somali NGOs' present role is emerging as one to support the mass movement towards peace and reconciliation. Moreover, relief and rehabilitation are vital obligations to rebuild a collective society in which every individual becomes a citizen. The Somali NGOs have all the right to voice the aspirations of the Somali people who are unwillingly caught in the present stateless and lawless situation.

Apparently, their roles of policy advocacy, development education and empowerment of the grassroots are currently much needed in Somalia/Somaliland. The consequences of collapse of the state creates special responsibilities for NGOs both in physical as well as moral terms. They offer one of the few threads of opportunity to strengthen local capacities that could at least empower and stimulate the participatory approach needed for recovery.

Briefly, the civil society groups such as women, intellectuals and professionals were able to reactivate up to a level through 1993 after two years of bloody civil war in Somalia. As a result, local NGOs, women's organizations, intellectual groups and professional associations have started some promising activities. The translation of such structures into workable bodies warrants further capacity-building inputs, training, methodologies, operating procedures, and management principles..

For instance, the formation of the Somali Professional Society for Agriculture, Livestock and Fisheries took place on 3 March 1993, in Mogadishu. The main objectives of this society are:

1. To maintain and advance the highest professional standards in the public interest;

2. to promote and further the interest of the profession and its members. To achieve this, the society is empowered to take certain specified steps.

Despite limited representation across the country, genuine attempts of social and professional reorganization have already contributed to the furtherance of the efforts towards a healthy Somalia. We should expect similar isolated activities both inside and outside the country. To improve on the current painful situation in Somalia, civil society groups must be empowered to play a role in the process of peace and recovery.

IV. The Nature, Objectives, and Constraints of the Local NGOs

Most of the emerging local NGOs are within the category of simple structures in which the founders also serve within the executive body. Such NGOs depend on affiliated professionals for their project preparation needs. A few have entrepreneurial or business background, operating under salaried structures and with a contractor's small project objectives. Such NGOs utilize better infrastructure for their operations and thereby tend to attract more projects and activities from the international community. Reportedly close to 940 Somali NGOs are registered or in the process of registration by the UNOSOM Humanitarian division.

Most of these NGOs have wide-range objectives and target areas. Basically, most of the women's NGOs have clear objectives, even if not well-documented. Their objectives and target areas are limited to social activities (health and education) and income generation for women such as handcraft development, etc. Notably, few local NGOs have so far proved capable. The few local NGOs that went into partnership with other international NGOs are lucky to have obtained a level of the necessary institutional capacity needs and joint action programs.

The absence of the necessary climate and infrastructure such as the financial institutions like banks, etc, has limited the progress of the Somali NGOs. Initially, it was helpful for local NGOs to receive outside funding for basic work in relief or rehabilitation. However, as the international agencies and NGOs continued to operate and gain experience in Somalia/Somaliland in the midst of the chaos, the Somali NGOs felt lower priority for relief and rehabilitation, and a higher priority to move on to basic social and economic development.

The local NGOs' worries of lack of involvement, weak coordination, absence of institutional building and training needs, etc. by UN operations and international NGOs were voiced in both the January and March, 1993 humanitarian conferences in Addis Ababa, as noted before. Both of the joint statements expressed their expectations of involvement in development as a sector in the Somali process of recovery and reconstruction.

As in the case of the NGOs, the outcome of the women's workshop held on lst March 1993 in Addis Ababa also exposed the extent to which Somali women and children were affected in Somalia's civil war and their worries concerning exclusion in relief and rehabilitation programs. Part of their appeal is quoted as:

we now appeal to the international community to assist Somalia Women's groups. PLEASE DO NOT EXCLUDE US. Instead, place us very high on your agenda. We are the ones who bear Somali children. The children are our future. We can be the catalyst in peace making.... Accept us and work with us for the future of Somalia.

Above the present lawlessness and insecure environment, any possible oversight of the Somali NGOs' vital role as facilitator or partners of relief and development may place them in the role of development trade unions. Their local participatory efforts and initiatives must be allowed to grow with the on-going international agencies and NGOs programs in Somalia. The Somali NGOs statement at the January Addis Ababa conference outlined the constraints against their development which is very briefly pinpointed at the conclusion.

For sure, there are inherent weaknesses in the Somali NGOs' development besides the capacity-building areas already raised, including the almost total lack of locally available fund-raising sources and the true knowledge of the non-profit organization as contributors to public well being. So far, an NGO as a voluntary body, is vague and less measurable than a profit organization for Somalis involved in present NGO activities.

In spite of the local NGOs' worries, we could ask whether international agencies and NGOs had some reason to rethink their modes of cooperation with the local NGOs. According to some sources within the international agencies and NGOs, they had uncertain feelings about entering into cooperation or partnership with all the local bodies during this period when accountability and evaluation of NGOs activities were not feasible. It was an environment where insecurity and political factionalism dominated the daily course of events.

In contrast, local NGOs have raised some cases of international NGO diversions and misuses, and pointed out that this period of uncertainty and confusion as risk-prone for both the national and international organizations in the humanitarian and rehabilitation operations of Somalia. They also argue that the mistakes noted so far in the few activities undertaken by local NGOs are relatively small.

It would be understandable if the international humanitarian offices were unable to meet some of their terms of references because of security concerns. Nobody could doubt that their physical coordination and inspection or evaluation of activities would have been initially very dangerous in Somalia. UNOSOM previously had no substantial resources for small scale-projects until late 1993. The amount of 160 million U.S. dollars raised in the Addis Ababa follow-up humanitarian conferences between 11-13 March 1993 was not adequate, reportedly because of donors' dissatisfaction with the level of stability in Somalia. The UNOSOM operation in Somalia was overwhelmed by military activities through 1993 as well.

Indirectly, UNOSOM operations facilitated a level of both improved security and humanitarian environment in some regions in Somalia. This change of environment has helped the activities of the agencies and NGOs at the field level. As a result, the focus of the international community's activities were shifted to some of the regions where relatively better security environment prevailed. The decisions reached at the Addis Ababa Humanitarian Conferences to reward peace at the local level was not fulfilled by UNOSOM nor other agencies as such. The case of Somaliland and other regions of Somalia at this time could be taken as examples.

Besides the loopholes raised during the review of the 1993 relief and rehabilitation program (presented at the March 1993 humanitarian Addis Ababa conference), shortcomings of duplication of efforts and poor coordination were also reported. However, the international NGOs' field activities both on relief and rehabilitation could not be undermined. Perhaps their performances lacked the necessary local contributions on broader community lines or even the essential formal national and regional relations; yet the overall results must be judged as highly effective.

During late 1993, UNOSOM Humanitarian Division reported that some funds were finally available for small-scale projects. A project guideline was also distributed to the local NGOs. This was a very good step that could have taken UNOSOM's humanitarian division to the professional and physical activities of the local NGOs. In principle, the active portion of the local NGOs was happy with the new guidelines as a basis for a healthy NGO competition.

However, there were problems rooted in the present status of Somalia as a stateless country and the still inherent problems and attitudes of fragmentation and factionalism in socio-political contexts. The controversial reinstitution of the district and regional councils by UNOSOM II could give the local development process a more solid footing than the previously centralized-only government option and the relevant attitudes to that. Beyond a doubt, there is already a conspicuous public inclination towards regional autonomy policies and practices for the rebirth of Somalia.

Optimistically, local NGOs must be assisted so that they may voluntarily grow with the aspirations of the people, without any institutional restrictions imposed by outside agencies. The required verticality in development should be facilitated so as to encourage the essential reorientation of the Somali people from clan based platforms to higher levels of integration. Professional local capacities must be allowed to progress and contribute to local development along broader lines, depending on the dynamics of Somali reconstruction and rehabilitation processes and policies.

According to local NGOs, certain points of the NGO guidelines in UNOSOM's humanitarian division, issued on 28 October 1993, did not reflect fully the present capacities of the indigenous NGOs. The information this guideline considered included the odds of the present Somalia situation regarding the local NGO operations and their larger numbers which appear less feasible for tangible community development action plans.

The involvement of the local formal and traditional authorities in the management board of the projects was, in principle, very fair. However, there were local NGOs' worries of how that will match with the day-to-day professional procedures of the project implementation activities. Local NGOs preferred to seek community participation themselves, given their own approaches subject to UNOSOM or other funding agency's monitoring and evaluation criteria.

Two main points follow noting themes in which local NGOs have shown most interest:

1. the NGO must secure inputs in kind which match the contributions of UNOSOM;

2. the NGO has to have resources to pay the salaries of its own regular employees.

The reaction of the local NGOs on these two points were serious. They asked

if any indigenous NGO or up to a level the international NGOs could cover from their funds or could meet the salaries of their project's staff from their funds or even solicit that from a poor country in the Third World like Somalia.

It is doubtful whether any single Somali NGO could pay the salaries of its core staff who offer all technical support services to the project cycle involved. Normally, the supervision and administration cost are planned within the project's budget components with cautious consideration of the non-profit making NGOs' philosophy. The technical, professional and administrative inputs of a particular project are essential for the overall growth of the country's physical and human development.

Inherent weaknesses of local NGOs' fund raising were accounted for in this paper. The Somali NGOs as a new phenomena and in consideration of the present socio-economic realities of the Somali society must have different treatment. Such conditionalities as criteria without prior organizational inputs might tend to frustrate NGO development and/or create unnecessary grievances and tensions.

V. Local NGO Coordinating Bodies

NGO coordinating bodies are member organizations established to provide common services and to strengthen the NGOs' managerial, information, government and resources agencies' relations. These organizations apply various names to themselves, from council to groupings or informally as "umbrellas" (Stremlau, *World Development*, Vol. 15, edited by Drabek, p. 213)."

In both stages (1980-1990 and 1990-1994) of Somali NGOs' development, attempts to initiate a forum, networking body, or consortium were tried. Because of the current fragmentation of Somalia into isolated regions in the hands of armed movements, factions and administrations, a national umbrella for local NGO coordination has not been possible.

However, parallel to the international NGOs consortium established in Mogadishu in October 1992, efforts to initiate a forum, network or consortium were made. The idea of forming a forum for a group of NGOs to discuss common areas of interest and to exchange information was in process since then. Another concrete step of networking local NGOs was discussed and adopted in the Oxfam American sponsored Orientation Workshop on NGOs for Somali Indigenous NGOs in Addis Ababa 22-27 October 1993. The twenty NGOs from Somaliland and Somalia decided, with their Ethiopian counterparts, to form networking structures for Somali participant NGOs:

> this relationship that NGOs consciously establish with other NGOs or groups of NGOs is networking...this learning and listening can be horizontal between two NGOs or vertical through coordinating body that member NGOs create (Asfaw, 1993, p. 46).

The international NGO consortium in Mogadishu was launched in October, 1992. It acts as a focus and working body for NGO activities, provides a forum for discussing working practices, facilitates payment and operational requirements, and is the representative body through which to channel and regulate issues with the UN and other bodies. Membership in the consortium and its links with operational NGO policy groups continues to grow. The Council of Somali Voluntary and Development Organization (COSVADA) was first established by the middle of 1990. Equally, the Somali NGOs Consortium (SNC) and the Somali NGOs Council were founded in July, 1994 in Mogadishu and Nairobi respectively. There are other regional networking organizations elsewhere as well.

The last quarter of 1994 has seen UNOSOM II operations shrinking from the regions and pulling out of Mogadishu. International NGOs and most of the UNOSOM humanitarian personnel have already left the country at the outset of the Rwanda Emergency Operations in early 1994. As a result, the activities of the Somali NGOs were affected. Naturally, the vacuum created by the closure of UNOSOM II operations and the failure on its attempts to facilitate Somalia's political reconciliation process will increase security and political tensions for some time.

Somalia is at a crossroads between a fallback to the scenario of 1991-1992 or a move forward to a realistic approach for comprehensive political reconciliation. Several situations are still unresolved: the political environment resulting from the October 1994 fighting in Hargeisa (Somaliland) between the forces loyal to President Egal and SNM Chairman, Abdirahman Tur; participation in the still unsuccessful reconciliation process for Somalia as of mid-1994 by the SNM and other northern political movements such as SDA, USF, and USP; the reaction of the Somaliland administration, entering into an agreement with the Somali Salvation Alliance headed by Ali Mahdi.

Generally, civil society's re-activation and development process which was markedly in progress throughout Somalia will suffer in the midst of the new vacuum. However, the future development of Somali NGOs into a viable sector could be considered as a promising new capacity for relief and community development. The new UN-consolidated appeal for Somalia, under which an amount of US $70,000,000 will be raised for Somalia's humanitarian activities during 1995, is a good sign of the international community's continued commitment, despite the still unyielding political process of this country.

The Somali NGOs coordinating bodies' initiatives for future vision of a consortium is part and parcel of the revival of the national civil society groups for democratic development. The tragic scenarios of the civil war through 1991-1994 in Somalia had devastated this segment of the society. The social groups for peace and democracy both inside and outside of the country have shown their need for an alternative national platform than the currently active clan based one in Somalia.

VI. Conclusion

The emergence of local Somali NGOs as a product of crisis and as a perception of need is a new phenomenon. The first set of the Somali local NGOs was mainly the outgrowth of the half million Somali-Ethiopian refugees influx into Somalia as a result of the 1977-1978 Somali-Ethiopian war in the Horn of Africa. Moreover, the change of political environment at that time, from socialist and public sector orientation after the war to private sector and free market development, has contributed to the embryonic growth of local NGOs capabilities in the country as a promising future nonprofit sector. Despite the attempts of the past regime to frustrate emerging local capabilities, the local NGOs have manifested a level of progress during 1980-1990.

Even though some NGOs were displaced during the deadly civil war in Somalia through 1991-1993, a new set of local NGOs has arisen out of the humanitarian assistance programs such as the kitchens, orphanages and self-help communities as well as some others with professional background that served the rehabilitation projects and programs of the international agencies and NGOs. The controversial broad-based efforts of the United Nations Operation for Somalia (UNOSOM) with the objective to empower the local social structures and the local support structures such as NGOs have also encouraged the growth of a sizeable number of Somali NGOs. Close to 940 NGOs were reportedly registered or in the process for registration by the UNOSOM Humanitarian Division throughout Somalia. The most active local NGOs in the country include the following categories:

1. professional NGOs;

2. extension of international NGOs in the form of partnerships;

3. NGOs with entrepreneurial background;

4 NGOs as an extension of relief capacities such as kitchen units and orphanages;

5. NGOs on the self-help group level working mostly at the district/regional levels; NGOs working as an umbrella for different branches such as the Somali National Partners (SNP) with up to twenty-three branches so far from the same geographical area;

6. NGOs as intellectual movements or women's associations.

Besides the absence of the necessary climate and infrastructure such as financial institutions like banks, etc., local NGOs have both strengths and constraints facing them in their present course of development as identified by a Multi-Donor Task Force, under the coordination of the World Bank (Somalia-Framework, 1993, p. 76).

Strengths of existing NGOs include:

1. an ability to mobilize manpower with special skills ranging from engineers, teachers, health professionals, to business managers;

2. an ability to mobilize women development managers as well as women in the community;

3. first- hand experience with all the local conditions;

4. acceptance as part of the community;

5. support and encouragement from the community and authorities.

Numerous constraints facing them have also been identified as:

1. limited experience in management;

2. limited structures and resources available in the country;

3. lack of experience while operating in an emergency situation;

4. institutional and management weakness;

5. limited financial and material resources and facilities;

6. lack of logistic capability to supervise the monitoring activities;

7. lack of communication facilities.

For the local NGOs, institutional development, both as a social movement for policy advocacy and grassroots development education, and also as a non-profit making development sector, demonstrates an immediate need for networking among the Somali NGOs in the country. There are already embryonic initiatives and activities in progress which hopefully will yield concrete fruits in the near future towards local NGOs networking and consortia building process. The founding of COSVADA, the Somali National Consortium and the Somali NGOs Council, based in Mogadishu and Nairobi, are good steps towards this goal.

Local NGO experience at the various isolated regions of the country have shown that there are a number of lessons and activities that the Somali NGOs could exchange if the necessary mechanisms for dissemination of information and coordination are put well in place. There are certain local NGOs which have developed skills in local fund raising or established income generating capacity. These capabilities could be replicated or set new examples for communication or exchange of experiences from the civil war years of factionalism and fragmentation.

From UNITAF to UNOSOM and finally Operation United Shield, the Somali political deadlock remains unresolved for the sixth year (1991-1996). However, the Somali people look forward to see their country in peace, enjoying a politically comprehensive settlement. The role of the Somali NGOs remains even more important than in the past, both during this interim period and for the future of the Somali people.

Bibliography

1. Asfaw, Z. (ed.), Orientation Workshop on NGOs for Somali Indigenous NGOs, 22-27 October 1993, Addis Ababa.

2. Drabek, Anne Gordon, (ed.) "World Development Alternatives: The Challenge for NGOs." *World Development* Vol. 15, 1987.

3. Elmi, Omar Salad, *The Somali Conflict and Current Causes*, 1992.

4. Fitzgibbon, Louis, *The Betrayal of the Somalis*, London, 1992.

5. Hancock, Graham, *Lords of Poverty*, 1991

6. Handbook of International NGO Programs in Somalia, March 1993, Second Edition, International NGO Consortium, Information Office, Mogadishu

7. Management Control in Non-Profit Organizations. Anthony/Young, 12th edition, 1988.

8 Multi-Donor Task Force, World Bank Draft Report, October 12, 1993.

9. Notes of Dr. Hussein M. Adam on Somali NGOs, 1980s.65. Notes on Afro-Action Experience 1991-1993.

10. Notes of the UN Emergency Unit and UN Agencies Reports, 1991-1993.

11. Partners in Development GSDR/USAID PVOs-NGOs, 1986.

12. War and Famine Indigenous Perspectives on the Horn of Africa. Institute of Peace and Conflict Studies, Conard Greble College, Waterloo, Ontario, Canada, March 1988.

13. *Seeking Somali Reunification*, Somalia, April, 1995.

CHAPTER TWENTY FOUR

A Proposal for Reorganizing the Health Sector in Somalia After the Emergency

Abdullahi M. Ahmed, Ranieri Guerra and Augusto Pinto

Abstract

The civil war in Somalia has destroyed the social, economic and political structure of the country. One of the most severely affected areas is the health sector. Health facilities and health training institutions were destroyed, equipment was looted and most of the health workers escaped to all parts of the world. Moreover, over two million Somalis fled to the neighboring countries in search of security and shelter.

In light of the above situation, this paper tackles two aspects of health organization in Somalia. First, it presents a protocol for planning repatriation of Somali refugees from the neighboring countries. Second, it attempts to develop a model to guide the reorganization of the health sector in Somalia after the emergency.

The returnees will go back to their districts of origin to avoid temporary hosting camps in the country. Information regarding the destination of the returnees will be collected from the refugee camps by means of direct interviewing. Moreover, the receptive capacity of the districts that will receive the returnees will be studied according to land-tenure, health system, cost of housing, road status and communications, and resident population's attitude towards returnees. According to the receptive capacity, interventions will focus on those areas defined as *at high risk* (lowest receptive capacity). Emergency funds will be allocated accordingly.

The proposed model suggests a focus on a district health system based on primary health care. The model illustrates the organization of a district health system, its health facilities, its staffing and the activities to be performed at each level. The structure is based on the traditional administrative division of the country into regions, districts, wards *(beel)* and village *(tuulo)*.

This model also elaborates on the health referral system. The district hospital is the center of the health delivery system. It will provide support to the peripheral health units, namely primary health care centers at *beel* level and dispensaries at *tuulo* level. Each district health system should be able to train health workers staffing its peripheral health units.

The revitalization of the health sector requires an initial investment from the international community. However, in the proposed organization model, community participation and self-sustainability as strategy will be the cornerstone of the health care delivery system.

I. Introduction

Before the civil war, Somalia was committed to primary health care (PHC) principles for its health care delivery (WHO/UNICEF, 1987). By the end of 1990, 10 out of the 18 regions had PHC programs that were supported by international or bilateral organizations (MOH, 1989).

In 1987, a global evaluation of PHC programs was carried out in the entire country to review the level of implementation of programs. One of the main obstacles was found to be lack of clear guidelines from the Ministry of Health (MOH) regarding the homogenization of different PHC programs in each region. Thus, there was little coordination among programs and each donor country or organization implemented as it considered appropriate (MOH, 1985; MOH/WHO, 1987; Branca and D'Arca, 1992).

The civil war has heavily destroyed the social, economic and political structure of the country; a severely affected area is the health sector that was already suffering from scarce resources (Tommasoli, 1993). The effects of the civil war on health and health-related sectors can be divided into three categories:

A. Effects on the Population's Health

The civil war seriously affected the health of the general population remaining in Somalia because of disruption to health care delivery systems, food and safe water provision, and distribution mechanisms. Moreover, people suffered from different war-related pathologies such as trauma and epidemics.

On the other hand, it is estimated that more than two million people have fled the country by land and sea. During these long journeys, many vulnerable people died from different causes, mainly accidents and lack of food and water. Those who reached refugee camps suffered especially from malnutrition and transmissible diseases, mainly due to crowding, unsafe water and poor sanitation (UNICEF, 1993).

B. Effects on Health Care Facilities

Before the civil war, many regions were implementing PHC programs and strengthening their district hospitals. The civil war forced almost all donor agencies to pull out their support to the Ministry of Health (MOH) in the implementation of PHC. Moreover, Somali health workers had to escape from their working places and fled abroad or to their regions of origin. The meager health facilities were either destroyed or misused. Medical instruments and equipment were looted in many hospitals and peripheral health units. Few health facilities are currently working.

C. Effects on the Health Training Institutions

Health workers represent the most important resource in the health care delivery system. Somalia had few institutions for training different health cadres. There was one medical school, established in 1973, that produced an average of 40 doctors per year, which has ensured one trained doctor for each district. Most of the school's equipment and instruments were looted. Currently it is closed.

For training nurses, midwives and paramedical staff, there were several institutions in Hargeisa and Mogadishu. Hargeisa nursing school was founded in 1964 and the two schools in Mogadishu were founded in 1970 and 1972 respectively. A new school in Kismayo was completed just before the civil war and before it could recruit its first intake. Unfortunately, all the nursing schools are idle and their facilities either damaged or used for other purposes.

In light of the above reality, this paper discusses how the health sector can be reorganized after the civil war. First, it presents a protocol for the repatriation of the displaced people. Second, it attempts to develop a long-term planning model for the reorganization of the health sector after the emergency based on PHC district health system.

II. Repatriation of Displaced People

The displaced people left their places of origin in search of security for their children and themselves. During the few times that there were signals of peace negotiations, voluntary repatriation took place. On these occasions, people returned (or booked themselves to return) to their places of origin. This is an indication that refugees are willing to go back to their districts.

Hence, repatriation should be planned and organized to accommodate returnees in the best situation. Moreover, the main objectives of planned repatriation are twofold. First, returnees go directly back to their districts, avoiding temporary hosting camps. Second, the information generated will be also used for all the resettlement programs including the reorganization of the health sector.

Information regarding the provenance and returnees' preferred destinations will be collected from the refugee camps in the neighboring countries and from the internally displaced people. Both qualitative and quantitative techniques will be used. A set of rapid appraisal and epidemiological techniques will be jointly applied as a means of collecting information in a simple, rapid, cost-contained, and reliable way (Pinto, *et al.*, 1993). Appropriate sampling can be applied countrywide according to geographical accessibility, transportation and area of origin of returning refugees. Anyway, the land extension, road-mining, remoteness and isolation of certain areas could constrain the process of data collection excluding some inaccessible areas from the study.

After collecting the information on the returnees' destination, the receptive capacity of the host districts will be measured according to the following categories: land-tenure, health system, cost of housing, road status and communications, and resident population's attitude towards returnees.

Each category will be defined by a score built around a set of indicators, including easy measurement and collection. The land-tenure system will be measured by availability and type of irrigation, use of fertilizers, type of agricultural tools used by the peasants, livestock, fishing and hunting practices, and presence of agro-industry. The health system will be measured through the actual status of health structures, checked with standard tools, the distribution of front-line health personnel still working on the territory, the degree of functioning of the drug distribution system and the preventive and curative activities still performed by health workers. Cost of housing will be expressed in local currency, according to the materials used for the house, either traditional (hut), or modern (bricks). The communications will include information about condition of local roads or pathways, eventual presence of mines, local situation of transportation network and time needed to travel from one place to another. The attitude towards returnees will investigate on the potential relationship between the returnees and the communities interested.

According to the receptive capacity thus defined, interventions will focus on the areas at high risk (lowest receptive capacity). Emergency funds will be allocated on the basis of the receptive capacity score. A comprehensive intervention will be planned based on this information.

III. Organization of the Health Sector

Besides the above-suggested protocol for collecting information on the nature of returnees and the receptive capacity of the districts that will receive them, other experiences and information should be for the reorganization of the health services in Somalia. An invaluable source of information is the structure and the experience from the PHC programs implemented before the civil war (MOH, 1985; Buschkens, 1990; Branca & D'Arca, 1992).

The current proposed reorganization of the health sector considers the pre-existing situation of the country with its health care delivery and administrative structure. The country is divided into regions, districts, wards (*Beel*) and villages (*Tuulo*). Each region is divided into 3-8 districts. The district population ranges between 20,000-100,000 and is divided into 3-5 wards. A ward consists of several villages of 500-2,000 people, sometimes scattered in a vast area, sometimes called smaller satellite villages. The model illustrates a district health system based on PHC. It shows health facilities, staffing level and activities at each level that represent the minimum requirements to perform satisfactorily.

A. Health Facilities

The proposed health facilities are based on the administrative division of a district. A village should contain a village health post (VHP) which consists of at least four rooms: a consultation room, a mother and child health (MCH) room, a dispensing room and a dressing and injection room. A ward should have a health center with seven rooms divided into a consultation room, a dressing and injection room, an MCH room, a maternity room, an observation room, a record keeping room and a store. Each district will have a referral hospital with 20-30 beds including male, female, maternity, pediatric and infectious wards. Obviously, a district hospital should contain rooms for the activities described above for a health center. Moreover, a district hospital should have a wing for administration and training activities.

The health facilities will be equipped according to the activities carried out at each level. In the next section, we will describe the health workers needed for each health unit.

B. Health Workers

Staffing varies according to the type of health facility and the activities to be performed at each level (Table 1). The VHP is staffed by two community health workers (CHWs) and two traditional birth attendants (TBAs). Both cadres are selected from the community and receive on-the-job training and orientation to carry out certain activities.

A health center requires at least three trained health workers, namely a nurse, a midwife and a sanitarian (health officer). These are intermediate school graduates who receive at least three years of training in a health institution.

A district hospital is the referral point of all district activities and consists of several departments. Thus, the staffing level should be higher in terms of training and quantity: a medical doctor, a number of trained nurses, midwives, paramedical staff and sanitarians form the core medical team; other staff members are health secretaries, auxiliaries and supporting staff.

TABLE 1

**Staffing Level of Health Facilities with the
Minimum Required Quantity**

Health Facility	Type of staff	Quantity
District Hospital	Medical officer	1
	Trained nurses	6
	Trained midwives	6
	Paramedical staff	5
	Sanitarians	3
	Health secretaries	3
	Auxiliary and supporting staff	20
Health Center	Trained nurse	1
	Trained midwife	1
	Sanitarian	1
	Auxiliaries and supporting staff	3
Village Health Post	Village health workers	2
	Traditional birth attendants	2
	Supporting staff	2

C. Main Activities at Each Health Level

Table 2 summarizes the activities of each health facility. The main task of the VHP is to offer preventive services in the areas of MCH (which includes the management of normal pregnancies and deliveries), family planning and immunization. The health workers should fulfil their tasks through health education, home visiting, etc. The only curative service at this level is treatment of the most common diseases and injuries using essential drugs following a national treatment protocol at outpatient level. Records of activities should be kept for the entire system using simple forms which can be passed onto the health centers. All cases that cannot be managed at this level should be referred to the upper levels (health center or district hospital) according to the flow-charts and decision tree which are validated and used.

At the health center level, there are trained staff that, in addition to all activities carried out in dispensaries, perform other managerial, medical and minor surgical activities. The diagnostic service is limited to parasitological analysis of feces and urine and to the determination of hemoglobin levels. Staff at this level supervise their dispensaries and provide continuing education to CHWs and TBAs. Data collected here will be tabulated and the summary of information submitted to the district. Difficult cases will be transferred to the district hospital according to the above-described mechanism.

The district medical officer is the head of a district health team composed of heads of health departments. The team's job is to manage all health activities and to supervise and support health workers at the peripheral health levels. The district team will be responsible for the training and continuing education of all its health workers except the medical officers. The preventive services also include environmental health and school health. The district hospital should deal with all medical and surgical (especially obstetrical and abdominal) cases. The hospital should have an X-ray department and a laboratory to carry out basic hematological, biochemical and serological tests according to the national guidelines. Difficult cases that need specialized diagnostic procedure and medical or surgical interventions will be transferred to the regional or national referral hospitals.

TABLE 2

Main Activities Carried Out at Each Health Level

Services	District Hospital	Health Center	Village Health Post
Preventive	- MCH - family planning -environmental health -school health	- MCH - family planning - environmental health	- MCH - family planning - environmental health
Curative	- medical - surgical - oral health - outpatient	- medical - minor surgery - outpatient	- outpatient
Diagnostic	- clinical laboratory - radiology	- clinical laboratory	Administrative/ Financial - supervision - record keeping - information system - issue of certificates - record keeping - information system & record keeping
Training	- nurses - paramed-ical - CHWs - TBAs	- CHWs - TBAs	

IV. Conclusions

Reorganization of the social and economic sectors in Somalia needs to be based on the realities developed in the last few years of civil war. Many things have changed and new realities have emerged. This has led us to recommendations to base the reorganization of the health sector on information regarding the refugees and the status of the remaining health resources both in terms of health personnel and health facilities.

The health policy of Somalia should be based on the district health system (WHO, 1988) and should stress the importance of rural people (Aden, 1994). The system can be implemented only through a sound PHC strategy. This requires decentralization of resource allocation and decision-making. Therefore, the district should be the focal point of the health care delivery (WHO, 1987; WHO, 1988). The suggested model gives the district the possibility of becoming self-sufficient by generating financial resources and by training its health workers including nurses, midwives and paramedical staff.

Most of the social and economic infrastructure has been destroyed during the civil war. Thus, its revival needs a strong and continuous participation of the community which is a basic component of the PHC approach. Reconstruction of facilities and remuneration of health workers will be on the shoulders of communities, according to conditions considered to be socially and economically feasible for each community.

The PHC program gives priority to the neediest classes of the society. It is clear from the activities to be carried out at each level of the health system that women and children's health are given priority. Furthermore, attention is given to the health of communities and families and not only to individual problems. Thus, health promotion and prevention are the cornerstone of this model.

The last remarks are on ways and means to identify the resources needed for implementing the proposed program and to find strategies to mobilize them. It is true that health facilities are destroyed and looted, many health workers are internally or externally displaced and state structures are not functioning. Therefore, revitalization of the health sector requires a huge initial investment from the international community. However, community participation and cost-sharing will be the basis of the health care delivery system in Somalia after the emergency.

Bibliography

Aden, A.S. (1994). *Studies for Health Planning in Rural Somalia: Community Perceptions and Epidemiological Data.* Umea. Umea University.

Branca, F.; D'Arca, R. (1992). *Salute per Tutti? Esperienze e Valutazioni da un'Area Rurale della Somalia.* Milan : Franco Angeli.

Buschkens, W.F.L. (1990). *Community Health in the Developing World: The Case of Somalia.* Assen: Van Gorcum & Company.

MOH (1985). *PHC Policies Implementation: Guidelines.* Mogadishu: MOH.

MOH (1989). *National Health Planning 1989-1992.* Mogadishu: MOH.

MOH/WHO (1987). *Joint PHC Review in Somalia.* Mogadishu: MOH.

Pinto, A., Zagaria, N., Guerra, R., Arcadu, G. and Babille, M. (1993). "Risk Assessment and Repatriation in Angola: Quantitative and Qualitative Techniques Combined for Better Decision-Making." In *Proceedings of the 2nd International Conference on Emergency Planning and Disaster Management.* Lancaster (UK), July 11-14, 1993, pages, 622-629. Lancaster: Lancaster University.

Tommasoli, M. (1993). *Somalia Sanità Difficile.* Rome: Istituto Italo Africano.

UNICEF (1993). *UNICEF assistance to Somalia. January - June 1993: Review of activities.* New York: UNICEF.

WHO (1987). *Report of the Interregional Meeting on Strengthening District Health Systems Based on Primary Health Care.* Harare, Zimbabwe, 3-7 August 1987. Geneva: WHO.

WHO (1988). *The Challenge of Implementation: District Health Systems for Primary Health Care.* WHO/SHS/DHS/8.1.Rev. Geneva: WHO.

WHO/UNICEF (1978). *Report of the International Conference of Primary Health Care.* Alma Ata, USSR, 6-10 September, HFA Series, No. 1. Geneva: WHO.

CHAPTER TWENTY FIVE

Teacher Education and Reconstruction in Somalia

George Urch

I. Introduction

Education is viewed by most Third World countries as a primary vehicle for their socio-economic and political development. The schools are expected to prepare knowledgeable and skilled people who understand their social responsibility, have the necessary capacity to assist in economic development and can provide future leadership for their country. The heavy responsibility placed on education is predicated on the assumption that without education, development will not occur. Most African nations have accepted this premise and governments have contributed substantial sums from their national treasury for the expansion of educational opportunity.

There is little doubt that a reconstituted and reconstructed Somalia also will view education as a major instrument to assist in its redevelopment. A new government must strike a balance among the demands for education, the needs of the state and the scarcity of resources. To accomplish this task, a set of policies must be developed and a prioritized plan devised to implement them.

At the center of educational reform should be a careful review of the education of teachers for they must be knowledgeable and receptive to the goals of a revitalized system of education. In many ways, teachers, rather than policies, will shape the reconstructed educational system. They will be the interpreters, implementors and conveyors of educational policy and they must move the policy into practice. It will be the teachers who are called upon to prepare a cadre of educated people who can participate in Somalia's redevelopment. Education must be made available for people in both rural and urban areas, as well as those who exist in the margins of their society.

II. Teacher Education

This paper will focus on the role of education in a reconstructed Somalia, and begin to ask questions of the new mission of Lafoole College of Education, Somali National University. In the past, Lafoole College was the English-speaking teacher training institution that prepared secondary school teachers. It was a part of Somali National University, but in several ways, both philosophically and physically, it operated as a separate institution. The new mission of the College has yet to be determined. However, it is assumed that its redevelopment and reorientation will be an important factor in determining the redirection of teacher education in the country.

To consider the new role of Lafoole College, this paper will pose a series of questions and explore some tentative answers in an attempt to help Somali educational leaders address key issues that surround a reconstructed educational system.

III. The Nation and Education

Before the civil war, the population of Somalia was estimated at 7.7 million. During the past three years approximately 400,000 people died through famine and war and 45% of the population was displaced (Putman and Noor, 1993: p.1). Somalis identify with clans and sub-clans that help bring a form of solidarity, but also can be a source of conflict. With nearly 80% of the population living in rural areas, the shifting world of clan politics continues to be a divisive force. The present conflict can be seen as a struggle among opposing clans that want to move into the power vacuum left when the central government collapsed in early in 1991.

However, there are several elements that can serve as a unifying force. Ethnically and culturally, Somalia is one of the most homogeneous countries in Africa. The people speak a common language and practice the same Islamic religion (Putman and Noor, 1993: p.2). For a period of time, education also was a binding force. In the early 1970's, the Somali language was put into written form and a Roman alphabet adopted.

Simultaneously, basic education, using the new Somali script, became compulsory and a national literacy campaign was launched. All government officials were required to learn the script. By 1990, the United Nations estimated that about one-fourth of the people were literate.

For a short period of time the Somali National University was viewed as a unifying institution. Founded in 1970, the University grew to include thirteen faculties with 800 faculty and 7,500 students (Lubbock, 1993; p.A29). Supported, in part, by external funds the University became a show-place for Somali culture with a special emphasis on language, art, poetry and song. However, by the time it closed early in 1991, faculty appointments and student placements were often used as rewards for loyalty to the ruling clan. Today, the University is just a shell. The campus has been stripped of anything of value, including windows, doors and interior plumbing (*Ibid*).

IV. New Opportunities

Since the 1960's, the main priority of educational policymakers on the African continent was to increase access to formal education. The reasoning was that educational expansion was necessary in order to show a commitment to equality. Perhaps this was the case in Somalia. Between 1960-1980 the total enrollment in Somali education at all levels increased from 25,000 to 318,000 (World Bank, 1988: p.130).

However, in the 1990's policymakers have not focused on expansion, but rather on relevance; the relations between an investment in education and the dividends it pays in political stability and socio-economic development. This could be a major concern in a reconstructed Somalia. Certainly, tension will occur between the need to emphasize a commitment to equality and the need to produce a small cadre of knowledgeable and skilled people to manage a new governmental structure. In addition, tension will emerge between educational needs and the need to supply resources for military defense as well as commercial enterprises.

The emerging political power will establish educational priorities. The new state will be the principal shaper of any structural change and evolving educational goals. There have been examples of other revolutionary governments in Africa that have recently emerged; Mozambique and Uganda being two such examples. In both cases, governments have emerged through armed conflict, crisis management and socio-economic upheaval. In both cases, the goals of education have been made clear. The new governments want political stability and acquiescence and they recognize that the people want to survive and prosper economically (Carnoy, 1990; Republic of Uganda, 1992). Perhaps the educational priorities of a reconstructed Somalia will be similar; the use of education as a tool to promote political allegiance while simultaneously, to equip the youth with the skills necessary for economic advancement. Whether these two overarching goals can be accomplished is still to be determined. There will certainly be major obstacles in its path.

V. Major Obstacles

Besides the obvious need to silence the guns, restore peace and reorganize a government with a national or semi-national identity, there are other major obstacles in the path of educational development. To begin, the relations between the Muslim religious leaders and the new government has yet to be determined. In the previous government religious schools, including those of Christian missionaries, were nationalized. Not known is whether a new government will need the support of Muslim clergy to help unite a disparate people; or whether clergy support will be based upon a greater role for religion in the schools (Urch, 1992: p. 98).

Another obstacle is the appalling condition of what has been left of the educational structure. The decline of the educational system began before the fighting escalated. By the mid-80's the nation's bureaucracy had begun to crumble and teachers were not being paid. As a consequence, teachers found employment elsewhere, schools closed and teaching material disappeared. In addition, during the armed conflict, school buildings were destroyed. In many ways, formal education in Somalia must begin all over again (Toll, 1993: p.10).

Perhaps the greatest obstacle to educational development a new government will face is the perception of a traumatized people. How much trust will there be? How can communities begin to rebuild and reorganize when dramatic change through renewed warfare could be around the corner? What new political alliances need to be forged? What will the new "political correctness" be for the emerging schools? What political engineering will take place? Will the loyalty of teachers become most important? Will the new revolutionary leaders demand overnight educational results that are not possible in the eyes of more traditional leaders? The combination of trauma, new leadership and trust must be confronted and reconciled by the schools.

VI. A New Structure

If there is one possible educational advantage that a reconstructed Somalia might have, it is the possibility that a completely different educational system could emerge; one that is more closely allied with the needs of the majority of the people rather than an elitist system inherited from a colonial master. The inherited system produced an educational pyramid that used primary and secondary education as a selecting devise in which a few students were permitted access to higher education.

Nations throughout the African continent have slowly moved away from the colonial model toward an educational structure that helps to establish and maintain indigenous cultural identity. In addition the new leaders want a system geared to meet the basic human needs of the majority of the people in order that the nation can move toward self-reliance. Examples of such systems exist on the African continent. They share certain characteristics in common. Among the most common are:

1. a decentralized system where the local community takes responsibility for some of the educational costs; and where the core curriculum at the primary level is adapted to the specific needs of the local community;

2. an emphasis on linking education with the world of work and promoting those local skills necessary for income-generating activities; in addition, the promotion of attitudes conducive to the development of good work habits;

3. the use of the local environment as a learning resource which includes bringing successful entrepreneurs into the schools, as part-time teachers, and sending students out to internships wherever available;

4. the infusion into the curriculum of those issues which are of great concern to local communities such as health, hygiene, nutrition, population and environmental education;

5. the strengthening of technology, science and mathematics in the curriculum, especially as it relates to local conditions: and

6. an orientation to the political goals and structure of the nation and respect for moral values.

Some educational activities in Somalia have already begun. More aid organizations are now moving resources into education. CONCERN, the Irish charity, has started 28 schools which offer basic education. In addition, UNESCO is in the process of establishing seven regional centers away from Mogadishu. Known as "Islands of Education for Peace," they are just beginning to address future plans. UNESCO is also preparing a program of school reconstruction needs and costs throughout the country (Toll, 1993: p. 10).

Somali educators, likewise, are becoming involved. Presently they are talking of a plan sponsored by U.S. agencies to bring faculty from the University of Massachusetts Center for International Education to organize specialized courses for teachers offered through Lafoole College of Education (Lubbock, 1993). However, education cannot and should not be left in the hands of outside agencies. While some intervening organizations are useful to begin the process, the ultimate decisions on the redirection of education must be left to the new educational leaders. It is hoped they will learn from the mistakes of others, but there is little guarantee.

VII. Lafoole College of Education

Whatever happens to a renewed Lafoole College of Education will be influenced by the reconstituted national educational goals and the curriculum that emanates from them. However there are some tentative questions that can be addressed so that the College is positioned to play a pivotal role in the education of teachers. Those questions include:

1. What tentative proposals can be made in order that Lafoole College can assist in preparing teachers that can address the new opportunities and help to overcome present obstacles?

2. How should the College be administered?

3. What qualifications should the faculty have?

4. What kind of students should be admitted?

5. What should the curriculum look like?

6. How can classroom instruction be strengthened?

7. Is there a role for an intervening institution?

VIII. External Assistance

What should be the role of external organizations and institutions in helping to redevelop the College? Can an outside university facilitate this redevelopment? Can the outside university draw upon past experience in Somalia? If so, how? Should Somali teacher educators work with an outside university to help identify problems and priorities? Can such a group analyze opportunities and formulate short and long term strategies? What resources can an outside institution bring to the College? What joint proposals are feasible?

IX. Summary

During the three year period 1986-89, the University of Massachusetts Center for International Education worked closely with the administrators and staff of Lafoole College in a staff development effort. A linkage relationship was maintained between the two institutions and Somali teacher educators pursued short term training and advanced education at the University of Massachusetts, Amherst, until the recent conflict escalated.

The three year Project was funded by the United States Information Agency under the title of the Teacher-Text-Technology Initiative. The primary goal of the project was to strengthen teacher education in mathematics, science and English. The University of Massachusetts Center for International Education is prepared to continue this relationship and expand on its mission, when, and if, the opportunity becomes available.

Often, the process of educational redevelopment is slow. While governments can exercise a strong influence in determining the purpose of education, teachers must identify with that purpose. At times there is a gap between what teachers expect from schooling and what the government wants. In spite of these constraints, nation-building still remains one of the primary reasons why governments support education. How teachers prepared at Lafoole College can best be utilized to help in the process of reconstruction in Somalia is the emerging challenge.

Bibliography

Martin Carnoy and Joel Samoff (1990), *Education and Social Transition in the Third World*. Princeton: Princeton University Press.

R.G. Havelock and A.M. Huberman (1977), *Solving Educational Problems: The Theory and Reality of Innovation in Developing Countries*. Paris: UNESCO.

Republic of Uganda (1992), *Government White Paper: Education for National Integration and Development*. Kampala: Government Printer.

Val D. Rust and Per Dalin (eds.) (1990), *Teachers and Teaching in the Developing World*. New York: Garland Publishing, Inc.

Joel Samoff, (1993), "The Reconstruction of Schooling in Africa" in *Comparative Education Review*. Vol. 37, No. 2, May, 1993.

Maria Teresa Tatto, D. Nielsen and W. Cummings (1991), *Comparing the Effects and Costs of Different Approaches for Educating Primary School Teachers: The Case of Sri Lanka*. Cambridge: Basic Research and Implementation in Developing Education Systems Project.

Katerina Toll, (1993), "Somalia: Starting From Scratch" in *UNESCO Sources*, No.49, July-August, 1993.

George E.F Urch,. (1992), *Education in Sub-Saharan Africa*. New York, Garland Publishing, Inc.

World Bank (1988), *Education in Sub-Saharan Africa: Policies for Adjustment, Revitalization and Expansion*. Washington, D.C.: The World Bank.

CHAPTER TWENTY SIX

Rebuilding Somalia: A Methodology that Starts from the Bottom

Richard Ford

I. Introduction

In recent years, the concept of the African nation state has been called into question. Some, such as Basil Davidson, argue that it was an externally imposed European paradigm that should never have been installed in the first place.[1] Others, such as several contributors to this volume,[2] suggest that the overwhelming need for solid grassroots institutions requires that one rebuild at local levels before worrying about restoring the nation state. Those who advocate a decentralized Somalia, such as many making recommendations in Chapter 41, suggest that strong local institutions are:

- consistent with earlier pastoral models;
- an essential step of state building that Italian and British colonial officers bypassed during the colonial period; and
- the only viable option for Somalia in the short-run, given present levels of destruction of the national infrastructure.

Therefore, they argue one should start with grassroots institutions, build slowly, and allow regional alliances and linkages to determine the nature of a new nation state.

If there is to be energetic, coordinated, and orderly rehabilitation of Somalia; if this restructuring is to take place in a methodical way with generally agreed upon procedures; if the new modes will respond both to majority needs and minority visions; and if the local units are to fit, one day, into a larger economic and political entity resembling a state, then there is need to devise explicit governance methodologies for local levels.

At the moment, political scientists, farmers, constitutional lawyers, female heads of households, development economists, politicians, private enterprise specialists, camel herders, planners, and technical advisors have little recent experience or theoretical models of how to implement such a decentralized plan. Any decentralization recently introduced in Africa -- for example, Sudan's *de facto* northern and southern divisions; Ethiopia's transitional state, Nigeria's multiple state system, or even Liberia's present spheres of influence governance -- was born out of political expediency and has arisen in response to specific military, political, or ethnic pressures.

This paper describes a GTZ field experiment in decentralized rehabilitation, launched in Northeastern Somalia in June, 1994. The project introduced decentralized planning and action through community-based data collection/analysis, ranking, planning, decision-making, implementation, monitoring, and evaluation. It was intended as a model for decentralized and grassroots action that would offer options for other Somali communities wishing to rebuild water, grazing, health, education, agriculture, marketing, income generation, and employment endeavors.

Even though events in the Northeast have overtaken the GTZ plan and while two vehicle hijackings forced the withdrawal of GTZ , the lessons of the experiment have taken root in the Northeast. The decentralized methodology is alive and well in several communities, through the work of a number of indigenous NGOs. This article reports on the initial findings of the experiment and suggests that additional field trials of similar approaches are an essential next step in rehabilitating Somalia, assuming that the grassroots and decentralized strategy becomes one possible approach to Somalia's reconstruction.

II. The Site and the Participatory Model

The field test was a training course for community-based and local NGO officers in Gardo District, Northeastern Somalia. The immediate community where the field work took place was a pastoral village, Jeded, which maintains a 400 m. deep borehole. A case study on the experiment is available in English and Somali from Clark University.[3]

Jeded is a village of nomads, typical of many pastoral communities dispersed throughout much of the central and northern regions of Somalia. Founded in 1954 because of a new well and good grazing, Jeded has become an important watering point and provisioning station for a large nomadic community. One elder estimated that over a million animals are watered at Jeded's borehole every year.

Jeded is a community of about 70 households with a bleak, hot, dry, dusty, windy and sometimes overwhelming landscape. Jeded's soil productivity is marginal. Rains are unreliable with a meager 50 mm (2 inches) per year of which upwards of 80 percent falls between April and September. As a result, villagers consistently complain of declining grass and tree cover, rapid runoff, flash floods, and severe soil erosion. Elders described a succession of droughts and famines that have afflicted the village since its founding. While it is hard to judge which droughts and famines were the most severe, all agreed that the years of 1954, 1968, 1974, 1983, and 1989 were especially difficult.

In spite of these hardships, the combination of a central location, a reliable water table, hundreds of nomads with thousand of animals, and scarcity of surface water elsewhere in the region makes Jeded a significant economic force. Italian colonial officials recognized these potentials when they drilled Jeded's first borehole in 1954.

Jeded's location (see map on next page) on the road to Bender Beila, a small fishing village on the Indian Ocean, gives it some commercial advantage. While there is only occasional traffic on the road, it is clear that Jeded is an important warehousing depot for the region. Two or three trucks appeared almost every day, usually bringing supplies of sugar, cooking oil, salt, cloth, and small personal items such as batteries, flashlights, matches, soap, and sandals. About half the trucks left empty; the other half carried goats, camels, and sheep to market, usually at the port of Bosaso, the regional capital 300 kms. to the north. Other important towns within a few hundred kms. in the Northeast are Garowe, Galkayo, and Iskushuban.

Jeded residents earn their living selling these commercial products and foodstuffs to the nomadic herdsmen who visit the village regularly. Goat herders schedule their grazing to include a watering stop at least once every two days and, in the very hot season, every day. Camel herders require water every 12 to 14 days for their herds and are far more independent than the small ruminant herders. The camel herders will range up to 100 or even 150 kms. from the borehole, making contact only as water needs demand it. Given these large numbers of animals and

Figure 1

Area Map

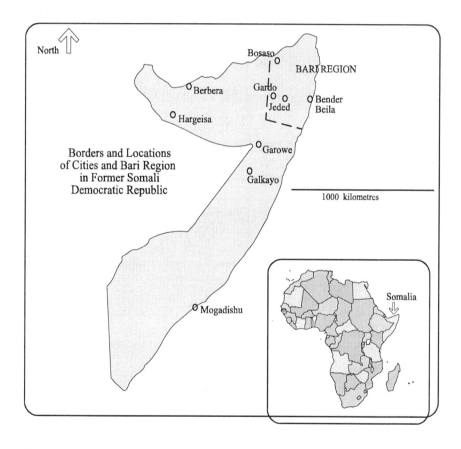

Borders and Locations
of Cities and Bari Region
in Former Somali
Democratic Republic

skimpy rainfall, there is little vegetation in or around Jeded.

The result of the deforestation and loss of vegetation is twofold. In the months of July and August, the winds are almost unbearable. Starting in mid-morning, the gusts bellow and blow with such force that it is impossible to do much of anything out doors. Even to walk across the village open spaces at midday or to try to cook lunch was difficult and, on some days, impossible.

The second problem is flooding. To think of a problem of floods with an annual rainfall of 50 mm. seems ironic. Yet it is a hard fact of life for Jeded. The rains that come in the months of April to June are intense and heavy. They drench the land and quickly create large pools. Jeded's chronic devegetation and loss of trees and grass cover provides no barrier to these pools and within half an hour, surging torrents of water cascade through the village. The hard soil just below the sandy surface absorbs water very slowly. The result is flash flooding which digs deep gullies into the soil, carries off what little vegetation may have survived the goats, and threatens to wash away even the sturdy stone houses in Jeded.

Thus, while the borehole water brings life to Jeded, it also brings death to the trees, vegetation, soils, and perhaps one day to the village itself. While residents are keenly aware of the problem and can articulate the relationship between the well and the resource degradation, they are in no position, household by household, to take initiatives to solve these problems. Issues that transcend the magnitude of an individual household require institutional structures to coordinate plans and policies at a larger scale. Normally the government would assume such responsibilities. Given the absence of any government authority, Jeded needs an alternative institutional structure through which, internally, they can organize groups of citizens. Such was the task of the GTZ exercise in community-based initiatives.

It is important, however, to note that the "government" is not totally lacking in Jeded. Like the rest of the Northeast, there is an informal acceptance of understandings about regional "management." The SSDF is looking after political affairs. Regional committees and councils are being formed. Yet technical and social services as well as conflict management, if available at all, are provided on mostly a voluntary basis. For example, a former veterinary officer lives in the next village and comes by to help with livestock inoculations; a teacher has stayed in the village and occasionally meets classes; the Koranic School thrives, but without payment to the teachers; women's groups exist though they rarely meet as there is no agenda to discuss; the village nurse is still available and receives medicines from UNICEF, but has no regular salary; and the water engineer has stayed on from earlier years to operate the pump -- and partly because he married a Jeded woman -- but earns money only when the livestock herders have cash to pay. Finally, a core group of elders manages the daily affairs of the community, including the borehole, yet has little formal authority to make decisions about things such as reforestation, health, employment creation, or community collaboration on flood control. Perhaps most significant, there are no government salaries nor is there any formal police organization or court of law.

It was in this setting that GTZ invited a team experienced in community management of productive resources to train local NGOs in community-based planning and to strengthen capacities of community groups to carry out the methodology. While the community-based action recognized the role of elders and clan leadership, and while it fully involved the clan leaders at every point in the discussions and decision making, it did not rely on the elders to carry out the actual implementation. Instead, it structured a set of community subcommittees and task forces to do the work. To see how these groups emerged, it will be helpful to consider their core methodology, known as Participatory Rural Appraisal (PRA).

III. About Participatory Rural Appraisal (PRA)

PRA is a new way to systematize a very old approach to rural development: community participation. It first appeared in Kenya in the 1980s as a response to the increasing failure rate of large, centrally financed, and technology importation projects of earlier decades. Instead of relying on central planners to decided what is useful and how to do it, PRA calls upon community institutions to become full and equal partners in development planning and action. PRA helps rural communities to support activities which they design and implement; strengthens local leadership and institutional management capacities; integrates sectors at the community level; and helps to build partnerships between local groups and development agencies external to the community. Three assumptions form the basis for PRA:

... farmers and pastoralists have knowledge and information: but it needs to be organized;

... villagers have resources: but they need to be mobilized;

... outside resources are available: but they need to be defined and invested in the context of village-identified priorities.

PRA uses techniques of data gathering, analysis and ranking derived from Rapid Rural Appraisal, including sketch maps, trend lines, time lines, transects, seasonal calendars, institutional diagrams, resource access ranking, and options assessment ranking. Further, PRA calls upon the Rapid Rural Appraisal criteria of productivity, sustainability, equitability, and stability to find solutions to problems the community identifies as its most severe. The solutions are then organized into Community Action Plans in which specific community groups are identified to carry out actual work or to initiate partnerships with external organizations that can provide the necessary technical, managerial or financial inputs.

The combination of community data analysis, ranking, planning, and implementation creates local "ownership" of the plan. Given the levels of interest in and commitment to such locally identified plans, the sustainability of PRA projects is considerable. While it is far too early in the life of PRA in the Northeast to make any long term assessments and while the withdrawal of GTZ, UNOSOM II and other donors from the Northeast makes formation of partnerships difficult, encouraging activities continue. For example, as a result of the initial PRA training, the US-based unit of a French NGO, ACIF (Organization Against Hunger), has conducted ten community assessments and implemented action plans, mostly in areas of water, health, and income generation.

The case studies mentioned earlier offer full details of the PRA experience, including descriptions of each of the exercises and how the action plan emerged from sometimes sticky discussions. This record is important and requires careful analysis though the present article provides only an overview.

IV. The Exercises and Lessons from Jeded

During three weeks in June-July, 1994 villagers met in small groups to gather and analyze data. For most of the meetings, the community was divided into three groups of about 25 each -- elders, women, and young men. The meetings were generally held in late afternoon or after dinner as the wind was too strong to hold group meetings inside or outside during the day. The purpose of the small group meetings was to organize information about Jeded into four large blocks -- spatial, temporal, institutional, and technical. In so far as possible, data were collected with visual instruments such as sketch maps, transects, trend lines, or institutional diagrams. The purpose of using visual instruments was to encourage those without literacy skills to join in as full members of the group. The team also made special points to work with Jeded's women in ways that would elicit maximum participation. For example, the 30 NGO staff

Figure 2

Trends in Jeded Village

Human Health

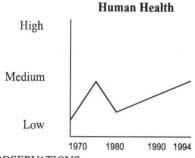

OBSERVATIONS:

1970-1975 - Good rains and no epidemics contributed to overall good health

1975-1980 - Dabadheer drought caused ill health and mortality

1980-1994 - Outbreaks of malaria due to heavy rains; infant mortality due to influx of displaced people from South; otherwise improving

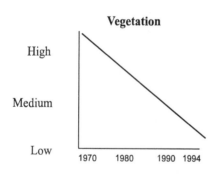

OBSERVATIONS:

1975-1994 - Establishment of the village, new water sources, and overgrazing have greatly reduced vegetation in Jeded and its surrounding area, leading to strong seasonal winds and dust

Note for both health and vegetation that the assessments are made independently of the overall political environment. It suggests that the people of Jeded are prepared to think and act on development themes, even though the political situation is not yet resolved. These are examples of important, indirect lessons coming from the community assessment exercises.

included eight women, so whenever possible the NGO women worked directly with the Jeded women.

Yet the actual information was not the most important part of data collection. As residents discussed the tasks, for example, on trends in vegetation or health, people talked about many things including views of why problems had emerged or what was working (for example, the borehole pump was regularly repaired and maintained, in spite of the difficult economic and transportation situation). Further, there were exchanges between different members of the smaller groups that clearly helped to spread understanding and empathy about many divergent and sometimes conflicting views within the small groups. Further, the small groups were announced as preliminary meetings to prepare for village-wide fora on analyzing the nature of Jeded's problems and considering which of these problems were of highest priority to the entire community.

By the middle of the second week, sufficient data had been collected and sorted to hold larger meetings. These were generally held at night because as many as 125 to 150 people would come. Considering that the village was only about 70 households, such attendance suggested there was interest in the topic. The goal of these plenary sessions was to exchange views between members of the small groups and to begin the process of ranking priorities and then setting an action plan in place.

Whereas meetings had gone smoothly in the small group sessions, such was not to be the case in the plenaries, especially when it came time to rank problems. One evening, with 125 men and women present, the discussions became heated. Two or three articulate women were emphasizing their need for income generation activities while the men spoke of need for greater support in veterinary services to care for their camels and goats. Even though the group was using a time-proven methodology of pairwise ranking, discussions reached an unusually high level of intensity. Finally, three of the elders -- in the midst of the discussion -- got up and left. Though their departure was quiet their comments as they reached the back of the group were not. One said, as he exited, that "having women participate with men on equal terms was *bullshit.*" Although the meeting continued and a ranking order of priorities emerged, the spirit was different as a result of the walkout.

The following morning a number of small groups met to talk about the events of the previous evening. Ironically, the most heated exchanges were among the 30 NGO staff members who were visitors to Jeded. One group, including both men and women, noted that it was astounding that the elders could be so reactionary on women's rights on the eve of the 21st century. Further, they observed it was a good opportunity for the visitors to tell the men that women's participation should be a given, not a special privilege. They wanted a confrontation with the elders as soon as a meeting could be arranged.

Yet this view was hardly a consensus among the NGO staff. Others, including both men and women, said that we outsiders owed the elders an apology even to think that women should help to rank priorities. Vocal group members urged that we call a meeting, apologize to the community for tampering with their cultural values, pack our bags, and go home.

Needless to say, the discussions swirled for the entire day when it was finally agreed that a small committee from the NGO group meet with the elders to see if a compromise position was possible. That evening and most of the next day, the mediation discussions moved forward. While the meetings with the elders were considerably less emotional than those among the NGO staff, it was clear that the issue of "who decides" lay at the core of the tension.

After some proposals, counter-proposals and eventual amendments, a management diagram, as noted on the next page, was accepted by the mediation committee. Each took the diagram back to his or her respective group and later a village-wide meeting was called to present the proposed settlement. While there were moments of tension and potential eruptions during the two days of discussion, by the end of the second day the prevailing sentiment was one of acceptance and feeling that a good arrangement had been reached.

The following day the entire group worked out details for the Community Action Plan, setting priorities of education and soil control to be responsibilities of the youth; animal health and jobs for the men to look after; human health and income generation as responsibilities of the women; and water and flood control of such magnitude that both men and women would share duties.

The intriguing part of the agreed management compromise was that the elders continued to be symbolically in charge of all activities. In fact the actual duties would reside with the youth, women and elders, all under the jurisdiction of the Jeded Village Steering Committee. The compromise structure was possible only because of the good will and rapport that had built up during data collection, group discussions, and analysis.

This brief excursion into Jeded's PRA suggests that adaptation of the community-based approach may have value for other Somali communities. It supports the proposition that decentralized action may be possible in Somalia, even in the absence of a state, so long as it is carried out within frameworks of structuring information, mobilizing resources, and building partnerships with outside entities. Such a tangible approach offers hope that priorities can be established within communities and that local groups can have the primary say in determining what will be done.

Figure 3

**STEERING COMMITTEE
AND TASK FORCES –
JEDED VILLAGE**

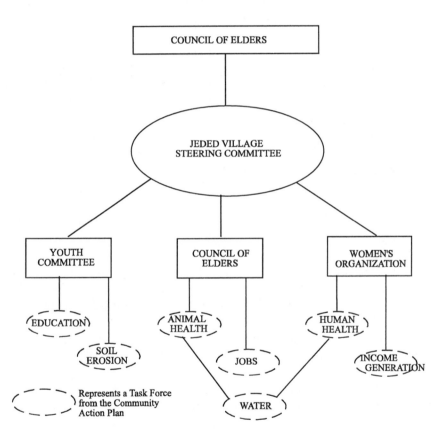

There are at least five additional and distinct messages to be considered as one reflects on the meaning and lessons learned from Jeded. They include:

Visual Exercises: Working with community groups through visual data collection instruments was highly effective. Creating sketch maps, trend lines, institutional analyses, ranking priorities, and other group/visual activities enabled community residents to express themselves freely and candidly. Given the potential tensions that might ensue as a result of events of the last few years, achieving candid discussions at an early stage is vital. The visual activities were a splendid way to get started.

Community Rapport: The community assessment team lived in the village for the duration of the appraisal. Taking meals, playing soccer (football) with the young people, visiting classes in the Koranic school, helping women with daily chores, and taking tea with the elders established another level of confidence and close working relationships. Given the tensions that had prevailed in much of the country for several years, such close interaction was greatly valued by the community. Even though there were a few "incidents" elsewhere in the district during the appraisal, Jeded was the epitome of calm.

Resolving Conflicts: As noted in the incident of men walking out of a meeting, Jeded was not without conflict. Issues of class, length of residence in the community, control of water, gender, grazing rights, and many other issues created tension -- as in any community in any part of the world. While community appraisals are not designed to resolve community conflicts, they are designed to encourage participation from a broadly based community constituency. In so far as broad participation anticipates or even heads off conflict, it is an important methodology to be used in mobilizing Somali communities.

Local Ownership: The Jeded appraisal led to an action plan, with priorities parallel to those noted in Figure 3. Without question, a broad cross-section of Jeded residents owned the plan. Because most of the action that will follow in such a community setting -- especially given the present political climate in Somalia -- will come from local resources, the principle of local ownership is of great significance. Whereas many communities have learned to prepare shopping lists for donors and NGOs, few have experience devising development agendas that they are prepared to support themselves. Local ownership of rehabilitation and local development holds the key to sustainability. The Jeded appraisals demonstrated that Somali communities can develop local ownership.

Strengthens Capacities of Community Institutions: As ownership is strengthened through community appraisals, so are capacities of local institutions. The very process of carrying out the appraisal suggests to communities that what they know and what they can do is important. The appraisal also contains modules which portray current institutional performance as well as what elements in the institution may be deficient. The use of community participation to diagnose institutional needs as well as to set remedial or developmental strategies in place to support these needs is important.

In summary, it was clear that the first two goals of the PRA exercise -- to organize the vast amounts of data already present in the community and to mobilize the considerable resources already available -- were fully achieved. It is less clear whether the people of Jeded have mobilized the resources of external organizations. While it is well established that other villages in the district, through ACIF, have planned and implemented several PRA action plans, the withdrawal of other donors creates uncertainty whether the full potential of community plans such as Jeded's will flourish.

V. Generalizations for Somalia

For Jeded and Somalia, six conclusions have emerged. The overall finding is that Somali pastoralists, women's groups, farmers, traders, and other rural residents have great resilience and capacities to undertake significant community-based projects. They have not always taken these initiatives in the past because many of the problems which they face are larger than individual households can manage. The villagers therefore need local organizations which: (1) transcend traditional clan or elder leadership without conflicting with those bodies and (2) enable households to join together to implement mutually agreed upon agendas. The model developed in the heat of two days discussion in Jeded may be one such example, though not a prescription. Thus, while community assessments, by themselves, are only part of the need, they do set the stage for additional action through:

♦   identifying priorities;
♦   reviewing which institutions are already active in the community;
♦   noting how to organize missing institutional capabilities;

◆   assessing what training or other institution building might be possible at community levels;
◆   determining what kind of indicators and participatory monitoring tools would be helpful to track project activity.

The six conclusions are presented here as generalizations which emerged from Jeded. They may apply to many other settings in Somalia and are therefore briefly summarized here. They are offered in more detail in the case study, *PRA With Somali Pastoralists* :

Development Without A State: *Development planning and action need not wait for creation of a new nation state in Somalia. Yet if community-based planning is to work effectively, it will need a structured and systematic approach such as PRA;*

PRA and Pastoralism: *Whereas previous PRAs in Africa and elsewhere have focused largely on agricultural and sedentary communities, Jeded's experience suggests it is equally applicable to pastoral groups.*

PRA in a Harsh and Isolated Environment: *Many examples exist of PRA helping communities that are fortunate enough to have basic resources. Yet examples of marginal ecosystems (Jeded receives 50 mm annual rainfall) are less known. The Jeded experience offered encouraging testimony that communities in even the most difficult environments can benefit from community-based planning and implementation.*

Monitoring and Evaluation: *Community-based development passes responsibility to increase production and sustain resources along to village institutions. While this task has usually meant data gathering, Jeded represents a new experiment in which local leaders use a Village Log Book, based on PRA data, for picking indicators, self monitoring and evaluation. Such local monitoring greatly increases ways in which community groups can track work of external groups and vice versa;*

Role of Women: *Somali women have special knowledge and skills which make Jeded's development and resource management plans more productive and sustainable. Working directly with women's groups and using PRA exercises which focused on women's needs created excellent rapport and a positive working relationship among women and men.*

Conflict Resolution: *Every community experiences conflict on differences in class, ethnicity, religion, caste, age, wealth, or race. The PRA approach does not necessarily resolve conflicts. However, by carrying out all elements of the PRA in an open, transparent and public environment, PRA has been able to help hostile groups set aside disputes. These conflicts are resolved not by direct mediation or negotiation but, instead, by helping all parties to see that cooperation benefits everyone.*

These conclusions raise an intriguing perspective about the role of PRA amid political instability and vulnerability or in the context of post-conflict development. Jeded does not exist independently of its larger political culture. While PRA may enable the village to make progress in solving local problems, the gains have no value if there is no supportive political mechanism into which the Jeded actions will fit. Somalia still needs some form of a state or federal structure, though its shape, duties, jurisdiction, revenue base, and accountability may be quite different from the model of nation state presently in place in much of Africa.

Perhaps the greatest challenge facing Somalia, Somaliland and Somalis all over the world is how to act immediately with community-based initiatives such as PRA -- we have convincing proof that such approaches work effectively in Somalia -- and then to design a national structure whose primary purpose is to support such initiatives. It would be a change, perhaps a refreshing breath of creativity, for a state to evolve with serving needs of local communities as one of its primary goals. It would be a magnificent example to the rest of the world that there can be both development and state formation based on "starting at the bottom." Community-based development offers a systematic methodology to do it.

Endnotes

1. Basil Davidson (1992), *The Black Man's Burden: The Curse of the Nation State in Africa*, 1996 (New York, MacMillan).

2. For example, see Chapter 16, "Somalia: Regional State or Cantonization of Clans?" by Ahmed Ashkir Botan or Chapter 23, "Somali NGOs: A Product of Crises," by Abdirahman Osman Raghe.

3. Contact: The Director, Program for International Development, Clark University, Worcester, MA 01610, USA and request either *PRA with Somali Pastoralists: Building Community Institutions for Africa's Twenty-First Century* or *PRA iyo Reer Guuraaga Soomaalida: Dhisidda Ruggo Beeleed ee Afrikada Qarniga 21aad.*

SECTION SEVEN

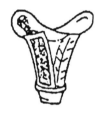

The Plight of
Somali Refugees

Summaries: Section Seven

Hamdi S. Mohamed (Chapter 27) is the first of three authors to explore the issues of Somali refugees outside of Somalia/Eastern Africa. This is the first time such papers have been presented at a Somali Studies International Association Congress. She notes the enormous and new vulnerability to which Somali women are subjected when they are torn from their culture. For example, she states that there were "hundreds if not thousands" of Somali women refugees raped in 1992-93, with the accompanying physical pain and damage, emotional trauma, and cultural destruction association with such acts. Beyond rape, she notes how women refugees in Canada have been subjected to abuse at home from male family members who themselves are often unemployed, frustrated and angry in their amorphous role of refugees.

Ladan Affi (Chapter 28), the second author to comment on the plight of overseas refugees, notes that the experience of 70,000 Somali refugees had been a new experience for Canada. The author pays particular attention to problems of single-parent mothers in dealing with immigration and citizenship forms, school officers, police, social workers, lawyers, landlords, and other figures with power over some aspect of their lives. She concludes with case examples of Somali women: (1) working together to change Canadian legislation, (2) organizing social clubs, (3) developing self-help societies, and (4) collaborating to improve housing conditions.

Hasan Adam Utteh (Chapter 29) offers a third article on the theme of the "Refugee Diaspora," this time to Europe. He too describes the cultural, political, and economic tensions which the refugees encounter. Family tensions build in the midst of these new challenges, often leading to divorce or separation. Of particular concern is the cultural identity of the youth who arrived too young to remember their Somali homeland. Their language, values, habits, diet, education, and friends, not surprisingly, are European, not Somali. Such reculturation makes the likelihood of repatriation slim. Thus, much of the new generation of Somalis may know very little about the Somali culture or way of life. He also discusses the costs incurred by sustaining *qaad (khat)* eating habits while in Europe.

Paul Goldsmith (Chapter 30) presents his perspectives on the considerable impact which the Somali upheaval has had on Kenya. From obvious changes such as the overwhelming influx of 800,000 refugees -- of which the poor went to camps and the more affluent immersed themselves into Nairobi's economic and social life -- to new roles for Somali women; to strengthened linkages between the Kenyan "Sijui" and the "Walendo" Somali Somalis; to an increase in the *miraa (qaad or khat)* trade -- all of these have left indelible impacts. But perhaps more important is the change in geopolitical relations in the Horn resulting from the demise of Somalia and the increasing awareness that many of the problems of both Somalis and Kenyans emanate from the very state structures that, in an ideal world, are intended to solve such problems.

CHAPTER TWENTY SEVEN

The Somali Refugee Women's Experience in Kenyan Refugee Camps and their Plight in Canada

Hamdi S. Mohamed

I. Introduction

In traditional Somalia, as in most other African countries, society defines a "good" woman as one who is under the protection of a male: a father, brother or husband. However, the refugee experience has fragmented families. Many Somali women are in refugee camps and have been resettled in the western countries such as Canada. For these women, their traditional network of male protection has been lost. Many men have been killed in the war, have left Somalia or have been caught up in the tragic civil conflict. As a result, women have been exposed to various threatening and violent experiences beyond their capacity to cope. In addition to stress and trauma associated with refugee experiences of women, and in the absence of "male protection," Somali women refugees are most vulnerable to sexual exploitation and violence such as rape and forced prostitution.

In this paper, I will examine the conditions and the experiences of

Somali refugee women, fleeing the brutal and bloody war in Somalia. I will also discuss women's dreams and aspirations in searching for a "Safe Haven" for themselves and their families, a dream which usually ends in disappointment. Women become disillusioned when they discover they have to face other sets of "new problems" in their new home. These "problems" -- racism, sexism, and violence -- have no cultural mechanisms within the Somali culture to assist women to deal with them.

Compounding these difficulties is the sudden transformation of the role and status of women. Somali women are defined primarily through their roles as mothers and wives, depending upon the support of their extended family and community. When thrust into the role of refugees, they become sole decision-makers, responsible for economic well-being in a very strange land, outside of their traditional cultural context.

It is within this context of Somali women's lives that I will base my analyses of the realities of life as a Somali woman in Canada. Amnesty International has characterized what is happening in Somalia as "a human rights disaster," where "individuals continue to be targeted for deliberate killings solely on the basis of their clan membership." In January, 1991, Siyad Barre's regime, which ruled Somalia with an iron fist for the past twenty-one years, was toppled and Somali women, men, children, and the elderly rejoiced, expecting a better government. However, it did not take long for everyone to realize that the situation would not improve. Presently, the situation is worse than anyone could ever imagine.

> Somalia is going through the most difficult period in its history. War and drought have devastated the whole nation. The country has yielded to anarchy. The state has ceased to exist, the support system (government institutions) has collapsed, and the country has fallen apart.[1]

Although the Somalis have profound historical and contemporary experience with tribal feuds, they have never witnessed a civil war of this magnitude. Historically, there was a legal system -- *"Xeer Soomaali"* -- in place which mediated among the warring factions and succeeded in bringing feuds to an end. As a result of the recent civil war, the traditional legal system was undermined and Somalia armed itself. In fact, there was a period during the civil war when "the bullets were cheaper than the bread" in the streets of Mogadishu.

Although everybody has suffered a casualty in the civil war, Somali women have paid the highest price. In addition to the fear of being killed or injured, starvation, injury, insecurity, and suffering the loss of loved ones, Somali women have become victims of everyday torture, sexual assault and rape. Contrary to men who were fighting to gain political power, to defend their clan and/or "honor," women felt they did not have anything to do with the civil war and needed to cope with the loss of their husbands, fathers, and sons, their traditional "male protection." Consequently, Somali women have become vulnerable to all sorts of dangers, the worst of which are, perhaps, rape and sexual assault.

At a workshop organized by OXFAM Canada, "Setting Development Priorities for the Health and Social Well-being of Somali Women and Children" held in Ottawa in October 1993, Dr. Nimo Abubakar, who recently returned from Somalia, reported that things are much worse than anybody can possibly imagine; "when the father took the gun for whatever reasons, mother does not have any help from anywhere." Women are responsible for taking care of the children who often need constant supervision as many children have been injured in the war. Bullets and landmines have resulted in injuries to children requiring amputation of legs and arms. With no medical help available, mothers must care for the children and provide assistance to heal the wounds. Often, the women are pregnant or breast-feeding and are themselves weak and in need of medical and health assistance.

In the hope of saving their families from the dangers of the civil war, Somali women make the decision to flee with their families to a "Safe Haven." To their dismay, they soon realized that the nightmare does not end after leaving Somalia. In the refugee camps, particularly the camps found in Kenya, Somali women are, once again, exposed to sexual harassment and rape. Although they have escaped the war in Somalia, the Somali women are not able to sleep in peace. In the Kenyan refugee camps, there is constant threat of rape and sexual assault. The rapists are both Somali bandits and Kenyan officials who are supposed to protect the camps from attack. Reports by the UNHCR have documented the fact that women are often sometimes raped repeatedly by many men. In some cases, especially in Mogadishu, "Rape Camps" have been organized where women are kept for months at a time and constantly raped.[2] Not only are the women assaulted and raped, but their attackers usually steal their meager belongings; the assailants, "made their tents collapse by cutting the holding ropes before they attacked. Later, they collected and took tents with them."[3]

Another complicating factor for women is the fact that they do not have recourse to laws or a legal system to protect them. In addition, they are too frightened to report the rapes and sexual assaults to the Kenyan police who are, in some cases, the perpetrators of the crimes; "those responsible for protecting them are often precisely those responsible for the gravest abuses."[4] Women must choose whether to report the crime in

light of the fact that there is, "no disciplinary action taken against police
or security guards accused of abuses." [5] In fact:

> the (Kenyan) police can rape, torture and kill refugees, safe in the
> knowledge that they will never be called to account.[6]

According to the office of the UNHCR, social workers and human
rights groups, there are hundreds, perhaps thousands of Somali refugee
women who have been raped over the last year.[7] Due to the fact that
women rarely report the rapes, only an estimated ten percent of the cases
of rape are reported.[8] There is reason to believe that the number is much
higher than estimated in the report. Fouzia Mussa, a UNHCR consultant
working with Somali refugee women who have suffered rape and sexual
violence, stated that "this is just the tip of the iceberg."[9]

One factor which makes the whole ordeal very hard to bear and
discuss is that Somalis are Muslim, and rape was relatively rare in
Somalia before the war. Within the Muslim religion, rape is ethically and
morally unacceptable. Women who are raped feel ashamed and do not
come forward except when medical assistance is required. Furthermore,
within Somali culture, women who are raped are blamed for the crime. As
such, many women have been abandoned by their husbands and families
and were marginalized within the community. The fear of this kind of
punishment has resulted in many women refusing to report the fact that
they have been raped. There is also a tremendous danger that women
who hide the incident may suffer psychological trauma and, in a case
where the woman has been infibulated, [10] the rapist must use a sharp
instrument such as knife or razor blades to open her up which usually
results in extensive bleeding, injury and infections;

> Sexual intercourse for women who have undergone this operation is
> painful, unless the opening is gradually expanded over a period of
> time, or they are recut to widen the opening. Rape becomes
> excruciatingly painful for the refugee women who have undergone
> the procedure. In some cases, *shiftas* preparing to rape a refugee
> woman have slit open her vagina with a knife before raping her.[11]

In addition, women who have undergone excision and have been victims
of rape, "may become permanently handicapped due to nerve and muscle
damage, or are rendered infertile."[12]

Victims of rape are faced with the double jeopardy of surviving rape
and sexual assault and being rejected by both her family and community.
Women who are raped are often not accepted back into the community

and are shunned. They reported feeling that "they have lost everything -- their chastity, their self esteem, their home and their will to live."[13] A sixteen-year old Somali woman who was raped stated that, "Now I am treated like a prostitute. The only thing I want now is to be buried alive and disappear from this world."[14] *Africa Watch* reported at least one case in which:

> ...[after the] husband discovered that she had been raped, he kicked her out of the compound where the family was living and took her belongings, including her food ration card. For approximately one month, she was sleeping in different places unable to collect her food ration. She was also forbidden by her husband from seeing her children.[15]

The number of women who have been raped has reached an alarming level. Collective and public rapes, often in front of family members -- husband, parents, and children -- are common occurrences and intended to humiliate women in front of their families. In many instances, the war has been used to humiliate and destroy women and men of certain clans. "In addition, assailants often attack the families of their victims... in at least one case a child suffered permanent brain damage after being beaten about the head with a rifle butt by her mother's attackers."[16] Sometimes, the victims' husbands were forced to watch their wives being raped:

> Most of the attacks carried out by bandits also involved assault on the victim's families (e.g. husbands, parents, and/or children) as well as assault. Thus, such attacks have resulted not only in the severe traumatization of the victims but also that of their families who have been forced to witness the violation of their loved ones.[17]

Aside from the physical damage and the psychological trauma, victims of rape carry with them an overwhelming feeling of guilt. Women usually feel that they must have done something to deserve being raped; that somehow the rape was their fault and that they could have prevented it. For the many who are able to speak of their experience, many more remain silent, withdrawn, and unable to share their humiliation.

II. Wife Abuse in Canada

Somali women have survived, along with their families, through very difficult and traumatic situations, in flight, in refugee camps, and in countries of asylum without any protection from men and little protection from organizations. They have witnessed and survived sexual assault, rape, torture, and loss of loved ones. Upon arrival in Canada, such violence does not disappear but changes form. In some cases, women must cope with abuse from their husbands.

Although wife assault existed in Somalia, there was a traditional legal system in place which protected women from such abuse. The system condemned men who mistreated their wives, and forced men to take responsibility for their action:

> If a wife is mistreated by her husband, it is a case of *Xeer* -- the women from the husband's clan who have married into the other clan will be treated in the same way; a clan known to have bad husbands runs the risk of being refused when looking for a new wife... A brother, father, uncle, cousin or the closest male relative is responsible for the protection of his female relatives. They will often force a man to divorce or will warn him fiercely if mistreatment is ever suspected.[18]

Somali women were aware of wife abuse and start warning their daughters against wife-beaters at a very early age. An example of this appears in the following song where a Somali mother promises her daughter she will not marry her off to a wife-abuser;

> When you reach marriageable age
> And if God keeps his approval
> A wicked mean and evil man
> A wife-beater, an intimidator
> To such a man (I promise) your hand won't go.[19]

When Somali women come to Canada they find that the traditional system of protection is not in place. Neither is there any family or community support they have come to depend upon. In addition, the men who used to support the family find themselves in stressful conditions including adjusting to a new country, norms and values of western society. Aside from these factors, men must also cope with the loss of their role as protector and provider of the family and the privileges that come with being the head of the household. As a result, men usually take out their anger and frustrations on their wives in the form of wife abuse.

Somali women have to cope with the trauma of losing their male companion and emotional partner, and from the loss or separation from her loved ones. As Amina Adan demonstrates in her article, "Women and

Words," the Somali man, under normal circumstances, "will prize her over everything... Somali men show, at most, respect to their mother and aunts, and they will give all their wealth, if need be, to a sister or a sister's child."[20]

> Perhaps it is the realization of this that gives the Somali woman her inner strength, for, in compensation for the rest of her hard life, she knows that surely, during one short phase of it, she will be prized above all else, and that for a glimpse of her, a man will travel on foot hundreds of miles, will risk his life (since her male kinfolk will inevitably object to the suitor), and in honor of her shadowed eyes and slender arms will think up lyrical verses comparable to Herrick and Marlow.[21]

Somali women suffer in silence in Canada. Women who are abused become prisoners in their own homes. They usually don't speak either of the official languages (English or French) and they are often not aware of services that are available for sexually assaulted women in the country of asylum or country of settlement. Thus, consequences of torture and rape are neither recognized nor treated properly. Violence against those at home occurs in every society, across class and racial boundaries. Yet, refugee women without work experience and lacking official language proficiency are in a much worse situation. A recently published report on violence against women correctly noted that:

> Systems don't work for immigrant women. These women have even less power than other women and are faced with discrimination, racism, and language disability.[22]

Isolated, these women can be trapped, especially when their husbands prevent them from having friends and deny them access to the larger community. For women who decide to leave abusive situations and go to battered women's shelters to find "protection," often this means coming in contact with other social services. This interaction and contact can be very stressful and lead the women to feel trapped in a miserable, unbearable situation of having to cope with racism and discrimination.

Social services in Canada have been designed to meet the needs of white, middle class women and are not equipped to address issues of accessibility, linguistic and cultural barriers and the realities of refugee women who have experienced mental and physical torture. Such services lack the cultural sensitivity and linguistic abilities to serve women from ethno-racial groups. As the above-mentioned report noted,

An example is the case of a policeman asking a Somali woman to show him the physical marks on her body as proof of the beating her husband allegedly inflicted on her. Such a request revealed a total disrespect for her religious beliefs, and her inability to comply with the police officer's request because those beliefs placed her under continued threat of abuse.[23]

Somali refugee women, more than ever, feel lonely and isolated within this system.

III. Conclusion

In the civil war in Somali, just like other wars in human history, women have become war casualties and rape has, unfortunately, become a common weapon of war. The London-based group, African Rights, calls the plight of Somali refugee women "the forgotten part of Somalia's tragedy." I would tend to agree . While I was conducting interviews for this paper, few Somali men or women were willing or comfortable to discuss this issue.

To some extent, there is a form of denial in accepting that such acts of violence can be found in the community. However, the question remains: will it go away if we do not talk about it? The answer is absolutely not. Sexual assault and rape cannot, and should not, be a fact of life for thousands of Somali women in Somalia, in the refugee camps, and in countries of resettlement such as Canada. This issue demands immediate attention and action. Ways and means should be found to stop these rapes and abuses. Medical assistance, support, counseling and material help should be make available to the victims of such violence.

There is an emergency need for educational programs promoting awareness and understanding of the plight of Somali refugee women whether they are in North America, Europe, Asia, refugee camps in Africa, or still in Somalia where the rape and genocide continues.

There is also need to educate the families of these women in terms of how to cope with the whole issue. There are many cases where husbands have left their wives because "they did not know how to deal with the whole thing," or, "they felt ashamed of it." Husbands should support their wives who have experienced sexual assault and violence and not fall back on the traditional attitudes which tend to punish women. Most victims and their families remain hidden, refusing to speak about their horrible experiences. They should not have to protect themselves behind a wall of silence!

Endnotes

1. Saeed Sheikh, "The Rise and Fall of Somali Nationalism," *Refugee, Canada's Periodical on Refugees,* vol.12, No.5, November-December 1992.

2. Fouzia, Musse. "Women Victims of Violence." Report for UNHCR, Nairobi, 1993.

3. *Ibid.* p. 4.

4. Africa Watch Women's Rights Project, Division of Human Rights Watch, "Seeking Refuge, Finding Terror: The Widespread Rape of Somali Women Refugees in North Eastern Kenya," vol.4, no.14, October 4, 1993, p.43.

5. *Ibid.* p .22

6. *Ibid.* p .22

7. *International Herald Tribune,* Oct. 2-3, 1993.

8. Africa Watch. p.7.

9. Mussa. "Women Victims", p. 1.

10. Infibulation is an operation where a young woman's clitoris, labia majora and labia minora are cut and then the rest of the vagina is stitched together. One of the reasons given to justify this operation is that it is believed that this will stop women from being raped or sexually active.

11. Africa Watch. p. 9.

12. Roberta Aitchison. "Reluctant Witnesses: The Sexual Abuse of Refugee Women in Djibouti." *Cultural Survival Quarterly.* 1984, vol.8, no. 2, p.27.

13. UNHCR. "Sexually Assaulted Refugee Women." Information Bulletin, October, 1993.

14. *Ibid.*

15. *Africa Watch,* p. 17.

16. Musse. "Women Victims." p .5.

17. *Ibid.* p .2.

18 Amina Adan. "Women and Words." *Ufahamu.* Spring 1981, vol.10, no. 3. p. 135.

19. *Ibid.* p. 124.

20. *Ibid.* p. 134.

21. Cited by Adan, p .134

22. Canadian Panel on Violence Against Women. Changing the Landscape: Ending Violence-- Achieving Equality. Minister of Supply and Services Canada: Canada, 1993. p. 85.

23. *Ibid.* p. 89-90.

Bibliography

Adan, Amina. "Women and Words" *Ufahamu, Journal of the African Activist Association,* Volume X, Number 3, Spring 1981.

Africa Watch Women's Rights Project, Division of Human Rights Watch, "Seeking Refuge, Finding Terror: The Widespread Rape of Somali Women Refugees in North Eastern Kenya", Volume 5, Number 13, October 4, 1993.

Aitchison, Roberta. "Reluctant Witnesses: The Sexual Abuse of Refugee Women in Djibouti." *Cultural Survival Quarterly,* vol. 8, no. 2, pp. 26-27.

Canadian Panel on Violence Against Women. Changing the Landscape: Ending Violence -- Achieving Equality. Ottawa: Minister of Supply and Services Canada, 1993.

Drummond, Tammerlin. "Crisis in Somalia; Kenya's Patience and Goodwill Run Out Amid Refugee Problems; Government Says Somali Gangs are Behind Wave of Violence." *The Houston Chronicle,* October 10, 1993.

Esipisu, Manoah. "Kenya Tolerates Rape of Somalis -- Rights Group." *The Reuter Library Report*, September 28, 1993.

Mbete, Chege. "Most Rape Victims Treated As Outcasts." *Calgary Herald,* September 13, 1993.

Musse, Fouzia. "Women Victims of Violence," Report for UNHCR, Nairobi, 1993.

Richburg, Keith B. "Threat of Rape Haunts Somali Refugee Women in Kenya," *International Herald Tribune,* Saturday-Sunday, October 2-3, 1993.

Sheikh Mohamed, Saeed. "The Rise and Fall of Somali Nationalism," Special Issue on Somalia, Vol. 12, No. 5, *Canada's Periodical on Refugees,* November-December, 1992.

UNHCR, "Sexually Assaulted Refugee Women," Information Bulletin, Nairobi: Public Information, October, 1993.

CHAPTER TWENTY EIGHT

The Somali Crisis in Canada: The Single Mother Phenomenon

Ladan Affi

Traditionally Canada has welcomed immigrants and refugees from around the world, particularly those of European heritage. Although the percentage of immigrants to Canada has remained relatively steady since World War II, their cultural backgrounds have not. Figures published by Statistics Canada reveal that the ethnic diversity of new Canadians has increased dramatically during the past decade.

Further, within the last few decades the composition of immigrants has changed dramatically, from approximately 80 percent from countries with European heritage to almost three-quarters from Asia, Africa, Latin America, and the Caribbean. Almost half of Canadian immigration now comes from Asia. Between 1971 and 1986 the number of Canadians who had been born in Africa, Asia, and Latin America grew by 340 percent.

Recently, there has been an increase of immigrants and refugee claimants from African countries such as Somalia, Ethiopia, Eritrea and the Sudan. Within 5 years, the Somali population in Ontario has increased by 613 percent. There are now 70,000 Somalis living in Canada, 13,000 of whom live in Ottawa.

Somalis first entered Canada in 1988 after the destruction of Northern Somalia, and in larger numbers in 1991, after the outbreak of civil war in the southern part of the country. The majority of refugees originally arrived in the United States and, after long and harsh cross examinations, received refugee status in Canada. It is estimated that the majority of Somali women in Canada are single mothers. The focus of this paper will encompass the problems that Somali single mothers face in the process of adapting to life in Canada. Major emphasis will be given to the immigration process, employment, systemic barriers and family disintegration in Canada.

"The growing Somali community is considered to be one of the most disadvantaged among the visible and ethnic minorities." The majority not only have had to cope with living in an alien culture without the traditional support system of the extended family, but also with not being able to speak either of the two official languages, English or French. Somalis experience a high rate of unemployment and, in general, struggle to survive. Settling as claimants, Somalis were ineligible for many government programs available to newcomers. For example, landed immigrants receive effective government programs established to assist them in integrating into Canada such as language classes and skill training. As such, many Somalis do not have access to such programs until their claims are settled. Women comprise about 60% of the total adult Somali population and are the most vulnerable sector of the community. Many have lost their husbands in the war, resulting in a great number of Somali families headed by single mothers. Single Somali women endure extreme obstacles in Canada including gender discrimination, language difficulties, and sole responsibility for child-rearing with a lack of any support system.

Somali single mothers must cope daily with doing the household chores, disciplining and raising children and often they have to take low paying unskilled jobs to help support family members, both in Canada and in Somalia. Once they enter the system, however, they quickly learn that the system was not designed for them.

Before entering into a discussion of the difficulties that Somali single mothers face, it is appropriate to elaborate on the principal causes of the "single-mother phenomena." There are several factors why there are many single mothers as heads of families. First, the Somalis who came as refugee claimants were predominantly women with many children and they chose to come to Canada because of its international image of helping and welcoming immigrants and refugees. For many, "Canada is the first exposure to Western culture for the vast majority of Somali women."

A second factor is that some of the women's spouses and children had to be left behind in Somalia. In many cases, women fled Somalia with false passports and could only bring the number of children stated on these passports. The financial issue of the cost to bring the children to Canada was also used as a factor to decide which children to bring. The decision of who would depart and who would stay is a most difficult one since there are mothers who leave young children behind in the hopes of sponsoring them, once they become permanent residents. This process however, on average, takes over one year and sometimes longer.

Third, the rate of divorce among Somali couples is incredibly high. The conflicts which arise are mainly due to the redefinition of traditional cultural roles between women and men and the stress of trying to cope in a foreign country. For example, women raise a family without the help of their husbands, yet it is the men who expect to be treated with respect and exert authority as heads of households as they once had in Somalia. These men are expecting to be obeyed without contributing very much to the well-being of the family.

In Somalia, men did not help their wives with household chores and caring for their children because there are many relatives helping then instead. In Canada, however, this kind of support from relatives does not exist, yet Somali men fail to understand that.

The result is an extremely high divorce rate. Marital break-ups are also often the result of there being no mechanism in Canada similar to the one in Somalia of mediation in the event of marital conflicts. Conflicts which might lead to divorce are often solved in Somalia, therefore saving the marriage. Another factor is lack of knowledge of Canadian law. For example, one Somali woman who was angry with her husband called the police but had no intention of charging him with anything. She had just wanted to teach him a lesson. She did not anticipate that the police would adopt harsh measures.

One of the most immediate issues that these women face on their arrival to Canada is the immigration process. First, women have to retain their own lawyer, attend numerous interviews with the authorities, write a coherent statement regarding why she should be considered a refugee and convince an immigration officer and the Immigration and Refugee Board of Canada that she has a legitimate claim. When making a refugee claim in Canada, the claimant has to remember exact dates and times of when events occurred. This is extremely difficult for Somalis who have a tendency not to put emphasis on how far they traveled from one city to another, or the date of when they left. This often leads to their claim being rejected due to inconsistencies or for lack of facts. Throughout this long process, the claimant is living with the uncertainty of what will happen to them and at the same time beginning the stressful process of appealing the negative decision. Women who have been raped or sexually assaulted are faced with yet a further barrier. Somali women are not likely to mention the rape or assault in the context of their claim or hearing. Yet without this information, the claim may be rejected. Women under such circumstance are forced to reveal the violations or choose to remain silent about what has happened to them, out of fear of being ostracized or blamed for the abuse within their community.

Canada introduced, in March 1993, gender guidelines which are intended to take such factors of the abuses women refugee claimants suffer into account. Unfortunately, the stigma of making a claim based on rape or sexual abuse in Somali society is so great that few Somali women have used the guidelines, although some would no doubt qualify. Another obstacle was created by the new immigration law, Bill C-86, which was implemented in February 1993. This Bill requires that claimants, even after being found to be convention refugees by the Immigration and Refugee Board, are still compelled by Immigration Canada to have documentation predating their entrance into Canada, in order to prove their identity. "Our primary concern is not to enter a situation where we are landing people and we don't know who they are." says Jim May, Chief of Immigrant and Visitor Operations. Since identity documents were not widely used in Somalia and since Somali women were less likely to own one, as they likely did not drive or work where documentation was needed, they might have no documents. This requirement directly affects women more than men because men often do have access to such documents. Also, refugees are usually fleeing dangerous situations and war conditions. Under these conditions, there is no available system to apply for documentation proving their identity. However, this is a reality that immigration officials fail to acknowledge. Refugees with their proper paperwork and documentation are rare.

Some Somali women have had their claims rejected on the basis that they could live in safe areas, inhabited by their children's clan. Although the clan system is strong in Somalia, many clans are at war and no area can be considered safe. Refugee women also face sexism from Immigration and Refugee Board officers as was the case of a Somali woman whom the Immigration officer referred to as "my dear lady," and also described her as "little lady." Such language is clearly sexist and patronizing. Some immigration officers even refer to Somali women's dress styles, conforming to Islamic Shari'ah, as outdated and backward. This type of attitude may influence how a woman's claim is decided.

Canada is no longer "a nation in which single-wage earners predominate;" single mothers feel the pressure more than two-parent families. Due to the fact that many Somali women are in a situation where they are the only adult in their family living in Canada, there are certain responsibilities that she alone must fulfill such as supporting family members back home by sending money, and trying to sponsor other family members into Canada. Sponsorship has been made somewhat more difficult under Canada's recently restricted immigration law which only allows sponsorship of spouses and children under 19 years of age. Parents and grandparents, minor age siblings, and adopted and orphaned children can be sponsored only if the sponsor is working. The Somali women are thus forced, due to "economic pressures, to take any jobs. These jobs, however, are usually low-paying and result in having to accept two or three part-time jobs in order to meet the minimum requirement for earned income set by immigration.

"Immigrant women experience extreme difficulty finding decent employment at every level of the Canadian labor force" and Somali women tend to face the additional hardships of "cultural and language barriers (Somali and Muslim) and discrimination (Black, female and Muslim)." The visibility of Somali women in terms of dress and behavior has major implications for both employment opportunities and access to services. The majority of Canadian employers inevitably ask for Canadian work experience and are not likely to acknowledge previous work and educational experience of refugees in their home countries. This forces "most immigrant women into jobs well below their overall skills and almost always below their potential." Women also lack work experience as they might not have worked in their home country.

Due to all these barriers, the majority of Somali women are employed in some form of domestic work because there is minimum language requirement and such "unskilled" jobs are available in greater numbers to women. Once women enter these menial jobs it is difficult, if not impossible, to escape this employment ghettos.

Since the lack of English or French language skills is often not considered a problem with such low-paying jobs, they do not have opportunities to improve their language skills at work. Women therefore remain ineligible for occupational training or upgrading. On the job, these women have few opportunities to learn the official languages because their fellow workers and supervisors usually do not speak to them and the work is done in isolation. The long hours and the exhausting nature of the work also make it extremely difficult for women to attend evening or weekend language classes. They are "caught in a self-perpetuating trap, which makes them vulnerable to exploitation."

Due to the breakdown of the traditional support systems available in Somali, abusive relationships among married couples as well as between parents and children is increasing in the Somali community. There are increasing incidents of violence within Somali families, "where stress may be high and where abused family members do not know their rights and/or sources of help." Marital conflict which sometimes becomes abusive, aside from being the result of power inequities in society between men and women, can also be attributed to several other factors. First, the political conflicts in Somalia are often transferred to Canada. The effects of this conflict are magnified, especially if the husband and wife are from different clans. This manifests itself in the form of who to send money to; should it be her clan or his? Her family or his? or should they spend it on their own needs?

Second, a large percentage of Somali men are unemployed due to the current recession and lack of recognition from employers of previous work experience as well as education. Somali women, on the other hand, are willing to take dead-end, low-paying jobs in order to support their family in Canada and abroad. This creates a role reversal as women become financially independent of their husbands. This results in men feeling alienated, useless, angry and frustrated, eventually, reaching a point where their frustrations are taken out on their wives and children. This leads many Somali women to look to the police for protection for themselves and their families.

There are also a large number of children who speak either English or French and have figured out how to use the system to their benefit and are also in many cases abusing their mothers. Somali children tend to believe that "they are deprived of the freedoms that Canadian children enjoy." This leads the children to threaten to call the police or the Children's Aid Society (CAS) and report abuse unless they get their way in the family. Police and CAS intervention is the nightmare of most Somali single mothers in Canada, as many who have had contact with such agencies have had their children taken away from them.

All of the above are only a fraction of the problems faced by Somali single mothers. Housing has also been identified as a major issue. Families on welfare are asked to provide the name of a co-signer who has an income of $50,000 or over. This criteria cannot be met by many Somali single mothers and they have no option but to enter shelters in order to qualify for subsidized housing from the Ottawa-Carleton Regional Housing Authority. This, in turn, has led to an influx of Somalis into certain areas of the city. Due to the increasing intolerance in Canada towards newcomers in general and towards the Somali community specifically, there has been an increase in conflict between

Somalis and white Canadians who have stereotyped Somalis as abusing the social assistance system. This conflict has manifested itself to the point where Somalis are increasingly facing individual and systemic racism which has made their integration much more difficult. In many cases, Somalis have been physically attacked and injured.

A poll done in 1993 by *Maclean's*, one of the leading magazines in Canada, revealed that there is increasing intolerance toward newcomers and found that "34 percent [of those interviewed] said that immigrants should be encouraged to "blend with larger society." Another previous poll done by *Maclean's* in 1990 indicated that "40 of the respondents ... said that new immigrants should be encouraged to maintain their distinct culture and ways." These are contradictory messages and most likely reflect the confused state of what multiculturalism means to Canadians.

Recently, the Somali community has faced increasing, systemic racism in the media and government, and from the general public. Many Somalis have been charged with collecting multiple claims for welfare in order to send money to their warlords of choice. Even though these allegations have been shown to be false, the Somali community continues to face the repercussions of such false reporting.

Despite these difficulties, the Somali community in Ottawa-Carleton has organized to assist their members. Several programs have been implemented to make life easier for community members. Some community health centers such as the Carlington Community Health Centre and the Sandy Hill Community Health Centre have hired Somali workers to do outreach and counsel Somali single mothers and the Somali community in general. Carlington Community Health Centre, for example, has a Somali women's program where the women get together, decide upon the topics to be discussed as well as who to invite as speakers. They have also attempted to recreate the support mechanism that they had in Somalia and have empowered themselves by finding out how the Canadian system works and how it can benefit them. Other governmental agencies including the three levels of government as well as non-governmental organizations have hired Somalis to render the services accessible and available.

Numerous heritage schools where the Somali language and culture is taught have also emerged in the area. Women get together on weekends to teach each other skills and exchange ideas. There are also increasing numbers of Somali religious elders who now do counseling in a way similar to that done in Somalia. During Ramadan, the holy month of fasting, Somali women organize locations to break the fast together and share prayers. During holidays such as Eid Al Fitr, women organize camps and picnics for the community to come together.

Somali women have not only tried to improve life in Canada for themselves but have had a positive impact on other refugees and immigrants in Canada. In 1991, a group of Somali women in Toronto who were part of a support group being offered by the Canadian Centre for Victims of Torture and facilitated by Fadumo Dirie, decided that one of their immediate needs was access to government housing which was not available to refugee claimants. The women did research, collected support from other agencies and members of the provincial parliament and then launched a lawsuit against the Housing Authority stating that they were being discriminated against. This has led to the law being changed to make all refugee claimants eligible for subsidized housing.

As the Somali community continues to face many problems in Canada, Somali women, as the majority of the adult population, will continue to play a major role in solving the above-stated problems. While Somalis have been victims of racism due to their vocal resistance to being discriminated against, they have become scape-goats in the media, which makes them vulnerable to even worse racism and discrimination. The Somali experience in places such as Ottawa has played a significant role in policy changes which have benefitted newcomers as a whole and which can be used as a model for organizing Somali communities in other parts of Canada.

Bibliography

Adan, Zeinab, "Somali Refugee Women in Canada" INSCAN, Vol. 6, No. 2/3 Ottawa: November 1992.

Boyd, Monica, "Immigrant Women in Canada: Profiles and Policies." Research Division, Immigration Canada and Status of Women Canada. Ottawa, March 1987.

Cairns, Alan C., *Charter Vs. Federalism: The Dilemma of Constitutional Reform.* Montreal: McGill-Queens University Press, 1992.

Ethnocultural Data Base, Policy Services Branch, Ministry of Citizens, *Ethnic Origins - 1991 Census Update.* Toronto, April 1993.

Hanafi, Ahmed, " Family Problems" INSCAN, Vol.7 No.2, Ottawa, November 1993.

McGowan, Sharon, "Immigrant Women in Canada: A Resource Handbook for Action." Vancouver, B.C.: Task Force on Immigrant Women, July 1982.

Wood, Nancy, "Immigration: A Reluctant Welcome" *Maclean's* Vol. 105, No.101, Ottawa, January 4, 1993.

CHAPTER TWENTY NINE

The Plight Of Somali Refugees in Europe, With Particular Reference to Germany (1993)

Hassan Adam Utteh[1]

I. Introduction

Since the dawn of history, the people of Somalia, traditionally a pastoral society, have freely enjoyed traveling to distant lands in search of greener pastures. Their conquering of neighboring and distant lands is well-known. Somali sea pirates, it is recorded, once sailed from the port of "Barbaria (Somaliland)" to Korfu, presently a Greek tourist resort island and "destroyed it entirely but were then wiped out by the Byzantines" in about l032.[2]

Although a detailed documented record of an ancient Somali settlement on a Greek island has not been established, aged sailors, mostly from the former British Somaliland, have been permanent residents in British harbors since the colonial era. These retired Somalis once sailed in His/Her Majesty's Navy and on various British cargo ships.

Today Somalis are found all over the world: in almost every Western European country, North America as well as in virtually almost every African country. There are Somalis in Australia, the Far East and even in South America, not to mention the neighboring Middle East where thousands were attracted by the oil boom. The hottest and the coldest corners of this earth could not hold them back!

Before Africa shook off the shackles of colonialism at a time when the colonial powers put strict control over the movement of their subjects, Somalis were known to have been globe-trotting. However, it should be realized that the early Somali adventurer's purpose was the search for temporary employment to enable him later to return home and establish a family within his rural nomadic community.

In the post-independence sixties, an influx of young Somalis moved to eastern and western Europe, the USA and as far as China for higher education. A large number, after completion of their studies, stayed in their respective Western countries of study because of the attractive opportunities and a comfortable better life in comparison with an unpredictable future back home. A government run by nepotistic leaders in Somalia could neither provide nor guarantee the procurement of prospective jobs for all the returning graduates. Worse still, the political situation at home was not conducive to attracting those highly qualified intellectuals whose services were urgently needed.

II. The Prevailing Problems and Their Outcome

A. The War

When the Northerners revolted against General Mohamed Siyad Barre's regime in the north in May, 1988, fifty to sixty thousand Isaaq were killed and nearly half a million fled to neighboring Ethiopia[3] while thousands of others who could afford it, headed for Europe, North America and as far as Australia as refugees. Within five years, these countries had taken in thousands of Somalis, mostly women and children, who previously had never left the area of their domicile.

In addition to the influx, a large number from the southern region (where the war had not yet reached), from neighboring Djibouti and from as far as Tanzania, Kenya, Uganda, Saudi Arabia, the United Arab Emirates, and the Arabian Gulf where the situation was not the worst, jumped onto the "refugee" bandwagon. They headed for Europe where, so the story was fabricated, Somali asylum seekers were being provided with free furnished apartments, new winter and summer clothes, free education, free medical treatment and lump sums of money to send home to their relatives! As a result, many Somalis sold their property and headed, *en mass*, to this new El Dorado, all claiming to belong to the victimized Isaaq clan! But when Siyad's regime was defeated in the north and the war spread to the south, thousands of southerners joined the exodus heading for neighboring Kenya and Tanzania while the rich headed overseas. This time, Somali "refugees" who landed overseas claimed to be either Darood or Hawiye victim of the conflict in the south!

Today we have thousands of displaced Somalis in the United Kingdom, Italy, North America and a large number in Holland, Germany, Sweden, Norway, Denmark, France, Belgium and in Finland. Hundreds more who were headed for Western Europe are believed to be stranded in Russia, Romania and Hungary.

B. *Qaad**

One of the major problems confronting the Somali male today -- whether in Africa or in Europe -- is his excessive consumption of *qaad* or *chaad*, botanically known as *Catha edulis*, a semi-drug plant mainly grown in Kenya, Ethiopia and Yemen and which, many chewers believe to have medical values against fever, coughs, general body illness, influenza, stomach aches and even against gonorrhea! Although one isn't really cured by chewing and swallowing the bitter sap of this plant, one "feels" relieved from his pains or even "elated" after excessive consumption of the drug. However, it has been scientifically established that the leaves and the bark of *Catha edulis* contain powerful narcotic alkaloids and that regular consumption of it destroys the body as well as one's mind causing sleeplessness at night (which results in many men being in bed the whole day!), impotence, dental decay, lack of appetite, fantasizing and negligence of one's family obligations.

It is addictive and a prolonged use can have dangerous and even fatal results. Its soaring price in Europe (it is imported by air from Kenya) certainly drains the meager income one receives for the maintenance of one's family. Consequently, 90 percent of Somali broken homes in Europe today could be linked to this drug. Therefore, its immediate prohibition in the whole of Europe and in Canada where it is also widely used is called for to eradicate this problem and remedy the situation. The Scandinavian countries, after women complained to the authorities, have already realized this and a strict control of its importation is exercised by the customs authorities. Countries such as Saudi Arabia impose severe penalties on those who smuggle it into the country.

---

* Also called *miraa* or *khat* in other chapters.

C. Idleness and Frustration

The European winter necessitates families -- large and small -- to huddle together in the small spaces provided, squatting in front of the TV set and getting on each other's nerves. This naturally breeds an aggressive attitude which sooner or later reaches a breaking point. A father who receives the same amount of money as his wife for sustenance loses his prestige and identity as the proud head of family who once earned the family's daily bread. He is reduced to a character who simply huddles within the family, hardly productive for his family in any respect. On the contrary, he becomes a "family burden" for, as tradition always demanded, he expects his commands to be obeyed and his wishes immediately fulfilled without questions or criticism. As a result, many wives who have been "enlightened" by their social workers that in Europe men and women are on an equal basis and that men must help women on their daily family chores, have legally sought separation from their male partners. This has not only resulted in the suffering of the children who, after separation and divorce, are legally kept by mothers but, in certain cases, it has had serious consequences.

For instance, in a small German town in the region of Northern Westfalia, one afternoon in later 1993, a Somali stabbed his wife to death in public at a traffic light while she was holding the hand of her child whom she had just picked up at the kindergarten because, according to his allegations, she had been unfaithful to him by having an affair with the German social worker who frequented the family. It is reported that because of the shock, the poor child has had incurable hiccups ever since. In the Netherlands, more than six Somalis -- males and females alike -- have so far committed suicide for various "maladies" which Somalis hardly suffered in their country: loneliness, depression, forced separation of husbands from their children and the denial of fathers to see their offsprings. A large number of young Somalis has sought the bottle as the only alternative means to drown their miseries, hence, the rising number of young alcoholics in the Somali community today. These are but a fraction of some of the "maladies" which have so far led many Somalis to suicide or for psychiatric treatment. Several who attempted suicide by throwing themselves from tall buildings are permanently crippled or paralyzed.

D. Lack of Employment

Since in many countries refugees are not allowed to work because the issuance of a work permit largely depends first on being officially recognized as a refugee -- a very rare case in Germany these days -- many Somali asylum seekers have been "migrating" from one country to another where, so the argument goes, "the possibility of being granted a refugee status and finally securing a job is better." However, these supposedly new "better and prospective" countries turn out to be worse than the former, hence, many frustrated males end up in *qaad*-chewing sessions or they simply abandon the family and return to the countries of their origin. Thus, today women play the leading role in assuming family responsibilities; they are coping with it alone in unfamiliar environments under difficult circumstances. Many are, therefore, questioning whether the overseas Somali male hasn't lost his sense of duty and responsibility towards his family.

E. New Arrivals and Their Experiences

Then there are those not-in-need families from the oil-rich Arab countries and from East Africa where their husbands were/are working and where many of them led comfortable lives. These, mostly women and children, on arrival were either dumped by their husbands at airports or they arrived alone -- to take care of themselves and apply for political asylum in strange unfamiliar countries. Wives and grown-up daughters whose movements were once strictly controlled under watchful eyes, found themselves in countries where, for the first time in their lives, they could not only move freely without any restriction but where, they were told, the law is in their favor! Results: some lonely neglected wives ended up having non-Somali boyfriends, mostly Europeans, an action which led to divorced wives accusing Somali males of negligence, irresponsibility, "hardly demonstrating neither tender love nor devotion to their families." Some of those who have "discovered" their new freedom of movement have gone to extremes, some returning home at very late hours and some having even the audacity of openly claiming to have been spending the night with "friends." Such behavior would be unthinkable for the orthodox Somali Muslims and to the once proud pastoralists who regard any uncircumcised non-Muslim as a *gaal* (unbeliever) who hardly deserves to defile the purity of his daughter!

F. Communication Problems

As a whole, grownups have little interest in learning the language nor will they bother to be trained in any of the accessible professions. It is the school attending children who quickly pick up the language of the host country. The sad result is that within a short period of time, children who easily forget their mother tongue, hardly communicate nor relate to their own parents who, themselves, are either perpetually watching the TV set or, in the case of the father, busy chewing *qaad* and doesn't want to be disturbed (*hadaarin*)!

G. Loss of Identity and Cultural Conflict

Today the Somali youth who arrived at his present domicile as a child hardly identifies himself with his Somali culture which he is unfamiliar with and which he finds even despised by many of his own people. It has been observed that in many Somali fatherless families, for instance, children have developed an inferiority complex. There are mothers who have been told by their own children not to escort or pick them up at school because they do not want to be seen or to be identified with their shabby-looking black mothers who "come from the poor black, hungry, war-torn continent where starvation and diseases are rampant!" Worse still, there are children who publicly avoid their parents or refuse to speak with them in the "primitive bush language," especially when they are with their friends. It will not be easy for children growing up in these environments where the media always portray Blacks as either a warring people or starving masses whose leaders are always globe-trotting to world capital, bowls in outstretched hands.

Culturally, most of the so-called modern urban "civilized" Somalis have either forgotten or they hardly have any positive regard for their culture and tradition. What Somalis seem to love most today is *everything foreign*, especially western values. To mention just one example, one has only to observe, for instance, how a modern Somali wedding is celebrated to confirm this statement. Gone are the days of Somali dances, (*ciyar Soomaali)* the recitation of *gabay* in praise of the bride and bridegroom. Gone are also the days of the bride wearing a full traditional Somali wedding dress with its full gear; in the case of the Northerners: *maro saddex qaad ah, bogor,* adorning herself with a *dhacle, tusbax cunnaabi ah* and *jiman* to match and the Somali makeup consisting of *xinne, cusbur, diib,* etc., while the bridegroom put on *laba go'oo caddeysan* and *kabo fay gamoor ah.* Almost gone also is the ceremonial opening of the *heedho,* formerly by the bridegroom himself symbolizing the young virgin bride,[5] later performed by young men who are related to the husband on the night of the *gaafka* under the watchful eyes of young maidens, a stick in hand, ready to whip them at the slightest break in the rules in their effort to untie the tricky knot, expertly tied by elderly women. Today, laments Asha H. Mohamed of Wapping, London, the *hedho* is not only exaggeratedly decorated with gold and money but it is even opened by women, contrary to tradition![6] During the night of the *gaafka,* traditional rhythmic *ciyar Soomaali* such as *batar, harimahee* or *Zylic* just to mention a few, used to be performed outside the *aqal laba deryaale ah* by both young males and young females till later in the night while women continuously ululated their tongues in appreciation.

The collapse of these traditional wedding practices is accompanied by adoption of the latest American dances -- *a la* Michael Jackson -- in expensive rented hotels. The poor couple has to dance in circles in the hall stepping on each other's toes for what, to them, must seem an eternity before other couples gather enough courage to join them on the floor to save them from their predicament! There are Somali women who even got married in church in spite of the fact that they are Muslims! The very expensive high creamy cake cut by both bride and bridegroom and then feeding each other a piece of the cake and the lily-white wedding gown for the bride and a dark suit for the bridegroom have, alas, replaced the beautiful Somali marriage ceremony and, for those who could afford it, the seven day's joyous wedding celebration of merry-making, feasting and dancing.

A young Somali who has been in Holland for less than a year recently visited a group of his old friends who, during their *qaad*-chewing session, were listening to Somali "hello" songs on a radio cassette. Surprised, he wondered why they were still listening to the "old backward primitive bush music" while an "educated" young Somali mother from Kenya could not help but recently remark about the "poor" quality of Somali music and wondered why Somalis don't simply use the European musical instruments instead of continuously banging the old "ugly" *kaban with the accompaniment of knocking of empty beer bottles!*

Urban parents are to blame for this sorry state of affairs and for their failure in fulfilling their obligatory elementary duties as tutors to firmly instill in their offsprings' young minds the pride of Somali culture, tradition and pride. Unless there is an immediate massive reorientation of the masses and reestablishment of the already destroyed Somali moral code and religious values, we might as well expect Somalis, within a few decades, to have lost the rich cultural traditions of their forefathers.

H. Attitude and Behavior

While Somalis in Europe cannot be accused of either robbing or raping, their I-couldn't-care-less attitude and their cheating behavior (*musug-maasaq)* have painted a negative picture of Somalis as an untrustworthy people. In Germany, Somali refugees are not only frowned upon in many areas, but are not entitled to have a telephone installed in their dwelling places unless a large sum of money is first deposited. The simple reason is that many of them are in the habit of "exploding" *(Qarxin!)* their telephones, as the terminology goes, meaning they make the longest calls in the history of telephoning and then vanish into thin air as soon as the bill soars to thousands, leaving the authorities concerned, perplexed and confused! Second, Somalis are known to have the habit of applying for a refugee status in various regions within a country or even in two or three neighboring countries to cash the monthly payment. Smuggling children, as well as adults, in and out of Somalia for large sums of money, even by Somalis already in possession of valid passports, has been a regular, prosperous booming business practiced even by mothers living in Kenya! Of course it cannot be generalized but, as the old saying goes, *a rotten apple spoils its neighbor!* Even Canadian officials have branded Somalis as "masters of confusion and misrepresentation" and that, among other things, they are

> a group of people (who) have demonstrated repeatedly that they can obtain and will readily use fraudulent and improperly issued documentation to facilitate their goals. This includes illegal immigration and welfare fraud. In addition, they are opportunists and masters of confusion unparalleled except by the Gypsies of Eastern and Western Europe.[7]

Second, the majority of Somalis are hardly grateful for the hospitality extended to them by their host countries. Their many complaints, nagging and abuse directed against their hosts are endless. They seem not to realize that they are lucky to be where they are today, namely overseas where they are at least safe, while thousands of their countrymen are either still crammed and languishing in over-crowded camps or have already succumbed to the ravaging hunger and diseases which swept the country, not to mention the thousands who have already perished or are daily victims of the still existing conflict between the warring clan factions.

II. Future Plans

The majority of Somalis abroad hardly entertain the idea of ever going back home to the nomadic way of life with which they grew up -- a life with which they are familiar. The abandonment of the nomadic way of life, it should be borne in mind, is the beginning of the end of Somali culture and tradition, for the pastoralists were the preservers of the rich Somali culture and tradition.

Many of the overseas Somali asylum-seekers believe that they are in their host countries to stay put. Many were even shocked to learn of the downfall of their tormenter General Mohamed Siyad Barre who was the cause of their misery and flight, knowing well that if peace is achieved back home the days of their sojourn in Europe would be numbered. As a matter of fact, the majority are hoping and praying for the day to dawn when their application for full recognition as refugees will be favorably considered, which will be a *sesame* for a permanent residence, leading later to a full citizenship.

When the news leaked, for instance, that a certain West European country was easily issuing refugee passports to Somali asylum-seekers, there was a commotion and a mass "migration" to that country. Host countries such as Germany, which had had a large number of Somali refugees, suddenly found themselves deserted while this particular country woke up to find itself thronged by hundreds more Somali mouths to feed, without knowing how they managed to enter the country in spite of strict control at borders and airports!

III. Conclusion

The thousands of Somali refugees outside Somalia/Somaliland in general, especially those in Europe, North America and Australia who have it better than their brothers and sisters in Kenya, Tanzania or Ethiopia should make up their minds as to what they intend to be in the future: Somalis or otherwise. Whatever their decision and their future plans, they must abandon their *naivete* and realize that host governments -- regional or national -- are no longer in a position to indefinitely spend their taxpayers' money on a large, non-productive group of people within their communities -- a group which is only there for consumption and not for production. Neither does the present behavior of many Somalis indicate that their future in Europe, where unemployment is soaring to millions and radicalism and racism are on the increase, help to win the sympathy of their host governments for favorable consideration of full citizenship -- the ultimate goal of almost every Somali refugee today. Even if granted, however, will they really feel at home in these countries, under these circumstances?

The only alternative is, therefore, a mass repatriation to their respective areas in Somalia/Somaliland as soon as peace is achieved and the international community grants them full recognition. This action will definitely not only cost a lot of money but will also be frowned upon by those who have already turned their backs on the Old Country. However, I believe it is the only solution which will ultimately be beneficial to all concerned, rather than allowing a large Somali community, which cannot be assimilated, remain in a country where they could later be a social problem. Granting long-term loans to former successful businessmen and farmers who lost their property in the war and offering incentives for the much needed Somali professionals and artisans who are now idle overseas is another step. Another strategy is encouragement of small industries in their respective countries and the improvement of the destroyed infrastructure. These actions should slowly improve their lot back home. Better still, after repatriation, the present host countries could do even better by maintaining these refugees in their own homelands at less expense for at least a certain period of time. This transition subsidy would allow the former refugees to readjust to their long forgotten environments and be preferable to the present, expensive arrangement where they will ultimately end up being neither Somalis nor real nationals of host countries.

Endnotes

1. Hassan Adam Utteh is a lecturer in the Institute of African Studies, University of Cologne, Germany.

2. My translation of Durrel's Lawrence 1963: *Schwarze Oliven, Insel der Phäaken,* p. 133, Rowohlt Verlag GmbH, Reinbek bei Hamburg, 1963, a German translation from the original English title *Prospero's Cell,* published by Faber and Faber Ltd., London WCl, 1945.

3. The Africa Watch Committee, 1990. *Somalia:* A Government at War With Its Own People. Testimonies About the Killings and the Conflict In the North, p. 3.

4. *Warsidaha Somaliland,* February, 1994, p. 17 quoting *The Weekly Review.*

5. Hanghe, Ahmed Artan: *The Arranged Marriage Among the Pastoral Somalis,* an unpublished Ms.

6. See *Warsidaha Somaliland,* February, 1994, p. 21.

7. *Warsidaha Somaliland*, February 1994, p. 16 quoting *The Weekly Journal* of 6 January, 1994.

Bibliography

Anonymous, 1945: The need for the control of *Khat.*, *Medical Journal Bd.* 22, 1,9-10.

Anonymous; 1956: Khat. *Bulletin on Narcotics*, United Nations 8, 6-13.

Braenden, O.J.; 1980: Research in the Chemical Composition of Khat. In Harris, L.S. (Ed) 1979: Problems of Drug Dependence. *Proceedings of the 41st. Annual Scientific Meeting.* The Committee on Problems of Drug Dependence. NIDA 27. DHEW Pub. No. (ADM) 80-901, Washington D.C.

Brooke, C.; 1968: *Khat* (Catha edulis): Its Production and Trade in the Middle East. *Geographical Journal* Vol. 126, 52-59.

Brücke, F. Th. von; 1941: Uber die Zentral-erregende Wirkung des Alkaloids Cathin, Arch. f. Exp. *Pathologie und Pharmakologie,* 198, 100-106.

Carrothers, J.C.; 1941: *Miraa* as a Cause of Insanity, East *African Medical Journal*, 4-6.

Hogaland, J.; 1975: Chewing Qat in Forgotten Arabia. *Washington Post* 10. Aug. 1975.

Kennedy, J.G.; Teague, J.; Fairbanks, L.; 1980: Qat Use In North Yemen and the Problem of Addiction: A Study in Medical Anthropology. *Culture, Medicine and Psychiatry*, 4, 311-344.

Margetts; E.L.; 1967: Miraa and Myrrh in East Africa -- Clinical Notes About Catha edulis. *Economic Botany* 21, 358-362.

Paris, R.; Moyse, H.; 1957: Essai de Caracterisation du Khat ou The des Abyssins (Catha edulis Forsk., Celastraceae) drogue recemment inscrite au tableau B., -- *Ann. Pharm. Francaise*, 15, 89-97.

Qedan, S.; 1972: Catha edulis, eine wenig bekannte Rausch - und Genubdroge, *Planta Medica* 21, 113-126.

Schopen, A.; 1978: Das Qat, Geschichte und Gebrauch des Genub-mittels Catha edulis Forsk. in der Arabischen Republik Jemen, Band 8, Franz Steiner Verlag GmbH, Wiesbaden.

Schorno, X.; Steinegger, E.; 1979: *The Phenylalkylamines of Catha edulis Forsk: The Absolute Configuration of Cathinone.* United Nations Document MNAR/3.

Stockman, R.; 1912: The Active Principles of Catha edulis. *Pharm. J. and Pharmacist* 35.

Watt, J.M.; Breyer-Brandwijk; 1962: *The Medical and Poisons Plants of Southern and Eastern Africa.* E and S. Livingstone Ltd., Edinburgh and London.

CHAPTER THIRTY

The Somali Impact on Kenya, 1990-1993: The View From Outside the Camps

Paul Goldsmith

I. Introduction

This report offers some perspectives on how the collapse of the Somali state and its aftermath affected the neighboring country of Kenya. The perspectives themselves are expressed in the form of various geographical and sectoral "viewpoints," based on ethnographic observation and informal interviews and conversations with various Kenyans and Somalis from different walks of life. I happened to be conducting research in Meru at the same time, and as a result the details of the "View from Meru" are more elaborate than those of the other sections. This is perhaps fitting insofar as the Somali diaspora has had a particularly pronounced effect on Meru's Nyambene region.

The disaster rising out of the decline and collapse of Siyad Barre's Somali government, the regional famine, and the internal strife that overtook Somalia received extensive and dramatic, if uneven, coverage from the international media. The publicity itself was an important factor in the multinational response to the crisis. Like Kafka's hunger artist, however, any single catastrophe captures and holds public attention for a limited time only. The Somalis displaced by the chaotic conditions in their country have been far from passive actors during the crisis phase, and the maladaptive political behaviors emanating out of Mogadishu should not distract us from the wider picture of adaptive societal responses catalyzed by state collapse.

These vignettes and the observations accompanying them hardly tell the whole story, but they do attempt to do justice to the proposition that African developmental processes encompass complex group interactions that cannot be reduced to the formal orthodoxies informing most state and donor-led developmental initiatives on one hand, and explanations of ethnic conflict based on the simple notion of tribalism. Events in Somalia triggered the flight of an estimated 800,000 Somali refugees into Kenya. The informal sector, i.e., societal domain, aspects of this phenomena are of significant interest to our understanding of wider regional processes in Africa. The Somali impact on Kenya reveals how the affairs of individual ethnic units and sovereign states converge within dynamic historical and contemporary processes proceeding on a regional basis.[1]

The composite picture assembled here also endeavors to extract some insights concerning the longer term influences of the crisis in Kenya, and how developments in Kenya feed back into the process of change within Somali society. We begin with a brief synopsis of Somali-Kenya international relations in order to establish a context for investigating other facets of what remains an evolving situation.

II. The View From the Kenya State

Kenya was experiencing its own problems during the period when Siyad Barre's government was collapsing. The Rift Valley ethnic cleansing campaigns suggested parallels with the more advanced state of ethnic conflicts manifesting within the Somalia region. The economy was sinking, and by 1992 it had reached its lowest point since the country gained independence in 1963. The government had become bellicose in its reaction to internal and external criticism, and the international donor community eventually severed aid flows, even though Daniel arap Moi's government grudgingly bowed to the pressure to institute a multi-party political system. Although President Moi sometimes pointed to the internal problems of Somalia and Ethiopia in his defense of the one-party state, the monolithic governance was responsible for setting in motion the underlying fissionary social forces in both countries. Their destructive manifestation in Somalia argues more for the adapting of the state to African conditions than the preservation of centralized political machinery.

The division of ethnic units within different states nevertheless creates its own difficulties. The core problem of modern Somali society parallels the dilemma of the Kurds, a culturally distinct population that found themselves at the intersection of five different countries. Kenya's ethnic Somali population has always been a critical factor in Kenya-Somali state relations. Kenya's Northeastern Province is one of the regions of greater Somalia represented by the five-pointed star imposed on the blue background of the Republic of Somalia's flag.[2] Ninety percent of the region's inhabitants voted for unification with Somalia in a 1960 British referendum on the issue prior to Kenyan independence. The referendum fueled expectations leading to the violent rebellion that erupted in 1963.

The Somali government initially supported the secession movement which, as an armed push for self-determination, was relatively short.[3] The government in Mogadishu withdrew logistical support after several years, and an agreement between Somalia and Kenya in 1969 formally ended the Somali government's tacit political support for the Kenyan Somali insurgency. The annexation of northeastern Kenya became a dead issue although *shifta* banditry in Kenya continued as an enduring phenomena, rising and falling with cycles of drought and political instability in the Horn.

Siyad Barre ruled Somalia from 1969 to 1991. Barre was known as an anti-nationalist, anti-Somali Youth League (the SYL was the organization at the forefront of the campaign for Somali independence) during his pre-independence tenure as a commandant in the colonial police force. He moved to the National Army after its formation in 1960. Lacking professional training, he used entrepreneurial skills, corruption, and the manipulation of personal alliances mirroring traditional patterns of clan interaction to advance his military career. The country's first president, Aden Abdalla Osman, was voted out in 1967. In 1969 a clique of army officers engineered the shift to military rule, replacing the popularly elected Somali government. Barre emerged at the head of the council of officers, and hung onto power tenaciously until driven out of the capital on January 26, 1991 by the joint forces of the United Somali Congress (USC) and the Somali Patriotic Movement (SPM).

Barre adopted an aggressive policy of scientific socialism and banned manifestations of traditional clanism in word and deed. Ideological differences and Somalia's strong links with the Eastern Block had kept Kenya-Somali relations on a tentative footing during the 1970s. The strained character of Kenya-Somalia relations during the Kenyatta era reinforced the discriminatory treatment of Kenya's ethnic Somalis. Periodic episodes like the revenge killings of several Kenyan civil servants by a notorious individual associated with *shifta* in 1978 precipitated a wave of retaliation against Kenya Somalis, and Kenyans of Somali origin have been the objects of a series of state polices over the years not extended to the population in general.[4]

Barre's hard-core socialism waned, and the Somali-Kenya relationship gradually improved after Moi succeeded to power in 1978. Moi diluted the strength of Kenyatta's entrenched power structure by increasing minority communities' political role in the government. The broadening of participation and state resource distribution extended some benefits to long-neglected Somali areas. The attempted air force coup of 1982 provided the turning point in the Somali community's relationship to the government. Major-General Mahmoud Mohamed, a veteran of the Kenya Army's anti-*shifta* campaigns, led the counterattack that ended the senior private-led cabal's short-lived reign of confusion in Nairobi; his loyalty and valor earned him credit for almost single-handedly saving the Moi government. He was placed in charge of the new "1982 Air Force," and his brother, Maalim Mohamed, was made a Minister of State in recognition. Somalis subsequently became more visible in the state administrative structure and civil service, and Kenya Somalis' *de facto* second class citizen status generally improved during the 1980s.

The elevation of Mahmoud and Maalim Mohamed had long-term ramifications for the state of Somali embedded lineage principles in Kenya. Members of the Mohamed brother's Ogaden clan were the principal beneficiaries of the government favors bestowed upon Kenyan Somalis. The Ogaden also occupied a central position in the greater Darood clan confederacy, which includes Barre's Marehan clan. The Somali President was personally affiliated with the Ogaden via his mother, and Somalis coined the term M-O-D alliance in reference to the prominent role of the Marehan, Ogaden, and Darood Dulbahante clan in the government of Somalia. The Kenya-Somali Ogaden linkage thus reinforced the positive trajectory of relations between Moi's and Barre's governments, but also planted the seed of Somali clan dynamics within Kenya society.

The Barre-Ogaden linkage in the government of Somalia had also been an instrumental factor in the first covert, then unconcealed support for the Western Somali Liberation Front (WSLF), which was formed to fight for Ogaden self-determination. The Ogaden conflict appears peripheral to Kenya Somali affairs during the 1990s, but the Ogaden War was the single most important event leading to the disintegration of the modern Somali polity. Recounting the chain of events precipitated by the Somali invasion of the Ogaden in 1977 provides the critical backdrop necessary for grasping the distinct Somali social dynamics that expanded to fill the social gap created by the collapse of the Somali state.

Unlike post-independent Kenya, independent Ethiopia was governed by groups historically hostile to the Somalis and never made a meaningful effort to integrate Somalis into national society. A series of commissions before Somali independence periodically fueled local aspirations of reuniting the Ogaden with Somalia proper. Ethiopian pressure insured that disputed borders remained outside the arena of international *realpolitik*. The Ogaden issue simmered in the background for a number of years while the region continued to be occupied by nomadic Somali Republic nationals who depended upon the seasonal grazing of the Ogaden in order to survive from year to year.

The WSLF was based in Mogadishu, and Siyad Barre handpicked its leaders and supervised its operations. But the Ogaden cause also enjoyed the universal support of Somali citizens, who were very much aware of its historical economic, social, and even linguistic importance as the home of some well-known national poets in a country where poetry is the national pastime. Ironically, this unified, cross-society support for the liberation of the Ogaden provided the political rupture that set the unraveling of Somali society in motion.

The 1977 WSLF invasion of the Ogaden grew out of the shifting international *status quo* in the Horn of Africa, following Haile Selassie's death in 1974. Mengistu Haile Mariam emerged at the top of the Dergue, the amorphous committee of army officers ruling the country after the revolution, after a conference room shootout in 1977. Mengistu then purged the Teferi Bante faction, who supported a more non-aligned foreign policy stance, and radically tilted the country's domestic and foreign policies to the left. The Carter administration cautiously shifted America's role in Africa's Horn region towards Somalia as Ethiopia emerged as Africa's premier Afro-Marxist state. The domestic turmoil accompanying Ethiopia's shifting internal configuration signified external opportunities for Somalia -- and the US government made known their intention not to resupply Ethiopia in the case of an invasion.

This amounted to a tacit green light for Barre's scheme, although open Western support was withheld in respect for the Organization for African Unity's (OAU) principle of territorial integrity. Western powers actually were prepared to give Somalia arms until Kenya, whose chronic security problems emanated from the Somali border voiced an uncompromising objection.[5] The WSLF initiated military operations in late 1976, and had the Ethiopian Army's Third Division on the run by June of 1977. Active support from Mogadishu in the form of Somali National Army regulars and equipment commenced on July 23. Soon the WSLF was in possession of the Ogaden and most of its towns and military bases, in addition to non-Somali patches of Arsi, Bale, and Sidamo. Only the Ethiopian garrisons at Harar and Dire Dawa were able to hold out.

The Somali military victories in the Ogaden contrasted with the Barre regime's inept maneuvers on the international political front. Barre's point men, appointed largely on the basis of nepotism, produced a string of public relations boondoggles. Somalia was diplomatically isolated in sub-Saharan Africa after violating the one article of the OAU charter -- the inviolability of colonial borders -- adhered to religiously by member states, and Barre managed to alienate potential allies in the form of the other Ethiopian liberation groups fighting for self determination. After openly supporting the invasion of the Ogaden, Barre blatantly lied about it in the international arena, giving the Soviets the excuse they needed to dump Somalia and embrace Ethiopia.[6] Barre's abrogation of the Soviet-Somali Friendship treaty on November 13, 1977 was a mere formality: the intricately planned Soviet airlift of troops, advisors and weapons to the Ogaden in support of embattled Ethiopian forces began two weeks later.

The Somalis never stood a chance against the vastly superior force, and by March 9, 1978, the Somali liberation of the Ogaden was history. Western powers limited their involvement to negotiating an orderly retreat for the Somali troops, thoroughly battered by the superior Soviet and Cuban forces. Hundreds of thousands of refugees followed their bloody tracks across the border.

The progressive, scientific socialism of Barre's Somali, for all intents and purposes, was also history from this point on. Barre censored the war's heroes from public recognition and largely left the wounded and crippled to their own devices. A month after the defeat, disillusioned officers of the Darood-Majerteen clan failed in a coup attempt, and were executed. Barre purged the military and recruited new troops on the basis of clan politics. After the war, Barre reverted back to a patrimonial form of governance. The armed forces were repoliticized, and friendship, marriage, regional background, business ties, and clan politics replaced the socialist ideology of the previous phase. Barre converted the three to four hundred million US dollars contributed by the Gulf States for the war effort into a personal slush fund. Barre rewarded clan-identified individuals that supported them while punishing those who did not. After years of institution building, the regime effectively shifted the process into reverse.

Barre encouraged clans loyal to him to establish armed militias, sowing the seeds of the current chaos. The circle of patronage increasingly narrowed to his immediate clan. The country's economy rapidly deteriorated. The economic boom in Saudi Arabia and the Gulf states, long a source of bilateral aid and personal remittances from overseas Somalis, was over. The country was saddled with large numbers of Ogaden refugees, and the international community was uneasy about aiding the regime.[7] Government machinery atrophied. The state administration was unable to respond effectively to World Bank and donor programs, and bureaucratic despondence and patronage forced much of the economy underground. As time went on any pretense toward administrative procedure was dispensed with: between 1984 and 1987 an estimated $1 billion in Italian aid went directly into the pockets of the Barre family and their Italian associates.[8]

Disillusioned members of the government defected to nascent liberation movements like the Somali Salvation Democratic Front (SSDF) based in Addis Ababa and the Somali National Movement (SNM) based in the northern homeland of the Isaaq confederacy. The government responded with a scorched earth campaign in the predominantly Majerteen inhabited Mudugh area. The north was to witness even more savage repression. Barre sent the army to the north to quell the SNM rebellion. Many Somali military commanders maneuvered to the best of their ability to exercise genuine restraint toward civilians. Not satisfied with a military victory, Barre hired mercenary pilots from Southern Africa to unleash aerial bombardments which killed tens of thousands of civilians and completely destroyed the town of Hargeisa and much of Burao. He intimidated the incipient Islamic movement by gunning down hundreds of worshipers as they were leaving Friday prayers in Mogadishu, dragged civilians from Isaaq areas of the north out of their homes in the middle of the night, and buried them in mass graves.

By the time he evacuated Mogadishu in a convoy of tanks and half-tracks on January 27, 1991, Barre was, in essence, reduced to the status of chief warlord of his Marehan clan. Repulsed by Mohamed Farah Aidid after a feeble attempt to retake Mogadishu, Siyad Barre and his personal entourage entered Kenya via the border town of Mandera with Aidid's soldiers hot on his heels.

The final collapse of Barre's government in January, 1991 presented both problems and opportunities for Moi's government in Kenya. The initial problem was the former Somali President himself. Barre's presence in Kenya was a daily embarrassment for the Kenya government, already on the defense because of its poor human rights record. Aidid's people showed their displeasure over Barre being in Kenya by shooting up Mandera on several occasions. Barre's entourage was sequestered in the Nairobi vicinity and his whereabouts were the source of rumors and intense speculation until a reporter with a telephoto lens exposed his residence at the posh Safari Park Hotel. Kenyans and Somalis alike were indignant when they found out the man responsible for his people's incalculable suffering was ensconced in exclusive 60,000 Kenya shillings a day haunts. The government's dilemma was compounded by the unwillingness of any other country to grant the Somali "father of knowledge" asylum. Nigeria's President, Ibrahim Babangida, eventually agreed to accept him in his capacity of "the current chair of the OAU."

The numbers of Somali refugees who began to enter Kenya in 1990 became an avalanche by 1991. The remains of Barre's tattered army, denied entry when the President's convoy crossed into Kenya, and highly mobile bandits, percolated across the border. An epidemic of bandit attacks that inscribed a wide arc roughly following the course of the Tana River from the northern Meru-Isiolo region to the coastal hinterland of Lamu District appeared related to the time required for the heavily armed former military to cross the sparsely populated arid rangelands of Kenya's Northern Frontier District. Kenyan security forces faced the logistical challenge of patrolling a long and remote international border, protecting the northern transport route passing through Marsabit to Moyale on the Kenya-Ethiopia border, and the vulnerable band of agricultural settlements stretching from eastern Ukambani to the coast.

Arrangements for the refugees themselves, in contrast, were handled mainly by international donors and various private voluntary organizations. The humanitarian refugee operations channeled resources that bolstered the sagging national economy. The emergency generated opportunities within the local transport, communications, and service sectors. Nairobi served as the base for a spectrum of relief organizations serving Kenya and most of Somalia itself. At its height the Somali crisis commanded one quarter of the International Committee of the Red Cross (ICRC) total budget. A sizeable portion of this and other international funds were spent in Kenya.

The financial flows accompanying the stream of refugees did not, however, alter the government's negative attitude towards the refugees themselves, which included Sudanese and Ethiopians in addition to the estimated 800,000 Somalis asylumed in the country in 1992. A select number of Somali citizens obtained Kenyan papers during the post-political pluralism campaign to boost the members of Kenya's ruling party, KANU. But little official action was taken as the reported cases of abusive and exploitive behavior perpetuated by security forces assigned to camps grew, reflecting the Kenya government's unconcealed desire to limit the stay of most refugees to the shortest term possible. The evidence for government hostility included policies of forcible repatriation, forced removal to camps, detention without charges or trial, and incidents of torture, beatings, killings, and rape by the security forces.[9] The extra population within Kenya's borders increased the demand for commodities already in short supply,[10] compounded existing security problems in rural and urban areas, and carried implications for a host of other long-term problems.

The adaptive capacity of Somali society in general often provides a marked contrast to the actions of the deceased Somali state, the United Nations, and the other nation-states that intervened into Somali affairs. There is, nevertheless, an organizational threshold that appears to act as an invisible barrier separating societal and state level processes. The incongruity of these domains embodies the essential quandary of the contemporary Somali condition. The specific qualities of the Somali diaspora in Kenya (and beyond) engendered a complex set of economic, ethnic, and political ramifications. The consequences cannot be represented in the broad macro state-formal sector -- statistical picture alone.

The war in southern Somalia highlighted the negative aspects of what the Somali scholar, Said S. Samatar of Rutgers University has described as "the schizophrenic social world" of the Somali. Samatar elaborates by referring to this as a social-biological configuration which imbues the Somali social universe with "an eerie Alice in Wonderland flavor of deception and hypocrisy," simply because an individual's best intentions and otherwise rational behavior is highly susceptible to corporate group pressure predicated on the geneo-socio-political logic of segmentary lineage. But outside Somalia, this underlying structure of Somali society functioned as a rather impressive and autocatalytic support system operating across several continents.

Members of the same *jilib*, subclan or sublineage units, retain especially strong reciprocal obligations to relatives, even if they are complete strangers who might share a common ancestor five or six generations removed. Consistent with its influence on many other aspects of Somali behavior, the segmentary system of kinship conditioned the movements of individuals comprising the exodus out of war-torn Somalia. The refugees themselves were a far from homogeneous population, many of whom were not in camps in the first place. This segment of the Somali refugee population in Kenya exerted the most complicated impact on the country.

III. The View From Kenyan Society: Nairobi

Kenyans were not as put off by the refugee invasion as one might expect, based on past civil relations. On the down side, there was increased banditry in parts of the country, additional competition for housing in Nairobi and Mombasa, and dollar-bearing refugees exerting upward pressure on the prices of a number of basic commodities in limited supply. On the upside, there were new business and employment opportunities and a general recognition that helping the victims of maladaptive governments was a moral obligation, and in view of the country's own internal conflicts, good karma as well. Kenyans could empathize with the refugees' plight, and wondered where they would flee themselves if the same calamity was visited upon them.

Refugees outside the camps generally paid their own way, circulating a significant portion of Somalia's foreign exchange into the Kenyan economy. Despite the association of Somalis with the "*shifta*" highwaymen in the bush, who preyed on Kenyans and Somalis alike without discrimination, the refugees were generally a well behaved and self-policing crowd. This, however, did not mean that the displaced Somalis ending up in Kenya did not leave the "schizophrenic," and other distinctive features of their culture behind them in Somalia. Proper examination of the manifestations emerging out of the intersection of Somali culture and the Kenyan environment entails further disaggregation of the Somali impact according to specific places and groups in Kenya.

The Somali refugees can be separated into three main categories. The wealthy urban dwellers, including well-off Hawiye businessmen from Mogadishu or Barre's Marehan kinspeople, found residence in Hurlingham and other upscale sections of Nairobi. Urban Somalis in East Africa are predominantly members of the Majerteen, Ogaden, and various Isaaq clans, and this served as a magnet for civilians fleeing the chaos in Mogadishu and the southern region of Somalia. Those refugees, fortunate to have some kind of clan or lineage connection with Kenyan Somalis congregated in Nairobi's Eastleigh area, already a major node within the Somali world network. Darood Somalis in particular were able to console themselves with the observation that, although they had lost the government in Mogadishu, they still had a "government chair" in Nairobi.[11] The poorest refugees, i.e., unconnected individuals or members of the "lower status" groups like the Rahanweyn, ended up in camps like Liboi and Utange.

Somalis refer to the internationalized city of Nairobi as "Half-London." In 1992 the downtown population of Half-London appeared to be at times half Somali, as refugees congregated around cafes and the Jamia mosque. People began calling the middle income Nairobi West housing estates "Mogadishu West." But it was lower middle class Eastleigh that naturally became the main base in Kenya for the Somali diaspora. The main part of Eastleigh, sections one and two, is a relatively compact grid some twenty blocks long and four blocks wide hosting the ethnic diversity of places like East London and culinary variety of Chicago's Clarke Street within a combined African truck stop, outdoor market settings.[12] Eastleigh was formerly a barrio of one-story, Bombay style flats, outdoor "jua kali" garages,[13] wooden kiosks manned by Nyambene Meru *miraa* (also known as *khat*) traders, with long distance double trailer lorries lining the streets. During the height of the influx, most every Somali household was overflowing with refugees. Lodgings were clogged with refugees willing to pay premium prices in foreign currency for housing. The refugees filled the mosques, chewed *miraa*, and congregated in large groups on various streets according to clan affiliations. The dollars they dumped into Eastleigh began to circulate. The large clothing market that sprang up on Wood Street, in the rear of section two, changed the area into a sprawling indoor-outdoor mall. Since the refugee influx, the ultimately unsustainable hospitality extended to refugees has slackened, while construction of numerous, stylish multi-story apartment buildings and refurbished business premises are beginning to give Eastleigh a slightly up-scale facade.

Social and economic interaction is not restricted to the greater Somali community. For one, the socially leveling institution of *miraa* consumption is known to facilitate interaction among individuals of diverse cultural, religious and economic backgrounds. Local businesses, many of which are Gikuyu owned, raked in profits. Entrepreneurs started Swahili classes for the refugees using simulations of real-life situations to teach students how to talk their way through police checks and barter in markets and shops. As the refugees became more integrated into their new environment, the local settings reassumed an appearance of normalcy. Then something happened to provoke a major police swoop that swept many refugees into a makeshift camp set up at the end of a runway at Jomo Kenyatta International Airport.

In August of 1992, a hand grenade concealed in a large tin of ghee exploded, damaging a lorry traveling from Garissa in Northeastern Province to Nairobi. The Rift Valley ethnic cleansing campaigns, targeting mainly Gikuyu farmers settled in Kalenjin areas to the west of Nakuru, were still festering when the incident alerted the authorities that the evolving Somali-Gikuyu commercial symbiosis very likely involved other cases of weapons smuggling. The sudden police deployment rounded up many unsuspecting Somalis in Nairobi neighborhoods who had grown accustomed to the *carte blanche* freedom of movement outside the refugee camps. The unlucky detainees, subjected to the continuous roar of jet traffic at the Embakasi camp, were then put in lorries and transported to bush camps. Although some managed to "wander" out of the camps in typical Somali fashion, and others purchased their freedom before being forcibly removed from Nairobi, the action underscored the problems of seeking asylum in Kenya.[14]

IV. The Sijui Point of View

Segmentary lineages provide social structures with an elastic internal system for reinforcing linkages among populations accustomed to periodic separation and reunion. Comparing lineages is a basic exercise whenever and wherever members of the same Somali tribal confederation meet.[15] But integration into Kenya's multi-ethnic and economically diversified society has weakened lineage influences among many of Kenya's Somalis, especially the urbanized. Some can still recite their forefathers' names fourteen or fifteen generations back, but others get lost after several generations. Frustrated (or fed up) part of the way into the genealogical chain, they have been known to exclaim "sijui!" (i.e., I don't know in Swahili). Thus, Somalis from Somalia started calling Kenyan Somalis "Sijuis." In response, Kenya's Sijui Somalis began to call the Somali nationals "Walendo," a Swahilicized, Anglicized derivation for people from Somaliland.

Walendos consider Sijuis to be culturally diluted and linguistically impoverished by Somali standards; the Sijuis often describe Walendos as unsophisticated, provincial, and tribalistic by their standards. Regardless, the support system still functions wherever Somalis meet. Kenya has a substantial Somali population, and the different clans of the two main refugee tribal groupings, the Darood and the Isaaq, are particularly well represented in urban areas. In their case, it is only a matter of time for a Somali in Kenya to meet up with some close or distant kin. Once they do, they are almost guaranteed to receive the assistance they need: Somalis retain a remarkable capacity for sharing their resources with their near and distant kin in this respect.

In addition to the pastoral population who fell within Kenya's borders, many Somalis came to East Africa via recruitment into the British army, as employees of Europeans during the colonial era, or as traders. The roots of contemporary Somalis in Kenya date back several generations, and the urban Somali population in Kenya are thoroughly Kenyanized despite the strength of their own culture. Clan identity is strong, but the integration into Kenyan society has largely vitiated tendencies towards internal tribal antagonism. Some Somali households in Eastleigh welcomed refugees regardless of their clan affiliation, and cases of Somalis taking Ethiopian refugees were not unheard of. Even so, new tensions erupted among groups who were accustomed to attending each others' weddings and social functions as the "Alice-in-Wonderland" qualities of the Somali social universe, exacerbated by the politics of Siyad Barre and civil strife, reasserted themselves with the "Walendo" Somali influx.

On the other hand, the situation revitalized dormant linkages. The widening diaspora has also carried some of Kenya's "Sijui" Somalis abroad to Western countries where they enjoy better economic opportunities and become reintegrated into the greater Somali community. Over the long run, the movement of Somali actions reconstitutes the original unitary and borderless nature of Somali society, but within a more cosmopolitan and international context mitigating the primordial loyalties of clan and lineage. This new stage in the evolution of Somali culture in external settings may prove to be a positive influence and source of material support for Somalia's reconstruction in the long run.

The reconfiguration of women's positions in society is another important cultural development emerging out of the crisis. Women and children were the most vulnerable segment of society victimized by the catastrophe not of their own making. Women adopted a more activist role as it unfolded, and women's initiatives to preserve a semblance of civil society stood out in stark contrast against the factional struggle for resources and political control waged by the male population. Women took to the streets with their children to stage a protest march in Hargeisa when clan conflict threatened to shatter the fragile peace in the nominally independent Somaliland Republic. The action was effective, forcing the antagonistic parties to step back from the brink. Sheer necessity prompted expanded participation in the economic realm, relief operations, and other services. This expanded role is another factor supporting the empowerment of women.

Shifting gender relations provoked different reactions as events inside Somalia contributed to deteriorating relations among Somali men and women outside the country. In the Greek play, Lysistrata, women exasperated with their menfolk's warring ways decide to withhold sex from them. Some Kenyan Somalis and Somali refugee women take things a step further by abandoning their men altogether. The manner in which patrilineal lineages sweep individuals into the primordial maelstrom against their will is, for some younger women, only a minor factor supporting a trend to seek out prospects outside their community. One Somali woman summed up the situation for me in plain terms, "Our men are good at doing the negative thing."

The Kenya environment has always provided Somali women greater scope for social mingling and intermarriage. Freedom from traditional

Somali gender relations, the attractions of a different social universe, and other perceived opportunities motivated a number of refugee women, once in Kenya, to respond in kind. Overall, the shift in women's status is one element in the general trend of social change accelerated by the crisis. Half-London, however, offered the option of stepping out of defined social orbits and into the sometimes glitzy world of Nairobi night life. The small but conspicuously visible minority of refugee women visited clubs like Nairobi's Florida 2000 or Mombasa's Bora Bora disco, where the well-paid expatriate is a prize who can bring lasting benefits to the woman and her family. The Western administrators and relief workers coming from the war and starvation zones serviced from Nairobi who joined the eclectic collection of foreigners and locals mixing it up at night spots added a feedback loop.

The significance was not lost on Walendo Somali men. A woman seen in the company of a foreign companion on Nairobi streets was often taunted by loitering Somali males with remarks ranging from "aren't we good enough for you?," to "whore!" or simply "Christian!" While the Somali crisis heightened tensions in these circumstances, over the long term alternatives to traditional arranged marriages is simply one more factor contributing to the amelioration of women's status and not a threat to the domestic foundation of Somali society.[16] The increased scope for other Western influences, however, may increase polarization along religious lines.

V. The View From Meru

The collapse of the state in Somalia led to an increase in *khat* consumption among Somalis everywhere. The expansion of the market for *khat*, or *miraa (Catha edulis,)* as it is known in Kenya,[17] has had an explicit economic impact in the Nyambene Range of northern Meru where it is grown comparable in ways to the coffee boom of 1977-78 in other small farm areas of the Mt. Kenya region. The social impact of *miraa* outside Meru invokes parallels with the controversy generated by the introduction of coffee in Arabia and Europe several centuries ago. As in the case of coffee, which was condemned, vilified, and controlled by the elites before entering the popular sphere of consumption, the phenomenon is excoriated by many of those not familiar with it, and praised by many of those who are. While this is not the place for a treatise on *Catha Edulis* consumption, it is also impossible to talk about it in economic terms without some preliminary clarifications concerning its consumption, especially in the current Somali context.

Miraa is a tree indigenous to highland areas of eastern Africa. The leaves and tender parts of new twigs are chewed to produce a mildly stimulatory "high." New growth from the tree contain concentrations of two active compounds that stimulate the cardiovascular system, cathine and cathinone. Cathine, or nor-pseudoephedrine, is an organic version of the active ingredient in most sudafed-type cold medications. Cathinone is a stronger phyto-chemical precursor of cathine that rapidly breaks down into cathine after harvest. The quality and strength of *khat* varies according to climatic and ecological conditions, the variety (many consumers are poor at distinguishing among the three main varieties of domesticated *Catha edulis*), and the age of the trees. The best *miraa* harvested from hundred year or more old trees of the slow growing "dark" variety cultivated in Kenya's Nyambene Hills is the metaphorical equivalent of a fine cognac. The "white" *miraa*, especially when harvested from young trees, is more akin to a cheap brandy.

Khat is classified by the UN as a non-narcotic natural amphetamine. The effort required to untie, strip, and chew enough of the twigs necessary to achieve an effect makes a labor-intensive substance to consume. Typically consumed in a social context, it produces a mildly euphoric and distinctly mental high which stimulates intellectual discourse and tends to inhibit physical activity. The latter aspect leads many local critics to equate it with laziness. In contrast to the influence of alcohol, under normal circumstances a *khat* chewer is much more likely to talk about killing someone than getting up and doing it.

Khat was exploited by the Western media to add a sensational element to the tragic events in Somalia, where it was equated with violence. A news item in *Africa Confidential* at the peak of Somalia's civil war reported that "for the gunmen and soldiers in what is a violent society, chewing gives them a focused edge." The US Assistant Secretary of State for Africa alluded to it around the same time in terms of "teenage *khat*-chewing Rambos getting pumped up for early evening raids" on the MacNeil-Lehrer news hour. Combat versions of the Toyota land cruiser, the war machine of choice in Africa ever since Hissene Habre used them to rout a more conventionally armed Libyan-backed force in northern Chad in 1988, manned by *khat*-chewing warrior herdsmen created a situation one foreign correspondent described as "Mad Max in Somalia" in a broadcast carried by Washington, D.C. based National Public Radio.

The drug-driven crime hypothesis prevalent in the West distracts from a true understanding of the forces operating in Somalia, and the *miraa* factor in the Nyambene agricultural economy. Just as Toyota is not a defense contractor, *miraa* is not a drug of war. *Catha edulis* is the substance of choice for alcohol eschewing Somalis as well as many other Muslim and non-Muslim peoples in Africa and Arabia. They chew in times of peace as well as times of war.

Many Somalis display a phenomenal appetite for *Khat*, although a traditional Somali-*miraa* legacy exists only in the northern Isaaq-inhabited region adjacent to the Jijiga-Harar Highlands of Ethiopia. Perishability and rapid loss of potency limits the economic half-life of most *khat* to forty-eight hours. Hostage to the transport infrastructure, *khat* consumption was limited to the regions proximate to where it was grown slow until fairly recently. Demand for Meru *miraa* by the British recruited Isaaq soldiers who later settled in Kenyan and Tanzanian urban centers as businessmen and transporters were one stream feeding the growth of *khat* as a social institution in East Africa during the 1950s. *Khat*, a natural aid to the traveler, suppressing hunger, and keeping sleep at a distance, also encouraged its popularity within the Somali-dominated long haul transport sector.

Consumption is nevertheless comparatively new in the war zones of southern Somalia -- Mogadishu and Benadir coastal towns, and the south-central interior. Siyad Barre understood the urban Somalis' affinity for *Catha edulis*, and seized upon it as political weapon. Barre banned the import of *khat* in 1981, and then allowed political allies to smuggle it into the country. Soon afterwards Meru *miraa* was being collected at a depot in Kaelo, deep in the Nyambenes, sent by land and air to Mandera on the Somali border. Camels transported the *miraa* from Mandera to pick up points twenty kilometers inside Somalia. Army land rovers then sped it on to Kismayo and Mogadishu, where it was marketed by individuals from clans supporting the government. The warlords in Somalia ended up using *miraa* in the same manner. Both Ali Mahdi and General Aidid controlled *miraa* import and distribution to generate revenue, and at one point it was one form of currency distributed as a reward and as a lever of control over the irregulars forming clan militias. A dependent variable in the post-state Somali political equation, its absence in Mogadishu and other areas would change relatively little.

Fresh *miraa* at bargain prices, for refugees who consumed it as a luxury item in Somalia, ranked high among the attractions of Half London and the coastal city of Mombasa. Demand in Kenya rose accordingly, while the overseas expansion of the Somali diaspora expanded nascent *miraa* markets in Europe, Canada, and the United States.[18] *Miraa* is a relatively slow-growing tree. It takes five years to produce the first small harvest and isn't considered mature in Meru until it approaches the half-century mark. The rapid increase in exports therefore boosted the value of Meru *miraa* quicker than the supply, and added a new dimension to the pre-existing marketing network.

The varying physical qualities and physiological effects of *miraa* influence market demand for different types of Nyambene *miraa*. The external Somali markets for Kenyan *miraa* prefer the white and kithara varieties produced in recently commercialized areas of *miraa* production outside the core area of Nyambene production. This *miraa* is stronger in the purely physical sense, keeps better, and is considerably cheaper than the high grades of *miraa* exported from Muringene market. Consequently, the war in Somalia directly increased the income flow in several economically undeveloped areas of the Nyambene on the periphery of the dominant Muringene-Laare market axis. Most of the *miraa* for London comes from the Athiru Gaiti area, on the lower side of Maua, the chief Nyambene commercial center; the Antubetwe Kiongo area deep in the interior. Other areas near the Ngaya forest provide most of the *miraa* for markets stretching from the towns and NFD camps of Northeastern Province to Somalia itself.

Unlike the established Meru-controlled marketing network based in Muringene and Laare markets, Somali traders are the main exporters and retailers in the new markets. This limits local involvement to production and packing in these distant but lucrative markets. Somali traders well-placed in the Isaaq-controlled London/North American network and the Darood-Hawiye-controlled Somalia network have reaped sizeable profits over a short period of time. Income from a variety of sources feed these market networks: salary employment in North America, welfare and refugee allowances in the British Isles and other parts of Europe, and in Somalia, an undetermined combination of legitimate and illegitimate resources harvested from the UN and international donor agencies operations, the profits from cannibalizing the country's private and public infrastructure in Mogadishu, and more conventional economic activities.

Whereas producers receive a high percentage in the range above sixty percent of the retail market value in the Meru marketing network, they receive approximately twenty percent or less of the London retail value of *miraa* — wholesalers, retailers, airlines, and taxes divide the lion's share of revenues in descending order. The overall economic effect in the Nyambenes is most noticeable in rapidly urbanizing Maua, where Somalis have grown into a visible presence. Fleets of new pickups and cruisers grace the main road, the on-going building boom proceeds unabated, and a crowd of Somali casuals attracted to the *miraa* itself and Maua high life as much as the employment are a new addition to the growing population of outsiders attracted to the town's informal service sector. Economic diversification in the areas of traditional production is gradually decreasing the overall importance of *miraa* in the commercial economy. Other considerations aside, the Somali markets have more than filled the income gap created by the precipitous decline of coffee, and are extending the economic diversification process to less commercialized areas beyond the traditional *miraa* belt and tea zones in the Nyambenes.

In return, Nyambene *miraa* helps Somalis recreate their social milieu wherever they are. A Somali *khat* gathering in London or Toronto is indistinguishable from one in Eastleigh. In terms of social structure, the Somalis are among the most pre-adapted of peoples for coping with an event that has scattered them across the globe. *Miraa* functions as a kind of social glue reinforcing the octopus-like Somali social network, and contributes to the social intercourse that boosts communication across the geographically scattered nodes of the reconfigured lineage grid. As in the examples of other socially consumed substances that have evolved apace with socio-economic change, *miraa* has become more important within the far-reaching developments altering the traditional foundation of Somali society.[19]

VI. The Regional Political Economy Perspective

Somalia has influenced the development of the post-communist "New World Order" to a degree unimaginable before 1991. Even if we attribute the fiasco perpetuated by General Aidid and Rear Admiral Howe to the idiosyncratic qualities of the two protagonists in the conflict, Operation Restore Hope demonstrated all too clearly the inherent political liabilities for individual national leaders who venture too far beyond the strictly utilitarian perception of national interests. Policy analysts and decision makers are unfortunately reluctant to disaggregate the problems that mitigated against generating a lasting political solution for the Somali conflict out of international humanitarian intervention -- with extremely negative consequences for the portion of humanity victimized by political conflict in Bosnia, Haiti, Rwanda, and other disasters waiting to happen. The unresolved problems of Somalia will nevertheless continue to exert a direct destabilizing impact on the regional political economy of eastern Africa.

For Kenya, the endemic threat to internal security on its northern frontiers has been aggravated by episodes of turbulence in Somalia. Since the conclusion of the *Shifta* War, the incidence of banditry in the NFD, Tana River, Lamu, and the outer fringes of Meru has recorded upsurges following conflict in Somalia like the Ogaden War, armed insurgence against the Barre regime, and the post-state civil war. Enforcing security is aggravated in the large region of Mandera, Wajir, and Garissa districts inhabited by the Kenya's pastoral Somali population -- who often are on the receiving end from both directions. It is not a situation conducive to easy solutions.

Coping with refugees added a twist to the security headache. Now the government was responsible for protecting Kenyan Somalis and Somalis from Somalia from attacks by both Kenya *shifta* and Somali "technicals." For a number of refugees and Kenyans, who were also hit hard by the drought, the security forces were a third threat.[20] To make matters worse, a violent conflict broke out between the Ajuran and Degodia clans in 1993. Some Kenyan Somalis became refugees in Ethiopia, and the availability of arms and ammunition had prompted Ajuran raids on the Waso Borana of Isiolo District, who had entered a temporary alliance with the Degodia. Since 1960, the combination of Somali raids and government policies destroyed the formerly prosperous southern Borana.[21] Needless to say, the chronic instability in Kenya's pastoral north has checked most development activities for some time.

The new government in Ethiopia has attempted to deal with a similar situation in its eastern regions in a more positive manner. Ethiopia was on the brink of disintegration several years ago. The internal Ethiopian situation appeared worse than that in Somalia prior to the campaign sweeping Mengistu's government away. The new government's policy of devolving authority to the regions seems to be working. The state allowed the Eritreans the choice of independence, preserved the unity of the territory remaining within Ethiopia, and coped with the Somali influx in a more humane manner than in Kenya -- according to reports of Somalis who have passed through both countries. A Somali scholar who traveled across the northern areas inhabited by Somalis in 1993 reported that the Ogaden is actually the most dynamic and economically active area in the region.[22]

Many underlying causes of conflict and instability in the NFD can be traced back to colonial policies early in this century.[23] Kenya's reliance on violent security operations, like the Ethiopian policies which led to the Ogaden conflict, only exacerbates a situation that greater local autonomy and national participation has proven to stabilize. Appreciation of the benefits conferred by their Kenyan nationality displaced irredentist sympathies long before the unraveling of Somalia and the resurgence of clanism removed all doubts. Repression of Somalis of any clan or nationality within the country's borders and separate treatment of Kenyans of Somali origin only encourages the continued life of separatist forces and the possibilities of a hostile future government in Mogadishu.

The crisis in Somalia generates social learning that may yet contribute to national governance approaches more supportive of regional economic development. The unholy alliance formed by the involuntary prerogatives of cultural forces and the intransigence of political actors certainly lend weight to Basil Davidson's conclusions about the importance of popular participation following his highly distilled historical analysis of the nation-state in Africa, written just prior to the collapse of the Somali state (published in 1992). In Africa, participation in social and economic networks are a countervailing influence on flawed political structures. In any event, Kenyans and Somalis share a common perception that their problems come more from their governments than from themselves.

In the case of Somali refugees, interactions outside the camps initially based on internal kinship-based networks have exposed them to cultural forces and led to wider societal contacts within and without the Somali polity. If the experience is sometimes cloaked in the usual cultural rhetoric, the linkages represent a growing social grid spanning political and ethnic borders. The highly mobile and keenly entrepreneurial nature of Somalis in particular augurs for potential economic flows among the countries where they have settled. Kenya stands to play a role in the eventual reconstruction of Somalia just as in the relief operations. Meru-Somali relations indicate that exchange based on interaction fosters mutual understanding while a host state-refugee relationship poisons it.

The refugee crisis reinforces coevolutionary processes characteristic of historical development across East Africa to the extent that social and economic linkages can reconfigure the relationships between societies defined mainly on the state level during most of this century. Somalia is perhaps the greatest single example of a developmental disaster. Western intervention, encompassing both ends of the ideological spectrum, contributed to outcomes culminating in a country's self-destruction.[24] The performance of the United Nations throughout the crisis similarly underscores the cold hard fact that ultimately local actors will have to cobble together their own viable solutions for regional problems. Just as Somalia is discovering how hard it is to cure itself, locally led initiatives generating a positive role for external agencies may do more for steering the UN towards reform over the long run than direct attempts to cure its internal maladies.

Endnotes

1. The regional dimension of African processes was one of the points emphasized by Hopkins (1986) in an essay exploring the incorrect assumptions guiding donor strategies in Africa.

2. The arbitrary colonial division of Africa in the late nineteenth century partitioned the Somali population into five different regions: the largest portion of Somali territory fell under Italian control; the British took the northern extension of Somaliland to insure a supply of livestock for their base at Aden; and the environs of the port of Djibouti became a French enclave. A large slice of Kenya's Northern Frontier District, formerly Galla territory conquered by the Somalis

during the nineteenth century fell under British administration, and the Ogaden region of Somalia's western flank was officially ceded to Ethiopia. The points represent British and Italian Somalia, unified at independence, and the unliberated territories of Ogaden in Ethiopia, Kenya's Northeastern Province, and the former French enclave of Djibouti.

3. *Shifta* is a Somali word for bandit.

4. Political persecution against Kenya's ethnic Somalis is reported in the Africa Watch publication, *Kenya: Taking Liberties (1991)*.

5. Barre's support for the Western Somali Liberation Front (WSLF) invasion of the Ogaden was later buoyed by military assistance from Saudi Arabia, Iran, Egypt, an alleged US $7 million in covert assistance from the CIA, and German material aid in acknowledgment of the Barre government's role in freeing passengers from a hijacked Lufthansa airliner during a stopover in Mogadishu.

6. When Barre tried to perpetuate the sham in Moscow, Andre Gromyko simply pinpointed on a map the positions of Somali army units deployed in the Ogaden.

7. Engagement with the outside world was limited to the refugee relief operations and the "Access Agreement" with the US, granting the Americans use of the Berbera naval facility in exchange for US $93m, $40m of which came in the form of military aid.

8. References to Somalia's internal conditions over this period is based on Galaydh (1990).

9. *The Nightmare Continues...Abuses Against Somali Refugees in Kenya*. September 1993 African Rights Report, London: pg. 50.

10. *Kenya Economic Survey 1993*. Nairobi: Government Printing House.

11. This is in reference to the Minister of State, Maalim Mohamed's position in the Kenya Government.

12. Spatially separated Eastleigh Section Three has more in common with other non-Somali middle to lower income neighborhoods of Nairobi's Eastlands estates. Eastleigh Section Seven, bridging Section Two and California Estate, is smaller and more Swahilicized neighborhood. I have yet to hear an explanation that accounts for the non-existent Sections Four, Five, and Six.

13. The term *jua kali*, referring to "hot sun" open air workshops, has become coterminous with Kenya's informal artisanal and manufacturing sector.

14. Many refugees were "parked" in Kenya while waiting for the lengthy process of obtaining asylum in Western countries where they had family already living.

Interviews and other activities related the processing of asylum requests and family-sponsored immigration applications were conducted in the camps. As a result, many Somalis commuted to the camps, especially Utange, in order to establish a camp residence although they resided elsewhere.

15. Lewis (1969) provides the most detailed study of Somali clans and lineages in his monograph on the Somali, Afar, and Saho.

16. News of what goes on outside reaches Mogadishu as surely as the *khat* does, and the incident where a young gunslinger in Mogadishu fatally shot a Red Cross employee who invited a young woman to his quarters, ostensibly to feed her, is indicative of the resentment and potential fundamentalist Islamic reaction to the westernization accompanying foreign interventions in Somalia.

17. Here, the term *miraa* is used in specific references to Kenya *Catha edulis*, and *khat* in other more general contexts.

18. US customs made cathine, one of the active alkaloids in *khat*, a Schedule Four controlled substance (equivalent to prescription medicines) in 1992. Canada and some other European countries have enacted similar restrictions.

19. Schivelbusch (1992) explores the general link between social consumption and economic change exemplified by the adoption of coffee, tea, tobacco, spices, and the shifts in alcohol use. Aytoun (1956) and Hattox (1985) examine the evolution of coffee and society. Mintz's (1985) and Varisco (1987) investigate the same thesis as it applies to the social aspects of Catha edulis consumption, and Cassanelli (1985) specifically addresses the historical relationship between *khat* and Somali society.

20. *Op. cit.* Africa Watch 1992.

21. Hogg (1980) chronicles the problems of the Waso Borano beginning with their internment in government camps and continuing to the present.

22. Personal communication, Dr. Ali Abdul Rahman Hersi.

23. Sobania's (1979) history of the Mt. Kulal region mentions unchecked immigration of Ethiopian Borana, arbitrary "tribal" borders, and the contribution of selective taxes to a sharp increase in pressure on NFD land carrying capacities by the 1920s.

24. Hancock's (1989) searing critique of the development industry highlights graphic examples of the UN and USAID in Somalia's development disaster.

Bibliography

Aytoun, E. (1956, *The Penny Universities: A History of the Coffee House.* London: Secken and Warburg.

Davidson, Basil (1992). *The Black Man's Burden: The Curse of the Nation State in Africa.* New York: MacMillan.

Hancock, Graham (1989). *Lords of Poverty.* Great Britain: MacMillan London Limited.

Hattox, R.S. (1985). *Coffee and Coffeehouse.* Seattle and London: University of Washington Press.

Hogg, Richard (1980). "Pastoralism and Impoverishment: The Case of the Isiolo Boran of Northern Kenya." *Disasters*, Vol. 4, No. 3: 299-310.

Hopkins, Antony G. (1986). "The World Bank in Africa: Historical Reflections on the African Present." *World Development*, Vol. 14, No. 12: 1473-1487.

Galaydh, Ali K. (1990). "Notes on the Somali State." *The Horn of Africa.*

Lewis, I.M. (1969). *Peoples of the Horn of Africa: Somali, Afar, and Saho.* London: International African Institute.

Mintz, Sydney (1986). *Sweetness and Power: The Place of Sugar in Modern History.* New York: Penguin Books.

Schivelbusch, Wolfgang (1992). *Tastes of Paradise: A Social History of Spices, Stimulants, and Intoxicants.* New York: Vintage Books.

Sobania, Neal (1979). *Background History of the Mt. Kulal Region.* Integrated Project for Arid Lands Report #A-2. Nairobi: UNESCO.

Weir, Shelagh (1985). *Qat and Yemen: Consumption and Social Change.* London: British Museum Publications.

SECTION EIGHT

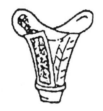

Horn of Africa Context - The Other Somalis

Summaries: Section Eight

Martin Doornbos (Chapter 31) traces the evolution of the Ogaden, in its political, ecological, social, and economic development. He describes a number of alternatives that might lead to settlement of the century-long border conflict: (1) adjust the borders through some form of internationally assisted negotiation; (2) seek the status of a separate state; and (3) create some form of decentralized and semi-autonomous unit within the context of a larger political entity, either through Ethiopia or perhaps some yet-to-be determined political unit. He suggests that whatever the solution, it will only be a lasting one if there is broad-based and intensive participation on the part of the people of the Ogaden.

John Markakis (Chapter 32) takes a different perspective from the previous articles. He looks at the internal politics of Ethiopia, somewhat independent of the variable of the Somali crisis. He traces the process which picked up the pieces remaining in Ethiopia when Mengistu Haile Mariam departed, with special attention to ethnic determinism. This process included the famous Addis conference of July, 1991, attended by 24 "nationality movements." The conference initiated a charter and governance model, based on ethnicity, which has survived violence, drought, famine, and election irregularities. Whether ethnicity is a long-term and valid principle for governance in Ethiopia, or whether it is merely a figment of the anthropological imagination, remains to be seen. To some extent, aging Somali dissidents found themselves running hard just to keep up with fast moving, Ethiopian events.

Peter Schraeder (Chapter 33), similar to Markakis (Chapter 32), writes of another internal political situation, this time in Djibouti. The specter of Djibouti seeking return to "Greater Somalia" looms in and out of focus, though for the moment, is a dead issue, given the demise of the Somali "mother state." Djibouti's primary recent political agenda, as determined by the Afars and Issas, has been the civil war (1991-1993). Schraeder concludes that President Gouled's persistent insensitivity to ethnic issues assures that the ethnic crisis and conflict will continue to simmer. The role of France and its troops in Djibouti is also discussed.

CHAPTER THIRTY ONE

The Ogaden After 1991: What are the Options?

Martin Doornbos

I. Background

To note that African state boundaries were demarcated in a highly arbitrary fashion is now virtually a commonplace which barely needs repeating. The same is true for the observation that during the late 19th century, the European scramble for territory left many population groups anomalously straddled across colonial and subsequently post-colonial boundaries, some of them subdivided or dislocated as a people, divorced from their traditional resource base or placed under hostile political powers as the case may be.

To be sure, the commonplace can be qualified by noting that there is nothing particularly "natural" about political boundaries anywhere, and that also in Europe, and elsewhere, boundaries have usually come into existence as the outcome of power confrontations rather than on the basis of ethnological surveys or social rights. In many cases, also, processes of adjustment and accommodation to new state boundaries have been occurring, causing earlier divisions to become largely obliterated through new centrifugal forces and absorbed within changing political and economic frameworks. In other instances, however, the interventions associated with colonial partition and repartition of territories have indeed created, accentuated or magnified social and political differences and laid the basis for profound and long-term conflicts.

The Ogaden region between Ethiopia and Somalia, now Region 5 within the new transitional Ethiopian framework, represents one such case: both the particular historical conditions under which the issue came into existence and the long-term consequences which it has given rise to have made it one of the most problematic examples of colonial partition. Two elements have made the Ogaden question politically more severe than most 'ordinary' instances of arbitrary boundary demarcation during colonial occupation. One was the circumstance that the main imperial power concerned, Britain, in 1897, chose to negate its obligations to which it was bound by an earlier protectorate treaty it had concluded with Somali notables from the Ogaden, by ceding (without the latter's knowledge, let alone consultation) the larger part of the region to its (and their) main rival power, Ethiopia's Emperor Menelik, who had been pressing to get part of the territorial cake to satiate his own interest in imperial aggrandizement. To place these Somali-speaking people under Ethiopian control was not merely an illegal act in light of the earlier treaty, but given the historical relations between the Somalis and the Ethiopian power-holders, it would have amounted to a morally unjustified act even if legal constraints to the transfer had been non-existent. The two-line letter from the British government to Menelik at the conclusion of the arrangements requesting his assurance that 'these tribes receive equitable treatment' (reproduced in FitzGibbon, 1985, p. 128) illustrates the hypocrisy involved in the diplomacy of (re-)partition.

The second circumstance which, in due course, worsened the conflict, lies in the fact that the region has always been essentially given over to migratory pastoralism, requiring physical mobility for access to grazing and markets unhindered by political boundaries. What is more, migratory pastoralism traditionally involved not only the Ogaden clan, who might consider themselves the `true' inhabitants of the region, but also members of the Isaaq, another Somali clan which traditionally used to frequent the Ogaden region, specifically its Haud pasture areas, for seasonal grazing (Markakis, 1989). In this respect, anybody could have predicted that a situation in which the pastoralists in the Ogaden might be cut off from their natural productive resources would, sooner or later, give rise to serious conflicts -- which has happened on not a few occasions.

There have been many confrontations in the region over the years; the resistance of Sayid Mohamed Abdille Hassan and his Dervish troops during the first decades of the century; during the Second World War with Britain and Italy involved (followed by the 1946 abortive Bevin-plan to re-unite all Somali territories); and especially in the Ogaden War (1977-78) involving the Western Somali Liberation Front, the Somali

Republic and Mengistu's Ethiopia (with massive Cuban and Soviet support). The confrontations have been described by various authors (FitzGibbon, 1982; Lewis, 1980; Markakis, 1989 and 1990) and need no recounting here. Suffice it to say that they have immensely deepened and complicated the issues concerned, including the question of possible alternative solutions. Nonetheless, in light of the dramatic shifts that recently have come about in the international power constellation concerning the Horn of Africa as a whole, it seems opportune to ask what new options, if any, might suggest themselves at the present junction. This paper seeks to briefly explore this question and to throw up some issues for reflection and debate.

II. Current Context

Against the background of the failures of armed interventions, representative organizations for the Ogaden such as the Ogaden National Liberation Front, the Ogadenia Action Group, or the Ogaden Relief Association, today take the reasonable stand that instead of serving as a passive object in the exploits and conflicts between its larger neighbors, the people of the Ogaden should themselves be put in a position to determine what its future political status should be. Recently this argument would seem to have been strengthened by the EPRDF's declaration that, in principle, all nationalities within Ethiopia ought to have and exercise the right of self-determination. Also, the current divisions within Somalia and the potentially enduring division of Somalia into two, a northern (ex-British) and a southern (ex-Italian) part, would seem to underscore the same position. Cognizant of the current interventionist mood in global politics, ideas among spokesmen for the Ogaden tend to converge on the possibility of a referendum supervised by the UN or with EEC observers. Basic is the principle that `the people should decide'.

If one accepts this as a point of departure, two preliminary observations seem in order. One is simply to note that if there were to be any referendum or plebiscite, the `people' cannot give their vote or opinion without having a proper prior question, or set of questions, placed before them. The formulation of such questions, reflecting as they should feasible options among which realistic choices can be made, will clearly be of utmost importance. For example, a possible referendum might not simply ask questions like "Would you favor remaining with Ethiopia, joining Somalia, or having an independent state?" but may need to attach important modalities for each of these options or probe into additional possibilities. To arrive at any adequately considered set of questions and corresponding options will clearly require a concerted preparatory exploration involving intensive political and diplomatic pre-work,. It will also require "voter education" on the part of leaders of a body such as the ONLF, and perhaps others. In other words, the basic principle that "the people will decide" is, by itself, insufficient and must always entail a similarly basic responsibility on the part of the political leadership in investigating and carefully formulating options which might be put before a possible referendum.

The second point is closely related and is to note how the present, i.e., post-1991, political situation in and around the Horn may possibly allow for openings and opportunities which were not available hitherto. These changed, and changing, conditions need careful examination and testing on their possible merits for the future of the Ogaden. Essentially, the international situation has changed in three major respects: the decline of superpower rivalry and the support it entailed for maintaining the *status quo* between centralizing state systems in the Horn; a general re-emphasis on and relative support for decentralization and democratization efforts throughout Africa; and as of 1991, an entirely new situation in Ethiopia and Somalia, which, at least in terms of their internal political balances and conflicts, represent radical departures from the preceding contexts. To develop future options for the Ogaden, therefore, requires a creative approach which explores this new constellation and examines what new departures it might allow or suggest.

III. Alternative Options

Within the changing international and regional context, what options seem, *a priori,* worth exploring? First, for all their interventionist mood, the superpowers and the international community generally do not seem keen to intervene in order to correct a 100-year old border dispute. Not too much should be expected of this particular route. Therefore, superpowers will be less interested than during the Cold War when, in principle, there was always a latent interest in reducing the opposite camp. On the other hand, the international circuit can provide important support if there is a chance of arriving at a settlement agreeable to all parties concerned.

Second, in view of the failure, by and large, of the model of the post-colonial African state, the pursuit of a full-fledged independent state alternative for Ogadenia *prima facie* might seem addressed perhaps to issues and solutions, that rather pertained to a previous period and situation. It is doubtful whether there would be the necessary international support for such an entity, though of course it can be explored.

If other options fail, it will naturally be a last resort. Perhaps more than anything else, the idea of a separate state with its own standard apparatus, personnel and powerholders, rules and regulations and, again, demarcated boundaries would seem to militate against the basic requirements and traditional social structure of the region, which essentially calls for open borders and cooperative arrangements facilitating pastoral mobility and trade relations. Instead, intellectuals from the Ogaden could make a crucial contribution to the current thinking about state and society in Africa by focusing first of all on the non-state sphere and critically examining in what ways extensions and renewals of pre-existing political arrangements could be developed to suit contemporary requirements. This would add substance and meaning to the contemporary interest in civil society, and help redirect the African political discourse away from the pros and cons of the central state and on to the potential merits of non-state political processes and arrangements. Conceivably such re-examinations could also produce well-argued demands for autonomy and self-government in a variety of spheres vital to the particular economic and social processes in the region.

Third, it goes without saying that the changed political situations in Ethiopia and Somalia -- or the Somali states -- must be carefully considered on their possible implications for the future status of the Ogaden. Undoubtedly political leaders from the Ogaden are deeply involved in such reconnaissance efforts. Historically, it is a rare if not unique moment, and perhaps implying an important opportunity to see virtually simultaneous changes in two rival states which have both been laying competitive claims on the Ogaden. This coincidence necessitates testing the ground, not only on two fronts, but also in two respects. Naturally, one may want to explore to what extent altered orientations, especially in Ethiopia, might allow for a change of political status for the Ogaden into either a semi-independent unit or even a transfer. Equally important -- and perhaps more realistic -- will be consideration in what respects the newly evolving situation, especially in Ethiopia, may satisfy the needs and aspirations of the people of the Ogaden, and enable them to engage in self-organization and autonomous development activities as required for their particular livelihood strategies. Of special importance in this connection will be realistically to face the question of potential resource conflicts especially between the Ogaden and the Isaaq clans, and to try and devise arrangements which may sustain equitable access to markets and grazing lands for both groups. At this particular juncture in the history of the Horn, therefore, it would appear crucial to investigate (and negotiate) necessary safeguards as regards the kind of conditions which can be laid down in this respect. Perhaps with appropriate international underwriting and guarantees, a basic aim could be to arrive at essential decentralization and autonomy for the Ogaden.

Fourth, it will be similarly important to recognize that the differentiation of political functions and structures is likely to occur at different levels. Specifically, it is conceivable that the transformation of state frameworks in the Horn generally will be progressively articulated in an "upward" as well as a "downward" movement: the latter taking the form of far-reaching and substantial autonomy and international recognition for various regions. The former would point to the increasing adherence of the logic and desirability of having common services and institutions at an overarching level, eventually, possibly becoming that of a confederal kind comprising a wider range of semi-independent political entities. In recent times, some leading political figures from different Horn countries have been coming out in favor of such evolution. Both these tendencies, "upward" as well as "downward", are of key political significance for the Ogaden. Among other things, they might create room for a (modest) role of its own among and between Ethiopia and Somalia. Clearly, therefore, there is every reason for leaders from the Ogaden to support such developments, or to try and initiate the process wherever possible. Solely focusing instead on the tabling of a claim for a national state might jeopardize chances of any such wide-ranging transformation and evolution and could amount to setting back the clock.

Fifth, within a context of the Horn as a whole, various additional arrangements may be needed to reach the same objectives of substantial autonomy, freedom of mobility, and appropriate frameworks of resource mobilization and exploitation. The joint running of common services in border regions, as currently practiced between various European countries (for example, between the Netherlands and Germany, and between Belgium and Luxemburg) is one such possibility. In the same vein, a graduate student from one of the Horn countries some years ago was making a case for functional, not territorial, administration for the Ogaden, under the joint responsibility of the two governments concerned. The idea still has merit. One aspect of this could be the granting of dual citizenship to the people of the Ogaden, and to others frequenting the region, as suggested by John Markakis. Again, with suitable international support one might contemplate entrusting such tasks to an appropriate supra-national body, on the model of an expanded IGADD, the Inter-Government Authority on Drought and Development based in Djibouti, which might be called upon to administer this and perhaps other regions on behalf of a larger number of concerned parties -- Horn governments, UNEP, and possibly with some sympathetic donor countries in an observer status.

IV. Concluding Remarks

The present historical conjuncture appears to offer ample opportunity, unprecedented as well as largely unexpected, for the people of the Ogaden to participate decisively in shaping their own future and to play an active role within the region of the Horn as a whole. Conceivably, the Ogaden and its people might evolve into playing a significant bridging role between Ethiopia and Somalia in lieu of constituting the key bone of contention which for so long has been keeping them divided.

In light of the history so full of arbitrariness and injustice to which the people of the Ogaden have been subjected, the case for the right of self-determination morally appears to be a strong one. It is important to bear in mind that the right of self-determination is a dynamic concept. Ways of exercising it include "the establishment of a sovereign and independent State, integration with an independent State or the emergence into any other political status freely determined by a people" (Declaration on Principles of International Law, United Nations General Assembly, 24 October 1970). This right has not been effectively gained in the case of the Ogaden, but in the realm of international law and inter-state relations it is already an asset of some kind to have a case like the present one to pursue - one which might get recognition in due course. This also implies, therefore, that any possible preparedness not to further pursue the case of self-determination (which presumably should itself be resting on a broad consensus within the region and would, it might be agreed, itself constitute a self-determination of sorts) already should yield substantial concessions in terms of autonomous institutional development.

Above all, however, it will be well to remember that for all the attention and effort that might be invested in getting a hearing for the case, it is of equal importance to consider the question as to what should be done with it in the (as yet hypothetical) event that it might become realizable. Surely, any such possible scenario must call for a good deal of constructive anticipatory thinking as to what institutional frameworks - if any - would seem most appropriate and desirable with respect to the rather unique conditions of the Ogaden region. *A priori* one would anticipate that a good and imaginative plan would stand every chance of attracting the support, including material assistance, from the EEC countries, especially UK, Italy or France, while probably also qualifying for longer-term international attention in its actual operation and execution. The most important primary task, no doubt, will be to listen carefully and analyze what the people of the Ogaden themselves would see as their priorities, given their social and economic requirements and conditions and relationships with their neighbors, and to translate that into possible options which can be formulated in terms that can be put to the vote.

Bibliography

FitzGibbon, Louis. 1982. *The Betrayal of the Somalis*. Rex Collins, London.

FitzGibbon, Louis. 1985. *The Evaded Duty*. Rex Collins, London.
Lewis, I.M. 1980. A Modern History of Somalia: Nation and State in the Horn of Africa. Longmanns, London.

Markakis, John. 1989. "The Isaaq-Ogaden Dispute" in Anders Hjort af Hörnas and M.A. Mohamed Salih (eds.) *Ecology and Politics: Environmental Stress and Security in Africa*. Scandinavian Institute of African Studies.

Markakis, John. 1990. *Nation and Class: Conflict in the Horn of Africa*. Zed Books, London.

CHAPTER THIRTY TWO

The Somali in the New Political Order of Ethiopia

John Markakis

I. Introduction

With the collapse of its military regime which ruled between 1974 and 1991, Ethiopia entered a season of political ferment. The collapse signaled the defeat of forces that had dominated Ethiopia throughout this century, and made possible the political self-assertion of subordinate and minority groups. Whether the end result of this process will be a fundamental and historic change in the political life of this country is as yet uncertain. In the meantime, many political organizations have emerged to represent long suppressed population groups, and they are claiming a share of power in a proposed decentralized state structure whose constituent units are ethnically defined. Among them are more than a dozen organizations claiming to represent the Somali people of Ethiopia.

Given their history of alienation and irredentism, Somali participation in the process, with its declared goal of restructuring the Ethiopian state on the basis of self-governing ethnic communities, came as a surprise. It was welcomed by the aspiring architects of the new state who came to power in Addis Ababa in May, 1991. The Ethiopian Peoples' Revolutionary Democratic Front (EPRDF), created and controlled by the Tigrai Peoples Liberation Front (TPLF), had a blueprint of the new political order ready before it came to power. Theoretically, this is based on the TPLF's own avowed commitment to national self-determination. From a practical viewpoint, since ethnicity had become the dominant force for political mobilization in Ethiopia during the violent reign of the military regime, especially mobilization of opposition groups, it could not be ignored. The participation of the Oromo Liberation Front (OLF), whose claim to represent the largest ethnic group in the country made it a key player, hinged on this point; that is, political recognition and self-government for ethnic groups. The representatives of the US government, who also took part in the preparation of a new government for Ethiopia, supported a strategy designed to entice most of the existing and potential political actors to participate. Indeed at the time, an appeal to ethnicity appeared to offer the only hope of foregoing the political consensus required by the new rulers, if they were to rule Ethiopia peacefully, and the EPRDF embraced it.

The victors in the Ethiopian civil war went to considerable lengths to ensure that representatives of the main ethnic groups and organizations could attend the Democratic and Peaceful Transitional Conference held in Addis Ababa in July, 1991, a little more than a month after the EPRDF came to power. Although it was felt there was little hope to secure Somali acceptance, nevertheless they asked for Sudanese help to locate representatives of the long moribund Western Somalia Liberation Front (WSLF). The Sudanese found them hiding in the midst of war-torn Mogadishu, fearing Hawiye revenge for their long association with Siyad Barre's regime and the mindless violence sweeping the Somali capital. They were flown to Khartoum, where they met with EPRDF representatives.

The leader of this delegation was none other than Abdi Nassir Sheikh Aden, veteran Ogadeni nationalist leader who began a long career as a founder and director of the subversive Ogaden Company for Trade and Industry in the 1950s, and who had been Siyad Barre's Secretary General of the WSLF since 1983. Another member of this group was Ugas Mohammed Abdi, a veteran of the 1963 uprising in the Ogaden and, at this time, defense chief of the WSLF. In Khartoum, they were shown the draft Charter for the transitional government of Ethiopia, a remarkably liberal document which guaranteed not only the right of nationalities to administer their own affairs, but also their right to independence, if they so wished. On this basis, the WSLF veterans accepted the invitation to attend the conference held in Addis Ababa in July, 1991.

They represented an organization that had no real presence within Ethiopia after the defeat of the Somali invasion of the Ogaden in 1978. Controlled and manipulated by the Siyad Barre regime, the WSLF had become a pawn in the domestic politics of the Somali Republic, and the Ogadeni were enrolled in the clan coalition which sustained that regime. Offices in the WSLF became a sinecure for compliant veterans, while younger and more militant members left the organization in disillusionment and many of them went abroad. Disillusion turned to outrage when Siyad Barre betrayed the cause of the Ogaden in a *quid pro quo* with Mengistu Haile Mariam, the Ethiopian dictator. When the two beleaguered tyrants met in January, 1986 under the auspices of the Inter-Governmental Authority on Drought and Development (IGADD) in Djibouti, they negotiated a deal that was sealed with a peace accord between the two countries, signed in April, 1988. Siyad Barre sold out the Ogaden in exchange for the expulsion of the Somali National Movement from Ethiopia. The fact that the WSLF was not even able to register a protest destroyed what little credibility it had left.

Mogadishu's unsubtle exploitation of Somali irredentism in Ethiopia and heavy-handed control of the WSLF had always been resented by many Ogadeni militants, but their attempts to resist had never succeeded, thanks to the efficiency of Siyad Barre's security services. Many attempts were made to form what was called a "front within the front," but none succeeded. It was not until the final betrayal by Siyad Barre that defectors from the WSLF were able to form an autonomous organization abroad.

The Ogaden National Liberation Front (ONLF) is said to have been formed in the Gulf in August, 1984, but a public announcement of its existence was not made until March, 1986, in Kuwait. Its founders were members of the WSLF, and some of them were its representatives in the states of the Gulf. Sheikh Ibrahim Abdulah, the chairman, was WSLF representative in Abu Dhabi. Abdulahi Mohammed Sadi, its most prominent member, was WSLF representative in Kuwait. In February, 1987, Abdulahi distributed ONLF documents at the Islamic Conference in Kuwait, and the Arab press took notice of its existence. Soon afterwards, he was expelled from Kuwait and found refuge in Norway.

The initial ONLF policy statement defined the Ogaden as "an oppressed nation colonized by Ethiopia," and pledged to establish "an independent Ogaden state with full sovereignty in line with the aspirations of its people." This was a departure from the irredentist aspirations of the WSLF, and for the next few years the ONLF struggled to get out of the shadow of the older movement and establish a distinct identity. The gradual unraveling of the Somali state into warring clan fiefdoms created a conducive climate for a reassessment of the merits of Somali irredentism and the assertion of Ogadeni political autonomy. However, the claims sometimes made by ONLF supporters of the sudden birth of an Ogadeni nation and its aspirations for independence seemed a bit premature, to say the least. The ONLF had yet to make its presence felt, when the military regime collapsed in Ethiopia, and was not invited to attend the conference in Addis Ababa in July, 1991. It seemed also that the ONLF had yet to make up its mind about the unfolding situation in Ethiopia. Ibrahim Abdulah, its chairman, a teacher educated in Arabia, was against involvement with the new regime in Addis Ababa. In a public meeting in Amsterdam held at the time of the Addis Ababa conference, and attended by the author, the ONLF members present openly disagreed among themselves about the position of their organization and its relationship with the WSLF.

The Democratic and Peaceful Transitional Conference of Ethiopia was held in Addis Ababa during 1-5 July 1991. It was attended by representatives of twenty-four "nationality movements." A few of these had existed prior to this time; such as the WSLF, which was allotted two seats. Most of the others were formed in Addis Ababa on the eve of the conference, at the behest of the EPRDF. Among the latter was an "Issa and Gadabursi Peoples' Movement" which was allotted one seat. Representatives of a few multi-ethnic political groups were included to make a total of eighty-seven participants. The EPRDF had thirty-two seats, and with the support of the OLF which had twelve seats, was in full control of the proceedings. The main task of the conference was to approve the Charter for the provisional government of Ethiopia, prepared by the EPRDF in collaboration with the OLF. In the preceding month, the EPRDF had managed to present its objectives to the leaders of the main groups, and while most thought them too good to be true, they were willing to give the new regime time to prove itself. Indeed, they had no other choice. In the conference, only one vote was cast against the resolution that accepted the referendum in Eritrea, and four abstentions were registered on the final vote on the Charter.

The Charter provided for the establishment of a Council of Representatives, which was more or less a replica of the conference, although provision was made for the inclusion of a few more ethnic groups. Each ethnic group was allotted a number of seats, and these were divided among the organizations claiming to represent it. The only condition was that they accept the Charter, and that their representatives had not been members of the defunct Party of the Working Peoples of Ethiopia set up by the previous regime, or its security apparatus. Although they bargained for more, the Somali were allotted four seats, of which the WSLF took three. The fourth went to the ONLF, whose leadership had gathered belatedly in Addis Ababa.

Both organizations share the same Ogadeni clan base, and their adherence to the charter signifies an identity of political objectives. Understandably, they came under pressure to unite, and pronouncements to that effect were made on several occasions in the months that followed. They opened a joint office in Addis Ababa after the conference, and resolved to call an "Ogadeni National Congress." Later, Abdi Nassir announced the two had a "unified leadership" and were working as one (*Ethiopian Herald* 28/3/1992). In reality, they were competing for political support among the Ogadeni, although only the ONLF appears to have made much of an effort.

The first ONLF congress was held in the Ogaden in February, 1992. It chose leadership in the form of a central and an executive committee, and Sheikh Ibrahim Abdulah as its chairman. Being essentially an exile organization, the ONLF was conscious of the need to cultivate support in the region, and exerted some effort in that direction. By contrast, while it has roots and a clear image in the Ogaden, the WSLF remained organizationally moribund. Abdi Nassir Sheikh Aden toured the region to rally support, but had little help. For example, Ugas Mohammed Abdi, WSLF spokesman in Addis Ababa and one of its representatives in the Council of Representatives, made not a single visit to the Ogaden, a region he had not entered since 1964.

Having adopted ethnicity as the guiding principle in the design of the new state, the new Ethiopian regime faced the task of delineating ethnic regions to serve as its constituent units. Given the fact that more than eighty distinct ethnic groups have been identified in Ethiopia, this was risking the opening of Pandora's box. However, the committee set up to demarcate the regions had its task made comparatively easy by work done under the previous regime, which had founded an Institute for the Study of Ethiopian Nationalities to prepare a regional self-administration scheme of its own that never materialized. The committee's report was discussed in the Council of Representatives in November, 1991. It was adopted with some revisions, and a provisional map appeared.

Using mainly linguistic criteria, the map divided Ethiopia into twelve ethnic regions plus two regions for the multi-ethnic cities of Addis Ababa and Harar. Nine of the regions contain a number of ethnic groups, and they are divided into zones and districts designed roughly to fit ethnic criteria. Only three regions are ethnically homogeneous; Region 5, the Somali region, being one of these. This region includes not only the Ogaden, but the area in the north bordering Djibouti, as well as southern Bale and part of southern Sidamo. The last two regions had been the domain of the Somali and Abo Liberation Front (SALF), which had a mixed constituency of Oromo and Somali and a blurred identity, and operated in tandem with the WSLF in the 1970s.

Like the WSLF, SALF in the 1990s was a phantom organization with no presence in Ethiopia, but it was not forgotten by the EPRDF. It asked the Sudanese to bring Wako Gutu, the legendary Oromo rebel leader, and some of his companions from Mogadishu to Addis Ababa in time for the July conference. After being briefed by EPRDF representatives in Khartoum, the veterans who had fought against Ethiopian rule for nearly three decades were forced to consider the political implications of ethnicity, something they were never troubled with before. With ethnicity now the cardinal principle of political organization, a mongrel like SALF had no place in the new scheme. Consequently, the Oromo were forced to part with their Somali comrades and choose a name with a clear ethnic image. They divided, some opting for the name Oromo Abo, while Wako and others chose United Oromo. They went to the conference, and later to the Council of Representatives separately with these names.

The regional delineation was a fair dispensation, and the Somali had no cause for complaint. Indeed, Ugas Mohammed Abdi, one of the WSLF members in the Council of Representatives, declared it "a victory for Somalis" (*Ethiopian Herald* 29/1/92). Region 5, the Somali region, shares an extensive border with Region 4, the Oromo region, which is the largest of all. Overlapping claims were inevitable, and when it came to the elections, which were based on this scheme, confusion and conflict were unavoidable. The map itself was withdrawn to contain the conflict. However, for the time being, the lid was kept on Pandora's box.

To put the self-government scheme into operation, elections were held at the local and regional levels in April and June, 1992 respectively. Intense political activity, an unprecedented experience in Ethiopia, preceded the elections. Political parties, nearly all claiming an ethnic identity, proliferated. The lead was given by the EPRDF, which had no intention of losing control of the political process it had initiated. It quickly promoted the formation of affiliated organizations in most regions of Ethiopia, invariably named "peoples democratic organizations" (PDOs). The prototype was the Oromo Peoples Democratic Organization (OPDO), founded even before the EPRDF came to power.

In many areas the PDOs competed with factions claiming to be the genuine representatives of their ethnic group. A plethora of organizations emerged to represent ethnic minorities that found themselves encapsulated in regions dominated by large ethnic groups. Only a few groups were formed to oppose ethnicity as a political principle and to defend Ethiopian unity. It should be noted that nearly all these political factions were little more than coteries of urban petty bourgeois elements and intellectuals, mostly resident in Addis Ababa. The number of school teachers involved in them is impressive. Actively assisted by the resources of the state, including the EPRDF guerrilla army, the PDOs harassed and intimidated the opposition, creating an atmosphere of crisis, and finally provoking the withdrawal of many opposition organizations from the elections, the suspension of elections in several areas, and earning the censure of international observers. Not surprisingly, the EPRDF and its affiliates swept the elections throughout the country, except in the Somali region.

Probably because it was deemed a hopeless venture, Region 5 was the only one where no attempt was made to set up a PDO affiliate, and the Somali were left to their own political devices. They reacted characteristically by forming more than a dozen clan and lineage-based groups to resist domination by the Ogadeni clan. Thirteen had registered with the Electoral Commission by mid-1992, and some more appeared later. They included the Issa and Gurgua Liberation Front, the Horiyal Democratic Front, the Ethiopian Somali Democratic Movement which claims to represent the Isaaq living in the Haud, the Democratic United Party which claims to represent the Hawiye of the southern Ogaden, the Democratic Action League formed by Issa, a group representing the Rer Barre cultivators in Kelafo, and another representing the Shekash clan which is dispersed throughout the Ogaden.

Two other groups sought to rally support across clan and lineage lines on the basis of Islam, as their names signify. An Islamic Solidarity party formed around a well-known and respected cleric, and pursued a moderate course for unity in line with Somali political tradition. It accepted the Charter, and maintained amicable relations with other Somali political factions. The Islamic Unity party belongs to the modern militant fundamentalist creed, preaches world Muslim unity, and is linked to similar organizations in the region. Led by relatively unknown persons, most of whom are thought to have been educated in the Arab region, it clashed violently with other Somali political factions in the period leading to the elections, and ultimately refused to participate.

There was no lack of incidents in the Somali region during this period, and not a few lives were lost, including that of a UNHCR employee who was killed in Gode. Drought and threatening famine made the situation worse. Tension reigned in many districts on the border between Regions 4 (Oromo) and 5 (Somali). At least eleven districts with mixed ethnic population became bones of contention. Tension reached a peak during voter registration, when people were asked to declare their ethnic identity, and each side tried to reinforce its claim on the basis of numbers. No election was held in three districts because of ethnic clashes, while the results in another eight were disputed. The city of Dire Dawa is claimed by the Somali as the capital of their region, but this claim is strongly opposed by the Oromo, and both sides were asked by the central government to desist until after the national elections scheduled to be held in 1994.

A major breakdown was averted, and the elections in Region 5 were probably the fairest in Ethiopia. Certainly, they produced the most diversified results. Out of 48 districts claimed by Region 5, elections were completed in 37, each district sending three representatives to the regional assembly. Out of the total of 111 seats, the ONLF won over 70, the WSLF 9, the Democratic Unity Party (Hawiye) 9, the Ethiopian Somali Democratic Movement (Isaaq) 7, the Islamic Solidarity 7, the Democratic Action League (Issa) 6, the Horiyal 3, and the Rer Barre 1.

The regional council met initially in Dire Dawa where it was addressed by the Ethiopian Prime Minister, Tamrat Layne, who said the event proved that "Ethiopian Somalis are Ethiopian citizens of Somali stock" (*Ethiopian Herald* 26/1/93). He also advised them not to press their claim to Dire Dawa at that time, and the assembly chose Gode as the temporary regional capital. The choice of this remote and isolated location, in preference to Jijiga for instance, was dictated by the fact that it lies deep in Ogadeni country. The assembly also chose a flag and a symbol for the region, but not a name, because the preference of the majority for the name Ogadenia is not accepted by the other clans.

The assembly elected a regional executive committee of nineteen members. Twelve of these, including the chairman and vice chairman came from the ONLF. Abdulahi Mohammed Sadi was elected chairman, that is, chief executive of the region. Forty-five years old, he is a graduate of the Somali National University and has pursued further studies abroad where he spent many years representing the WSLF. Seven seats went to other parties, except for the Rer Barre and Horiyal factions. The members of the executive committee were divided into a number of committees in charge of regional affairs. According to the transitional scheme, only foreign affairs, defense, and external economic cooperation are excluded from the mandate of the regional government.

Decentralized schemes tend toward complexity and duplication. Region 5 is divided into 48 districts, which are the administrative units (*woreda*) of the former provincial administration. Each of these elects its own executive committee of nine persons, three of whom comprise the chairman, vice chairman and secretary of the district, while the other six are divided into two committees in charge of social services and development, respectively. A number of districts are grouped together to form zones, of which Region 5 has nine. Zonal administrative committees comprise members of the regional council elected in the districts within each zone. In order to enable the regions to fulfil their responsibilities, the central government proposed to transfer all assets, personnel, records, etc., from the central ministries and other state agencies to the regional governments. The chairman of Region 5 and other members of the regional executive committee spent the early part of 1993 in Addis Ababa searching for these assets and negotiating their transfer to the region. They were grimly amused to discover that most of the assets and much of the personnel assigned to the provincial administration of the Ogaden by former Ethiopian regimes could not be traced.

Finding trained personnel promised to be a major problem. Although little was said officially on the subject, it was assumed that regional administration employees ought, at least, to be familiar with the local language. Potentially, this could evolve into an ethnic barrier in regional administration employment. At any rate, there couldn't be many trained non-Somali Ethiopians who would consider working in Gode. Nevertheless, by mid-1993, the regional administration had managed to put together a skeleton professional staff of about one hundred Somali. The police commissioner is a former military chief of the ONLF. He is responsible for establishing an all-Somali police force under the sole authority of the regional government. The head of education is a former dean of the Somali National University. The choice of language, having been left to the regions, Region 5 decided to use the Somali language and Latin alphabet at the primary level and English at the secondary. So far, no provision has been made for teaching Amharic, still the language of the government in Ethiopia. One woman has been included in the regional executive committee. Asked what responsibility had been assigned to her, the regional chairman replied with a straight face, "industry."

The Somali regional government faces a formidable task in any field of development it chooses to embark. Even by Ethiopian standards, the region over which it rules is isolated and impoverished. Gode, the capital, is not even connected by telephone with the rest of the country, nor by any modern transport links. The only potential resource available are the natural gas fields discovered in Kalubo and Hilala south of Gode. Developed with Soviet Union assistance under the military regime, they are now part of a World Bank project that awaits the approval of the central government. The previous regime also built a 3,000 hectares cotton farm in Gode, and a dam for irrigation and hydroelectric power on the Shebelle River. Finally, there is a modern military air base at Gode built by the United States under the Haile Selassie regime to bring Somalia within reach of the Ethiopian air force.

The pastoralist economy of the region has been undermined by two decades of intermittent war, repeated and massive population displacement, the interruption of trade with and through Somalia, the influx of refugees from that country, and frequent drought. Famine was a constant threat during the past two years. No taxes were collected by the state during this period anywhere in Ethiopia, and the budget of regional governments was met by central government subsidy. From now on, however, the regions are expected to raise their own revenue through taxation, and this will present the government of Region 5 with a delicate problem, given the weak economic situation of the pastoralists and their strong aversion to taxation.

The region has already experienced its first internal political upheaval. In July, 1993, when the chairman of the regional council returned to Gode after a prolonged stay in Addis Ababa, he was accused of misappropriating funds granted by the central government to the region, and he, together with the entire regional executive committee were removed from office. A new executive committee was elected, headed by Hassan Jire Qalinle, an ONLF member and former pilot of Somali Airlines.

II. Prospects

There is an air of unreality about events in Ethiopia these days. The dawn of a brave new political world in this afflicted corner of Africa is something most people find difficult to take seriously. A number of questions hang over the experiment that is being tried. The first concerns Pandora's familiar box. Despite the fact that it is an essential factor in political practice throughout Africa, and it could hardly be otherwise. Ethnicity has never been considered a suitable principle in statecraft design because of its alleged divisive nature. The new regime in Ethiopia argues that what has proven to be divisive, in fact, is the attempt to deny ethnicity the political recognition it merits.

Given the proven impossibility of determining its essence, the first question -- insistently raised nowadays by a new generation of social anthropologists, whose predecessors invented the concept -- is whether the ethnic group in truth is a figment of the anthropological imagination rather than a social fact. In Ethiopia, the problem of definition has been sidestepped by making language the criterion of ethnic identity. This raises a second question, which is whether "ethnic" groups thus defined have the demographic coherence, social integrity, shared material base, and the political solidarity required to make them suitable building blocks of a larger political structure. If not, then intra-ethnic, rather than inter-ethnic, conflict is likely to be the order of the day.

Signs of this have already appeared in Ethiopia, and not only in the predictable political fragmentation of the Somali along clan lines. Similar splintering along regional and lineage lines, as well as religion and dialect has effected other ethnic groups, and it seems likely to acquire momentum as communities mobilize to fight for resources that are coming under regional control. Self-government is meaningless unless it produces tangible material results, and there hangs a third question, which is, "how can the poorest and least developed country in the world support what is probably the most complex, delicate and expensive system of government?"

These questions do not touch upon the intentions of the regime in power. There are many in Ethiopia who doubt its sincerity, and for them such questions are academic. According to one school of thought, to which most aspiring "ethnic" politicians frustrated by the maneuvers of the PDOs belong, maintains that the new scheme is but the latest ploy used by the Abyssinians of the north to retain control of the imperial state; albeit this time under Tigrayan hegemony. Whereas, the imperial regime invoked God, and the military trusted in Marx, the Tigrayans resorted to tribalism in order to divide and rule. This is the line taken by the Oromo Liberation Front, for instance. There are many others who reject ethnicity and regard the present scheme as the prelude to the disintegration of Ethiopia. They also see it as a ploy by the regime to retain power.

The existence and breadth of the opposition raises a final question, which is whether the new regime can retain control of the country for long, whatever its intentions might be. For example, while it managed to outmaneuver and reduce the OLF to political impotence for the time being, it is far from certain that it can win lasting political support from the vast Oromo population through the Oromo Peoples Democratic Organization. The same applies to many other ethnic groups. If it fails to do so, then it will have to resort to force to retain power, and the experiment will be over.

The Somali politicians in Ethiopia are sensitive to the manifold ambiguities of the situation, but they don't display any ambivalence towards regional self-administration. They appear determined to gain as much as possible from the scheme, and profess hope for the future. Only the Islamic Unity faction came out against it. Asked how he can reconcile a life-long struggle against Ethiopia with his present position in the Council of Representatives, Ugas Mohammed Abdi replied with his own question: to wit, "isn't this what we fought for all along?" Understandably, pan-Somali unity is not a subject fit for discussion anywhere these days. Moreover, if the relative strength of the ONLF means anything, it could be that irredentism is losing favor among the Somali in Ethiopia. That could not be simply because the idea at present seems farcical, but also because it had long become clear that the struggle of the Somali in Ethiopia for political freedom was futile as long as it was perceived as a territorial dispute between Ethiopia and Somalia. This was an argument used by the ONLF to good effect.

Endnotes

The data presented in this paper were gathered during the summer of 1993 in Ethiopia. Most of it came from interviews with persons referred to in these pages. Those who wish to know more about the background of organizations and events mentioned here can consult Markakis, J., *National and Class Conflict in the Horn of Africa*, (Cambridge University Press, 1987; Zed Press, 1989).

Note also that the following short item by John Markakis is an update on the situation of the Somali in Ethiopia as of the end of 1996. It is reprinted here with permission of the *Review of African Political Economy* (#70, 1996).

The Somali in Ethiopia: An Update

Persuading the Somali living in Ethiopia to shed their irredentist aspirations and the dream of Greater Somalia was a conspicuous initial success for the regime that came to power in that country in 1991 (see *ROAPE* 59, 1994). Undoubtedly, the disintegration of the Somali state itself had something to do with it. Be that as it may, the Somali apparently accepted the offer of self-government within a decentralized Ethiopian state and plunged enthusiastically into political competition for control of their regional government. They did this in characteristic Somali fashion: each clan produced its own political party, and soon there were more than a dozen. The Ogaden, the dominant clan in the region that traditionally bore its name, was initially represented by two organizations.

The veteran Western Somalia Liberation Front (WSLF), founded in the mid-1970s, was now overshadowed by the Ogaden National Liberation Front (ONLF), formed a decade later by defectors from the WSLF who had exchanged Somali irredentism with Ogaden nationalism and aspired to set up their own state. Two Islamic organizations also made their appearance - one representing militant fundamentalism, the other the traditional religious leadership. While both aspired to transcend clan boundaries, their support, as their names indicate, came mainly from the Ogaden clan. The formal name of the first is Ogaden Islamic Union, and of the second Islamic Solidarity Party - Western Somalia - Ogaden.

In the first elections for the regional government, held in 1992, the ONLF won around 70 seats and the WSLF 10 out of a total of 110 seats in the regional assembly. With an additional 7 seats won by Tadamun (Solidarity), the traditionalist Islamic party, the Ogaden commanded an absolute majority in the regional assembly and took control of the regional government. Both the president and vice-president of the region were ONLF members, and the Front also dominated the regional executive. The ONLF's commitment to the new order in Ethiopia was not solid. Its chairman, Sheikh Ibrahim Abdalla, a graduate of Islamic jurisprudence from the University of Riyadh, was reluctant to accept Ethiopian sovereignty, and stayed in Saudi Arabia. In his absence, Abdulahi Mohammed Sadi, a former WSLF member and one of the founders of the ONLF, became president of what was at the time Region 5. He avowed to test Ethiopian intentions and, if necessary, to exercise their right to self-determination. Relations between the two leaders were far from smooth, and the ONLF was riven with factionalism. By contrast, the fundamentalist Islamic group made no secret of its opposition to any collaboration with Ethiopia's rulers, and refused to take part in the elections.

The Somali claimed Dire Dawa, the most important town in southeast Ethiopia, for their regional capital, but this claim was strongly contested by the Oromo. The central government settled the issue by making Dire Dawa a separate self-governing entity, The ONLF then chose Gode, at the western end of the Somali region, as the capital. A remote and inaccessible township, of some 12,000 inhabitants, bereft of road connections and facilities, including telephones, it lies deep in Ogaden clan territory.

Hussein Mohamed Adam observed (*ROAPE* 54, 1992) that Somali society is obsessively preoccupied with "the issue of equality and recognition on the part of individuals, families, sub-clans, clans and clan families," and the most common *causus belli* of clan conflict is the rise of one clan to a position of dominance. Not surprisingly, Ogaden control of the regional government united all the other clans in opposition, and they set about to derail the newly-established regional administration. They took advantage of the fact that the regional leadership spent several months in early 1993 in Addis Ababa, arranging for the transfer of government personnel, assets and records to Region 5, and incurring sizable hotel bills and other expenses. When they returned to Gode in July, they were accused of fund misappropriation by the Ministry of Justice in Addis Ababa. The entire regional executive was replaced, and the regional president, Abdulahi Mohammed Sadi, was thrown in prison. When he was released on bail, he fled abroad.

He was replaced by Hassan Jire Qalinle, a former pilot of the Police Air Wing in Somalia. He had been elected as a member of the WSLF and switched to the ONLF afterwards. In February 1994, the assembly of Region 5 met in Jijiga, and in an outburst against alleged interference of the central government in Somali regional affairs, it voted to exercise the right to self-determination, i.e. secession. Less than two months later, Hassan Jire and his deputy were removed for "preventing the people of the region from enjoying the benefits of the transitional period" (*Ethiopian Herald*, 9 April 1994). He was replaced by Abdurahman Ugaz Mahmud, who had been director of the Relief and Rehabilitation Commission branch in Gode. An Ogaden clansman, he was supported by the members of the other clans because he was not a member of the ONLF. In August of that year, nearly all the bureau heads and their deputies in the regional administration were dismissed for corruption. Abdurahman himself was dismissed in December 1994 for "obstructing development projects" (*Ethiopian Herald*, 6 December 1994). The vice-president, Ahmed Makahil Hussein, also an Ogaden clansman, became acting president.

Needless to say, there was precious little sign of development in the region during these years. On the other hand, the political struggles intensified and the stakes were raised recklessly. The opposition clans strove to forge a united front against the Ogaden, encouraged by the central government's growing disenchantment with the ONLF. Initially, the government wisely stayed out of Somali regional affairs, and had not sponsored an affiliate political organization in Region 5, as it did nearly everywhere else in Ethiopia. However, it soon began to have second thoughts. Lacking firm leadership and direction, the ONLF spoke with many voices, some calling for secession and others for acceptance of the reformed Ethiopian state. The central government was involved in the removal of three successive Somali regional presidents, none of whom stayed in office more than seven months. A number of regional officials and ONLF members were also imprisoned. All were charged with embezzlement of funds, abuse of authority and sundry other crimes. This effectively crippled the regional administration, alienating the Ogaden clansmen, and provoked sporadic clashes between government forces and members of the ONLF. Itihad, which was threatening insurrection, eagerly joined the hostilities.

The effort to unite the opposition bore fruit early in February, 1994 with the formation of the Ethiopian Somali Democratic League (ESDL) at a meeting held at Hurso military training camp near Dire Dawa, which lasted three days and was addressed by then Prime Minister Tamrat Layne. He was accompanied by two Somali members of his cabinet, who became president and secretary general of the new party. The president, Abdul Majid Hussein, was educated in Ethiopia and Europe and had been an international civil servant before becoming Minister of External Economic Cooperation in Ethiopia. He is an Isaaq, a clan which has been feuding violently for decades with the Ogaden over possession of the Haud pasturelands along the eastern border. Samsudin Ahmed, the secretary general of ESDL, is a Gadabursi, and was a civil servant in Addis Ababa before becoming vice-minister of the Ministry of Mineral Resources and Energy. Neither of them had previous connection with Somali nationalist and clan politics. The ESDL claimed twelve clans, including the Ogaden, were represented in its Executive Committee.

The day before the Hurso meeting began, then President Meles Zenawi addressed a gathering of Somali elders and politicians in Harar urging them to cooperate. He pointedly warned that the right of secession was to be exercised "by the people and the nation, not a political party or clan" (*Ethiopia Herald*, 11 February 1994). Meles returned to the region in January, 1995 to address a conference on peace and development in Kebri Dehar. The leadership of most groups attended, including a delegation of the ONLF led by Abdirazak Tibba, a member of its executive committee. There they signed an agreement to keep the peace and participate in the elections. Itihad stayed away.

The Ogaden now made an effort to close ranks in the face of the massed clan opposition. The WSLF, which had come out unequivocally against secession, joined with Tadamun to form the Western Somali Democratic Party (WSDP) in 1994. The ONLF was invited to join, and a delegation led by Omar Nur, a legendary WSLF commander in the 1970s, engaged in discussions. They proved fruitless, however, allegedly because Hassan Jire, who had earlier returned to the WSLF, was made leader of the WSDP.

National and regional elections were held again in mid-1995. The ESDL contested all the districts in the region with candidates chosen for their local clan ties, and had the advantage of ample funds and the backing of the ruling Ethiopian Peoples Revolutionary Democratic Front (EPRDF). Prior to the elections, some Ogaden constituencies were merged, giving rise to charges of gerrymandering. The task of the ESDL was made easier by an ONLF split on the issue of participation. Having visited the region in 1993-4, Sheikh Ibrahim Abdalla returned to Saudi Arabia and remained opposed to participation. Shortly before the elections, a splinter group led by Bashir Abdi Hassan registered as the 'legal' ONLF and proceeded to contest the elections. That it was doing so under adverse conditions was made clear when the National Elections Board twice warned its officials in the Somali region not to obstruct the registration of ONLF candidates, and balloting had to be postponed for nearly a month in some regions due to ONLF protests. Familiar incidents were reported in the course of the elections; ballot boxes in some polling stations disappeared; elsewhere they were found full before balloting began. The results in three districts became the subject of investigation, and there was a storm of protest from the losers. Of the 139 seats in the regional assembly, the ESDL won 75, the 'legal' ONLF 18, the WSDP 15 and 24 seats went to independents. ESDL also won 23 seats in the Federal Assembly out of the 25 assigned to the Somali region, the WSDP 1, and 1 was won by an independent.

Now came the turn of the Ogaden to have a try at derailing a regional government controlled by other clans. The 'legal' ONLF and the WSDP members refused to take their seats in the regional assembly until the investigation of the results in the three contested districts was concluded. They claimed the assembly lacked a quorum because it mustered only 54 out of its full membership of 139. Ahmed Makahil Hussein, the former acting president who was re-elected in 1995, refused to vacate his office. He was arrested and is now in prison awaiting trail. Id Tahir, the new regional president, who is from the Isaaq clan, claimed that 76 members were in attendance in the first brief session of the regional assembly. The first act of the new regional government was to shift the capital from Gode to Jijiga in the east. A larger (about 30,000 pop.) and lively trade center, Jijiga lies outside Ogaden clan territory and near Isaaq grounds. Region 5 was officially named the Somali National Administrative Region.

The new political order in Ethiopia does not seem to have affected the categorical imperative of Somali political practice, which is clanishness. Opposition to the threat of Ogaden dominance is what brought the other clans together in the ESDL. It was to be expected that having gained the upper hand, the ESDL itself would become the arena for clan rivalry. In order to delay the inevitable, the League has not called a meeting of either its congress or its central committee since its founding. Although it is supposed to meet every six months, the regional assembly did not meet for the second time until September, 1996. Nor has the region held elections for local administration, as have the other regions in Ethiopia. Nonetheless, there have been several announced defections from the ESDL during this time. Marginalized in the new political order, the Ogaden clan turned defiant once again. With its leadership in prison or abroad, the 'illegal' ONLF drifted on a collision course with the central government. In June, 1996, an agreement was announced in London between this group and the Oromo Liberation Front, an organization that has flirted with secession and has declared war on the regime in Ethiopia. The two agreed to coordinate their activities in the "diplomatic, political and military fields." Similar agreements are said to have been concluded with Itihad and the Islamic Front for the Liberation of Oromia.

It was also inevitable that Isaaq prominence would make it the target of other clans. On 8 July 1996, there was an attempt to assassinate the ESDL chairman, Abdul Majid Hussein. He survived multiple wounds, while two of his bodyguards were killed. A spokesman for Itihad in Mogadishu claimed the fundamentalist group was responsible. Afterwards, the Ethiopian authorities arrested numerous Ogaden political activists, including members of the regional assembly. Among the latter were Sheikh Abdi Nassir Sheikh, the long-time secretary general of the WSLF, and Colonel Ibrahim Aden Dolal, former political commissioner of the Somali armed forces. All told, six regional assembly members are in prison in Jijiga.

Itihad appears to be the main problem for the Ethiopian government, which blames this fundamentalist group for attacks against its soldiers in the Ogaden and several hotel bombings in Addis Ababa and other towns. Itihad is closely linked to its sister movement in Somalia, whose stronghold is the Gedo region in southern Somalia across the border from Ethiopia. Itihad established bases there to carry out crossborder raids into the Ogaden. Ethiopians know from long experience that it is futile to chase guerrilla bands in this vast, arid region, if they find sanctuary on the other side of the border. Consequently, the Ethiopians recently carried the fight into the Gedo region with ground and air attacks. They seemed to have found an ally in the Somali National Front, a Marehan clan organization which competes with the fundamentalists for control of Gedo. Tragically, the dark shadow of war is falling once more over the Ogaden, a region that has known little peace for more than three decades.

CHAPTER THIRTY THREE

Origins and Unfolding of the Civil War in Djibouti

Peter J. Schraeder

I. Introduction

In November, 1991, the outbreak of civil war shattered the metaphor of Djibouti as the "eye of the hurricane" in the Horn of Africa. Amidst growing pressures for democratization and rising popular dissatisfaction with an increasingly authoritarian regime headed by Hassan Gouled Aptidon, the Front pour le Restauration de l'Unité et la Democratie (FRUD -- Front for the Restoration of Unity and Democracy) launched a military offensive that led to the capture and control of a significant portion of national territory. Nineteen months later, a counter-offensive led by the significantly expanded Djiboutian Armed Forces successfully broke the military back of the FRUD and led to the reestablishment of central government control over the majority of its territory.

As is the case with victors in the aftermath of most conflicts, either civil or international, the Gouled regime continues to present a self-serving version of what occurred in Djibouti from November, 1991 to July, 1993. Specifically, the Gouled regime has sought to rewrite history by claiming that the opposition forces simply constituted "bandits" or "terrorists" who at best were engaged in what can be characterized as an "insurrection" or a "rebellion," as opposed to a legitimate opposition military force that had been involved in a civil war.

What at first glance may seem to constitute a rather innocuous terminological debate has significant international implications, most notably within the economic realm. For example, several companies -- especially those owned by current or past members of the Gouled regime -- are currently seeking insurance payouts from Western-based insurance companies for installations destroyed during the civil war.

If it is determined that a state of civil war existed in Djibouti at the time that these installations were destroyed, some of these insurance companies are not liable and no payments will be made. To the contrary, if what occurred in Djibouti was the act of terrorists or bandits, individuals -- some legitimate and some not -- stand to benefit. Terminology, thus, plays an important role in both the political and economic historiography of Djibouti.

The primary purpose of this paper is to explore the origins and unfolding conflict in Djibouti from 1977 to 1994, with a special focus on explaining why the level of hostilities from November, 1991 to July, 1993 did indeed constitute a civil war in the international legal sense of the term. Nine "war-risk" terms are mentioned throughout the article, particularly within the conclusion, and are based on an analysis of international legal texts and dictionaries. These eight terms include (1) mutiny; (2) sabotage; (3) terrorism; (4) coup d'etat; (5) ethnic conflict; (6) insurrection; (7) rebellion; (8) revolution; and (9) civil war.

II. The Ethnic Dimension of Djiboutian Politics

Djibouti is an ethnically diverse country where population statistics are subject to controversy and range from conservative estimates of roughly 330,000 to official Djiboutian government estimates of 520,000. The Afar and Issa peoples comprise the two dominant ethnic groups which historically inhabited the territory. A subgroup of the Somali people, the Issas constitute the largest ethnic group (roughly 33 percent of the population) and inhabit the southern one-third of the country below the Gulf of Tadjoura and east of the Djibouti-Addis Ababa railway. Divided by the arbitrary imposition of colonial borders, the Issa people spill over into both the secessionist Somaliland Republic (the northern portion of Somalia that declared its independence in 1991) and Ethiopia where they number 50,000 and 230,000, respectively.

The Afars, also known as the Danakil, constitute the second largest ethnic group (roughly 20 percent of the population) and inhabit the northern two-thirds of the country above the Gulf of Tadjoura and west of the Djibouti-Addis Ababa railway. Also divided by ill-conceived colonial boundaries, the Afars spill over into the southern portion of the territory controlled by the Republic of Eritrea and extend westward as far as the Ethiopian town of Nazreth in numbers that surpass 600,000. The territory inhabited by the Afar peoples in the Horn of Africa is often referred to as the "Afar triangle."

The remainder of Djibouti's population is divided among five major groups (largely living in Djibouti City) which were not historically indigenous to the area. The Gadaboursis (15 percent) and Isaaqs (13.3 percent), also subgroupings of the Somali peoples, migrated from northern Somalia during the twentieth century. They were attracted by work associated with the construction of the Djibouti-Addis Ababa railway and the expansion of the port at Djibouti City. Arabs, particularly Yemenis, constitute a third major group. Largely working in the commercial sector of Djibouti City, they constitute approximately 6 percent of the overall population. A fourth group, comprising approximately 4 percent of the population, includes a large number (roughly 10,000) of French and other European nationals who work at nearly all administrative levels of the Djiboutian government. Of particular significance are the nearly 3,500 French troops and family members (a total of 6,000) maintained by the French government on Djiboutian territory since independence in 1977. Finally, fluctuating numbers of refugees and illegal economic migrants from both Ethiopia and Somalia have periodically comprised upwards of 10-15 percent of the country's population at any given time. This final grouping has strained the limited capacities of the Djiboutian government, contributing to often acrimonious political debates and international controversy.

In addition to sharing a common nomadic tradition that places a high value on livestock and virtues of bravery and individualism, a strong adherence to the Islamic faith, and an oral tradition that holds singers and poets in high esteem, the country's two dominant ethnic groups -- the Afars and the Issas -- have maintained strong social networks that form the basis of everyday life, especially within the rural areas. The Issas maintain an especially egalitarian form of social organization based on clan membership in which all "men" are considered equal, and each has the right to voice his opinion about the affairs of his clan. As such, decisions are arrived at through consensus. The Issas are divided into three major clan families, two of which are further subdivided by several subclans. The Abgal clan family, which accounts for three-quarters of all Issas in the Horn of Africa and two-thirds of those living in Djibouti, includes the following four sub-clans: Yonis-Moussa, Saad-Moussa, Mamassan and Ourweine. The Dalol clan family, which accounts for only one-fourth of all Issas and roughly one-third of those living in

Djibouti, is similarly divided among three sub-clans: the Fourlaba, Horrone, and Walaldon. The Wardick constitutes the final Issa clan family represented in Djibouti, and is believed to be the result of mixed Somali/Afar unions. Although very few in number, the Wardick derive their prestige from the fact that the Ugas, the spiritual leader of the Issa group, is chosen from this clan family.

Despite a similar emphasis on clan membership as the basis for everyday life, the Afar maintain a hierarchical form of social organization that derives from traditional chiefdoms and sultanates, such as the still existing Tadjoura Sultanate. Decisions and debate among the Afars, unlike among the more egalitarian Issas, are more the reserve of recognized leaders and the heads of clans. For example, the sultans of Afar sultanates historically made decisions based on the advice of viziers and councils composed of the heads of sub-clans and notables. In this regard, there is an important distinction between the so-called "noble" Asaihimera ("red") clans and the lowland Adohimera ("white") clans. Among the five major clans represented in Djibouti are the Adarassoul and the Debne, both of which are prevalent in the Dikhil region; the Adail and Badoita-Mela, which are located in the region of Obock; and the Hassoba, which is representative of the Tadjoura region.

III. Independence and the Creation of the Djiboutian Polity

In a significant change in the pro-Afar policies that dominated French political thinking prior to Djibouti's independence in 1977, the first Djiboutian government of the independence era reflected an important shift in French involvement in internal Djiboutian politics: Hassan Gouled Aptidon, an Issa Somali and leader of the Ligue Populaire Africaine pour l'Indépendance (LPAI -- African Popular League for Independence), became the first President of the Republic, and Ahmed Dini, an Afar and Secretary-General of the LPAI, assumed the position of Prime Minister. Similar to actions taken by the majority of African leaders during the post-World War II period, Gouled oversaw the strengthening of a single-party system increasingly subject to his personal control and restrictive of popular debate.

According to the National Mobilization Law passed by the National Assembly in October, 1981, for example, Djibouti officially transformed itself into a single-party political system in which the only legal party prior to 1992 was the state-endorsed Rassemblement Populaire pour le Progrès (RPP -- Popular Assembly for Progress). As such, only those politicians approved by the RPP were allowed to present themselves as part of a single-party slate during election periods. It is at least partially (some would say completely) for this reason that Gouled -- the only choice offered to the electorate -- received an overwhelming number of votes cast in presidential elections held in 1981 (84.66 percent) and 1987 (87.42 percent).

The Office of the President was further strengthened by the fact that Djibouti's army and security forces fall under the direct control of the president as commander-in-chief. Throughout the 1980s, the Djiboutian National Army numbered approximately 2,600 soldiers, including a 900-strong infantry commando regiment, a 200-strong armored company, an 800-strong frontier commando unit, and a 300-strong gendarmerie force. In addition, internal security forces numbered approximately 1,400, inclusive of 1,200 members of the National Security Force. These Djiboutian forces were buttressed by nearly 3,500 French soldiers stationed throughout the country who fell under the command of the Commanding Officer of French Forces in Djibouti. Although the majority (2,757) of these soldiers were associated with the French Army, including the 13th Demi-Brigade of the French Foreign Legion, the French Air Force (840 personnel) and Navy (134 personnel) also were represented. Djibouti permits the existence of one of the few remaining French bases on African soil.

Gouled's power was further strengthened by a political system that prior to 1992 lacked a formal constitution. As a result, the functioning of the system was based on a series of *ad hoc* rulings issued by the Office of the President, as well as laws passed by the sixty-five-member National Assembly -- a body presided over by a prime minister who, in turn, was appointed by the president. Yet despite his far-reaching powers, Gouled consistently sought to craft a ruling coalition inclusive of all groups but which nonetheless ensured control by the Issa ethnic group. In an unwritten power-sharing agreement worked out prior to independence and maintained ever since, the office of the president was occupied by an Issa and the office of prime minister was occupied by an Afar. Afar politicians who have occupied the office of prime minister include Ahmed Dini (1977-78), Abdallah M. Kamil (1978), and Barkat Gourad Hamadou (1978-present).

Gouled's desire to maintain an ethnic balance in politics also played a role in elections governing membership in the National Assembly. Under another power-sharing agreement worked out prior to independence, the sixty-five-seat National Assembly was divided along ethnic lines. Whereas Issas and others of Somali origin (Gadaboursis and Isaaqs) were guaranteed a plurality of thirty-three seats, the Afars were apportioned the slightly smaller number of thirty seats. (The Arab portion of the population was guaranteed two seats.) A major complaint of Afar opposition candidates concerning this arrangement was that the single slate of candidates presented to the public was chosen and approved by the Issa-dominated RPP, ensuring the selection of Afar candidates who potentially were more beholden to Gouled than to their own people. In any case, the slate of candidates presented to the voting public in the 1982 and 1987 legislative elections were overwhelmingly approved by margins of 90 and 87 percent, respectively.

An important aspect of Djibouti's political system has been the often disruptive impact of external, and particularly regional events. This problem stems from the simple fact that, while many Djiboutian Afars feel a special affinity for their counterparts in Ethiopia, as well as often strong feelings for and against the central governments that have held power in Addis Ababa, many Djiboutian nationals with ethnic ties to Somalia historically have been captivated by the thought of Djibouti becoming part of a "Greater Somalia" in which all Somalis in the Horn of Africa would become part of a Somali state. During the 1977-78 Ogaden War between Ethiopia and Somalia, for example, these affinities were manifested by Djiboutian nationals taking arms against each other through clandestine movements supported by both Ethiopia and Somalia.

In a more recent manifestation of this phenomenon, the civil conflict between the (now deposed) government of Mohammed Siyad Barre and a host of guerrilla movements committed to his overthrow spilled over during 1989 and 1990 into the Djiboutian capital. Violent ethnic fighting broke out in Balbala, a large shanty town on the outskirts of Djibouti City, between the Gadaboursi and Issa communities. This conflict occurred because Gadaboursis living in Somalia, who tended to side with the Siyad government and were recruited to serve in the Somali military, had taken part in repression targeted against Issas in northern Somalia who, in turn, tended to support the Somali National Movement (SNM), a guerrilla movement which was seeking to overthrow the Somali government. In all such cases, Gouled has not hesitated to exert pressure on targeted ethnic groups considered to be a threat to the security of the state.

Despite Gouled's efforts to maintain some degree of ethnic balance within the government, the Afars increasingly felt slighted by a regime in which the Issas dominated the civil service, the armed forces and the RPP. Issa domination was favored by the simple fact that they constitute the largest ethnic group and that their power base, Djibouti City, remains the political and economic center of the country. As a result, many Afars felt that those among them, such as Prime Minister Hamadou, who have accepted positions with the Gouled government, were corrupt and inept officials who merely serve as "window dressing" for an Issa-dominated government rather than serving the legitimate needs of their own people.

Afar dissatisfaction increasingly was transformed into a guerrilla insurgency or "rebellion" whose goal was to overthrow the Gouled regime by force. For example, in 1979 the leaders of two Ethiopian-supported guerrilla movements -- the "Mouvement Populaire de Libération" (MPL -- Popular Movement of Liberation) and the "Union Nationale pour l'Indépendance" (UNI -- National Union for Independence) -- created a joint military organization, the "Front Démocratique pour la Libération de Djibouti" (FDLD -- Democratic Front for the Liberation of Djibouti). In the political realm, former Prime Minister Ahmed Dini attempted to break the monopoly of the ruling RPP in 1981 by forming the "Parti Populaire Djiboutien" (PPD -- Djiboutian Popular Party), an opposition political party which was quickly outlawed by the Gouled regime. The net result of more vocal Afar opposition was an escalating cycle of violence in which military attacks by Afar guerrillas was countered by government repression, particularly within the northern Afar-inhabited territories.

Although the Gouled regime was able to stifle Afar demands for greater political power within the political system during the immediate post-independence era, the end of the Cold War and the decline of single-party rule in both Eastern Europe and the former Soviet Union, led to growing pressures for multiparty politics throughout Africa, inclusive of Djibouti, by the end of the 1980s. The most notable aspect of this trend was growing dissatisfaction within Gouled's own ethnic group over the authoritarian nature of single-party rule in Djibouti. For example, Mohamed Moussa Kahin, former director of planning and economic adviser to Gouled, clandestinely formed the "Mouvement pour l'Unité et la Démocratie" (MUD -- Movement for Unity and Democracy), an organization committed to the introduction of a multiparty political system. Kahin's actions especially were significant as he represented the first senior member of Gouled's ethnic group (Issa) and clan (Mamassan) to break openly with the government. Similarly, Aden Robleh Awaleh, an Issa of the Yonis-Moussa clan who fled Djibouti in order to avoid life imprisonment amidst charges of having fostered political destabilization, formed the "Mouvement Nationale Djiboutien pour l'Instauration de la Démocratie" (MNDID -- Djiboutian National Movement for the Installation of Democracy). Finally, in a move designed to unify the opposition in its quest for a multiparty political system, both the Issa-based MNDID and the Afar-based FDLD formed a joint organization known as the "Union des Mouvements Démocratiques" (UMD -- Union of Democratic Movements) in January, 1990. The UMD claimed that it was seeking to "unite all ethnic groups and different political persuasions within the country" so as "to put an end to the chaotic situation which the people of Djibouti are in due to their tribal and obscurantist regime."

Rather than entertaining the idea of multiparty politics, however, the Gouled regime increasingly resorted to authoritarian tactics at the beginning of the 1980s to silence opponents. As documented in its first major report related to Djibouti, Amnesty International concluded in July, 1991 that various methods of torture were being employed by the security forces against a variety of opposition figures. After the October, 1990 terrorist bombing of the Café de Paris in which a French child was killed and fourteen people were injured, over 200 members of the Gadaboursi ethnic group were arrested and tortured. Similarly, in the aftermath of a military attack against a government military barracks in Tadjoura, hundreds of Afars were arrested and tortured after being charged with seeking to overthrow the government. Among the most prominent of those arrested was Ali Aref Bourhan, a member of the Hassoba sub-clan from Tadjoura who was one of the French-favored leaders of the territory prior to 1977. "The government said 11 years ago that torture would be stopped, but the evidence shows that it is still happening," Amnesty International declared on November 6, 1991. "We're again calling on the government to urgently tackle both the problem of torture and other human rights issues."

IV. The Djiboutian Civil War

Rising frustrations within the Afar community reached a turning point in November, 1991 when the "Front pour le Restauration de l'Unité et la Démocratie" (FRUD -- Front for the Restoration of Unity and Democracy), a military force of approximately 3,000 guerrilla fighters primarily from the Afar ethnic group, launched a sustained military offensive that eventually captured all the major areas in the north except for the towns of Tadjoura and Obock. Signalling the end of Djibouti's special status as the "eye of the hurricane" in the Horn of Africa, the offensive was initiated by Afar leaders calling for the removal of the Gouled regime and the installation of a multiparty political system. Indeed, the military leaders of the FRUD undoubtedly sought to duplicate the outcomes of civil wars in neighboring Somalia and Ethiopia which had led to the overthrow of the Siyad and Mengistu regimes during the first half of 1991. As for the Djiboutian government, it declared a state of emergency, arrested hundreds of Afars in the northern region, ordered the mobilization of the entire population, and, most important, invoked a Franco-Djiboutian defense treaty signed in 1977 that provided for French aid in the event that Djibouti was threatened with "external" aggression.

An extremely controversial aspect of the Gouled government's position was whether the military operations of the FRUD constituted illegitimate external aggression or legitimate internally based military operations -- the implications of which would determine the legality of French intervention under the Franco-Djiboutian defense treaty. The Gouled government predictably accused the FRUD of being an externally based (i.e., illegitimate) invasion force which was threatening Djibouti's sovereignty. Similarly, the FRUD predictably replied that it constituted an internally based (i.e., legitimate) military force deserving of the status of belligerency. As a result, whereas the Djiboutian government demanded swift intervention on the part of France to contain FRUD military advances, the FRUD requested French military restraint, as well as humanitarian aid and possible mediation between the two sides of the conflict.

As is the case in any politically charged debate when military forces are clashing on the battlefield, both sides of the argument contained some element of truth. In support of the argument that the FRUD constituted an indigenous military organization as opposed to a foreign invading force, it is clear that the leadership of the FRUD was composed primarily of disaffected members of the Afar community from within Djibouti (although, as was noted above, leaders within the Issa community also became critical of the Gouled regime). For example, the first president of the FRUD was Mohamed Adoyta Youssouf, an Afar who served as the secretary general of the FDLD and was a member of the executive committee of the MPL. Similarly, the first spokesperson of the FRUD in Djibouti City was Abbate Ebo Adou, a medical practitioner and veteran Afar opposition figure. Moreover, the FRUD enjoyed widespread popular support within the Afar-inhabited areas of northern Djibouti -- especially among disaffected youth more prone to seek redress by military means.

Despite significant levels of elite and popular support for the FRUD within Djibouti, it is also clear that at least a portion (exact figures are unobtainable) of the roughly 3,000 guerrillas came from Afar-inhabited territories of both Ethiopia and Eritrea. This situation was at least partially due to the large numbers of government troops, refugees, and, most significant, light arms and weaponry that streamed into Djibouti in the aftermath of Mengistu's overthrow in May, 1991. It is important to note, however, the difference between the movement across borders of guerrilla fighters based on ethnicity and the provision of aid by external governments or movements. In this regard, if one attempted to find a basis for the argument that the FRUD was an externally supplied invasion force, one immediately ran into the dilemma of actually finding a foreign power which was seeking to overthrow the Gouled government by military means.

An obvious turn to the Afar Liberation Front (ALF) based in Ethiopia was problematic because one of the sporadically stated platforms of this group -- the creation of a secessionist "greater Afar" country out of portions of present-day Djibouti, Ethiopia, and Eritrea -- ran counter to the FRUD's repeatedly stated goal of maintaining the territorial integrity of Djibouti. Sporadic tension between the goals of Afar leadership in Ethiopia and Djibouti had been fueled by the fact that many of the FRUD leadership perceived the ALF as constituting a largely backward, traditionalist, and illiterate organization led by corrupt, self-serving politicians, such as Sultan Ali Mirah, the ALF leader who originally was placed in power by Ethiopian leader Haile Selassie. Moreover, it has been argued that the FRUD leadership was concerned that the creation of a "greater Afar" country would lead to financial demands from the impoverished Afar-inhabited areas of Ethiopia and Eritrea, thereby contributing to the decline of resources, and thus of the standard of living, available to Afar leaders and their respective constituencies in Djibouti. "The FRUD leadership is used to access to hospitals where one can get care, schools where people get taught, and telephones that work, and they don't want to lose that," explained Gérard Prunier, an analyst associated with the Paris-based Center de Recherches Africaines. "There is a strong sense among the FRUD leadership that an independent Afar country would be a financial basket case and, fully cognizant of the dire straits in which Djibouti's neighbors find themselves, that the proper course is to seek change within the existing boundaries of Djibouti."

Other regional actors were also unlikely proponents of a FRUD military victory. Both Eritrea (governed by the Eritrean People's Liberation Front -- EPLF) and the guerrilla leadership of Ethiopia (subsumed under the banner of the Ethiopian People's Revolutionary Democratic Front -- EPRDF) opposed a FRUD military victory due to a concern that overturning the Gouled government would strengthen separatist Afar movements within their territories. The secessionist Somaliland Republic was similarly opposed to the FRUD due to a desire to maintain a working relationship with the Gouled regime. Finally, despite the fact that Yemen allowed the FRUD to establish an office in the capital, Sanaa, Yemeni leaders did not favor a military solution, and instead offered to serve as neutral mediators between the FRUD and the Gouled regime. In short, the Djiboutian civil war initially was an internal conflict in which an internally-based leadership lacked external military patrons, but nonetheless, enjoyed the support of an undetermined number of migratory soldiers and a ready supply of light weapons from black markets in neighboring Somalia, Eritrea, and Ethiopia.

It is the latter interpretation of the civil war which initially guided

French foreign policy toward the Gouled regime and created somewhat of a crisis for Franco-Djiboutian relations. In the early stages of the FRUD offensive, French officials strongly tied to the Socialist Party, such as Ministre Délégué des Affaires Étrangères Alain Vivien, emphasized that French military forces would not become involved in what was perceived in Paris as an internal civil war between the Gouled government and the Afar opposition. France instead offered to act as a neutral mediator in negotiations, ideally leading to the creation of a multiparty political system. This demand of the opposition was also the growing preference of French specialists increasingly weary with the corrupt and authoritarian practices of the Gouled regime. In order to achieve such an outcome, it was believed that, as part of a general cease-fire arrangement, the FRUD had to renounce the achievement of its aims by military means, at the same time that the Gouled government had to recognize the FRUD as a legitimate politico-military force. In essence, France was *de facto* recognizing the belligerency status of the FRUD -- i.e., that a situation of civil war existed in the country, and only an even-handed policy could peacefully resolve the conflict (thereby protecting French interests in the region). Although French policy became less neutral and more explicitly pro-Gouled in February, 1992 when French troops were ordered into Dikhil to prevent the advancing FRUD military forces from occupying the town and opening a major southern front (the net result of which might have been a FRUD victory in the civil war), the French continued to pressure the Gouled regime to seek a negotiated end to the civil war and to fashion a more inclusive multiparty political system.

Initially unwilling to heed French overtures and compromise with the FRUD opposition, the Gouled regime instead sought to bolster the Djiboutian Armed Forces and achieve a military victory by reportedly recruiting trained guerrilla fighters among the Issa populations residing in Ethiopia and Somalia, as well as some former Isaaq fighters from the SNM. One outcome of this general trend toward the militarization of policy was a massacre in the Arhiba district of Djibouti City in which at least thirty were killed and eighty were reportedly wounded by government security forces on December 18, 1991. "According to eyewitness reports," noted an Amnesty International report of the incident, "the security forces rounded-up over 100 people in searches and identity checks before dawn and then shot people who refused orders to enter trucks to be driven away or who tried to escape." "One Afar member of the security forces was apparently executed himself," the report continued, "when he refused to fire on fleeing civilians."

The Arhiba massacre served as a significant turning point in the Djiboutian civil war in two major respects. First, less than twenty-four hours after it occurred, Gouled for the first time announced his willingness to entertain the idea of establishing some sort of multiparty political system. Toward this end, the president charged a committee with preparing the country's first post-independence constitution that would be submitted to a popular referendum as soon as six months after completion. Although opposition figures rightfully questioned whether this simply constituted a delaying tactic -- Gouled announced, for example, that such a referendum could only be held after the "foreign" invaders had withdrawn from Djibouti -- the actions of the regime nonetheless opened up a process of political reform which could prove increasingly difficult for the Gouled regime to control in the long term.

A second major outcome of the Arhiba massacre was growing dissension at the highest levels of the Gouled regime. For example, in an effort clearly designed to cause a crisis of governance, the minister of health, Mohamed Djama Elabe, accused his government of being incapable of solving the country's ills, denounced the "war logic" that seemed to prevail at the highest levels of the Gouled regime, and resigned his post. He subsequently formed a political organization, the "Mouvement pour la Paix et la Réconciliation" (MPR -- Movement for Peace and Reconciliation), that rejected the militancy of both the Gouled regime and the FRUD, and sought instead to build a trans-ethnic opposition coalition. Elabe's resignation carried a lot of weight due to his status as France's favored candidate to succeed Gouled as president of Djibouti. (A member of the Fourlaba subclan of the Issa ethnic group, Elabe is well respected among the Afar, and therefore is potentially capable of building a coalition that could transcend ethnic lines.) However, the mass resignations that were expected to follow that of Elabe did not materialize, although the prestige of the Gouled government obviously had been challenged and even weakened.

The combination of military pressure from the FRUD, political pressure from the civilian opposition, and diplomatic pressure from France led the Gouled regime to undertake a process of political reform designed to seek an accommodation with the Afar opposition. In response to a FRUD declaration on February 28, 1992, which established a unilateral cease-fire and underscored a commitment to French mediation, for example, the Gouled regime the very next day released from detention Dr. Abatte, the former spokesperson of the FRUD, and partially lifted an economic blockade of the north, as witnessed by the reestablishment of sea transport connecting Djibouti City with Obock and Tadjoura. On April 6, 1992, Gouled announced the outlines of a draft constitution that eventually provided for administrative decentralization, freedom of the press, the protection of human rights, and the creation of a multiparty political system that would be limited to no more than four political parties. Following the Djiboutian Council of Ministers' passage on April 23 of a limited amnesty for those who had participated in acts against the government since November, 1991 (the beginning of the FRUD military offensive), the proposed constitution was presented to the voters in the form of a referendum on September 4. According to the government, over 96 percent of those taking part in the referendum (roughly 75 percent of all registered voters) voted in favor of adopting the new constitution.

This process of reform was significantly marred, however, due to the refusal of the Gouled regime to do no more than what critics perceived as the cosmetic "patching up" of a "dictatorial and tribal-based regime." One of the earliest complaints of critics revolved around Gouled's clear intention to design the constitution and carry out the referendum process with little if any input from either the civilian or armed opposition groups in Djibouti. As a result, a variety of opposition figures met in Paris from June 20 to 24, 1992, to create an umbrella organization, the "Front Uni de l'Opposition Djiboutienne" (FUOD -- United Front of Djiboutian Opposition), that could mount a trans-ethnic challenge to the Gouled regime. Among those organizations which participated in the June meeting were the FRUD as led by former Prime Minister Ahmed Dini; the trans-ethnic MRP as led by Elabe, one of the strongest Issa contenders for future presidential elections; the "Union Démocratique Djiboutienne" (UDD -- Djiboutian Democratic Union), a Gadaboursi movement represented by Mohamed Moussa Ainache; the "Mouvement National Djiboutien" (MND -- Djiboutian National Movement), an Isaaq organization represented by Sallam Mahmoud; the "Front des Forces Démocratiques" (FFD -- Front of Democratic Forces), an Issa-based grouping represented by Omar Elmi Kaireh; the largely Arab-based "Mouvement pour le Salut et la Reconstruction" (MSR -- Movement for Safety and Reconstruction) headed by Galal Abdourahman; and the Djiboutian human rights organization, "Association pour la Défense des Droits de l'Homme et de la Liberté (ADDHL -- Association for the Defense of Human Rights and Liberty).

The so-called "Paris Accords" which emerged from the June, 1992 meeting outlined a variety of opposition demands that seriously called into question the reform process initiated by the Gouled regime. Most significantly, the accords called for the creation of a transitional government that would be led by a prime minister chosen from the ranks of the opposition -- a proposal immediately dismissed by President Gouled. In terms of Gouled's proposed constitution, the opposition was particularly concerned that the executive branch of government remained far too strong. Specifically, neither the office of the prime minister nor the legislature were endowed with any special prerogatives, such as oversight of presidential appointments at the cabinet level, that would allow them to significantly question or oversee executive branch policies. As a result of these concerns, approximately 50 percent of Djibouti's voting-age population heeded the demands of the FRUD, the FUOD, and the legislative opposition, and boycotted the referendum. In short, a significant portion of the opposition firmly believed that participation in a referendum on a constitution "prepared and approved by the President alone, without any discussion with anyone else" in essence constituted a "vote for his [Gouled's] dictatorship."

The constitutional referendum and the legislative and presidential elections were neither free nor fair. Rather, they were intended to provide the appearance of democracy, while ensuring the maintenance of the political status quo. Significantly marred by electoral fraud and another FRUD-inspired boycott that was heeded by approximately 50 percent of the voting-age population (primarily within the Afar community), these electoral contests not surprisingly led to victory for the ruling RPP and President Gouled. Held on December 18, 1992, the legislative elections resulted in a complete sweep of all sixty-five seats of the National Assembly by Gouled's ruling RPP party (which obtained 72 percent of the popular vote). In the presidential elections held on May 7, 1993, Gouled emerged victorious with 60.71 percent of the popular vote. The remainder of the votes were split primarily among the candidates of two Issa-based opposition parties legalized by the Gouled regime: Mohamed Djama Elabe, an Issa who heads the Party of Democratic Renewal (PRD -- receiving 22.03 percent of the votes), and Aden Robleh Awaleh, an Issa who heads the Democratic National Party (PND -- receiving 12.29 percent of the vote).

As predicted by most foreign observers, Gouled's ephemeral "victory" at both the legislative and presidential levels was followed by a government military offensive in July, 1993 that severely damaged the military integrity and effectiveness of the FRUD as a unified military force. Having quintupled to a force size of approximately 15,000 troops (at the expense of the government incurring huge budget deficits and foreign debts), the Djiboutian Armed Forces not only retook the major towns held by the FRUD in the northern portion of the country, but also overran the two main rebel bases of Randa and Assa Geyla. This successful military operation marked the end of the Djiboutian civil war as the scattered remnants of the FRUD were forced to return to the hit-and-run tactics of a guerrilla insurgency.

The FRUD's defeat in the face of overwhelming military force also led to the splintering of the political opposition to the Gouled regime.

First, a second meeting of the FUOD in Addis Ababa from January 19 to 23, 1994, that called for the "continuation and reinforcement of armed conflict," was not attended by the leadership of the two Issa-dominated opposition political parties (the PND and the PRD), suggesting a growing split between the Issas and the other ethnic groups within the country, most notably the Afar (although Isaaq, Arab, and Gadaboursi parties supported the declaration of continued armed conflict). Second, and more damaging to the FRUD military effort, is a growing split among the Afar opposition. Specifically, Afar faction leader Ougoureh Kifleh Ahmed not only opened up separate peace talks with the Gouled regime, but successfully forced a reshuffling of the FRUD's executive committee at the beginning of July, 1994. This led to the marginalization of the old leadership, most notably ex-President Ahmed Dini, who were attempting to maintain their control over the organization from exile in Ethiopia.

V. The Djiboutian Civil War in Perspective

The preceding analysis clearly demonstrates that Djibouti was engulfed in civil war during a twenty-one month period from November, 1991 to July, 1993. Unlike more limited forms of civil conflict, most notably ethnic conflict, insurrection, or rebellion (also referred to as guerrilla insurgency), the Djiboutian civil war reached a level of intensity equivalent to conflicts between states; two major armies -- at their height surpassing 3,000 soldiers for the FRUD and over 15,000 soldiers for the government forces -- opposed each other over an extended period of time in a country whose population figures range only from 330,000 to 520,000. Indeed, although one can argue that ethnicity played a major role in this conflict (i.e., an Afar-dominated FRUD opposing an Issa dominated government) the guerrilla forces of the FRUD were nonetheless supported by other ethnic groups in the country, just as the government forces recruited from among non-Issa clans and ethnicities. Equally important, the FRUD established an effective government and military organization that controlled more than 50 percent of Djibouti's territory at the height of its political and military operations. In this regard, it was only the movement of French military forces into the town of Dikhil that prevented the FRUD from opening a major southern front which potentially would have led to the defeat of the Djiboutian Armed Forces and the overthrow of the Gouled regime. The creation of a buffer zone in essence bought the Gouled regime the precious commodity of time that enabled it to quintuple the size of its military forces and enact minor political reforms, both of which contributed to the military defeat of FRUD forces in set battles and the splintering of the political coalition that once supported the overthrow of the Gouled regime through military means. As was the case during the period immediately preceding the FRUD offensive of November, 1991, the post-July, 1993 period is marked by a lesser form of conflict known as rebellion in which guerrilla bands control little territory and are forced to adopt hit-and-run tactics.

The deployment of French military forces to Dikhil further underscores that civil wars are rarely decided solely by indigenous forces. Indeed, when the FRUD attempted to expand military operations into southwestern Djibouti, French mediator Paul Dijoud, Directeur des Affaires Africaines et Malgaches within the French Ministry of Foreign Affairs, announced that victory by military means was "futile" and that a "peace mission" of French troops was positioning itself within the region to ensure the maintenance of the *status quo*. Yet despite its unwillingness to permit the military overthrow of the Gouled regime, the French government nonetheless accorded the FRUD military forces a certain level of legitimacy by *de facto* recognizing that a state of belligerency existed. Specifically, pressure was placed upon the Gouled regime to recognize the legitimacy of the FRUD, and to undertake a process of political reform designed to seek a negotiated end to the civil war. However, an unwillingness to allow the FRUD to capitalize on its military momentum ensured an initial military stalemate in the Djiboutian civil war that ultimately facilitated a military victory by government forces resupplied from abroad. Indeed, unlike its initial reaction to the outbreak of civil war in Djibouti (i.e., non-military involvement in an internal conflict), as of this writing it appears that the French government is going to err on the side of supporting the Gouled regime as long as President Gouled continues to make some effort at seeking a political compromise with opposition forces within the country. Regardless of French policy, however, continued intransigence on the part of Gouled to allow for the creation of a truly free and fair democratic system simply delays the potential emergence of another civil war that may be even bloodier and more costly than that of the November, 1991-July, 1993 period.

---

* The main essay constitutes a revised and updated version of Peter J. Schraeder, "Ethnic Politics in Djibouti: From `Eye of the Hurricane' to `Boiling Cauldron'." *African Affairs*, vol. 92 (1993): 203-21.

Bibliography

Kemp, Peter (1976) *The Oxford Companion to Ships and the Sea*. Oxford: Oxford University Press.

Krieger, Joel, et al. (1993) *The Oxford Companion to Politics of the World*. New York: Oxford University Press.

McGowan, Pat, and Thomas H. Johnson (1986) "Sixty Coups in Thirty Years -- Further Evidence Regarding African Military Coups d'État" 24, 3: 539-46.

Plano, Jack C., and Roy Olton (1988) *The International Relations Dictionary*. (4th ed.) Santa Barbara, CA: ABC-Clio.

Raymond, Walter John (1992) *Dictionary of Politics*. (7th ed.) Lawrenceville, VA: Brunswick Publishing.

Skocpol, Theda (1979) *States and Social Revolutions: A Comparative Analysis of France, Russia and China*. Cambridge and New York: Cambridge University Press.

Scruton, Roger (1982) *A Dictionary of Political Thought*. New York: Harper and Row.

Shafritz, Jay, Phil Williams, and Ronald S. Calinger (1993) *The Dictionary of 20th Century World Politics*. New York: Henry Holt and Company.

von Glahn, Gerhard (1986) *Law Among Nations*. (6th ed.). New York: Macmillan Publishing.

SECTION NINE

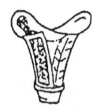

The Somali Crisis Within an International Context

Summaries: Section Nine

Ahmed Qassim Ali (Chapter 34) reviews the role which foreign governments, mostly the USSR, Italy, and the US played in post-independence Somalia. He notes that the Soviets focused on military hardware and ineffective economic assistance. The US contributed $500 million mostly in large-scale economic aid and military equipment which Siyad used against his own people. The Italian assistance become so deeply intertwined with internal Italian politics and corrupt aid to Italian corporations that it had little positive impact on Somalia. Following the collapse of Siyad, Ali finds the assistance from all donors mostly too little too late.

Giampaolo Calchi Novati (Chapter 35) describes the Italian involvement in Africa in general and the Horn in particular, from the 1880s. Instability and shifts in priorities among Italian governments, combined with a highly volatile situation in Ethiopia, Somalia, and Eritrea, led to many shifts in policy toward the Horn. By the 1980s, Somalia was Italy's last hope to maintain a presence in the Horn and the government therefore lent full support to Siyad Barre. Siyad's collapse in 1991 dashed even this thin strand of achieving Italy's elusive goal of influence in Africa. Novati concludes that the Somali people have suffered overwhelming problems, many of which were exacerbated by the weakness and inexperience of the Italian colonial and post-colonial presence.

Maria Brons Bongartz (Chapter 36) begins with the delineation of peace-keeping and peace enforcement and then develops four arguments about whether the UN military intervention into Somalia in December, 1992 was justified. She then reviews the performance of the UN mission, including its successes and failures. The chapter concludes with an attempt to portray how the UN could still be a viable instrument in the process leading to reconciliation, peace and rehabilitation.

Edmond J. Keller (Chapter 37) writes from the perspective of African-Americans on the events of Somalia. He makes four proposals: (1) implement an arms embargo; (2) reopen the issue of African state sovereignty and when it is appropriate for the OAU to intervene in the internal affairs of an African state; (3) urge that external organizations (UN, OAU) assist African states to deal with issues of shifting sovereignty; and (4) rebuild Somali society from the bottom up, not through externally imposed concepts of the nation state.

CHAPTER THIRTY FOUR

The Foreign Factor In the Somali Tragedy

Ahmed Qassim Ali

I. The Military Dictatorship

It has become a common cliché of the international media to describe the Somali situation simply as a product of the Cold War, without indicating the internal and external forces responsible for the tragedy. Some authors who undeservedly are quoted as the main authorities on Somalia more simplistically have attributed the responsibility of the situation in Somalia to the "nature of the Somalis" and "segmentation curse" of Somali society.

Undoubtedly, the responsibility for the present Somali tragedy lies in the first place on Somalis themselves. It is the consequence of the criminal policy of the military regime, led by Mohamed Siyad Barre, his clique, and a handful of power greedy war criminals who have transformed a legitimate popular insurrection against tyranny into a senseless power struggle and a destructive savage war. These are not the only parties responsible for the tragedy. There are others who have contributed at different levels and degrees to the exacerbation and degeneration of the Somali plight which has cost so much in lives and property.[1]

The following analysis deals with the relationship of foreign governments with the Somali problem, the extent to which they have contributed to the conservation and the fall of the dictatorial regime, and finally, their attitude toward the Somali tragedy after the fall of dictator

Siyad Barre. But before we undertake this analysis it would be worthwhile to review briefly the domestic and foreign policies practiced by the regime that these governments have had to deal with.

II. The Domestic Policy of the Military Regime

From the beginning, the Military Regime abolished all existing constitutional rights and guarantees and replaced them with its arbitrary authority which resulted in one of the most horrendous human rights abuses in the world. The dictatorial regime, led by Mohamed Siyad Barre, cared only about the maintenance of its power. Its domestic policy was totally geared to protect the stability of illegitimate institutions. Citizens were prevented from exercising their basic rights. Their lives and property were constantly under threat. The NSS (National Security Service) was empowered to perpetrate all sorts of injustice: detention, torture, summary execution and political persecution. Citizens were deprived of the right of *habeas corpus* and thus became victims of the most abusive restraints on personal liberties. A neofascist judicial system based on gross application of the infamous Law 54 for "safeguarding national security" was established in the country. Loyal practitioners without law backgrounds were appointed justices. Almost the entire population became victim of the abuses of a tyrannical power who saw in every man and woman a potential threat to its existence. Only a small minority, an inner circle of the Military Regime and the dictator's clan affiliation were to benefit from economic and social privileges with a level of corruption unprecedented in modern Somali history.

The meager resources of the government were devoted primarily to the creation and strengthening of the repressive apparatus. The administration of the regions and districts was entrusted to loyal individuals whose merits were gauged only on their repressive capability. In the name of socialism and development, the whole national economy was stabilized and privately owned properties and businesses were confiscated. In the rural agricultural area, private lands and facilities were confiscated for unproductive state farms. A law which forced farmers to sell all their harvest was introduced. Marketing of agricultural products was the sole privilege of ADC (Agricultural Development Corporation) and farmers were compelled to buy their own produce at higher prices. Such practice had a deleterious effect on a mainly subsistence agriculture. The nomadic population was taxed to "participate in the development of the country" when their livestock and their very existence were at the mercy of unpredictable weather and recurrent droughts. The urban areas had no better luck with the whole economy controlled by the state. As the rural population was growing poorer, rural youth were flocking to the towns and cities. The latter lacked basic amenities. Education became a business of the state alone and even private foreign language schools were closed. The posts of managers of the state enterprises were given on the basis of loyalty or clan affiliation with disastrous consequences.

The sacred law of Siyad Barre was "divide and rule" which he inherited from the colonial system which shaped his personality during his long years of service and training as a colonial intelligence officer. Making treasure of his peculiar training, Siyad Barre practiced the division of the people, used contra opposition and rivalry, and stirred up trouble among the rural nomadic population inside and outside Somalia's boundaries. Periodically, he would single out and crack down on a region, clan, subclan or social group and label it "a threat to national stability." He used repressive, paramilitary agents, all with permission, to kill, torture, arrest civilians and to destroy livestock and water points.

III. The Foreign Policy of the Military Regime

The Military Regime did not have a consistent foreign policy and international relations were not geared to pursue the achievement and the preservation of national interests. Since its early stage, the Somali people abhorred the foreign policy of the Military Regime and disassociated itself from it. Basically, the foreign policy of Siyad Barre's regime was founded on servility toward foreign powers. The Military Regime soon subjugated the country to the Soviet Union in return for obsolete arms and an army of military advisors and trainers. The Soviet Union was not eager to finance development projects unless they fit its plans of exploitation. This servile attitude culminated with the signature of the Somali-Soviet friendship treaty in July, 1974 which made out of the national territory a large military facility for the superpower. A similar attitude but of lesser magnitude, which was evidenced by the about-face of Siyad Barre, culminated in the "underselling" of the main ports and the national coast to the US in 1980.

In the 1970s, the Military Regime maintained its ties with EEC (Economic European Community) countries and Italy, from which it was seeking economic support. In these years the Military Regime, with the intention to profit from financial support from Arab countries while helping to expand Soviet influence in the area, stirred the banners of pan-Arabism, pan-Africanism and "non-alliance" rhetoric, but its foreign policy remained inconsistent and without compass.

In the Military Regime, Mohamed Siyad Barre, not accountable to anyone, was the only one responsible for foreign policy. After he deposed Omar Arteh Ghalib from the post of foreign minister, Siyad Barre appointed his brother who held the post from 1975 until almost the end of the regime. The latter was known for his incompetence as a diplomat. The diplomats entrusted with conducting foreign relations and representing the state abroad were chosen from Siyad's entourage and among his clansmen, regardless of their acquaintance with the art of diplomacy and foreign policy.

As far as the "Somali territories" are concerned, a fair solution of their problems has never been a genuine concern of the Military Regime which maintained a gigantic army, mainly for the repression and control of the Somali people inside the republic. Contrary to common belief, the adventure of the war of 1977 was not the result of a consistent policy of realization of the aspirations of the Somali population, but an attempt by the regime to stir nationalistic fervor and thus strengthen its position internally. In fact, from the beginning, the Military Regime suppressed the movement for the self-determination of Western Somalia and persecuted members and leaders of the movement.

IV. The International Relations of the Regime

In the heyday of the Military Regime, Mogadishu hosted more than thirty embassies and missions while the Military Regime had about forty embassies scattered over four continents. The great number of "diplomats" abroad indicates the maladministration of the Military Regime. These diplomats were chosen not on the basis of their competence but, as with all other nominations, their selection was based on the degree of loyalty and the proximity to the dictator's extended family and only a few of them were worth the name of diplomat. Though draining precious hard currency, most of these embassies were not swimming in wealth and were not able to pay their rent and the bills punctually. For many, since there were not many foreign relations to conduct, the holiday abroad and a petty business in hard currency were worth the trouble and the humiliation of dealing with the whims of an incompetent foreign minister and his brother. It was a common belief among many Somalis that the foreign minister used an evaluation method based on the size of the banquet held in his honor and the petty favors done for relatives and *protégés*. The "actual" foreign relations were carried out according to the whims of Siyad Barre. The Military Regime was a very unpopular dictatorship with a bankrupt economy. For such a regime, outside support to prolong its rule was essential.

Until 1988, the year when the Military Regime savagely leveled the major towns of the north, causing more than 50,000 deaths and 500,000 refugees, only a handful of the foreign states with accredited diplomatic missions in Mogadishu had a "cold relationship" with the Military Regime. Some of these governments provided political support and others provided economic and/or military support to a "government at war with its own people." Few of these states cared about the fate of the millions of Somalis who were experiencing the worst dictatorship in Africa and perhaps in the world. For instance, Japan provided economic support, and some Arab countries provided economic and political support. But the provision of military support was the privilege of the Soviet Union replaced by the US in the 1980s, Italy, Germany and some Arab countries such as Egypt, Libya, Iraq, Saudi Arabia and the UAE. These countries supplied funds, arms, ammunition, military technical assistance and military training. To the regime, the military assistance provided through these bilateral relationships was not enough; therefore, it became an addicted customer to the arms black markets. As a matter of fact, when Siyad Barre fled Mogadishu in January, 1991, a shipment of light arms and ammunition was ready to reach the country. After payment, the shipment arrived at the port of Mogadishu, where it was looted by various armed thugs.

In the following paragraphs we will examine the individual relationships of some countries with the military regime.

V. The Soviet Union

The Soviet Union was primarily responsible for the militarization of the country and the deterioration of the livelihood of the Somali population in the 1970s. The then superpower virtually colonized the country and there was no sector of the economy or section of the population left out of its control. In less than a decade, the army grew by 175 percent and its cost grew by over 600 percent.[2] Soviet experts from *Gosplan* (State Planning) overtook the planning institutions of the country and produced an economic catastrophe. It brought an economy based on state farms, state factories, nationalization of trade, banks and businesses which contributed to further debt in the country. When the Soviets "crossed the border" to switch alliances, Somalia was left with an external debt equal to more than half of its GNP, which at that time was around $1.2 billion.

VI. The Italian Government

The colonial power in Somalia's past and devoted ally of Siyad Barre, Italy occupies a unique position in the political, economic and military support of the dictatorial regime. Italy occupied southern Somalia until 1941 as a colonial power and returned in 1950, sent by the UN to prepare the country for its indcpendence as a UN trusteeship. After independence and especially after 1963 when the new Somali Republic severed its diplomatic relations with the UK, Italy dominated the political life of the country. Even during the Soviet period, Italy was the closest partner after the USSR. When Moscow switched alliances in the Horn of Africa, Italy regained its primary role in Somalia. Emilio Colombo, then foreign minister, visited Somalia in 1981 to sign a program of assistance. But mainly due to the effort of the Italian Socialist Party, which in the 1980s occupied in Somalia the place of the Christian Democrats and the Italian Communist Party, a new era started for relations between the Military Regime and Italy. Military and economic aid started flowing to Siyad Barre in an unprecedented manner. Italian Socialist dignitaries and government members began to feel at home in Mogadishu. Paolo Pillitteri, a socialist former Chairman of the Italian-Somali Chamber of Commerce (which secured a great deal of investment in Somalia) and later on mayor of Milan, greeted the new era with the publication of a pamphlet on Somalia. The book was introduced by Bettino Craxi himself who indulged in praising the dictator and describing him as a "wise leader in the post-Sadat era."[3]

In the 1980s, Italy increased its aid to Third World countries in order to extend its foreign market. It was also in this period that a great deal of public funds were funneled into private companies. With Law 38 in 1980 and the institution of DIPCO (Department of Cooperation) with extensive powers at the Ministry for Foreign Affairs Italy became a member of the family of "big donors" jumping from the 13th place to the 5th. In 1983, when Craxi became prime minister, Giulio Andreotti was selected for the *Farnesina* (Foreign Affairs). Craxi and Andreotti found DIPCO not flexible enough for emergency situations and expeditious disbursements. In 1985 with Law 73 the FAI (Fondo Aiuti Italiano-Italian; Fund for Aid) was established. FAI was authorized to spend the record amount of two trillion lira in eighteen months. A socialist professor of economics, Francesco Forte, was appointed as the head of FAI and was given exceptional powers. Today, the judges of *mani pulite* (clean hands) are investigating Craxi, Andreotti and Gianni de Michelis — the socialist minister who replaced Andreotti — for mismanagement of FAI funds. Gianni De Michelis, named by the Italian press *Attila*, will be remembered for his attachment to the dictator whom he defended until the last day of his rule. The funds became easy profits for a few, top Italian contractors such as Ansaldo, Sadelmi, FIAT, Astaldi, Cogefar, etc.[4]

With the establishment of FAI, the process of financing projects was made very easy for private contractors. In order to have access to FAI funds, it was enough to show written approval of the recipient of projects conceived, prepared and tailored to the needs of the contractor. In 1985, Bettino Craxi visited Mogadishu to announce the pledge of 0.5 trillion lira. Most of the FAI funds went to the Garoe-Bosaso road which, during commissioning, had a price escalation of 100 billion lira. FAI projects were "cathedrals in the desert" and neither were based on the real needs of the country nor on sound economic and technical feasibility studies. Parallel to the grant projects, Italy also pushed a few commercial loan projects which were lucrative for Italian companies such as the fertilizer factory which cost $75 million, of which one million dollars went into the pockets of Siyad Barre.[5] Despite the opposition of the Ministry of Planning, the factory was implemented and never went into production for lack of power *inter alia*. Its urea would have been about three times more expensive than the imported one. Another example was Gizoma, an animal fattening facility, which at the beginning was a commercial loan but later was taken over by FAI. Gizoma, a useless project which partly duplicated a USAID- financed facility located at a distance of about forty miles, was solely conceived for the benefit of an Italian company.

In 1985, when the SNM (Somali National Movement) was launching its strikes against the regime, Italy sent a special military mission called DIATMA (Delegazione Italiana Tecnico Militare Aeronautica-Italian Military and Air Force Technical Mission) consisting of more than fifty military experts in Somalia to militarily support the regime. During the period 1979-85, Italy assisted Siyad Barre with armaments whose value exceeded $550 million including M47 tanks, Fiat APCs and Mll3, airplanes, helicopters, heavy military trucks, ammunition, etc.[6] This occurred in a period in which Siyad Barre was at war only with his own people. Repression of the resistance was going on in different regions such as the Northwest, central region and Bokol, but Italy chose to stand at Siyad Barre's side against the Somali people.

Even when the armed struggle in the north became fierce and the news of the repression against towns and villages in the Northwest echoed throughout the whole world and most western countries were distancing themselves from the regime, Italy further increased its political, economic and military support to the dictatorship. Italian dignitaries and government officials visited Mogadishu. The Italian president of the Republic, Francesco Cossiga, paid a visit to Mogadishu in February, 1989, i.e., after Siyad Barre had destroyed Hargeisa, Burao and other centers in the north causing thousands of deaths and hundreds of thousands of refugees.

In 1989, Giulio Andreotti became prime minister and Gianni De

Michelis went to the *Farnesina*, and the Italian commitment to the preservation of the regime increased. Despite the outcry of the Italian Radical Party and other opposition parties to stop the support to a regime at war with his own people and in whose prisons many innocents were dying, the Italian government continued to support the regime. The opposition also requested the government to shed light on how funds were spent in Somalia. Italian assistance continued, even after the decision by the Parliament to stop it. In mid-1990 a contract was awarded to Ansaldo to implement a diesel power house in northern Mogadishu with the value of 33 billion lira.

The Italian government supported the dictator until his last days and cared less about the lives of more than 1,500 members of the Italian community of which about five hundred had invested genuinely in the country and opted to live permanently in Somalia. In 1989 and 1990, a series of attacks on foreigners were carried out by unknowns and by the regime. In July, 1989, the Bishop of Mogadishu was shot on the stairway of the cathedral. The assassination is believed to have been commissioned by the regime because of the Bishop's personal relationship with USC (United Somali Congress). In 1990, an Italian biologist was assassinated in a prison cell belonging to the 77th division of the Army. These episodes and the general situation of Somalia did not persuade the Italian foreign minister to refrain from supporting Siyad Barre. The Italian Parliament intervened to suspend Italian assistance to the Military Regime in mid-1990. On January 8, 1991, a few days before the dictator was forced to leave the capital, the Italian ambassador proposed to USC to stop fighting and attend an Italian-sponsored negotiation with the dictator to be held in Cairo or Rome in July 1991. This act led many people to conclude that Italy believed in the invincibility of Siyad Barre, perhaps because of the amount of arms supplied to him.

VII. The United States

The relationship between the US and Somalia deteriorated after the installation of the Military Regime in 1969. For a decade this relationship was reduced to the formal presence of a diplomatic mission in Mogadishu and Washington. The Military Regime participated in the Cold War in full swing on behalf of the Kremlin. In the early 1970s the Military Regime, dizzied by Soviet generosity in arms and military advisors which reached a peak of 4,000 men, undertook a senseless anti-American rhetoric which echoed in Somalia and in all forums to which the regime had access. Somali citizens were in danger even for their genuine ties with the US such as training, culture, business, marriage, etc., unless they publicly repudiated the US and showed loyalty to the regime. US officials and citizens, too, had their freedom and contacts restricted in Somalia. Obtaining a Somali visa became arduous for US passport holders.

During the Carter administration when Siyad Barre was planning his war with Ethiopia, the Military Regime approached Washington in the hopes of military backing. It was a widespread opinion in the Horn of Africa at that time that Siyad Barre did obtain a promise of arms from the Carter administration. However, according to David A. Korn and Paul B. Heinze, such a promise never took place. After the 1977 fiasco and in the early 1980s, the US administration was more than willing to counteract the Soviet presence in the Horn of Africa, and thus supported Siyad Barre, who for the occasion elected himself president after he printed a constitution, "as an outpost of the Free World." Heinze wrote that the US "was ready to turn a blind eye on internal conditions in Somalia." Korn wrote on the attitude of the Reagan administration toward Somalia: "[Reagan] came to office persuaded that its predecessor had failed to stand up for its friends and make itself respected by its adversaries. Here was an opportunity to show Somalia that the United States could be counted on and to demonstrate to Ethiopia that the United States' restraint in arming Somalia was not to be construed as a sign of weakness or as a license for Ethiopia to work its will with its southern neighbor." This attitude, according to the author, clearly contrasted with the Carter attitude which, "wanted to establish an American position in Somalia and recognized that this would inevitably entail the United States becoming a supplier of arms to Somalia, but it was not going to supply Somalia so that Somalia could resume the pursuit of its irredentism ambitions."[7]

In August, 1980, Siyad Barre signed an agreement with Washington for the use of naval and air facilities in Somalia in return for $65 million in military assistance at the rate of $20 million annually. In 1981, Siyad Barre visited Washington to seek more support and arms. As a result of his visit, a military delegation led by an American admiral attended the 12th celebration of the "October Revolution" in Mogadishu. After the attacks of Balanballe and Goldogob — in the central regions -- by joint forces of SSDF (Somali Salvation Democratic Front) and Ethiopia and the occupation of these localities by the same forces, the Reagan administration airlifted to Mogadishu arms and ammunition in the value of $5.5 million and another shipment of $10 million followed. The arms delivered included APCs, tanks, TOW missiles and ammunition. The Reagan Administration authorized Italy, Egypt, Saudi Arabia, and United Arab Emirates (UAE) to transfer old tanks, artillery pieces and other equipment. American military training centers opened their doors to officers of the Military Regime, and US military and civilian experts flowed into Somalia. USAID restarted its economic assistance to Somalia, funding projects in agriculture, livestock and other sectors. During the decade 1980-1989, US aid totaled roughly $500 million. Siyad used US arms and ammunition to repress and kill Somali citizens with great embarrassment to the Reagan Administration in 1988. American assistance was suspended only in late 1989 when the Military Regime was almost collapsing and most of the regions were under the control of rebel forces and when there were enough American arms in Somalia. These arms were used by the regime during the insurgence of Mogadishu. Even after the dictator fled Mogadishu, American arms such as the jeep-mounted recoilless 106 mm cannon played a major role in the destruction of the capital.

VIII. Other Western Countries

The EEC economically supported the Military Regime from the outset but assistance was increased in the 1980s. The EEC never encouraged its member states to suspend their aid to the Military Regime even after it had come to wage an open conflict with its people and human rights organizations and the European media had denounced its atrocities.

France and West Germany, too, supplied a great deal of political, economic and military support to the Military Regime. After Palestinians hijacked a Lufthansa plane to Mogadishu and the regime authorized the German anti-terrorist unit to intervene and save the hostages, Bonn increased its ties and assistance to the Military Regime. Nevertheless, France and Germany were among the first countries to distance themselves after the repression increased sharply in the northern and central regions and human rights violations of the Military Regime were publicly denounced by the international media.

IX. The Arab Countries

Most of the Arab countries had good ties with the regime because the Military Regime, since its early stages, paid lip service to the Arab cause and Palestinian support pretending to care about Arab problems. Two factors influenced the close Somali-Arab relationship which resulted in Somalia's entrance into the Arab League. First, most of the young officers who participated in the *coup d'état* were graduates from Egyptian and Iraqi academies and also a number of civilians in the Military Regime machine such as Omar Arteh Ghalib (foreign minister, 1970-1975) were favorable to the Arab League. Second, it was the years of the petro-dollars boom and the rich Arab Gulf countries had given employment opportunities for Somali workers and economic assistance to the regime. In 1974, Somalia was accepted as a full member of the Arab League, and the ties between the League members and Somalia increased. Saudi Arabia and United Arab Emirates financed several development projects. Siyad also benefitted from these countries for military assistance. In fact, Italian sources agree that during 1979-83, the Military Regime purchased about $500 million in arms (with the help of Arab petro-dollars), becoming the third most important client of the Italian arms industry.[8] The regime also increased its pro-Arab rhetoric and, above all, provided a cheap vote for some rich Arab countries in all international forums. This irritated regimes like Assad's and Gaddafi's who often showed hostility to the Military Regime. But unstable Gaddafi shifted alliances several times. After an initial flirtation with the Military Regime, Libya abandoned the regime when it became socialist and displayed Marx, Engels and Lenin portraits instead of the Koran and the Green Book. When SSDF started its guerrilla movement, Libya supplied arms and assistance to it. But in the final days of the regime when Siyad Barre was engaged in the most cruel war against his people, Tripoli assisted the military regime and supplied arms and even chemical weapons used in the north. Ironically, after the fall of the Military Regime, Libya was the first country to supply the Somali people with a large amount of relief aid.

The two Yemens had a different attitude towards Somalia. The South, an ally of Moscow, acted in two phases. When the Military Regime was allied to the Soviet Union, the two anti-popular regimes had good relations. Later, South Yemen established an alliance with Ethiopia. During the 1977 war, South Yemen aided the Ethiopian regime politically and militarily. Aden provided pilots and other assistance, angering the Somali people who had a historic relationship with Aden. Aden was also instrumental to Moscow and Cuba's plan to conciliate Mogadishu and Addis Ababa in Moscow's interest, proposing a confederation of all the states of the area including South Yemen. North Yemen who did not support wholeheartedly the Military Regime can claim a more consistent relationship with Somalia. In the late 1980s, North Yemen assisted all opposition movements by publicly allowing them to open offices in the country to the great dismay of the Military Regime.

X. The World and Post-Siyad Somalia

From 1989, Siyad Barre's army continued its devastation in the central regions, stronghold of the United Somali Congress (USC). It destroyed villages, livestock and water points in the hopes of undermining the support of the armed struggle. This devastation caused a mass exodus to the south, especially to Mogadishu. Thousands of displaced youth joined the USC militia or just formed groups, *sacbooley*, following the fighters in the hope of getting arms from defeated soldiers. After the capture of Mogadishu, the United Somali Congress was unable to handle the problem of the militia and the thousands of youth who had previously fled to Mogadishu. Feeding and providing them with other basic needs was out of USC's reach. When the hopes for a conference for national reconciliation faded away because of the shortsightedness of USC-Mogadishu leadership, the situation indeed became desperate. USC did not have any plan for such an explosive situation. The clashes with the remnants of Siyad Barre and their presence in the south of the country worsened the situation, for USC did not dare to disband the militia. From that time on, USC was dependent upon a countless armed voluntary militia without any source of subsistence. Soon a factional split prevailed throughout USC and two strong militias and a cluster of clan militia with shifting poles infested the entire southern Somalia. It became impossible to find a political solution to the deep crisis and the struggle for power. For USC factions, the only way to keep the militias mobilized was to close one eye to looting. Looting became the pay and soon became a way of life and after that a business. No faction was immune to this disease. The situation deteriorated further when the power struggle inside USC got polarized and led to continuous armed confrontation.

The port of Mogadishu was inoperative due to the factional conflict and uncontrolled clan thugs. The control of the food lifelines was important because of the scarcity of food and relief from outside since the international community, except for a few private non-governmental organizations (NGOs), preferred to take a wait-and-see attitude. The 1991 sorghum harvest in the Upper Juba was good, and Mogadishu businessmen supplemented the trickle of food relief with imported food. In the beginning, they tried to keep prices as low as possible. Nevertheless, with the general unemployment and looting, most of the population was unable to afford food from the market at any price. After the conflict of November, 1991 between USC factions, the situation got totally out of control and an immense tragedy made known by the media to the whole world took place. Minor clashes took place in July and September but the worst of the confrontation started on November 17 and continued until February, 1992. A cease fire brokered by James Jonah, special envoy of the UN, was reached only in February, 1992. Thousands of people were decimated by aimless artillery used irresponsibly, and by famine and disease. Those who escaped death by fleeing the country met death on the sea, on unsafe and overcrowded boats; on the land without food and shelter in defense from looters; and even at international borders where they were rejected or kept in inhumane conditions.[9]

The inter-riverine region, especially Bay and the Lower Shabelle and Juba, were devastated in 1991 by the remnants of Siyad Barre, *faqash*, who also looted their grain stocks and their livestock. The local population organized themselves under the Somali Democratic Movement (SDM) and freed Baidoa and Bay region with the help of Bakool. Again in September 1991, the Bay region was occupied by the *faqash* who committed the most horrible criminal acts of the whole Somali tragedy. The SDM-Bay, tired of waiting for fuel and ammunition that never came from their ally Ali Mahdi, split into two factions. The alliance with USC-Aidid and SSNM (Southern SNM) produced the Somali National Alliance (SNA) whose armed force was called Somali Liberation Army (SLA). The assistance from the SLA brought about liberation, but the political aftermath was disastrous. Power struggles broke out among SDM factions. The SLA militia behaved like an occupation force in the inter-riverine region. Uncontrolled armed bandits became widespread creating terror in the region. From *deyr* rains of 1991, farms were not cropped because of war, insecurity, and drought. The inter-riverine region was stricken by the drought in 1992 while the region remained isolated from the port and the capital because of USC factional fights. The masses in the inter-riverine region suffered immensely from a terrible human-made tragedy.

XI. The Attitude Of the International Community

The cry of the Somali people and the voice of the opposition movements remained unheard by those governments that supported the Military Regime politically, economically and militarily. Although sometimes representatives of the opposition were allowed to hold press conferences in Rome, London, Frankfurt, etc., it is unfortunate that these governments did not want to help the opposition movements.

After mid-1990, when the Military Regime lost control of most of the regions and the flames of the armed struggle were close to the capital, Italy called on Egypt for a joint effort to mediate between the opposition and the regime, a step which to many seemed an attempt to rescue the dictator rather than to help the Somali people.

The US, which on many other occasions supported armed opposition movements such as UNITA in Angola, the Contras in Nicaragua, the Afghan Mujahidiin, etc., did not even open a dialogue with the Somali opposition. Except Italy, which stayed with the dictator until his last days, all western governments who were close to Mogadishu preferred to take a "wait-and-see" attitude. That did not help the Somali people. The Bush Administration did not want to do for Somalia what was done later for Ethiopia.

Similarly, the Arab and African countries that could play a role in the coordination of the opposition movements took the same attitude as the western powers by whom they were inspired. The cynical attitude of these "brotherly and friendly" governments continued even after the fall of Siyad Barre and despite the apparent failure of the opposition movements to cooperate in establishing a transitional government. Two years after the fall of the Military Regime, the Somali novelist Nuruddin Farah, referring to the attitude of these countries, wrote in the *New York Times* accusing them "for watching with mind-boggling indifference while Somalis destroyed themselves, while the country collapsed into absolute anarchy -- the worst of its kind." With great bitterness he lamented: "I will spare you my outrage at the Arab, the Muslim and the non-aligned league of which Somalia is a member. They are not worth my brothers."[10]

But if the western and other governments have abandoned Somalia to her helpless fate, the army of reporters of the international media, distracted in the past by the Gulf war and then by the Yugoslav war, continued to report at length about the Somali plight caused by war, famine and banditry in the towns and remote villages of the Upper Juba. Despite the attention of the newspapers, Somalia was still not getting the world's attention. What made the difference were the pictures. The TV brought, via satellite, dramatic images from Somalia to the overfed viewers of the developed countries. Stories and pictures of starving children and images of emaciated mothers darted into the consciousness of the viewers, proving once more the power of TV's visual imagery and color pictures. Enzo Biagi declared that it was not the death that struck him but "the life that is not lived." Jack Kelly wrote in September, 1992 in the columns of *USA Today* about a three year old girl in Baidoa: "The girl, name unknown, grasped her mother... 'you can take my food' she said combing her hair with her hand. But it was too late. The mother was dead. And no one had the heart to tell the child."[12]

Under pressure from appeals by the relief agencies, moved by these images, congressmen, politicians, movie stars and government officials visited Somalia. Nancy Kassenbaum was the first US senator to visit Somalia. Bernard Kouchner, French minister for health and humanitarian affairs, visited Somalia in October. Lynda Chalker, UK minister for foreign aid and the German foreign minister followed. Douglas Hurd, leading a *troika* of foreign ministers including the Danish foreign minister, was sent by the EEC. Mary Robinsen, the President of the

Republic of Ireland, visited in early October and upon her return made a dramatic, tearful statement in Nairobi. George Bush broke his indifferent silence when asked by a journalist during the Presidential debate in St. Louis in September 1992 if he had ever seen those pictures, Bush replied: "...The pictures,..., the little skinny arms. And it just wrenched the heart of any American."

For the Somali people, caught by the plight, the world's response appeared as "too little, too late" making them believe that the world had no heart just like the dictator and the warring factions.

In the following paragraphs we will examine the attitude of the closest western countries and the UN which was delegated to deal with Somalia's tragedy after the fall of the dictatorship.

XII. The Italian Government

Some time after Siyad Barre was ousted and Ali Mahdi Mohamed was installed by his faction in Mogadishu as an interim president, the Italian government sent its ambassador to Mogadishu. Mario Sica, a maladroit diplomat appointed by Gianni De Michelis, started in mid-1991 a frenetic senseless diplomacy which worsened the already bad relationships among the Somali factions. On the other hand, he was not able or willing to provide badly-needed humanitarian relief. Sica was followed by Under-Secretary Umberto Plaja who promised relief aid to Somalia, and Sica himself reiterated that Italy had allocated unlimited funds for Somalia. He also promised the reestablishment of the international communication system with an emergency one until the main system could be repaired.[13]

In the following months Ambassador Sica engaged his diplomatic activity, flying to and from Mogadishu, Kismayo, Bosaso, Berbera, Nairobi and Rome and in less than six months was able to spend $30 million providing Somalia with less than 2,000 tons of materials. His diplomacy and attitude angered all Somali factions because it lacked transparency. The Italian historian Angelo Del Boca described the Italian relief as follows: "...[A] thousand ton or so consisting of food, medicine and fuel first dumped at Mogadishu, Berbera and Kismayo by plane and then by ship." Sica was reinforced with Undersecretary Raffaelli who also visited Berbera to meet with SNM (Somali National Movement) leaders without any results.[14]

During his first visit to Mogadishu, Sica blamed Farah Aidid for some press releases in early 1991 made by his representative in London, discouraging support to the Interim Government. On the other hand, Aidid accused him of interference in Somali affairs and the unwillingness to provide humanitarian relief. The hostility between Aidid and Craxi was well-known in Italy and in Somalia since Aidid sued Craxi and Pillitteri and others in the Italian court in a civil case concerning commission fees on projects. The court in Italy has postponed the hearing several times since 1989 and only in 1990 ruled in favor of Craxi.

Sica did not cease to travel in all directions without any tangible results. Del Boca reported in his book that according to Sica between January 17 and July 30 he made ten visits to Mogadishu, eight to Berbera, four to Kismayo and two to Bosaso and Garoe. Del Boca concluded that "It is legitimate to have some doubts about the validity of the good offices offered by Italy. It must be pointed out that the Italian intervention would have credibility and effectiveness if it was carried out by new diplomats that had no rapport with the regime of Siyad Barre" and "As far as the legitimacy of the Italian peace mission it was repeatedly questioned by the major armed movements who often considered it an inappropriate interference and appealed to the Italian government to refrain from missions other than humanitarian ones."[15]

At the end of October 1991, "the Barest Affair" took place. Andrea Barest, Christian Democrat Undersecretary to *Farnesina*, undertook an ill-planned visit to Mogadishu. His arrival angered Aidid, who was not informed and the tower told Barest's plane that because of sudden fights which had erupted in the capital, his plane could not land. On November 17, hostilities broke out between the two USC factions and during the fights the Italian Embassy was looted. The Italian government considered these facts as an "insult" and in November 1991 decided to interrupt all relations with Somalia, including humanitarian assistance. This attitude of the Italian government angered most Italians and the press criticized it. Del Boca called the Italian attitude "a defeat of intelligence." He wrote: "Once again, as in the past, we assisted in the defeat of intelligence. Intelligence as intuition, competence, capability of intervening in an emergency and making a difference in history."[16]

It took one year for the Italian government to reopen Somalia's case. After one year, Emilio Colombo -- new foreign minister -- paid a visit to Somalia on September 7, 1992 after the Somali tragedy had echoed all over the world. A new ambassador who attempted to pursue a more "balanced diplomacy" replaced Mario Sica. Before his departure from Rome, Emilio Colombo pledged that Italy would play an active role in the Somali tragedy. He also promised that the Italian government would investigate the issue, denounced by a UN agency, of alleged illegal dumping of more than one million metric tons of toxic wastes in Somali waters by an Italian firm. During his visit, Colombo met with both Ali Mahdi and Farah Aidid.

The new Italian initiative was overshadowed, on one hand, by the SEGA-initiative of the UN-US in Somalia and on the other hand it drowned in the chronic Italian political, constitutional and financial crisis. With its deep crisis, Italy was not in a position to commit itself to a peace offensive in Somalia. Since the eruption of the Somali crisis, Italy, "the sick man of Europe," changed three premiers, three foreign ministers, three ambassadors, one president of the republic; had a constitutional crisis, and had experienced *tangentopoli* (kickback city), the worst corruption scandal in its history which affected, among others, two former premiers who are under investigation by the judges of *mani pulite* (clean hands).

Nevertheless, when Operation Restore Hope was implemented, the Italian government, to everyone's surprise, insisted on joining UNITAF forces. Italy was previously advised by the US not to participate in these forces. Emilio Colombo, in an interview with the Italian major newspaper *Il Corriere della Sera*, announced that Italy would not remain behind when the American and French troops were involved. In the same interview, Sig. Colombo defended the support of the Italian government to Siyad Barre as legitimate in the era of the Cold War.[17]

In the meantime, the Giuliano D'Amato administration resigned and an independent prime minister, Carlo D'Azeglio Ciampi, was chosen to lead the 52nd administration of Italy since World War II. But Ciampi's government was not well-positioned to play an active role in Somalia. After a period of low profile, the Italian troops in Somalia twice became the center of wide attention. The first incident occurred, in the spring of 1990, when Italian forces became involved in widespread human rights violations and abuses. In June 1990, the Italian magazine *Epoca* published under the title of "These Images Tell Everything" shocking pictures of gross abuses and violence against Somali citizens by Italian soldiers. The issue was discussed in the Parliament.

Nevertheless, the Italian government claimed a more leading role for *Italfor* in the peacekeeping operations. The Italian officers were totally disappointed when they found that they ranked fourth in decision-making in UNOSOM II for matters concerning intelligence, perhaps because of the position of the Italian language in southern Somalia. After May 4, General Bruno Loi made known to the UN that he had to consult Rome on all matters. The Italian defense minister had previously requested that Italy be given a post of command in the peacekeeping force in Somalia. According to the Italian press, the Americans let the Italians believe that their request would be met. Instead, on July 14, Kofi Annan requested the removal of General Loi. According to *Il Corriere della Sera,* the answer to the Italian request actually came before Kofi Annan from Madelaine

Albright in Mogadishu when she praised the leadership of General Bir whom the Italians were hoping to replace. However, until the incident of the "Pasta Factory" checkpoint on July 2, when three Italian soldiers were killed and twenty wounded, *Italfor* was very proud of the use of force in the Italian style. The latter differs from the "Pentagon doctrine" which relies on overwhelming the "enemy" with superior power fire and leaves no room for waving the carrot. The Italian style is based on the philosophy that Italians are even in war *"brava gente."*[18] General Giampiero Rossi, the Italian commander (replaced later with Gen. B. Loi) stressed in *Epoca* in mid-May 1990 that they "impose peace with force." On that occasion, Rossi complained that the UN distributed decisional roles ignoring "the logic of political military" and that "Mogadishu was given to Pakistanis who do nothing and called in Egyptians and Nigerians who are not welcomed by the Somalis." On June 17 when the UN forces made their worst retaliatory attack, the Italian forces participated in the operations. *Il Corriere della Sera* compared the violence of the attack to that against Libya in 1986 and the missiles against Baghdad in January 1990. The Italian defense minister Fabio Fabbri stated that: "We could not fail to participate in the executive phase of what the UN command had assigned to us." He also added: "[Italy] has requested and obtained the participation of our commanders in the decision-making process." This was confirmed by Gen. Bruno Loi who in an interview with the newspaper stated that he was properly consulted by UNOSOM: "The consultation was satisfactory, I expressed my opinion which after all was that of the Italian Defense Ministry and the Chief of Staff." Beniamino Andreatta, the new Italian foreign minister, also declared: "It is not possible to build a state amid flowers and fanfare without the use of force. The precious gift of building a state, to help a country to build one, is a risky operation.[19]

It is hard to believe that the Italian disagreement with the UN policy in Somalia is founded entirely on concerns about the well-being of the Somali people. In essence, the Italians had behaved in July in the same way the Americans behaved in October 1990, i.e., using the UN as a scapegoat. But in the UN American muscles count more.

XIII. The United States of America

The United States was noticeably absent from the Somali scene after the ouster of Siyad Barre. For a short time, some US embassy staff were in Nairobi, and some AID officials visited Mogadishu and delivered little, untimely, and ill-planned relief. A shipment of a few thousand tons of sorghum sent when Somalia had a good sorghum harvest, was dumped by a ship at Mombasa port, claiming that was its contract obligation. During the fights in January, 1991, Mogadishu and the surrounding area survived with the beans that the US donated to the regime, convincing Somalis that the US was more generous with the dictator than with the people of Somalia. After the November, 1991 clashes, again the US abandoned Somalia. In fact, for two years the Somali issue "did not move beyond the realm of the Assistant Secretary of African Affairs, Herman J. Cohen.[20] The Bush Administration was down playing the Somali case at the Security Council.

Nevertheless, American private relief organizations and a medical team assisted and shared with the Somali people the hardship of the war and famine. But American relief agencies received few donations for Somalia from the American citizens perhaps because of the economic recession. By August, 1992, agencies had received less than one million dollars compared to the $410 million in contributions to Ethiopia between October, 1984 and March, 1985.[21]

Already in mid-January 1992, Senators Nancy Kassenbaum, Paul Simon and others appealed to the Bush Administration to take the Somali matter before the Security Council of the UN. In mid-1992, the Somali tragedy was on the front pages and on TV screens. It was the time of TV images and photos from Somalia. In July 1992 the White House made a statement on Somalia declaring that the US stood ready to do its part to support the proposal of Secretary General Boutros Boutros-Ghali to mobilize the international community for Somalia. The White House claimed that the Administration had committed $63 million over the past two years. After only two weeks, it announced that the US would airlift relief into the interior regions of Somalia and northeast Kenya to the refugees.[22] On that occasion, the White House claimed that the total American contribution to Somali relief to that date had exceeded $76 million and pledged to intensify US effort. Immediately after, an additional $10 million to be spent within a short time was announced.[23]

Even though statements were not totally clear, it suggested that things were now moving quickly. Only one day after the White House made the above statement, a stronger one, articulated in five points, appeared:

> 1. the Defense Department will begin emergency airlift operations to deliver food to Somalia and to the Somali refugees in Kenya;
> 2. consultations will begin with the UN to seek a Security Council resolution for additional measures to ensure that humanitarian relief can be delivered;
> 3. a donor's conference will convene with the participation of

the Somali factions;

4. an additional 145,000 tons of American food will be made available for Somalia; and

5. Andrew Natsios is appointed Special Coordinator for the Somali Relief.[24]

With this operation, named "Operation Provide Relief," the US was determined to abandon totally its previous position and take a leading role in the Somali situation. This drastic change in the position of the Bush Administration for the last eighteen months came as a surprise to many political observers. But the real surprise came when the Bush Administration announced "Operation Restore Hope" at the end of November, 1992. Considering the nature of the intervention and the anticipated lack of hostility to the mission and thus an "easy success," the Administration did not encounter resistance from lawmakers. Congressional leaders expressed agreement and no "War Power Resolution" was evoked even though the operation was dispatching 28,000 US troops.

The US offer also passed smoothly at the Security Council of the UN and gained unanimous support because, as Henry Kissinger, former Secretary of State explained: "....the approval was for an American proposal presented on a take-it-or-leave-it basis. Since the US clearly preferred the first stage to be unilateral, other countries were risking the entire prospect of an international effort by refusing it."

There is no doubt that George Bush saw in Somalia an opportunity that militarily appeared to be easy success and yet would obtain huge approval from every corner of the nation. Even though the decision took place after the fate of the elections was decided it was a graceful act by George Bush whose campaign was based on the "character issue" of the future commander in chief of the US forces. Perhaps, if the Bush Administration had given the same importance earlier to the Somali situation, success could have been achieved with lesser military might.

The Los Angeles Times added spice to the matter when it asserted that the "oil factor" played a role in Bush's decision to respond to Somalia's emergency. Oil has been discovered in the north and oil companies did not hesitate to sign contracts for further oil prospecting with the Somaliland government. According to Conoco, it achieved "a very good show" of oil also in the south. In fact, the Conoco staff never abandoned Somalia and its General Manager stressed "We stayed because of Somalia's potential for the company and to protect our assets."[25] The Italian daily *La Repubblica* went even further in asserting that the American decisions were influenced by oil. "Four of the 'seven sisters' -- the major US oil companies -- have concessions to drill in two-thirds of the country."[26]

The Clinton Administration also showed strong determination to continue the US role in Somalia, even though many Americans were not convinced that the operation was worth the risk. While the responsibility of sending troops to Somalia lay with the Bush Administration, it surprised many that the Clinton Administration totally endorsed all the mistakes of the UN. But the mystery disappears when we think that the UN is not an independent body from the US. In fact, with all its ineffectiveness and cumbersome bureaucracy, the UN is executing in Somalia a program that is "a US baby." As a matter of fact, the real decision-making and the military striking power of the peacekeeping operations in Somalia are American.

Perhaps Somalia was chosen randomly as a guinea pig for a post-Cold War peacekeeping test. No matter, whatever role was initially planned for Somalia, today it became unequivocally a place to test the UN-US partnership in peacekeeping. How much can be carried out directly by the US and how much can be left to an empowered UN multinational umbrella is being experimented today in Somalia. *The Economist* commented cynically in December 1992 that "America, after all, is not exactly unilateralist: it likes the UN to bless what it is doing and other rich countries to cough up men or cash" for its role of "world cop."[27]

But the massacre of October 3, 1990 partially aborted the "Somali ordeal" because certain foreign policy issues resurfaced. Accidentally, Somalia rekindled issues that Americans had believed they had finally left behind. Somalia rekindled the President's war power issue and the specter of Vietnam. The debate following the October episode led to the popular and congressional demand to get out of Somalia which put the Administration in a very difficult situation. Despite the confusion around the Somali intervention, two conclusions can be drawn. First, US companies will be the first to benefit from eventual oil and the US will not allow, like it did in the 1980s, "unfriendly" countries such as Iraq to carry out their plans for the extraction of uranium in central Somalia. Second, the future of peacekeeping operations and military interventions in regional affairs in the post-Cold War era was being shaped during operations in Somalia.

XIV. The United Nations

The UN evacuated during the insurrection of Mogadishu in January, 1991. Considering the magnitude of the fights in the capital, the evacuation was reasonable. But the UN returned to Somalia only after the tragedy had reached unthinkable levels. However, the UN, in its public statements, claimed that its "humanitarian efforts" were restarted after only two months. This claim does not reflect reality since the UN returned to Somalia in January, 1992, when Undersecretary James Jonah was entrusted with brokering peace by the former Secretary-General of the UN. Not only did the UN abandon Somalia to its fate, it did not acknowledge the crisis to the world. In fact, the private relief agencies and human rights organizations have rightly attributed much of the deterioration of the situation in Somalia to the UN. Africa Watch, for instance, stressed that "the UN's refusal to acknowledge the crisis also played a large part." The UN did not actively participate in the peace effort which led to the Djibouti conference. At the conference, the UN was represented by the office of the UNDP (UN Development Program) in Djibouti. When the US, in December 1991, needed a UN plane for food delivery, the UN refused because Somalia was an unsafe place. As far as its agencies were concerned, none of them had an office in Somalia before 1993.[28]

The Jonah mission, though successful in brokering a cease fire agreement between warring USC factions, was a failure. James Jonah worked most of the time in New York and Addis Ababa, and he remained in Mogadishu only a few days. In March, 1990, when the agreement on how to implement the cease-fire was signed, Jonah "instead of urging stepped-up relief on the heels of the cease-fire, recommended only a technical assessment of Somalia's peacekeeping and relief needs and the deployment of UN observers."[29]

The image of the UN improved greatly when the Algerian diplomat Mohammed Sahnoun was appointed at the end of April 1992 as a UN Special Envoy to Somalia. Then followed Resolution 751 of the Security Council on April 1992 which established the UN operation in Somalia called UNOSOM to help end hostilities and maintain the cease-fire throughout the country in order to promote reconciliation and provide humanitarian assistance. However, Sahnoun's Somali ordeal was interrupted because, frustrated by the UN bureaucracy, he grew critical of the organization. He then was forced to resign. In November, Sahnoun was replaced by an Iraqi, UN bureaucrat Ismat Kittani, and the UN abandoned "Sahnoun's approach" centered on the belief that peace and reconciliation can only come if a genuine Somali effort is strengthened by a facilitating, consistent, and never-tiring honest diplomacy. Sahnoun quickly grasped the aspiration of the Somali people and understood fully that the struggle and armed banditry involved only a small fraction of the people the majority of whom wanted peace and stability. In addition, a large number of personalities, national leaders (such as the first president of Somalia), elders, intellectuals and women were endeavoring to persuade the faction leaders to accept peace. "Sahnoun's performance remains the highest of the UN's relations with Somalia since 1990, and that his tenure ended bitterly is more a comment on the UN's approach to Somalia than on Sahnoun's considerable achievement."[30]

After Sahnoun stepped down, the UN endeavor was bound to lead to the occupation of Somalia to implement the multi-billion "industry of peacekeeping" very dear to Boutros Boutros-Ghali who explained his philosophy in his essay "Empowering the United Nation" at the end of 1992.[31] The gigantic bureaucratic machine of the UN was responsible for removing Sahnoun and putting Somalia under a UN transitional rule which can lead to a foreign sponsored Somali government. The road to military intervention was made inevitable once Sahnoun's idea of limited deployment of blue helmets in key points in Somalia, combined with effective diplomacy, was abandoned. Also many NGOs are of the opinion that the UN bureaucracy jeopardized peace initiatives as well as the humanitarian relief. J. Stevenson concluded his analysis on Operation Restore Hope as follows: "In fact, the expensive American initiative would have been unnecessary had the UN not fired Sahnoun; rendering a political solution impossible at the moment of Somalia's most critical need."[32] Boutros Boutros-Ghali, despite his accusation of the Western World to only care about the "rich man's war" in Yugoslavia and his numerous reports and resolutions, failed to give a try to Sahnoun's diplomacy.

While the humanitarian situation was degenerating in Somalia, the UN was escalating ineffective resolutions at the Security Council. It is hard to keep track of the number of resolutions adopted in 1992 alone. Resolution 733, for instance sanctioned a complete arms embargo to Somalia but it was never implemented and arms flowed from Kenya to Siyad Barre's remnants. Resolution 767 of July 27 followed Resolution 751 which established UNOSOM and called for airlifted relief to Somalia. Resolution 771 requested an increase in UNOSOM forces of up to 3,500 men and was followed by Resolution 775 which welcomed the US offer to airlift relief aid. In the meantime, the security situation in Somalia deteriorated, especially in the inter-riverine region which made it impossible for humanitarian aid to flow to the needy unless heavily armed protection was secured. Paid armed guards hired locally to escort the food convoys became ineffective. Extortion, banditry, looting, killing, and other crimes became widespread compelling thousands of civilians to flee by land and sea.

The UN saw the acceptance of the conditions laid down by the US for Operation Restore Hope, and Resolution 794 as a remedy. From December 9, 1992 until May 4, 1993 UNITAF (American led Task Force) took over UNOSOM During this period, UN diplomacy was guided by White House officials. Robert Oakley, former US ambassador in Somalia in the early 1980s, manipulated the political situation in order to withdraw the US forces as early as possible. Under Operation Restore Hope, relief convoys moved safely and reached the main centers. Thanks to the NRC (National Reconciliation Conference) held in Addis Ababa in March, the future of Somalia looked brighter and the US could withdraw the marines, taking credit for having achieved its declared objectives.

While Somalia was waiting for the implementation of the fragile agreement reached at Addis Ababa in March 1993, by the fifteen factions, the situation escalated dramatically in early June when twenty-four Pakistani soldiers were killed in an ill-planned operation of "peace enforcement." UNOSOM never admitted the plain truth that sending a contingent into a hostile zone without sufficient evaluation of the risks involved and without providing appropriate measures for its retrieval in case of emergency was putting the lives of the men in jeopardy. If a Somali faction failed to comply with the terms of the agreement it signed with the other fourteen factions, it was up to these factions to denounce the violation and suggest how to implement the agreement. But the UN did not bother with legalities because UNOSOM *de facto* considered Somalia under its administration. In fact, the following day, it already had in hand Resolution 837 of the Security Council authorizing UNOSOM forces to retaliate against the SNA (Somali National Alliance). Violence broke out and escalated, indefinitely postponing the Somali peace initiatives. Militiamen and civilians were killed by the hundreds, more blue helmets and even foreign journalists also lost their lives. Ultra-sophisticated weapons were employed, creating a climate of terror. As the operation was proving to be ineffective, the Pentagon doctrine prevailed and more weapons and special troops were brought in. The UN abandoned everything else in Somalia and focused on a manhunt for Mohamed Farah Aidid after it issued posters with rewards as was the custom in the "wild west." Despite the widespread criticism from the international media and the public, the manhunt continued while civilians, mainly women and children, were dying and being injured. This state of affairs continued until October, when several helicopters were downed and an entire contingent of elite US rangers of one hundred men were wounded or killed. This incident constituted a turning point because the images shown on the screens in America undermined the operation.

Many Somalis believed that UNOSOM and UNITAF would help peace in Somalia by disarming the militias and uncontrolled thugs even after the UN had castigated Sahnoun for his well-founded criticism of the UN bureaucracy and its slowness and indifference to the violence of

Somali bandits. Soon the hope was dashed, first, by Robert Oakley who refused to disarm militias. Then the Somali people placed their faith in UNOSOM II in the hope of disarmament. But once again, they were disappointed. Rakiya Omar and Alex de Waal concluded in their recent article: "By now the single biggest error of the occupation had also become apparent: there were no checks on the behavior of the troops, nor were there any procedures for redress."[33] There were no self-criticism or admission of errors: there were only retaliation, and retaliation is only revenge and it is the negation of rationality. It led only to peril.

XV. Conclusion

Undoubtedly, the responsibility for the present Somali tragedy lies, in the first place, with Somalis themselves. The military dictatorship survived and prolonged its reign of terror with the help of the international community who provided political, economic, and military support. While some governments distanced themselves from the Military Regime when the situation deteriorated beyond remedy, others such as the Italian government chose to stay with the dictator against the Somali people. After the ouster of the dictatorship, Somalia sank into chaos because of the failure of the opposition movements to establish a transitional rule. During this crucial period, the international community abandoned Somalia and kept a "wait-and-see" attitude. In the eyes of the Somali people, caught by the plight, the response of the world at the end of 1992 appeared as "too little, too late." The UN failed in making peace in Somalia. The UN proved to be slow in relief operations, intolerant to criticism and bureaucratic. Its failure in achieving a political solution paved the road to the military occupation of Somalia. The UN is greatly responsible for the present stalemate in Somalia.

Peace in Somalia cannot be imposed by force; it can only come from a genuine Somali effort. The international community should facilitate the process of reconciliation and provide humanitarian aid.

Endnotes

1. Ali, Ahmed Q. "Predicament of Somali Studies". Paper presented at the 35th Annual Meeting of African Studies Association, Seattle, 1992.

2. Heinze, Paul B. *The Horn of Africa: From War to Peace*. London, MacMillan, 1991, p. 103.

3. Pellettieri, Paolo, *Somalia 1981*, Milano: Segarco, 1981.

4. Petrucci, Pietro. "Che Affare quei Poveri". *L'Espresso*, November 29, 1992.

5. Petrucci, Pietro. "La Loro Africa". *L'Espresso* September 6, 1992. See also: Del Boca, Angelo, op. cit. p. 43.

6. Del Boca, Angelo, *Una Sconfitta dell'Intelligencza, Italia a Somalia*, Bari: Latorza, 199,. p. 35.

7. Heinze, Paul B., *The Horn of Africa: From War to Peace*, London: Macmillan, 1991, p. 154. See also: Korn, David A., Ethiopia, The United States, and the Soviet Union, Beckenham (UK): Croom Helm, 1986, pp. 74-77.

8. Petrucci, P., *Somalia la Nostra Vergogna*, Rome, Iceberg 2, 1991, p. 197.

9. For the plight of Somali refugees, see: Africa Watch, *Seeking Refuge, Finding Terror*, October, 1990. African Rights, *The Nightmare Continues... Abuses Against Somali Refugees in Kenya*, September 1993.

10. Farah, N., "Praise the Marines? I Suppose So," *New York Times,* December 28, 1992.

11. Biagi, Enzo, *La Stampa,* August 29, 1992.

12. Kelly, Jack, *USA Today*, September 9, 1992.

13. The funds mentioned are 300 billion lira from FAI funds allocated to Somalia in 1990.

14. Del Boca, op. cit., p. 82.

15. *Ibid.*, p. 106.

16. *Ibid.*, p. 108.

17. *Il Corriere della Sera*, December 6, 1992.

18. *Ibid.*, July 4, 1990. See also *L'Espresso*, July 25, 1990.

19. *Il Corriere della Sera,* June 13, 1990. See also *Epoca*, June 29, 1990.

20. *The New York Times,* August 30, 1992.

21. *Los Angeles Times,* August 19, 1992.

22. *Weekly Compilation of Presidential Documents*, Vol. 28, #31, August 3, 1992, p. 1341.

23. *Ibid.*, #33, August 17, 1992, p. 1437.

24. *Ibid.*, p. 1441.

25. Fineman, Mark, "The Oil Factor in Somalia." *Los Angeles Times,* January 18, 1990.

26. *La Repubblica,* August 3, 1990.

27. World Cop, *The Economist,* December 19, 1992.

28. *The New York Times,* December 11, 1992.

29. Stevensen, Jonathan, "Hope Restored in Somalia?" *Foreign Policy,* #91, Summer 1990, p. 144.

30. Human Rights Watch, *The Lost Agenda and UN Field Operations*, New York: Human Rights Watch, June 1990, p. 119.

31. Boutros-Ghali, Boutros, "Empowering the United Nations." *Foreign Affairs*, Vol. 71, #5, p. 89.

32. Stevensen, J., op. cit., p. 151.

33. Rakiya Omaar & de Waal, Alex," Somali Resentment," Pacific News Service, in *The Arizona Daily Star*, October 3, 1990.

CHAPTER THIRTY FIVE

Italy and Somalia: Unbearable Lightness of an Influence

Giampaolo Calchi Novati

I. Introduction

The unfinished tragedy in Somalia -- from the setback of the military regime led by Siyad Barre to the political and ecological catastrophe which followed the breakthrough of its overthrow -- had the effect, *inter alia*, to put in evidence objectives, ambitions and limits of the Italian approach to the facts of Somalia and the Horn at large. Like in past opportunities, Italy tried to combine different options, avoiding as much and as long as possible to commit herself in a sharp and excluding choice. The outcome was a behavior that, regardless of its merits, was incapable to draw all the consequences from the premises and the perspicuity of an analysis that in principle was better founded and motivated than the policy carried out by the multinational force under the aegis of the US personnel and the pervasive leadership of the UN Secretary General, Boutros Boutros-Ghali.

The purpose of this paper is to identify and explain such a contradiction through the story of Italy's policy towards Somalia in the three periods in which it can be roughly divided: colonial administration, trusteeship on behalf of the United Nations after World War II, and bilateral relationships and cooperation with the independent Somali state.

II. Italian Colonial Policy

A paradox of the Italian colonial policy was the striking contrast between first priority aims and the actual results produced. The Mediterranean, with its familiar towns, harbors and cultures, and plenty of Italians transplanted from the poor, overpopulated countryside of the peninsula, was the main target of any desirable expansion, but historical circumstances forced Italy to divert her attention and emigration streams toward far-away, unknown and hostile lands on the Red Sea. Minister Mancini, in 1885, adroitly formulated a bizarre aphorism in a bid to convince a disoriented public opinion and a doubtful Parliament: "The Red Sea is the key to the Mediterranean." So from the outset, Italian colonial dreams competed with interests, almost making Italian authorities lose a sense of proportion.

When, at the beginning of the age of imperialism, Italy was solicited to intervene in Africa, the government of the time studied the case with a caution that seemed excessive to detractors. The government was concerned with refraining from false steps. It was just in North Africa, i.e., in Tunisia and Egypt, that the Italian government's attitude was more prudent, giving the impression that even good opportunities were being missed. Cairoli did not check the French occupation of Tunis and Mancini preferred to decline the British offer to dispatch an expeditionary force against Urabi Pasha's nationalist uprising. Rationality came first. Africa did not deserve wasting Italian resources. Italy was committed to building a nation, to setting up an integrated economy and to creating a reliable network of alliances at a European level. Yet in the region of the Red Sea, awareness and caution were swept away and action was based less on reflection. In 1882, the Italian state replaced the commercial firm Rubattino in the ownership of the Assab settlement installations by signing a bilateral agreement. In 1885, Mancini, author of well-known writings defending the basic rights of peoples and nations, employed force to conquer Massawa, ignoring the claims of Turkey, Egypt and local authorities. With the same mix of boldness and superficiality, Italy embarked into a wide penetration in Somaliland first via initiatives of commercial companies and then performing, as a state, the tasks of subjugation, unification and administration.

Italian territorial expansion in East Africa during the hectic years of partition of the Black Continent reached its climax in the military confrontation with Menelik's power and his staunch decision to fight for the autonomy of the Empire. The Italian defeat at Adowa turned into a sort of stain of blame all nationalists pledged to delete from the records of the Motherland, no matter which profits they expected to obtain by such a redemption. Obsession with Adowa had a strong impact on the fascist fatal determination to relaunch outdated colonial adventures in Africa. Mussolini focused his rhetoric on the Mediterranean, the Mare Nostrum of ancient Rome's historical memory, but again the target of his aggressiveness was Ethiopia, exploiting a skirmish across the sands of The Ogaden. The Ethiopian War and the founding of Africa Orientale Italiana (AOI) brought popularity to the Duce and spelled success for fascism, making it easier to heal some of the negative impact of the Great Depression in the Italian economy.

Italy lacked the financial and technical resources, as well as the time, to effect a real transformation of the economy and society of AOI, but from their headquarters within Haile Selassie's Palace Italian administrators had hoped to achieve more far-reaching goals than mere imperialism. They figured out to believe that it was possible to change the very soul of Ethiopia by manipulating the hierarchical balance of power among nations and elites. Deputy General Governor Cerulli had always cherished the ambition to promote the peripheral nomadic Muslim peoples at the expense of the Semitized Christian plateau dwellers, in order to gradually wear down Abyssinian resistance. In this framework, we have to evaluate the fatal decision to carve out the Ogaden from the Ethiopian empire and to administer it together with Somalia, giving new impetus and legitimization to pan-Somalist myth but, despite her virtual dominance, without supporting this territory and sovereignty manipulation with the necessary authority in order to make the merging effective and lasting.

During World War II, Italy was defeated and in 1941 lost all her possessions in East Africa, surrendering to British troops and to the Emperor's army. AOI foundered and ceased to exist only five years after it had been pompously proclaimed. Italian defeat was mostly due to military inferiority on the battlefield. Worse than that, Italy left behind in Africa no credible element -- influence, prestige -- to pave the way to a return in any form whatsoever. The dismal reality was that Italy had been unable to set up any structure of mutual partnership and complicity which normally had been the result of European colonialism and which had often proved stronger and more resilient than direct colonial administration. Also, the accomplishment of the responsibility of the trustee power in Somalia abided by and resented this inferiority status.

The terms of the Peace Treaty seemed to leave Italy no hope; they flatly demanded a formal renunciation of all her colonies. Yet the Italian government did its utmost to fulfill a deep, and in a way foolish, desire to reacquire at least partially her African Empire. The final destiny of the colonies would be determined by the four big powers; if no deal was struck by September, 1948 the United Nations would have to treat the question. Long and tough negotiations followed. Italy's residual aspirations, on one hand, and the impending East-West confrontation on the other, prevailed, overriding or baffling the rights of African peoples.

On the agenda of Italian foreign policy in the aftermath of World War II, the colonial issue was second only to the dispute with Yugoslavia over Trieste. Government and opposition alike were committed to rescuing at least some colonies, even as a trusteeship. It was considered a matter of honor and national pride. Nobody could at that time foresee that within a few years the African continent would be rapidly and entirely decolonized. In the meantime, Italy wished to preserve the privileges and property of the "coloni," particularly in Eritrea (beside Libya).

The political parties which were going to build the post-fascist democratic state in Italy shared the same broad principles: lip service to anti-colonial feelings and nationalist aspirations which could easily become expansionist appetites. Italy prided herself on her colonial patrimony. Even the left-wing parties were sensitive to the idea of Italy's right to "return" to Africa on the ground that Italian presence in Africa had been sustained by the work of the Italians rather than by capital investment. Colonies, after all, were a good electoral issue.

Italy was not a member of the UN; her position during the debate at the General Assembly was consequently fairly difficult. The former colonies, which were considered either Arab countries or closely associated with the Muslim world, relied on the support of the Arab League, that claimed their independence at once or after a short period of administration under the aegis of the United Nations. East-West conflict hardly left any room for the Italian delegation to maneuver and to achieve its purpose. The main concern of the powers engaged in the Cold War was to prevent a widening of the counterpart's influence into the "grey areas" of the Third World-to-be. Britain and the United States were aware that opposition to Italy had spread throughout the Horn and feared that a pro-Italian verdict at the UN would step up unrest and riots which Italy was unlikely to play down. The Soviet government was now thoroughly sympathetic with the anti-colonial cause and in its mind the African territories were no exception. Italy was compelled to rely, above all, on the friendship of the Latin American countries with their twenty votes in UN bodies.

Playing too many cards and pursuing too many ends altogether, Italy failed to obtain the expected compensations and lost almost everything. The outcome of the UN debate was disappointing in comparison with

Italian expectations, unless the real goals of Italian policy were not in Africa, but in Europe. Only poor and neglected Somalia -- where Italian settlers were less numerous than in any other Italian possession -- was assigned to Italian administration as a trusteeship territory for a ten-year period. The demarcation of the Somali boundary as well was bound to push Italy into a collision course with Emperor Haile Selassie, who had advanced a claim on Somalia even though with less emphasis than that on Eritrea. The interminable "good neighbors" question with Ethiopia had not been solved and ran the risk of becoming as divisive an issue as it had in the past. The Emperor demonstrated a spirit of forgiveness and reconciliation but was reluctant to open the way back to Italian supremacy in the Horn.

The shadows in the relations between Italy and Ethiopia during the long bargaining in view of a normalization of political and diplomatic relations were due mostly to Italy's insistence on the full respect of Eritrea's autonomy. In contrast, Ethiopia maintained that Italy was not entitled to look after the implementation of UN resolutions and disregarded any criticism. The contrast highlights Italy's incapacity to reconcile different and possibly contradictory stakes. Did she mean to restore an implicit form of colonialism in the Horn (Somalia, Eritrea)? Or did Italy aim at going ahead and opening a fresh chapter in her policy in Africa by advocating the rights of the newly independent African states and by accepting a relation with Ethiopia on the basis of a genuine equality? And in unearthing Ethiopia's interference, either in Eritrea or Somalia, did Italy protect the national rights of the African nations or was she just selfishly worried that decolonization or the absorption of her former colonies into the Empire would jeopardize Italian settlers' interests and business?

III. The Italian Trust Administration

The Italian Trust Administration of Somalia (AFIS, according to the Italian acronym) was a challenge for Italy. AFIS had to show Italy's new democratic look. The decisive step turned out to be reconciliation with the most militant offspring of Somali nationalism, the Somali Youth League (SYL). Regardless of the past hatred and prejudices, the two parties were bound to work hand in hand as the result of their converging interests.

For her part, Italy was confident that the government of SYL -- a mix of traditionalism, ethnicity and modernization within the frame of semi-representative institutions -- would be doomed to rely on financial assistance from Italy because of the backwardness of a country craving for goods, cash and know-how. The former colony on the Indian Ocean that merged with former British Somaliland after independence, in 1960, was the main -- indeed sole -- nation to benefit from Italian aid during the sixties and seventies. Harmony would have been perfect if Italy had undertaken to provide the arms and military training Somalis desperately needed to endorse their Greater Somalia design; despite the traditionally pro-Somali leanings of Italian diplomacy, the Italian government rejected the package deal put forward by the Somali government, clearly showing its opposition to pan-Somali irredentism, that threatened the territorial integrity of Ethiopia and other neighboring countries. As a conservative power, Italy did not want to stimulate instability in the periphery.

The military takeover in October, 1969 caused the replacement of the elite with which Italy had shaped the Somali state. Most of the high officers who seized power in Mogadishu had been trained in the Soviet Union and they were supposed to be loyal to socialism and Moscow's will rather than to Western values and Italy's influence. However, Mohamed Siyad Barre had spent many years in Italian military academies and had been pushed to the top of the military hierarchy by Italian officials. In the cabinet, there were ministers with Italian university degrees. As far as political ascendancy is concerned, it was well-known that some of them were close to the Italian Communist Party (PCI). Did socialist ideals which prevailed in the revolutionary regime stem, after all, from the former metropolitan power despite unorthodox channels?

Faced with a radical and anti-Western regime that turned to the Soviet Union for sophisticated military equipment, the Italian government preferred to remain in touch with Somalia so as not to deliver it into the hands of the Eastern bloc, given the bipolar symmetry. A prolonged financial injection and technical assistance were intended to create economic linkages and, in the long run, political solidarity or complicity. Running the Somali National University provided Italy with a powerful leverage to influence the leading class, intelligentsia and administrators.

Italy believed that her assistance was far more palatable to nationalistic forces in Africa than American or British aid. Developing countries had nothing to fear from a middle-size power like Italy. Her weakness on an international scale became a modest but significant asset; Italy could not be suspected of embarking on neocolonial or neo-imperialist schemes. What is more striking is that the demise of Western influence in a Third World country was likely to foster Italian political self-promotion as the last resort for the West. Italy stood out among the leading donors to Somalia even during the embargo imposed by the United States to retaliate against the use of ships flying the Somali flag to supply North Vietnam, but she did officially stop supplying military equipment until after the Ogaden War. Among the African nations, Somalia, together with Nigeria, was the main buyer of Italian arms in the eighties and ranked sixth among customers from all the developing countries.

In a stretch of time of about five years -- from the coup of the Free Officers led by Moammar Gadhafi in Libya to the revolutionary upheaval in Somalia and the overthrow of the Ethiopian monarchy -- all the former Italian colonies passed through drastic changes that propelled the radicalized segments of the armed forces to power. It is questionable whether it was a simple coincidence. For sure, Italy proved to be a negligible factor in the political ups and downs of territories theoretically under her own influence.

Officially, Italy was committed to a policy of strict equidistance -- between Somalia and Ethiopia or between Ethiopia and Eritrea -- without espousing the cause of either. This multi-faceted cooperation -- within the framework of a more comprehensive Italian commitment to the region of East Africa -- was meant to soften the intransigent stances of the rival states (or guerrilla movements) and to foster Italy's mediation. In the meantime, Italy's cooperation helped turn the efforts of the nations towards development rather than the arms race.

The Italian government itself, however, was racked by feuds, which made Italy's warnings and her apparent goodwill far less effective. The two major partners in the cabinet coalition, Christian Democrats (D.C.) and Socialists (P.S.I.), patronized both Ethiopia and Somalia. Equidistance was pursued also in the Eritrean case, formally recognizing the unity of Ethiopia on one hand, and flirting with separatism and hosting semiofficial rallies of Eritrean students and exiles in Italy on the other.

Contrasts came out in the open during the 1977-1978 crisis. Because of the rift over its decision to send the regular army into the Ogaden, Somalia made a u-turn and severed its friendly relations with Moscow. Siyad Barre's startling initiative was judged (and agreed to) by the standards of the Cold War rather than by the merits of The Ogaden question. The Socialist Party especially supported Somalia's adventurism in the name of their anti-Soviet feelings. For its part, the government reiterated its commitment to preventing Ethiopia's disintegration. Furthermore, Italy -- as a minor partner with a widespread and long-standing knowledge of the regional problems and less compromised with imperialism -- reckoned that the interruption of the relations between the Dergue and the United States might widen her scope for action and enhance possibilities of mediation. Basically Italy pretended to be neutral: friend to all, enemy to none. Italy sought to side with the states of the Horn in their tormented evolution without being strait-jacketed by the East-West alignments and in a sense taking her distance from them. This did not keep Italy from attending meetings with Western allies to coordinate their action vis-a-vis the Soviet and Cuban counter-offensive in the Ogaden.

Italy was so tightly entangled in the Horn that the Somali-Ethiopian conflict affected not only the government but the main opposition party as well. Despite its solid attachment to the Unitarian rules of "democratic centralism," the PCI was split between a pro-Somali lobby led by the future secretary-general, Achille Occhetto (then married to a young Somali actress) and the bureaucracy of the External Relations Department which were more and more disappointed by the Somali regime's performance and were, instead, gambling on the revolutionary boost of the Dergue and of Mengistu Haile Mariam personally.

The Eritrean issue was the occasion for even more marked and resounding contrasts, which again passed across the coalition in power and the individual parties. While Pan-Somali claims could be regarded as a threat to the stability of a state, Eritrean warfare was widely considered a legitimate struggle for national liberation against an anomalous form of internal colonialism. Which principle -- self-determination of peoples or territorial integrity of states -- ought to be supported if the two were not compatible?

The Horn of Africa has always been included among the priorities of Italian policy in the Third World. However, it was hard to say how important the various states actually were because Italy did not stake out her strategic perimeter. To preserve historical links and the legacies of her dominance, Italy did not dare cheer both governments and oppositions. Apart from the political stake, this comprehensive and ubiquitous stance, buttered with the doubtful generosity of financial and technical assistance, was designed to secure a privileged place in markets which were relatively important for Italian export.

IV. Somali Turmoil and Italian Policy

The potential or imaginary advantages Italy boasted in the Horn evaporated all at once when the 1990-1991 turmoil disrupted the established regimes, first in Somalia and then in Ethiopia, giving way to the *de facto* independence of Eritrea and the beginning of a period of civil strife and disintegration in Somalia. Italian policy had always considered the state as the proper term of reference, but the first victim of the crisis was the state, which collapsed or even committed suicide. The crux of the question -- consent, effectiveness, viability -- shifted from the regimes to the states putting them in a very dreary crisis. Africa too was experiencing the effects of the great mutation that occurred in the world overturning the legitimacy, insofar uncontested, of the nation-states including the pseudo-national states born of decolonization. Was a centralized and bureaucratic state emulating Western models the best solution for societies, like the Somali one, dominated by the individualistic and clannish ethos of a nomadic people? Was such a state the best way to provide for a peaceful *modus vivendi* among different linguistic and ethnic groups in the multinational Ethiopia?

While Somalia was ravaged by civil war, hastening the downfall of Siyad Barre's regime in a dramatic crescendo of bloodshed and despair, Italy sought once more to manage the crisis by offering her good offices. The aim was to effect an orderly transfer of power to a large coalition of forces, parties and persons in which Siyad Barre would continue to play an important transition role in order to avoid, it was argued, a dangerous power vacuum. A self-fulfilled prophecy. Siyad's enemies firmly refused to join such a deal, pleading that the President should be personally responsible for crimes, malpractices and political chaos. An eleventh hour reconciliation conference, co-chaired by Italy and Egypt, was called in Cairo but it was doomed from the start and at the last minute was canceled. General Aidid wouldn't forget the activism of Boutros Boutros-Ghali, then foreign minister of Egypt, to "save" Siyad. The flight of Siyad Barre from Mogadishu deprived Italy of her best card. The setback was definitive. A regime Italy had tried stubbornly to preserve for over twenty years as a token of stability, was in shambles. The University, the jewel of Italian technical assistance, was destroyed and vandalized. Italy was aghast and bitter; the subsequent backlash could have wiped away all the care and interest for the whole Horn.

Lacking any viable alternative, Italy had to watch as a passive by-stander the last battle for the control of the capital city. The Italian embassy was the last to be evacuated: a sign of responsibility and of the strong will to stay on, perhaps a pledge for the future, but also the evidence -- at least in the perception of Siyad Barre's opponents -- of a special link with the fate of the dying regime. Italy had been the last Western country to suspend economic aid to Somalia as well.

The unstable coalition set up from among the liberation fronts that seized power in Mogadishu in January, 1991 left hardly any room for Italy's mediation, as anarchy and wild reprisals erupted in the whole country. Italy could hope for rewards in return for the support given in the past to the United Somali Congress (USC.) which had been founded in Rome; but the connection with the new leaders was precarious and finally because of the split between the military and the political wings, and between Ali Mahdi and General Aidid, the United Somali Congress was the main contender in the civil warfare. Moreover, Italy had always had difficulty in dealing with the northern, Anglophone Somalis, possibly more docile to the British sirens. As a matter of fact, Italy failed to secure the participation of the Somali National Movement in the meeting with the provisional organization formed by the United Somali Congress and in the end, the Isaaq movement decided to secede.

Not withstanding, Italy was asked to supply emergency aid and was prepared to reoccupy her traditional position in Somalia. Was it possible to help Somalia without interfering in its domestic affairs and precipitating an escalation? Given President Ali Mahdi's isolation, receiving international aid might be the most immediate form of diplomatic recognition for him. On October 29, 1991, an Italian aircraft which carried humanitarian aid with Undersecretary Andrea Borruso on board was prevented from landing by the fire from General Aidid's militias. A fierce battle raged between the two rival factions of the leading USC. The Italian expedition had been badly conceived and conducted even worse; the Ministry of Foreign Affairs did not even arrange the rescue flight in coordination with Mario Raffaelli, who was mediating behind the scenes on behalf of the Italian government. Was this a new chapter in the feud between the Christian Democracy (to which Borruso belonged) and P.S.I. (the party of Raffaelli and Foreign Minister De Michelis) in commanding Italian policy in the Horn?

When the United States and then the United Nations decided to intervene in Somalia, Italy was compelled by its own rhetoric to send her troops to Mogadishu. Usually the former colonial powers are kept out of UN emergency forces intervening in the Third World. Italy's self-nomination was immediately ill-resented by the American government generating a misunderstanding which would never end. Possibly the US was reluctant willingly to take a partner with a better expertise on the local reality, assisted by old and new clients, in a stronger position to draw economic and political advantages.

Italy restarted her all-embracing activity dealing with the factions and their military chiefs. The landing of the troops with the Tricolore was welcomed by Ali Mahdi and sharply rebuffed by Aidid but shortly, the adroit diplomacy of Rome's would-be ambassador and of the commander in charge of the Italian military unit had conquered even the most controversial and ambitious Somali warlord. The bitter strife with the United States and Boutros Boutros-Ghali on the best line to follow in order to urge a respite from violence and prepare a national agreement avoiding the use of force was won by Italy as far as the political outcome, but actually was lost because of the obvious superiority of her competitors on the political arena. The rehabilitation of Aidid after his unilateral ostracism was perhaps a moral acknowledgment for the Italian attitude and yet it came too late to reinstate a distrustful Italy which was resigned to give up her elusive "grandeur" dreams.

V. Italian Hegemony

From its earliest contacts with Africa, Italy had pursued and to some extent achieved a sort of hegemony in the Horn. Italian explorers and geographers were followed by missionaries, and then ethnologists and historians. The immense amount of scientific knowledge about lands, peoples, languages and civilizations became part of the overall cultural wealth but was exploited above all by the Italian state to gain its place in world competition for resources and markets. Ethiopia has always been the main goal of Italian colonialism.

However, as Italy was a second class power -- the last of the big powers or the first of the small ones -- she was not able to comply with the tasks of power on a regional scale. Even colonial conquests have been facilitated by the complacent neglect of her informal ally, Britain. For her part, Italy could not challenge France and Britain. Italian colonialism could not afford to carry out the social, economic and institutional transformations that usually went along with colonialism; this is why it is conventionally defined as demographic colonialism, to stress the special function of settlers rather than finance and investments.

The defeat in the Second World War deprived Italy of her colonial possessions. Italy tried nevertheless to seek a role to play in the new Africa. Where else but in the Horn? Would the big powers accept Italy's request to continue to be present in Africa, at least in the pre-fascist colonies? Italy was aware of her expertise and wanted to contribute to the accomplishment of what Italian post-colonial thinking called Eurafrica, a close association between Africa and Europe (or the West when imperatives and blocs of the Cold War spread throughout the Black Continent). In whatever way, nothing could make up for Italy's deficiencies in the current restructuring of African markets and polity.

This rapid screening of Italian conduct from the Peace Treaty to the latest tragedies in the Horn has shown how Italy was bypassed and eventually overcome by major internal and international events and how she failed to keep the peace. The reasons for the limits of Italy's African policy can be summarized under three sub-headings:

1. Italy tried to make up for her weakness by multiplying the initiatives and appeasing various partners at the same time. This

strategy led to contradictions between counteracting players (Somalia vs Ethiopia, self-determination vs integrity of states and empires, sympathy with liberation fronts vs cooperation with governments, Ali Mahdi vs Aidid, etc.). In the end, Italy unable to manage. It is nearly impossible to ascertain whether Italy intended to deal with states, nations, territories, peoples, political forces, classes or leaders, to respect the local expectations, to perform a design of stability or to pursue her own interests. The expedient was more often to delay a definitive choice or a synthesis of the possible options preaching general "conciliation" (of contraries?).

2. Apart from the continuing confusion concerning the goals of her policy, Italy employed improper means. Given the sharp polarization of the Italian political system, not only was any bipartisan policy not feasible -- that is, a policy shared both by government and opposition -- but the government itself was divided. The result was rather a "partisan bi-policy." The parties of the majority coalition -- and sometimes even organized factions within a single party -- differed widely in their attitudes. Therefore, they concentrated their efforts and the funds made available by the official aid policy on a specific partner or issue, expecting profits in terms of political obedience, cronyism, lawful or illicit economic returns, etc. This made it far more difficult to express a positive approach according to the African nations' rights and to the regional balance of power. In the last Somali crisis as well, Italy baffled the discipline of the international operation, made use of unfair means in order to cherish her collaborators, justifying the reputation of Machiavelli's country and risking to damage a cause that was essentially right and well-founded.

3. Finally, with the crumbling of the military regimes, Italian authorities and private and public enterprise indulgently supported *de facto* allies because of its inferiority. Italy could not go it alone. Due to her limited resources, she could hardly support the local forces in rearranging their political institutions and economies in the era of globalization. Pretending to appreciate Italian neutrality, Aidid cheated because Aidid himself was careful to aim at major and not minor targets.

Africa is discovering that it lacks the force to obtain the benefits of interdependence that other developing countries have been able to grasp. So far, former Italian possessions have been more vulnerable than other African nations because of their greater isolation from the main economic and financial trends and technological innovations, again as the result of the weakness of their traditional patron. In Somalia and in Ethiopia, ravaged by war and drought, the traumas of the transition have brought catastrophe to the state. The Italian influence was not a valid bulwark against such a crisis. It is likely that the Somali military factions and the new government will nevertheless seek Italian cooperation, because of historical links and acquaintance. However, their stabilization and sustainable development will depend in the long run on factors that are beyond the scope of Italian possibilities, and that require at least a European dimension that, for reasons of selfishness, Italy has, thus far, failed to facilitate with any real energy.

CHAPTER THIRTY SIX

The United Nations
Intervention in Somalia

Maria Brons Bongartz

Introduction

The paper develops four arguments about whether the UN military intervention into Somalia in December 1992 was justified.

I. The Risks of Military Intervention in Chronic Internal Conflicts: Peace Keeping And Peace-Making Debate

In 1956, Dag Hammarskjold, the second UN Secretary General, introduced the concept of peace-keeping into the United Nations vocabulary and set of activities. The concept stipulates that UN peace-keeping missions are only implementable if the conflicting parties agree to accept the mission, or at least do not resist. They are not meant to bring about concrete solutions to conflicts, but rather to limit conflict-induced violence and loss of life by building buffer-zones, to assist in keeping cease-fire-agreements and to support humanitarian relief operations. Dag Hammarskjold's peace-keeping model instituted a new perception of the UN potentialities and capabilities in the field of international security (Czempiel, 1986).

Peace-keeping missions, as referred to in Chapter VI of the Charter, have to be perceived as supporting factors to United Nations-sponsored negotiations between warring sides. Peace-making, on the other hand, means peace-enforcement under a war situation. Peace-enforcement is expressed in chapter VII of the Charter of the United Nations. It refers to "collective security" on which the League of Nations and later on the United Nations were originally created to secure world peace. In the event that world-peace and international or regional security is threatened, intervention by a multilateral UN force under UN command is justified.

Peace-enforcement is highly problematic to implement while maintaining the goal of impartiality of UN forces. It is also highly vulnerable to abuse by some of the parties involved in the conflict. The use of coercion involves the risk of being drawn into the conflict or of being accused of partiality by stepping out of peace-enforcement into the muddy arena of war-making (Conroy, 1994). Moreover, in a sensitive and highly politicized environment, the very structure and composition of the UN intervention force is of crucial importance to its acceptability by the warring parties.

II. Is the Move From Peace-Keeping to Peace-Making Justified?

The justification for the UN peace-making mission in Somalia has been questionable from the beginning. It is crucial to understand several factors concerning the genesis of the Somali crisis:

1. The crisis in Somalia is a product of a civil war led against the dictatorship of Siyad Barre, whose regime - in power since 1969 - had grossly violated human rights and used excessive coercion against the opposition.

2. One major characteristic of the late Siyad Barre regime was the extensive exploitation of clan-differences within Somali society (Bongartz, 1991). The opposition groups and today's political factions were accordingly rooted in different clans or sub-clans.

3. Detention, rapes and mass-killings along clan lines were committed by government forces throughout the 1980s and with special intensity in the North of the country since 1988 (Africa Watch, 1990).

4. Mass starvation, famine and massive refugee movements across the border to Ethiopia (in 1988:326,808; in 1990:431,266; Brons *et al.*, 1993), at a later stage and to a lesser extent to Kenya, Djibouti and Yemen, posed an additional threat to the stability of the already conflict -riddled region of the Horn of Africa.

By and large, the arguments given by the UN to justify its intervention in Somalia could be refuted for several objective reasons, including:

A. Threat to Regional Peace and Stability

The Secretary-General of the UN, Boutros Boutros-Ghali, in his letter of November 29, 1992, requested that the Security Council move from peace-keeping to peace-enforcement. He argued that,

> At present no government exists in Somalia that could request and allow such use of force. It would therefore be necessary for the Security Council to make a determination under Article 39 of the Charter that a threat to the peace exists, as a result of the repercussions of the Somali conflict on the entire region, and to decide what measures should be taken to maintain international peace and security.

In light of the experiences of the people of the Horn of Africa in the last two decades, the `threat to regional peace and stability' argument seems weak. The Somali-Ethiopian war in 1977/78 and the ongoing hostilities between the two countries throughout the 1980s, equally well backed by the American and the Soviet superpowers, posed a permanent threat to regional stability. Even in its heyday, the refugee crisis produced about 750,000 Somali-Ethiopian refugees in Somalia who destabilized the region. The suppression of the political and economic aspirations of the Somali-Ethiopians (in the Ogaden) by the Mengistu regime and of the Isaaq-Somali in Northern Somalia by the Barre regime had destabilized these areas throughout the 1980s.

Relative to that, the years 1991 and 1992 revealed comparative regional stability resulting from: 1) the successful achievement of Eritrean independence; 2) the political transformation in Ethiopia (the advance of the EPRDF forces and their quest for democratic rights for all nationalities) and the granting of regional autonomy to Region 5; the 'Somali' region in Southeast Ethiopia; and 3) relative political stability in the self-declared independent Republic of Somaliland in 1991. These developments removed the presence of intensive warfare in the Horn.

Therefore, many tend to assert that the Secretary-General's argument could only be understood from his narrow national political background as a former Egyptian foreign-policy-maker. In this perspective, a political vacuum in the Horn and a possible splitting up of the Somali Republic into two separate political and economic entities is considered a possible threat to the position and influence of Egypt in the region of Northeast Africa (Brons, 1993).

B. Human Rights Violations

In the Security Council's resolution 794 (3.12.1992), a link was made between the "magnitude of the human tragedy caused by the conflict in Somalia" and the "threat to international peace and security." Major human rights violations were, for the first time, in international (customary) law linked with Chapter VII to justify a "humanitarian military UN intervention".

However, the `human rights violation'-argument could have been applied to the situation in Somalia since 1988. As mentioned earlier, repeated atrocities and the incidence of state-sponsored, clan-based genocide against the Isaaq population in Northern Somalia was rampant. Bombardment of civilian targets, mass-killings and destruction of the sources of livelihood were reported by human rights organizations such as Africa Watch and Amnesty International, as well as by the United States State Department Report, "Why Somalis Flee?," as early as 1988/89. Nevertheless, diplomatic, political and economic contacts as well as economic and military aid flowed not only from the United States, as comprehensively reported by Gejdenson (1990), but also from Somalia's closest protegee, Italy. These flows continued until shortly before the fall and flight of Siyad Barre from Mogadishu.

It is argued among international lawyers that the emergence of an international humanitarian law, i.e. the link between human rights and international military intervention in accordance with chapter VII, questions the very legitimacy of governments who violate and commit large-scale human rights abuses. The people of the world should be acknowledged as the "true subjects of international law" rather than states, which still present the "formal subjects of international law" (Fielding, 1994). Thereby, a direct link between the individual and an international human rights authority should surpass the violating state.

The problem with this argument is that it is out of touch with the reality of the international system, which is based on respect for the sovereignty of nation-states - as alien as this notion may have been revealed to be during the last decade or so. In the case of Somalia, the government of Siyad Barre was internationally recognized until the very end, despite well-established knowledge of human rights violations. Likewise, in January 1991, the interim government of Ali Mahdi was at first internationally recognized, despite its lack of wide acceptance by large sectors of the Somali political factions. One serious problem with the UNOSOM mandate was that it hastily attempted to re-establish, as soon as possible, a national council without acknowledging that a genuine rebuilding of the political community needed to be undertaken at its own rhythm and speed (Normark, 1994).

Simultaneously, the UN denied Somaliland and its elected government (in a national reconciliation conference hosting representatives from all regions and all clans in Northern Somalia) recognition and a fair chance of a UN-supervised national referendum (Brons, 1993). This episode questions whether the intention of the UN in the Somali situation was to deal with the right of the people, or the right of the "juridical shell" (Jackson, 1992, p.90) of nation-states. Political considerations of UN member states with their own national or regional-political interests, which then come into the forefront of a discussion on certain issues, cannot be dismissed as seemingly detached from humanitarian concerns.

C. No Authorities for the Negotiation of Peace-Keeping

The main argument to move from peace-keeping to peace-enforcement was, according to the Secretary General's letter of November 29, 1992, that "there are at present very few authorities in Somalia with whom a peace-keeping force can safely negotiate an agreed basis for its operation." The UN approach, up to that time, had followed a low-profile, two-sided decentralized line, including a minimal peace-keeping force, partially operating and controlling the airport and harbor to protect relief food, and focusing on negotiations with the leaders of the military factions as well as the elders from different regions in Southern and Central Somalia.

This decentralized approach was a pragmatic adaptation to the reality created by the break-down of the central government authority and the disintegration of the whole country into traditional clan-based power enclaves. Its continuation would have enabled the UN slowly to marginalize the warlords and empower the traditionally accepted representatives of Somali communities and clans (Normark, 1994). A Somali traditional peace-keeping process is lengthy and could extend to several months between conflicting Somali clans. There was no doubt that Somali-type negotiations would have resulted in long-term peace reconciliation processes. This should ideally have included various military, political, religious and community leaders, a process which the UN peace-keeping mission could hardly entertain (financially and considering the need for specialized political manpower) or find agreeable to its regulations, style and domain of operation.

D. Mass Starvation

In the end, the mass starvation of the Somali population, exposed by the media during August/September 1992, gave currency to the need for speedy action including the deployment of more troops with a peace-enforcement mandate. This course of events had occurred with disregard to the warlords' possible reactions. NGOs had been blackmailed by the warlords and thus, indirectly, contributed to the prolongation of the conflict by paying them immense sums of protection money. The lucrative protection rewards gained from the NGOs came to a halt with the arrival of UNITAF, and the food delivery situation improved rapidly.

The UNITAF mandate "to establish as soon as possible a secure environment for humanitarian relief operations in Somalia" (Res. 794) was fulfilled in a short span of time. However, it should be highlighted that the UN had earlier played its part in the deterioration of the famine situation by recalling all its agencies out of Somalia in January 1991 and not returning until autumn 1992. The UN's early withdrawal denied it the opportunity to monitor the food delivery situation. Under such circumstances, agreements with the actual power-holders in the respective regions to secure that the UN humanitarian agencies, following their own request, be accompanied by UN peace-keeping units with an extended mandate for self-defense, could have been made in due time.

III. UN Mission on the Balance: Successes and Failures

A. The Humanitarian Mandate

UNITAF forces controlled the airport and harbor and with them the major inlets and store-facilities of food aid. They specifically accompanied the NGOs and secured their feeding stations in and around the capital. The food crisis thus was reasonably controlled. The extended UN mandate enabled it to save many lives, especially those of the war refugees who had fled to the capital when fighting intensified in the Southern Lower Juba and Shabelle regions, in a short space of time. Many farmers were chased away from their land or lost all the subsistence basis of secure livelihood as grain and livestock were looted.

However, even with the improvement in food deliveries, the death rates did not immediately drop. First, the majority of the weakest -- the elderly, the ill and the children under five -- had already died during the months before the intervention. Second, many undernourished people in the countryside, but even inside the capital, remained outside the reach of the relief programs. Third, epidemic diseases, the main reason for death, were not adequately addressed by the relief programs (*Africa Rights*, 1993).

Nevertheless, in the humanitarian field, food delivery and medical care improvements were made in the months following the initial intervention, so that feeding stations were operational in most major southern and central Somalia towns. Medical teams accompanying the UN soldiers opened field hospitals for local citizens.

B. Lack of a Political Mandate

Failures of the UN mission have to be seen in the context of its approach to the Somali problem. Even though there was no central government authority, there was not a political vacuum in Somalia. The warlords had become a ghastly reality to reckon with. The Somali crisis was narrowly defined by Resolution 794 as a purely humanitarian problem. Hence, the mandate did not address in detail other complementary objectives for a successful intervention or appropriate means for achieving these objectives. Initially, there was a complete absence of discussion on issues such as:

1. Disarmament and rehabilitation programs, especially for fighters and young men.

2. Resettlement of internal refugees and displaced peoples, including the difficult task of settlement of land ownership rights and rehabilitation programs for farmers in the Southern region.

3. A bottom-up approach to political reconciliation, strengthening traditional political forces in the Somali society and marginalizing the "warlords".

4. Integration of civilian, "non-warlord" Somalis into all humanitarian operations as well as military control.

5.Control of military forces, confidence-building and thereby keeping to the imperative of impartiality.

The credibility won during the first weeks of UNITAF operations was lost through inconsistent disarmament (Africa Rights, 1993) and the paying of more attention to political and military leaders during operations in the country as well as during UN-sponsored reconciliation meetings (Normark, 1994). The neglect of civilian Somalis by UNITAF and UNOSOM II, who had offered in vain their expertise and good-will, was perceived as a humiliation for the Somalis (Gassem, 1994). The UN forces were frightened of and alienated from Somali society after ambush attacks had claimed UN casualties, and UN soldiers were increasingly criticized for their inhumane treatment and attacks of innocent civilians (Gassem, 1994; Omar, de Waal, 1994).

C. Risks of Premature, Top-down Reconstruction of Political Structures

The UNOSOM II political branch gave high priority to political reconciliation and reconstruction of administrative structures. Fast solutions were sought not only by the UN, considering the high costs of its operation (HAB, 2/94; Prendergast, 1994), but also by the main power players of both rival factions. This is especially true for the Southern regions where the rich farmland is situated, belonging traditionally to minority clans. Being already expropriated under the Siyad Barre regime, the so-called liberation brought about just another "master" (*Africa Rights*, 1994). Similar power-imbalances prevail in the Kismayo area. Therefore, even though the establishment of district councils, in accordance with the Addis Ababa agreement of March 27, 1993, was a step towards bottom-up empowerment of the people, it was met with scepticism and suspicion by some of the military faction leaders. Premature elections would have caused a manifestation of clan power-balances, before the rightful owners of the respective areas had been given the chance to reclaim their lands (Africa Rights, 1994).

D. Lack of Impartiality

The loss of impartiality in the UNOSOM military operations, especially after the June 5 and October 3, 1993 killings of UN soldiers, was widely discussed and criticized by various parties. Only after quite some time, and the UN military command in Somalia realized its failures in this respect, did the UN withdraw the death penalty on General Mohamed Farah Aidid and reformulate its mandate (Res. 897, January 1994), which no longer included provisions on forcible disarmament.

Still, in its whole approach to the Somali crisis, the UN created unspoken alliances of convenience (Prendergast, 1994). Such tendencies were made obvious by the UN approach towards Somaliland: the UN's consistent unwillingness to acknowledge the peace and reconciliation progresses in Somaliland; the denial of the right of self-determination for the people of former British-Somaliland and disinterest in supporting a national referendum on the question of independence; the denial of financial or material assistance for the ongoing demobilization of former militiamen and for the re-establishment of a police force. All these are clear signs of double standards from the side of the UN leadership (Brons, 1993; Warsame, Brons, 1994). The role of the Secretary-General in this context, who, in accordance with Article 99 of the UN Charter, made extensive use of his right to initiate debate over issues and developments threatening world peace, and thereby determined, to a certain extent, the scale of discussion of the Somali crisis (Wembou, 1993; Elmi, 1992).

In the Republic of Somalia, the UN seemed to have coped better with the Manifesto-group around Ali Mahdi (Hawiye, close to Italian and Egyptian influence), than with the SNA-alliance under Mohamed Farah Aidid. Similar unbalanced treatment was seen in Kismayo, when, once, Morgan (former member of Barre-government) was not hindered in taking Kismayo, while Omar Jess (SPM) had to cope with retaliating UN soldiers. More striking is the possibly unintended neglect of minority clans from the Digil and Rahanweyn, the Bantu and the coastal people, such as Bajuunis and Brawanis.

In conclusion, the very clans or political power-groups which played a significant role in the corruption and subsequent destruction of the Somali state and government structures since independence, are yet again in the forefront of the struggle for state power. With no significant economic resources in their traditional clan strongholds, they are out to dominate the minority clans in the south -- the Rahanweyn and other groups from the inter-riverine rich agricultural lands and the coastal people with resource endowments such as those around the important southern harbor of Kismayo. By insisting on the integration of Somaliland into Somalia, they aim, as well, to keep control over the major livestock export routes to the Arabian peninsula and the consumer goods harbor at Berbera, traditionally resources of the Isaaq.

IV. Prospects for UN Support In Reconciliation And Rehabilitation

In March 1995, the UNOSOM military wing finally withdrew its troops from Somalia. However, the main political objective of establishing a central government and a system of law and order throughout the whole country, was not met. Peace-enforcement failed blatantly, resulting in a death toll of 135 on the side of the peace-keepers and a many times larger number of Somali fighters and civilians (HAB, 2/1995). During 1993/1994, reconciliation conferences were held on different political levels, within the international arena in Addis Ababa, as well as in various regional settings and among local communities. While agreements reached on the global political level were mostly failures, those reached at the regional and local level often proved to be successful in establishing reconciliatory relationships between opposing clans and groups within the communities. Those successes, however, cannot merely be attributed to UNOSOM. They were often reached despite differences with UNOSOM policies. Where community leaders took a peace initiative without outside pressure concerning time allocation and the choice of subject matters, the outcome had all chances of a long lasting mutual agreement. Hence, at the time when the UN was pulling out in March 1995, the situation in most of the Somali countryside was quite promising. Only in and around the capital, where the UNOSOM military presence had been most dense and conflict-perpetuating, and indeed had become "part of the problem" (S. Illing, EU special envoy, 24.3.1995 (Reuters), in HAB 2/95), reconciliation was far from reality. However, this cannot solely be blamed on the conduct of the UNOSOM presence, but must be understood in light of a general tendency in African politics, that whomever controls the capital is internally in charge and internationally a recipient of merits and recognition which, in return, consolidates the thin power base. Therefore, the fight over power and control in Mogadishu is the fiercest. The military presence and involvement of

UNOSOM in the power-struggle in Mogadishu has therefore exhibited the most damaging results such as a complication and prolongation of the civil war.

An evaluation of efforts aiming at peace-making in Somalia since January 1991 reveals that there is no way other than a "bottom-up"-approach, beginning with villages and sub-clans, where grievances and traditional disputes over political power as well as economic rights are known up to the last detail. Contemplating a future constitutional framework for Somalia would certainly reveal that there is no need for a centralized state structure. What could be useful for Somalia to consider is a genuine process of institution building, aiming at a federal structure on the national level.

As Martin Doornbos, Mohamed Salih and I argue elsewhere in relation to the Ethiopian-Somali, the newly emerging political institutions have to reflect identity patterns as perceived by the very people who are supposed to be represented. Whether these identity patterns refer back to traditional local community structures, such as religious and elders-committees, or rather rely on "modern" constituencies such as women and youth organizations, remains to be seen. A broader institutional and political framework could grow out of inter-regional peace and cooperation accords. In light of the academic discourses on the redefinition of the Somali nation, however, it would not be wise to advocate the reconstruction of the pre-war "nation-state."

Concerning the political reconciliation process outlined above, the UN and the international community would be wise to play an indirect and supporting role in order not to be drawn into the conflict again. Concerning the Somali people who wish to prevent recurrence of such events, their solutions would be more balanced as no outside agency would have tilted power in favor of one or another local group.

It should be recognized that the UN has a role to play and is dearly welcomed in post-war rehabilitation activities. However, political reconciliation and economic and social rehabilitation are two sides of the same coin, especially in the case of state and/or donor resource allocation and in matters such as land and grazing rights. It was often heard that the presence of aid agencies had fueled the fighting, and this not only as a security requirement for aid agencies which partially financed the war, but also because of the supply of the very resources the different parties were fighting over. In that context and with the close cooperation between UN agencies and NGOs in mind, the establishment of a "code of conduct" by the Somali Aid Coordination Body (SACB) is promising and may contribute to the avoidance of the return to the days of dependence on various faction leaders' whims. However, UN and NGO personnel, involved in assisting with planning and implementation of development and rehabilitation, especially in the agricultural sector, in health care, vocational and administrative training, must be aware of the importance of the participation of those vested with the trust of local power structures. Attention should equally be given to long-term consequences of their projects on the balance of power within the clan-based structure of Somali society. Should such matters not carefully been attended to, then even noble humanitarian rehabilitation efforts would hamper any development towards a genuine peace and reconciliation in Somalia.

My own recommendations and others which were proposed elsewhere (Gassem, 1994; Africa Rights, 1994; Prendergast, 1994; Mohamed Salih, Wohlgemuth, Uppsala Forum, 1994) pertain to the necessity of a grassroots approach to political reconciliation. However, some preconditions to that approach have to be met first, and the UN, especially UNHCR has a vital role to play in that respect. An integrated repatriation program for refugees, returnees and displaced persons including the whole Somali region, southern and central Somalia as well as Somaliland and the Somali Region 5 in southeast Ethiopia is needed. Only if an improvement of conditions for self-sufficient livelihood has taken place in all these areas in the Horn, supported, where necessary, by agricultural inputs, such as seeds, pumps etc., by veterinary services and the cleaning of wells in the livestock sector and vocational training and job-creation, people would be encouraged to go back home to areas of their origin and/or family-affiliation or simply of their preference. Only when the Somali people stop "being on the move" can social stability be restored. As long as major population shifts are expected, no premature establishment of representational political bodies, such as district and regional councils, should take place. Referring to the minority-clans, especially those in the inter-riverine areas, the actual power holders should be persuaded to consider minority rights over land ownership through UN/NGOs project implementation in the agricultural sector in order to avoid a stipulation of unequal power balances.

A second precondition for repatriation, economic rehabilitation and finally reconciliation is the provision of security. Only in a secure environment will people go back to where they want and farm and graze their animals without risk. In that respect, the following measures should get funding priority by the UN and other organizations:

1. The creation of law and order, the reestablishment of a police force, courts and jails;

2. Gradual, but largely spontaneous disarmament, through incentives carried out by the Somalis themselves, combined with rehabilitation programs to motivate the militia to return to civilian life and end militia service and banditry;

3. UN financed and eventually organized patrol of water and firewood sources and transport lines to increase security, especially to protect women from rape;

4. The clearance of land mines.

Finally, referring back to the integrated regional approach, the UN in cooperation with NGOs should follow the international community and its representative body to promote a UN-supervised referendum in Somaliland. This would enable funding and operationalization of the above mentioned programs in that particular area. A referendum would clarify the question of independence for Somaliland and thereby stabilize the region politically. In the long term, this would open the way to larger economic and political cooperation.

Bibliography

Africa Watch (1990) *Somalia. A Government at War with its own People*, Washington, London, (January 1990).

African Rights (1993) *Somalia. Operation Restore Hope: A Preliminary Assessment*, London (May 1993).

African Rights (1993) *Land Tenure, the creation of famine and prospects for peace in Somalia*, Discussion Paper No.1, London, (Oct. 1993).

Amnesty International (1988) *Somalia. A Long-Term Human Rights Crisis*, London.

Bongartz, Maria (1991) *Somalia im Burgerkrieg. Ursachen und Perspektiven des innenpolitischen Konflikts*, Hamburg, Institut fur Afrikakunde.

Brons, Maria; Woldeyesus Elisa; Mandefro Tegegn; M. A. Mohamed Salih (1993) "War and the Somali Refugees in Eastern Hararghe, Ethiopia", in: T. Tvedt (ed.), _Conflicts in the Horn of Africa: Human and Ecological Consequences of Warfare_, Uppsala, EPOS, Uppsala University.

Brons, Maria (1993) _Somaliland. Zwei Jahre nach der Unabhangigkeitserklarung_, Hamburg, Institut fur Afrikakunde.

Conroy, Richard W. (1994) "From Peace-Keeping to Peace-Enforcement: Lessons from the Case of Somalia," paper presented at the 7th Annual Meeting of the Academic Council on the UN System: _'Approaching Fifty: The United Nations from Europe'_, The Hague, 23-25 June 1994.

Czempiel, Ernst-Otto (1986) "Konzepte der Kriegsverhutung: Friedenssicherung im Rahmen der Internationalen Organisation", in: P. J. Opitz, V. Rittberger (eds.) _Forum der Welt. 40 Jahre Vereinte Nationen,_ Bonn, Bundeszentrale f. politische Bildung.

Elmi, Omer Salad (1992) _The Somali Conflict and the undercurrent causes_, Mogadishu (Dec. 1992), Beeldeeq Printing Press.

Fieldings, Lois E. (1994) "The Evolving Legal Parameters For Intervention by the Security Council under Chapter VII to Protect Human Rights", paper presented at the 7th Annual Meeting of the Academic Council on the UN System: `Approaching Fifty: The United Nations from Europe'_, The Hague, 23-25 June 1994.

Gassem, Mariam Arif (1994) _Hostages. The People Who Kidnapped Themselves_, Mogadishu, Central Graphic Services/Nairobi.

Gejdenson, Sam (1990) "Congress makes U.S. foreign policy. Somalia: A Case Study", in: _The American University Journal of international Law and Policy_, Vol 5 (1990), No.4.

Gersony, Robert (1990) "Why Somalis Flee: a Synthesis of Conflict Experience in Northern Somalia by Somali Refugees, Displaced Persons and Others", in: _International Journal of Refugee Law_, Vol 2 (1990), No.1.

Jackson, Robert H, (1992) "The Security Dilemma in Africa" in: Job, Brian (ed.) _The Insecurity Dilemma_, Boulder, London (Lynne Rienner).

Lewis, I.M. (1961) _A Pastoral Democracy_, London, New York, Toronto, Oxford University Press.

Life & Peace Institute (1995) _Horn of Africa Bulletin_, Uppsala, Vol. 6, Nr. 2,

March-April 1994; Vol. 7, Nr. 2, March-April 1995.

Normark, Sture (1994) "Life and Peace Institute in cooperation with UNOSOM political division", in: Mohamed Salih, M. A., Lennart Wohlgemuth (eds.), *Crisis Management and the Politics of Reconciliation in Somalia. Statements from the Uppsala Forum, 17-19 January 1994*, Uppsala, (Scandinavian Institute of African Studies).

Omar, Rakiya, Alex de Waal (1994) "Document V: Somalia. Human Rights Abuse by the United nations Force" in: Mohamed Salih, M. A., Lennart Wohlgemuth, *Crisis Management and the Politics of Reconciliation in Somalia. Statements from the Uppsala Forum, 17-19 January 1994*, Uppsala, (Scandinavian Institute of African Studies).

Prendergast, John (1994) *The Bones of our Children are not yet buried: The Looming spectre of famine and massive human rights abuse in Somalia*, Washington, Centre of Concern.

Wembou, Michel-Cyr Djiena (1993) "Validite et portee de la resolution 794 (1992) du Conseil de Securite", in: *African Journal of International and Comparative Law*, Vol 5 (1993), No.2.

Warsame, Amina; Brons, Maria (1994) "Somaliland. A State in Pursuit of Peace and Stability", in: Mohamed Salih, M. A., Lennart Wohlgemuth (eds.), *Crisis Management and the Politics of Reconciliation in Somalia. Statements from the Uppsala Forum, 17-19 January 1994*, Uppsala, (Scandinavian Institute of African Studies).

CHAPTER THIRTY SEVEN

African-Americans and the Somali Crisis

Edmond J. Keller

As an African-American scholar with a long standing and intimate relationship with the countries and the people of the Horn of Africa, I have always felt a special need to educate my kinspeople about current situations in the region. I am most known for my work on Ethiopia and Eritrea, but developments over the past decade and a half have made it very clear to me that every country in the Horn is intimately connected with every other country in the region. That being said, I frankly have to admit that I, and scholars like me, have not done a good job of educating the African- American community about the crisis in the Horn, apart from the situation in Ethiopia. This was brought home to me over the past several months as I spoke to people about the Somali crisis.

African-Americans, like others, were shocked into at least acknowledging that there was an African country known as Somalia, by the graphic pictures broadcast over television, showing the devastating impact of drought, famine and civil war on the Somali people. Nobody seemed to want or feel the need to understand how things got to be the way they are. They simply saw the tragedy and either wanted to help or were puzzled by the apparent anarchy that had come to characterize Somali society.

Unfortunately, the picture of Somalia that African- Americans--and the American public as a whole--have observed over the past two years is that of a pathological society that needed somehow to be healed. The first problem was seen as a humanitarian one. People had to be alleviated of famine and they had to be able to live in security. George Bush claimed that the United States had a moral obligation to help the Somali people recover from drought and famine. He was less committed to the long- term security of the Somali people. What was more, Bush and others making US policy in the Horn, as well as the US media, focused mainly on the symptoms of the problem, and did not project into the future to consider what might happen if the root of the problem was not adequately addressed.

I would contend that this was a major mistake. It has resulted in the quagmire we now see. What I think is that the US policymakers need to back up a bit and try to understand the real essence of the problem. Such steps are necessary to devise a realistic solution to the Somali problem.

I am often struck by the fact that no matter how much US policymakers and the public in general talk about the Somali crisis, nobody traces the problem back to the Cold War competition of the superpowers in the Horn. This competition began in earnest in the mid-1970s and ended only in the early 1990s. In the process, the armies of Ethiopia and Somalia grew exponentially as each country tried to hedge against possible invasion by the other. When the 1977-78 Ogaden War failed to result in a Somali victory, the regional war gave way to an internal war as President Mohammed Siyad Barre attempted to liquidate potential opponents and to strengthen his and his clan family's position of power and domination.

Barre presided over a rentier state, relying on resources he extracted from the Somali population and on foreign assistance. Rather than these resources being poured back into development projects, they either ended up in the coffers of the military or the pockets of Barre and his supporters.

The most notable feature of the Somali civil war was its destructiveness. The amount of arms in Somalia had proliferated to such an extent that opposition forces were able to meet the army of Siyad Barre on its own terms. By January 1991, the Barre regime had succumbed to a multi-front military onslaught by several opposition movements. Ironically, African-Americans, and Americans in general, seemed oblivious to the massive destruction and human suffering that had been wrought as Barre struggled to cling to power. They hardly noticed when the Republic of Somaliland declared its independence. They focused in only when anarchy came to grip Mogadishu, forcing foreigners to leave the country and creating massive dislocations of innocent civilians.

It was not until the fall of 1991 that Americans and the world at large came to a realization that something had to be done to address the human catastrophe that Somalia had become. The question was, "How should help be provided?"

The answer was the United Nations sponsored and the US dominated "Operation Restore Hope." Although people felt that military intervention would have to facilitate the humanitarian mission, nobody quite knew what was in store. The American military has always miscalculated the problems that it might face when it intervenes militarily into Third World situations. They are always looking for the "surgical operation," the "quick fix," but every problem is not like Grenada, or Libya or Iraq. Some problems are like Lebanon, if not like Vietnam.

Bush felt that American troops could intervene, create a safe condition for the humanitarian mission, and then withdraw. He continued to hold to this assumption even as UN Secretary General Boutros Boutros-Ghali made it clear that the UN would stop at nothing short of gluing Somalia back together again. He wanted to make Somalia whole again, and thus to preserve its sovereignty and territorial integrity. However, there was the rub. The UN had its agenda and the US had its own; yet, they were operating under the same banner.

At first, it looked like the political solution was more important to the UN than the military one, but when Boutros-Ghali relieved his special envoy to Somalia, the Algerian diplomat Mohamed Sahnoun, of his duties, the military option seemed to become paramount. The idea was to preserve Somalia as a coherent nation-state at all cost. Boutros-Ghali did not, and does not, seem to realize that the situation is such that traditional social control mechanisms in Somalia have been severely ruptured and the nation-state has virtually ceased to exist.

In this situation, the first order of priority would seem to be the reestablishment of social control mechanisms, and the whole question of remaking the Somali nation-state should be placed on a very distant back burner. Hopefully, we are now returning to this point. If the talks in Addis Ababa lead to the creation of some local space in which the Somali can begin to put their society back together, much will have been accomplished. What now seems to be realized is that Africans will have to help Africans find solutions to African problems. What then, should be the role -- if any -- of the UN and the US?

There is now a need for a different US political approach to the crisis. It is my view that the Africa lobby -- particularly the African-American lobby -- needs to gain a better understanding of the complexity of the Somali situation, and put that understanding into language that the average citizen can understand. Then it will be in a better position to take a leadership role in pressing for a clearly defined US position on the Somali crisis and its resolution.

Elements in this new policy approach would include:

1. A proactive and enforced arms embargo in border zones of the Horn (Aren't you amazed at the firepower that exists in Somalia today. There is a reason for this. The borders with Kenya and Ethiopia are porous and the flow of weapons into Somalia continues to be brisk. The US should be able to use leverage over Kenya, Ethiopia and its friends who continue to sell weapons to the various parties in the Somali conflict. Arms providers are driven by their own greed and self-interest rather than by humanitarian concerns for the Somali people.)

2. A second thing that needs to be done is to encourage the Organization of African Unity to come to terms with the changed realities of the African (and indeed the world) state system. Eritrea and Somalia make it abundantly clear that the whole question of the sovereignty of African states needs to be revisited. The OAU needs to establish new norms of intervention into the most severe incidents of domestic conflict. It needs to intervene in such situations in a diplomatic way before domestic crises spill over and become regionalized or internationalized and harder to manage. The good offices of African leaders are not sufficient. A permanent OAU mechanism for conflict avoidance, preventive diplomacy, conflict management and resolution is sorely needed.

3. Countries like the US and organizations like the UN and OAU should provide resources and the support needed to allow Africans to develop the capacity to appropriately address the changed situation as it relates to state sovereignty and the norms of intervention.

4. There is a need for public education on the Somali situation and for public pressure on US policymakers to proactively work to induce a lasting peace in Somalia and the Horn in general, and to assist in the reconstruction of Somali society. Alternatives to warlordism need to be provided through inducements such as education, employment, and economic opportunity for the Somali people. The first step in this direction would be a demonstration on the part of Somali elites of their political will to prioritize peace and reconstruction above all else. The issue of piecing the nation-state back together can wait. The priority should be on creating a viable Somali society. The issue at hand is the creation of conditions

conducive to building Somali society from the bottom up. Our policymakers need to know this. We African-Americans need to tell them and we need to hold them accountable for following through.

SECTION TEN

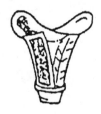

The Post-Congress Symposium: Selected Presentations

Summaries: Section Ten

Charles S. Weiss (Chapter 38), speaking on behalf of the College of the Holy Cross, opened a follow-up workshop to the December, 1993 International Congress. In his short welcoming address, he traced the history of Holy Cross College -- the host institution -- with special attention to the college's special connections with Africa and Africans.

Ambassador Robert Oakley (Chapter 39) was a first-hand participant in the events in Somalia, having served earlier as Ambassador and then as US representative during 1992 and part of 1993. His comments in this article are a transcript of a keynote address about how the US became involved in the December, 1992 military intervention and, in particular, how initial relations among the warlords and the US military were reasonable, open, and almost trusting. Work had begun, using Somali talent, to establish a police force, legal services, health services, women's groups, and other local organizations. Yet the situation deteriorated when external nations and international organizations determined that Somalis somehow quickly join together to form a national government. And what happened after that is too well known to repeat here.

John Prendergast (Chapter 40) reviews the Somali experience with famine and emergency food distribution. He determines that the issue of banditry was of less concern than the way warlords used food aid as a political weapon. Given these political issues, it was not possible to establish criteria for distribution. As a result WFP and the international NGOs often gave food to anyone who wanted it. At the same time, he notes that there are many local coping strategies that can be called upon in time of future famine. Although these strategies vary by clan and subcultural groupings, they represent an important resource in time of future response. Prendergast concludes that these were many examples of where agencies did an effective job in delivering food. Yet after all the food was distributed, there was little success in converting the food aid into rehabilitation, development, human rights protection, or in organizing viable political institutions.

The **Recommendations** (Chapter 41) include the perspectives of four working groups, representing a broad cross-section of Somali society, as well as European and North American Somali specialists. While these recommendations have no formal standing in any governmental or international organization, they do represent the collective wisdom of scholars, practitioners, former government officials, and informed donor and NGOs officers. They are submitted here to move forward the dialogue toward reaching accord among the different political elements in Somalia/Somaliland. While these recommendations, by themselves, will not solve the problems of Somalia/Somaliland, they are an important step in analyzing past events and using the findings to inform policy and action for the future. In Chapter Five, historian Charles Geshekter quoted a well known Russian historian, Vassily Osipovich Kluchevsky. In summarizing the final chapter in this volume of collected essays dedicated to "mending rips in the Somali sky," it is perhaps fitting to revisit that quotation:

> History teaches nothing. It only punishes us severely
> for not learning its lessons.

CHAPTER THIRTY EIGHT

Opening Remarks: Somali Studies Symposium

Charles S. Weiss
College of the Holy Cross

Thank you, Professor Adam. It is truly my pleasure to welcome all of you to the College of the Holy Cross--some of you I welcome to campus for the second time.

As you know, Holy Cross hosted the Fifth International Congress of Somali Studies in December of 1993. It was a very special event for the College--we learned a great deal about Somalia, the beauty and strength of its people and their struggle. We hope that you found Holy Cross then, and that will find it now, to be a friendly, hospitable and enjoyable environment. If there is any way that I may be of service to you, please just ask me directly and I'll do my best to help.

The 1993 Congress was particularly meaningful to me. Not only did I attend most sessions, but I even joined a panel discussion about the psychology of power, greed and violence. Never in my wildest dreams did I, a neuroscientist who studied rat brains for most of my career, expect to ever speak about issues relating to Somalia.

My interest in Somali studies came not through my readings, or television or because of famine and civil strife. Rather, my interest developed because of one very persistent and charismatic man--a man who taught me about NGOs and PVOs (acronyms I had never heard before), a man who introduced me to the concept, not just of development, but of sustainable, indigenous development, a man who has insatiable drive and energy and who taught me much about fund-raising. Certainly, you know I am speaking of my friend, my colleague -- Dr. Hussein Adam.

On one of my most memorable trips with Hussein, we were visiting the United Nations, asking for money, what else? "Hussein," I said, "how do we do this?" He put it simply, "we will just go and ask them for it, that's all." While I had been at the UN many times as a tourist, that day I was behind the scenes where no tourists ever go. We went for lunch into the Ambassador's Lounge -- a large two-level room full of smoke where they served strong coffee, straight alcohol and sweets. This room, I recall, was used in an Alfred Hitchcock film a few decades ago. As soon as we entered, people of all colors and accents came to see Hussein. "Do you know who you are with?" they asked me. Seeing the vacant look in my eyes, they then told me much about Hussein and indeed I was impressed anew and remain impressed by this man. I am not here to give a testimonial to my friend but I must tell you that this year he was granted tenure by the College. We hope he will spend his career with us at Holy Cross and continue to be happy and productive here.

I do wish to take a few moments to tell you about this place, the College of the Holy Cross. Holy Cross is a Jesuit, co-educational, liberal arts college founded 152 years ago. Among its first graduates--in fact, our very first valedictorian--was an African-American man named James Healy. He went on to become the Catholic Church's first African-American Bishop. His brother, who attended Holy Cross, became the president of Georgetown University.

Holy Cross has about 2,600 students equally divided between men and women. The majority of our students ranked in the top 10% of their high school classes. Particularly noteworthy is the dedication shown by our students to helping others--a fact that was recognized with a Point-of-Light by President Bush. At the same time, over one-third of our students participate in NCAA intercollegiate athletics.

Holy Cross offers majors in eighteen disciplines as well as concentrations or minors in many other fields including Peace and Conflict Studies, International Studies, Women's Studies and African-American Studies. Our 210 full-time faculty are as prolific in writing, composing, performing, and exhibiting their work as any faculty in the nation. I know of no better cadre of teachers, of truly brilliant teachers, than at Holy Cross.

In recent years, Holy Cross has been consistently recognized as one of the finest colleges in the nation. Ranked among the top twenty-five national liberal arts colleges (along with Williams, Amherst, Bowdoin, Wellesley, etc.), Holy Cross is the only school in this group with a clear and present religious affiliation. This distinction is most significant to everyone who studies, learns, teaches and works here. As stated in the Mission Statement we, as faculty, crafted several years ago:

> Holy Cross has sought to educate students who, as leaders in business, professional, and civic life, would live by the highest intellectual and ethical standards. In service of this ideal, Holy Cross endeavors to create an environment in which integrated learning is a shared responsibility, pursued in the classroom and laboratory, studio and theater, residence and chapel. Shared responsibility for the life and governance of the College should lead all its members to make the best of their own talents, to work together, to be sensitive to one another, and to seek justice within and beyond the Holy Cross community."

These are not mere words, they are guideposts for those of us who choose to participate in the life of Holy Cross. Several years ago, Hussein, several colleagues from Catholic Relief Services, and I met at my office to plan a conference on sustainable development in Somalia (and of course to plan how to raise the funds for it). For some reason, after coming back into my office, my attention was called to the fact that here were members of Christian, Jewish and Islamic traditions working through a Catholic agency, at a Catholic College to bring people together to discuss sustaining the development of an African nation. I thought, "how remarkable?" But upon reflection, I also thought,"How usual, how regular, how Holy Cross this is?"

For it is usual and expected, at Holy Cross, to ask "What are our obligations to one another? What is our special responsibility to the world's poor and disenfranchised? How do we engage in dialogue which will allow us to remain open to a sense of the whole -- calling us to transcend ourselves and challenging us to find our common humanity? As a Jesuit College, the cultivation of intellectual, social, religious and ethical refinement is not an end in itself. Rather, it means educating young people to be truly concerned about human welfare, about making our economies more just, and about placing men and women in public office who are honest and honorable. Holy Cross "educates men and women for others" and we live out this powerful statement in very real ways. We are proud, for example, that a very significant number of

Fortune 500 companies are headed by Holy Cross alumni, imbued with this great tradition.

Things are, of course, not perfect here on the hill. In particular, I look forward to the day when people of all colors are so much a part of campus life that I simply don't notice. I wait for the day that I can say "how usual, how regular, how Holy Cross." That day, I believe, is coming soon.

Let me close by saying how delighted we are that you are here working on such an important issue. I hope that you find your room accommodations suitable, the food to your liking and the community to be welcoming. Do take some time to walk around campus, visit the library and the art gallery, and see our gardens and sculptures. Finally, I would be remiss if I did not call to your attention the generosity of the United States Institute of Peace which has provided to Hussein and the College a generous grant which is supporting this meeting and the publication of materials from the Congress.

Best wishes on a successful meeting. Thank you very much.

CHAPTER THIRTY NINE

"Look, We've Got To Do Something"

Ambassador Robert Oakley

Let me begin by saying thank you to Dr. Hussein Adam, not only for persuading me to come to Holy Cross, but also thank you for persisting. And let me also thank all of you for working to convey knowledge of Somalia to others. It is a challenging task because Somalia is a very complicated country to understand. Even Somalis do not understand all aspects of their country. For example, if one is an expert on plans in Somalia, it means the expertise holds only for one's own plan, not for anybody else's. Yet in spite of Somali individualism, attempts such as this conference to press for more knowledge, for better understanding among all parties, and to seek exchanges of these understandings are all highly important goals. Hence, the work you are doing to break down stereotypes and misunderstandings is essential, especially in a civil war-ravaged environment such as Somalia.

We all need to think about other ways of doing this, and one idea that occurred to me, Hussein, is to try to take advantage of Somalia's participation in the Olympic Games next year. Somalia is a rich country, a civilized country, a country that's always been active in sports. One might seek Somali expatriate participation in and around the Olympics, and think about how that can best be done. It would perhaps provide an opportunity to change Somalia's image. Because there's going to be so much publicity around the games, it would provide an exceptional opportunity to further work that has begun at meetings such as this one. I think they are supposed to start training in Atlanta this summer and remain for a whole year.

All of you in this room, and all the Somalis in North America, ought to think about how one could take advantage of such an opportunity as the Olympics. To encourage it, see who's coming from Somalia. If the best people are not coming, see if there's not a way to get them here. Bob Gosende [assistant to Ambassador Oakley during 1992] and I worked hard on sports while we were out there, and for a while it looked like it was going quite well. At one stage we had 30,000 Mogadishu residents come to a soccer match from all over the city. They walked in, very peacefully, and, after the game, walked out, very peacefully. Competition was intense between the different teams, including US military officers playing on the US team -- that was something. Education, health, business and other areas where I think there's still the possibility of doing things between Somalia and the United States can pay off in terms of understanding Somalia in this country, and in terms of doing something inside Somalia. These are important steps.

Someone suggested I talk about what went wrong in Somalia. I will do that very, very briefly, because I want to spend as much time answering your questions as I do conveying whatever thoughts I might have. Somalia is perhaps the first and the most vivid example of what has come to be called a failed state, and the efforts of the international community to rebuild the failed state -- which did not succeed. There was one that preceded it -- Afghanistan -- that did not get as much publicity as Somalia, perhaps because the involvement never achieved the same level of intensity.

There have been many other failed states where international communities perhaps have not made quite as big or as visible an effort, but where the same problems have prevailed: too many people, too few resources, bad governments, new communications raising expectations and new forms of protest. But all these things have come together in many countries around the world and produced a tremendous loss of faith in government. In the US, the government is seen as bad. Even stable nations such as Italy and Japan are experiencing major transformations in expectations in governance..

So you find that Yugoslavia is broken up into three pieces. In situations, whether it is Chechenya or Liberia or what used to be Somalia, you find a return to ethnic groups, religious groups, or racial/tribal or clan groups. And there are plenty of demagogues around to exploit this for their own purposes. But much of the agenda is not religion or ethnicity or tribal identity. Instead, it is politics. Add in these other elements, which is easy to do these days, and the situation becomes explosive. Therefore, it's more dangerous and more prevalent as we approach the 21st century. But in Somalia, as you know better than I, General Siyad's authoritarianism became more and more unacceptable to more and more Somalis. Eventually, you had the civil war. Battles against Siyad's army blew back and forth, devastating the countryside. Then when he was finally pushed out, you began to have battles to see who was going to succeed. Those battles continued, though some say that by late summer of 1992, the war was, in fact, over. Therefore, what was all this US intervention about anyway?

I was thinking that the pause for breath to rearm, and to some degree the efforts of Mohammed Sahnoun, created a temporary calm. At the same time, the US was landing in December. Morgan was moving on Kismayo, and Baidoa. The war was about to resume in both places, although it had temporarily stopped in Baidoa, which was a centerpiece not only in famine and fighting, but also the showplace for CNN.

So, looking at this situation, President Bush said, "look, we've got to do something." And he was not alone. Even the Pentagon people finally dropped their reservations about involvement, partly because they felt that the former Yugoslavia/Bosnia was beyond their capabilities, or the international community's capabilities to handle the military, political, and humanitarian aspects of the situation. The Pentagon felt that they could provide what you might call a "blanket of foam" which would be powerful enough to put the Somali fire out and give people a chance. And they were right, and they transformed the old Weinbarger/Powell doctrine into something different by combining it with humanitarian operations in a systematic way, something they had stumbled into in Turkey and Northern Iraq. They complemented the military by bringing in a political component -- namely me, Bob Gosende and a handful of other people who understood enough about Somalia -- to provide general guidance.

President Bush could not, as a lame duck president, come up with an overall plan for Somalia. There are people who criticize saying that without an overall plan the situation was bound to go wrong. Well, he was a lame duck president. He confined his list of objectives to immediate and short-term goals. He very clearly spelled them out though the UN Secretary General and many Somalis did not like them. He assumed that the best we could do was to stop the fighting, allow the humanitarian operation to proceed, provide protection for the humanitarian operations, and create a situation in which the UN could come in for a longer term. President Bush assumed that his successor and the new Congress would set the longer term US policy. We were well aware that a lame duck president could not determine long term goals as they would probably not be sustained with new leadership.

While we were there, with the help of Bob Gosende and a lot of others, we branched out a bit, locally because we received no plan from the United Nations. Many of you are students of Africa. There was an overall plan for Namibia; an overall plan for Angola, which did not work very well; an overall plan for Mozambique, which did. In Central America there was sensible planning, including things like police forces, disarmament, demobilization, new jobs for militias -- a lot of things of that sort. For some reason, there was no comprehensive approach to the problem of Somalia from the United Nations. And Washington was not able to generate one, not at that stage.

So we did what we could. We eventually got permission to use local resources and set up a police force. We got the top leaders -- military and political -- from the two most powerful groups in Mogadishu to let it happen and to set up a ten-man control commission. It was reasonably confident and reasonably neutral. The police force was created in such a way that the police who lived in the northern part of Mogadishu were working in the southern part. Those who lived in the south were working in the north, at their own insistence. This was allowed. The joint commission of political and military leaders all said, "We want this to happen, will you, Ambassador Oakley, convince General Aidid to let it go forward?"

We worked with women's groups, journalists, law professors, teachers, doctors, nurses, and with NGOs. Some sort of civil society was slowly returning. We adopted this approach because we felt it made the most sense in Somalia. Because we had been there before and because we did not know that much about the complex details of local issues, we encouraged Somalis to do things for themselves, with our help. We refrained from saying, "do it this way, do it that way." On many occasions, people would come in with disputes and we would say fine, "we'll get the other person in this dispute here, and we'll help, but we are not going to be the judge, we cannot be. We'll never know the truth of the matter, and if we make a value judgment as to who's right and who's wrong, it won't work. So you've got to find a more local way to do it."

There were a number of occasions in which they did. With property or houses that had been taken by factional groups, many were returned to their owners through the joint commission, after they had ineffectively attempted to get them back by force. How interesting that when force failed, sometimes turning to the joint political committees, the joint security committees, the police, the religious leaders, and the clan leaders, that people would work together to restore the property to its original owners. Probably 150 houses were returned peacefully through this process.

Where things began to go wrong -- and I've thought a lot about this -- was in Addis Ababa during the political and military elite conferences where the Somalis began to look at things from the point of view of the international community. They sensed that international bodies wanted Somalis to form a new government. We wanted all these formal structures of the state. These were not necessarily the goals of the Somalis. The Addis convention came up with a number of resolutions and recommendations, as they had been encouraged to do -- by African leaders, by the United Nations, by other countries. But in creating this structure, curiously enough, it did two things which I think became very distorting and contributed to problems rather than moving toward solutions. It created a situation in which everyone was looking at a government which was going to be formed. Who was going to be in charge of that government? We knew that Ali Mahdi had already named himself interim president. And we knew that Aidid felt that fate somehow destined him to take the place of Siyad Barre, a man whom he took credit for having overthrown. So there were at least two contenders. Even more important was the fact that there was a government being created, that the international community was going to recognize it, and that the international community was also going to recognize a leader. That was a point of conflict that the Addis meeting brought home, not something in the far distant future, but something soon and immediate. We tried to encourage local governments to set up district and regional councils, in whatever way they wanted. "Whatever way they wanted" was by the traditional Somali way, and different parts of the country set up their own councils in many different ways. So that we would have something to work with, both on the security side and on the developmental side, the outside agencies demanded a structure. And then the United Nations, and others said, "OK, here's the formal structure." We are now going to see to it that this structure is implemented. People then began to look at the implementation in terms of their own values and goals, and some Somalis were able to make more sympathetic presentations than others. Aidid's effort to gain power, blatant as it was, turned many off. Officials said "this man is anti-democratic."

If you examine, for example, attitudes toward local councils, I would not say that Ali Mahdi's people were no better than Aidid's. They all wanted to appoint their people to the local councils, all over the country. They did not want the local leadership to come up from the bottom. They wanted to make sure that the people at the top could say, "I'm the leader of the movement, therefore, the local council out there's going to respond to me." That was not confined to Aidid, but Aidid was much more blatant and aggressive in pushing his approach. That was his style. He therefore became the bad guy, the opponent of this new democracy, the democracy that was the vision of the Clinton administration.

During those early months of rehabilitation, things seemed to be getting off to a good start; Somalia hovered on the horizon as the international community's first successful test case to rebuild a failed state. The Secretary General of the United Nations, as we know, had his own ideas about Somalia. These ideas go back, I think, to the times of his ancestors, the pharaohs, not merely to his years as Minister of Foreign Affairs for the Egyptian government. Not that the Secretary General felt that Aidid was a bad guy, rather he thought Aidid was anti-democratic. He felt he was a bad guy for being an enemy of Boutros Boutros-Ghali of Egypt. In any event, this great enthusiasm took place, everyone rushing toward this wonderful first case where the United Nations is going to solve the problems of a failed state. And they did not know anything about Somalia, nothing. Moreover, the foam blanket -- the upper hand -- the fair degree of security which had been generated in many parts of the country, began to slip.

The last thing the US marine generals told the Pakistani generals who were taking over responsibility for South Mogadishu -- and this was just one small part of the problem -- "no matter what you may hear from General Bir, or the Secretary General's special representative, Admiral Howe, or from anyone else, there are two things you must do: keep your patrols on the street all night, and have daily dialogue with the SNA (General Aidid's coalition)."

The Pakistanis did neither. They did not feel capable of patrolling at night, they felt that it was too dangerous. Aidid was the bad guy, therefore he was not someone you could trust or talk to.

We found there were any number of people within his movement who were sensible, though not without difficulty. And there were some very nasty ones who are still there. But there are also some very, very positive ones who, periodically, would take us aside and say, "Hey, look out for this and that. Let's work together to deal with this nasty problem in our own movement, because we know it's going to put our movement and Somalia in a very bad situation. It might get us all killed, because you all are so powerful militarily, and so alert." So we found that there was a general movement in both the Aidid and Ali Mahdi groups that were working to stay together. But this working relationship was allowed to slip, because the movement began to shift back. Then as a struggle surfaced, the Addis Ababa conference became an opportunity to move in a different direction, the wrong direction. The reaction arose because of this competition for leadership and competition for power in and amongst Somalis.

Then there was a succession of bad things: bang bang! The 5th of June, the Secretary General's three person committee visited and said "Yes, this was within the UN mandate, but it's extremely provocative, and extremely unwise." If you talked to the marines, they'll say, "Hey, when we went to a weapons compound, first we only went by helicopter. But we knew there were very rough, very nasty people in that compound, that storage depot. If we occasionally made the point that we could go on foot, we sent word several days in advance that we would get hold of the commander as well as his superiors within the Aidid organization. We would have a long talk and agree on a date and a time. Then we would go together. We did not expect to find anything, but that way it was all agreed. We made no surprise visits to that very, very troublesome spot." So that was the approach before June 5, 1993.

After that, the international community, led by the US, took great umbrage saying "Oh this is terrible, look what's happened, we've been attacked, we have to stop this because this is not only bad for Somalia, but it upsets our global plans of using UN peacekeepers." Then the US became fully engaged. You had the US helicopter gun ships ambushed on the 12th of July, which is at least as vicious an ambush as what happened to the Pakistanis on the 5th of June. But deliberately, without warning, getting the maximum number of SNA leaders in one place and firing missiles at them does not lead to a peaceful resolution to Somalia's problems. Not if you know the Somalis. So it went on from there.

And we all know what happened on the third of October, 1993.

One last serious opportunity to pull the country back together, I believe, was in December, 1993, when after great difficulty with the Secretary General, and to some degree with our own government, we were able to get everybody together in Addis Ababa for humanitarian talks. And we got Aidid out of his bunker -- physically and mentally -- at least he was talking to people. And the civil war has not resumed. You all know that better than I. It does not mean the country's peaceful, but starvation has not resumed either. And whether Somalia can put itself together -- I do not know. Outsiders do not understand Somalia well enough to do it and the mere attempt by outsiders to do it for Somalia is guaranteed to produce a negative result. But that's where we are today, and that's how I see what happened.

CHAPTER FORTY

Preventing Future Famine in Somalia

John Prendergast

I. Preface

Current capacity to respond to major Somali food insecurity depends much less on international NGOs than it did in 1992–93. Then, the international NGO community delivered upwards of 90% of the food for Somalia. But WFP's role and the involvement of Somali NGOs have since grown to a much larger ratio of commodities, since many of the emergency-oriented NGOs departed, and still more NGOs fled the growing insecurity. The issue in 1994-95 was one of food security rather than direct feeding. Physical security will become the predominant factor to determine whether famine returns. It will become the critical factor in allowing humanitarian aid to move and, more importantly, people to plant, store, and market food.[1]

Before UNOSOM left, Ken Menkhaus attributed continuing food shortages largely to the interveners' inability to control banditry, including theft of :

villagers' harvests and ... food aid once military escorts leave the scene ... predatory banditry in parts of the inter-riverine region, which in some cases has approached alarming forms of quasi-enslavement...and the rising number of armed attacks on NGOs and UN agencies.[2]

If Somalia again faces major food shortages, it must draw significant lessons from the 1992–94 intervention. Perhaps one of the most important is that the price of food plummeted before the UNITAF intervention in response to the U.S. airlift and increased internal production. These lower prices indicate improved supply, and increased poorer Somalis' access to food and strengthened their ability to avoid distress sales of livestock.

Some observers claim that the large troop presence has hurt relations between international NGOs and the local communities they serve. One NGO official bemoans,

> The NGOs [no longer] need[ed] to have the extensive links with the community they [had] needed before the troops came in. After the troops came, they had a buffer. Now a few loose cannons can throw grenades into an NGO compound and the elders don't care because their links with NGOs are weakened.

There is much better information now on food security throughout southern Somalia. Somali organizations, WFP, FAO, and the NGO Consortium are working together to provide early warning information, as well as consistent monitoring by tracking market prices and grain production. USAID and the EC are interested in helping to fund a food security task force. The donors also showed interest in placing a full-time agronomist and economist in southern Somalia's 12 regions.

Disturbingly, the 1993-1994 output of food grains was sixty percent below the average annual pre-war output, and represented only one-third of the production of the harvests of a year ago, according to WFP/FAO assessments. In mid-1994, WFP was providing assistance to approximately 274,000 people in 9 centers around Somalia through institutional feeding, supplementary feeding, targeted dry feeding, food for work, resettlement and monetization. Nearly half of all WFP activities took place in Mogadishu, Middle and Lower Shabelle, and southern Hiraan. Most importantly, eighty percent of all activities were implemented by Somali NGOs. UNICEF was supporting 73 supplementary feeding centers which served 53,000 women and children. The numbers began rising again in May 1994, due to increased prices because of poor harvests combined with continuing insecurity which disrupts commercial movement of grain.[3]

Furthermore, one donor government official noted that NGOs which pulled out in 1994 often did so because of security problems and the lack of reaction on the part of local Somali communities to either "prevent these incidents or pursue the guilty parties." The same official noted that some NGOs are planning to return to the extensive hiring of Somali guards. Furthermore, NGOs which desired to move to longer-term development are faced with bureaucratic and regulatory constraints going from using (in the case of US money) OFDA funds to DFA resources. The official recommended, "If [the US Agency for International Development] is to be able to respond reasonably to protracted, structural relief cases like Somalia, it must have multi-year funding sources that have the same `notwithstanding' flexibility as OFDA/IDA funds."

II. Looting and Diversion

Menkhaus observed as early as mid-1991 that relief operations were constrained by the diversion of food aid, the targeting by militias or bandits of communities which receive food aid, the difficulty of targeting aid to the most vulnerable, the predicament of preventing the location of operations from leading to perceptions of favoring particular sub-clans, food aid's sustenance of warring factions, and the difficulty of withholding aid because of the immediate impact on the most vulnerable.[4]

ICRC officials claim that when the UNITAF forces landed, they were losing only 5-20% of the commodities they were bringing in. They acknowledge that in the beginning, this figure was much higher, but, according to one official, "We invested a lot in understanding the reasons for diversion and in improving management. Management is what helps reach the most vulnerable."[5]

To prevent major famine, donors must squarely address the issues of diversion and looting. Many analysts have seen large-scale looting as simply an extension of years of dependency on and theft of international aid. The appropriate response depends on the nature of the looting: organized, large-scale, commercial activity; or petty "have gun, take penicillin" banditry.[6] Those responsible for major diversion are often the businessmen who own the trucks, as one NGO official notes:

> The political structures of the militias are usually not able to contain the avarice of the businessmen. The businessmen support whomever will help them.

The Murosade businessmen illustrate how business interests can create famine. This group controlled a substantial part of Mogadishu's commercial flow in 1991 until Aidid's forces hit them at the end of the year because they were selling arms to the Abgal. After Aidid took them out, the Murosade began shooting at ships approaching Mogadishu's port in order to keep prices artificially high for the food they had in the market. They also retaliated against Aidid. Murosade in Afgoi blocked food convoys from Mogadishu to Baidoa, an Aidid stronghold.

In Baidoa itself in 1992 the looting was fairly organized by the militias in the town and at the airport. By mid-1993, the looting was much more random as smaller bandit groups replaced the militias as the primary problem.[7]

One crucial factor in responding to food crises is to understand whether mitigating ties exist between civilians and those diverting aid in the region. Menkhaus warned in mid-1991 that in Lower Juba,

> no `social contract' of clan affiliation and obligation exists between the occupying forces, who are ethnic Somalis, and the villagers, who are not; there is thus little likelihood that diverted food aid will trickle down to the villagers. Diverted food aid has, however, reached many of the town dwellers and displaced persons in the region....[8]

III. Lessons Learned

Most analysts agree in retrospect that it was a major mistake to overfocus on Mogadishu, both in terms of project activity as well as in concentrating most of UNOSOM's capacity in a centralized manner in South Mogadishu, Aidid's stronghold.

It is also important to recognize that Somali society is stratified not only **between** but **within** sub-clans. Most communities encompass substantial income and resource differentials, and the better off largely survived the 1991–92 famine: Lance Salisbury of Catholic Relief Services described "people ... existing on leaves and nuts in the same village as people selling surplus grain in Quansa Dhere [a district in Bay]."[9] Conversely, Isaaq and Marehan populations survived their 1991 exodus from Mogadishu because richer community members cared for the poorer.

It is critical to understand the importance of, and regional differences in, family and kinship in order to respond to future famine. Extended families are not as prevalent or important in Bay Region, for example, as elsewhere in southern Somalia. (The Rahanweyn have been sedentary much longer than most other Somali communities and came to have less need for extensive extended families. Also, the colonial-era advent of wage labor provided another pressure on the maintenance of extended families.) The Bay Rahanweyn thus lacked the mutual-support safety nets that sustained many communities at the height of the crisis.

Another important issue is Somali farmers' practice of monetizing their crops after harvest and then buying back grain after depleting their personal stocks. During 1993-4, merchants bought up much of the marketed grain in Bay Region, sold it in Luuq and Mogadishu, and then charged Bay farmers exorbitant prices for grain. "The merchants are playing the market forces," says one NGO representative. Acute food insecurity resulted by early 1994 in Quansa Dhere district. One NGO reported that prices rose from 400 shillings per kilo in mid-1993 to 3,000 in January 1994. CRS had to restart food distribution. Another NGO official described the merchants' exploitation of the intersection of markets and food aid, in which even some District Council members participate:

> The merchants didn't have to loot. They bought surpluses, hoarded them, and even exported some to the Arabian peninsula. As long as food is being pumped in, the merchants can buy it up cheap and hoard or sell it. The Rahanweyn are viewed as superfluous.

A further important factor is urbanization. In the 1980s, Somalia's percentage of urbanization overtook Kenya's and Ethiopia's.[10] Policies that discriminated against rural areas and producers were the main culprit. Rural instability and banditry in the last 3 years added fuel. Serving these newly urbanized populations is one element of the policy puzzle, but eventually providing incentives to reverse the rural-urban shift is more important given the unsustainability of present trends in terms of employment, food security, environment, and social services. Escalating urbanization make food and cash-for-work critical in mitigating famine. OFDA's famine mitigation resources should be deployed in Somalia within a broader preventive framework.

UNOSOM's policy of providing rehabilitation resources only to areas deemed secure was immediately problematic. "When Admiral Howe came [to Baidoa] and said he would reward Bay for its security, we immediately saw an upsurge in violence," according to an NGO official. "The same thing happened in Bakool, when the MDM official was assassinated in Wajid." The hand grenade attacks on compounds and similar tactics were intended to disrupt peaceful development processes to prevent aid flows to those regions. Furthermore, Habar Gedir forces of the SNA attacked some areas because the NGOs in those areas had pulled out of Habar Gedir areas, punishing them for their withdrawal.

Further complications ensue when one group feels left out of processes in their home area. Again in Bay, the Hiraan sub-clan of the Rahanweyn felt that the Leyson sub-clan had principally benefitted from resource flows to Bay since major food distributions began. The Hiraan had become the dominant economic group under Barre but felt cut out when some international NGOs primarily developed security arrangements with Leyson elders. The resulting tensions erupted into inter-sub-clan fighting north of Baidoa, and the Leyson destroyed some Hiraan villages.

In Somalia, as in most other places, donors cannot target vulnerables within a larger community without providing the larger community some corollary benefit. In January, 1992, an aid official posted to Merca recounted an incident in which bandits from Mogadishu who felt left out of the aid distributions looted and killed 20 people who were literally starving. "The lesson we learned was that we had to feed everyone." That extreme example illustrates the need for sensitivity about who will be (or perceive themselves as) winners and losers when donors introduce external resources into a volatile, polarized situation. Every charitable act has political ramifications.

Furthermore, a food-aid-first strategy is inappropriate except in extreme food deficits. An ICRC official comments, "We must hold the Somalis responsible. We should not have the unconditional dumping of food. Blank checks create major problems."

Donors must greatly improve their understanding of the survival strategies of the most vulnerable in order to support these strategies when feasible. So-called "survival strategies" often erode the base for future survival. These include the sale of important assets such as livestock and personal items (jewelry, utensils), and the depletion of community assets such as forest cover.

Other survival strategies better deserve and allow support. Survival foods are an example. "The [Gosha] populations in Kismayo went to the (Juba) Valley to get bananas and mangos which were growing wildly," according to Awil Bashir Ahmed, UNICEF nutritional officer in Kismayo.[11] "That's why at times they were better off than the Tunis, who were helpless." The pastoral Tunis were unprepared to forage for survival when displaced and stripped of all their livestock.

MSF-Belgium concluded that the 29 UNHCR Quick Impact

Projects (QUIPS) around Kismayo positively affected nutritional levels in the latter half of 1993. They injected cash into the local economy, creating demand for commodities and thereby increasing market activity.[12] Nutrition levels were also impacted by increased food deliveries by WFP, UNICEF, and MSF feeding programs, the absence of epidemics, increased locally produced food in the markets, and a reduction of internal displacees in Kismayo.

Many agencies have had difficulties moving to rehabilitation. Food-for-work, for example, has been difficult to implement because of the prior dumping of food commodities without reciprocal requirements. "We were delivering food to people that could have been productive," according to one official. The town of Wajit in Bakool Region was receiving five planes a day at 15 metric tons per flight in late 1992. "There was no need for that much food," the official concludes. "The communities were paralyzed; they would not do anything because they expected the handout." Future food assistance should clearly be tied to some activity -- preferably one that reinforces production.

Relatedly, prior aid imposes political costs. When ICRC ceased its delivery of nearly 1,000 tons of food per month to Kismayo in early 1993, no one was in a position to continue such volume. WFP delivered 50 tons of food the next month and suffered constant demonstrations and stonings. In Mogadishu, Admiral Howe pushed certain NGOs to continue general distributions well after need ended in order "to keep the streets quiet." One NGO official reported, "We wanted to stop, but Howe told us not to." Future food assistance should clearly be tied to some activity -- preferably one that reinforces production.

When the emergency response began to escalate in 1992, agencies rarely coordinated cost-containment. "Agencies were coming in with lots of cash," remarked a former official of an aid agency. "They all wanted their personal stamp on their operations. They would pay at twice the rate the last agency paid for transport, housing and security. Huge inflation resulted for everyone." Unsustainable costs have led agencies to suffer violence against personnel in 1993 and 1994 and to draw down or withdraw altogether. The above aid official suggested standardizing costs at the outset of emergencies. Donors should require inter-agency coordination to set uniform costs if another emergency requires scaling up.

In Xoddur in the latter half of 1992, agencies were handing over approximately 2,000 bags of food per month to militia men -- perhaps 30% of the total. They also paid for security.

The early stages of the intervention entailed little to no training of

Somalis and no emphasis (beyond rhetorical) on building local capacity. Subsequent rectification has been limited by international agencies' *modus operandi* with Somali NGO partners; i.e., providing immediate operational funds -- instead of slowly building capacity through training -- in order to respond visibly to perceived problems. Rebuilding the Somali primary health care and surveillance system by funding and training Somalis in a Somali-managed system is much more critical than funding dozens of small local NGO fiefdoms and replicating the worst aspects of the uncoordinated international emergency response system.

Now that funding is quickly drying up for Somalia, some of the international NGO–run hospitals and programs face critical inabilities to continue services. Unsustainability is a major problem in the aftermaths of many emergencies in which curative initiatives superseded preventive ones.

Rural rehabilitation and recovery should be the primary objective of humanitarian interventions in Somalia. Agencies must prioritize initiatives to restore rural communities' subsistence and recreate wealth-producing opportunities through ecologically sound agricultural and pastoral activities over urban-focused interventions that become magnets for the marginalized.

Wisner notes, "The Somali people have a long tradition of consultation, debate, and consensual decision making, especially during times of stress."[13] Whatever interventions are attempted should feed into and build on these local processes and the local capacities (organization, energy, skill) of the communities assisted.

IV. Rehabilitating Agriculture and Fishing

The principal crop for Juba Valley small holders is maize, used to make *soor*, the region's staple porridge. Sesame planted using flood recession techniques has been the major cash crop for 30 years. Intercropping is widespread, but land scarcity has reduced fallowing.[14]

The International Rescue Committee is rehabilitating rainwater catchment areas, the major rural source of water, in the northern Valley. Oxfam and Swedish Church Relief have provided crucial emergency water packages to meet immediate needs. "Both approaches are appropriate, given the diversity of need," according to the water coordinator for an NGO. Further support should be provided to Somali communities that practice flood irrigation, a skill with enormous potential for expansion.

Oxfam-UK and SCF-US have prioritized the rehabilitation of

irrigation for small-scale farmers. Inputs for successful programs include (1) clearing canals, (2) the provision of tools, and (3) perhpas food-for-work to clean secondary canals, a donor-funded internal purchase program to buy surplus inputs for pumps, and access to seed.[15] The irrigated sub-sector produced over half of the total output of grains before the war, approximately 700,000 tons annually.[16]

Oxfam-UK turned over Juba valley seed distribution to FAO. By late 1993 much of the agricultural activity in the valley was cash crops --- sesame, sorghum, and tobacco. The plantations were inoperable, with no financial backers in sight to reconstruct them. Many village cooperatives had formed to address land reclamation, irrigation, and labor constraints in a labor-intensive area.[17]

World Concern distributes seeds and tools in Gelib and Bua'ale Districts to sedentary populations and returnees. Outside of these activities, seed is relatively scarce in the Valley.

Support for dryland farming is equally critical. "To date, various Somali governments have not applied the same vigor to improving dryland farming as they have to supporting irrigation," observes Wisner.[18] Regardless, there is evidence that integrated food security programs have worked in Somalia. A USAID evaluation of 17 years of soil and water conservation projects found that yields doubled in areas in which bunding was encouraged and practiced, and that increases of 50 percent held up over time.[19] Rainfed agriculture, despite very low yields, still produced roughly 30% of total crop output. Most of these farmers are agro-pastoral. Besides herd restocking, these families need seed, tools, and assistance in rehabilitating water supplies.[20]

One priority for those NGOs and donors who remain engaged in Somalia is to study the potential of the former plantations for alternative production, such as rice for domestic consumption and fruits for export to the Middle East.[21]

Security for transporting goods to market is critical for restoring a measure of self-reliance and creating opportunities to invest in asset- and wealth-building activities. Road disrepair, unavailable transport, and insecurity are three major impediments to functional marketing systems. Donors have not fully explored the potential for using external start-up financing to help ex-militia play roles in creating transport and security cooperatives to move produce.[22]

Donors should prioritize continual distribution of fishing equipment for two reasons. In the event of continuing conflict, populations in flight can retain a means to get food if they stay near any body of water. If stability spreads, communities can fish either to supplement their diets or produce for the market.

Revolving loans for small-scale fishing by local fishing associations would be another valuable input. Inputs needed are materials to rehabilitate boats, nets, tools, and motors.[23]

V. Rehabilitating Livestock

The livestock sector should also be an ongoing priority. The FAO estimated that 171,000 metric tons of meat were produced for local consumption before the war. The average prewar annual consumption of every Somali was 17.9 kg of meat and 237 liters of milk. Livestock production has provided the bulk of foreign exchange and employment since the 1960s.[24] Southern Somalia herds are probably half or less their late-1980s levels. The usual coping/restocking mechanisms -- loans of stock repaid in kind from progeny -- no longer function in many areas.[25] In contrast, an SCF-UK survey found Somaliland's 1993 livestock exports higher than in prewar years.[26]

Training and retraining a cadre of Somali veterinary workers to create a national vaccination system would contribute invaluably not only to food security but also to wealth creation and asset building. Reconstructing former quarantine stations in Berbera, Bosaso, Mogadishu, and Kismayo (most cattle went through the latter two) would be a further priority.

Those (agro-)pastoralists whose entire herds have been wiped out present special challenges. As early as September, 1992, Fred Cuny advocated exploring restocking options:

> Unfortunately, there is no source of animals in the Western food aid programs. Thus, the proceeds from the monetization program should be used to support livestock recovery and redistribution activities on a priority basis.[27]

Green estimates that core herds would cost $2,000 for the larger herds and $1,200 for the smaller ones. The current impossibility of traditional intra-family restocking loans suggests revolving loan projects for kin-groups. Sheep, goats, and cattle can all be purchased regionally. The cost-benefit calculation must include the cost of maintaining perpetual relief assistance for those newly dependent families. Green estimated the comparative numbers in 1993 at $80 million to rehabilitate 25,000 nomadic and 25,000 agro-pastoral families versus continued relief programs for 400,000 displaced persons "whose livelihoods cannot be rehabilitated."[28] Although camels are much better suited to the Somali environment than cattle, the camel-cattle ratio has greatly shifted in favor of the latter.[29]

Since the early 1900s the invasion of commercial capital has slowly eroded the traditional Somali pastoral life. Increased ecological degradation and vulnerability of pastoralists have resulted. Merchants and those controlling the State have exploited pastoralists. Price decreases for exports in the 1980s led to a decline in the standard of living/subsistence for pastoralists, lower profits for merchants, and less foreign exchange for the Barre regime. Most ominously, according to Abdi Samatar, is that "the ecological ruin of the Somali range is rendering precapitalist pastoral knowledge and management systems defunct or incapable of sustaining this form of commercial pastoral production."[30] Any support of the livestock sector should maximize nomadic participation in environmental management and stock protection and marketing.

VI. Postscript from Post-Intervention Somalia: March 1995

The widely predicted escalation of the Somali civil war after UNOSOM (the United Nations Operation in Somalia) troops withdrew in February has still not transpired. For the extraordinary amounts of financial and diplomatic resources expended by UNOSOM, its legacy is surprisingly small. Now that the international forces have departed, significant internal trends in Somalia have emerged which provide promise that a series of uneasy truces throughout the country may actually hold up for some time to come.

Nevertheless, these truces have not obviated the primary legacy of the vicious civil war which is thought to have resulted in the deaths of a quarter to a half million people: a geographical realignment of many Somali population groups which resulted in forced displacement, extrajudicial execution, mass rape, and asset transfer (land, livestock, and grain reserves) based primarily on sub-clan affiliation. As they do throughout the world, women and children are the first to suffer when fighting intensifies.

Lawlessness puts the Bantu communities and other minorities at increased risk of parasitic looting by the "*Mooryaan*," the bandits. Extortion is a way of livelihood for the "*Mooryaan*" now and a fact of life for the Bantu and other farming communities. They are nothing more than classic mafia rackets -- pay us to protect you from us. Villages are randomly looted; the looting is certainly more frequent than before the war, but much less than in its height in 1991-92. The extortion is probably the equivalent of much more than pre-war government taxation. There are cases of forced labor and forced displacement, and rape is also common, but the exact scale is difficult to pinpoint. The forced labor and looting is pure opportunism by the "Mooryaan." The forced displacement is part of a decades-long pattern of expropriation of the best farmland along the rivers by more powerful groups.

In the last year, forced displacement has taken many forms. The Abgal routed the Murosade out of the Medina neighborhood of Mogadishu, and the Murosade, in turn, burned many of the Abgal homes in neighboring Bermuda. But most of the displacement in Somalia was caused by Habar Gedir advances, pushing Biyaamal leaders (bureaucrats, elders, and the sultan) out of Merca and the Hawaadle from Mogadishu South, Belet Weyne, Bulo Berti, Jalalaxi, and Lower Shebelle. Those displaced correspond to those who present a military or political challenge to the Habar Gedir. For example, when the Hawaadle attacked Habar Gedir-occupied Belet Weyne on December 26, 1994, the latter responded by destroying two Hawaadle villages, Badeere and Bowholle in Hiran Region.

Some Bantu have been pushed from the west to the east side of the Juba River, primarily by Ogadeni "Mooryaan" looking to expand their territory. One official observed, "Bantu vulnerability lies in the lack of control of the militias, who do the looting."

Perhaps a third to a half of the Bantu population has disappeared from the Juba Valley. They either died or remain displaced. The Bantu also have fewer employment opportunities than before the war. In the Lower Shebelle, Bantu workers earn somewhere between 5,000 and 20,000 Somali Shillings ($1-$4) per day working for the plantation owners who sell to Dole and Somalifruit, the two multinational companies buying fruit in Lower Shebelle. In the social structure of Somalia, the Bantu have always suffered a *de facto* apartheid situation in which deep-rooted discrimination is a constant.

The Rahanweyn in Gedo are permanently displaced by default. In 1991-92, the fighting displaced them. When they went back to their lands they found them taken over by the Marehan. This expropriation is fueled by the desire of the Marehan to acquire the best farmland next to the Juba river all the way down to Bua'ale in Middle Juba. The Rahanweyn often leave their women and children in the displaced camps in Bardera (perhaps 10,000 displaced around Bardera) while the men go cultivate. This is due to Rahanweyn families having to diversify income because they are now farming more marginal lands.

The Rahanweyn in Bay are steadily recovering from the civil war. Their future security is in part dependent on whether the Habar Gedir believe they can get what they need from Bay without attacking; i.e., if their free trade access continues, there may be little rationale to militarily occupying the area, which would mean facing strong local opposition -- both armed and unarmed -- as well as international condemnation. In 1991, there were few people in Bay who were armed. In 1995, everyone has arms and the Leyson sub-clan has a small army. Crops are being sold to buy guns this month. The Rahanweyn in Bay still may be no match for the marauding pastoralist militias, but they won't be the pushover they were in 1991-92.

Just as powerlessness has its element of vulnerability, so too does potency. If a group fights and loses, it immediately becomes extremely vulnerable to repercussions from the victor. More broadly, when intense fighting erupts, everyone in a sense becomes vulnerable, as market structures collapse and livelihoods are destroyed.

The International Organization for Migration estimates that roughly 60% to 80% of the internally displaced in Mogadishu are women and children. Staff members found some of the worst organized camps they had witnessed in the world. On the other hand, another Non-Governmental Organization (NGO) found very well organized camps with rigid structures and micro-societies which include chiefs, mosques, and Koranic schools, and a better nutritional situation than the resident population. The picture is murky for the overall situation of the displaced. No comprehensive information base exists, despite a whole division of UNOSOM being devoted to resettlement.

The only human rights protection extant in Somalia today is the clan structure. The clan, in a sense, protects rights. Most are armed so there is restraint due to the potential for clanic retaliation -- the MAD principle (Mutually Assured Destruction) writ small. The human rights crisis occurred in 1990-92 in the context of large armies engaged in major territorial advances who preyed on defenseless subsistence agro-pastoral populations who could not retaliate. This same factor still leaves some communities with no "human rights defense," but some have armed themselves (Rahanweyn) and others provide a useful function (Bantu labor), so there are built-in restraints governing the human rights situation today.

The level of immunizations is still too low to contain any epidemic. The coverage for measles is below 50%. No health structure or system exists in many places, despite progress by UNICEF and many NGOs. Furthermore, security remains the main constraint to increased production and trade, so progress is obviously tenuously perched. On the other hand, two bumper harvests have begun to put money back in people's hands, and herds are naturally regenerating rapidly. Therefore, barring a major eruption in the smoldering war, most communities will slowly but steadily see an improvement in their situation.

Although Somalia represents a potential minefield of intra-and inter-clanic conflicts, the departure of UNOSOM has allowed locally-owned economic, social and political processes to emerge and flourish. Driven by economic self-interest, war weariness, and a re-emergence of traditional authorities at the expense of the militia leaders, the imperatives for peace inherent in some of these indigenous processes hold great promise for the future of the Somali people, if not for the future of a Somali state.

Endnotes

1. USAID, "Food Security Issues and INGOs in Southern Somalia," March 9, 1994, p.1.

2. Menkhaus (1), p. 153.

3. UN DHA, June Information Report, July 13, 1994, p. 2.

4. Menkhaus (2), p. 42.

5. Interview with Geoff Loane.

6. Interview with Stephen Tomlin, International Medical Corps, March 24, 1994.

7. Interview with Lance Salisbury, Catholic Relief Services- Baidoa, March 24, 1994.

8. Menkhaus (2), p. vi.

9. Interview with Lance Salisbury.

10. Wisner in Samatar, p.29.

11. Interview, March 27, 1994.

12. G.A.D. Barret, December 18, 1993, p.5.

13. Wisner in Samatar, p. 57.

14. Menkhaus, p.3.

15. Green, p. 10.

16. *Ibid*, p. 11.

17. G.A.D. Barret, p.9.

18. Wisner in Samatar, p. 41.

19. J.W. McCarthy, "A Soil and Water Conservation Project in Two Sites: Seventeen Years Later", AID Project Impact Evaluation Report, No. 62, 1985, quoted by Wisner.

20. Green, p. 12.

21. *Ibid*, p. 11.

22. Obura, p. 4.

23. Green, p. 14.

24. Abdi Samatar in Samatar, p. 67.

25. Green, p. 9.

26. Information provided at a meeting of the NGO Consortia in Mogadishu, March 30, 1994.

27. Fred Cuny, "The Functioning of Village Markets in Strife-Torn Areas of Somalia," unpublished mimeo, September 22, 1992, p.3.

28. Green, p. 13.

29. Wisner in Samatar, pp. 47-48.

30. Abdi Samatar in Samatar, p. 72.

CHAPTER FORTY ONE

Recommendations

At the end of the Post-Congress symposium, participants broke into small groups to consider lessons learned from the Somali experience. Given their rich body of knowledge as well as direct experience from many perspectives -- former government officers, NGO officials, donor representatives, academics, and given that they included many different political viewpoints from within and outside Somalia, it was a propitious time to reflect on what had happened and what might be done. The delegates prepared a number of recommendations.

This chapter contains a condensed version of all of the groups' recommendations, broken into four categories. The first are general considerations, designed to set overall policy and program guidelines for rehabilitation. The second, and longest section deals with short, medium, and long-term economic and human rehabilitation. The third set comes from a group particularly concerned about conflict resolution and bringing a healing process to all the people of Somalia. The fourth group was concerned primarily with the Northwest -- Somaliland -- and offered recommendations specific to their needs. While there is some duplication among the four clusters of recommendations, the overlap has been preserved in the editing as a means to bring emphasis to particular points.

I. GENERAL RECOMMENDATIONS

Donor Policies

External Aid: The Somali people hold the key to their future. Solutions imposed from outside are bound to fail. Yet external assistance, free from coercion, bias or arrogance is essential in rebuilding the lives of millions of displaced Somalis;

Equitable Allocations of Aid: International relief and development assistance should be provided to all parts of the country, primarily through local community organizations. It was noted that Somaliland and the northeast region had received very little international aid.

Scale

Local to Regional: Grassroots, local and regional level structures need strengthening if lasting peace is to be achieved. As local groups feel confident, possibilities will then emerge to find political mechanisms that hold regions together;

Regional Views: The shape of the new government(s) should be decided by democratic processes, with the people of the North enjoying the right of self-determination if that is their preference.

Peoples' Participation

Minority Rights: Somali society has neglected rights of minorities. Somalia's minority communities have legitimate demands which should be respected, including political institutions, language/culture and human rights;

Focus on Democracy: International assistance should support programs that develop democratic institutions and their ability for: constitution making, education, open elections and local capacity building;

Human Rights: Respect for human rights is an essential component of peace and reconciliation and a necessary basis for a Somali state, or states.

Somali Culture

Traditional Values: International agencies should respect traditional Somali political institutions and values. Institution-building is best facilitated from the bottom-up rather than by imposition of alien political visions installed in a top-down mode;

Elders and Local Leaders: The role of elders, clan heads, and religious leaders needs to be studied. Their expertise in traditional conflict resolution methods needs greater encouragement and their leadership in related matters needs strengthening;

Islamic Values: Traditional Islamic values of peace, fairness, and justice form a base for moral reintegration of Somalia. However, Islamic fundamentalism is not a positive force in the country at this period in time. Disruptive foreign agendas often come wrapped in the guise of Islamic fundamentalism; there is need for local and international vigilance.

Keeping the Peace

Demobilization: All parties should cooperate for disarmament and demobilization, using approaches such as vocational training, settlement, training of local police and the revival of courts and legal authorities;

Arms Restraint: International arms embargoes must be enforced, with particular attention to Kenyan sources.

Extending Social Services

Women's Groups: Special support should go to women's organizations so they can assume prominent roles in rebuilding civil society. Women should be empowered to participate actively at every level of the emerging democratic process;

NGOs: International and local non-governmental organizations deserve full recognition for their important role in humanitarian assistance and rehabilitation. Special support and encouragement should be given to Somali NGOs that continue to provide relief, reconstruction and conflict resolution programs;

Education: Formal and non-formal education programs require support. Such education should go beyond literacy and job skills to include training in non-violence, tolerance and dialogue.

Reconstruction

Educated Core: The Somali educated strata--at home and abroad--must strive to cooperate through the formation of professional associations;

Focus on Healing: A Truth and Reconciliation Commission(s) should be established to inform Somalis of the serious crimes committed and to facilitate a genuine healing process;

Horn of Africa Perspective: The increasing cooperation among IGADD member states -- Ethiopia, Eritrea, Djibouti, Uganda, Kenya, (Somalia) and Sudan -- has been highlighted and appreciated. The international community should support and enhance such efforts to encourage regional cooperation in the face of mounting economic and political pressures.

II. ECONOMIC RECONSTRUCTION AND REHABILITATION

Recommendations for reconstruction and rehabilitation contain three major proposed interventions: (A) Regeneration of the Economy: Immediate Action; (B) Creating an Economic Environment Conducive to Recovery: Medium-Term Action; (C) Building National Capacity: The Longer View. The following are proposed:

A. Regeneration of the Economy: Immediate Action

A joint effort is needed for Somalis, international organizations and donor countries to assess the current economic situation for immediate regeneration of the economy. This may involve the following steps:

• utilize Somali business groups to administer financial expenditures for relief, emergency, and future rehabilitation;

• adopt procedures to involve Somalis in all aspects of designing and administering relief and recovery, both for the present and future;

- assess urban commodity markets and their linkages with regional markets;

- study the potential role of exchange markets as reconstruction, production, and domestic/foreign trade expand;

- examine ways to generate income for public works in the absence of a formal government;

- establish public services for the "interim" period;

- restore financial services such as letters of credit, transfer payments and deposit facilities to assist traders;

- offer limited central bank functions in areas of exchange intervention and influencing money supply;

- devise strategies to deal with issues unique to Somalia such as: reintegration of "Boy Soldiers," assistance to informal sector, credit facilities to small farmers, support for female-headed single families and help for the urban poor.

B. Creating An Economic Environment Conducive to Recovery: Medium-Term Action

There is dire need to create a sustainable macro-economic framework that can promote successful rehabilitation for the medium-term.

- assess mechanisms to generate public revenues including direct and indirect taxation, import duties, and revenues such as fees for public services;

- introduce viable and self-sustaining credit schemes, especially in production, trade, housing and resettlement activities;

- establish financial intermediaries, including a commercial banking system to facilitate transfer of payments and safe-keeping of deposits;

- assist the informal sector in Somalia. It is currently the most active provider of employment in Somalia.

C. Building National Capacity: The Longer View

Building long-term national capacity and focusing on human development will sustain programs started during rehabilitation and reconstruction. This means empowering people to take charge of their destiny. International donors can facilitate such a process, fostering sustainable human development.

Human development is not limited only to social sectors (health, education and nutrition). It also places great importance on how these capabilities are employed. Therefore, free participation in social, political and economic decision making is vitally important. Human development does not have a uniform agenda for every country. Indeed, Somalia needs its own focus to put people in the center of their own development agenda in order to create an open-ended process for inclusion of national aspirations and desires.

C-1 The Structure

Since independence, there has been a government superstructure with non-traditional characteristics, inspired by colonial administrative modes. Political power, despite such administrative structures, was formed on the basis of tribal coalitions. In order to overcome the existing "institutional vacuum," Somalia needs to concentrate on the resumption and restructuring of four important sets of institutions: political, legal, financial and civil. Building national capacity in Somalia is a formidable task. It must fill a large gap created by the ruins of the last four and a half years of civil unrest as well as by neglect of decades of its governing administration. These areas include:

- *Political Institutions*: Political participation in the governance of their country/community is a crucial prerequisite for achieving a higher degree of development. Building political institutions for Somalia is not to erect a political ideology, as this is purely an internal matter. Rather, political institutions are needed to provide services in the following areas:

  a. for representation at community, local and national levels;

  b. for media ownership and management;

  c. for establishing entities which defend the right of individuals and groups to have access to free, non-violent political participation.

- *Legal Institutions*: Rule of law is an essential component of a civilized society. The prevailing anarchy in Somalia eroded the basis of any written law in the country. In certain areas, lawlessness caused a rebuke of traditions which had prevailed for centuries. Among the many existing problems, the lack of a constitution is a major stumbling block. Nonetheless, stopping and doing nothing is a greater problem. The building of legal institutions requires information about every aspect of Somali society. The task of institution building in this area can focus on the following:

a. public administrative institutions which embrace the development of public sector administrative machinery and training of their technical staff in all levels of local, regional and later at the national level;

b. private sector, management organizations and professional development institutions which tackle the development and training of qualified professional managers and other technical expertise of the non-government sector for the present and the future Somalia.

- *Financial Institutions*: Finances require immediate attention, as noted earlier. Lack of financial institutions has crippled business activities, inflicted damage to the production capacities in rural and urban sectors and made it impossible to have any regular and systematic public service delivery as there has not been any public revenue generation to secure such services. The areas of reconstruction and rehabilitation of a viable financial structure include the following:

a. public revenue-generating institutions at all levels of local communities and later, on at the national level;

b. institutions tackling financial mediation, provision of credit for investment in all areas of production and trade, and safe-keeping of savings.

- *Social Sector and Civil Institutions*: Improving social sector takes the center stage in any Human Development Program. The current situation in Somalia is desperate. However, the history of neglect extends to the entire period of the 1980s. Deterioration of health, decline in the school enrollment, reduction in the number of caring teachers and the fast erosion of all means of social safety nets happened during the 1980s. Rebuilding social institutions requires a major mobilization in Somalia. It includes the following:

a. rehabilitation of educational institutions at all levels of primary and secondary schooling will involve a thorough assessment of the most urgent needs as well as institution building for the longer term. Needs include management (retraining of teachers, mobilizing communities, community-based education, restoration of schools (primary, secondary, and adult). There is also need for peace education to create hope and confidence in the future instead of fear and despair. The work involves forming youth clubs, orienting youth toward positive attitudes, and teaching younger generations about the values of peace and human rights;

b. rehabilitation is needed of technical training institutions. These include technical schools and vocational training centers. Curriculum development, training technical teachers and building managerial skills are among the most important needs;

c. rehabilitation of post-secondary institutions, including management institutions and universities is another priority. This is a longer term program which can be tackled at a regional and national level later on, as the country returns to normalcy;

d. rehabilitation of health, sanitation and nutrition institutions at all levels will be necessary. The already fragile health manpower received a bigger blow during the crisis. The immediate goal is to utilize existing professional Somali manpower which may be scattered throughout the regions. The goal is to strengthen existing institutions and develop further capacity in potable water, sanitation facilities, disease control, nutrition, and inoculation;

e. strengthening community capacities at the local and regional level will help to deal with social emergencies, especially poverty alleviation. In terms of training, there is a tremendous need for preparing community social workers and other technical staff that can provide services for the deprived strata of the society. The relevant areas for the immediate future include strengthening the existing and establishing new institutions for reintegration of "Boy Solders," assisting single women as heads of family, and caring for orphans and other socially disadvantaged groups.

C-2 The Approach to National Capacity Building

In the absence of any functioning government in Somalia, the program can embark on an approach compatible with the existing political environment. The approach must generate national capacity-building to foster sustainable economic development in Somalia. The outline of such an approach includes:

- **Decentralization**: a decentralized and broad-based institutional foundation. Such a political power structure may be justified on the following grounds:

  a. the traditional structure of Somali society and the political development of the last four and a half years indicate that a decentralized power base is the most likely scenario to succeed;

  b. empowering people to take charge of their own destiny is the unavoidable ingredient of a successful strategy for strengthening national capacities;

  c. decentralization of political power does not necessarily mean weakening of national unity. It merely means a more efficient method of governing a society by the people who are bound together by the virtue of their own culture, social heritage or economic considerations.

- **Institution Building**: institutions are needed to strengthen political freedom through emphasizing personal security for peaceful political activity; allow for rule of law; support freedom of expression and legal guarantees for all; and encourage economic and political participation of all the people.

- **Private Sector Focus**: promote the role of the private sector by providing a higher degree of professional competence and managerial capabilities.

- **Utilize Local Resources**: put great emphasis on the utilization of internal resources in all areas and functions for capacity building. This is an important element contributing to the creation of a self-sustained program.

- **Realistic Investments**: avoid committing Somalis in developing activities which are beyond their institutional, technical and financial capacity in a foreseeable future.

- **Social Benefit**: seek tangible social benefit in excess of the social cost and pursue a clear order of preference for implementing projects/activities. In certain cases there may be justifiable ground for simply looking at cost recovery as a selection criterion as cost recovery continues to be an important element of sustainability;

- **Maintain Regional Balance**: address the historic imbalances in the allocation of resources for the development of the regional capacity.

- **Equity**: reach all segments of society and create greater opportunity for the lower strata, minorities, and women. Attention is also important for returning refugees, displaced peoples, and other specially deprived groups.

- **Environment:** safeguarding the environment is a necessary element of a sustainable development. In the context of Somalia, the abject poverty of the overwhelming majority of its population is the biggest threat to the environment.

C-3 Implementation Provisions: The Process

The objectives and the principles of national capacity building have been highlighted in the foregoing sections. The approach, as explained, creates a framework for human development programs compatible with the evolving social and political conditions. The central issue in a successful program is the "relevance" and the "pragmatism" pursued in laying down the provisions for its implementation. A human development approach, as argued before, should not be seen as a mere training program. It should create an environment conducive to equitable social development and economic growth. The program thus relates to the economic, social and political policy agenda as well as trying to prepare people to be technically more productive. As there is no nationally accepted government in Somalia who could be in charge of developing a national strategy, one has to rely on a collective effort of donors, international organizations and the central involvement of Somalis as the main architect.

III. CONFLICT RESOLUTION AND MINORITY RIGHTS

We believe that every conflict is resolvable unless one or a few of the parties involved either goes about the conflict resolution ineffectively or does not want to resolve the conflict. However, we support the theory that says, "do not waste too much time dealing with the symptoms; instead, deal with the disease itself." In the Somali conflict, dealing with the disease itself is like finding a magic button that transmits currents of electricity into people's minds and behaviors. Such buttons are hard to find. Most Somalis have suffered tragically from the current catastrophe. However, those from minority communities such as Somalis of Bantu origins, have experienced worse forms of violence than others.

The vast majority of Somalis vehemently support the mythic methodology that "tradition" will resolve the Somali conflict, regardless of its complexity. Well, four years of misery and mystery have passed by under a state of anarchy and we see no elder with a solution to the looming atrocities and wanton human rights abuses. Besides, we see no elder who has been able to silence the booming guns and technicals that are traumatizing the unarmed groups. Therefore, our conclusion about the Somali traditional method of resolving conflict implies failure, because we are still in the middle of the militia mire.

People assure us that because something has always been done in a certain way, it somehow means it is the best way. Yet it may not automatically be the best. It may have been appropriate for the past and for a particular group, but is it appropriate today? Tradition certainly has its place and value in Somali society, but in resolving a conflict of this magnitude, we need to rely mostly on effective skills. Let us learn from the past in order to lay down a solid and fortified foundation for the future.

We are optimistic that a solution can be found to this man-made crisis in Somalia, as soon as we begin systematic manumission to the victims and still vulnerable groups, despite all of the ramifications and recalcitrance of the warlords to the peace process. We therefore recommend the following to begin the conflict resolution process:

- **Reconciliation**: The reconciliation process must be reinforced, although it is one of the most complicated and delicate segments in the entire process, given the unhealed wounds from killing, rape, torture, robbery and destruction which a few ruthless warlords engineered . Most of the agony of Somalia has impacted innocent people who did not participate in atrocities for power struggles. Their hatred and pain cannot be reconciled easily. War victims have lost faith, human dignity, and self-esteem. Inclusion of every clan/tribe in the process of reconciliation is pivotal;

- **Disarmament:** An immediate and thorough disarmament is essential. However it should not be implemented unilaterally. Instead, disarmament should engulf every arsenal of every callous warlord. Without full participation, the credibility and value of the efforts of the peace process committee will be in vain;

- **Representation:** Since Somalia is a nation that holds together people from different traditions, cultures, destinies, values, and languages, it would be wise to consider the Belgian constitutional system. This system would provide a fair representation to every Somali community, whether a minority or a majority. It would be ideal to transform Somalia's current constitution of simple majority rule with strong control from a highly centralized state into a federation of cultural, regional, and linguistic communities. Political authority and responsibility can be divided among the three levels of government -- federal, regional, and community level. The federal government's powers should be restricted to matters of foreign affairs, national defense, internal security, social security, resources, and taxation. Regional powers should be restricted to socio-economic issues, such as environment, housing, and employment. Community powers should be restricted to cultural and person-related matters, including education, health care, and disability and welfare policy;

- **Decentralization:** Cantonization, as in Switzerland, is another option that might help Somalia's total lack of infrastructure. Cantonization is the division of the country into small political cities which govern themselves. The canton system would give every city/town in Somalia the authority to rule and control its internal affairs without the interference of the central government. Besides, the canton system would facilitate the participation of the minority and the oppressed in Somalia and allow them to contribute and gain in the prosperity of their nation;

- **Democracy:** Somalia needs to create a unique democracy that accommodates all the important and relevant aspects of our lives. By democracy, we are not referring simply to slogans of multi-partisanship, of official opposition parties, or of regular elections of leaders. By democracy, we mean a system of government where the people have a right to elect their leaders from their community whether it is under a political party arrangement or not. Along with the freedom to elect leaders comes freedom from government harassment. Tolerance is a key element of democracy, as is compromise. Therefore, in the process of creating a new constitution, people of all ages from all locations and both sexes must be included. The creation of this constitution may draw inspiration from a combination of three elements: the Islamic Religion, the cultural traditions from different Somali communities, and selected concepts and practices from the global democratic system;

- **Minority Rights**: Naturally, democracy gives the right of decision making to the majority, but also provides rights, security, and freedom for the minority. Under democracy, the majority should rule and the minority should be protected. However, in the Somali case there is no guarantee that the rights and freedom of the minority will be protected. It is, therefore, only fair that the constitution guarantee key positions in executive, administration, and political institutions to members from minority communities, as well as an adequate number of representatives in the future parliament, in order to give minority groups a voice of their own;

- **Politics of Inclusion**: The situations in Somalia, Rwanda, and Burundi offer good examples of the bankruptcy of the politics of exclusion. Any political system that seeks to run a nation by excluding groups of people, whether the group is racial, tribal, religious or regional, is destined to run into violent opposition. The solution is inclusion, or what President Yoweri Museveni of Uganda calls a broad-based administration, a system of government in which divergent and even opposed and hostile groups are given a chance to work together in the administration of the nation;

- **Return Looted Property:** all looted properties must be returned to their rightful owners, including the illegally obtained farms and land tenure documents;

- **Trials for Offenders:** all alleged criminals and extortionists who instigated killings and other criminal activities must be brought to trial before a human rights court of law and made to pay for their criminally destructive behavior.

IV. RECOMMENDATIONS ON SOMALIA AND SOMALILAND

Within this symposium, some believe that Somalia's long-term interest will best be served by restoring the single state; others believe that two states should exist, restoring the previous temporary independence of the north, ex-British Somaliland. Yet others believe that the best approach is a confederation between North and South. Most believe that, at least for the moment, resolution of this problem should be given secondary importance. The Symposium Workshop Group in favor of independence for Somaliland went on to draft and adopt the following general statement and included five specific recommendations.

The idea of Somaliland underscores an opportunity of enormous historic significance. It is pregnant with much potential that includes: identification of common critical development issues; imagining and building an effective democratic process and institutions; marshaling human talent and natural resources; and establishing a new and intelligent dialogue with neighboring communities and the world society. In short, its brief history facilitates a real possibility to create a new and traditionally inspired community.

But to capture this promise expeditiously and wisely requires careful, concentrated and sustained attention and effort. Consequently, we strongly and urgently suggest the following as crucial and immediate steps to be taken:

- **Cease Fire:** an immediate cease-fire and cessation of hostilities and a return to the means of solving problems through democratic dialogue and compromise;

- **Constitutional Development:** strengthening and enforcing the process of constitutional development until a system of plural democracy evolves. In this process, special attention must be paid to the complementary role of political institutions and traditional leadership as an autonomous body;

- **Decentralization:** decentralizing effective decision-making is a _sine qua non_ for a non-authoritarian political and economic development. The people and government of Somaliland are urged to continue and advance the laudable steps they have already taken in this regard;

- **Statehood:** restoration of the statehood of Somaliland must be legitimized through the constitutional development mentioned earlier, culminating in a referendum in which all the people of Somaliland participate. Simultaneously there is need to conduct dialogue and formulate cooperation with neighboring Somali regions, including Somalia, and other countries of the Horn; and

• **Overseas Somali Communities**: urging the Somaliland community in the diaspora to organize itself formally into associations that promote the welfare and development of their peoples.

Notes on Contributors

Hassan Adam is a lecturer in Swahili and Somali at the Institute of African Studies, University of Cologne, Cologne, Germany.

Hussein M. Adam is Associate Professor of Political Science at the College of the Holy Cross, Worcester, Massachusetts and the founding President of the Somali Studies International Association (SSIA) and Coordinator of the Fifth International Congress of Somali Studies.

Ladan Affi is an independent Somali researcher in Ottawa, Canada.

Abdullahi M. Ahmed is a Somali researcher in the field of health, based in Rome, Italy.

Ahmed Qassim Ali is an independent Somali researcher based in Pheonix, Arizona.

Ahmed Ashkir Botan is a former Minister of Higher Education in Somalia, currently living in The Netherlands.

The Reverend John Brooks, SJ, is President Emeritus of the College of the Holy Cross, Worcester, Massachusetts.

Maria Brons Bongartz is Associate Researcher at the University of Groningen, The Netherlands.

Lee V. Cassanelli is Professor of History at the University of Pennsylvania and Program Chair for the Fifth International Congress of Somali Studies.

Jamshid Damooei worked for the United Nations in Somalia and currently teaches economics at the California Lutheran University.

Martin Doornbos is Professor of Political Science at the Institute of Social Studies, The Hague, The Netherlands.

Omar Eno is an independent Somali researcher living in Toronto, Canada.

Ahmed Yusuf Farah is a Somali social anthropologist working with the United Nations Development Program in Addis Ababa.

Ricahrd Ford is Professor of History and International Development and Director of the Center for Community-Based Development, Clark University, Worcester, Massachusetts.

Charles Geshekter is Professor of History at California State University at Chico and Co-Coordinator of the First International Congress of Somali Studies in Mogadishu Somalia.

Ranieri Guerra, lives in Rome Italy and specializes in health research.

Amina Sharif Hassan works for the Rexdale Women's Center in Toronto, Canada.

Bernhard Helander is Editor of the Somali News Update (SNU) and teaches anthropology at the University of Uppsala, Sweden.

Shamis Hussein is an independent Somali consultant living in London, United Kingdom.

Mohamud A. Jama works for the United Nations in New York.

Edmond J. Keller is Professor of Political Science and Director of the African Studies Center at the University of California, Los Angeles.

Hilarie Kelly teaches social anthropology at UCLA.

I.M. Lewis is Professor of Anthropology at the London School of Economics and Political Science, University of London and Honorary Director of the International Africa Institute.

Abdalla Omar Mansur, a former Deputy Dean of the Faculty of Languages at the Somali National University, is currently affiliated with the University of Rome.

Roland Marchal is a researcher at the Center for African Studies at the National Center for Scientific Research (CNRS) in Paris.

John Markakis is Professor of History and Political Science at the University of Crete, Greece.

Ali A. Mazrui is Albert Schweitzer Professor and Director for Global Cultural Studies at the State University of New York (SUNY) at Binghamton, New York.

Abdi-asis M. Mohamed is an independent Somali researcher living in London, United Kingdom.

Hamdi Mohamed is a doctoral candidate at the University of Ottawa, Ottawa, Canada.

Mohamed-Abdi Mohamed is a Somali anthropologist and Co-Founder of the European Association of Somali Studies. He currently lives in Besancon, France.

Mohamed Haji Mukhtar is Associate Professor of African history, Department of Social and Behavioral Sciences, Savannah State College, Savannah, Georgia.

Giampaolo Calchi Novati is Professor of Political Science at the University of Urbino, Italy.

Robert Oakley served as Ambassador and later as Special Envoy of Presidents Bush and Clinton to Somalia. He is currently affiliated with the National Defense University in Washington, DC.

John Prendergast is a US Institute of Peace fellow at the National Security Council; a Visiting Fellow at the University of Maryland's Center for International Development and Conflict Management; and former Horn of Africa Project Director at the Center for Concern.

Agusto Pinto specializes in health research from Rome, Italy.

Abdirahman Osman Raghe was involved in the establishment of the Somali Unit for Research on Emergencies and Rural Development (SURERD) and currently lives in Toronto, Canada.

Mohamed M. Sahnoun, former Algerian Ambassador and OAU official, served as Special Representative of the United Nations Secretary General to Somalia in 1992.

Ibrahim Meygag Samater is a former Planning Minister in Somalia. He later served as Chair of the Somali National Movement (SNM) and of the Interim National Assembly in Somaliland.

Said S. Samatar is Professor of History at the Rutgers State University in Newark, New Jersey.

Peter J. Schraeder is Associate Professor of Political Science at Loyola University in Chicago.

Ann Seidman is Professor of International Development at Clark University in Worcester, Massachusetts.

Robert Seidman is Professor of Law at Boston University in Boston.

Mohamed Aden Sheikh is former Somali Minister of Information, currently living in Turin, Italy.

David Smock is Director of the Grants Program at the United States Institute of Peace (USIP), Washington, DC.

George Urch is Professor of Education at the University of Massachusetts, Amherst.

Frank Vellaccio, former Vice President and Dean of the College, is currently Provost of the College of the Holy Cross, Worcester, MA.

Charles S. Weiss is a Professor of Psychology and Director of Research Grants at the College of the Holy Cross, Worcester, MA.

Bibliography

Adam, Hussein M. "Somalia: Militarism, Warlordism or Democracy?" *Review of African Political Economy* 54 (July 1992): 11-26.

_____. "Rethinking Somali Politics." *Proceedings of the Sixth Michigan State University Conference on North East Africa.* East Lansing: Michigan State University, 23-25 April 1992.

_____. Somalia: A Terrible Beauty Being Born?" In *Collapsed States: The Disintegration and Restoration of Legitimate Authority.* Edited by I. William Zartman. (Boulder, CO: Lynne Reinner Publishers, 1995).

_____. "Clan Conflicts and Democratization in Somalia." In *Ethnic Conflict and Democratization in Africa.* Edited by Harvey Glickman. (Altanta, GA: The African Studies Association Press, 1995).

_____. "Formation and Recognition of States: Somaliland in Contrast to Eritrea." *Review of African Political Economy* 59 (March 1994): 21-38.

_____. "Islam and Politics in Somalia." *Journal of Islamic Studies.* 6:2 (1995): 189-221.

Adan, Amina. "Women and Words," *Ufahama, Journal of the African Activist Association.* X:3 (Spring 1981).

_____. "Somali Women From 1800 to the Present." Paper written for Dr. Chris Ehret, University of California, Los Angeles.

African Rights. *Land Tenure, the Creation of Famine, and Prospects for Peace in Somalia.* Discussion paper No. 1. (London: Africa Rights, October 1993).

_____. *Somalia. Operation Restore Hope: A Preliminary Assessment.* (London: Africa Rights, May 1993).

Africa Watch Women's Rights Project, Division of Human Rights
Watch. "Seeking Refuge, Finding Terror: The Widespread Rape of
Somali Women Refugees in North Eastern Kenya," 5:13 (4 October
1993).

Africa Watch. *Somalia Beyond the Warlords: The Need for a Verdict
on Human Rights Abuses*. (New York: Africa Watch, March 1993).

Ahmed, A. (Ed.) *The Invention of Somalia*. (Trenton, NJ: Red Sea
Press, 1995).

_____. *Daybreak is Near*. (Trenton, NJ: Red Sea Press, 1996).

Amnesty International. *Somalia: A Human Rights Disaster*. (London:
Amnesty International, 1992).

_____. *Somalia: A Long-Term Human Rights Crisis*. (London:
Amnesty International, 1988).

_____. *Somalia: The July 1989 Jezira Beach Massacre*. (London:
Amnesty International, 1990).

Amoo, S. *The OAU and African Conflicts: Past Successes, Present
Paralysis and Future Perspectives*. (Fairfax, VA: George Mason
University Institute of Conflict Analysis and Resolution, May 1992).

Andrezjewski, B.W. "Somali Literature." In *Literatures in African
Languages*. Edited by B.W. Andrezjewski et al. (Cambridge:
Cambridge University Press, 1987).

_____. "Reflections on the Nature and Social Function of Somali
Proverbs," *African Language Review* 7 (1968): 74-85.

_____, and Lewis, I.M. *Somali Poetry: An Introduction*. (Oxford:
Clarendon Press, 1964).

_____, Galal, H.M. "A Somali Poetic Combat." African Studies
Center, Report of 1963, Michigan State University, East Lansing.

Aronson, D. "Kinsmen and Comrades: Towards a Class Analysis of the Somali Pastoral Sector." *Nomadic Peoples* 7 (1982):14-24.

Askar, Ahmed Omer. *Sharks and Soldiers*. (Finland: publisher n.a., 1992).

Assefa, H. and Khadiagala, G. (editors) *Conflict and Conflict Resolution in the Horn of Africa*. (Washington, DC: Brookings Institution, 1994).

Barakat, Halim. *The Arab World: Society, Culture and State*. (Berkeley: University of California Press, 1993).

Barre, A. *Salient Aspects of Somalia's Foreign Policy: Selected Speeches*. (Mogadishu: Ministry of Foreign Affairs, 1978).

Barre, M. "Speech to the Nation on October 21, 1979." In *African Contemporary Record, 1980*. Edited by C. Legum. (London: African Publishing Company, 1980).

Bongartz, Maria (Brons). *The Civil War in Somalia: Its Genesis and Dynamics*. (Uppsala: Scandinavian Institute of African Studies, 1991).

_____. *Somalia im Burgerkreig: Ursachen und Perspektiven des innenpolitischen Konflikts*. (Hamburg: Institut fur Afrikakunde, 1991).

_____. *Somaliland: Zwei Jahre nach der Unabhangigkeitserklarung*. (Hamburg: Institut fur Afrikakunde, 1993).

Boutros-Ghali, B. *An Agenda for Peace*. (New York: United Nations, 1992).

_____. "Empowering the United Nations." *Foreign Affairs* 71:5, (1992/1993).

Bredvold, L. and Ross, R. (editors). *The Philosophy of Edmund Burke*. (Ann Arbor: University of Michigan Press, 1960).

Brickhill, Jeremy. *Disarmament and Demobilization in Somaliland.* (Northwestern Somalia: n.p., 22 April 1994).

Bull, Hedley. *The Anarchical Society.* (New York: Columbia University Press, 1977).

Buschkens, W.F.L. *Community Health in the Developing World: The Case of Somalia.* (Assen: Van Gorcum & Company, 1990).

Cassanelli, L. *The Shaping of Somali Society: Reconstruction of the History of a Pastoral People, 1600-1900.* (Philadelphia: University of Pennsylvania Press, 1982).

Castagno, A. "Somali Republic." In *Political Parties and National Integration in Tropical Africa.* Edited by J. Coleman and C. Rosberg, Jr. (Berkeley: University of California Press, 1964).

Clark, Jeffrey. "Debacle in Somalia," *Foreign Affairs*, 72:1 (1993).

Clark, J. *The U.S. Government, Humanitarian Assistance and the New World Order: A Call for a New Approach.* (Washington, DC: US Committee for Refugees Issue Brief, September 1991).

Cohen, R. "The State in Africa." *Review of African Political Economy* 5 (1976): 1-3.

Cuny, Fred. "The Functioning of Village Markets in Strife-Torn Areas of Somalia." Unpublished mime,. (22 September, 1992).

Damooei, Jamshid. *Moving Towards Creation of a Conducive Economic Environment for Reconstruction and Rehabilitation in Somalia.* (New York: UNDP, 1993).

_____. *An Outline for UNDP Fifth Country Programme: A Medium-Run Programme (1991-1993).* (New York: UNDP, 1991).

Davidson, Basil, *The Black Man's Burden: Africa and the Curse of the Nation-State.* (New York: Times Books, 1992).

_____. "Somalia in 1975: Some Notes and Impressions." *Issue* 5:1 (1975): 19-26.

Deng, F. and Zartman, I.W., (editors). *Conflict Resolution in Africa.* (Washington, DC: The Brookings Institution, 1991).

De Waal, A. *Famine that Kills.* (Oxford: Clarendon Press, 1989).

Drysdale, John. "Somalia: The Only Way Forward," *Journal of the Anglo-Somali Society.* (Winter 1992/3).

_____. *Somalia: Problems of Rebuilding a Nation.* (Hove: Quantum Books, 1992).

_____. *Somaliland 1991: Report and Reference.* (Hove, England: Global-Stats, Ltd., 1991).

_____. *The Somali Dispute.* (London: Pall Mall Press, 1964).

_____. *Whatever Happened to Somalia? A Tale of Tragic Blunders* (London: Haan Associates, 1994).

Farzin, Hossein Y. *Food Import Dependence in Somalia.* World Bank Discussion Papers No. 23. (Washington, DC: World Bank, 1988).

Fenet, A. "Djibouti: Mini-State on the Horn of Africa." In *Horn of Africa: From "Scramble for Africa" to East-West Conflict.* (Bonn:Forschungsinstitut der Friedrich Ebert Stiftung, 1986): 59-69.

Fineman, Mark. "The Oil Factor in Somalia." *Los Angeles Times.* (18 January 1993).

FitzGibbon, Louis. *The Evaded Duty.* (London: Rex Collins, 1982).

_____. *The Betrayal of the Somalis.* (London: Rex Collins, 1982).

Gassem, Mariam Arif. *Hostages: The People Who Kidnapped Themselves.* (Mogadishu: Central Graphic Services/Nairobi, 1994).

Gelb, L. "Shoot to Feed Somalia." *New York Times.* (19 November 1992): A27.

Ghalib, Jama Mohamed. *The Cost of Dictatorship: The Somali Experience.* (New York: Lilian Barber Press, 1995).

Gerlach, J. "A U.N. Army for the New World Order?" *Orbis* (spring 1993): 233-6.

Gersony, R. *Why Somalis Flee: Synthesis of Accounts of Conflict Experience in Northern Somalia.* (Washington, DC: United States Department of State, August 1989).

Geshekter, C. "Anti-Colonialism and Class Formation: The Eastern Horn of Africa, 1920-1950." Paper presented at the Second International Congress of Somali Studies, Hamburg, August 1993.

_____. "Entrepreneurs, Livestock and Politics: British Somaliland, 1920-1950." In *Entreprises et Entrepreneurs en Afrique: XIXe et XXe Siecle.* Edited by C. Coquery-Vidrovitch. (Paris: Editions L'Harmattan, 1983).

Green, Reginal Herbold. *Somalia: Towards Reconstruction, Rehabilitation, Restructuring.* (New York: UNICEF, 1993).

Gyerye, K. *An Essay on African Philosophical Thought.* (Cambridge: Cambridge University Press, 1987).

Hay, Margaret Jean and Stichter, Sharon, (editors). *African Women South of the Sahara.* (New York: Longman, 1984).

Hancock, Graham. *Lords of Poverty.* (Great Britain: MacMillan London Ltd., 1989).

Helander, B. "The Hubeer in the Land of Plenty: Land Labour and Vulnerability among a Rahanweyn Clan." In *Production and Politics in Southern Somalia.* Edited by C. Besteman and L.V. Cassanelli. (Boulder: Westview, 1994).

_____. "Who is Starving?" *Somali News Update.* 1:28 (1992).

_____. "The Slaughtered Camel: Coping with Fictitious Descent Among the Hubeer of Southern Somalia." (Unpublished Doctoral Thesis, Uppsala University, Sweden, 1988).

Held, D. *Political Theory and the Modern State: Essays on State, Power, and Democracy.* (Stanford: Stanford University Press, 1989).

_____. *Models of Democracy.* (Stanford: Stanford University Press, 1989).

Heinze, Paul. *The Horn of Africa: From War to Peace.* (New York: St. Martin's Press, 1991).

Hess, Robert. *Italian Colonialism in Somalia.* (Chicago: University of Chicago Press, 1966).

Hodgkin, T. "The African Middle Class," *Corona* (March 1956):88.

Huntington, Samuel. *The Third Wave: Democratization in the Late Twentieth Century.* (Tulsa: University of Oklahoma Press, 1991).

Human Rights Watch. *The Lost Agenda and UN Field Operations.* (New York: Human Rights Watch, June 1993).

International Labor Office. *Economic Transformation in a Socialist Framework.* (Addis Ababa: Jobs and Skills Programme for Africa, 1977).

International Monetary Fund. *Somalia - Recent Economic Developments.* (Washington, DC: IMF, 1983,1985,1987,1988,1989).

_____. *Supplement to the Staff Report for 1988.* Article IV, Consultation (Washington, DC: IMF, 3 June 1988).

Iye, Ali Moussa. *Le Verdict de L'Arbre (Go'aankii Geedka): Le Xeer Issa Etude d'une Democratic Pastorale.* (Djibouti: n.p. 1990).

Jackson, R. *Quasi-States: Sovereignty, International Relations and the Third World*. Edited by A. Kohli. (Princeton: Princeton University Press, 1986).

Jamal, V. "Somalia: Survival in a 'Doomed' Economy." *International Labour Review*. 127:6 (1988): 783-812.

_____. *Nomads, Farmers and Townsmen: Incomes and Inequality in Somalia*. (Addis Ababa: ILO Working Paper, 1981).

_____. "Nomads and Farmers: Incomes and Rural Poverty in Somalia." In *Agrarian Policies and Rural Poverty in Africa*. Edited by D. Ghai and S. Radwan. (Geneva: International Labor Office, 1983).

Johnson, J. *Heellooy, Heellooy: The Development of the Genre Heello in Modern Somali Poetry*. (Bloomingon: Indiana University Press, 1974).

Kaplan, I., et al. *Area Handbook for Somalia*. (Washington, DC: US Government Printing Office, 1987).

Kapteijns, L. *Women and the Somali Pastoral Tradition: Corporate Kinship and Capitalist Transformation in Northern Somalia*. (Working Paper No. 153. Boston: Boston University African Studies Center, 1991).

_____, and Spaulding, J. "Counsels of Despair: Social Vignettes of 19th Century Colonial Aden." (Forthcoming).

_____. "Class Formation and Gender in Precolonial Somali Society: A Research Agenda." *Northeast African Studies* 11:1 (1989):19-38.

Kelly, Hilarie. "Orma-Somali Culture Shaping the Juba-Tana Region." In *Proceedings of the Second International Congress of Somali Studies*. Volume VI. Edited by Thomas Labahn. (Hamburg, Germany: Helmut Buske Verlag, 1984): 13-38.

Khaldun, Ibn. *The Muqaddimah: An Introduction to History*. Trs. F. Rosenthal. (Princeton: Princeton University Press, 1967).

Laitin, D. "The Political Crisis in Somalia." *Horn of Africa* 5:2 (1982): 60-64.

_____, and Samatar, S. *Somalia: Nation in Search of a State.* (Boulder: Westview Press, 1987).

_____. "Somalia's Military Government and Scientific Socialism." In *Socialism and Sub-Saharan Africa: A New Assessment.* Edited by C. Rosberg and T. Callaghy. (Berkeley: Institute for International Studies, 1979).

Lawrence, M. *A Tree for Poverty.* (Nairobi: Eagle Press, 1954).

Lefebure, Jeffery A. *Arms for the Horn: US Security Policy in Ethiopia and Somalia 1953-1991.* (Pittsburgh: University of Pittsburgh Press, 1991).

Legum, C. "Somali Liberation Songs." *Journal of Modern African Studies* 1:4 (October 1987): 503-519.

Lewis, I.M. *Blood and Bone: The Call of Kinship in Somali Society.* (Trenton, NJ: Red Sea Press, 1994).

_____. *Understanding Somalia: Guide to Culture, History and Social Institution.* (London: Haan Associates, 1993).

_____. "Misunderstanding the Somali Crisis," *Anthropology Today*, 9:4 (August 1993).

_____. *A Modern History of Somalia.* (Boulder: Westview Press, 1988).

_____. *A Pastoral Democracy: A Study of Pastoralism and Politics Among the Northern Somali of the Horn of Africa.* (London: Oxford University Press, 1981).

_____. *Peoples of the Horn of Africa: Somali, Afar, and Saho.* (London: International African Institute, 1969).

_____. "Integration of the Somali Republic." In *African Integration and Disintegration*. Edited by Arthur Hazelwood. (London: University Press, 1967).

_____. "Lineage Continuity and Modern Commerce in Northern Somaliland." In *Markets in Africa*. Edited by P. Bohannan and G. Dalton. (Evanston: Northwestern University Press, 1962).

Lyons, T. "The Horn of Africa Regional Politics: A Hobbesian World." In *The Dynamics of Regional Politics*. Edited by H. Wiggins. (New York: Columbia University Press, 1992).

Makdisi, J. *Beirut Fragments: A War Memoir*. (New York: Persea Books, 1990).

Markakis, John. *National and Class Conflict in the Horn of Africa*. (London: Zed Books, 1990).

_____. "The Ishaq-Ogaden Dispute." In *Ecology and Politics: Environmental Stress and Security in Africa*. Edited by A Hjort af Ornas and M. Salih. (Stockholm: Scandinavian Institute for African Studies, 1989).

Markovitz, I.L. *Power and Class in Africa*. (Engelwood Cliffs, NJ: Prentice-Hall, 1977).

Melander, G. *Refugees in Somalia*. Research Report No. 56. (Uppsala: andinavian Institute of African Studies, 1980).

Migdal, Joel. *Strong Societies and Weak States*. (Princeton: Princeton University Press, 1988).

Mohamed Salih, M.A. and Wohlgemuth, Lennart, (editors). *Crisis Management and the Politics of Reconciliation in Somalia: Statements from the Uppsala Forum, 17-19 January 1994*. (Uppsala: Scandinavian Institute of African Studies, 1994).

Mohamoud, O. "Somalia: Crisis and Decay in an Authoritarian Regime." *Horn of Africa*. 4:3 (1981):7-11.

National Academy of Sciences. *Scientists and Human Rights in Somalia.* (Washington, DC: National Academy Press, 1988).

Nozick, R. *Anarchy, State and Utopia.* (New York: Basic Books, 1974).

Omaar, R. and de Waal, A. *Somalia, Operation Restore Hope: A Preliminary Assessment.* (London: Africa Rights, 1993).'

Omar, Mohamed Osman. *The Road to Zero: Somalia's Self-Destruction* (London: Haan Associates, 1992).

Perlez, J. "How One Family, Some of it, Survives." *New York Times* (16 November 1992): A3.

Physicians for Human Rights. "Somalia: No Mercy in Mogadishu." (Washington, DC: Africa Watch, 26 March 1992).

Prendergast, John. "Somalia's Silent Slaughter," *America* (24 March 1990).

_____. *The Gun Talks Louder than the Voice: Somalia's Continuing Cycle of Violence.* (Washington, DC: Center for Concern, July 1994).

_____. *The Bones of Our Children are Not Yet Buried: The Looming Spectre of Famine and Massive Human Rights Abuse in Somalia.* (Washington, DC: Center for Concern, 1994).

Republic of Somalia. *French Somaliland: A Classic Colonial Case.* (Mogadishu: n.p. 1965).

_____. *Somalia: A Divided Nation Seeking Reunification.* (Mogadishu: Ministry of Information, 1965).

_____. Planning and Coordinating Commission for Economic and Social Development, *First Five-Year Plan, 1963-67.* (Mogadishu: Ministry of Planning, July 1963).

Reusse, E. "Somalia's Nomadic Livestock Economy: Its Response to a Profitable Export Opportunity." *World Animal Review* 43 (1982): 2-11.

Riker, W. *Liberalism Against Populism.* (San Francisco: W.H. Freeman, 1982).

Rirash, M.A. "Camel Herding and Its Effects on Somali Literature." In *Camels and Development: Sustainable Production in African Drylands.* edited by A. Hjort af Ornas. (Uppsala: Scandinavian Institute of African Studies, 1988).

Rothchild, D. And Chazan, N., (editors). *The Precarious Balance.* (Boulder: Westview Press, 1988).

Ruiz, H. *Beyond the Headlines: Refugees in the Horn.* (Washington, DC: US Committee for the Refugees, 1988).

Samatar, Abdi. "Destruction of State and Society: Beyond the Tribal Convention." *Journal of Modern Africa Studies* 30:4 (1992): 625-641.

_____. "Social Classes and Economic Restructuring in Pastoral Africa: The Somali Experience." *African Studies Review* 35:1 (1992): 101-128.

_____. *The State and Rural Transformations in Northern Somalia 1884-1986.* (Madison: University of Wisconsin Press, 1989).

_____, Salisbury, L. and Bascom, J. "The Political Economy of Livestock Marketing in Somalia." *African Economic History* 17 (1988): 81-97.

_____. "Merchant Capital, International Livestock Trade and Pastoral Development in Somalia." *Canadian Journal of African Studies* 21:3 (1987):355-374.

Samatar, Abdi and Samatar, Ahmed Ismail. "The Material Roots of the Suspended African State: Arguments from Somalia." *Journal of Modern African Studies* 25:4 (1987): 669-690.

Samatar, Ahmed Ismail, (editor). *The Somali Challenge: From Catastrophe to Renewal?* (Boulder: Lynne Reinner Publishers, 1994).

_____. "Under Siege: Blood, Power, and the Somali State." In *Conflict and Conflict resolution in the Horn of Africa*. Edited by H. Assefa and G. Khadiagala. (Washington, DC: The Brookings Institution, forthcoming).

_____. "Somali Studies: Towards an Alternative Epistemology." *Northeast African Studies* 11:1 (1989): 3-17.

_____. *Socialist Somalia: Rhetoric and Reality*. (London: Zed Books, 1988).

_____. "Somalia's Impasse: State Power and Dissident Politics." *Third World Quarterly* 9:3 (July 1987): 871-890.

_____, (editor). "Somalia: Crises of State and Society." Special issue, *Africa Today* 32:3 (1985): 5-70.

Samatar, Said. *Somalia: A Nation in Turmoil*. A Minority Rights Report. (London: The Minority Rights Group, 1991).

_____. "The Somali Dilemma: Nation in Search of a State." In *Partitioned Africans: Ethnic Relations Across Africa's International Boundaries, 1884-1984*. Edited by A. Asiwaju. (New York: St. Martin's Press, 1985).

_____. *Oral Poetry and Somali Nationalism*. (Cambridge: Cambridge University Press, 1982).

Schraeder. P. "Ethnic Politics in Djibouti: From 'Eye of the Hurricane' to 'Boiling Cauldron'." *African Affairs* 92:367 (April 1993):203-221.

Sheikh, Mohamed Aden. *Arrivederci a Mogadiscio*. (Roma: Edizioni Associate, 1991).

Sheikh Mohamed, Saeed. "The Rise and Fall of Somali Nationalism," Special Issue on Somalia, *Canada's Periodical on Refugees*. 12:5 (Nov.-Dec. 1992).

Sklar, R. "Developmental Democracy." *Comparative Studies in Society and History* 29:4 (October 1987): 686-714.

Somali Republic. *The Somali Peninsula: A New Light on Imperial Motives*. (London: Ministry of Foreign Affairs, 1962).

Somali Democratic Republic. *National Development Strategy and Programme, 1989-91*. (Mogadishu: Ministry of National Planning, 1989).

_____. *Go From My Country*. (Mogadishu: Ministry of Foreign Affairs, 1978).

"Somali PM on Threat to Bomb Capital." *The Nation* (Nairobi, 4 January 1991):1.

"Somalia: Death by Looting." *The Economist* (18 July 1992):41.

"Somalia: Nasty, Brutish, Split." *The Economist* (7 September 1991):42.

"Somalia: One State or Two?" *Africa Confidential* 32:12 (14 June 1991): 5-6.

Stevenson, Jonathan. "Hope Restored in Somalia?" *Foreign Policy* 19 (Summer 1993).

Swift, J. "Why are Rural People Vulnerable to Famine?" *IDS Bulletin* 20:2 (1989): 8-15.

_____. "The Development of Livestock Trading in a Pastoral Economy: The Somali Case." In *Pastoral Production and Society: Proceedings of the International Meeting on Nomadic Pastoralism*. (Cambridge: Cambridge University Press, 1979).

_____. "Pastoral Development in Somalia: Herding Cooperatives as a Strategy Against Desertification and Famine." In *Desertification: Environmental Degradation In and Around Arid Lands*. Edited by M. Glantz. (Boulder: Westview Press, 1977).

Thompson, V. and Adloff, R. *Djibouti and the Horn of Africa*. (Stanford: Stanford University Press, 1978).

Tilly, Charles. "War Making and State Making as Organized Crime." In *Bringing the State Back In*. Edited by P. Evans, D. Rueschemeyer, and T. Skocpol. (Cambridge: Cambridge University Press 1985).

Tolba, M.K. "Disposal of Hazardous Wastes in Somalia." United Nations Environmental Program (UNEP) News Release, Statement by UNEP Executive Director, (Nairobi, 9 September 1992).

Touval, Saadia. *Somali Nationalism*. (Cambridge: Harvard University Press, 1963).

Turton, E.R. "Somali Resistance to Colonial Rule and the Development of Somali Political Activity in Kenya 1893-1960," *The Journal of African History*, XIII (1972).

Tyler. *Somalia: Case Study on Rural Poverty*, (Rome: FAO, WCARD In-depth Studies No.7, 1983).

United Somali Party. *Crisis in Somalia: A Call for Peace and Stability - A United Somali Party (USP) Perspective*. (N.p.: United Somali Party, March 1992).

United States, Department of State. "Address by Chester Crocker, Assistant Secretary for African Affairs, before the Baltimore Council on Foreign Relations." *Current Policy* 431:4 (28 October 1982).

Vietorisz, Thomas. *Regional Variation, Economic Specialization and Income Distribution in Somalia*. (Somalia: USAID, 1987).

Vail, Leroy, editor. *The Creation of Tribalism in Southern Africa*. (Berkeley: University of California Press, 1989).

Wallace, B. "Somali War Draws Scribes, Hustlers." *Africa News* (26 October - 8 November 1992):2.

Woodward, D.J. and Stockton, G. *A Study of the Profitability of Somali Exports.* (Mogadishu: US Agency for International Development, 1989).

World Bank. *Somalia: Crisis in the Public Expenditure Management.* (Washington, DC: World Bank, 1990).

_____. *Somalia and Public Enterprise Reform.* (Washington, DC: World Bank, 1987).

Young, Crawford. "Patterns of Social Conflict: State, Class, and Ethnicity." *Daedalus* (Spring 1992):72.

_____, (editor). *The Rising Tide of Cultural Pluralism: The Nation-State at Bay?* (Madison: University of Wisconsin Press, 1993).

Zartman, I.W. *Ripe for Resolution.* (Oxford: Oxford University Press, 1990).

Zolberg, Aristide. "The Spectre of Anarchy: African States Verging on Dissolution," *Dissent* 39:3 (summer 1992).

INDEX

The Red Sea Press, Inc.

11-D Princess Rd., Lawrenceville, NJ 08648-2319

(609) 844-9583 p FAX: (609) 844-0198

P.O. Box 48, Asmara, ERITREA p Tel:. +291-1-120707, Fax: +291-1-123369

P.O. Box 40634, Addis Ababa, ETHIOPIA p Tel:. +251-1-651073, Fax: +251-1-651100

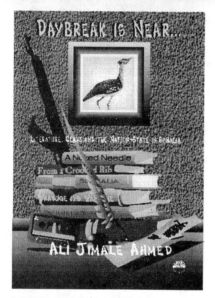

Daybreak is Near . . .
Literature, Clans and the Nation-State of Somalia
Ali Jimale Ahmed

1-56902-022-1 hc $59.95

1-56902-023-X pb $18.95

The author of this important study takes a unique approach to examine the role literature has played in Somali society of the past half century. He examines Somali literature, both written and oral, to trace the development of Somali nationalism, and seeks explanations for the disintegration of the post-colonial Somali nation-state. In the tradition of Edward Said, Ali Jimale Ahmed tells us that "the literary text does not only describe existing conceptions of society, but it also captures key events in Somali history in their inchoate forms. As such, the literary text, as Belinsky states, can be read as 'the pulse of a nation's inner life.'" Dr. Ahmed demonstrates his perspective with unparalleled mastery and skill by citing numerous evidence from diverse sources such as Somali prose and fiction, Nuruddin Farah's novels, Somali theater and Somali poetic duels, touching also on the liberating role of orature and cassette culture in Somali society. The author initiates a rigorous dialectical discourse on Somali literature and politics. This book will not only have a lasting and positive impact in the study of African literature, but more importantly, it will contribute immensely to the current debate within the Somali community, as the nation struggles to find a way out of its current tragedy.

Ali Jimale Ahmed is Associate Professor in the Department of Comparative literature at Queens College and at the Graduate Center of the City University of New York. He is the editor of *The Invention of Somalia* (RSP 1995) and co-edited (with Taddesse Adera) *Silence is Not Golden: A Critical Anthology of Ethiopian Literature* (RSP 1995). Prof. Ahmed is also the president of the Somali Studies association of North America.

The Red Sea Press, Inc.
11-D Princess Rd., Lawrenceville, NJ 08648-2319
(609) 844-9583 p FAX: (609) 844-0198
P.O. Box 48, Asmara, ERITREA p Tel:. +291-1-120707, Fax: +291-1-123369
P.O. Box 40634, Addis Ababa, ETHIOPIA p Tel:. +251-1-651073, Fax: +251-1-651100

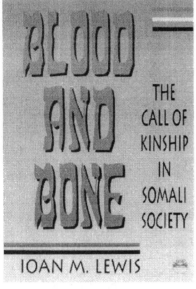

Blood and Bone
The Call of Kinship in Somali Society

Ioan M. Lewis

In Somali political culture, clan solidarity is represented by the evocative symbols of blood and bone — immutable natural endowments inherent in kinship traced through the father in the male line. This book explores the extraordinary persistence and resilience of these age-old loyalties. Grounded in the traditional life of the pastoral nomad, kinship is a multipurpose resource, the basis of the individual's social, political and economic security. Outside the local pastoral economy, it has proved equally adaptable in organizing labor migration and livestock trading in the gulf states. It survived and even flourished under the anti-clan regime of "scientific Socialism" of 1970s Somalia, and played a crucial role in the most successful recent Somali guerilla movement. Above all, it dominates the 1990s crisis of the Somali state.

This analysis, which challenges contemporary anthropological understanding of kinship structures, is based on over forty years' of research on the Somali people.

Ioan M. Lewis has been professor of Anthropology at The London School of Economics since 1969 and is also consultative director of the International African Institute. He has taught social anthropology in Africa, Asia, Nothern America and Europe, and has written eighteen books--five on different aspects of Somali cultures and society. He is widely regarded as one of the world's foremost authorities on Somali studies, and as a leading British social anthropologist.

0-932415-92-X *hc* $49.95
0-932415-93-8 *pb* $16.95

The Red Sea Press, Inc.
11-D Princess Rd., Lawrenceville, NJ 08648-2319
(609) 844-9583 p FAX: (609) 844-0198
P.O. Box 48, Asmara, ERITREA p Tel:. +291-1-120707, Fax: +291-1-123369
P.O. Box 40634, Addis Ababa, ETHIOPIA p Tel:. +251-1-651073, Fax: +251-1-651100

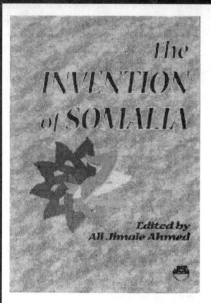

The Invention of Somalia

Edited by Ali Jimale Ahmed

The Somali civil war had caught many people by surprise. How was it possible that a nation that had so much in common—or so it seemed—could suddenly "snap" and easily descend into such a fratricidal binge and mayhem? What had become of the Somali "national character" that was enshrined in the national lore and propagated in books by both Somali and non-Somali scholars? How did "homogeneity," stubbornly and unbeknownst to anyone, degenerate into the worst forms of mosaic fiefdoms? This book is the first real attempt by scholars on Somalia to identify and analyze the basic assumptions, which had informed the construction of the now debunked

0-932415-98-9 *hc* $49.95
0-932415-99-7 *pb* $16.95

Somali myth. The authors do not only suggest alternative ways of seeing and interpreting existing data, but also initiate and propose new ways of reading Somali past and present. This new way of reading is not born on the heels of the disintegration of the Somali State. Rather the seminal thesis of the book—that Somali a had indeed come to a sticking place both in terms of ideas and of state power—has its origins in a paper read at the University of Southern California (USC) in 1983 by one of the contributors to the volume.

The relevance of findings in this anthology is not only limited to the Somali experience, but is germane to the discussion of any country where so much energy had gone into the analysis of a single myth variant in a nation's history.

Ali Jimale Ahmed is Associate Professor in the Department of Comparative literature at Queens College and at the Graduate Center of the City University of New York. He is the author of *Daybreak is Near...: Literature, Clans and the Nation-State in Somalia* (RSP 1996) and co-edited (with Taddesse Adera) *Silence is Not Golden: A Critical Anthology of Ethiopian Literature* (RSP 1995). Prof. Ahmed is also the president of the Somali Studies association of North America.

The Red Sea Press, Inc.
11-D Princess Rd., Lawrenceville, NJ 08648-2319
(609) 844-9583 p FAX: (609) 844-0198
P.O. Box 48, Asmara, ERITREA p Tel:. +291-1-120707, Fax: +291-1-123369
P.O. Box 40634, Addis Ababa, ETHIOPIA p Tel:. +251-1-651073, Fax: +251-1-651100

The Last Camel: True Stories of Somalia
Jeanne D'Haem

The Last Camel is a collection of stories about the people who live in a little village in Northern Somalia. These are compelling tales about African spirits, clever women, untouchable *Midgaans*, sagacious elders who struggle with modern technology, bandits, and a few goats. The tales are told by young American Peace Corps teacher who lived alone in the village of Arabsiyo in Northern Somalia in the late 60s. The book reveals the complex hearts and minds of the Somali people because it was written by a young woman who slept among the camels, spoke the language, starved, smiled, and savored life in Africa.

1-56902-040-X *hc* $59.95
1-56902-041-8 *pb* $18.95

Jeanne D'Haem was a Peace Corps volunteer in Somalia in 1968. She was posted to the village of Arabsiyo in Northern Somaliland, where she learned to speack Somali and was adopted by the villagers and was made a member of the Sa'ad Musa tribe. D'Haem has a Ph.D. from New York University and is a public school administrator in New Jersey.

In the Shadow of Conquest:
Islam in colonial Northeast Africa

Edited by Said S. Samatar

There are two questions designed to facilitate the reader's appreciation of the order and character of the essays presented in this book: What did the societies treated here have in common during the period under consideration? And to what extent did this commonality shape or condition the character of their response when they faced a transregional crisis—the Euro-Christian conquest? A self-evident answer is that the vast majority of those societies were Muslim. The closing decades of the 19th century engulfed the Muslims of Northeast Africa in a series of traumatizing

0-932415-69-5 *hc* $39.95
0-932415-70-9 *pb* $12.95

events attendant upon European (and in the case of the Horn of Africa, Ethiopian) occupation. The essays in this volume present case studies dealing with the aspects of, rather than a common Muslim response to, the onset of European conquest.

Said S. Samatar is a professor of History at Rutgers University. He is the author of *Oral Poetry and Somali Nationalism: The Case of Sayyid Mohammed 'Abdille Hassan.*

The Red Sea Press, Inc.

11-D Princess Rd., Lawrenceville, NJ 08648-2319
(609) 844-9583 □ FAX: (609) 844-0198

P.O. Box 48, Asmara, ERITREA □ Tel:. +291-1-120707, Fax: 291-123369
P.O. Box 40634, Addis Ababa, ETHIOPIA □ Tel:. +251-1-651073 Fax: +251-1-651100

TO ORDER:
SEND $4.00 POSTAGE FOR FIRST BOOK, AND $1.00 FOR EACH ADDITIONAL BOOK

		Price	ISBN	Qty.	Amount
Dayreak is Near. . .	Hc	$59.95	1-56902-022-1		
Literatures, Clans and the Nation-State in Somalia	Pb	$18.95	1-56902-023-X		
Blood and Bone	Hc	$49.95	0-932415-92-X		
The Call of kinship in Somali Society	Pb	$14.95	0-932415-93-8		
The Last Camel	Hc	$59.95	1-56902-040-X		
True Stories About Somalia	Pb	$18.95	1-56902-041-8		
The Invention of Somalia	Hc	$49.95	0-932415-98-9		
	Pb	$16.95	0-932415-99-7		
In The Shadow of Conquest	Hc	$39.95	0-932415-69-5		
Islam in Colonial Northeast frica	Pb	$12.95	0-932415-70-9		

Please make checks or money order payable to: The Red Sea Press, Inc.

Yes, we accept □ Discover □ Diners Club □ Visa □ Master Card
□ American Express (*indicate which card*)

Name _____   Subtotal _____

Address _____   Shipping & Handling _____

City _____ . State _____ Zip _____

Telephone ( ) _____   NJ Residents Add 6% Sales Tax _____

Credit Card Number _____ Expiration Date _____

X Signature _____   TOTAL _____

RSP

Visit our new website at http: www.africanworld.com
e-mail address: awprsp@castle.net